Counselling Psychology

BPS Textbooks in Psychology

BPS Wiley presents a comprehensive and authoritative series covering everything a student needs in order to complete an undergraduate degree in psychology. Refreshingly written to consider more than North American research, this series is the first to give a truly international perspective. Written by the very best names in the field, the series offers an extensive range of titles from introductory level through to final year optional modules, and every text fully complies with the BPS syllabus in the topic. No other series bears the BPS seal of approval!

Many of the books are supported by a companion website, featuring additional resource materials for both instructors and students, designed to encourage critical thinking, and providing for all your course lecturing and testing needs.

For other titles in this series, please go to http://psychsource.bps.org.uk.

Counselling Psychology
A Textbook for Study and Practice

Edited by

DAVID MURPHY

The University of Nottingham
Nottingham, UK

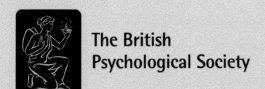
The British
Psychological Society

WILEY

This edition first published 2017 by the British Psychological Society and John Wiley & Sons Ltd

© 2017 John Wiley & Sons Ltd

Registered Offices
John Wiley & Sons, Inc., 111 River Street, Hoboken, NJ 07030, USA
John Wiley & Sons Ltd, The Atrium, Southern Gate, Chichester, West Sussex, PO19 8SQ, UK

Editorial Office
The Atrium, Southern Gate, Chichester, West Sussex, PO19 8SQ, UK

For details of our global editorial offices, customer services, and more information about Wiley products visit us at www.wiley.com.

Wiley also publishes its books in a variety of electronic formats and by print-on-demand. Some content that appears in standard print versions of this book may not be available in other formats.

Library of Congress Cataloging-in-Publication Data
Names: Murphy, David, 1970 October 27- editor. | British Psychological
  Society, issuing body.
Title: Counselling psychology : a textbook for study and practice / edited by
  David Murphy, The University of Nottingham, Nottingham, UK.
Description: Chichester, West Sussex, UK ; Hoboken, NJ : John Wiley & Sons,
  2017. | Series: BPS textbooks in psychology ; 2380 | Includes index. |
  Published on behalf by the British Psychological Society. |
Identifiers: LCCN 2017012484 (print) | LCCN 2017026725 (ebook) | ISBN
  9781119106845 (pdf) | ISBN 9781119106838 (epub) | ISBN 9781119106852
  (cloth) | ISBN 9781119106869 (pbk.)
Subjects: LCSH: Counselling psychology.
Classification: LCC BF636.6 (ebook) | LCC BF636.6 .C67584 2017 (print) | DDC
  158.3—dc23
LC record available at https://lccn.loc.gov/2017012484

Cover image: © Ralf Hiemisch/Gettyimages
Cover design by Wiley

Set in size 11/12.5 and Dante by Spi Global, Chennai, India
Printed by CPI Group (UK) Ltd, Croydon CR0 4YY

10 9 8 7 6 5 4 3 2 1

The British Psychological Society's free Research Digest email service rounds up the latest research and relates it to your syllabus in a user-friendly way. To subscribe go to http://www.researchdigest.org.uk or send a blank e-mail to subscribe-rd@lists.bps.org.uk.

For Lisa, Ellie, Megan and Joseph.

Brief Contents

About the Contributors   xix
Foreword   xxvii

PART 1   Introduction and Foundations   1

CHAPTER   1 Introduction to the Textbook on Counselling
                 Psychology   3
                 David Murphy

CHAPTER   2 A History of British Counselling Psychology   8
                 Alan Frankland

CHAPTER   3 Counselling Psychology: Assumptions, Challenges,
                 and Aspirations   22
                 Stephen Joseph

CHAPTER   4 Philosophical Issues in Counselling Psychology   36
                 Simon du Plock

PART 2   Approaches to Counselling Psychology   53

CHAPTER   5 Existential Counselling Psychology   55
                 Elaine Kasket

CHAPTER   6 Person-Centred Experiential Counselling Psychology   72
                 David Murphy

CHAPTER   7 Psychodynamic Counselling Psychology   88
                 Andrea Halewood

CHAPTER   8 Cognitive-Behavioural Counselling Psychology   104
                 Windy Dryden

CHAPTER   9 Transpersonal Counselling Psychology   120
                 John Rowan

CHAPTER 10 Pluralistic Counselling Psychology   134
                 Terry Hanley, Laura Anne Winter, John McLeod, and Mick Cooper

CHAPTER 11 Psychotherapy Integration for Counselling Psychology   150
                 Michael J. Lambert and John C. Norcross

PART 3   **Working with Client Groups**   169

CHAPTER 12   Counselling Psychology for Children and Young People   171
Terry Hanley, Jasmina Frzina, and Nafeesa Nizami

CHAPTER 13   Counselling Psychologists Working with People
with Special Needs and Disabilities   185
Anne Emerson

CHAPTER 14   Counselling Psychology for Clients with
Asperger Syndrome   200
Anja Rutten

CHAPTER 15   Counselling Psychology for Trauma in Emergency
Services Occupations   214
Noreen Tehrani

PART 4   **Socio-cultural Issues**   229

CHAPTER 16   Sexualities in Counselling Psychology   231
Eric E. Arnold and Melanie E. Brewster

CHAPTER 17   Social Class in Counselling Psychology   249
William Ming Liu and Alex J. Colbow

CHAPTER 18   Issues of Race and Ethnicity in Counselling Psychology   265
Ohemaa Nkansa-Dwamena

CHAPTER 19   Gender in Counselling Psychology   281
Meg-John Barker and Christina Richards

PART 5   **Professional Issues**   297

CHAPTER 20   Developing Ethical Awareness Whilst Training
to Be a Counselling Psychologist   299
Pam James

CHAPTER 21   Practice Ethics for Counselling Psychology   315
Dee Danchev

CHAPTER 22   The Politics of Counselling Psychology   330
Colin Feltham and Richard House

CHAPTER 23   Supervision in Counselling Psychology   346
Mary Creaner and Ladislav Timulak

CHAPTER 24   Training in Counselling Psychology   361
Ewan Gillon, Ladislav Timulak, and Mary Creaner

PART 6   **Research in Counselling Psychology**   377

CHAPTER 25   Research Ethics in Counselling Psychology   379
Dee Danchev

CHAPTER 26 An Introduction to Qualitative Research
in Counselling Psychology   394
John McLeod

CHAPTER 27 An Introduction to Quantitative Research
in Counselling Psychology   408
Duncan Cramer

CHAPTER 28 Hermeneutic Single Case Efficacy Design
for Counselling Psychology   425
Robert Elliott and Mark Widdowson

CHAPTER 29 Theory-Building Case Studies for Counselling
Psychology   439
William B. Stiles

Index   **453**

Contents

About the Contributors   xix
Foreword   xxvii

PART 1   Introduction and Foundations   1

CHAPTER 1 Introduction to the Textbook on Counselling
                Psychology   3
                David Murphy

CHAPTER 2 A History of British Counselling Psychology   8
                Alan Frankland

                Introduction   9
                A Founding Figure   10
                The Institutional History   11
                And How Has It Grown Since?   15
                And Now?   16

CHAPTER 3 Counselling Psychology: Assumptions, Challenges,
                and Aspirations   22
                Stephen Joseph

                Introduction   23
                The Assumptions of Counselling Psychology in Relation
                to the Medical Ideology   24
                Challenges to Counselling Psychology   28
                Looking to the Future of Counselling Psychology   31
                Conclusion   33

CHAPTER 4 Philosophical Issues in Counselling Psychology   36
                Simon du Plock

                A Personal Perspective   37
                So What Do We Mean When We Use the Word
                "Philosophy"?   38
                The Relationship between Philosophy and Therapy   40
                The Place of Philosophy in Counselling Psychology   41
                A Philosophically Informed Knowledge Base
                for Counselling Psychology   43
                A Philosophical Rather Than a Medical Perspective
                on What it Means to Be Well   45
                A Philosophical Perspective on Movement
                and Exercise   47
                Conclusion   49

PART 2   Approaches to Counselling Psychology   53

CHAPTER 5 Existential Counselling Psychology   55
Elaine Kasket

Introduction   56
Ontological Assumptions: Image of the Person   57
Epistemologies: The Ways of Knowing within
Existential Therapy   58
Guiding Principles: Core Theoretical Assumptions   59
Nature and Understanding of Psychological Distress   61
The Role and Place of the Therapeutic Relationship   62
Therapist, Client, and Relational Contributions
to Effective Existential Therapy   63
Contemporary Adaptations, Developments, and Extensions
of the Existential Approach   65
Future Orientations   68
Conclusion   69

CHAPTER 6 Person-Centred Experiential Counselling Psychology 72
David Murphy

Introduction   73
Ontological Assumptions: Image of the Person   74
Epistemology: Ways of Knowing   75
Guiding Principles and Core Assumptions   75
Nature and Understanding of Psychological Distress   77
The Role and Place of the Therapeutic Relationship   79
Therapist, Client, and Relational Contributions
to Effective Person-Centred Experiential Counselling
Psychology   80
Adaptations, Developments, and Extensions
of Original Approach   81
Future Orientations   84
Conclusion   84

CHAPTER 7 Psychodynamic Counselling Psychology   88
Andrea Halewood

Introduction   89
Ontological Assumptions: Image of the Person   89
Epistemologies: The Ways of Knowing   90
Guiding Principles: Core Theoretical Assumptions   91
Nature and Understanding of Psychological Distress   92
The Role and Place of the Therapeutic Relationship   93
Therapist, Client, and Relational Contributions
to Effective Psychodynamic Therapy   94
Contemporary Adaptations, Developments,
Extensions   95
Future Orientations   99
Conclusion   100

CHAPTER 8 Cognitive-Behavioural Counselling Psychology 104
Windy Dryden

Introduction 105
Ontological Assumptions: Image of the Person 105
Epistemologies: The Ways of Knowing 106
Guiding Principles: Core Theoretical Assumptions 107
Nature and Understanding of Psychological Distress 108
The Role and Place of the Therapeutic Relationship 110
Therapist, Client, and Relational Contributions to
Effective Cognitive-Behavioural Therapy 111
Contemporary Adaptations, Developments, Extensions 113
Future Orientations 116
Conclusion 117

CHAPTER 9 Transpersonal Counselling Psychology 120
John Rowan

Introduction 121
Ontological Assumptions: Image of the Person 121
Epistemologies: Ways of Knowing in Transpersonal
Counselling Psychology 122
Guiding Principles and Core Theoretical
Assumptions 123
Nature and Understanding of Psychological
Distress 124
The Role and Place of the Therapeutic Relationship 125
Therapist, Client, and Relational Contributions
to Effective Transpersonal Counselling Psychology 127
Contemporary Adaptations, Developments, Extensions 129
Future Orientations 131
Conclusion 131

CHAPTER 10 Pluralistic Counselling Psychology 134
Terry Hanley, Laura Anne Winter, John McLeod, and Mick Cooper

Introduction 135
Ontological Assumptions: Image of the Person 136
Epistemologies: Ways of Knowing 136
Guiding Principles: Core Theoretical Assumptions 137
Nature and Understanding of Psychological Distress 138
The Role and Place of the Therapeutic Relationship 139
Therapist, Client, and Relational Contributions
to Effective Pluralistic Counselling Psychology 140
Contemporary Adaptations, Developments, Extensions 141
Future Orientations 145
Conclusion 146

CHAPTER 11 Psychotherapy Integration for Counselling Psychology 150
Michael J. Lambert and John C. Norcross

Introduction 151
Varieties of Integration 152

Ontological Assumptions: Image of the Person 155
Epistemologies: Ways of Knowing 155
Guiding Principles and Core Theoretical Assumptions 156
Nature and Understanding of Psychological Distress 158
The Role and Place of the Therapeutic Relationship 159
Therapist, Client, and Relational Contributions to
Effective Counselling Psychology 161
Contemporary Adaptations, Developments, Extensions 162
Conclusions and Future Directions 164

PART 3   **Working with Client Groups**   **169**

CHAPTER 12   Counselling Psychology for Children and
Young People 171
Terry Hanley, Jasmina Frzina, and Nafeesa Nizami

Introduction 172
Background and Scope of Work for Counselling
Psychologists Working with Children and Young People 172
Guiding Principles for Practitioners 174
Conceptualizing Distress for this Group 176
Common Issues 177
Review of Evidence-based Methods 178
Legal and Ethical Issues and Relevant Frameworks
for Reference 179
Conclusion 182

CHAPTER 13   Counselling Psychologists Working with People
with Special Needs and Disabilities 185
Anne Emerson

Introduction 186
Models of Disability 187
Guiding Principles for Practitioners 187
Conceptualizing Distress 191
Counselling Psychology Approaches for SND 194
Conclusion 196

CHAPTER 14   Counselling Psychology for Clients with Asperger
Syndrome 200
Anja Rutten

Introduction 201
Autism and Asperger Syndrome 201
Diagnostic Labels 202
Considering Autism as Counselling Psychologists 202
Is Autism a Disability? 203
Person-First Language or Not? 204
Autistic People's Distress 204
Therapeutic Work with Clients with Asperger Syndrome 205
Experiences of Therapy 207
Conclusion 209

CHAPTER 15 Counselling Psychology for Trauma in Emergency
Services Occupations   214
Noreen Tehrani

Introduction   215
The Nature of Traumatic Exposure in Organizations   215
The Impact of Trauma on Emergency Service Personnel   217
High Risk Roles and Duty of Care   218
Early Trauma Interventions   220
Trauma Therapy   222
Conclusion   226

PART 4   Socio-cultural Issues   229

CHAPTER 16 Sexualities in Counselling Psychology   231
Eric E. Arnold and Melanie E. Brewster

Introduction   232
Diverse Sexual Practices   232
Unpacking the Alphabet Soup: LGB Identities   233
Identity Intersectionality in a Multicultural World   235
Minority Stress and Marginalization   238
Identity Development   238
Experiences in School and Work   239
Intimacy and Families   240
Physical Health in LGB Communities   241
Mental Health   242

CHAPTER 17 Social Class in Counselling Psychology   249
William Ming Liu and Alex J. Colbow

Introduction   250
Social Class and Psychological Distress   251
Counselling Psychology as a Transmitter of Classism   253
What Students and Clinicians Can Do   256
Upward Mobility Bias   258
Conclusion   260

CHAPTER 18 Issues of Race and Ethnicity in Counselling
Psychology   265
Ohemaa Nkansa-Dwamena

Introduction   266
Dialogue and Narrative: How Does Counselling
Think About Race and Ethnicity?   267
Privilege, Prejudice, Bias, and Race   269
Challenging Stereotypes   270
Clinical Practice: How Do We Engage with Race
and Ethnicity?   271
Working Across the Lifespan: History in Race
and Ethnicity   274
Conclusion   278

CHAPTER 19 Gender in Counselling Psychology   281
Meg-John Barker and Christina Richards

Introduction   282
Understanding Gender   283
Counselling Psychology with Cisgender Women and Men   286
Counselling Psychology with Trans Men and Women   288
Counselling Psychology with Nonbinary People   290
Conclusion   293

PART 5   Professional Issues   297

CHAPTER 20 Developing Ethical Awareness Whilst Training
to Be a Counselling Psychologist   299
Pam James

Introduction   300
Question 1: What is Working Ethically?   300
Question 2: Why is it Necessary to Have Codes
of Practice and What Are They?   302
Question 3: What is the Specific Nature of Counselling
Psychology Training?   304
Question 4: Does the Way of Working Ethically
Change from Pre- to Postqualification?   306
General Learning Points for the Development
of a Personal Ethical Awareness   312
Conclusion   312

CHAPTER 21 Practice Ethics for Counselling Psychology   315
Dee Danchev

Introduction   316
Trust   316
Codes, Principles, and Virtues   317
Dilemmas and Structures for Solving Dilemmas   318
Are There Ethical Differences Among Therapeutic
Orientations?   322
Responsibility   322
Online Counselling   323
What Are Unethical Actions?   325
Practice Supervision   325

CHAPTER 22 The Politics of Counselling Psychology   330
Colin Feltham and Richard House

Introduction   331
Politics and Counselling Psychologists   331
Alignment with Marginalized and Oppressed Groups   334
Professional Politics   336
Wider Applications of Counselling Psychology Theory,
and Crossovers   339
Conclusion   341

CHAPTER 23 Supervision in Counselling Psychology 346
Mary Creaner and Ladislav Timulak

Introduction 347
Defining Supervision in Counselling Psychology 347
The Relationship in Counselling Psychology Supervision 349
Models of Supervision in Counselling Psychology 351
Supervision Competencies 352
Supervision Training for Counselling Psychologists 353
Multicultural and Diversity Issues in Supervision 354
Posttraining Supervision in Counselling Psychology 354
Future Directions for Supervision in Counselling
Psychology 355

CHAPTER 24 Training in Counselling Psychology 361
Ewan Gillon, Ladislav Timulak, and Mary Creaner

Introduction 362
The Structure of Counselling Psychology Training
in the UK 362
The Organization of Counselling Psychology Training
in the UK 364
Training Standards in Counselling Psychology
Internationally 369
Developing the Training Agenda in the UK 372
Conclusion 373

PART 6 Research in Counselling Psychology 377

CHAPTER 25 Research Ethics in Counselling Psychology 379
Dee Danchev

Introduction 380
Historical Context 380
The Ethics of the Researcher and Their Positioning 381
The Participant's Perspective 383
The Use of Incentives 384
Informed Consent 385
Deception 387
Anonymity 387
Online Research 388
Research Method, Analysis, and Reporting Findings 388
Aftercare of Participants 389
Dissemination and the Research Afterlife 389
Researcher Self-care 390
Conclusion 391

CHAPTER 26 An Introduction to Qualitative Research
in Counselling Psychology 394
John McLeod

Introduction 395
Epistemologies: Ways of Knowing 395

Guiding Principles   397
What Questions Can Be Asked in Qualitative
Psychological Research?   398
Key Research Methods   399
Sampling   400
Approaches to Analysing Data   402
Conclusion   405

CHAPTER 27 An Introduction to Quantitative Research
in Counselling Psychology   408
Duncan Cramer

Introduction   409
Why Use Quantitative Research Methods?   409
Guiding Principles and Core Methodological
Assumptions   411
Major Types of Experimental Designs   412
Questions That Can Be Asked in Quantitative
Psychological Research   413
Key Research Methods   414
Sampling   416
Sample Research Study Example   420
Conclusion   422

CHAPTER 28 Hermeneutic Single Case Efficacy Design
for Counselling Psychology   425
Robert Elliott and Mark Widdowson

Introduction   426
Epistemologies: Ways of Knowing   426
Guiding Principles and Assumptions   428
Research Questions Addressed   429
Key Research Methods   430
Sampling   432
Approaches to Analysing Data   432
HSCED Examples   434
Conclusion: Strengths and Limitations of HSCED   435

CHAPTER 29 Theory-Building Case Studies for Counselling
Psychology   439
William B. Stiles

Introduction   440
How Theory-building Research Works   440
How to Do Theory-building Case Studies   445
Conclusion   451

Index   **453**

About the Contributors

Eric E. Arnold MEd Teachers College, Columbia University. He is currently in private practice as a licensed mental health counsellor in New York, New York. Mr Arnold's research focuses on HIV / AIDS prevention.

Meg-John Barker PhD, is a writer, therapist, and activist-academic specializing in sex, gender, and relationships. Their popular books include the (anti-)self-help relationship book *Rewriting the Rules*, *The Secrets of Enduring Love* (with Jacqui Gabb), *Queer: A Graphic History* (with Julia Scheele, Icon Books, 2016), and *Enjoy Sex, How, When and If You Want To* (with Justin Hancock, Icon Books, 2016). Meg-John is a senior lecturer in psychology at the Open University and has published many academic books and papers on topics including nonmonogamous relationships, sadomasochism, counselling, and mindfulness, as well as co-founding the journal *Psychology and Sexuality* and the activist-research organization BiUK. They were the lead author of *The Bisexuality Report*—which has informed UK policy and practice around bisexuality—and are currently co-editing a book on nonbinary gender with similar aims in that area. They are involved in running many public events on sexuality and relationships, including *Sense about Sex* and *Critical Sexology*. Meg-John is a United Kingdom Counselling and Psychotherapy (UKCP) accredited psychotherapist working with gender, sexually, and relationship diverse (GSRD) clients, and they blog about all these matters on www.rewriting-the-rules.com.

Melanie E. Brewster PhD, is a Psychology and Education Professor at Teachers College, Columbia University. Her research focuses on marginalized groups and examines how experiences of discrimination and stigma may shape the mental health of minority group members (e.g., LGBTQ individuals, atheists, people of colour). Dr Brewster also examines potential resilience factors, such as bicultural self-efficacy and cognitive flexibility, that may promote the mental health of minority individuals.

Alex J. Colbow PhD, received his doctorate from the University of Iowa's counselling psychology programme. He is completing his internship at Purdue University. His research interests include social class, gender, tele-mental health, and academic success.

Mick Cooper DPhil, is a Professor of Counselling Psychology at the University of Roehampton and a chartered counselling psychologist. Mick is author and editor of a range of texts on person-centred, existential, and relational approaches to therapy, including *Existential Therapies* (2nd ed., Sage, 2017), *Working at Relational Depth in Counselling and Psychotherapy* (with Dave Mearns, Sage, 2005), and *Pluralistic Counselling and Psychotherapy* (with John McLeod, Sage, 2011). Mick has also led a range of research studies exploring the process and outcomes of humanistic counselling with young people. Mick's latest book is *Existential Psychotherapy and Counselling: Contributions to a Pluralistic Practice* (Sage, 2015).

Duncan Cramer BSc, PhD, ABPsS, chartered psychologist, is Emeritus Professor of Psychological Health. After graduating from University College London in 1969 in psychology, he completed his PhD in 1973 with Hans Eysenck on his theory of personality at the Institute of Psychiatry in London. He then lectured for 3 years in the Psychology Department at Queen's University Belfast before coming to the Social Sciences Department at Loughborough University in 1977 and retiring in 2013. His research interests and publications include such topics as mental health, personality, personal relationships, organizational commitment, psychotherapy, and counselling. He has been a past Joint Editor (1995–2000) and Associate Editor (1993–1995, 2000–2001) of the *British Journal of Medical Psychology* and its successor *Psychology and Psychotherapy* (2002–2010) as well as an Associate Editor of the *Journal of Social and Personal Relationships* (2004–2009). His authored books include *Personality and Psychotherapy* (Open University Press, 1992), *Close Relationships* (Arnold, 1998), *Advanced Quantitative Data Analysis* (Open University Press, 2003), *Sage Dictionary of Statistics* (with Dennis Howitt, Sage, 2004), *Research Methods in Psychology* (with Dennis Howitt, 5th ed., Prentice Hall, 2017), *Understanding Statistics in Psychology* (with Dennis Howitt, 7th ed., Prentice Hall, 2018), *Introduction to SPSS in Psychology* (with Dennis Howitt, 7th ed., Prentice Hall, 2018), and *Quantitative Data Analysis with IBM SPSS Statistics 17, 18 and 19* (with Alan Bryman, Routledge, 2011). He has also co-edited *Inappropriate Relationships* (with Robin Goodwin, Lawrence Erlbaum Associates, 2002) and *Positive Psychology of Love* (with Mahzad Hojjat, Oxford University Press, 2013).

Mary Creaner DPsych, is an Assistant Professor and Research Co-ordinator with the doctorate programme in counselling psychology and Course Director of the MSc in clinical supervision, Trinity College Dublin. She is an accredited therapist and clinical supervisor with the Irish Association for Counselling and Psychotherapy (IACP), and a member of the American Psychological Association (APA). Mary is a supervision consultant and trainer to statutory and voluntary agencies and has been involved in developing and delivering a variety of postgraduate, professional development training, and adult education programmes for over 25 years. Mary has a particular interest in supervision practice, training, and research. Among her publications is the text book, *Getting the Best Out of Supervision in Counselling and Therapy* (Sage, 2014). She has been a guest editor for a special section on 'Current trends in clinical supervision' (2014) with *Counselling Psychology Quarterly* (CPQ).

Dee Danchev PhD, is a Health and Care Professions Council (HCPC) registered counselling psychologist and a British Psychological Society (BPS) chartered psychologist. She worked as a university counsellor for over 20 years, first at Keele University, then as Head of Counselling, Health Advice and Disability at the University of the Arts, London, and finally as Pastoral Advisor at Nuffield College, Oxford University. She has also had a parallel career in counsellor and counselling psychologist training at Keele University, City University, London, and Oxford University, and has served as Chair of the BPS Counselling Psychology Qualifications Board.

Windy Dryden PhD, is Emeritus Professor of Psychotherapeutic Studies at Goldsmiths University of London, and is a Fellow of the British Psychological Society. He has authored or edited more than 215 books, including the second editions of *Counselling in a Nutshell* (Sage, 2011) and *Rational Emotive Behaviour Therapy: Distinctive Features* (Routledge, 2015). In addition, he edits 20 book series in the area of counselling and psychotherapy, including the *Distinctive Features in CBT* series (Routledge) and the *Counselling in a Nutshell* series (Sage). His major interests are in rational emotive behaviour therapy and CBT; single session interventions; the interface between counselling and coaching; pluralism in counselling and psychotherapy; writing short, accessible self-help books for the general public; and demonstrating therapy live in front of an audience.

Robert Elliott PhD, is Professor of Counselling at the University of Strathclyde, and Professor Emeritus of Psychology at the University of Toledo. He has served as co-editor of the journals *Psychotherapy Research* and *Person-Centered and Experiential Psychotherapies*. He is co-author of three books, including *Facilitating Emotional Change* (with Les Greenberg and Laura Rice, Guilford Press, 1997), *Learning Emotion-Focused Therapy* (with Jeanne Watson, Rhonda Goldman, and Les Greenberg, APA, 2003), and *Research Methods in Clinical Psychology* (with Chris Barker and Nancy Pistrang, 3rd ed., APA, 2015) as well as more than 150 journal articles and book chapters. In 2008 he received the Distinguished Research Career Award from the Society for Psychotherapy Research and the Carl Rogers Award from the Division of Humanistic Psychology of the APA.

Anne Emerson PhD, worked as a speech and language therapist with children and adults with communication impairment and intellectual disability, as a teacher in further education, and advocate for families, before becoming a researcher. She is currently Associate Professor of Special and Inclusive Education at the University of Nottingham. Her research interests include augmentative and alternative communication approaches, the development of engagement, and the impact of special needs on self-esteem and behaviour. Most recent work has been with families of children with significant disabilities or health conditions, investigating resilience and coping in parents.

Colin Feltham is Emeritus Professor of Critical Counselling Studies, Sheffield Hallam University, and teaches part-time at the University of Southern Denmark. His many publications include *Counselling and Counselling Psychology: A Critical Examination* (PCCS Books, 2013), *Depressive Realism: Interdisciplinary Perspectives* (Routledge, 2017), and *The Sage Handbook of Counselling and Psychotherapy* (edited with Terry Hanley and Laura Winter, 4th ed., Sage, forthcoming). His research interests include anthropathology, depressive realism, death, and aspects of evolutionary psychology.

Alan Frankland is a Consultant Counselling Psychologist (chartered by BPS and registered by HCPC) who has been in practice and working as a trainer and writer in the field of psychotherapy since the last years of the 1970s. Formerly Head of the Division of Counselling and Psychotherapy at Nottingham Trent University, he currently works independently in Nottingham (APSI) and London (Apsilon) as a therapist and supervisor, and examines for the BPS Qualification in Counselling Psychology as well as being involved in the MSc in the Person Centred Approach with Sherwood Psychotherapy Training Institute (SPTI) in

Nottingham. In the past he was active on several committees of both BACP (elected as a Fellow mainly related to his work on accreditation) and the BPS, including time on the Society's Board of Directors (2000–2) and in chairing roles in the Division of Counselling Psychology (1997–2001). His professional experience as a therapist has mostly been in the voluntary sector and in independent practice, but he also worked in a jobshare mainly working on issues to do with counselling psychologists in a large London Trust in the NHS (2005–8). He was Stipendiary Registrar for Counselling Psychology within the BPS from 2002 to 2008.

Jasmina Frzina DCounPsych, CPsychol, is an HCPC registered counselling psychologist and Visiting Lecturer at the University of Manchester. Currently she is the Lead of Psychological Services in a private hospital. Her clinical practice has predominantly been with adults, young people, and their families in an inpatient setting. Previously she has worked in NHS Primary Care settings with couples, and individuals diagnosed with moderate and severe mental health problems. She is also the Chair of the North West BPS Branch of Division of Counselling Psychology. Her special interest is relational approaches to therapy and client's experience.

Ewan Gillon PhD, is Professor of Counselling Psychology at Glasgow Caledonian University, where he established and directed the first doctorate in counselling psychology in Scotland. He has a long-standing interest in postgraduate education and training, particularly at doctorate level, and is presently leading the development of a doctoral framework in applied psychology. Ewan has a strong commitment to counselling psychology practice and is Clinical Director of First Psychology Scotland, an independent psychology and counselling business with eight centres nationally. He has written widely on a range of issues in the counselling psychology field and comments regularly on psychological issues in the media. In addition to his work in the counselling psychology field, Ewan is a General Member of the Mental Health Tribunal (Scotland).

Andrea Halewood CPsychol, is a Senior Lecturer in Counselling Psychology at the University of the West of England (UWE) and a Visiting Lecturer at Warwick University. Prior to working at UWE, she was the Programme Co-ordinator of the Counselling Psychology Programmes at Roehampton University. She has worked in Primary Care as a practice counsellor, in Secondary Care as part of a Crisis Response Nursing Team, and at King's College Hospital as a research psychologist. She is a chartered psychologist/psychodynamic psychotherapist in private practice, and her main research and clinical interests are relational approaches to psychotherapy and critical perspectives on the medical model of mental health.

Terry Hanley PhD, CPsychol, AFBPsS, is the Programme Director for the doctorate in counselling psychology at the University of Manchester. He has a keen interest in training therapists in research skills and is a co-author of *Introducing Counselling and Psychotherapy Research* (with Clare Lennie and William West, Sage, 2013). Additionally, his own therapeutic practice and research has primarily focused around work with young people and young adults, a topic on which he is also lead editor of the text *Adolescent Counselling Psychology* (Routledge, 2013). He is a HCPC registered counselling psychologist and presently works as a therapist with the organization Freedom from Torture, providing psychological support to a football therapy project.

Richard House PhD, is a chartered psychologist, an educational consultant, and a long-time writer/campaigner on childhood issues and Steiner education. Formerly Senior Lecturer in Psychotherapy (Roehampton University) and Education Studies (Winchester) and ex-editor of *Self and Society* journal, Richard's 12 books include *Therapy Beyond Modernity* (Karnac, 2003), *Against and For CBT* (with Del Loewenthal, PCCS, 2008), *Too Much, Too Soon?—Early Learning and the Erosion of Childhood* (Hawthorn, 2011), and *Humanistic Psychology: Current Trends, Future Prospects* (with David Kalisch and Jennifer Maidman, Routledge, 2017). Research interests include critical perspectives on technology, holistic education, and postmodernity and new paradigm science.

Pam James PhD, is a chartered and HCPC registered counselling psychologist and a registered psychologist specializing in psychotherapy (senior practitioner). She was Chair of the BPS Qualification in Counselling Psychology for 6 years and after an appropriate gap is again in that role. She has also been twice Chair of the BPS Division of Counselling Psychology. She held lecturing and management posts at Liverpool John Moores University for 25 years, where she was awarded Professor of Counselling Psychology in 2000; she also worked in NHS Adult Mental Health for 10 years. Currently, she has a private practice in Southport and is Chair of the BPS Special Group for Independent Practitioners. Her doctoral thesis was in learning and she remains interested in the learning process per se, including the process of change whilst in the therapeutic relationship. She has recently co-authored *Common Presenting Issues in Psychotherapeutic Practice* (with Barbara Douglas, Sage, 2013).

Stephen Joseph PhD, is a professor in the School of Education at the University of Nottingham where he is the convenor of the counselling teaching group. He is a senior practitioner of the British Psychological Society's register of psychologists specialising in psychotherapy and an HCPC registered health and counselling psychologist. Interested in the study of human flourishing, Stephen is the editor of *Positive Psychology in Practice: Promoting human flourishing in work, health, education, and everyday life* (Wiley, 2015). His latest book is *Authentic: How to be yourself and why it matters* (Piatkus/Little, Brown, 2016).

Elaine Kasket DCPsych, C.Psychol, is an HCPC registered counselling psychologist, a private practitioner, and an academic who has written extensively about the field of counselling psychology and about her primary area of research, which is bereavement in the digital age. She is a Principal Lecturer and the Head of Programmes for Counselling Psychology at Regent's University London, where the existential-phenomenological approach is the core model taught. She is the author of *How to Become a Counselling Psychologist* (Routledge, 2017).

Michael J. Lambert, PhD, is a former Professor of Psychology, Department of Psychology and Susa Young Gates University Professor, Brigham Young University, Provo, Utah, USA.

John McLeod PhD, is Visiting Professor at the Department of Psychology, University of Oslo, and the Institute of Integrative Counselling and Psychotherapy, Dublin. He has published widely on a range of topics in counselling and psychotherapy, with a particular interest in the development of flexible, collaborative approaches to therapy that are informed by cultural awareness and relevant research evidence.

William Ming Liu PhD, is Professor of Counselling Psychology at the University of Iowa. His research interests are in social class and classism, men and masculinity, and multicultural competencies. He has been identified as one of the most frequent producers of research in the psychology of men and masculinity and most cited in multicultural competency research. He received the Emerging Leader award from the Committee on Socioeconomic Status (APA), Emerging Young Professional Award (Division 45, APA), and the Researcher of the Year Award (Division 51, APA). He is an editor of the *Handbook of Multicultural Competencies in Counseling and Psychology* (with Donald B. Pope-Davis, Hardin L. K. Coleman, and Rebecca L. Toporek, Sage, 2003), an editor of *Culturally Responsive Counseling with Asian American Men* (with Derek Kenji Iwamoto and Martin H. Chae, Routledge, 2010), the author of *Social Class and Classism in the Helping Professions: Research, Theory, and Practice* (Sage, 2011), and the editor of the *Handbook of Social Class in Counseling* (Oxford, 2013).

David Murphy PhD, CPsychol, AFBPsS, is a Full Member of the British Psychological Society Division of Counselling Psychology, a person-centred experiential psychotherapist on the BPS Register of Psychologists Specialising in Psychotherapy and has a particular interest in the field of counselling and education and the effects of psychological trauma. He is the Course Director for the Master's program in Person-Centred Experiential Counselling and Psychotherapy at the University of Nottingham, UK. He previously held the position of Honorary Psychologist in Psychotherapy at the Centre for Trauma, Resilience and Growth, Nottinghamshire Healthcare NHS Trust.

Nafeesa Nizami (Naz) BSc (Hons), MSc, Reg. MBACP (Accred) is a psychotherapist and trainer. She is currently working in the areas of couples, young peoples, parents/families, groups, bilingual and Improving Access to Psychological Therapies (IAPT) therapy for a national charity. Her clinical background includes having worked in the NHS and within Child Protection for the past 10 years. Nafeesa is currently undertaking her PhD at the University of Manchester. Her research focuses on deconstructing pre-trial therapy; exploring the relationship between law, therapy, and sexual abuse through discourse analysis. She has a keen interest in the areas of mental health, social justice, politics, ethics, philosophy, poststructuralism, colonial studies, childhood studies, and feminist theories.

Ohemaa Nkansa-Dwamena DPsych, is an HCPC registered and BPS accredited counselling psychologist. She is an Associate Fellow of the BPS and co-founder of the Black and Asian Counselling Psychologists group (under the umbrella of the Division of Counselling Psychology). Dr Nkansa-Dwamena currently holds clinical positions at the London School of Economics in the student well-being and staff counselling services. She is also a Visiting Lecturer at City University and works in private practice. She has over 10 years' experience in the mental health field, with varied work in both the public and charity sectors. This has included work with adults and children from diverse backgrounds in forensic, NHS Primary and Secondary Care settings. Her research interests include multiple identity negotiation (in relation to individuals from

Black Minority Ethnic (BME) backgrounds), culture and diversity in the therapeutic process, and sameness and difference and its implications for counselling psychology.

John C. Norcross PhD, ABPP, is Distinguished Professor of Psychology at the University of Scranton, Adjunct Professor of Psychiatry at SUNY Upstate Medical University, and a board-certified clinical psychologist. Dr Norcross has co-written or edited 20 books, including the *Handbook of Clinical Psychology* (with Gary R. VandenBos, APA, 2016), *Supervision Essentials for Integrative Psychotherapy* (with Leah M. Popple, APA, 2016), *Clinician's Guide to Evidence-Based Practice in Behavioral Health* (2008), *Psychotherapy Relationships that Work* (OUP USA, 2012), *Leaving It at the Office: Psychotherapist Self-Care* (with James D. Guy Jr, Guilford Press, 2007), and the *Handbook of Psychotherapy Integration* (with Marvin R. Goldfried, OUP USA, 2005). He has served as President of the APA Division of Clinical Psychology, the APA Division of Psychotherapy, and the Society for the Exploration of Psychotherapy Integration.

Simon du Plock PhD, is Professor and Faculty Head for Post-Qualification and Professional Doctorates at the Metanoia Institute, London, where he directs counselling psychology and psychotherapy research doctorates jointly with Middlesex University. He is a chartered counselling psychologist, an Associate Fellow of the BPS, and a founding member of the BPS Register of Psychologists Specialising in Psychotherapy. He is also a Fellow of the Royal Society for Medicine and a UKCP registered psychotherapist. He lectures internationally on aspects of existential therapy and became, in 2006, the first Western therapist to be made an Honorary Member of the East European Association for Existential Therapy, in recognition of his contribution to the development of collaboration between East and West European existential psychotherapy. He has authored over 80 book chapters and papers in peer-reviewed academic journals, and has edited the journal of the British Society for Existential Analysis since 1993.

Christina Richards BSc (Hons), MSc, DCPsych, CPsychol, MBACP (Accred.) AFBPsS is an HCPC registered doctor of counselling psychology and an Associate Fellow of the BPS. She is also an accredited psychotherapist with BACP. She represents the East Midlands to NHS England's Clinical Reference Group (CRG) on Gender Identity Services, and is one of the few psychologists recognized by HM Courts and Tribunals Service as a specialist in the field of gender dysphoria, thus allowing her to prepare medical reports for the Gender Recognition Panel.

John Rowan PhD, has been a member of the BPS Counselling Psychology Division since its inception. He was a contributor to the volume 'Counselling Psychology' (Petruska Clarkson, 1998) and has an abiding interest in the field. He is a Fellow of the BPS and a founding member of the Association of Humanistic Psychology Practitioners.

Anja Rutten MSc, has worked as an academic in counsellor training, a therapist, and manager in various settings including higher education, the private and voluntary sector, and an NHS commissioned service. She has worked extensively with autistic adults and young people and their families. As a therapist experienced in working with autistic clients, Anja has offered numerous workshops across the UK. Anja's research interests are in therapeutic experiences of clients with Asperger syndrome, and in person-centred/experiential counselling for this client group.

William B. Stiles PhD, is Professor Emeritus of Psychology, Miami University, Oxford, Ohio, USA, and Adjunct Professor of Psychology at Appalachian State University, Boone, North Carolina, USA. He has been President of Division 29 (Psychotherapy) of the APA and of the Society for Psychotherapy Research. He has served as editor of *Psychotherapy Research* and *Person-Centered and Experiential Psychotherapies*. He has published more than 300 journal articles and book chapters, most dealing with psychotherapy, verbal interaction, and research methods.

Noreen Tehrani PhD, is a chartered occupational, health, counselling, coaching and trauma psychologist. She formed her company in 1997 to assist organizations and employees to maximize their effectiveness and efficiency. Noreen has combined her commercial, psychological, and counselling knowledge and experience to develop an approach to supporting employees, which meets the needs of both the organization and the employees. For the past 10 years she has concentrated on dealing with traumatic events in organizations, and has worked with emergency services and charities to address primary and secondary traumatic exposure.

Ladislav Timulak PhD, is Associate Professor at Trinity College Dublin. He is Course Director of the Doctorate in Counselling Psychology. Ladislav (Laco for short; read Latso) is involved in the training of counselling psychologists and various psychotherapy trainings as well. Laco is both an academic and practitioner. His main research interest is psychotherapy research, particularly the development of emotion-focused therapy. He is currently developing this form of therapy for generalized anxiety disorder. He has written five books, over 60 peer-reviewed papers, and various chapters in both his native language, Slovak, and in English. His most recent book is *Transforming Emotional Pain in Psychotherapy* (Routledge, 2015).

Mark Widdowson PhD, is a teaching and supervising transactional analyst and a UKCP registered psychotherapist. He is a Senior Lecturer in Counselling and Psychotherapy at the University of Salford. Mark has specialized in investigating the effectiveness of transactional analysis, primarily using Hermeneutic Single Case Efficacy Design (HSCED). He is the author of *Transactional Analysis for Depression: A Step-By-Step Treatment Manual* (Routledge, 2015).

Laura Winter DCounPsych, chartered psychologist, is an HCPC registered counselling psychologist and lecturer based at the University of Manchester. Her research interests include social justice, and in particular the impact of economic and relational equality on well-being and education. Previous work has included exploring social justice within counselling and educational psychology, the impact of welfare reform on families, and the way in which schools are supporting emotional well-being in the context of austerity. Her clinical practice has predominantly been based within NHS Primary Care settings, working with individuals who have been diagnosed with "moderate" and "severe" "mental health problems."

Foreword
ERNESTO SPINELLI

Towards the end of one of his BBC4 television programmes, the eminent British physicist, Professor Jim Al-Khalili concluded that: "[i]n sum: all the complexity of the universe emerges from mindless simple rules rules repeated over and over again. But as powerful as this process is, it is also inherently unpredictable" (Al-Khalili, 2009).

Professor Al-Khalili's remark serves to remind us of the ever-present and irresolvable "tension" that exists at the very heart of scientific enquiry. It is that foundational tension between explanation and understanding, which is exemplified by the (seemingly interminable) debate between natural science research and human science research.

It was Wilhelm Dilthey who first coined this distinction. Its aim was to clarify "the methodological difference between explanation and understanding" (Makkreel, 1995, p. 203, quoted in Cohn, 2002, p. 114). As Rudolf Makkreel clarified:

> The natural sciences seek causal explanations of nature—connecting the discrete representations of outer experience through hypothetical generalizations. The human sciences aim at an understanding . . . that articulates the typical structures of life given in lived experience. Finding living experience to be inherently connected and meaningful.
>
> (Makkreel, 1995, p. 203, quoted in Cohn, 2002, p. 114)

Dilthey argued that these different endeavours require different methodologies and lead researchers to very different terrains. For example, the natural science stance, which remains the dominant attitude towards psychology research, examines psychological variables by: (a) reducing them to observable, quantifiable elements; (b) utilizing controlled experimental design; and (c) seeking verification via replication. The human science view, on the other hand, argues that its way of engaging in investigation highlights issues centred upon *meaning*. As such, it

> cannot be accomplished by observing the individual as a complex mechanism geared to respond to certain conditions in regular ways; rather we have to get inside the forms of life and the socially normative regularities in which the person's activity has taken shape. This requires . . . [a]n empathic and imaginative identification with the subject.
>
> (Gillett, 1995, p. 112)

In short, natural science and human science approaches cannot truly be "mixed and matched," nor can they be conjoined together. Instead, held side by side, they express a "tension of polarities" that demands acknowledgement and acceptance. This conclusion does not usually sit well with determined advocates of either side. Each, in turn, might seek to diminish and dismiss whatever might be gleaned from either explanation or understanding. As such, those psychologists who favour a human science approach tend to accuse natural science approaches of failing to address the central questions of psychology and instead of "transforming" these central questions so that they conform to the dictates of a natural science paradigm. So, for instance, "[s]adness cannot be measured—but the tears which are formed as a result of psychosomatic connections can be examined quantitatively in various ways" (Heidegger, 2001, p. 105, quoted in Cohn, 2002, p. 53). In similar fashion, psychological advocates of a natural science perspective tend to accuse human science approaches of promoting qualitative research that leads to the logical "dead end" of an ongoing relative reality where all meaning statements, views, and positions are to be treated and respected as being of equal value and merit—and, hence, lacking in any scientific worth.

Putting aside whatever is one's preferred view, we can see that the "deeper strategy" adopted by each competing stance is the same: to reduce, if not entirely remove, the existing tension via an act of exclusion. Attempts at such strategies have been, and continue to be, made throughout the whole history of psychology. One would think that, by now, we would have seen through such and agreed to a different strategy.

I state all this because, perhaps uniquely, since its origins, counselling psychology within the British Psychological Society (BPS) has both recognized and acknowledged (possibly even celebrated) the inevitable tension between explanation and understanding as expressed by the divide between natural and human sciences, or, more specifically, between quantitative and qualitative research. Indeed, BPS counselling psychology's explicit advocacy of a "scientist-practitioner model" served to highlight this recognition and to make plain that counselling psychologists were prepared to work (and play) with the potential and possibilities of that tension. And that, in doing so, BPS counselling psychology could highlight its distinctiveness in relation to other psychological categories and divisions, as well as contribute to the general advancement of psychological insight and knowledge.

This was, and remains, a grand aim that, it must be said, continually runs the risk of being forgotten, misused, and minimized when presented to those in charge of programme funding or of potential employment. Nonetheless, in many ways, counselling psychology's identity and purpose pretty much rest upon its "way of meeting" that persistent tension. Its upholding of the diversity of theories and practices within counselling psychology exemplifies an attitude that seeks to include rather than to remove, and to respect and value heterogeneity rather than insist upon uniformity of thought and practice. The challenges that counselling psychology must face in order to maintain this stance are as plentiful as they are ever-present. Yet if the distinctiveness of counselling psychology is to be retained, there is, truly, nothing to be done other than to face such tensions and, perhaps, in doing so, thrive through them.

Happily, texts such as this one which you hold in your hands (in some form or other) do much to remind us of what counselling psychology seeks to express and provide, and why we might want to continue to cherish its aims and ambitions as well as make them our own. Its broad aim is to infuse—or perhaps rekindle—that sense of excitement, possibility, and commitment that counselling psychology can generate. Like all good texts, it invites us to return to it again and again so that, each time we might emerge with more adequate explanations and deeper understanding.

REFERENCES

Al-Khalili, J. (2009). *The secret life of chaos*. Documentary film directed by N. Stacey and produced by Furnace Ltd for BBC Television.

Cohn, H. W. (2002). *Heidegger and the roots of existential therapy*. London: Continuum.

Gillett, G. (1995). The philosophical foundations of qualitative psychology, *The Psychologist*, *8* (3), 111–114.

Heidegger, M. (2001). *Zollikon seminars: Protocols-conversations-letters*. Evanston, IL: Northwestern University Press.

Makkreel, R. A. (1995). *The Cambridge dictionary of philosophy* (R. Audi, Ed.). Cambridge: Cambridge University Press.

NOTE

Professor Ernesto Spinelli is a Fellow of the BPS and in 2000 was awarded the BPS Division of Counselling Psychology Award for Outstanding Contributions to the Advancement of the Profession. It was his honour to serve as Chair of that same Division between 1996 and 1999. His most recent text, *Practising Existential Therapy: The Relational World*, 2nd edition (Sage, 2015), has been widely praised as a major contribution to the advancement of existential theory and practice.

Counselling Psychology

1 Introduction to the Textbook on Counselling Psychology

DAVID MURPHY

LEARNING OUTCOMES

BY THE END OF THIS CHAPTER YOU SHOULD BE ABLE TO ANSWER THE FOLLOWING KEY QUESTIONS:

1. What is counselling psychology?
2. What are the main approaches to counselling psychology?
3. What key issues does counselling psychology engage with in practice?

This textbook is for anyone with an interest in counselling psychology. When I was an undergraduate psychology student I learned about the different divisions in the British Psychological Society (BPS) and the important differences in the work that people do within different psychologist roles. I came to realize that my passion was in psychotherapy. This interest in psychotherapy had started prior to being an undergraduate and was stimulated by a reading of both Freud's *Interpretation of Dreams* and Carl Rogers's *On Becoming a Person*. These two books had a profound impact on me, although each in quite different

Counselling Psychology: A Textbook for Study and Practice, First Edition. Edited by David Murphy.
© 2017 John Wiley & Sons Ltd. Published 2017 by John Wiley & Sons Ltd.

4 INTRODUCTION AND FOUNDATIONS

ways. It was the practice of psychotherapy, and the humanistic psychology of Carl Rogers, which seemed to call me closer and provided the motivation to discover more. I realized that counselling psychology was where I needed to be. This journey to counselling psychology began in the early 1990s and it's very satisfying to have the chance to contribute this book to the professional field of counselling psychology.

After undergraduate studies I took the independent route to chartered psychologist status, achieving full membership of the Division of Counselling Psychology. This involved completing the BPS Qualification in Counselling Psychology. In completing this qualification I elected to commit to an extensive training in person-centred therapy, and undertook further training to become a person-centred group facilitator. I also trained in interpersonal psychotherapy (IPT) and completed supervision training, and developed a personal interest in the experiential approaches to education and psychotherapy. The journey was long, hard, and expensive. So why am I telling you this? It's because I hope that if you are reading this and are yet to make the journey towards qualification as a counselling psychologist, you will be able to use the book to help and accompany you through your own journey. Counselling psychology is a profession that can be rich in the satisfaction it brings and it is a great privilege to share in the lives of our clients; I hope that this book might offer some companionship to you in your training.

The aim of this book is to provide a textbook that can be a companion to studying counselling psychology at both undergraduate and postgraduate levels. I hope you will find many valuable insights if you are a qualified practitioner too. Counselling psychology in the UK is a lively and thriving profession. It is also, in my experience, an inclusive professional group and I hope that this book will speak to everyone with an interest in counselling psychology. Together with my contributing authors we have created an engaging text that is both personal and academically rigorous in an accessible format.

Inclusion is an important feature of the book. The origins of counselling psychology lie firmly in the field of humanistic psychology, which considers the therapeutic relationship as central. Our success in therapy is reliant on the relationships we build with our clients. Within these relationships counselling psychologists are able to draw on their skills and high level of competency and creativity to find the best ways to support their clients towards personal change and growth. This relationship paradigm must always be identified as a radical alternative from and reaction to the pernicious effects of the medical model ideology. The medical model ideology is all too dominant in the field of professional psychology. Counselling psychology must actively work against the medical model ideology. Counselling psychology's potential for shaping the wider field of applied psychology comes with a great deal of responsibility. It is the task of counselling psychology, in my view, to humanize the psychological professions.

There are a number of ways in which counselling psychology can take up this responsibility. The key activity of counselling psychology is psychotherapy. Psychotherapy has to be protected as something that exists beyond being a "health profession." More radical counselling psychologists, for example, might see themselves less as "health practitioners" and instead see psychotherapy as something that cannot be confined to the field of "health care." Health care, at least in the field of mental health care, is not concerned with human growth and development. It is concerned with repair, with restoration, fixing, and addressing deficits in functioning. To many this might sound perfectly acceptable. For counselling psychology this is not satisfactory. It is restrictive to put such limits around our human potential, and to focus only on deficits, problems, and fixing things does just this. Instead counselling psychology is based on the growth paradigm rather than a deficit paradigm. Whilst existing mental health services are based on the deficit paradigm, counselling psychologists are concerned with growth, with reaching human potential with full functioning, and thereby offer a radical alternative to any other application of psychology.

There are, however, some challenges facing counselling psychology. We need to address the issue of eclecticism and pluralism. A varied and evolving counselling psychology field is essential to our ongoing growth. The creative tensions that exist within our community can and do give rise to new developments and exciting ways forward. What we must be cautious about, however, is imposing eclecticism and pluralism onto the field rather than seeing them as emergent from the field. To configure the field of counselling psychology by supposing that eclecticism and pluralism are right for everyone is to create a new dogma. To impose eclecticism and pluralism upon all practitioners forces a situation where everyone must be all things to all people. In this book a wide range of approaches to counselling psychology, of issues and contexts, are explored as well as a range of research approaches presented. This is because counselling psychology is inherently pluralistic in the sense that it offers a broad range of ways of practising. But this is different to saying that everyone needs to be "a bit of everything" themselves. This book intends to convey the richness in how diverse our approaches are from one another. It intentionally does not state or support the notion that every counselling psychologist must/should/ought be doing everything.

Individual counselling psychologists can retain their right to professional self-determination and to practise an approach to psychotherapy to which they are best suited. Counselling psychology has nothing to fear from this. Perhaps it is the existential, person-centred experiential and psychodynamic practitioners who are most likely to remain true to their original models. Integrative, pluralistic and cognitive-behavioural therapists already have practice methods that are integrative. The integrative and pluralistic approaches will readily adapt therapy to what the therapist thinks will be most effective for the client depending on the therapist's understanding of the client's problems. There is a risk, though, of the practitioners of those approaches moving towards the medical model ideology without having realized it (see Chapter 3).

This book is organized into six parts containing 29 chapters. The parts provide a map to help guide readers through the book. All chapters have been contributed by leading figures with years of experience in the field of counselling psychology practice, research, and education.

Part 1 focuses on introducing and providing an overview of the foundations of counselling psychology. To outline these chapters in more detail, we begin by setting counselling psychology in context historically, paradigmatically, and philosophically with chapters from Frankland (Chapter 2), Joseph (Chapter 3), and du Plock (Chapter 4), respectively.

Then, in Part 2, there is a series of chapters that each considers a different therapeutic approach counselling psychologists might practice. These include existential counselling psychology in Chapter 5 (Kasket). Chapter 6 is on person-centred experiential (Murphy), Chapter 7 is on the psychodynamic (Halewood), and Chapter 8 is on the transpersonal (Rowan) approach. Chapter 9 introduces cognitive-behavioural (Dryden), and Chapter 10 pluralistic (Hanley, Winter, McLeod, and Cooper), and finally Chapter 11 is on integrative counselling psychology (Lambert and Norcross). Each of these chapters offers an overview of the philosophical underpinnings, the theory of distress, and the theory of therapy in counselling psychology, and offers a case example showing how the approach can be practised.

In Part 3 you will find chapters on client groups. Chapter 12 is where Hanley, Frizina, and Nizami focus on working with children and young people. Next in Chapter 13 Emerson offers a chapter on working with people with special needs and disabilities. Then, in Chapter 14, Rutten provides a chapter for counselling psychologists working with people with Asperger syndrome. Trauma is increasingly recognized in the emergency services and Tehrani covers working with this client group in a chapter reporting on her trauma support programme with emergency service personnel (Chapter 15).

This is followed by Part 4 containing chapters on the socio-cultural issues associated with counselling psychology. Arnold and Brewster consider sexualities in Chapter 16, and in Chapter 17, Liu and Colbow consider social class. In Chapter 18 Nkansa-Dwamena considers issues of race and ethnicity, and in Chapter 19 Barker and Richards consider issues of gender in counselling psychology. Each of these issues warrants a chapter in its own right; however, counselling psychologists also need to develop a complex and sophisticated understanding of how issues of sexuality, social class, race and ethnicity, and gender all intersect. Consequently, throughout this section an intersectional approach is taken.

Part 5 considers professional issues, and in Chapter 20 James focuses on the development of a personal ethics during training, whilst in Chapter 21 Danchev looks at developing a practice ethics to support decision making. In Chapter 22 Feltham and House explore the issues of power and politics as they relate to counselling psychology. Maintaining an awareness of the process of our work with clients is important, and Creaner and Timulak consider supervision for counselling psychologists in Chapter 23, and Gillon, Timulak, and Creaner focus on training counselling psychologists in Chapter 24. Counselling psychologists are also trained as researchers and are able to investigate the process of how therapy works as well as how well therapy works.

Finally, Part 6 looks at research in counselling psychology. In Chapter 25 Danchev considers research ethics. In Chapter 26 McLeod outlines qualitative research approaches, followed by Chapter 27, where Cramer gives an overview of quantitative approaches. The final two chapters focus on case study research. In Chapter 28 Elliott and Widdowson present the Hermeneutic Single Case

Efficacy Design approach, and this is followed by Chapter 29 in which Stiles presents the Theory Building Case Study method.

I hope you will find that the chapters in this book offer you an excellent resource, whether as students completing modules on undergraduate programmes, or graduates completing professional counselling psychology training. I'm sure there will be something too for those completing doctoral degrees and wanting to explore the full range of issues associated with counselling psychology, or practitioners conducting research into their counselling psychology practice.

Counselling Psychology

ALAN FRANKLAND

CHAPTER OUTLINE

INTRODUCTION 9

A FOUNDING FIGURE 10

THE INSTITUTIONAL HISTORY 11

AND HOW HAS IT GROWN SINCE? 15

AND NOW? 16

LEARNING OUTCOMES

BY THE END OF THIS CHAPTER YOU SHOULD BE ABLE TO ANSWER THE FOLLOWING KEY QUESTIONS:

1. What has been accepted as the major model or "grand theory" of the history of counselling psychology and how may it be questioned?

2. In what ways might Carl Rogers' biography be seen to illustrate a more organic "maelstrom" approach to this history?

3. What has been the course of development of counselling psychology in the UK both within the British Psychological Society (BPS) and in other spheres such as the universities, publishing and so on?

Counselling Psychology: A Textbook for Study and Practice, First Edition. Edited by David Murphy.
© 2017 John Wiley & Sons Ltd. Published 2017 by John Wiley & Sons Ltd.

INTRODUCTION

Show your workings: Although my first degree included some historical studies, I avoided the history of psychology module (taking the perhaps ignorant view that Boring [Boring, 1950] was boring) and I do not see myself in any sense as a historian. I came to this chapter with the apparently straightforward intention of simply telling the story of the development of counselling psychology as I saw it, drawing on an overview of events and pre-existing accounts and only incidentally on my experience as a participant in some of the processes. As a psychologist I am, of course, aware that there is no such thing as an objective account: there is bound to be some interaction between the perceiver and what is perceived, but I originally thought the task required me to minimize these effects and to attempt to be a chronicler (in the way of early writers, sometimes described as traditional narrative historians). In the event I discovered that is not what I wanted to do, nor was really capable of. As I thought and wrote about what I have been part of for something more than 40 years I realized my interest was not just to chronicle, but to comment, to identify patterns and trends where I saw them and sometimes to disagree with the accepted view of how this all came about. Although this still leaves me in the narrative approach to history I understand that this is what historiographers call the modern narrative style.

Almost from the time I was invited to contribute this chapter I had an idea that the history of counselling psychology in the UK had been somewhat unhelpfully presented to date as the coming together (through combat or wedlock) of two *separate* forces—the steady beat of modernist empirical psychology and the more romantic philosophical phenomenological and experiential forces that underlay the new psychotherapies of the 1960s and beyond. When Ray Woolfe wrote what he called the institutional history of counselling psychology (Woolfe, 1996), giving an account of the formal development and legitimization of counselling psychology within the British Psychological Society (BPS), that was his reading of the intellectual and practical vectors that make up the discipline and it has come to be the accepted truth, the dominant grand narrative about our origins. I am not sure it's the most helpful way to see it and am offering a different, somewhat less polarized (and hence less grand?) narrative here.

Because of my discomfort with the view of separate forces coming together I initially thought to completely break away from the institutional history (except for a brief paragraph or two inserted to give a sense of the key points in time) and concentrate on the argument that counselling psychology as much as any other branch of psychology, whether academic and conceptual or "applied"/ professional, comes out of a maelstrom of ideas and practices which is always much more organic and indeterminate than the imagery of just two competing forces suggests. It seemed to me impossible to imagine a psychology that is not always and inevitably both conceptual/abstract and practical, both steadily experimental and speculative, both scientific and imaginative; for where do testable hypotheses come from if there is no speculation and how do we extend our science and realize its technical and humane implications without imagination?

I went over a number of ways to demonstrate the essential reality of the organic maelstrom, thinking about the early studies of perception, or the later development of behaviourism and some aspects of modern neuropsychology or how this thesis might be illustrated through the biographies of a number of innovatory psychologists, but quickly came to realize that each of such themes would be a more major project than is required here. And yet . . . the biographical idea might offer a way forward and, linked with some observation of the institutional history and of the conceptual and practical developments that have been going on throughout my working life, it might provide a structure for this chapter.

A FOUNDING FIGURE

Despite my marked distaste for hero worship and hagiography, I do not doubt that Carl Rogers is one of the great figures of 20th century psychology and it happens that his personal biography well illustrates the notion that ideas in our discipline arise from an organic whole not a mechanistic ding-dong between competing elements. I am struck by how often professional psychologists (a good few even within counselling psychology) are unaware of the importance and true influence of Rogers' contributions to our discipline (not least because his work is sometimes airbrushed out of DPsych training programmes). Moreover, they seem to be unaware that his understandings of psychotherapeutic process arise from a complex whole which is *at one and the same time* scientific and imaginative, empirical and humanistic, because these are not exclusive constructs. Many think of Rogers just as a woolly idealist and a dreamer whose speculations about helping relationships somehow came up with potentially useful ideas about the core conditions necessary in a relationship that are likely to promote therapeutic change. Whilst there was undoubtedly some idealism and imagination and much conviction and energy expended on relating and promoting relationship as an essential for change towards a more humane society, there is so much more to it/him than this dismissive (not to say ignorant) account would suggest.

Carl Rogers was born in 1902 and raised (in his own words) in a "home marked by close family ties (and) a strict . . . religious and ethical atmosphere" (Rogers, 1961). From 1914 the family lived on a farm because of Rogers' father's concern to keep his children from what he considered to be undesirable aspects of suburban life and because of his interest in scientific agriculture. Perhaps for want of other activities the young Rogers ploughed his way through texts on this topic, learning about scientific method and experimentation as well as rearing livestock himself from an early age and realizing "some of the joys and frustrations of the scientist as he tries to observe nature" entailed in becoming an authority on local night-flying moths (Rogers, 1961, cited in Kirschenbaum & Henderson, 1992, p. 8). As a young adult Rogers set out, naturally enough with such a background, to study agronomy, but then (perhaps equally unsur-prisingly given the importance of faith in this family's life) came to the view that he had a vocation for the ministry. In the end neither path would fulfil his potential. In 1922 he had experiences of meeting what to him seemed like good people but with profoundly different views than those he had been raised with and he experienced this as leading him away from the orthodoxy of his parents. Although he continued towards ministry for a couple more years he also took more and more courses in psychology and moved towards a career in child guid-ance, which eventually led to his career as a psychologist, both as a practitioner and academic. Although something of an outsider in the discipline for some years (perhaps because he was more interested in people than rats, and because his studies included naturalistic observation as much as experimentation and statistical manipulation) he also became part of the psychological mainstream, the first President of the American Academy of Psychotherapists, later also President of the American Psychological Association (APA). He received the APA Distinguished Scientific Contribution Award the first year it was given as well as becoming, towards the end of his career, the first person to also receive the APA Distinguished Professional Contribution Award (Kirshenbaum & Henderson, 1992).

Rogers' ideas about the helping relationship and his exploration of therapy and later of what became known as "encounter groups" was certainly imagina-tive and innovative but it was also scientific and at times painstaking (e.g., he pioneered the detailed analysis of taped recordings of real therapeutic encoun-ters). His intellectual biography illustrates pretty well the point I am trying to make about psychology (and in this case what may be key aspects of counsel-ling psychology), arising not from separate elements being melded together but rather from a more organic whole.

Although I have to admit that Rogers himself sometimes wrote about his intellectual life as a struggle between competing elements, and, writing as his biographer, Howard Kirschenbaum identifies Rogers' capacity as a syn-thesizer as a key strength (Kirschenbaum, 2007), I think it more productive to see his life and that of our discipline without necessarily falling into this bipolar frame of reference. Rogers' life and intellectual development became mirrored in so many aspects of his work, not so much a matter of separate entities in collision but organic processes in motion as illustrated in central constructs like experience/experiencing as an alternative to the construct of seeing cognition and affect as separate often opposed elements of our internal world—or the emphasis on growth and actualization (becoming), inherently organic constructs.

THE INSTITUTIONAL HISTORY

Nevertheless it is, as we have seen, the bipolar view that predominates in the currently more widely accepted "grand" narrative about counselling psychol-ogy in the UK. This is evident when it is suggested that, some 35 years ago, practitioners of counselling and psychotherapy with initial qualifications in psychology but primarily basing their work on humanistic values and concern for their clients as individuals, as people, began to make an attempt to reconcile their work with formal psychology (as exemplified in the UK by the BPS). Taken to represent both professional standing and a positivist/modernist/scientific view of the discipline—this ongoing attempt it is claimed has given us the new (sub)discipline and practice of counselling psychology. This view of our history does seem to be enshrined in BPS documentation about counselling psychology, which quite frequently represents the emergent (sub)discipline as bringing together separate elements. For example, the Guidelines for Professional Practice in Counselling Psychology reflect the notion of a wedding in suggesting that the discipline attempts to "develop models of practice and research which marry the scientific demand for rigorous empirical enquiry with a firm value base" (BPS, 2005, p. 1) (with value base in this instance arguably being a kind of short-hand for matters that are not established by empirical enquiry!).

As already mentioned, in his early, influential, and formative text on the discipline, Woolfe (1996) set out what he described as the "institutional history" of counselling psychology in the UK, which may have been responsible for the power of this narrative in our discipline (although the rest of his chapter on our origins takes a broader perspective and is much more nuanced). In the same vein in a chapter published in 2003 (Frankland, 2003, p. 669) I too wrote of the sense that "as Counselling Psychologists we have already forged quite a robust way of holding together some quite traditional aspects of scientific psychology and a more personal and radical sense of the importance of feelings and experience." Ramsey-Wade in a more recent article (2014) refers back to Woolfe's institutional history too, which suggests that this reading of our origins with its bipolar tendency has become accepted as the essential truth that somehow explains counselling psychology today.

Whilst clearly preferring an organic model it is nonetheless apparent to me that we do need an "institutional history" looking at the development of the discipline and the organizational framework in which it took place but what I shall present here is perhaps differently framed from Woolfe's account.

The birth date of counselling psychology within the profession of psychology in the UK is widely accepted as being in 1982 when the BPS agreed to establish a Counselling Psychology Section. But what came before at an institutional/organizational level?

There was already within the Society a quite well-established Psychotherapy Section, largely meeting the interests and needs of clinical psychologists who had undergone and practised various (mostly psychodynamic) psychotherapies in both NHS and independent settings. The need for a separate Counselling Psychology Section stemmed, to a great extent, from those people who were not clinical psychologists but who experienced themselves as having an identity as psychologists or an allegiance to psychology (as the subject of their academic qualifications at undergraduate level at least) whilst having practice experiences and qualifications in counselling, rehabilitation, and related fields both in and on the edge of the NHS, and outside the NHS in student services, early employee assistance programmes, and welfare at work schemes, as well as aspects of guidance and counselling in the voluntary sector and independent practice. Many of the early movers in the field were also working in higher education as academics, trainers, and counsellors. Some of these people had been active through the latter part of the 1970s in meetings and publications linked with the Psychology and Psychotherapy Association, an organization with its roots in both academic and clinical psychology founded by those who wanted to "create a new vision of Psychology one which places the person—personal experience, personal relationships and personal action—at the centre of its concern" (Parry, 1982, p. 3). Others might have seen themselves as part of the antipsychiatry movement or were linked with the Association of Humanistic Psychology or with the journal *Self and Society* (the *European Journal of Humanistic Psychology*). Still others (although there would have been significant overlaps) probably found their professional identity as counsellors and were active in BAC—the British Association for Counselling. There would then have been some fairly radical perspectives around this initial step (both politically and in terms of humanistic models and values) as well as some who we might describe as more rebellious than radical—people who were unwilling to accept the status quo of professional organization and identity even though their practice and employment might in other ways have been fairly mainstream.

Whatever their antecedents, through the 1980s the initial grouping around/within the Counselling Psychology Section began to really cohere and to push for something more—the probable intention of at least some in the Section right from the start. It was the wish of many members that the Section should not just exist as a meeting place or an interest group but should begin formally to define a professional identity. This development was not unproblematic within the BPS and met with some opposition both from the administration of the Society and some within clinical psychology and the Psychotherapy Section. The angst and arguments stemmed largely from the difficulties the new body appeared to have in defining a field of interest and activity that was clear of the interests and influences of the existing groups—both professionally and practically. Eventually a separate enough field of interest was identified (although it is arguable that some of this was smoke and mirrors) and a core of Section members began to work towards an even stronger identity for counselling psychology. Never an unopposed journey because of anxieties in various parts of the Society about too broad a definition of psychology, it has to be said there were many clinical psychologists and members of the Psychotherapy Section and others in the wider Society who were actively supportive of the growing desire in counselling psychology not only to develop the more radical human science perspectives but also a potential professional status.

The formal structures required by the Society for such developments were gradually approved so that by 1989 the Society had agreed that the Section could become a Special Group that acknowledged the desire and began to provide the means for establishing a core of counselling psychologist members who were eligible for registration by the Society as chartered psychologists, which would enable the establishment of a Division of Counselling Psychology (a Division being that subset of the Society representing not just an interest in a particular area of the discipline, but recognizing a professional practitioner identity). With the existence of the Special Group, the Society established a Diploma in Counselling Psychology of an equivalent standard to that required for entrance to other Divisions so that by 1994 with a number of members having achieved the Diploma (or, for most of us, a Statement of Equivalence to the Diploma) the Division of Counselling Psychology was established.

However, it would be a mistake to see UK counselling psychology as only developing within one institution—the BPS. Similar disciplines and professional groups have been active throughout the world (particularly in the USA) for a considerable period (about 30 years) before there was much movement on this front in the UK (Munley et al., 2004). Although it can be argued that the roots of North American "counseling psychology" were originally as much in the traditions of educational and child guidance (Rogers' initial work setting) as in psychotherapeutic counselling (which was the prime influence in the UK), the existence of the discipline and practice within institutions elsewhere clearly stimulated developments here, and a number of figures who helped develop both counselling and counselling psychology in the UK had at least part of their education and training in North America.

Although it may be less obvious, because of language differences and other cultural factors, the development of counselling psychology in the UK has probably also been influenced from quite early days by European practitioners and writers, who found that their way of thinking and qualifications (although generally translated as "clinical" psychology) had more in common with UK counselling psychology than with BPS-recognized clinical psychology in the UK. It is arguable that then, as now, what passes for clinical psychology training in the UK is actually training for a particular kind of psychological practice in the NHS and that it might be more accurate to call such practitioners "NHS psychologists" rather than clinical psychologists. So strongly under the influence of a medical model of psychological pathology and well-being (see Chapter 3, this volume) such psychology is not often associated with phenomenological and existential ideas, which alongside psychodynamic and existential concepts have been quite strongly represented in "clinical" psychology training in Continental Europe.

It is also the case that from the late 1980s outside the Society, but influenced by developments there, and often stimulated by the same people, the university sector was gradually putting together training opportunities for this developing field. For example, the doctorate programme at Surrey University, the first full practitioner doctorate in counselling psychology, was established by the latter part of the 1990s and this followed a number of postgraduate diploma and Master's programmes in the university sector (e.g., at City University) designed to provide training in this area and to fulfil, in part or as a whole, the requirements that were being developed by the BPS. It is probably through the universities that the presence of US and continental psychologists had its most direct influence on the developing discipline. Many of the departments that took up early training in this area had (and still have) staff from North America and Continental Europe who contributed significantly to these programmes.

It seems that a similar dynamic to that between the universities and the growing profession was taking place with regard to journals and publishing. Whilst the newsletters and reviews from the developing BPS bodies gradually evolved into the Division's *Counselling Psychology Review* (by 1989), outside the Society the *Counselling Psychology Quarterly* was developed as an international journal independent of BPS and first appeared in 1988. By 1996 the field was sufficiently established for the first major textbook *The Handbook of Counselling Psychology* (1996) to appear.

Summary: from the late 1970s to the early 1990s the UK saw the gradual establishment of counselling psychology as a formal professional identity within the BPS, with training routes being established by the Society and in the wider higher education context, and the establishment of new journals and hence the beginnings of a literature of its own. Although this development has often been characterized as a marriage between scientific and humanistic elements in psychology and psychotherapy this development was never really a case of one or the other but was an organic development from the fertile growth of all aspects of postwar psychology.

AND HOW HAS IT GROWN SINCE?

A quick review of the early BPS journals shows some of the early topics of discussion. Although a number of early colleagues in BPS counselling psychology whose main interest was not strictly psychotherapy (but included work in rehabilitation, the growth movement, aspects of management, and consulting inter alia), these topics are not strongly featured even in the early journals. It is evident that UK counselling psychology quite quickly settled into what it is today—fairly tightly focused on psychotherapy, even if that is broadly defined. In the early journals there are a variety of studies of the therapeutic work individual counselling psychologists were doing, and areas of specialized interest and research (evident in *CPR* up to this day) but the journals from this period (and an occasional papers volume published as late as 1996) still suggest a very young body seeking its identity with discussions of how counselling psychology is (and is not) different from other parts of the psychotherapeutic helping professions and whether or not we can demonstrate the effectiveness of therapy. This may not have been exclusively the result of the "youth" of counselling psychology, it may also be an effect of the pressure being felt in all the helping professions by the (Conservative) government's insistence on seeking to introduce into this field occupational standards based on competences (largely described in behavioural terms), which many of us suspected were intended to curb the liberal professions every bit as much as they were to protect the public by ensuring an adequately trained and qualified workforce, which was their stated purpose.

As we moved towards the later 1990s and into the first years of the 21st century the journals, and my memory (I was Chair of the Division during this period) suggest that issues about identity were still recurrent and hotly debated, but these were often part of issues about equality (in job opportunities and pay) and about training and development. Again this would have been partly stimulated by factors specific to counselling psychology and partly to wider debates such as the growing discourse about statutory registration of the psychotherapy professions that was getting underway at this time. It was also evident by this time, following an extensive membership survey that Robert Bor carried out for the Division in 1998 that nearly half of the counselling psychologists who were members of BPS were employed by or derived a significant part of their income from NHS work. This potentially expanded the debate amongst counselling psychologists about models of working, training, and readiness to practice, particularly in statutory and NHS settings. In informal discussions this still comes up (as the "mini-clini" issue) about the direction of the Division and of counselling psychology training. Some, claiming to be "realists" arguing that if NHS practice is where most counselling psychologists are heading then (like clinical psychology before us) training and the thrust of the Division's work in the BPS and nationally must be to develop (and protect) workers in such roles. Others (sometimes cast as mere traditionalists or "idealists") continue to argue for a more independent sense of the work and the way it is ethically, politically, and conceptually framed to maintain a radical and questioning edge particularly about the medical model and the potentially mechanistic manualization of "therapy." If we are to make a real and continuing contribution to the people we see then we need to ensure that we stay true to our more radical origins, to stay more on the edge as a critical force and stimulant for change. The fact is that the NHS has been buying in counselling psychologists from our earliest days because we provide something different, if we try too hard and allow ourselves to become mini-clinis we lose not only our edge but our USP.

AND NOW?

My impression is that these latter themes and struggles will keep going in some form. For many counselling psychologists coming into training the predominant interest has increasingly (but far from exclusively) become the acquisition of skills that will enable them to gain employment and work effectively in statutory and organizational settings, particularly the NHS. Of course there are NHS counselling psychologists seeking a full career and development in that context, but it is worth noting that many counselling psychologists who work in NHS settings also maintain practice interests in nonstatutory and independent settings, and many still see their NHS work as a stepping stone towards independent practice. Of course the current developments in the internal narrative of counselling psychology are strongly influenced by employment opportunities, themselves strongly influenced by the government initiative on Improving Access to Psychological Therapies (formally inaugurated in October 2007), which has seen, nationally, a swing towards models of therapy that appear to have produced validated clinical outcomes (based on Randomized Clinical Trials [RCTs]) and has pushed (often rather limited visions of) cognitive-behavioural therapy (CBT) up the counselling psychology agenda. Since it is possible to see CBT, particularly in its early incarnations, as representing a rather limited, modernist, and mechanistic therapeutic technology, this has produced tensions for many counselling psychologists committed to relational and phenomenological ways of working. It is interesting that growing as we do from the same soil the debates and conferences of the Division have almost simultaneously thrown up two interwoven strands. One is a strong pluralistic discourse based on both critical science perspectives that question the predominance of RCT as the sole evidential base for complex relational activities like psychological therapies and a humanistic concern that the ordinary humanity in relationships between help seekers and providers does not get lost in standardized and manualized brief work. Whilst there is good evidence that CBT and other brief interventions can be helpful to some clients, especially when contained in a strong relational frame—such interventions undoubtedly miss others who need more discursive and phenomenological therapy to promote sustained change, who will gain access to a psychological therapy only to discover that it is too restricted to work for them.

If the organic model of the growth and development of counselling psychology that I have proposed is a more helpful narrative than the bipolar models of marriage or combat, then I think it would predict the continuation of the current move towards a postmodern pluralistic discourse for counselling psychology, although we clearly need to take care that this pluralism is not just a disguise for a rather weak and potentially undermining eclecticism (see Chapter 3 for the reasons that such pluralism/eclecticism might prove problematic). The organic perspective simultaneously draws from the whole of the pool neither excluding nor privileging science or craft, technology, or relational inspiration, but allowing each practitioner to draw on what is right for them and their clients in the particular circumstances and environments in which they are engaged (this position is in fact the very situation that Rogers (1957) outlined in his integrative statement on the necessary and sufficient conditions for therapeutic change). It removes the need to argue that one approach is right and accepts that different clients in different situations will call for different interventions from different therapists.

Sitting quite comfortably within this pluralistic discourse, most if not all those who identify as counselling psychologists today would, I think, see what they do as having at its core a relational, nondoctrinaire, flexible way of working that respects the uniqueness of each of the people they are working with, drawing insights from several theoretical models of psychotherapeutic processes and change, and having respect for what a broad range of empirical evidence shows. Although there are still signs from time to time within counselling psychology of some acerbic antipathy between schools and models, and concern that conceptual rigour may be lost in a loose eclecticism, I think generally we have moved beyond factionalism based on theoretical models towards an acceptance that a model is just a model and the factors that guide our choices as practitioners should probably owe more to core values that underpin counselling psychology and a framework for good practice than the claims of a particular school of thought.

This mutual acceptance looked shaky for a while, with the NHS Improving Access to Psychological Therapies (IAPT) agenda seeming to dominate other views, allowing early (possibly rather brash and mechanistic) versions of CBT to dominate the training and best-practice agendas. However as CBT gets both more sophisticated and pays more attention to the relational aspects that were always present in its cognitive roots, it becomes once again a genuinely therapeutic approach. Third- and fourth-wave CBT (with developments into mindfulness and branches such as acceptance and commitment therapy) move us away from most mechanistic and authoritarian practice and a bald acceptance of diagnostics and the medical model, towards practice that may be structured and sometimes authoritative but sits more comfortably within the more phenomenological flow of counselling psychology.

I hope the discipline will not become afraid of controversy and debating difference but as a practitioner whose conceptual map is quite strongly influenced by humanistic models and in particular by aspects of the person-centred approach (PCA), I am more comfortable when I do not have to constantly justify a relational stance and the merits and validity of a phenomenological, non-diagnostic more nondirective approach. In the past counselling psychologists from a PCA perspective have found themselves misunderstood (or criticized from a position of ignorance) by colleagues seeking to create the ascendancy of CBT or maintain that of psychodynamic models. One aspect of such debates (within therapy as a whole) has been some sharpening of how PCA presents itself as credible and evidential although, as suggested earlier, there is still, in some quarters, a shocking ignorance of PCA concepts, and the position is often criticized on the basis of misrepresentations and oversimplifications rather than on the breadth and depth of the conceptual apparatus and evidence that it offers. As the NHS espouses more patient-centred models of care and recovery, and especially with the development of particular focused therapies and techniques within health settings like motivational interviewing and counselling for depression, there seems to be some more room for ideas evolving from the PCA, although this is not without risks when the fundamental model is not being taught or properly critiqued so that what is being offered becomes divorced from its key values to become almost a skills check list rather than a way of being with clients.

I think that some adherence to the intricacies and certainties of psychodynamic conceptualizations is waning within the therapy world as a whole and certainly in counselling psychology. I suspect the lack of an evidential basis for the broad model is to some extent at play here but it may also be that as more psychologically evidenced ideas, developed from particular areas of psychodynamic work, come to the fore (I am thinking particularly of attachment theory here), some of the more recondite material is getting by-passed or framed in different language and used in more integrated ways. In a culture so profoundly affected by psychodynamic thought that we come across ideas like defence mechanisms and unconscious motivations being used in popular literature and drama, it is hard to believe that the influence for better or worse of this way of formulating ideas about human distress and healing will be lost completely. Later developments of psychodynamic thinking such as transactional analysis seem to have a continued popularity in the world of counselling and consultancy but interestingly do not appear to impact counselling psychology practice much as they do not get much coverage in training (again perhaps because of the absence of much of an evidential basis). I think it also arguable that the increasing currency of philosophically based therapeutic models (existential and phenomenological therapies), which often incorporate or draw on psychodynamic ways of working with clients, are taking the place of some psychoanalytic thinking and teaching.

Jungian constructs, though, clearly have some appeal for psychologists from a range of humanistic and transpersonal backgrounds as they have been influential in the development of these areas and provide some conceptual tools for dealing with the mysterious and uncertain issues of creativity, faith, and spirituality, which (perhaps surprisingly) have come back into focus partly because of the interest in Eastern psychologies and mystical traditions now current amongst some CBT practitioners. I am not sure how much transpersonal work actually gets into counselling psychology training or practice although its presence is surely felt whenever broad humanistic models come into play.

It seems to me that the need for evidentially based concepts and theories as well as the sudden rapid growth in the field of neuropsychology means that both within the broader enterprise of counselling and psychotherapy and in counselling psychology in particular there is an interest in and great expectations of this field. Whilst there is a danger in believing that if we know more of the physiology and biochemistry of experience we will have straightforward answers to human dysfunction and distress, there is new knowledge in a number of areas (effects of deprivation on neurological development, mirror neurones, post-traumatic responses) that may vindicate some therapeutic approaches, or guide us in how we work therapeutically through relationships, as well as potentially leading to new interventions in psychotherapy as well as psychopharmacology. It is not conceivable to me that this field of study will be omitted from the professional training and thinking of all counselling psychologists within the next decade. It may provide a powerful basis for integrative modelling for some, although that is not without risk in that it may again foster the illusion of scientific certainty at a time when we need to maintain our sense of uncertainty and creativity to ensure that we fulfil the potential richness of this field of enquiry for our work.

How all these fields of enquiry, knowledge, and theory can be held together will remain problematic for counselling psychology (as well as the broader area of counselling and psychotherapy). Until recently I have tended to argue that what is needed for each practitioner is a conceptual overview that creates consistency between underlying assumptions and conceptual frameworks; that it is not enough (indeed is unacceptably lax) to just go with a personal selection of an eclectic toolbox of ideas and strategies/interventions on the basis of aiming to do what works and what suits each practitioner's style and core values. However, the more I examine my own work (after nearly 40 years' practice) and particularly having tried to make sense of using some cognitive theory concepts and strategies alongside (or within) a phenomenological and relational way of working, I have come to the view that one can work with integrity without such conceptual consistency—that the consistency comes through values and intentions and is based on actions not abstractions. I find this adequate now and in many ways consistent with a postmodern pluralist position. I know there are many colleagues within counselling psychology who would not agree with this position, still wanting conceptual consistency, but there are also many others taking the even more pragmatic line of general eclecticism.

Perhaps the content of the *Counselling Psychology Review* current at the time of writing best gives the sense of the present breadth and feel of the situation in the discipline, with papers each growing out of both humane and scientific interests not as an artificial tension but as an organic whole: a rigorous outcome study of pluralistic therapy for depression by Mick Cooper and others, a narrative review of compassion focused therapy by Elaine Beaumont and Caroline Hollins Martin, and a grounded theory exploration by Catherine Atnas, Martin Milton, and Stephanie Archer, of the experiences of trans men making the decision to change, appear alongside papers on the ethical issues related to vicarious traumatization for psychologists working with trauma from Amirah Iqbal, and an important paper on neuroscience and counselling psychology by David Goss. The closing paper, like the first is also on a pluralistic/integrative model of working and comes from the newest contributor (with the article that won the 2014 Trainee Prize). Lucy Longhurst writes from her position as a trainee in an NHS psychiatric setting who has been able to put together a way of working that combines aspects of existential therapy, acceptance and commitment therapy and CBT, and to write about this way of practising through an imaginative composite case study. Enough said?

SUGGESTED FURTHER READING

Douglas, B., Woolfe, R., Strawbridge, S., Kasket, E., & Galbraith, V. (2016). *The handbook of counselling psychology* (4th ed.). London: Sage.
This book is a useful source for counselling psychology students and complements the current volume.
Kirschenbaum, H. (2007). *The life and work of Carl Rogers*. Ross-on-Wye: PCCS.
This book provides an excellent background to Carl Rogers—the psychologist whose work has had perhaps the greatest influence on counselling psychology.

REFERENCES

Boring, E. G. (1950). *The history of experimental psychology* (2nd ed.). New York: Appleton-Century-Crofts.
BPS (British Psychological Society) (2005). *Guidelines for professional practice in counselling psychology*. Leicester: BPS.
Frankland, A. M. (2003). Counselling psychology: The next ten years. In R. Woolfe, W. Dryden, & S. Strawbridge (Eds.), *Handbook of counselling psychology* (pp. 656–670). London: Sage.
Kirschenbaum, H. (2007). *The life and work of Carl Rogers*. Ross-on-Wye: PCCS.
Kirschenbaum, H., & Henderson, V. L. (Eds.) (1990). *The Carl Rogers reader*. London: Constable.
Munley, P. H., Duncan, L. E., McDonnell, K. A., & Sauer, E. M. (2004). Counseling psychology in the United States of America. *Counselling Psychology Quarterly, 17*(3), 247–271.
Parry, G. (1982). Editorial. *Changes, 1*(1), 3.

Ramsey-Wade, C. (2014). UK counselling psychology training placements: Where are we now? *Counselling Psychology Review, 29*(3), 4–16.

Rogers, C. R. (1957). The necessary and sufficient conditions of therapeutic personality change. *Journal of Consulting Psychology, 21*(2), 95–103.

Rogers, C. R. (1961). *On becoming a person: A therapist's view of psychotherapy*. London: Constable.

Woolfe, R. (1996). The nature of counselling psychology. In R. Woolfe, W. Dryden, & S. Strawbridge (Eds.), *Handbook of counselling psychology* (pp. 3–20). London: Sage.

3 Counselling Psychology: Assumptions, Challenges, and Aspirations

STEPHEN JOSEPH

CHAPTER OUTLINE

INTRODUCTION 23

THE ASSUMPTIONS OF COUNSELLING
PSYCHOLOGY IN RELATION TO THE MEDICAL
IDEOLOGY 24
    Acknowledgement of Social Processes 26
    The Central Role of the Client 27
    Focus on Strengths and Wellness 27

CHALLENGES TO COUNSELLING
PSYCHOLOGY 28

LOOKING TO THE FUTURE OF COUNSELLING
PSYCHOLOGY 31

CONCLUSION 33

LEARNING OUTCOMES

BY THE END OF THIS CHAPTER YOU SHOULD
BE ABLE TO ANSWER THE FOLLOWING KEY
QUESTIONS:

1. What are the main defining features of the
   medical model?

2. In what ways does counselling psychology
   differ from medical model approaches
   to therapy?

3. What are the challenges for the
   future development of counselling
   psychology?

Counselling Psychology: A Textbook for Study and Practice, First Edition. Edited by David Murphy.
© 2017 John Wiley & Sons Ltd. Published 2017 by John Wiley & Sons Ltd.

INTRODUCTION

> Are clients best assisted when the difficulty is accurately diagnosed and an intervention is made to reduce or remove the difficulty? Or, are they best served when the assessment and intervention process assists clients in identifying their own personal strengths and resources, then reinforces these strengths and resources within the intervention, so that they can serve to prevent future distress? The response to this question is part of the historical differentiation between clinical and counseling psychology, in which clinical psychology has emphasised diagnosis and treatment of disorders, and counseling psychology has emphasized normal development. (Altmaier and Rasheed Ali, 2012, p. 4)

In the history of applied psychology, the first clinical practitioners worked under the direction of psychiatrists. The main role of these early clinical psychologists was to administer tests rather than conduct therapy, which was carried out by the psychiatrists themselves, who at that time were influenced by psychoanalysis and trained in medicine. As such, this led clinical psychologists to adopt the methods and assumptions of their psychiatric counterparts. Maddux and Lopez (2015) discuss how these early influences led clinical psychology to become grounded in the medical ideology from the outset. Later in 1950 the standards for clinical psychology training at the American Psychological Association conference in Boulder, Colorado, further consolidated the medical ideology underpinning clinical psychology—this was, said Albee (2000), the "fatal flaw" that has "distorted and damaged the development of clinical psychology ever since" (p. 247). In contrast, and as the above quote by Altmaier and Rasheed Ali (2012) makes clear, counselling psychology has had its own unique approach to helping people that emphasizes "normal" development as opposed to diagnosis and treatment. The reason for this difference is that the origins of counselling psychology lie not in a concern with mental disorder but with helping people find their vocation in life.

In this chapter I will examine the three assumptions underpinning counselling psychology that have traditionally distinguished it from clinical psychology. These are: (a) its acknowledgement of the social processes that influence people, (b) its collaborative approach to client work in which the client is seen as the best expert on themselves, and (c) its emphasis on constructive and healthy functioning. However, I will argue that recent years have seen a shift in the values of counselling psychology away from these three assumptions and towards the medical ideology. As a result there is now a need for counselling psychology to reorient itself towards its original stance. First, I will discuss these three assumptions of counselling psychology in relation to the medical ideology. Second, I will examine the challenges to counselling psychology. Third, I will discuss the ways forward for counselling psychology to find its own distinctive voice.

Counselling psychology acknowledges the social processes that influence people.

Counselling psychology involves a collaborative approach to client work in which the client is seen as the best expert on themselves.

Counselling psychology places emphasis on constructive and healthy functioning.

THE ASSUMPTIONS OF COUNSELLING PSYCHOLOGY IN RELATION TO THE MEDICAL IDEOLOGY

Broadly speaking, the profession of psychology remains influenced by the medical ideology. To explain the medical ideology it is helpful to imagine our own experiences when, for example, we go to see the medical practitioner with an ailment such as stomach pains. We are likely to be uncertain what the cause of our pain is and anxious for our practitioner to accurately identify the problem and quickly provide the correct solution. To do this, the practitioner needs to be an expert diagnostician. They need to examine us in order to identify our specific symptoms in order to diagnose the most likely cause. As such they need to have knowledge of the likely conditions we may be suffering from and the symptoms of each. They will ask us questions about the nature of our pain, its location, duration, and physically examine us for bruises, swelling, and so on. Having reached a diagnosis, they are in a position to prescribe the correct treatment. The treatment will depend on what condition they think we are suffering from.

The diagnostician is a scientist practitioner in the sense that the diagnosis is a hypothesis. Only the right treatment will make a difference. As such, our practitioner will need to monitor us for a period of time to see if our symptoms abate. If our symptoms do abate this would seem to confirm their initial hypothesis. If our symptoms do not abate then they will develop a new hypothesis that explains our continued symptoms and provide a new prescription. This process continues until we are symptom free. An incorrect diagnosis could be the difference between life and death for us. As such, the more skilled the practitioner is, the better a diagnostician they are.

By adopting the medical ideology within psychology, the assumption is that psychological problems are like medical problems: they too require expert diagnosis in order to prescribe the right treatment. Such a way of thinking is illustrated when one looks through many of the standard textbooks in clinical and abnormal psychology (e.g., Kring, Johnson, Davidson, & Neale, 2015). Typically, the chapters of such books are structured by disorder. Each chapter introduces the reader to the research on, for example, anxiety disorders, somatoform and dissociative disorders, mood disorders, schizophrenia, substance-related disorders, sexual disorders, personality disorders, and so on. The purpose is to show the novice that these are the various conditions that a person can suffer from and what the appropriate treatments are for each specific disorder. The implication of the diagnostic system is that each client is treated as representative of the category to which they are assigned by diagnosis. Generations of graduates have now been inculcated in this way of thinking such that it has become deeply ingrained among today's psychologists.

The professional clinician is trained in the use of the American Psychiatric Association's Diagnostic and Statistical Manual of Mental Disorders, which is now in its fifth edition (American Psychiatric Association, 2013) and which describes the range of psychiatric disorders and the detailed procedure for the diagnosis of each. For each diagnostic category there are various psychometric tests that are available to aid in the diagnostic procedure and to facilitate research. Diagnostic categories provide a common language for researchers as they examine the causes, correlates, and most effective treatments for each disorder. As such, the most influential research strategy in clinical psychology is driven by the diagnostic process as information is sought to understand each disorder and to determine which treatments are most effective.

For many psychologists engaged in such research as that described above, it is a taken-for-granted assumption that this is the best way to proceed if we are to advance knowledge of psychological suffering and how best to provide help to people. So taken for granted is this assumption that the alternative ways of thinking are rarely acknowledged. Some contemporary clinical psychologists are now beginning to question their reliance on the medical ideology and the language of disorder and deficit, and are searching for alternatives (Division of Clinical Psychology, 2015), seemingly unaware that this was the intellectual space that the profession of counselling psychology traditionally occupied.

In contrast to textbooks on clinical psychology, books on counselling psychology (such as this volume) do not tend to provide an overview of the different so called disorders and their specific treatments. Instead they provide discussions on how counselling psychology relates to different personal and social contexts, such as ethnicity, gender, social class, sexuality (e.g., Altmaier & Hansen, 2012), and as with this book grapple with the question of theories that offer alternative paradigmatic ways of thinking to the medical ideology.

Theoretical perspectives in counselling psychology have traditionally been derived from humanistic, existential, and social psychological literatures that do not adopt psychiatric terminology but offer alternative ways of understanding how humans come to be distressed and dysfunctional, often as a disruption in normal developmental processes (e.g., Joseph, 2017).

As such, one of the differences in humanistic, existential, and social theories is that they tend to downplay relative to psychiatry the role of biological and genetic factors as the cause of distress and dysfunction. It is in this sense that perhaps most counselling psychologists understand themselves as challenging the medical model. But this is an oversimplified and misleading view of how the medical ideology is expressed in practice.

When a biological or genetic origin is implied, the more accurate term would be the biomedical model. However, as should be clear from the above description of the medical model, it is entirely possible to reject biological or genetic causes but still operate with a medical ideology in which it is assumed that the therapist needs to be an expert diagnostician in order to prescribe the correct treatment. As such, those who think the medical model necessarily implies the biomedical model may in their own way perceive themselves as challenging the medical model simply because they reject biological and genetic causes while condoning the medical ideology in their practice.

There are three defining features of the medical model in practice:

1. The focus on the individual. In the medical model the origins of distress and dysfunction are seen as within the person.
2. The role of the practitioner as expert on what the patient needs. In the medical model it is the practitioner who knows what is best for the patient.
3. The emphasis on distress and dysfunction. In the medical model the clinician is interested in what is weak and defective about people.

Counselling psychology has since its beginnings emphasized three themes that are in direct opposition to these three features of the medical model.

1. Counselling psychologists are concerned with the social systems of family and community and how other external forces can be understood to be acting on the person.
2. Counselling psychologists focus on the client as expert on what is best for them and seek to form collaborative relationships as an essential part of the therapeutic process.
3. Counselling psychologists are interested in the constructive and healthy potential of people.

As such counselling psychology has traditionally presented a genuine challenge to the medical model in these three ways: by looking to health and wellness, seeking to understand the social processes, and taking the stance that people are the best experts on themselves.

Acknowledgement of Social Processes

As we have seen, a central feature of the medical ideology is that it locates the source of people's problems within them. In psychiatry, for example, biological causes are often sought. Clinical psychology developed in the context of being servant to psychiatry and it is not surprising therefore that it inculcated these ideas of looking within the person for the origin of their difficulties. Clinical psychologists may not emphasize biological factors to the same degree but they do focus on cognitive processes that are internal to the person. In contrast, counselling psychology did not emerge in the shadow of psychiatry. Rather, its origins can be traced to the Division of Personnel and Guidance Psychologists, which then became the Division of Counseling and Guidance, finally giving rise in 1955 to the Division of Counseling Psychology. In the UK it was in the 1980s that counselling psychology was established (Steffan, Vossler, & Joseph, 2015; see also Chapter 2, this volume, for a history of counselling psychology in the UK).

As discussed earlier in Chapter 2 of this volume, one of the major influences in the development of counselling psychology was the work of Carl Rogers, who challenged the traditional medical ideology by emphasizing the social psychological processes underpinning distress and dysfunction. Rogers described how normal human development could be thwarted by controlling and conditional socialization processes (Rogers, 1951). In this way the medical model was never at the core of counselling psychology. As counselling psychology developed it was also influenced by political developments such as the Civil Rights Movement and feminism, thus emerging as a discipline that promotes core values of diversity, multiculturalism, and social justice (Lane & Corrie, 2006). Traditionally, therefore, counselling psychology places much emphasis on socially relevant processes and understanding how these influence experiences of distress and dysfunction.

The Central Role of the Client

As already mentioned, in adopting the diagnostic system each client is treated as representative of the category to which they are assigned by diagnosis. This may of course be entirely appropriate from the perspective of the medical ideology when dealing with physical complaints, but for the counselling psychologist informed by humanistic and existential perspectives such a view is incompatible with the need to understand each person as unique and to see the world from the client's point of view. The emergence of this line of thought was explicitly influenced by humanistic psychology, and most notably the client-centred school of thought developed by Carl Rogers. In the cultural context of the time, in which it was assumed that the therapist had the expertise on the client's mental world, it represented a challenge to the establishment of the day to consider that people might be their own best experts. Rogers originally referred to his approach as *non-directive therapy*. He described it as non-directive therapy because it was the therapist's task to follow the client's lead, thus challenging the then dominant therapist-directed approach of psychiatry and psychoanalysis. Rather than the therapist directing the course of therapy by using interpretative methods to derive solutions for the patient, Rogers turned the notion of the therapist as the expert upside down, such that the therapist followed the client, helping them to uncover their own solutions (Rogers, 1951).

As such, whereas the medical model requires the therapist to be expert over the client in knowing what questions to ask in order to determine what is best for the client, influenced by Rogers, the counselling psychologist aims to help clients understand for themselves what they need and how to move forward in life.

Focus on Strengths and Wellness

Given its roots the early focus of counselling psychology was on nurturing people's strengths and talents, ideas that were bolstered by the humanistic psychologists whose nonmedical approach included asking what made for the fully functioning life. "Fully functioning" was the term Rogers used to describe what it was that therapy freed people to move towards. It was not a description of the absence of negative qualities but a description of positive qualities. For example, one of the characteristics of the fully functioning person is that he or she lives in harmony with others and experiences the rewards of mutual positive regard. Another is that he or she is open to experience (Rogers, 1961).

CHALLENGES TO COUNSELLING PSYCHOLOGY

It is only when all three of these three alternative assumptions discussed above are simultaneously held that the medical ideology is fully challenged. In Rogers' person-centred approach, all three of these assumptions are held: distress and dysfunction are thought to arise from social processes, the client is their own best expert on what direction to take, and when provided with the right supportive environment will move in a direction towards becoming more fully functioning (Joseph, 2015). However, these three challenges to the medical ideology that are so tightly interwoven within the person-centred approach have become separated within counselling psychology as it has come to develop in the UK in the shadow of clinical psychology.

Typically, counselling psychology seems to have held more strongly to its assumptions about the social world and the importance of social justice as its defining feature than it has with the other two assumptions. In this way counselling psychologists may perceive themselves as challenging the medical ideology when in fact they are condoning it. For example, it may be that in emphasizing the social, they perceive themselves as challenging the medical ideology with its focus on the individual but nonetheless they focus on pathology and also take the role of expert. It is not surprising that such a situation may have arisen. In recent years these origins and three distinctive features of counselling psychology have increasingly become overshadowed by the immediate demands on practitioners and training courses from employers and funding agencies to offer interventions based on notions of pathology and cure, and to focus more on remedial ways of thinking.

To gain employment in NHS contexts, counselling psychologists needed to compete with their clinical colleagues and be able to demonstrate skills compatible with medical model thinking. The theories and practices of counselling psychology drawn originally from humanistic and existential psychology do not use the terminology of psychiatry. Although humanistic and existential theories offer alternative explanations that account for the same phenomena, when seen from within the medical ideology such alternative theories are seen as lacking in explanatory power and therapeutic effectiveness. This is likely a misperception of the traditional theories underpinning counselling psychology, and a misrepresentation of the theories (e.g., Joseph, 2017) and the evidence on therapeutic effectiveness of relationship-based therapies (Murphy & Joseph, 2016). It has nonetheless been a factor that has led counselling psychologists and training courses to accommodate working practices explicitly associated with the medical model and to look to other theories and therapies traditionally associated with the medical ideology.

In doing so, counselling psychologists have successfully enhanced their employability and gained prestige (Steffan et al., 2015). There has been a notable increase in employment opportunities for the younger generation of counselling psychologists, and as opportunities or employment have opened up the profession of counselling psychology has responded in ways that have served to further move it towards even more medicalized ways of thinking.

The medical dominance and the need to equip trainees for work in a medicalized setting has influenced training provision in counselling psychology, but such shifts have been subtle and may go unrecognized as such. For example, one way in which the medical ideology is currently played out in counselling psychology training and practice is in the notion that the counselling psychologist should have a breadth of expertise in multiple therapeutic approaches. This can be seen in its training in different approaches to therapy. One of the developments that now characterizes UK counselling psychology training is the requirement of an understanding and level of skills in a range of therapeutic approaches, often including cognitive-behavioural, systems-based, psychodynamic, and humanistic approaches to therapy.

These different therapeutic approaches have very different ontological positions that simply cannot be reconciled (Wood & Joseph, 2007). For example, the psychodynamic approach rests on the notion that human beings are essentially destructive and therapy is a way of curtailing those impulses, and humanistic psychology provides the view that human nature is essentially constructive and that therapy is a way to free those impulses (Joseph, 2008). One may be able to draw on *techniques* associated with psychodynamic therapy and then humanistic therapy from moment to moment but it is not possible for a therapist to move back and forth from one ontological position to another in a meaningful and therapeutically helpful way.

Learning different techniques may seem to represent an eclectic diversity and it has become popular to draw on techniques derived from across the variety of therapies. Contemporarily some therapists refer to this as a pluralistic way of working (Cooper & McLeod, 2011). However, this has come to mean different things to different people, a form of technical eclecticism for some and an approach to integration for others (See Chapter 10 and Chapter 11, this volume).

Another way of thinking about pluralistic ways of working is to consider one's stance on taking the expert role. There are essentially only two meta-theoretical stances that a therapist can take on the issue of expertise: either they assume themselves expert in the direction that the client needs to take (e.g., as traditionally a psychodynamic therapist would) or they assume the client is their own best expert (e.g., as traditionally a person-centred therapist would). As we have seen, counselling psychology traditionally adopted this latter position because it rejected the medical model, but in more recent years has shifted towards the former as it competes with clinical psychology in the context of a limited and medically influenced job market. However, the notion that counselling psychologists need to be knowledgeable in different approaches can be viewed from either meta-theoretical perspective.

Insofar as the therapist perceives that they need to be equipped to provide the "correct" form of therapy for the client, eclectic diversity has had the unfortunate side effect of promoting a medicalized way of working. The therapist may not be using formal psychiatric diagnosis in order to prescribe a specific treatment, but if the therapist sees their task as identifying which form of therapy (e.g., cognitive-behavioural, psychodynamic, humanistic) is best suited to a client's difficulties, they are essentially doing the same thing. They are in essence making a diagnosis and providing the "correct" prescription.

Diagnosis and prescription are terms that many counselling psychologists will not identify with and as such may not have viewed themselves as medical model practitioners. But, seen this way, the identification by the therapist that the client would benefit most from a particular form of intervention would be described as operating within a medical model, even though there is no formal use of psychiatric diagnosis. The above description of how counselling psychologists may sometimes operate within the medical model is of course different to how other psychologists using more formal systems of diagnosis and prescription may operate, but it is nonetheless a description of medical model practice. As such, it is clear that although many counselling psychologists do not use formal psychiatric systems of diagnosis or look to biological origins, they are in fact operating within the medical model in the sense that they are taking on the role of expert in that they understand their task is to identify the problems so as to be able to offer suggestions for intervention.

In contrast, those therapists whose notion of pluralistic practice is to adopt a way of working that follows the client, to listen to how the client identifies the problem areas to work on, and what might best help, and then drawing on techniques that may be associated with one therapeutic approach or another, is working within the traditional counselling psychology approach of the client as their own best expert.

The argument above is that, while it may be useful to be knowledgeable about different techniques drawn from a variety of therapeutic approaches, how one employs these in practice is always based on one's ontological stance and in this sense there is a difference between learning different approaches to therapy and learning different techniques that can be used coherently within one approach to therapy.

Likewise, the same argument can be applied to the notion of formulation (Division of Clinical Psychology, 2011). Formulation is a broad concept, perhaps best considered as a continuum. At one extreme it is akin to medical model practice as the therapist takes the lead in formulating the problem and offering the solution. At the other extreme it is akin to person-centred practice insofar as the client takes the lead in understanding their situation and drives the therapeutic process forward. Formulation takes place in the space between these two extremes (see Figure 3.1).

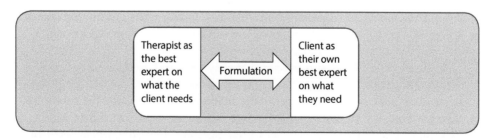

FIGURE 3.1 *The locus of expertise influences formulation.*

As such, formulation as an approach to making sense of the client's distress and mental health difficulties addresses many of the concerns associated with diagnosis, but it does not necessarily imply a nonmedical approach. There will inevitably be a difference in the use of formulation between any two practitioners depending on whether they see themselves or the client as the best expert on what the client is experiencing and what they need. Some might argue that this is to misunderstand how formulation is a collaborative process, but ultimately even the most collaborative process will be slanted one way or the other, if one considers how the concept is introduced, whether the conversation is directed by the therapist or the client, how the formulation is used, and, most importantly, the attitude of the therapist.

In each and every moment of therapy there is a direction that arises either from the therapist or from the client. When endeavouring to work collaboratively the therapist may move in and out of the role of the expert, at the expense of the client's ability to be their own best expert. Even in such a seemingly collaborative statement as "tell me what you hope to get from therapy and why it is that you've come and we can see what kind of interventions might be helpful" the therapist has subtly positioned themselves as the expert. Whenever therapy is guided by a professional-as-expert stance, formulation simply becomes another form of medical model practice, insofar as it requires the practitioner to apply their expert knowledge to understand the clients' problems in such a way as to recommend the best course of treatment.

As we look more towards the right hand side of Figure 3.1, the power in the relationship to determine the direction of the therapy shifts to the client. No longer would the therapist introduce the notion of formulation with the intention of using it as a way to determine what form of intervention might best help. The therapist is now following the client's lead. The able therapist will be responsive to meeting the needs of the client as determined by the client in the moment-by-moment interaction between the two of them. Instead of using formulation from an expert stance to determine what type of therapy or intervention to provide, therapy consists of the client engaging in their own formulation.

LOOKING TO THE FUTURE OF COUNSELLING PSYCHOLOGY

In these ways described above, there have been subtle shifts towards more medicalized ways of working within counselling psychology. This is not a criticism of training counselling psychologists to be knowledgeable about and skilled in the use of techniques drawn from humanistic, systemic, psychodynamic, and cognitive-behavioural approaches, but to emphasize the need to be clear about the ontological stance from which techniques are employed. While it may be possible to use techniques associated with different approaches at different points during therapy, the danger is that this can slide into a subtle expression of the medical ideology.

There is no need for a profession of psychology that takes such an ideological position because we already have it. It is clinical psychology. The point of counselling psychology was that it was different. However, the gulf between clinical and counselling psychology seems to be diminishing. It is in this sense that counselling psychology needs to re-evaluate its ontological position. I have discussed this above in relation to its stance on the role of expert, but there is also a need to look to the other assumptions that once made it distinct.

Given these influences on counselling psychology to adopt a more medical model it is no longer clear that its emphasis is on the promotion of health and well-being. Humanistic approaches to therapy have always emphasized fully functioning behaviour and the promotion of strengths and well-being, but as counselling psychology has looked to pluralistic practice within NHS contexts there has also been a shift to the language of disorder and deficit. Ironically, this has coincided with the rise of positive psychology. Both counselling and positive psychology are similarly rooted in what could broadly be termed the humanistic-existential-phenomenological paradigm (Robbins, 2015).

At the turn of the millennium the positive psychology movement started out with its own distinct identity as "a science of positive subjective experience, positive individual traits and positive institutions" (Seligman & Csikszentmihalyi, 2000, p. 5). Seeking to counter the dominant concern of 20th-century psychology with mental illness rather than well-being, positive psychology has succeeded in putting the study of well-being and human strengths back on the agenda of psychological science. Attention to positive psychology offers a new impetus for the profession of counselling psychology to help it regain sight of its traditional emphasis on well-being (Lopez et al., 2006; Vossler, Steffen, & Joseph, 2015).

Training programmes could be revised to contain specific information on assessment and interventions from a positive psychological perspective, such as the use of gratitude (Bono, Krakauer, & Froh, 2015), posttraumatic growth (Joseph, 2011), developing a sense of coherence (Vossler, 2012), and the client's strengths (Gerstein, 2006). Trainees should be encouraged to develop a balanced therapeutic approach with equal attention to problems and strengths and resources (Rashid, 2015; Scheel, Klenz Davis, & Henderson, 2012). This will involve new interest by counselling psychologists in how clients move towards states of well-being and flourishing, how to facilitate these in different clinical contexts and to develop new ways of understanding clinical issues from a nonpathological viewpoint (Joseph & Wood, 2010). Positive psychology has succeeded where counselling psychology has failed in promoting the notion of well-being and optimal functioning as central to what we should aspire to as applied psychologists. However, in positioning itself as a challenge to the medical ideology it has only done so in relation to that one assumption while largely maintaining a focus on the practitioner as expert and on the individual processes. Thus, looking to positive psychology can provide some corrective balance for the profession of counselling psychology, but if counselling psychology is to return to its original stance it must go further.

In response to the shift towards a medicalized, deficits model, there have been voices in recent years calling for counselling psychology to reaffirm its identity and re-orient its practice to the roots of the profession (e.g. Mollen, Ethington, & Ridley, 2006; Robitschek & Woodson, 2006). The above discussion offers some points for consideration as to how counselling psychology may be able to move forward in ways that reconnect it with its original vision.

CONCLUSION

The immediate concern must be the education of the future generation of counselling psychologists. There seems to be a need to assess and revise the educational strategies and underlying philosophy for training programmes. The most important task for counselling psychology in reshaping its agenda is not so much about the skills and techniques drawn from the different approaches that could be learned and practised, but rather going back to the origins of the discipline to re-examine its distinctive ontological stance.

SELECTED FURTHER READING

Cain, D. J., Keenan, K., & Rubin, S. (eds.). (2016). *Humanistic psychotherapies: Handbook of research and practice* (2nd ed.). Washington, DC: American Psychological Association.
This recent handbook summarizes research in the humanistic tradition and may be helpful to counselling psychologists in reconnecting with nonpathological ways of thinking and working and the current evidence.

Joseph, S (Ed.). (2015). *Positive psychology in practice: Promoting human flourishing in work, health, education and everyday life* (2nd ed.). Hoboken, NJ: John Wiley & Sons.
This is a key text on applied positive psychology that counselling psychologists may find helpful in reorienting themselves to the idea that their task is to help cultivate strengths and help people to become more fully functioning.

Worsley, R., & Joseph, S. (Eds.) (2007). *Person-centred practice: Case studies in positive psychology*. Ross-on-Wye: PCCS books.
This is a helpful book for trainees who wish to understand client-led as opposed to expert-led approaches to therapy.

REFERENCES

Albee, G. W. (2000). The Boulder model's fatal flaw. *American Psychologist, 55*, 247–248.
Altmaier, E. M., & Hansen, J. C. (Eds.) (2012). *The Oxford handbook of counseling psychology*. New York: Oxford University Press.
Altmeier, E. M., & Rasheed Ali, S. (2012). A view across the life span of counseling psychology. In E. M. Altmaier & Jo-Ida C. Hansen (Eds.), *The Oxford handbook of counseling psychology* (pp. 3–7). Oxford: Oxford University Press.
American Psychiatric Association (2013). *Diagnostic and statistical manual of mental disorders* (5th ed.). Washington, DC: American Psychiatric Press.

Bono, G., Krakauer, M., & Froh, J. J. (2015). The power and practice of gratitude. In S. Joseph (Ed.), *Positive psychology in practice: Promoting human flourishing in work, health, education and everyday life* (2nd ed., pp. 559–575). Hoboken, NJ: John Wiley & Sons.

Cooper, M., & McLeod, J. (2011). *Pluralistic counselling and psychotherapy*. London: Sage.

Division of Clinical Psychology (2011). *Guidelines on psychological formulation*. Leicester: British Psychological Society.

Division of Clinical Psychology (2015). *Guidelines on language in relation to functional psychiatric diagnosis*. Leicester: British Psychological Society.

Gerstein, L. H. (2006). Counseling psychology's commitment to strengths: Rhetoric or reality? *The Counseling Psychologist, 34*, 276–292.

Joseph, S. (2008). Psychotherapy's inescapable assumptions about human nature. *Counselling Psychology Review, 23*, 34–40.

Joseph, S. (2011). *What doesn't kill us: The new psychology of posttraumatic growth*. New York: Basic Books..

Joseph, S. (2015). *Positive therapy: Building bridges between positive psychology and person-centred psychotherapy* (2nd ed.). London: Routledge.

Joseph, S., (Ed.) (2017). *The Handbook of Person-centred therapy and mental health: Theory, research, and practice*. Ross-on-Wye: PCCS Books.

Joseph, S., & Wood, A. (2010). Assessment of positive functioning in clinical psychology: Theoretical and practical issues. *Clinical Psychology Review, 30*, 830–838.

Kring, A. M., Johnson. S. L., Davidson, G. C., & Neale, J. M. (2015). *Abnormal psychology* (13th ed.). Hoboken, NJ: John Wiley & Sons.

Lane, D., & Corrie, S. (2006). Counselling psychology: Its influences and future. *Counselling Psychology Review, 21*(1), 12–24.

Lopez, S. J., Magyar-Moe, J. L, Petersen, S. E., Ryder, J. A., Krieshok, T. S., O'Byrne, K. K., Lichtenberg, J. W., & Fry, N. A. (2006) Counseling psychology's focus on positive aspects of human functioning. *The Counseling Psychologist, 34*, 205–227.

Maddux, J. E., & Lopez, S. J. (2015). Toward a positive clinical psychology: Deconstructing the illness ideology and constructing an ideology of human strengths and potential. In S. Joseph (Ed.), *Positive psychology in practice: Promoting human flourishing in work, health, education, and everyday life* (pp. 411–427). Hoboken, NJ: John Wiley & Sons.

Mollen, D., Ethington, L. L., & Ridley, C. R. (2006). Positive psychology: Considerations and implications for counseling psychology. *The Counseling Psychologist, 34*, 304–312.

Murphy, D., & Joseph, S. (2016). Person-centred therapy: Past, present, and future orientations. In D. J. Cain., K. Keenan., & S. Rubin (Eds.), *Humanistic psychotherapies: Handbook of research and practice* (2nd ed., pp. 185–218). Washington, DC: American Psychological Association.

Rashid, T. (2015). Strength-based assessment. In S. Joseph (Ed.), *Positive psychology in practice: Promoting human flourishing in work, health, education and everyday life* (2nd ed., pp. 519–542). Hoboken, NJ: John Wiley & Sons.

Robbins, B. D. (2015). Building bridges between humanistic and positive psychology. In S. Joseph (Ed.), *Positive psychology in practice: Promoting human flourishing in work, health, education and everyday life* (2nd ed., pp. 31–45). Hoboken, NJ: John Wiley & Sons.

Robitschek, C., & Woodson, S.J. (2006). Vocational psychology: Using one of counseling psychology's strengths to foster human strength. *The Counseling Psychologist, 34*, 260–275.

Rogers, C. R. (1951). *Client-centered therapy. Its current practice, implications and theory*. Boston, MA: Houghton Mifflin.

Rogers, C.R. (1961). *On becoming a person: A therapist's view of psychotherapy*. London: Constable.

Scheel, M.J., Klentz Davis, C., & Henderson, J. D. (2012). Therapist use of client strengths: A qualitative study of positive processes. *The Counseling Psychologist, 41*, 392–427.

Seligman, M. E. G., & Csikszentmihalyi, M. (2000). Positive psychology: An introduction. *American Psychologist, 55*(1), 5–14.

Steffen, E., Vossler, A., & Joseph, S. (2015). From shared roots to fruitful collaboration: How counselling psychology can benefit from (re)connecting with positive psychology. *Counselling Psychology Review, 30*, 1–11.

Vossler, A. (2012). Salutogenesis and the sense of coherence: Promoting health and resilience in counselling and psychotherapy. *Counselling Psychology Review, 27*(3), 68–78.

Vossler, A., Steffen, A., & Joseph, S. (2015). The relationship between counselling psychology and positive psychology. In S. Joseph (Ed.), *Positive psychology in practice: Promoting human flourishing in work, health, education and everyday life* (2nd ed., pp. 429–442). Hoboken, NJ: John Wiley & Sons.

Wood, A., & Joseph, S. (2007). Grand theories of psychology can not be reconciled: A comment on McAdams and Pals. *American Psychologist, 62*, 57–58.

Woolfe, R. (2012). Risorgimento: A history of counselling psychology in Britain. *Counselling Psychology Review, 27*(4), 72–78.

4 Philosophical Issues in Counselling Psychology

SIMON DU PLOCK

CHAPTER OUTLINE

A PERSONAL PERSPECTIVE 37

SO WHAT DO WE MEAN WHEN WE USE THE WORD "PHILOSOPHY"? 38

THE RELATIONSHIP BETWEEN PHILOSOPHY AND THERAPY 40

THE PLACE OF PHILOSOPHY IN COUNSELLING PSYCHOLOGY 41

A PHILOSOPHICALLY INFORMED KNOWLEDGE

BASE FOR COUNSELLING PSYCHOLOGY 43

A PHILOSOPHICAL RATHER THAN A MEDICAL PERSPECTIVE ON WHAT IT MEANS TO BE WELL 45

A PHILOSOPHICAL PERSPECTIVE ON MOVEMENT AND EXERCISE 47

CONCLUSION 49

LEARNING OUTCOMES

BY THE END OF THIS CHAPTER YOU SHOULD BE ABLE TO ANSWER THE FOLLOWING KEY QUESTIONS:

1. What do counselling psychologists mean when they use the term "philosophy"?

2. What are the principal philosophical issues that have influenced the development of counselling psychology?

3. How does this philosophical underpinning make counselling psychology distinct from other approaches to psychotherapy?

Counselling Psychology: A Textbook for Study and Practice, First Edition. Edited by David Murphy.
© 2017 John Wiley & Sons Ltd. Published 2017 by John Wiley & Sons Ltd.

A PERSONAL PERSPECTIVE

Given that philosophy is most simply defined as a theory or attitude that acts as a guiding principle for behaviour, we can quickly appreciate that all of us, as we negotiate our way through our worlds, do so with some sort of philosophy in mind. We are, then, all philosophers to the extent that we make sense of our world and act in accordance with a set of values, beliefs, and expectations about life. So the notion of the neutral, objective author of a chapter of this type is as implausible as the notion of the neutral, objective researcher or counselling psychologist. In both cases, they have a *position*. In both cases the illumination they can provide depends upon who they are—or perhaps *where* they are—in relation to the client or the topic under consideration. I have found it helpful to conceptualize this "whereness," following May's notion (1983, p. 163) that asking clients *where* they are is more revealing than asking them *how* they are, in terms of "research trajectory." The term "research trajectory" indicates the angle at which the researcher enters into an explorative process. The angle at which one enters the field of enquiry determines what is illuminated. As this trajectory serves to privilege some aspects of the phenomenon under consideration, and will obscure others, it is important for the researcher to both be aware of their subjective stance at the outset of their research, and to be transparent about this to their audience. Readers familiar with Heidegger may recognize something of his notion of "a clearing in the forest" in my thinking here, and will understand that my position is unashamedly philosophical from the start.

Rejecting the possibility of being a neutral investigator, I need to describe briefly my own trajectory in relation to philosophy and counselling psychology. My first degree was in philosophy, psychology, sociology, and statistics. The course was specifically designed to encourage students to think about how each discipline provided intellectual tools that could be utilized to understand society. While the degree gave me Graduate Basis for Chartered Membership of the British Psychological Society (BPS) and, hence, a route to training as a counselling psychologist, the discipline was in its infancy and my interests led me instead to undertake sociological research on police recruitment and training and, later, statistical research on union and professional association membership patterns in the NHS. More than a decade passed before, in the aftermath of a personal existential crisis, I rediscovered existential philosophy and embarked on training in existential-phenomenological psychotherapy. I was tremendously fortunate to find myself in one of the first cohorts of the Master's in psychology of therapy at Regent's College (now Regent's University), and was there inspired by Professor Emmy van Deurzen and Professor Ernesto Spinelli, both of whom I later worked with. Emmy van Deurzen's fundamentally philosophical approach to psychotherapy, and her emphasis on "problems of living" rather than psychopathology, chimed with my own personal and academic experience—in particular, my earlier work in therapeutic communities, and involvement in gay politics. This was a period when it still seemed possible to talk about "counter-culture" without a hint of irony, and to question the validity of dominant ideologies. I remember reading R. D. Laing's controversial work on sanity and madness, and, in common with many of my peers, recognizing my own family dynamics, and, in some small way, feeling that I too had direct experience of "breakdown" as "break through."

With hindsight I can see that my immersion in this world was, then, as much about personal development and consciousness raising as it was about mastering a set of skills and techniques. As I write this I am aware of feeling almost defensive—is it appropriately "professional" to talk about "finding one-self" rather than expound psychological theories? I have to remind myself that research consistently points to the helping relationship in clinical work as the most significant component in a successful therapy encounter; counselling psychologists need to develop an understanding of both the self and their own sense of self in order to exercise flexibility, judgement, intuition, and imagination in the appropriate use of the various dimensions of a therapeutic relationship. The radical aim of counselling psychology, to engage with all the complexities of the client's world as fully as possible and "to respect and validate the Other in the totality of their being" (Cooper, 2009, p. 121), promised a more democratic, less expert-led way of working with clients (as shown in Chapter 2 and Chapter 3, this volume).

As van Deurzen (2015, p. 69) expresses it:

> Our founding zeal was rooted in our desire to reclaim psychology for a more human and philosophical way of working with individuals, preserving a more gentle and real interpersonal relationship with our clients.

Here was an opportunity for the "wounded healers," those who had first-hand experience of being labelled and pathologized by the medical model, to provide an alternative perspective on psychological health care—one that attempted to look fairly and squarely at the human condition, and that emphasized dis-ease over disease. In 2004/5 Ernesto Spinelli and I designed a doctorate in counselling psychology programme, which I subsequently led. This was unique at that time as it was the first BPS accredited programme to have an existential-phenomenological core philosophy. Since then there has been much debate within counselling psychology about the significance of the existential paradigm for counselling psychology, and the value of an existential sensibility "as a trans-theoretical attitude in counselling psychology practice" (Steffen & Hanley, 2014, p. 3), and about the extent to which an existential-phenomenological perspective may provide "a meta-model of human existence" (Milton et al., 2002, p. 17). Such a perspective can now be found to varying degrees in every UK counselling psychology training programme.

Having set out my personal and professional route into counselling psychology, I want to examine the place of philosophy in counselling psychology.

SO WHAT DO WE MEAN WHEN WE USE THE WORD "PHILOSOPHY"?

Philosophy has often been associated in the popular mind with the ivory towers of academe, and British and North American philosophical schools, which typically have conducted philosophy via the analysis of concepts, rather than

PHILOSOPHICAL ISSUES IN COUNSELLING PSYCHOLOGY 39

engagement with lived experience. This may lead us to regard it as, at best, irrelevant to the practice of counselling psychology, and, at worst, a distraction from our core activity of providing psychological therapy. However, open any handbook on the theory and practice of therapeutic work and the chances are that material related to "philosophy" will appear fairly early on. Discussion of philosophy may be explicit and prominent or it may be implicitly woven throughout, but either way any detailed description of a therapeutic approach will necessarily include some engagement with philosophy, if for no other reason than that key philosophical issues such as autonomy and free choice, the nature of the self, epistemology, ontology, and values and morals, are all also the foundation of therapy. While we may not hold this fully in our awareness as we go about our day-to-day practice, a moment's reflection will convince us that it is so.

The etymological root of the word "philosophy" is to be found in two Ancient Greek words: "phylos," meaning "to love," and "sophie," translated as "wisdom." Philosophy, then, means "love of wisdom." The definition of philosophy offered by the *Oxford Companion to Philosophy* provides a succinct clarification of what is intended by this:

> Philosophy is rationally critical thinking of a more or less systematic kind about the general nature of the world (metaphysics or theory of existence), the justification of belief (epistemology or theory of knowledge) and the conduct of life (ethics or theory of value). Each of the three elements in this list has a non-philosophical counterpart, from which it is distinguished by its explicitly rational and critical way of proceeding and by its systematic nature. Everyone has some general conception of the nature of the world in which they live and their place in it. Metaphysics replaces the unargued assumptions embodied in such a conception with a rational and organized body of beliefs about the world as a whole. Everyone has occasion to doubt and question beliefs, their own and those of others, with more or less success and without any theory of what they are doing. Epistemology seeks by argument to make explicit the rules of correct belief formation. Everyone governs their conduct by directing it to desired or valued ends. Ethics, or moral philosophy, in its most inclusive sense, seeks to articulate, in rationally systematic form, the rules or principles involved.

(Honderich, 2005, p. 309)

So we can see that the "wisdom" to which "philosophy" refers, is to be found in the systematic interrogation of the way we make sense of the world in which we live; as Socrates is credited with saying "The unexamined life is not worth living." Orlans and Van Scoyoc (2009), reflecting on the relationship between philosophy and counselling psychology, draw on the *Oxford English Dictionary* to state that "The word 'philosophy' can be used in a number of different ways, ranging from 'the study of the fundamental nature of knowledge, reality and existence' to 'a theory or attitude which guides one's behaviour" (p. 21). Honderich, in his description of philosophy, makes clear the way in which it embraces both the theoretical and the practical.

THE RELATIONSHIP BETWEEN PHILOSOPHY AND THERAPY

The etymology of the term "psychotherapy," the key activity for most counselling psychologists, deriving from Ancient Greek *psyche* (breath, spirit, soul) and *therapeia* (healing; medical treatment), reminds us that the entity we call therapy is informed by questions about what it means to be human, and that the positions we adopt in response to these questions have profound implications for the way we envisage therapeutic practice. I noticed in my time as a trainer on various therapy programmes that students generally found the etymology of psychotherapy uplifting and aspirational—who would not want to be associated with such a noble endeavour, and one with such an inspiring lineage? Other terms central to philosophy, most notably "ontology" and "epistemology" seem more difficult to grasp. Their meaning, perhaps, feels both more complex and more theoretical, in the sense of being to do with metaphysics, the branch of philosophy that deals with first principles of things, including abstract concepts such as being, knowing, identity, time, and space.

Whenever two or more therapists meet for the first time the question "what's your therapeutic orientation?" arises pretty quickly, and an exchange of views about what it means to be human naturally follows in one form or another. These interlocutors might not regard themselves as engaged in a philosophical discussion, but it is clear that they are. It is a truism that every therapeutic approach, from psychoanalysis to behaviourism, is founded on, and constantly draws upon, its own philosophical conception of the nature of human beings. With regard to my own theoretical orientation, I have noted just how deep the philosophical roots go:

> Most existential therapists recognize that this philosophical search for a better and wiser life was initiated several millennia ago by Athenian and Roman philosophers: like Socrates, Plato, Aristotle, Epicurus, Cicero, Lucretius, Epictetus, Marcus Aurelius and Plotinus; and that this search for existential wisdom was duplicated across the world, by philosophers such as: Confucius, Lao Tse, Buddha and many others.

(du Plock & van Deurzen, 2015, p. 7)

Not only the theory, but the methods too are explicitly philosophical, "existential therapists often use the phenomenological method, which provides existential thought with a practical way of investigating the world" (du Plock & van Deurzen, 2015, p. 7).

It might be objected that little can be concluded from the example of a theoretical approach that quite intentionally names itself after a well-known school of academic philosophy, but it is interesting to note that those approaches, most notably the cognitive and behavioural approaches, which initially seem to distance themselves from any specifically philosophical position and, in effect, appear to adopt the rejection of academic philosophy as one of their defining characteristics, only come to espouse a more specific philosophical stance when they go to great lengths to justify their methods by direct reference to their model of what it means to be human.

Sanders, writing about cognitive-behavioural therapy, explicitly identifies its empiricism as a distinct advantage in an economic climate that values efficiently identifying and attaining goals (2010, p. 121). Empiricism is the theory that all knowledge is based on experience derived from the senses. Stimulated by the rise of experimental science, it developed in the 17th and 18th centuries, expounded in particular by John Locke, George Berkeley, and David Hume. Empiricism can be contrasted with phenomenalism, the doctrine that human knowledge is confined to or founded on the realities or appearances presented to the senses. Philosophy, then, is inescapable, and the only danger lies in disregarding this fact. While practitioners almost certainly do not use philosophical teachings in their daily work, the way they understand human existence, and human nature, informs their way of being with clients.

THE PLACE OF PHILOSOPHY IN COUNSELLING PSYCHOLOGY

While clinical psychology emerged in medical settings, and to this day uses the language of patient and treatment, we need to be aware that increasing emphasis on prevention rather than cure, evidence-based practice, and interventions such as mindfulness have, to some extent, blurred the sharp distinctions between clinical and counselling psychology (see Chapter 3 for a fuller discussion of the clinical and counselling psychology disciplinary boundaries). It nevertheless remains true that what Woolfe et al. (2010, p. 10), calls "an interactive alternative" is not widely embraced by clinical psychology. Duffy (1990) emphasizes the development orientation of counselling psychology, in which crises and problems such as grieving, illness, and separation are perceived not as evidence of pathology but as normative human experiences that pose a challenge of developmental adaptation. The focus, then, is on the development of the self, and on psycho-educational interventions that can facilitate this.

The emergence of counselling psychology is often seen as an alternative to the somewhat mechanistic view of human beings inherent in more traditional psychological paradigms based upon a conventional model of the nature of science. It does not logically follow though, and it would not be accurate to assert, that counselling psychology eschews rigour. Elton Wilson (1994) attempts to position counselling psychology positively and in doing so offers the following definition:

> counselling psychology is a branch of post-graduate applied psychology dedicated to the use of the counselling relationship to test out a wide range of concepts and methods in alliance with clients, who are themselves potential consumers of the knowledge generated by the shared research projects.

(1994, p. 5)

She comments that the particularly distinctive feature of this definition is its location of the cooperative research project at the heart of professional practice.

Van Deurzen-Smith argues that the philosophical underpinnings of counselling psychology lie in "the immense gap left open by a psychology too devoted to narrow scientific principles to pay proper attention to what it means to be human" (1990, p. 9). She contends that psychology has lost its ability to function as an art. If the objective of the counselling psychologist is to help people to lead lives that are more fulfilled, one enters inevitably into the realms of morals and ideology, subjects that are the domain of philosophy rather than science. If we accept this line of reasoning, she suggests that the methods and insights of philosophy such as those of systematic thinking and dialogue, argument, logical analysis, and dialectical processing are more useful than the search for objective facts that characterize experimental psychology.

This is an important point, and in reflecting on philosophical issues in counselling psychology we would do well to consider both the losses and the gains when therapists lay claim to the professional status of "psychologist." Van Deurzen's 1990 paper, presented at the First Annual Conference of the Special Group in Counselling Psychology, continues to be relevant. It warned, as she expressed it, of "the fundamental contradictions and pitfalls that are to be found underneath the smooth presentations of this new discipline of Counselling Psychology" (1990, p. 8). It is not merely interesting to think about the extent to which contemporary counselling psychology has managed, by enormous effort and tenacity, to attain a position broadly similar in the health care field to that of clinical psychology. It is vital, I would contend, to adopt a philosophical position in order to question whether, in the process, it has found itself adopting much of the methodology and many of the values of the experimental psychology which, at the outset, it strongly critiqued.

A challenge to counselling psychology and counselling psychologists is to maintain and indeed expand upon forms of practice that uphold our focus on what it means to be human, rather than allow ourselves to be pulled ever more closely into the orbit of clinical psychology and, in the process, dilute what makes our offering distinctive. The title of this chapter, with its focus on "philosophical issues" rather than on "*the* philosophy" of counselling psychology, alerts us to the reality, and in some senses, the defining characteristic, of our discipline: that it is one fundamentally concerned with holding, or attempting to hold, the tension between a spectrum of competing and perhaps incompatible interests and knowledge communities. The first, most significant, and, in some respects, most easily overlooked philosophical issue is indicated in the very name of the discipline. "Counselling psychology," far from being an uncontentious descriptor, in fact signals an attempt to do something fundamentally radical. This has been recognized by the Training Committee in Counselling Psychology (TCCP) when it stipulates that trainings seeking BPS accreditation should identify their "Core Philosophy." As Orlans and Van Scoyoc (2009, p. 21) state:

> over many years of social and intellectual development mainstream psychology became divorced from its parent discipline of philosophy and it seems to have fallen to the field of counselling psychology to consider and manage some form of re-integration.

What do they mean here by "philosophy"? TCCP guidelines talk about "conceptual basis" and allow for an articulation on quite a wide continuum. The overall aim is in challenging courses and individuals to reflect more deeply on the basis to their work, and to encourage both those involved in designing training programmes, and their students/trainees, to engage in a process of reflexivity.

A PHILOSOPHICALLY INFORMED KNOWLEDGE BASE FOR COUNSELLING PSYCHOLOGY

While it might be said, and indeed is often argued in our postmodern world, that none of the disciplines rests on an indisputable bedrock of agreed knowledge, counselling psychology has always been marked out by the richness and diversity of its competing knowledge claims. The truth of this is immediately evident when we ask what constitutes the knowledge base of counselling psychology. A cursory glance at the mission statements of each of the UK counselling psychology programmes reveals a wide range of therapeutic orientations. They are, though, at least in theory, united by a common mission. As Martin (2006, p. 35) expresses it:

> We are in touch with our radical roots, our phenomenological understanding of human experience, the importance of the inter-subjective, the dangers of labelling. Above all else we affirm the potentially curative properties of the therapeutic relationship in the context of a material and social world.

We should celebrate our distinctive alternative voice in the family of psychotherapies in 21st-century UK psychological health care, a voice—or perhaps more accurately an array of voices—that emphasize subjectivity, values, and the context of the person alongside the problem-solving and medical-based interventions most frequently offered by applied psychologies. The annual conferences of the Division of Counselling Psychology, and the pages of the *Counselling Psychology Review*, are characterized by a breadth and richness of contributions to research and debate that attests to our desire to explore, engage creatively, and, dare we say even "play" with notions of psychological health and well-being. This "free thinking" aspect is in no way detrimental to our professional activities—rather it sits at their core. It acts as a compass, we might even say conscience, by which we steer our path.

Counselling psychology from its inception has been distinguished by its recognition of the quality of the therapeutic relationship as a crucial factor in clinical practice. We were pioneers in this respect and we can be proud to have played our part in foregrounding this vital aspect of therapy. We need, though, to be cautious in claiming this as our distinctive characteristic since, for a variety of reasons, awareness of the importance of relationship has now received wide recognition, including among clinical psychologists.

It might be suggested, though, that our adoption of scientist-practitioner and human science models of enquiry, and our holistic perspective on what it means to be human, allow us to engage with the notion of relationship in a new and distinctive manner. This permits us to throw our considerable professional weight (we should not forget that in terms of numbers, we constitute the largest Division within the BPS), into the ring as advocates of relationship not only in terms of the therapeutic relationship, but also in its broader, even broadest sense as what defines us as human beings. We might think here of Heidegger's contention of relationship as a given of human existence, that human being is always being *with*.

It might be suggested that counselling psychologists could have some very significant role in opening up this—perhaps intellectual-seeming—notion of human being to make it relevant for the way we in our society conceptualize psychological well-being and disease. I want to pursue this notion of relationship and use it to consider how we as counselling psychologists may be in a privileged position to comment on the experience of being a person in 21st-century Britain.

It is possible to identify a groundswell of initiatives that each strive towards a democratization of the UK psychological health culture, attempting to engage not just with illness, but with what defines us as human beings. In doing so, they move away from medical/scientific approaches that have historically informed psychological health care, and attempt to develop an understanding of psychological problems that are not reliant on the disease model as applied to physical illness. As Joyce McDougal (1990) recognized in her book, *A Plea for a Measure of Abnormality*, while physical health may be defined—arguably—as the absence of physical disease, mental health is certainly not merely the absence of mental illness, however defined.

The medical model continues to be highly influential, but it is increasingly challenged by a more educated rights-conscious public, many of whom will have an awareness of critiques of pharmacology, psychiatry, and psychoanalysis, though this last is increasingly a cultural phenomenon rather than a therapeutic possibility. It is also challenged to some extent by the recent emergence of philosophical counselling, coaching, and mentoring, and sports therapies, which position themselves to respond to demand for psychologically informed personal and professional development. As Joseph argues:

> Coaching psychology provides a new way of thinking about psychological practice and how we can facilitate optimal functioning. Coaching psychology contrasts with traditional psychological approaches which have been concerned with alleviating distress and dysfunction.

> (Joseph, 2005, p. 3)

The emphasis on the customer and their choice and on consumer status which characterizes current health care policy has begun to enable service users to voice their dissatisfaction with expert scientific knowledge. Those who are financially able have increasingly sought out alternatives from among the numerous different approaches available in the private health care market place. What such people have in common is a desire for individual attention for their very own personal distress. At the same time, they are increasingly unlikely to view this as a symptom of individual psychopathology requiring medication.

It is no surprise, then, that existential texts with titles such as *Everyday Mysteries*, *Demystifying Therapy*, *Tales of Un-Knowing*, and *Paradox and Passion* have found a considerable readership beyond the therapeutic community and among the general public. One of the earliest of these kinds of books is Rogers' 1961 text *On Becoming a Person*, which was addressed as much to the mass public as it was to academic psychology, and which spoke of philosophical issues and connected counselling psychology to the public consciousness. Interest in the contribution of philosophy in general to psychological well-being appears to be in the ascendant, and a number of academic philosophers have responded to this with texts designed to promote the relevance of their discipline to problems of living (Blackburn, 1999, 2001; Grayling, 2003). Familiarity with such initiatives may constitute an important element of continuing professional development, and a useful resource for us, helping to sustain us in holistic practice. Such challenges to the traditional medical model perspective on psychological distress, while very significant, are probably not, though, in the awareness of the majority of the public who consume the self-help literature that has grown exponentially in the UK over the past quarter-century.

Though these writers hold varying positions on the desirability or otherwise of psychotherapy, each is concerned to open up debate on the meaning and significance of psychological distress. Each presents a picture of psychological health care in which all—professionals, consumers, and the currently nonconsuming general public—struggle to reach a greater understanding of what it means to be human and to engage with problems of living.

A PHILOSOPHICAL RATHER THAN A MEDICAL PERSPECTIVE ON WHAT IT MEANS TO BE WELL

Counselling psychologists are particularly well placed to engage with this movement towards a philosophical rather than medical perspective on what it means to be well. Existential-phenomenological practitioners have been concerned to make explicit connections with philosophical thought and have traced the roots not only of this approach but of therapy generally back to philosophical movements in the Ancient World. An awareness of Greek and Roman philosophy is relevant to the project of therapy regardless of our individual orientations as counselling psychologists. For the philosophical schools of Greece and Rome—the Cynics, Skeptics, Epicureans, and

Stoics—philosophy entailed a pragmatic engagement with human misery. Where, though, does this suffering originate? These philosophers have no doubt: it originates in faulty thinking and mistaken values—in particular excessive emphasis on money, competition, status, and material goods. They come from society: individual beliefs, judgements, and desires, and even people's emotional repertoires can be deformed by the corrupting influence of their society. Even a brief glance at the practice of Hellenistic philosophy is likely to convince us as ethical counselling psychologists of its differences as much as its similarity to our own work. On the positive side, we may be impressed by the motives of these philosophers, and their formulation of arguments tailored to individual temperament. On the negative side we are likely to find their emphasis on instruction of a compliant recipient of wisdom somewhat alarming. We would not want to attempt to follow Socrates' example and set ourselves up as a counter-culture of philosopher kings; instead we might argue there is a pressing need to provide a perspective on contemporary society that identifies the effects of the worst excesses of consumerism and materialism and supports people in their efforts to find ways to help *themselves* counter some of the more toxic aspects of contemporary life—preferably ways that are inexpensive and provide a sense of mastery and agency where there was previously a sense of helplessness or passivity, mirroring Freud's psychoanalytic project of "transforming . . . hysterical misery into common unhappiness" (Breuer & Freud, 1893–1895/1955, p. 305).

Smail, in his *Power, Interest and Psychology* (2005) refers to the erosion of communal living (signalled by Thatcher's position that "There's no such thing as society, only individuals and families"), and the glorification of selfishness and competition that characterizes the contemporary West. He argues that deciding what sort of world we want to live in is an ethical choice. As psychologists, we have a responsibility to consider how mechanisms of power and interest impact upon the subjective experience of individuals. There is a pressing need for us to shift away from technical individualistic treatment of distress, and move towards a position that addresses the interconnectivity of different levels of power and authority. Counselling psychologists have made significant contributions to debate on issues of social injustice, the manifestations of power, and the importance of giving voice to the oppressed, culture (Eleftheriadou, 2010; Lofthouse, 2010), gender (Tindall, Robinson, & Kagan, 2010), diagnosis (Milton, 2012), and sexuality (du Plock, 1997; Hicks, 2010; Milton, Coyle, & Legg, 2002; Spinelli, 1997).

Insofar as we have created in counselling psychology a space for diverse views and debate, we can introduce ideas of an eccentric nature—"eccentric" in the etymological sense of being "outside the centre," being marginal or liminal. In clinical work it is often this eccentric perspective—the stance that asks not "why," but "why not?"—which frequently assists clients in their pursuit of clarity about their own way of being in the world. A liminal position enables us to throw light onto different parts of the client's world, while a central position may tend to reinforce the normative, the status quo, sedimenting the client's sense of being in some way marginal or mistaken in their worldview, rather than allowing it to simply come into view as fully as possible.

A PHILOSOPHICAL PERSPECTIVE ON MOVEMENT AND EXERCISE

I think we can learn a lot from the philosophers, and not always in the most obvious ways. Kierkegaard, for instance, was remarkably prescient in his awareness of the therapeutic value of physical exercise. Walking was important for Kierkegaard for both physical and metaphysical reasons: it was his form of daily exercise and it kept him in touch with his society, it was also his way of keeping abreast of political discussion. It was a symbol of movement itself. Writing to his young niece he urges:

> Above all, do not lose your desire to walk: every day I walk myself into a state of well-being and walk away from every illness; I have walked myself into my best thoughts, and I know of no thought so burdensome that one cannot walk away from it . . . in walking one gets as close to well-being as possible, even if one does not quite reach it . . . Health and salvation can be found only in motion.
>
> (Poole & Stangerup, 1989, p. 69)

We might say there is something obsessive in Kierkegaard's attitude to walking, but I can speculate he would find the notion of driving to work, sitting at a computer much of the day, and then going to a designated site where you would walk or run on a machine, to a background of disco muzak bizarre in the extreme. For Kierkegaard physical exercise is an integral part of community life, not a way of sculpting a body.

Henry David Thoreau chimes with these sentiments in 19th-century North America, writing in *Walking and the Wild* (1851):

> I think that I cannot preserve my health and spirits, unless I spend four hours a day at least sauntering through the woods, and over the hills and fields, absolutely free from all worldly engagements.
>
> (In Miller, 2006, p. 211)

Richard Mabey, the author of *Flora Britannica* and the remarkable autobiographical *Nature Cure*, reminds us that a respect

> for the curative properties of nature goes back as far as written history. If you expose yourself to the healing currents of the outdoors, the theory goes, your ill-health will be rinsed away. The Romans had a saying, *"solvitur ambulando"*, which means, roughly, "you can work it out by walking", including your own emotional tangles.
>
> (2005, p. 223).

Mass pilgrimages were regular occurrences in the medieval world and if we know our Chaucer at all, we know the journey was at least as important as the destination. Walking in the countryside was held to be particularly beneficial, and the movement and freedom of expression seem intimately related. "The country, by the gentleness and variety of its landscapes," wrote the philosopher Michel Foucault, wins melancholics from their single obsession "by taking them away from their places that might revive the memory of their sufferings" (Mabey, 2005, pp. 223–224).

Mabey makes the connection between nature and language and identity, when he says:

> We constantly refer back to the natural world to try to discover who we are. Nature is the most potent source of metaphors to describe and explain our behavior and feelings. It is the root and branch of our language. We sing like birds, blossom like flowers, stand like oaks . . . in using the facility of language, the thing we believe most separates us from nature, we are constantly pulled back to its, and our, origins. In that sense all natural metaphors are miniature creation myths, allusions to how things came to be, and a confirmation of the unity of life.

> (2005, pp. 19–20)

We cannot always, of course, be walking in nature, and counselling psychologists must always take the situation of their client into consideration. But even leaving aside the difficulty of this for urban populations, each of these writers is concerned with the attainment of a certain balance in life: they see having a relationship with the physical world as an element of good living, what the Greeks termed *eudaimonia*, as important as our relationship with our fellow human beings.

A CASE VIGNETTE

I am constantly mindful of the therapeutic benefits of encouraging clients to reflect seriously not merely on their presenting symptoms, but also on their way of making sense of the world—the personal philosophy that guides their thoughts and actions. Sometimes I will encourage this using Socratic questioning, but quite often I find it useful to draw more explicitly on philosophical concepts to assist clients to clarify their values and beliefs. Isabel (not her real name), came to see me saying that she was unhappy in her marriage, but could not bring herself to leave her partner. She was mystified by what she experienced as her inability to act. What was she to do?

A reductionistic application of existential-phenomenological theory might lead a practitioner to attempt to bring her to an understanding that she is choosing to stay in the marriage, and is in bad faith when she tells herself (and the therapist) that she cannot leave. My curiosity about the client's worldview, though, led me to explore her conception of freedom more deeply. In the course of several sessions I gained the impression that she could not act because, in some sense, she was not *ready* to act. Her lack of readiness seemed to me to be related to her confusion about the nature of freedom. She exclaimed that she wanted to be free of the marriage, but she did not have much conception of what this might actually entail. I was reminded of the relatively simple distinction the philosopher Lehav (1998) makes between two conceptions of freedom: "negative freedom" or "freedom-from," and "positive freedom" or "freedom-for." Negative freedom means the absence of limitations. Positive freedom means being free to commit to doing what we find meaningful and significant. When Isabel and I began to explore not just what she wanted to be rid of, but more positively what she might want to commit to do with her freedom, she found that she was able to recapture her agency.

CONCLUSION

My objective in referring to a wide range of observations about the nature of human beings, and how to live a flourishing life is in part to remind us of the practical relevance of Van Deurzen's argument that what makes counselling psychology distinctive is its potential to engage with "the heroic, the historic, the sublime, the absurd, the impossible, the unknown . . . the mystery of life and of mankind" (1990, p. 9). The intervening years have seen the development of a scientist-practitioner identity that enables us to position ourselves in more democratic ways in relation to those struggling with problems of living, but the balance between art and science remains an uneasy one. It may be argued that counselling psychology's debates about art and science have to some extent missed out an engagement with the humanities—by which I mean the wealth of thought about the human condition to be found not only in academic philosophy, but also in literature, religion, music, history, and languages. As Sarah Churchwell argues:

> When we stopped being citizens and began to think of ourselves—or rather, each other—only as consumers, we relinquished thousands of years of human development. . . . Even in instrumentalist terms, the humanities represent 5,000 years of free research and development in what it means to be human. I think we should use that.

(Churchwell, 2014)

Counselling psychology, with its ability from our holistic tradition to stand above technology and manualization, offers one way of using this fabulous resource. A philosophical overview which draws its vitality from a wide range of disciplines that seek to address what it means to be human enables us to assist those struggling with problems of living in an effective and direct manner.

SUGGESTED FURTHER READING

du Plock, S. (2006). Just what is it that makes contemporary counselling psychology so different, so appealing? *Counselling Psychology Review, 21*(3), 22–33.
Spinelli, E. (1994). *Demystifying therapy*. London: Constable.

REFERENCES

Blackburn, S. (1999). *Think. A compelling introduction to philosophy*. Oxford: Oxford University Press.
Blackburn, S. (2001). *Being good. A short introduction to ethics*. Oxford: Oxford University Press.
Breuer, J., & Freud, S. (1955). Studies on hysteria. In J. Strachey (Ed. & Trans.), *Standard edition of the complete psychological works of Sigmund Freud* (Vol. 2, pp. 1–305). London: Hogarth Press (original work published 1893–1895).

Churchwell, S. (2014, November 13). Sarah Churchwell: Why the humanities matter. *Times Higher Education* [online]. Retrieved from https://www.timeshighereducation.com/churchwell/humanities (accessed April 4, 2016).

Cooper, M. (2009). Welcoming the Other: Actualising the humanistic ethic at the core of counselling psychology practice. *Counselling Psychology Review, 24*(3&4), 119–129.

Duffy, M. (1990). Counselling psychology USA, patterns of continuity and change. *Counselling Psychology Review, 5*(3), 9–18.

du Plock, S. (1997). Sexual misconceptions: A critique of gay affirmative therapy and some thoughts on an existential-phenomenological theory of sexual orientation. *Existential Analysis, 8*, 56–71.

du Plock, S., & Van Deurzen, E. (2015). The historical development and future of existential therapy. *International Journal of Psychotherapy, 19*(1), 5–14.

Eleftheriadou, Z. (2010). Cross-cultural counselling psychology. In R. Woolfe, S. Strawbridge, B. Douglas, & W. Dryden (Eds.), *Handbook of counselling psychology* (3rd ed., pp. 195–212). London: Sage.

Elton Wilson, J. (1994) Current trends in counselling psychology. *Counselling Psychology Review, 9*(4), 5–12.

Grayling, A. C. (2003). *What is good? The search for the best way to live.* London: Weidenfeld & Nicolson.

Hicks, C. (2010). Counselling psychology contributions to understanding sexuality. In M. Milton (ed.), *Therapy and beyond: Counselling psychology contributions to therapeutic and social issues* (pp. 243–258). Chichester: Wiley Blackwell.

Honderich, T. (Ed.) (2005). *The Oxford companion to philosophy.* Oxford: Oxford University Press.

Joseph, S. (2005). Person-centred coaching psychology. *The Coaching Psychologist, 2*(2), 3–5.

Lehav, R. (1998) On the possibility of dialogue between philosophical counselling and existential psychotherapy. *Existential Analysis, 9*(1), 129–144.

Lofthouse, J. (2010). The "R" word. In M. Milton (Ed.), *Therapy and beyond: Counselling psychology contributions to therapeutic and social issues.* (pp. 229–242). Chichester: Wiley Blackwell.

Mabey, R. (2005). *Nature cure.* London: Chatto & Windus.

Martin, P. (2006). Different, dynamic and determined—the powerful force of counselling psychology in the helping professions. *Counselling Psychology Review, 21*(3), 34–38.

May, R. (1983). *The discovery of being: Writings in existential psychology.* London: W. W. Norton.

McDougal, J. (1990). *Plea for a measure of abnormality.* London: Free Association Books.

Miller, S. (2006). *Conversation. A history of a declining art.* London: Yale University Press.

Milton, M. (Ed.) (2012). *Diagnosis and beyond: Counselling psychology contributions to understanding human distress.* Ross-on-Wye: PCCS Books.

Milton, M., Charles, L., Judd, D., O'Brien, M., Tipney, A., & Turner, A. (2002). The existential-phenomenological paradigm: The importance for psychotherapy integration. *Counselling Psychology Review, 17*(2), 4–22.

Milton, M., Coyle, A., & Legg, C. (2002). Lesbian and gay affirmative psychotherapy: Defining the domain. In A. Coyle & C. Kitzinger (Eds.), *Lesbian and gay psychology: New perspectives* (pp. 175–197). Malden: Blackwell Publishing.

Orlans, V., & Van Scoyoc, S. (2009). *A short introduction to counselling psychology.* London: Sage.

Poole, R. & Stangerup, H. (Eds.) (1989). *A Kierkegaard reader. Texts and narratives.* London: Fourth Estate.

Sanders, D. (2010). Cognitive and behavioural approaches. In, R. Woolde, S. Strawbridge, B. Douglas, & W. Dryden (Eds.) *Handbook of counselling psychology* (3rd ed.) London: Sage.

Smail, D. (2005). *Power, interest and psychology. Elements of a social materialist understanding of distress.* Ross-on-Wye: PCCS Books.

Spinelli, E. (1997). Human sexuality and existential-phenomenological inquiry. *Counselling Psychology Review, 12*(4), 170–178.

Steffen, E. & Hanley, T. (2014). A moment to pause and reflect on the significance of the existential paradigm for counselling psychology. *Counselling Psychology Review, 29*(2), 3–7.

Tindall, C., Robinson, J., & Kagan, C. (2010). Feminist perspectives. In R. Woolfe, S. Strawbridge, B. Douglas, & W. Dryden (Eds.), *Handbook of counselling psychology* (3rd ed., pp. 195–212). London: Sage.

van Deurzen, E. (1990). Philosophical underpinnings of counselling psychology. *Newsletter of the Special Group in Counselling Psychology, 5*(2), 8–12.

van Deurzen, E. (2015). Response to Steffen, Vossler and Joseph—From shared roots to fruitful collaboration: How counselling psychology can benefit from reconnecting with positive psychology. *Counselling Psychology Review, 30*(3), 69–72.

Woolfe, R., Strawbridge, S., Douglas, B., & Dryden, W. (Eds.) (2010). *Handbook of counselling psychology* (3rd ed.). London: Sage.

PART 2 Approaches to Counselling Psychology

Psychology

ELAINE KASKET

CHAPTER OUTLINE

INTRODUCTION 56

ONTOLOGICAL ASSUMPTIONS: IMAGE
OF THE PERSON 57

EPISTEMOLOGIES: THE WAYS OF KNOWING
WITHIN EXISTENTIAL THERAPY 58

GUIDING PRINCIPLES: CORE THEORETICAL
ASSUMPTIONS 59
    The Physical Dimension 60
    The Social and Self Dimensions 60
    The Spiritual Dimension 61

NATURE AND UNDERSTANDING
OF PSYCHOLOGICAL DISTRESS 61

THE ROLE AND PLACE OF THE THERAPEUTIC
RELATIONSHIP 62

THERAPIST, CLIENT, AND RELATIONAL
CONTRIBUTIONS TO EFFECTIVE EXISTENTIAL
THERAPY 63

CONTEMPORARY ADAPTATIONS,
DEVELOPMENTS, AND EXTENSIONS OF THE
EXISTENTIAL APPROACH 65

FUTURE ORIENTATIONS 68

CONCLUSION 69

Counselling Psychology: A Textbook for Study and Practice, First Edition. Edited by David Murphy.
© 2017 John Wiley & Sons Ltd. Published 2017 by John Wiley & Sons Ltd.

LEARNING OUTCOMES

BY THE END OF THIS CHAPTER YOU SHOULD BE ABLE TO ANSWER THE FOLLOWING KEY QUESTIONS:

1. It could be argued that some of the assumptions and practices of existential psychotherapy are difficult to reconcile with psychology. In what ways is this so?

2. What are the components of the phenomenological method, and why is each of them important in existential work?

3. Describe the nature and role of the therapeutic relationship within existentially orientated psychotherapy.

INTRODUCTION

While a relatively small proportion of counselling psychologists formally train in existential psychotherapy as their core model, far more count existentialism as a strong influence on their work with clients. This makes complete sense, for while existential philosophy and psychological science do not always mix well, existential ideas chime more harmoniously with counselling psychology than with any other branch of applied psychology. This chapter seeks to orientate the reader to the main features of existential psychotherapy, but be warned: "existential therapy" or "the existential approach" is a slippery creature that eludes easy capture and study, a many-headed hydra rather than a neatly contained, unitary therapeutic approach.

On the broadest level, existential therapy is complicated because it unabashedly engages with the paradoxes and dilemmas of a phenomenon that is as broad and deep as you can imagine—human existence itself. Adding to the complexity, it boasts many branches and schools, constituting a "rich tapestry" (Cooper, 2003, p. 1). Furthermore, each existential therapist practices in his or her own way, and consequently there are as many existential approaches as there are existential practitioners (Iacovou & Weixel-Dixon, 2015). This uniqueness runs deeper still, however. As one well-known existential practitioner put it, "There is no client *as such*. If two therapists meet the same client, it is not the same client" (Cohn, 1997, p. 33). By extension, just as it is never the same client, it is never the same therapist, and each encounter is unique.

We should not become so focused on the individual pixels that we lose sight of the bigger picture, however, for common threads connect all existential practitioners. In this chapter, therefore, we consider the broad underlying assumptions, principles, and therapeutic strategies of existential approaches. We also look at some of the main variations of existential practice, and think about what its future might be.

ONTOLOGICAL ASSUMPTIONS: IMAGE OF THE PERSON

"In this world nothing can be said to be certain," said Benjamin Franklin, "except death and taxes." While the founding father of the United States only thought of two, the founders of existential philosophy counted several more human universals, to include being born or "thrown" into existence, existing within a mortal, physical body, existing within a physical world, and existing with other beings. Strings of hyphens are sometimes employed to express the idea that human existence, or Being, is embedded within inescapable contexts (Manafi, 2010): Being-towards-death, Being-in-a-body, Being-in-the-world, and Being-with-others. This is related to existentialists' rejection of the idea of a fixed, core "self": how could the nature of a being remain constant when it is constantly moving through time, experiencing things that alter it? This is the meaning behind the maxim "Existence precedes essence" (Sartre, 1943).

While *existential* givens are shared amongst all humans, each individual is thrown into a set of unique circumstances, or *situational* givens. The taxes to which Ben Franklin referred are a situational given, provided you live in a place and time in which being taxed is a fact of life, although the existential given of freedom means you may choose not to pay. Being a carbon-based life form in a physical body is an existential given, but your genotype is a situational one. Every human is a Being-in-the-world-with-others, but your bit of the world and the particular set of others you encounter are particular to you.

Human existence is seen, therefore, as paradoxical: the existential position is an ontological Möbius strip that manages to be concurrently absolutist and relativist. While existence has certain immutable givens, there is no inherent, universal meaning, and as subjective creatures we each make our own sense of life and experiences. We are always connected to others, and yet are also fundamentally isolated within our unique meaning-making and perceiving. We are to some extent determined by our universal and situational givens, and yet are ultimately free to respond to those givens. Victor Frankl refers to this balance when he says,

> Man is not *fully* conditioned and determined but rather he determines himself whether he gives in to conditions or stands up to them. . . . What he becomes— *within the limits of endowment and environment*—he has made out of himself. [emphases added]

> (Frankl, 1963, 206, 213)

Anxiety, viewed by some other therapeutic disciplines as a psychopathology, is considered an inescapable byproduct of our confrontation with the existential and situational givens of our lives (May, 1996).

The freedom to be "self-determining" can be seen as a positive, but it is important to note that existentialism's "self-determining" human is not the same as humanistic therapy's "self-actualizing" human. The inherently socially constructive and moral human of Carl Rogers' philosophy grows and flourishes in the "right" conditions, and even in adverse ones will strive for the light, as in his metaphor of the potato sprout. While existentialism recognizes certain universal aspects of being a person—primarily involving our subservience to natural laws—fundamental goodness is not one of them, and one criticism of existential philosophy is that it is,

> essentially amoral. In emphasising human freedom, the self-creation of values . . . it has been argued that existential thought is an ethic-less, "anything goes" philosophy in which values such as justice, equality and beneficence can no longer be privileged over their opposites.

(Cooper, 2003, p. 31)

On the other hand, as Crowe (2004) has argued, it may be a misperception of existentialism to accuse it of "anything goes" moral relativism just because each person is able to choose his or her own moral priorities. "[The] realisation of the need to value freedom extends not only to our own freedom, but also to the freedom of others," Crowe says. "Sartre's conception of human self-realisation centres on the need to recognise the capacity for meaningful choice in both ourselves and others. . . . [O]ur moral choices are not unrestricted." Once again, existential philosophy eludes reductive and simplistic understandings!

EPISTEMOLOGIES: THE WAYS OF KNOWING WITHIN EXISTENTIAL THERAPY

Existential therapeutic practice is rooted in the ideas of a collection of European philosophers: Kierkegaard, Nietzsche, Heidegger, Sartre, de Beauvoir, and Merleau-Ponty chief amongst them. Although these key figures developed and promulgated the ideas outlined in the previous section, often within influential but dense early 20th-century philosophical treatises such as *Being and Time* (Heidegger, 1927), *Being and Nothingness* (Sartre, 1943), and *The Phenomenology of Perception* (Merleau-Ponty, 1962), they did not apply them to psychotherapy, which during that time was only in its infancy.

Enter Swiss psychiatrist Ludwig Binswanger, who studied under Freud and was troubled by what he saw as Freud's overly scientific, objectifying way of understanding human nature. Binswanger did not feel that people could be studied like organisms under a microscope or reduced to component parts; neither did he feel that they could be determined by their pasts or understood independent of their unique contexts. In the existential philosophy of Heidegger, Binswanger found a *phenomenological* way of thinking about psychopathology.

Phenomenology refers to the study of human experience and consciousness from an individual, first-person point of view, and Binswanger argued that this was the most appropriate stance from which to see and understand the individual sufferer's way of being-in the-world (Cooper, 2003). Scientific knowledge, psychological theories, and any other form of fore-understanding only get in the way of understanding each person in their unique appearing. Binswanger's protégé Medard Boss followed his mentor's trajectory but focused on application of this theory to psychotherapeutic practice. Incorporating Heidegger's term for the human entity, *Dasein* ("Being-there"), he developed *Daseinsanalysis*, the first form of existential psychotherapy.

It is for good reason that existential psychotherapies are often referred to as *existential-phenomenological*. Whatever differences or variations there may be amongst existential practitioners, phenomenology unites them: "[I]f therapists are not engaging phenomenologically with their clients and drawing on aspects of existential philosophy to frame their responses, then they are not practising existential therapy" (Langdridge, 2010, p. 126). In trying to stay as close as possible to the client's world, existential practitioners employ the *phenomenological method*, a disciplined approach to interaction and enquiry that aims to allow the client's lived experience to shine forth. (More about the phenomenological method will be described later in the chapter.) Existential practitioners aim to get their own ways of knowing "out of the way" so that the *client's* ways of knowing take centre stage. Existential therapies are therefore often considered "antitheory," and this sometimes proves a tricky area for existentially orientated applied psychologists, who find themselves pulled between a theoretical pillar and evidence-based post.

GUIDING PRINCIPLES: CORE THEORETICAL ASSUMPTIONS

Again, "theory" is a potentially controversial word here. One definition of theory reads "A supposition or a system of ideas intended to explain something, especially one based on general principles independent of the thing to be explained" (Oxford Dictionaries, n.d.). While existential philosophy embraces the notion of universal givens, these are fundamentally interwoven and uniquely expressed through each human being rather than being "independent," and approaching persons as "things to be explained" is a perceived feature of medico-scientific psychological thinking that existentially orientated psychotherapists reject.

The universal givens, which have already received some attention in this chapter, have been presented using varying terminology and in different combinations by various existential philosophers, but they include Being-in-the-world, Being-in-the-world-with-others, embodiment, "thrownness" into the world (also known as "facticity"), finitude, and death. These aspects of our existence represent fundamental constituents of what it is to exist, and as stated above, they are the so-called *ontological* dimensions of our lives, the common denominators of humanity. The additional universal givens of freedom and responsibility (Yalom, 1980) mean that people respond variably to universal givens such as natural laws and the inescapable physical conditions in which they exist, and we build subjective meanings from the fundamentally meaningless existence into which we are thrown at birth—this is the idiosyncratic, *ontic* dimension of each of our lives. Paradoxically, we are as different as we are the same; and existential thought and therapy are concerned with these two levels of existence. In unpacking the further theoretical underpinnings of existential therapy, it may be useful to employ the dimensions of existence as laid out by philosopher and practitioner Emmy van Deurzen (2002): the physical dimension, the social dimension, the dimension of self, and the spiritual dimension (van Deurzen-Smith, 1997).

The Physical Dimension

We exist in a physical body, in a physical world. Our embodiment both facilitates and limits us. It gives us power and the ability to act in the world, but it also renders us vulnerable: to viruses, cancers, heat, cold, gravity, earthquakes, floods, hurtling objects. We depend on oxygen, healthy blood, functioning internal organs. Our nervous systems underpin our consciousness, which reaches out into the world to engage with people and objects and to make meaning of that engagement with them—a process termed *intentionality*. The ultimate limitation of our embodiment is finitude, our inevitable physical death. While awareness of our eventual death can be significant cause of anxiety, there is a flip side: "Only to the extent that we are aware of our fragility and mortality, are we capable of savouring the life that we have" (van Deurzen-Smith, 1997, p. 111).

The Social and Self Dimensions

Existential thinking sees human beings as fundamentally relational; it is virtually impossible to consider the self and the other independently of one another. From the moment of birth, others gaze upon us, respond to us, evaluate us, and give us messages about ourselves; your sense of "me" is a complex patchwork tapestry woven from the threads of countless others' perceptions of and responses to you, and in turn, you are influencing their sense of who *they* are. This continually running two-way interpretative process between ourselves and others is termed *intersubjectivity*, and it is a primary reason that our sense of self fluctuates and changes from context to context. My overall sense of myself is that I am a good lecturer; however, if a room full of students perceives me as a poor teacher, then in that moment I see myself as one. On a better day, my self-perception shifts back again. Often, in an attempt to manage the anxiety of all of this shifting and groundlessness, we subscribe to dogmas and objectify ourselves and others, seeing people as having fixed, predictable, knowable qualities. Sartre termed this tendency *bad faith*.

The Spiritual Dimension

We are thrown into a fundamentally meaningless existence, but we are fundamentally meaning-making creatures, ever toiling to create a values-driven life. Meaning is bound up with human existence to such an extent that to succumb to an overwhelming sense of meaninglessness, and to have no hope of finding meaning, is often to desire death. The spiritual realm of existence does not just refer to religiosity, but to our overall engagement with values, ethics, and purpose, our seeking out of a valued and meaningful existence.

NATURE AND UNDERSTANDING OF PSYCHOLOGICAL DISTRESS

Registered counselling psychologists in the UK are expected to situate and understand a client's distress through the process of psychological formulation (HCPC, 2015), and here we arrive at another sticky wicket: "Existential therapy doesn't have at its base a theory of psychology designed to explain and treat human distress" (Iacovou & Weixel-Dixon, 2015, p. xvii). Some existentially orientated practitioners may instinctively shy away from the notion of formulation, associating it with explanation, prediction, and objectification; however, a formulation that is collaboratively co-constructed between therapist and client, "concerned with the personal meaning to the [client] of the events and experiences of their lives" (DCP, 2011, p. 7), can certainly be consistent with existential practice. It is likely, however, that an existential formulation will draw on philosophy as much as psychology, providing a philosophical narrative to cast light on the nature of the client's suffering.

If counselling psychologists take a critical stance to notions of psychopathology and generally steer clear of diagnostic taxonomies, existentially orientated practitioners tend to take an even stronger position: "A fundamental tenet of existential counselling and psychotherapy is a rejection of psychopathology and psychiatric diagnosis" (Langdridge, 2010, p. 134). The writings of the "anti-psychiatry movement" such as *The Myth of Mental Illness* (Szasz, 2010) and *Sanity, Madness and the Family* (Esterson & Laing, 1964), proposing "madness" and "mental illness" as being socially triggered or entirely socially constructed phenomena, nearly always form part of the core readings list on existential training programmes.

Instead of seeing phenomena that we term "anxiety," "depression," or "psychosis" as biomedical "things," the existential approach conceives of them as understandable human responses to confrontations with givens of existence. Anxiety, for example, is seen as an inevitable byproduct of living, a consequence of being thrown into a world that is not of our choosing; of having to continually exercise our freedom to make choices, without ever being able to fully predict the outcome; and of knowing that our life is moving inexorably towards death, at a moment and under circumstances that may also not be of our choosing (Cohn, 1997). Depression is seen as a response to encountering fore-closed possibilities, or to feeling constrained from acting in a valued direction. We sometimes suffer feelings of depression as a response to *existential anxiety*—the awareness that we are not living the life that we might wish, or all the experiences in life that may be possible and desirable for us. Existential approaches even resist the medicalization of more uncommon human experiences such as "schizophrenia" or "psychosis"; explored openly and phenomenologically, for example, auditory hallucinations of voice-hearers are often discovered to be comprehensible and meaningful (Romme, Escher, Dillon, Corstens, & Morris, 2009). "[T]he philosophical framework within which existential thera-pists try to understand their disturbances applies to 'psychotic' clients as much as it does to other clients" (Cohn, 1997, p. 109).

THE ROLE AND PLACE OF THE THERAPEUTIC RELATIONSHIP

Irvin Yalom's mantra flows through the work of all existential practitioners: "It's the relationship that heals, the relationship that heals, the relationship that heals" (1989, p. 91). While many therapeutic traditions see the relationship as centrally important to the therapeutic enterprise (Cooper, 2015), existential philosophy's emphasis on our fundamentally relational nature translates into a therapeutic approach that is particularly relationally focused. Of course, a rela-tionship can have many qualities, and a therapist could relate to a client by dominating them, interpreting them, guiding them, soothing them, befriending them, arguing with them, passively listening to them, and so on. The common metaphor employed to describe the relationship between therapist and client in existential therapy, however, is that of "fellow travellers" (Yalom, 2001, p. 6). The therapist is not mystified or elevated as a sage: "Existential psychotherapy is a relationship between two people . . . an encounter, a meeting of souls. In this meeting each person is just as important as the other" (van Deurzen & Adams, 2011, p. 27). Yalom emphasizes the mutual humanness and fallibil-ity present in the encounter when he describes psychotherapy as "a personal discussion between two people, one of them more anxious than the other" (Yalom, 2001, p. 108).

In the case illustration later in this chapter, I present my work with a young bereaved woman, Martina, who was concerned that she was not "grieving cor-rectly." In a different kind of therapy, being knowledgeable about bereavement theories, I could have easily assumed the role of expert. I could have taken a psycho-educative role, explaining how other, empirically supported concep-tualizations of bereavement have largely superseded stage models. I could have taught her to reduce her symptoms of anxiety, perhaps using cognitive-behavioural techniques. Working existentially, however, I made no attempt to question or explain Martina's experience in the way she was seeking to do to herself; instead, I travelled with her, seeking to get as "experience near" as I could, trying to "understand the experience of grief through the eyes of those immersed in it" (Iacovou & Weixel-Dixon, p. 28). Through this kind of relating, experiencing my unquestioning acceptance of the validity of *her* experience, Martina became able to accept it herself.

Existential therapists draw a distinction between "I-It" and "I-Thou" interactions, categories of relating originally conceptualized by the philosopher and theologian Martin Buber (1878–1965). The kind of objectifying stance that Ludwig Binswanger felt that he saw in Sigmund Freud's approach is the essence of "I-It" relating. When we are in this mode, we stand apart from the other, gazing upon them with an interpretative, analytic, observing type of intention. In this position, we tend to take a "doing-to" approach to the object of our study, tinkering with it through various interventions, predicting its behaviour, and engineering particular outcomes. The alternative is "I-Thou" relating, in which we stand alongside the other, assuming the "fellow traveller" role of which Yalom spoke. As fellow travellers, therapist and client together look at the client's experience. Rather than "doing to," the fellow traveller is focused upon "being with," and understanding and healing are a collaborative process. "We journey with our clients as they explore and experience their world: listening to what they see and feel, reflecting it back, asking questions, and providing companionship and support" (Cooper, 2015, p. 27).

THERAPIST, CLIENT, AND RELATIONAL CONTRIBUTIONS TO EFFECTIVE EXISTENTIAL THERAPY

So if existential therapists eschew the "expert" role, privileging the client's truth instead, what does the therapeutic relationship look like? What form does the therapeutic dialogue take? Heidegger uses a Greek word—*aletheia*—which is variously translated as "truth," "disclosure," or even "shining forth," as a light in a clearing. Rather than being the shiner of the light or the determiner of the truth, the therapist aims to be a guardian of the clearing, helping to create the conditions where the client's experience can come out of the shadows and be explored and understood. Phenomenologically oriented questioning is governed by three main "rules," all followed in service of being able to "stand alongside" the client's experience as much as possible.

The rule of "epoche" is sometimes referred to as "bracketing." The therapist endeavours to "bracket" all assumptions, predictions, expectations—in short, anything that could get in the way of more fully understanding the client's experience. As humans always come equipped with learnings and assumptions, through which they engage with the world, it is understood that epoche is something that is never fully achieved, but in existential practice it is striven for, for "even when bracketing is not likely or feasible, the very recognition of bias lessens its impact upon our immediate experience" (Spinelli, 1989, p. 17). In the therapeutic encounter, even if the existential practitioner is carrying theories or assumptions based on psychological theory or past experience, he or she attempts to bracket these.

The second rule, the rule of description, is captured by the simple maxim, "Describe, don't explain" (Spinelli, 1989, p. 17). Keeping this mantra in mind not only centres the therapist in the "I-Thou" relationship described above, it encourages the client to reflect more deeply on aspects of their experience, in a way that increases self-awareness and, consequently, freedom. Imagine a client who has had painful experiences in relationships, but who avoids exploring the meaning of this for her. "Things happen," she says. "Nobody's fault. Just bad luck." Employing this stock explanation avoids awareness of feeling; it denies responsibility and agency; it prevents understanding. Ultimately, distancing herself in this way limits her ability to respond freely and openly to relationships with others. In existential therapy, she would be encouraged to *describe* her experiences and their meaning for her, attending to things that have long been "unreflected." Through this process, the client better understands her relating; in so doing, she acquires more freedom to choose her responses to others, from a wiser and more aware place.

The rule of horizontalization (or equalization) guides the therapist to avoid placing hierarchies of importance on all the things the client brings, to "treat each initially as having equal value or significance" (Spinelli, 1989, p. 18). By seeing all of the client's experience as having validity and potential significance (rather than arbitrarily privileging certain things and ignoring others), we can explore more of the whole picture, accessing important and useful understandings in the process. For example, if I am particularly interested in people's fear of death, I could find myself paying inordinate attention to death anxiety every time it seems to rear its head, unilaterally deciding that it should be a primary focus of therapy. Blindly following this preference would be the opposite of horizontalization.

Whilst bracketing preconceptions, privileging description, and applying horisontalization/equalization, existential therapists typically engage in *Socratic dialogue*—also referred to as *guided discovery*—with their clients. Professing ignorance of whatever topic was under discussion, the Ancient Greek philosopher Socrates instead engaged in sustained, thoughtful, curious questioning to encourage his students to examine their own assumptions, to explore their own ideas, and, ultimately, to answer their own questions. This method supports the therapeutic process in a number of ways: helping clients to become aware of and live in accordance with their values; working with clients' experience directly rather than as viewed through theory and abstract concepts; encouraging clients to experience and accept their "negative" feelings; assisting clients to explore all aspects of their being, noticing how interconnected they are; and generally helping clients to be more open to life's possibilities and potentials (Cooper, 2003).

CONTEMPORARY ADAPTATIONS, DEVELOPMENTS, AND EXTENSIONS OF THE EXISTENTIAL APPROACH

As noted in the introduction to this chapter, there is no unitary "existential therapy," although certain elements unite all existential approaches, such as phenomenological engagement with clients and rootedness in existential philosophy. In the book *Existential Therapies* (2003), the British counselling psychologist Mick Cooper provides a comprehensive yet succinct overview of the various schools of existential therapy, and the interested reader is referred to this text for a more thoroughgoing review. The main schools of existential therapy, as laid out by Cooper, are the original Daseinsanalysis of Binswanger and Boss; the meaning-focused logotherapy of Viennese psychiatrist Viktor Frankl; the American existential-humanistic school represented by Rollo May and Irvin Yalom; the existentially influenced approach of finding meaning in madness represented by Scottish psychiatrist/antipsychiatrist R. D. Laing; the British School of existential analysis birthed by counselling psychologists Emmy van Deurzen and Ernesto Spinelli; and brief existential therapies as covered by American psychologist James Bugental and British school-linked psychotherapists Freddie and Alison Strasser.

In the UK, the political, economic, and organizational forces governing mental health provision in the UK act as primary drivers of contemporary adaptations to existential practice. The current climate is characterized by an emphasis on therapeutic efficacy and measurement of outcome. In order for something to be measured, it has to be clearly defined; hence, therapies that better lend themselves to definition and manualization are thriving, with cognitive-behavioural therapies dominating government-funded psychological services. Existentially orientated practitioners now grapple with the dilemma of how—and whether—to adapt or evolve with the dominant systems. This will be discussed further in the "Future Orientations" section below, but first, a clinical example of an existentially orientated approach with one bereaved client.

CLINICAL EXAMPLE

Martina (not her real name) was a 25-year-old woman who made an appointment with me 2 months after the death of her mother, saying that her bereavement was preventing her being able to focus and function optimally at her job. Having consulted stage models of grief, she felt that she was not progressing through the stages properly, or sufficiently quickly. Her contact in Human Resources planted the seed that perhaps after 2 months' time Martina's grief might be "turning into something else," like depression. Conflicting reports of personal bereavement experiences from various well-meaning colleagues had confused Martina about how she was "supposed to feel," and recently she had been particularly alarmed when one colleague said, "It's something that you never fully get over." Martina very much wanted to get over it and wondered about the possibility of anti-depressant medication to lift her mood and help her "get control of her emotions."

Relevant Context

Martina was an only child who relied on her mother. "We were the best of friends," she said of Josie. "We told each other everything." Unfortunately, Josie gradually began to drink heavily and batted away her daughter's attempts at intervention. Martina's worst fears were realized when Josie was diagnosed with cancer, linked to excessive alcohol use. Only 7 weeks passed between diagnosis and death. Martina was devastated. She wrestled with feelings of isolation; with sadness and grief so overwhelming that she could not look at photographs or possessions of her mother's; with disbelief and shock at her mother's being gone; with anger at her mother for having "drunk herself to death"; with guilt over her anger; with frustration at colleagues for saying "the wrong things"; with helplessness in the face of her feelings; and with a conviction that life was not meaningful without her mother.

Existential Formulation

Martina came to therapy having been thrown into touch with one of the more difficult existential givens of the physical world: death. In existential philosophy, the reality of life's finitude is one of the primary drivers of existential anxiety. Confronted with the incontrovertible situation of her loss, Martina's response was to fight against it in various ways. While on one hand she was under no illusion that her mother had died, on the other she struggled to accept it: "it shouldn't have happened to her, she seemed so healthy." Martina was also desperate to rid herself of the overwhelming anxiety and grief she was experiencing. Attempting to gain control over her experience, she resorted to explanations, theories of grief, and predictions about its "typical"

course. Finding herself unable to adhere to these templates, she was beset by even more anxiety and even shame that she could not "pull herself together."

Therapeutic Work

As a counselling psychologist knowledgeable about bereavement theory, I know research evidence does not support orderly progression through stages of grief—the expectations against which Martina was measuring herself. Instead, the newer theories of grief situate it as a fluid, highly idiosyncratic process; this view is strongly aligned with the existential view of highly individual responses to universal givens. When seeing bereaved clients, the approach that usually seems to fit the best is an existential one.

Martina initially felt that she would find some relief by knowing whether her grief was "normal," and she sought my opinion on this. I could have given her an answer straight away from an "expert" position, saying for example that everyone grieves differently, but this would not have been effective as guided discovery. Through Socratic questioning, I gently challenged Martina's expectations that her experience—or her father's—would or should conform to a certain template.

MARTINA: *I'm confused about what's right. I'm too sad. It's been too long . . . should I be feeling this bad still?*

ELAINE: *What do you mean by "too long"?*

MARTINA: *I don't know. Is it normal that I'm crying every day? I mean, my father's just getting on with it.*

ELAINE: *And his just getting on with it . . . does that seem more "right"?*

MARTINA: *No. No, not at all. That bothers me, too. It's like she never existed. I feel like he should be more upset.*

ELAINE: *So your response and your father's response to your mother's death are really quite different?*

MARTINA: *Oh, god, very.*

ELAINE: *What do you make of that?*

MARTINA: *Well, you know, that's just the way he is. He's not like me at all. He doesn't show his feelings; he never has. He's quite traditional. English.*

ELAINE: *Not like you at all ... mm. I guess I'm wondering whether it actually would have surprised you if you and your father had reacted in the same way.*

MARTINA: *[pause] It would have, actually.*

This dialogue drew attention to the understandably different ways in which she and her father were responding to death, gently challenging Martina's sedimented idea that there must be "right" and "wrong" ways to grieve, if only she could work it out. This not only promoted acceptance of her own experience, she also felt less pressure to persuade her "stiff upper lip" father to respond to his bereavement in a "more emotional" way, recognizing her father's freedom to choose his response to his own bereavement. Conceiving of grief as an individual response to a universal given also helped Martina critically question the idea that her grief was "tipping over into depression" just because it had been 2 months since her loss.

In the next phase of our work, Martina spoke about the guilt she felt over not having been able to save her mother from her self-destructive behaviour. In a social situation, one might respond to someone expressing such guilt with explicit reassurance, or with challenging Martina's belief that she was to blame. In the context of therapy, however, I encouraged exploration of not just the guilt, but of any other aspects of Martina's experience that were being avoided.

MARTINA: *I was the only person who knew how much of a problem she had, how much she was drinking. I was the only one in a position to stop her. It was kind of my responsibility. And, god, I tried ...*

ELAINE: *Mmm. You did. You did try.*

MARTINA: *I tried everything I knew to do.*

ELAINE: *And yet ...*

MARTINA: *Nothing worked. Nothing helped.*

ELAINE: *What was that like for you? You knew everything. You were as close to her as anyone. And yet ...*

MARTINA: *It was the most maddening, frustrating, frightening thing ever. Especially when it was killing her, and I knew she knew that. And I was really ... I was really ... no. Never mind.*

ELAINE *[GENTLY]*: *You were really ...*

[pause]

MARTINA *[QUIETLY]*: *... angry with her. [sharp intake of breath—crying]*

ELAINE *[SOFTLY]*: *Angry with her. [pause] That's part of it too. You took a sharp breath there. That seems a hard part of it for you.*

MARTINA: *[nods]*

[Silence for a while together]

In this excerpt, through encouraging descriptive exploration of what she was experiencing, I helped Martina reflect on how difficult it was for her to confront the limits of her control, and I showed an acceptance of and curiosity about all her feelings, not judging any of these as right or wrong. The more Martina was able to adopt a similar attitude, the more her shame and guilt diminished, and with this Martina moved towards a greater acceptance of her mother's death.

In the latter stage of therapy, Martina began considering how she could derive some sense of meaning or purpose in her mother's death. Shying away from suggestion-making or advice-giving, I used guided discovery to help her think this through. Ultimately Martina decided that she wanted to become involved with a charitable organization that provided education and support about alcohol-related liver disease. She planned to participate in a charity run in her mother's memory as well as becoming more significantly involved by volunteering her time and public relations experience. We ended therapy after 10 sessions. While Martina was not "over" her loss, she no longer felt that getting past her grief was necessary in order to exist.

FUTURE ORIENTATIONS

As du Plock (2010) observed in the third edition of *The Handbook of Counselling Psychology*, "The current political climate presents humanistic therapists with a number of challenges, principally with regard to engaging with demands for evidence-based practice" (p. 147). Alongside Gestalt and person-centred therapies, du Plock counted existential-phenomenological as being a core member of the family of humanistic therapies, and there is no question that latter-day developments in UK mental health service provision have profoundly changed the landscape for both counselling psychologists and existential psychotherapists. These include the rising focus on evidence-based practice that du Plock identified, with its focus on outcome measurement and demonstrable results. The past decade has also witnessed the nationwide implementation of Improving Access to Psychological Therapies (IAPT), which largely limits its offerings to those randomized controlled trial (RCT)-supported therapeutic approaches that come recommended by the National Institute for Health and Care Excellence (NICE). Finally, 2009 saw the introduction of statutory regulation for practitioner psychologists, with competencies for each type of psychology set by the Health and Care Professions Council (HCPC) and enshrined in standards of proficiency that registrants must meet.

In light of the above developments, practitioner psychologists and the programmes that train them have evolved and adapted in order to survive. Keeping a weather eye on future employability for its graduates, at least one existentially orientated doctoral programme in counselling psychology requires its trainees to have a clinical placement in the NHS before graduating. Common standards of proficiency for a practitioner psychologist must be met in order to qualify, irrespective of how well they sit with traditional existential-phenomenological thought, but it is notable that the counselling psychology-specific competencies often reference "critical evaluation," as though to provide a tentative, questioning counterpoint to the more definitive flavour of some of the overarching competencies.

No unified position exists on how to meet the above challenges; tensions crackle and debates rage amongst counselling psychologists and existential practitioners alike. While some advocate cooperation with and adaptation to the structures and standards involved in contemporary mental health service provision (e.g., Cooper, 2011; Rayner & Vitali, 2014), others have employed the Sartrean concept of "bad faith" when they warn against getting into bed with purveyors of evidence-based therapies (Rogers, Maidman, & House, 2011). While some see existential therapy as integrate-able with mainstream approaches, and as sitting comfortably within the pluralistic ethos of counselling psychology, others (such as influential existential thinker and practitioner, Ernesto Spinelli) "[argue] that the principles of existential therapy are so radical and unique that they cannot be simply combined with more mainstream perspectives" (Cooper, 2015, p. 7).

On counselling psychology doctoral programmes where the existential-phenomenological approach is the core model, trainees scratch their heads over whether they can or "should" do existential formulations. They find their existential values and practices challenged by their placements within the NHS. Some are sufficiently flummoxed that they undertake doctoral research to further understand how such a juxtaposition can work, such as one trainee study that sifts through how existential therapists manage to practise brief existential psychotherapy within NHS primary care (Koebbel, 2016). Interestingly, the newer publications about existential therapy seem to reflect and respond to the current service provision climate, guiding practitioners towards how they might exist and work within these contexts. For example, in contrast to the older, more anti-technique generation of texts about existential approaches, newer books are often unabashedly practical, referencing "skills" and "techniques" (e.g., *Skills in Existential Counselling and Psychotherapy* from van Deurzen & Adams, 2011, and *Existential Therapy: 100 Key Points and Techniques* from Iacovou & Weixel-Dixon, 2015). Others emphasize the connection between *au courant* pluralism and existential thought and practice (see Cooper, 2015; Manafi, 2010). The debates may go on, but it seems apparent that as mental health provision structures and regulations in the UK continue to evolve, existential approaches and counselling psychology will need to change alongside them, lest they become exclusively relegated to the realm of independent practice, or disappear altogether.

CONCLUSION

Orlans and van Scoyoc (2009), in their *Short Introduction to Counselling Psychology*, argue that the tricky business of defining counselling psychology is largely down to "the gradual separation of mainstream psychology from its parent discipline of philosophy" (p. vii). This widening gulf is perhaps most clearly apparent for existentially orientated practitioners, who despite their diversity share at least one common denominator: "they base their work primarily on philosophy rather than on psychology" (van Deurzen & Adams, 2011, p. 1). In light of this inherent tension, even the deceptively simple title of this chapter— "Existential Counselling Psychology"—could be viewed as at least paradoxical, and perhaps even controversial. In addition, the title may sit strangely for other reason: A registered counselling psychologist is obliged to adopt a pluralistic stance, developed through multimodal training and formalized in the *Standards of Proficiency*: "Registrant [counselling] psychologists must . . . be able to implement therapeutic interventions based on a range of evidence-based models of formal psychological therapy" (HCPC, 2015, p. 24). Existential counselling psychology, therefore, may seem a bit of a misnomer. If one defines one's approach as exclusively existential, does one remain a true counselling psychologist?

Debates and questions around definition aside, however, counselling psychology's very roots are embedded in existential philosophy, and despite many contextual changes, its continuing connection to those roots is clear. Even for those practitioners who never offer formal existential therapy, the core values and assumptions they hold as counselling psychologists owe everything to existentialism: the emphasis on values, subjectivity, and intersubjectivity; the phenomenological approach to enquiry and interaction; the resistance to privileging any one way of knowing; and the focus on the individual in context.

SUGGESTED FURTHER READING

The first two books listed are recent overviews of existential thought and practice that are accessible and clear; the third considers existential practice within counselling psychology specifically.

Cooper, M. (2015). *Existential psychotherapy and counselling: Contributions to a pluralistic practice*. London: Sage.

Iacovou, S., & Weixel-Dixon, K. (2015). *Existential therapy: 100 key points and techniques*. Hove: Routledge.

Manafi, E. (2010). Existential-phenomenological contributions to counselling psychology's relational framework. Chichester: Wiley-Blackwell.

REFERENCES

Cohn, H. W. (1997). *Existential thought and therapeutic practice: An introduction to existential psychotherapy*. London: Sage.

Cooper, M. (2003). *Existential therapies*. London: Sage.

Cooper, M. (2011). Meeting the demand for evidence-based practice. *Therapy Today, 22*(4), 10–16.

Cooper, M. (2015). *Existential psychotherapy and counselling: Contributions to a pluralistic practice*. London: Sage.

Crowe, J. (2004). Is an existentialist ethics possible? *Philosophy Now (47)*. Retrieved from https://philosophynow.org/issues/47/Is_an_Existentialist_Ethics_Possible (accessed February 28, 2017).

DCP (Division of Clinical Psychology) (2011). Good practice guidelines on the use of psychological formulation. Leicester: The British Psychological Society.

du Plock, S. (2010). Humanistic approaches. In R. Woolfe, S. Strawbridge, B. Douglas, & W. Dryden (Eds.), *The Handbook of Counselling Psychology* (3rd ed., pp. 130–150). London: Sage.

Esterson, A., & Laing, R. D. (1964). *Sanity, madness and the family*. London: Penguin.

Frankl, V. (1963). *Man's search for meaning*. New York: Washington Square Press.

HCPC (Health and Care Professions Council) (2015). *Standards of proficiency: Practitioner psychologists*. London: Health and Care Professions Council.

Heidegger, M. (1927 [1962]). *Being and time* (J. Macquarrie & E. Robinson, Trans.). Oxford: Blackwell.

Iacovou, S., & Weixel-Dixon, K. (2015). *Existential therapy: 100 key points and techniques*. Hove: Routledge.

Koebbel, C. (2016). *Talking about life in a serious way: Existential-phenomenological therapeutic practice in primary care*. (Unpublished doctoral thesis.) New School of Psychotherapy and Counselling Psychology, London.

Langdridge, D. (2010). Existential psychotherapy. In M. Barker & A. Vossler (Eds.), *Understanding counselling and psychotherapy*. London: The Open University/Sage.

Manafi, E. (2010). Existential-phenomenological contributions to counselling psychology's relational framework. In M. Milton (Ed.), *Therapy and beyond: Counselling psychology contributions to therapeutic and social issues* (pp. 21–39). Chichester: Wiley-Blackwell.

May, R. (1996). *The meaning of anxiety* (rev. ed.). New York: W.W. Norton & Company.

Merleau-Ponty, M. (1962). *Phenomenology of perception* (C. Smith, Trans.). London: Routledge.

Orlans, V., & van Scoyoc, S. (2009). *A short introduction to counselling psychology*. London: Sage.

Oxford Dictionaries(n.d.). Theory. Retrieved from http://www.oxforddictionaries.com/definition/english/theory (accessed February 28, 2017).

Rayner, M., & Vitali, D. (2014). CORE blimey: Existential therapy scores GOALS! *Existential Analysis, 25*(2), 296.

Rogers, A., Maidman, J., & House, R. (2011). The bad faith of evidence-based practice: Beyond counsels of despair. *Therapy Today, 22*(6), 26.

Romme, M., Escher, S., Dillon, J., Corstens, D., & Morris, M. (2009). *Living with voices: 50 stories of recovery*. Ross-on-Wye: PCCS Books.

Sartre, J. P. (1943 [1958]). *Being and nothingness* (H. E. Barnes, Trans.). London: Metheun & Co. Ltd.

Spinelli, E. (1989). *The interpreted world: An introduction to phenomenological psychology*. London: Sage.

Szasz, T. (2010). *The myth of mental illness: Foundations of a theory of personal conduct* (revised ed.). Glasgow: HarperCollins Publishers.

van Deurzen, E. (2002). *Existential counselling and psychotherapy in practice* (2nd ed.). London: Sage.

van Deurzen, E., & Adams, M. (2011). *Skills in existential counselling and psychotherapy*. London: Sage.

van Deurzen-Smith, E. (1997). *Everyday mysteries: Existential dimensions of psychotherapy*. London: Routledge.

Yalom, I. (1980). *Existential psychotherapy*. New York: Basic Books.

Yalom, I. (2001). *The gift of therapy*. London: Piatkus Books Ltd.

Yalom, I. (1989). *Love's executioner and other tales of psychotherapy*. London: Penguin.

6 Person-Centred Experiential Counselling Psychology

DAVID MURPHY

CHAPTER OUTLINE

INTRODUCTION 73

ONTOLOGICAL ASSUMPTIONS: IMAGE OF THE PERSON 74

EPISTEMOLOGY: WAYS OF KNOWING 75

GUIDING PRINCIPLES AND CORE ASSUMPTIONS 75

NATURE AND UNDERSTANDING OF PSYCHOLOGICAL DISTRESS 77

THE ROLE AND PLACE OF THE THERAPEUTIC RELATIONSHIP 79

THERAPIST, CLIENT, AND RELATIONAL CONTRIBUTIONS TO EFFECTIVE PERSON-CENTRED EXPERIENTIAL COUNSELLING PSYCHOLOGY 80

ADAPTATIONS, DEVELOPMENTS, AND EXTENSIONS OF ORIGINAL APPROACH 81
    Focusing Oriented Therapy 81
    Pre-therapy 81
    Emotion Focused Therapy 82

FUTURE ORIENTATIONS 84

CONCLUSION 84

Counselling Psychology: A Textbook for Study and Practice, First Edition. Edited by David Murphy.
© 2017 John Wiley & Sons Ltd. Published 2017 by John Wiley & Sons Ltd.

LEARNING OUTCOMES

BY THE END OF THIS CHAPTER YOU SHOULD BE ABLE TO ANSWER THE FOLLOWING KEY QUESTIONS

1. What are the main philosophical and theoretical ideas underpinning the person-centred experiential approach to counselling psychology?

2. In what ways does person-centred experiential counselling psychology differ from other approaches?

3. What are the main issues for practice in the area of person-centred experiential counselling psychology?

INTRODUCTION

This chapter presents the person-centred experiential approach to counselling psychology. Sanders (2012) has referred to the wide array of person-centred "and" experiential psychotherapies as representing many "tribes" within one approach. The term *person-centred experiential* (PCE) is used in this chapter to represent a contemporary psychotherapy at the very nexus of the array. Bringing the person-centred together with the experiential in a single term, person-centred experiential, intentionally serves to demonstrate both how person-centred therapy is inherently experiential and that person-centred experiential is a contemporary psychotherapy distinct from the classical client-centred approach. In making explicit the experiential it also illuminates that the focus of therapeutic work is on the client's internal subjective phenomenological *experiencing* of life. However, putting the term "person-centred" up front serves to acknowledge that the client is always their own best expert and is able to direct both the content and process of therapy in a constructive direction.

The wide array (or tribes) of the person-centred and experiential therapies includes, for example, classical client-centred therapy (based exclusively on empathic understanding responses made to clients, Brodley, 1996), dialogical (Schmid, 2006) and pragmatic (Cain, 2010) person-centred therapy, emotion focused therapy (Elliott & Greenberg, 2001), and focusing oriented therapy (Gendlin, 1996). Each of these approaches was founded upon the work of American psychologist Carl Rogers. Becoming a person-centred experiential counselling psychologist involves a thorough and rigorous training that will demand an in-depth consideration of the concept of experiencing and experiential work. In training the central focus is on cultivating a particular *way-of-being* that is unique to each counselling psychologist. Because developing a way-of-being is the central aim of the therapeutic training, each individual cultivates their own *personal style* as a therapist (Rennie, 1998). Whilst most counselling psychology training courses will provide some basic training in person-centred experiential therapies, due to the demands of meeting standards in prescriptive curricula, it is more likely that the independent route to qualification will provide the best route to becoming a person-centred experiential counselling psychologist.

The person-centred approach was founded by Carl Rogers during the 1940s and 1950s. Since then the approach has developed and grown into one of the most widely practised forms of therapy. Essential to the person-centred experiential approach is the necessity and sufficiency of a therapeutic relationship between client and therapist to bring about constructive personality change. The therapist is trusted to develop their own way of working within the relational framework set out by Rogers (1951). Rogers (1986, pp. 3–4) stated the person-centred approach "encourages those who incorporate these values to develop their own special and unique ways of being, their own ways of implementing this shared philosophy."

Despite recent moves towards pluralistic eclecticism and broad-based theoretical integration within counselling psychology and psychotherapy more generally, person-centred experiential therapy is practised amongst counselling psychologists that affirmatively recognize the primary importance of the therapeutic relationship conditions (these are discussed below in more detail). Hence, the person-centred experiential approach is a powerful, radical approach to therapy that respects the client's right to self-determination and trusts in the client's capacities for self-direction and constructive growth. In this chapter I will consider the underlying assumptions that inform the approach, the guiding principles, the theory of distress, and theory of therapy. I will also present a case example, consider contemporary developments, and explore future directions for application.

ONTOLOGICAL ASSUMPTIONS: IMAGE OF THE PERSON

Person-centred experiential counselling psychology is based on an ontological assumption of what *is* a *person*; the view held is radically different to those underpinning the behavioural, cognitive or psychoanalytic schools. Rogers (1957a, p. 201) described the nature of a person as basically trustworthy, suggesting that the basic characteristics and potentials, of a person are

> towards development, differentiation, cooperative relationships; whose life tends to move from dependence to independence; whose impulses tend naturally to harmonise into a complex and changing pattern of self-regulation; whose total character is such as to tend to preserve himself and his species, and perhaps to move towards its further evolution.

Lietaer (2002) extends this by suggesting the image of a person means to be both *proactive* and *reactive*, and is driven by a tendency towards actualization. A person, he suggests, has a *margin of freedom* and is therefore not completely determined; is *pro-social*; and lives in a tension between *autonomy* and *belonging*.

Schmid (2003) has further emphasized the organismic perspective. He suggests that the term *person*-centred rests on the image of the person as having both a substantial (physical organism) and relational (social) dimension. Substantial refers to the "independence and uniqueness, freedom and dignity, unity, sovereignty and self-determination, responsibility, human rights" of a person. The relational dimension highlights the importance of "relationship, dialogue, partnership, connection with the world, interconnectedness and community" (Schmid, 2013, p. 68).

EPISTEMOLOGY: WAYS OF KNOWING

Person-centred experiential counselling psychology is firmly grounded in the concept of experiencing. It is the client's subjective sense of their experience that therapists aim to empathically understand. The approach suggests that the best vantage point from which to know the client's experience is from the client's own *internal frame of reference* (Rogers, 1951). The therapist is concerned with the phenomenology of the client's subjective experience.

Subjective experience is considered to be reality. Reality as perceived is dependent on interaction with others and the environment. The person-centred experiential approach is concerned with *experiencing* and the meaning that is given to experience, consequently it could be argued that the person-centred experiential approach is based on realist epistemology. Rogers (1961, p. 22) made a very particular point in suggesting that *experience* was the most reliable and valid, even the "highest authority" in terms of data and knowledge.

GUIDING PRINCIPLES AND CORE ASSUMPTIONS

Person-centred experiential counselling psychology supports the idea of an actualizing tendency (Rogers, 1963) as a basic tendency in every living organism, including humans, to maintain or enhance itself (Rogers, 1951). Originally, the actualizing tendency was proposed as the sole source of motivation responsible for all growth and development. It was hypothesized that the actualizing tendency could account for the observation that organisms continue to strive to fulfil their potential, even when environmental conditions are not conducive for growth.

The person-centred experiential approach holds the image of the person as basically trustworthy. Linking this to the actualizing tendency suggests that when social environmental conditions are conducive for growth, the actualizing tendency provides the motivation for the person to grow in ways that are socially constructive. This is not the same as saying that people are intrinsically *good*. People are equally able to develop, act, and behave in destructive ways. As the theory suggests it is the *interaction* of the person with the social environmental conditions that determines optimal growth.

Rogers's (1951) proposal that a person can be trusted to grow in a constructive direction remains a radical proposition and was a departure from the dominant views of analytic psychology and the emerging behaviourism at the time. Even today none of the other major schools of psychology holds this belief in human nature as a fundamental underlying premise to their work. The implication for person-centred experiential counselling psychology is that in therapy it is the client who is trusted to know what is best for them, to know what they need to focus on and bring forward in therapy. As Rogers (1961, pp. 11–12) said

> it is the client who knows what hurts, what directions to go, what problems are crucial, what experiences have been deeply buried. It began to occur to me that unless I had a need to demonstrate my own cleverness and learning, I would do better to rely upon the client for the direction of movement in the process.

The following table was adapted from Rogers (1951) by Murphy and Hayes (2015, pp. 297–298) and sets out some of the key propositions to understanding the person, development, and therapy from within the approach.

1.	All individuals (organisms) exist in a continually changing world of experience (phenomenal field) of which they are the centre.
2.	The individual organism reacts to the (phenomenal) field as it is experienced and perceived. This perceptual field is "reality" for the individual.
3.	The individual reacts as an organized whole to this phenomenal field. If one part of the organism is affected then this in turn has a knock on effect for all other parts. The theory is that organisms are holistic.
4.	The organism has one basic tendency and striving—to actualize, maintain, and enhance the experiencing organism.
5.	Behaviour is basically the goal-directed attempt of the organism to satisfy its needs as experienced, in the field as perceived.
6.	Emotion accompanies and facilitates behaviour. The type and intensity of the emotion is related to the perceived need and significance of the behaviour for the maintenance and enhancement of the individual.
7.	The internal frame of reference of the individual provides the best point of reference for understanding behaviour.
8.	A portion of the experience of the organism becomes known as the self.
9.	As a result of interaction with the environment, and particularly as a result of being evaluated in interactions with others, the structure of self is formed.
10.	Values attach to experiences, and the values that are a part of the self-structure, can be values experienced directly by the organism, or values that are introjected or taken in from others, but perceived in distorted fashion, as if they had been experienced directly.
11.	As experiences occur in the life of the individual, they are either (a) symbolized, perceived, and organized into some relationship to the self; (b) ignored because there is no perceived relationship to the self-structure; (c) denied symbolization or given a distorted symbolization because the experience is inconsistent with the structure of the self. Thus, we may see our experiences as relevant and integrate them or ignore them as irrelevant. If we experience something that does not fit with our self-concept, we may deny it to awareness or distort it to make it fit.
12.	Mostly people adopt ways of behaving consistent with the concept of self.
13.	Behaviour may be brought about by organic experiences and needs that have not been symbolized. Such behaviour may be inconsistent with the structure of the self; in such instances the behaviour is not "owned" by the individual. In other words, we may behave as a result of experiences or needs that we have denied. These behaviours may conflict with our self-concept so we refuse to accept that we are doing it.

14.	*Psychological maladjustment exists when we experience something that does not fit self-concept and when the experience is incongruent with the self, there is a basic or potential psychological tension.*
15.	*Psychological adjustment exists when our actions and experiences fit with our self-concepts.*
16.	*Any experience that is inconsistent with the organization or structure of self may be perceived as a threat. The greater the threat the more rigid the self-structure becomes.*
17.	*When threat to the self-structure is removed experiences that were previously inconsistent may be perceived and assimilated into the self-structure.*
18.	*As the individual becomes integrated they are more understanding and accepting of others.*
19.	*The individual gradually replaces a value system—based largely upon distorted introjections—with organismic valuing.*

NATURE AND UNDERSTANDING OF PSYCHOLOGICAL DISTRESS

Person-centred experiential counselling psychology conceives distress as the development of conditions of worth that become linked to processing difficulties (Hook & Murphy, 2016). This is based on Rogers's (1951, 1959) theory of personality development. The approach does not categorize or diagnose clients' problems as in the medical model (see Chapter 3, this volume). The approach recognizes the importance of embodied felt senses (Gendlin, 1962) and the role of emotion processing (Greenberg, Elliot, & Rice, 1993) as advances of theory from within the experiential paradigm.

Distress in the person-centred experiential approach acknowledges that Rogers' original theory was an organismic psychology that proposed people have the capacity to know what is most constructive for them. This capacity is referred to as the organismic valuing process. During infancy we are able to evaluate and, within reasonable limits, act in accord with our intrinsic valuing of experience. Consider, for example, a baby and how they can one moment be enjoying their feed. Once satiated they quite visibly look disgusted at the prospect at having to ingest more of the same. They know when they have had enough.

As the infant develops part of the direct experience of the organism becomes differentiated and forms a self-concept. The ideal environment for development is when the infant receives genuine understanding and warmth in a consistent and unconditional way. If this is available to the infant regardless of their preferences and individually selected choices then they have the best chance of developing their potential. However, it is unrealistic to expect caregivers to be capable of maintaining such an unconditionally accepting attitude all of the time. Consequently, the developing infant comes to experience some of their preferences, actions, or behaviours, as being more or less acceptable to their significant social others. As a result of the inconsistency in unconditional positive regard from the caregiver, the infant receives the message they are more worthwhile, acceptable, or loveable under certain conditions. As a child depends on their caregiving environment for safety and healthy development, they quickly learn that they can behave in ways that prompt a more favourable response from caregivers.

Rogers' (1957b, 1959) theory developed the ideas of unconditional positive self-regard, unconditional positive regard, and conditional positive regard and conditions of worth. It was hypothesized that the extent to which one can experience unconditional positive regard towards another is dependent upon the level of unconditional positive self-regard that is experienced. Hence, we are limited in our acceptance of others by the extent of our own unconditional self-acceptance. This is a very important concept for the person-centred experiential counselling psychologist and places a great emphasis on the rationale for personal development work during training.

A consequence of conditional acceptance is the development of conditions of worth. Conditions of worth develop when we take on the values associated with experiences that others reinforce when others' valuing is inconsistent with our intrinsic organismic valuing. Once these values are introjected and become firmly embedded within the self-structure, we then act in accord with the introjected values. Once this process of losing contact with our organismic valuing has occurred we will act in accord with our conditions of worth and not our intrinsic valuing of experience. The result of the development of conditions of worth is an externalized value system that is at odds with the organismic valuing system. The external valuing system of conditions of worth overrides the organismic valuing system. In addition to introjecting those values of significant social others, the social and cultural environment can also be a source of introjected values.

In person-centred experiential theory conditions of worth mediate the relationship between direct experience and the processing of symbolization of experience (Hook & Murphy, 2016). Processing as described by Warner (2005) involves an individual pausing and attending to a situation, staying with the emerging experience, holding it in attention without judgement, sensing new, spontaneous emotional and physical feeling responses, along with any triggered images and memories (Hook & Murphy, 2016). Processing and conditions of worth are linked to one another. Conditions of worth are formed at a deep level in the personality; at the level at which experience is filtered through the senses. Therefore, it is conditions of worth that influence the processing of symbolization of experience. Processing is what we "do" to information as it passes through our conditions of worth. Where conditions of worth point to a more stable and consistent conceptualization of the personality, processing provides a dynamic and fluid element to personality. Person-centred experiential counselling psychologists work to help clients become aware of their conditions of worth and of the way experiences are processed. This work takes place within the therapeutic relationship.

THE ROLE AND PLACE OF THE THERAPEUTIC RELATIONSHIP

The therapeutic relationship in person-centred experiential counselling psychology is the core of both practice and theory. Rogers' (1957b) hypothesis of six necessary and sufficient conditions has become ubiquitous in the field of psychotherapy. The conditions are, arguably, one of the single most researched hypothesis in the field of psychotherapy. The hypothesis claims that the relationship conditions are both necessary and sufficient for constructive therapeutic change to occur and has proved to be a robust predictor of outcome (Bozarth, 1998) whether that is in generic therapeutic settings or in therapy for discrete categories of distress (Elliott et al., 2013) and for severe distress (Rogers, Gendlin, Keisler, & Truax, 1967). Time after time, the relationship factors seem to outpredict specific interventions (Wampold et al., 1997; Wampold, Minami, Baskin, & Tierney, 2002; Zuroff & Blatt, 2006).

According to Rogers' (1957b) statement the six conditions are:

1. Two persons are in psychological contact.
2. The first, termed the client, is in a state of incongruence, being vulnerable or anxious.
3. The second person, termed the therapist, is congruent or integrated in the relationship.
4. The therapist experiences unconditional positive regard for the client.
5. The therapist experiences an empathic understanding of the client's internal frame of reference and endeavours to communicate this experience to the client.
6. The communication to the client of the therapist's empathic understanding and unconditional positive regard is, to a minimal degree, achieved.

Bohart and Tallman (1999) proposed the client as an active self-healing agent in therapy. One important construct in person-centred experiential theory is nondirectivity. Many person-centred experiential counselling psychologists will maintain a nondirective *attitude*. Grant (1990) referred to two types of nondirectivity. First, is instrumental nondirectivity, which is perhaps best considered as a technique. The therapist maintains an instrumental nondirective stance *in order to* make something happen for the client (e.g., with the intent for the client to grow). Alternately, principled nondirectivity is about not trying to make anything *specific* happen for the client, so growth happens as a fortunate consequence of the therapist's unwavering respect for the client's right to self-determination (Murphy & Hayes, 2015). In principled nondirectivity, the therapist is adopting an ethical stance in relation to the client.

It is important to be clear that a nondirective attitude on behalf of the therapist does not mean there is no direction to therapy. Attempting to clarify the often misunderstood use of the term nondirective Shlien (2003, p. 219) said, "there is indeed direction, but that the direction is prompted and determined *by the client*. It was never intended to mean 'therapist directed.'"

THERAPIST, CLIENT, AND RELATIONAL CONTRIBUTIONS TO EFFECTIVE PERSON-CENTRED EXPERIENTIAL COUNSELLING PSYCHOLOGY

Within person-centred experiential counselling psychology the primary approach involves the therapist empathically following their client by developing a deep empathic understanding of the client's experiences from within the client's internal frame of reference. Empathy was described by Rogers (1959, p. 210) as "to perceive the internal frame of reference of another with accuracy, and with the emotional components and meanings which pertain thereto, as if one were the other person, but without ever losing the 'as if' condition." It is important to be absolutely clear of the meaning of empathy in person-centred experiential approach. This is because nearly all forms of therapy, including those in this book, will claim empathy as part of the therapist role. However, Rogers developed empathy as being much more than part of a role. Empathy is a *way of being* (Rogers, 1975). Empathy in person-centred experiential therapy has many dimensions to it.

Schmid (2001) suggests that empathy is akin to the art of not knowing, in that the therapist is required to be completely open, without assumptions or intentions to explain clients' problems. Therapists' empathy is never in order to achieve some other goal than to understand the client. In person-centred experiential counselling psychology therapists respond to clients through empathic following; a creative and dynamic process in which the therapist finds ways of communicating to the client their understanding of how it is to be the client in this moment. Empathic following responds to both the client's relation to their experience and the direction the client is moving. Self-agency focused empathic reflections are central to the person-centred experiential approach (Murphy, Elliott, & Carrick, 2016).

Rogers (1959, p. 208) defined the therapist experience of unconditional positive regard as "if the self-experiences of another are perceived by me in such a way that no self-experience can be discriminated as more or less worthy of positive regard than any other, then I am experiencing unconditional positive regard for this individual." This is a key therapeutic relationship factor.

The third key therapeutic relationship factor in person-centred experiential therapy is the therapist congruence. Congruence refers to the authenticity of the therapist's empathic understanding and unconditional positive regard for the client. The therapist is congruent in the relationship to the client when they are accurately symbolizing their experiencing of the client's internal frame of reference and also experiencing unconditional positive regard towards the client.

Clients in person-centred experiential counselling psychology are considered to be the expert on their experiencing. They are trusted to direct both the content and process of therapy and are considered to be intrinsically motivated towards growth. In therapy, the client comes to understand themselves more fully, to experience an inner freedom where they are relieved of the effects of conditions of worth and are able to process experiences with greater fluidity and smoothness. The direction is towards being fully functioning.

ADAPTATIONS, DEVELOPMENTS, AND EXTENSIONS OF ORIGINAL APPROACH

There have been a range of adaptations, developments, and extensions of Rogers' original client-centred therapy. These now fall under the broad umbrella of person-centred "and" experiential therapies. The most well-known of these are outlined below, however, a helpful and in-depth review of the approaches can be found in Sanders (2012).

Focusing Oriented Therapy

Eugene Gendlin was a close colleague of Rogers at the University of Chicago Counselling Center in the 1950s. Gendlin's interest was in the concept of experiencing, and he concentrated on understating the inner experiencing of the client and how that experience is given expression (Purton, 2013). Gendlin proposed an approach that focuses on the moments when a client goes inwards to check their experiences to find the correct expression; in such moments he suggested that clients seemed to be trying to get a better sense of their experiencing. Gendlin's approach aims to support clients to make contact with this "felt sense." He termed his approach "focusing" and considered it a simple therapeutic technique that could be useful to everyone, regardless of whether they were a therapist or client. Purton (2013) asserted that focusing is not distinct from person-centred therapy and argued that focusing is what clients actually do in effective person-centred therapy.

Pre-therapy

The first of Rogers' (1957b) six necessary and sufficient conditions is that the client and therapist must be in psychological contact. Very distressed clients might have difficulty in establishing psychological contact, such as when they may be unaware of their surroundings. Gary Prouty (1976, 1994) first introduced his approach, pre-therapy, as a theory of psychological contact. The pre-therapy approach provides a helpful method of practice, a description of client internal function, and a description of measurable behaviours.

Pre-therapy extends person-centred experiential therapists' work to clients who have been unable to communicate in a straightforward way. Prouty argued that often considered "meaningless statements" uttered by the clients when experiencing a psychosis, did in fact have relevance and sometimes even pointed to the aetiology of the psychosis (Prouty, 1994). Thus, what had been considered evidence of mental illness by psychiatrists could actually be the route to the client's health; the client's very words and actions hold the key to unlocking their growth potential.

The evidence in support of person-centred work with clients experiencing psychosis is promising (Elliott, Greenberg, Watson, Timulak, & Freire, 2013). Likewise, the preliminary research findings also support contact work as facilitating client contact and the development of therapeutic relationships (Dekeyser, Prouty, & Elliott, 2008).

Emotion Focused Therapy

Emotion focused therapy (EFT) was developed originally by Laura Rice, Les Greenberg, and Robert Elliott (Greenberg, Rice, & Elliott, 1993). The approach has extended the theory of emotion from the original person-centred theory, which paid only minimal attention to the role of emotions in processing. EFT has integrated techniques such as the two-chair and empty-chair experiments to facilitate the resolution of splits, or unfinished business, respectively. EFT has become a well-established form of therapy receiving wide empirical support in a range of client populations (Elliott et al., 2013).

A number of other important approaches have emerged within the person-centred family. For example, process-based person-centred therapy (Worsley, 2001), pragmatic person-centred therapy (Cain, 2010), pluralistic person-centred therapy (Cooper & McLeod, 2011), dialogical person-centred therapy (Schmid, 2003) and integrative person-centred therapy (Bohart, 2012). In addition, a number of theoretical developments are also being advanced, such as relational depth theory (Mearns & Cooper, 2005; Knox, Murphy, Wiggins, & Cooper, 2013), configurations of self (Mearns & Thorne, 2000), mutuality (Murphy, 2010, Murphy & Cramer, 20144) as examples. A fuller exploration of these developments can be found in Murphy and Joseph's (2015) comprehensive review of the person-centred approach.

CLINICAL EXAMPLE

Daniel was a 31-year-old male client of northern European origin. Daniel had come to therapy following the recent loss of his position as a local council representative, a situation that had arisen through a series of interpersonal disputes. Daniel was distressed by the loss and he reported the events were symbolic of a pattern to his life. He expressed that his interpersonal difficulties were perhaps related to past traumatic events from his childhood, but that he was not clear why his childhood might still affect him so many years later. He disclosed in the early sessions that as a child he had been placed into care at age 9. After a series of failed foster placements, at age 12, and after his grandmother had recovered from a serious illness, she was eventually made his legally adoptive parent. He lived with her until he moved into rented accommodation in his mid-20s. Daniel's main employment was as civil servant working as a clerk in a benefits office.

Daniel disclosed quite early on in therapy an unusual experience of vomiting. He said that he would vomit regularly, several times throughout the day. Nothing in particular seemed to cause him to vomit; rather, it would happen spontaneously. Doctors were unable to find a medical cause yet prescribed antisickness medication; this seemed to have little positive effect and after 24 hr the vomiting returned. Daniel was self-medicating with various over-the-counter treatments for indigestion or other stomach and bowel complaints. He persisted with his search for a medical explanation all the way through to receiving a referral for a series of invasive exploratory tests. However, these provided no explanation for his sickness.

In parallel to his search for a medical and physical explanation, in-therapy discussions centred on events from childhood. This mainly pointed to a significant traumatic event when he had been force fed. Each time Daniel mentioned this traumatic event he got distressed. He was perplexed as to why anyone would want to do this to a child. His search for an explanation was important to him. As therapy progressed the exploration of the traumatic event, and his physical symptoms of sickness, were gradually presented in a more integrated form. He began to consider the possibility that there might be a connection between his vomiting and his past experience of having been force fed. His belief in finding a medical cause also started to loosen.

In therapy I maintained close empathic following of Daniel's moment-by-moment experiencing. By receiving deep empathic following he gained a deeper understanding of himself and of how he processed experiences. For example, he became more aware of how he responds when under pressure. He became aware of how, due to conditions of worth of not being acceptable, or wanted, or good enough, he would sometimes say things that were for the purpose of impressing others. He became aware that this sometimes alienated others, or made them think he was being inappropriate. In therapy he gradually became more open and accepting that he had had a difficult and challenging life. Being more open meant he could process experiences in the here-and-now of therapy and made connections between his current experiences and to childhood experiences. As he moved inwards and became more deeply known to himself he was able to accept more of himself, of his limitations and his potentials. He began to regulate his behaviour in new situations as he perceived them as less threatening and found that he got an increasingly positive response from others.

Approximately 6 months into therapy Daniel, explicitly albeit very tentatively, for the first time, explored that his experience of vomiting could be related to past experiences of abuse. This was a pivotal moment. After revisiting this idea several times over the next few weeks Daniel talked about his vomiting in more detail. This included more exploration of emotional experiences, such as feeling anxious and feeling stressed shortly before vomiting but not really knowing why. As he went into the experience of anxiety he realized he sometimes felt stressed and occasionally noticed a strange taste in his mouth prior to being aware that he felt anxious and began vomiting. These sessions were when he started to find new meanings to his experiences.

These explorations deepened his awareness and eventually a fuller experiencing in awareness occurred; Daniel came to realize he was deeply distressed by the experience of having been force fed. Not only this but that he could conceive the possibility that these disturbing memories from the past were having such a severe impact on his processing of current experience that he would sometimes be physically sick. Even though there is no "hard evidence" that this is indeed true, Daniel seemed in himself to be sure. His *experience* told him that these phenomena were linked. Following this he changed his behaviour. He put a stop to pursuing his doctor for an explanation. He did not request any more invasive physical testing and ceased his self-medication. He trusted himself again and physically he seemed more relaxed. In therapy his manner changed to becoming more reflective, less defensive, and he tried less to impress others. His valuing of himself was more internally located and he was more open to his experiences and to understanding in greater depth his own self.

FUTURE ORIENTATIONS

The future of person-centred experiential therapy looks promising. One recent development is the Counselling for Depression (CfD) (Sanders & Hill, 2014) approach, which provides grounds for counselling psychologists working within the person-centred experiential approach in the statutory health sector. The NHS and the National Institute for Clinical Excellence have recently supported the development CfD and the approach is now recognized as an evidence-based high-intensity therapy and alternative to cognitive-behavioural therapy.

Person-centred experiential therapy is also considered effective for working with children and young people. There are studies reporting the effectiveness of the approach within this client group (Hölldampf, Behr, & Crawford, 2010; McArthur, Cooper, & Berdondini, 2013). Perhaps one of the most significant areas of development has been in the field of posttraumatic growth, where person-centred experiential theory has contributed significantly to the understanding of reactions to trauma (Joseph & Linley, 2005). Building on this work of person-centred experiential theory reaching into mainstream psychology, Joseph and Murphy (2013a, 2013b) have presented the approach to the field of positive psychology.

CONCLUSION

In this chapter I have presented the person-centred experiential approach to counselling psychology as a radical alternative to the medical model expert-led approaches to psychotherapy. The approach is based on the inherent organismic wisdom of the individual and their intrinsic socially constructive potential and the tendency to actualize towards the fulfilment of this potential under fertile social and relational conditions. The person-centred experiential approach to counselling psychology is a good fit for those who do not feel the need to be experts and who have a basic trust in the humanity of their clients.

SUGGESTED FURTHER READING

Cooper, M., O'Hara, M., Schmid, P. F., & Bohart, A. C. (Eds.). *The handbook of person-centred psychotherapy and counselling* (2nd ed.). Basingstoke: Palgrave MacMillan.

Murphy, D., & Joseph, S. (2015). Person-centered therapy: Past, present and future orientations. In D. Cain, K. Keenan, & S. Rubin (Eds.), *Handbook of humanistic psychotherapies* (2nd ed.). Washington, DC: American Psychological Association.

Rogers, C. R. (1959). A theory of therapy, personality, and interpersonal relationships as developed in the client-centered framework. In S. Koch (Ed.), *Psychology: A study of a science. Vol. 3: Formulations of the person and the social context* (pp. 184–256). New York: McGraw-Hill.

REFERENCES

Bohart, A. C. (2012). Can you be integrative and a person-centered therapist at the same time? *Person-Centered and Experiential Psychotherapies, 11*(1), 1–13.

Bohart, A. C., & Tallman, K. (1999). *How clients make therapy work: The process of active self-healing.* Washington, DC: American Psychological Association.

Bozarth, J. (1998). *Person-centred therapy: A revolutionary paradigm.* Ross-on-Wye: PCCS Books.

Brodley, B. T. (1996). Empathic understanding and feelings in client-centered therapy. *Person-Centered Journal, 3*(1), 22–30.

Cain, D. J. (2010). *Person-centered psychotherapies.* Washington, DC: American Psychological Association.

Cain, D.J. (2013). Integration in person-centred psychotherapies. In M. Cooper, M. O'Hara, P. F. Schmid, & A. C. Bohart (Eds.), *The handbook of person-centred psychotherapy and counselling* (2nd ed.). Basingstoke: Palgrave MacMillan.

Cooper, M., & McLeod, J. (2011). Person-centred therapy: A pluralistic perspective. *Person-Centered and Experiential Psychotherapies, 10,* 210–223.

Dekeyser, M., Prouty, G., & Elliott, R. (2008). Pre-therapy process and outcome: A review of research instruments and findings. *Person-Centered and Experiential Psychotherapies, 7,* 37–52.

Elliott, R., & Greenberg, L. S. (2001). Process-experiential psychotherapy. In D. J. Cain & J. Seeman (Eds.), *Humanistic psychotherapies: Handbook of research and practice* (pp. 279–306). Washington, DC: American Psychological Association.

Elliott, R., Greenberg, L. S., Watson, J., Timulak, L., & Freire, B. (2013). Research on humanistic-experiential psychotherapies. In M. J. Lambert (Ed.), *Bergin and Garfield's Handbook of psychotherapy and behavior change* (6th ed.), pp.495–538. New York, NY: Wiley & Sons.

Gendlin, E. T. (1962). *Experiencing and the creation of meaning. A philosophical and psychological approach to the subjective.* New York: Free Press of Glencoe.

Gendlin, E. T. (1996). *Focusing oriented psychotherapy: A manual for the experiential method.* New York: Guilford Press.

Grant, B. (1990). Principled and instrumental nondirectiveness in person-centered and client-centered therapy. *Person-Centered Review, 5,* Feb. Reprinted in D. J. Cain (Ed.), (2002) *Classics in the person-centered approach.* Ross-on-Wye: PCCS Books.

Greenberg, L. S., Rice, L. N., & Elliott, R. (1993). *Facilitating emotional change: The moment by-moment process.* New York: Guilford Press.

Hölldampf, D., Behr, M., & Crawford, I. (2010). Effectiveness of person-centered and experiential psychotherapies with children and young people: A review of outcome studies. In M. Cooper, J. C. Watson, and D. Hölladampf (Eds.), *Person-centered and experiential therapies work: A review of the research on counseling, psychotherapy and related practices* (pp. 16–24). Ross-on-Wye: PCCS Books.

Hook, L., & Murphy, D. (2016). Related but not replaceable: a response to Warner's reworking of person-centered personality theory. *Person-Centered and Experiential Psychotherapies, 15,* 285–299.

Joseph, S., & Linley, P. A. (2005). Positive adjustment to threatening events: An organismic valuing theory of growth through adversity. *Review of General Psychology, 9,* 262–280.

Joseph, S., & Murphy, D. (2013a). Person-centered theory encountering mainstream psychology: Building bridges and looking to the future. In J. H. D. Cornelius-White, R. Motschnig-Pitrik., & M. Lux (Eds.), *Interdisciplinary handbook of the person-centered approach: Research and theory* (pp. 213–226). Springer: New York.

Joseph, S., & Murphy, D. (2013b). Person-centered approach, positive psychology and relational helping: Building bridges. *Journal of Humanistic Psychology, 53*, 26–51. DOI: 10.1177/0022167812436426.

Knox, R., Murphy, D., Wiggins, S., & Cooper, M. (2012). *Relational depth: New perspectives and developments.* Basingstoke: Palgrave MacMillan.

Lietaer, G. (2002). The client-centered/experiential paradigm in psychotherapy: Development and identity. In J. C. Watson, R. N. Goldman, & M. S. Warner (Eds.), *Client-centered and experiential psychotherapy in the 21st century: Advances in theory, research and practice.* Ross-on-Wye: PCCS Books.

McArthur, K., Cooper, M., & Berdondini, L. (2013). School-based humanistic counseling for psychological distress in young people: Pilot randomized controlled trial. *Psychotherapy Research, 23*(3), 355–365.

Mearns, D., & Cooper, M. (2005). *Working at relational depth in counselling and psychotherapy.* London: Sage.

Mearns, D., & Thone, B. (2000). *New developments in person-centred therapy.* London: Sage.

Murphy, D. (2010). *Psychotherapy as mutual encounter: A study of therapeutic conditions.* Unpublished doctoral dissertation. Retrieved from http://hdl.handle.net/2134/6627 (accessed February 28, 2017).

Murphy, D., & Cramer, D. (2014). Mutuality of Rogers's therapeutic conditions and treatment progress in the first three psychotherapy sessions. *Psychotherapy Research, 26*, 651–661. DOI: org/10.1080/10503307.2013.87405

Murphy, D., Elliott, R., & Carrick, L. (2016). Identifying therapist competences in early stages of person-centered and emotion focused psychotherapy for socially anxious and traumatised client. Paper presented to World Association for Person-Centered and Experiential Psychotherapy and Counselling, New York, July.

Murphy, D., & Hayes, K. (2015). Person-centered therapy. In H. E. A. Tinsley, S. H. Lease, & N. S. Giffin Wiersma (Eds.), *Contemporary theory and practice of counselling and psychotherapy* (pp. 295–232). New York: Sage.

Murphy, D., & Joseph, S. (2015). Person-centered therapy: Past, present and future orientations. In D. Cain, K. Keenan, & S. Rubin (Eds.), *Handbook of humanistic psychotherapies* (2nd ed.). Washington, DC: American Psychological Association.

Prouty, G. (1976). Pre-therapy, a method of treating pre- expressive psychotic and retarded patients. *Psychotherapy; Theory, Research and Practice, 13*(3), 290–295.

Prouty, G. (1994). *Theoretical evolutions in person-centred therapy. Applications to schizophrenic and retarded psychosis.* New York: Praeger.

Purton, C. (2013). Focusing-oriented therapy. In P. Sanders (Ed.), *The tribes of the person-centred nation: An introduction to the schools of therapy related to the person-centred approach* (2nd ed., pp. 47–69). Ross-on-Wye: PCCS Books.

Rennie, D. L. (1998). *Person-centred therapy: An experiential approach.* London: Sage.

Rogers, C. R. (1951). *Client-centered therapy: Its current practice, implication and theory.* Boston, MA: Houghton Mifflin.

Rogers, C. R. (1957a). A note on the nature of man. *Journal of Consulting Psychology, 4*(3), 199–203.

Rogers, C. R. (1957b). The necessary and sufficient conditions of therapeutic personality change. *Journal of Consulting Psychology, 21*(2), 95–103.

Rogers, C. R. (1959). A theory of therapy, personality, and interpersonal relationships as developed in the client-centered framework. In S. Koch (Ed.), *Psychology: A study of a science. Vol. 3: Formulations of the person and the social context* (pp. 184–256). New York: McGraw-Hill.

Rogers, C. R. (1961). *On becoming a person.* London: Constable.

Rogers, C. R. (1963). The actualizing tendency in relation to "motives" and to consciousness. In M. R. Jones (Ed.), Nebraska symposium on motivation (pp. 1–24). Lincoln, NE: University of Nebraska Press.

Rogers, C. R. (1975). Empathic: An unappreciated way of being. *Counseling Psychologist, 5*(2), 2–10.

Rogers, C. R. (1986). A comment from Carl Rogers. *Person-Centered Review, 1,* 3–5.

Rogers, C. R., Gendlin, E. T., Keisler, D. J., & Truax, C. (1967). *The therapeutic relationship with schizophrenics.* Madison, WI: The University of Wisconsin Press.

Sanders, P. (2012). *The tribes of the person-centred nation: An introduction to the schools of therapy related to the person-centred approach* (2nd ed.). Ross-on-Wye: PCCS Books.

Sanders, P., & Hill, A. (2014). *Counselling for depression.* London: Sage.

Schmid, P. F. (2001). Comprehension: The art of not-knowing. Dialogical and ethical perspectives on empathy as dialogue in personal and person-centered relationships. In S. Haugh & T. Merry (Eds.), *Rogers's therapeutic conditions: Evolution, theory and practice, Vol 2: Empathy,* pp. 53–71. Ross-on-Wye, England: PCCS Books.

Schmid, P. F. (2003). The Characteristics of a Person-Centered Approach to Therapy and Counseling: Criteria for identity and coherence. *Person-Centered & Experiential Psychotherapies, 2*(2), 104-120. https://doi.org/10.1080/14779757.2003.9688301

Schmid, P. F. (2005). Authenticity and alienation: Towards an understanding of the person beyond the categories of order and disorder. In S. Joseph & R. Worsley (eds), *Person-centred psychopathology: A positive psychology of mental health.* Ross-on-Wye: PCCS Books.

Schmid, P. F. (2006). The challenge of the Other: Towards dialogical person-centered psychotherapy and counseling. *Person-Centered and Experiential Psychotherapies, 5,* 241–245.

Schmid, P. F. (2013). The anthropological, relational and ethical foundations of person-centred therapy. In M. Cooper, M. O'Hara, P. F. Schmid, & A. C. Bohart (Eds.), *The handbook of person-centred psychotherapy and counselling* (2nd edn). Basingstoke: Palgrave MacMillan.

Shlien, J. (2003). Untitled and uneasy. In P. Sanders (Ed.), *To lead an honorable life: Invitations to think about client-centered therapy and the person-centered approach. A collection of the work of John M. Shlien* (pp. 173–190). Ross-on-Wye: PCCS Books.

Standal, S. (1954) *The need for positive regard: A contribution to client-centered theory.* Unpublished PhD thesis, University of Chicago.

Wampold, B. E., Minami, T., Baskin, T. W., & Tierney, S. C. (2002). A meta-(re)analysis of the effects of cognitive therapy versus "other therapies" for depression. *Journal of Affective Disorders, 68,* 159–165.

Wampold, B. E., Mondin, G. W., Moody, M., Stich, F., Benson, K., & Ahn, H. (1997). A meta-analysis of outcome studies comparing bona fide psychotherapies: Empirically, "All must have prizes." *Psychological Bulletin, 122*(3), 203–215.

Warner, M. S. (2005). A person-centered view of human nature, wellness and psychopathology. In S. Joseph and R. Worsley (Eds.), *Person-centred Psychopathology.* Ross-on-Wye: PCCS Books.

Worsley, R. (2001). *Process work in person-centred therapy: Phenomenological and existential perspectives.* Basingstoke: Palgrave.

Zuroff, D. C., & Blatt, S. J. (2006). The therapeutic relationship in the brief treatment of depression: Contributions to clinical improvement and enhanced adaptive capacities. *Journal of Consulting and Clinical Psychology, 74,* 130–140.

Counselling Psychology

ANDREA HALEWOOD

CHAPTER OUTLINE

INTRODUCTION 89

ONTOLOGICAL ASSUMPTIONS: IMAGE OF THE PERSON 89

EPISTEMOLOGIES: THE WAYS OF KNOWING 90

GUIDING PRINCIPLES: CORE THEORETICAL ASSUMPTIONS 91

NATURE AND UNDERSTANDING OF PSYCHOLOGICAL DISTRESS 92

THE ROLE AND PLACE OF THE THERAPEUTIC RELATIONSHIP 93

THERAPIST, CLIENT, AND RELATIONAL CONTRIBUTIONS TO EFFECTIVE PSYCHODYNAMIC THERAPY 94

CONTEMPORARY ADAPTATIONS, DEVELOPMENTS, EXTENSIONS 95

FUTURE ORIENTATIONS 99

CONCLUSION 100

LEARNING OUTCOMES

BY THE END OF THIS CHAPTER YOU SHOULD BE ABLE TO ANSWER THE FOLLOWING KEY QUESTIONS:

1. What are the main philosophical and theoretical assumptions underpinning the psychodynamic approach?

2. In what key ways does the relational model diverge from the "classical" psychoanalytic approach?

3. What are the main issues for practice in the area of psychodynamic counselling psychology?

Counselling Psychology: A Textbook for Study and Practice, First Edition. Edited by David Murphy.
© 2017 John Wiley & Sons Ltd. Published 2017 by John Wiley & Sons Ltd.

INTRODUCTION

The psychodynamic model is often associated with a remote therapeutic attitude, obscurantist language, and bizarre metaphorical concepts, and is therefore often approached with some trepidation by trainees. As Bornstein (1988) has noted, psychology textbooks tend to give precedence to Freud's more outlandish speculations rather than presenting more mainstream psychodynamic concepts and developments, and psychoanalysis is routinely presented as archaic and redundant. Consequently, as Kahn observes, teaching Freud's ideas often feels like an exercise in public relations (Kahn, 1991). However, the psychodynamic model is not a homogenous perspective (although many of its critics may present it as such) and there have been fundamental developments in theory, practice, and research over the past 100 years. Since the 1980s a relational paradigm has evolved, one that integrates Freud's ideas with those from a number of schools within psychoanalysis: object relations psychology, interpersonal psychoanalysis, and self psychology (Greenberg & Mitchell, 1983). This is argued to be "a distinctly new tradition" (Mitchell & Aron, 1999) and one that is becoming increasingly influential (Mills, 2005). It is also one that fits well with the postmodern philosophy of counselling psychology, particularly the centrality of the therapeutic relationship and the focus on subjectivity and intersubjectivity. In this chapter I will chart the development from the "classical" approach, which focuses more, though not exclusively, on the realm of the intrapsychic (i.e., the psychological processes that occur within the individual), through to a relational model which hypothesizes that relationships with others, both internalized and external, are the key elements of human experience and development. As well as presenting the basic theoretical framework and underlying assumptions of this approach, I will consider a case example, contemporary developments, and future directions.

It is important to distinguish between the terms "psychoanalytic" and "psychodynamic" when referring to clinical practice; both forms of therapy draw on psychoanalytic principles but the frequency of the sessions differs. Psychodynamic counselling psychologists are more likely to offer weekly sessions, whereas psychoanalysts may offer up to five sessions a week, which impacts the depth of the work and the therapeutic focus. Jacobs' (1988) general definition of the term "psychodynamic" is a useful one: "what particularly distinguishes the term 'psychodynamic' is that the activity of the psyche is not confined to relating to people, or to objects outside of the self. . . . Activity also takes place within the psyche, in relation to itself" (pp. 4–5).

ONTOLOGICAL ASSUMPTIONS: IMAGE OF THE PERSON

In his initial topographic model of the human mind Freud outlined the fundamental premise of psychodynamic theory: that human thoughts, affective states, and motivation appear to be largely determined by unconscious forces as evidenced by dreams, slips of the tongue, and psychological symptoms originating from repressed unconscious material (Freud, 1900). The individual is driven by instinctual impulses—primitive sexual and aggressive drives that push for expression and in doing so clash with the social world and internalized social rules. This clash leads to internal conflict between instinctual impulses and the defences against them, and, according to Freud's later structural theory (Freud, 1923a), between the id, ego, and superego. An intrapsychic compromise therefore needs to be reached, yet as Greenberg (1996) notes "this is always a tragic compromise" (p. 89) that impacts personality development.

Drive theory was challenged in the 1940s by object relations theorists such as Winnicott, Fairbairn, Guntrip, and Bowlby, who argued that the individual is motivated by the need for relationships; drives such as sexuality and aggression were conceptualized as operating *within relationships* rather than *within the person* (Mitchell, 1988). For object relations and relational theorists, the focus is on the quality of the individual's early relationships—on the ways in which these influence personality development and psychopathology as well as relationships with others and with the self.

EPISTEMOLOGIES: THE WAYS OF KNOWING

Freud argued that the basic elements of psychoanalysis were observations conducted during the analytic process and claimed that the purpose of psychoanalysis was the discovery of the role of the unconscious within mental life. Although he described his theories as "constructions" (Freud, 1937) it has been suggested that he perceived them as objective facts (Leary, 1994). However, it is important to reiterate that Freud was first and foremost a neurobiologist, "a discoverer rather than a healer" (Wachtel, 2008, p. 28); his initial aim was to develop a neuropsychological model of the mind (Borden, 2009). Furthermore, psychoanalysis developed at a time when modernism and positivism were dominant philosophies (Gergen, 1991); consequently, a central tenet of the "classical" perspective is the conviction that there is something within the client that can be observed and interpreted. This positivist perspective was challenged by Sullivan (amongst others), founder of the interpersonal school of psychoanalysis, who argued that the therapist, far from being a neutral and objective observer of the client, is instead a "participant observer" and should therefore focus more on the *interactional* than the *intrapsychic*, that is, what is going on in the client's current relationships, including the therapeutic relationship (Sullivan, 1940). As Mitchell (2000) observes, the "classical vision of the analytic situation as comprised of one mind providing content for an interpreter" (i.e. a "one person" approach) became increasingly untenable. A "two-person" epistemology suggests instead that the therapist cannot isolate the client's psychological structures or experiences from the relational context.

The relational approach adopts a constructionist epistemology; the focus is on how client and therapist collaboratively "co-construct" experiences within the therapeutic encounter, rather than on the search for an objective reality which is interpreted by the expert therapist. Acknowledging their role as "participant observers" (Sullivan, 1940), rather than as "scientist-therapists" (McNamee & Gergen,1992) relational therapists hold that absolute objectivity is impossible: the perceptions and experiences of both client and therapist are seen as being influenced by the subjectivity of the other. As Mitchell (1988) puts it "analytic enquiry entails a participation in, and an observation, uncovering and transformation of, these relationships and their internal representations" (p. 3). A two-person psychology is therefore required.

GUIDING PRINCIPLES: CORE THEORETICAL ASSUMPTIONS

While psychoanalytic theory and practice have developed since Freud's time, many of the core concepts remain, most significantly the construct of the dynamic unconscious. Freud (1926c) defined psychoanalysis as the science of unconscious mental processes and hypothesized a series of defences that enable the individual to regulate his anxiety by rendering unconscious those needs, desires, and feelings that lead to conflict both within the individual and with others around him. While the earliest theory of defences focused more on maintaining internal equilibrium, contemporary theories conceptualize defence mechanisms arising in the context of close relationships with important others; defences may protect the self-esteem of an individual rather than protecting him or her from becoming conscious of anxiety-provoking thoughts or ideas (Cooper, 1998). Sandler (1976) notes how certain kinds of defensive processes, for example, *projection* and *projective identification*, are manifested within the therapeutic relationship; clients unconsciously invite the therapist to respond towards them in ways that others have done in the past, or in ways that the client did with important others, while at the same time the client enacts roles that others engaged in with him. For example, the therapist might notice an anxious need to get everything right when working with a client who had a perfectionist parent, or that the client is acting towards the therapist *as if* they were a perfectionist. It is through the recognition of these repeated "enactments" in the therapeutic relationship that relational templates, patterns, and conflicts can be reflected on and ultimately revised.

Enactments can be anticipated to a certain degree if the therapist considers who they may be, or are likely to become, in the *transference*; transference can be understood as the client's expectations about, and ways of relating to others that are established during childhood and carried forward. For example, a client with a critical mother may unconsciously carry with her an expectation that others will behave towards her critically, an expectation that will often engender in others a critical response. By working with the transference the therapist helps the client to understand, in the here and now, just how enduring their relational templates are.

Transference was initially conceived of by Freud as a process occurring in the mind of the patient, without being influenced by the therapist. He theorized that if the analyst were appropriately neutral and anonymous then the transference would spontaneously unfold and would not be distorted by the personality of the analyst. A relational "two-person" understanding acknowledges that the personality of the therapist will impact the client's expectations about them. For example, if the client is concerned that the therapist appears uninterested, rather than interpreting this as purely being about the client, the therapist will consider what the client might be picking up on, possibly something about which the therapist is unconscious. Central to a relational, two-person model is the notion that who, and how, the therapist is, will be highly relevant for the client.

Countertransference was originally conceptualized by Freud (1910d) as the therapist's response to the client's transference. He cautioned that it interfered with the therapist's objective observation of the patient and therefore needed to be mastered. Ferenczi (1933 [1980]) was the first to assert that countertransference facilitated the process of therapy, and that both analyst and client were joint participants in this process. Following Ferenczi a two-person understanding of the transference/countertransference dynamic is that it is an interactive process co-constructed between client and therapist and as such is an invaluable interpretative tool in psychodynamic work; one that provides unique insights into the client's unconscious patterns of relating. As such, if noted and reflected on, countertransference is a valuable source of insight for the therapist too; one that invariably leads to increased self-awareness. However, as Lenthall (1995) points out, countertransference is invariably most powerful when the client's unconscious projections resonate with the therapist's unconscious vulnerabilities as I will illustrate in the clinical example below.

NATURE AND UNDERSTANDING OF PSYCHOLOGICAL DISTRESS

Freud originally linked some forms of psychological distress to early trauma, specifically sexual trauma; he became convinced that his "hysterical" patients (i.e., patients presenting with physical symptoms with no obvious neurological cause) had been exposed to seductive behaviour as children and that repressed memories were the cause of their symptoms. However, he lost faith in his "seduction hypothesis" for a number of reasons: first, he came to doubt the prevalence of sexual abuse he encountered in his clinical practice, and second, during the course of his own self-analysis, his repressed sexual feelings towards his mother led him to acknowledge infantile sexuality from which he constructed the Oedipus complex. This revision led Freud to privilege the role of repressed unconscious fantasy over interpersonal factors in the development of neurosis. Masson (1984), contending that Freud's original view was correct, accuses Freud of professional cowardice for abandoning the seduction hypothesis. However, as Robinson (1993) points out, Freud's shift from the highly controversial theory of infantile seduction to an even more contentious theory—that of infantile sexuality—can hardly be considered a career move.

Freud now contended that *all* individuals suffered from conflicted sexual impulses, and the sexual drive, rather than trauma, was conceptualized as the source of all conflict. This shift did not go unopposed; contemporaries of Freud, most notably Ferenczi, continued to argue that neurotic symptoms and psychopathology were primarily caused by emotional and sexual trauma in childhood (Ferenczi, 1933 [1980]). Object relations theorists, such as Fairbairn (1974), Guntrip (1971), and Winnicott (1960, 1965), later expanded trauma to include the parents' chronic failure to meet the psychological needs of the child; Winnicott theorized that the mother who is too intrusive, too stimulating, or lacking in attunement fails to protect the infant and allow psychological growth and health. Kohut (1977) maintained that parental failures to empathize with their children and the responses of their children to these failures resulted in a weakened or damaged sense of self. Bowlby's attachment theory (Bowlby, 1979) provided empirical confirmation of these observations, while interpersonalists such as Horney (1950), Fromm (1962), and Sullivan (1953) added that social forces also need to be considered in the formation of personality. From a two-person relational perspective, psychopathology (or to use Sullivan's less pejorative term, "problems with living") is seen as reflective of problems in relations with others; problems that also impact on how the individual relates to himself. For example, an individual with a critical parent will tend to see others as critical (projection), respond to others *as if* they are being critical (projective identification) thereby often evoking a critical response, and invariably relate to himself critically (turning against the self). Formulations of psychopathology focus on these inner representations of self and others and how these impact the individual. From this perspective the tendency to repeat problematic interactions indicates an effort to preserve familiar patterns of relating and ways of being in the interpersonal field no matter how problematic these patterns are.

THE ROLE AND PLACE OF THE THERAPEUTIC RELATIONSHIP

Psychodynamic therapy involves attending to these problematic relationship patterns, and, through participating in them (both consciously and unconsciously) helping clients to recognize, understand, and revise them. This endeavour is central to all psychodynamic schools, however, the neutrality of the classical analytic approach in which the analyst remained attentive, but essentially uninvolved in the relationship has been both challenged and revised. Ferenczi (1933 [1980]) argued that adopting an authority position created a hierarchical relationship and urged analysts to offer "maternal friendliness" rather than "intellectual explanations" (p. 160). Ferenczi's focus on the therapeutic relationship, on the "rule of empathy," and on the central importance of countertransference anticipated later developments in contemporary relational approaches, as did his interest in a more active and experiential therapeutic approach.

As outlined above, Sullivan (1940) conceptualized the analyst as a "participant observer" in the interactive field of the therapeutic situation, that is, while observing the client's relational patterns the therapist is also engaged in the interpersonal process. Sullivan argued that the more the client can come to understand their own interpersonal patterns of behaviour, the more he or she can learn to disrupt maladaptive patterns and develop more satisfactory ways of relating to others leading to "a satisfactory expansion of the self" (p. 205).

It has been suggested that Jung's "early dissents" from psychoanalysis prefigured the relational model (Greenberg, 1996). Jung emphasized the ways in which both client and therapist influence each other, both consciously and unconsciously, thereby anticipating the later focus on the reciprocal nature of the transference/countertransference process:

> For two personalities to meet is like mixing two different chemical substances: if there is any combination at all, both are transformed. In any effective psychological treatment, the doctor is bound to influence the patient; but this influence can only take place if the patient has a reciprocal influence on the doctor. You can exert no influence if you are not susceptible to influence.

(Jung, 1929 [1966], p. 71)

Over time an awareness of the need for (as well as the inevitability of) the therapist's involvement in the relationship began to develop: countertransference (Heimann, 1950), projective identification (Bion, 1959; Klein, 1946), and empathy (Kohut, 1977; Sullivan,1940) all became increasingly important theoretical and clinical concepts from the 1940s onwards. The idea that both therapist and client contributed to, and were affected by, relational dynamics (Loewald, 1970 [1980]; Sandler, 1976) gained increasing acceptance leading to a move away from the hierarchical towards a recognition of the mutual.

THERAPIST, CLIENT, AND RELATIONAL CONTRIBUTIONS TO EFFECTIVE PSYCHO-DYNAMIC THERAPY

As outlined above, within the classical psychoanalytic tradition a central therapeutic strategy would be the focus on an inner world which might not be accessible to the client, yet which can be theorized and interpreted by the therapist. This has been described as a "one-person psychology" (Wachtel, 2008)— the focus in on the intrapsychic world of the client—what goes on in his or her mind and the instinctual drives and the defences against anxiety that have protected the client from experiences or situations which otherwise may have been unmanageable or overwhelming. In order to allow free associations to unfold spontaneously the analyst remains neutral, not interfering with this self-contained process.

A two-person relational perspective is more concerned with "mutuality" (Aron, 1991 [1999], 1996) and intersubjectivity; both therapist and client are seen as actively engaged in the therapeutic endeavour and the therapist's use of him or herself is at the heart of this process. Consequently, a high degree of self-awareness is required; the psychodynamic therapist believes that what she or he brings to the therapy relationship is significant and must be brought to awareness and understood (via self-reflection and supervision), lest this be projected onto (or more damagingly into) the client. In this model, the therapeutic relationship and the transference/countertransference are always contributed to by both participants in the interaction and both will be impacted by it.

When considering personality development, the psychodynamic counselling psychologist attempts to understand their client's present patterns in the light of their past relational experiences and early environment, and what they have learned to defend against and adapt to. The therapeutic process will provide many opportunities for observing how clients' early patterns are repeated again and again in the therapeutic relationship and in the outside world; drawing clients' attention to these patterns provides opportunities for reflecting on them, and if necessary, revising them. As Sullivan (1940) puts it "one achieves mental health to the extent that one becomes aware of one's interpersonal relations" (p. 102). It is essential though to acknowledge how profoundly disorienting the prospect of change can be—this will often entail changing identity, lifestyle, and style of relating to self and others, and as such, as Sullivan points out, can feel like an attack on the core self (Sullivan, 1940). It is therefore important to respect clients' understandable resistance to change and to pace the work accordingly.

CONTEMPORARY ADAPTATIONS, DEVELOPMENTS, EXTENSIONS

The relational model outlined above has extended the traditional psychodynamic approach in a number of ways, but it has been argued that these developments are epistemological and clinical rather than theoretical (Mills, 2005). The traditional view of the analyst's authority and expertise, as well as the objectivist principles that underpin them, have been questioned by relational theorists, who emphasize the influence of the therapist in the therapeutic encounter to a greater degree, and question what can be objectively known. Within this frame clinical observations are viewed more as constructions within an intersubjective process rather than as objective facts. Therefore, the two-person therapist needs to attend carefully to what he or she observes in *both* participants in the therapeutic encounter. This requires a high degree of self-awareness as well as the courage and determination to explore previously disowned aspects of the self in supervision and in therapy.

However, while relational therapists clearly embrace a fundamentally different epistemological position to classical analysts in terms of practice, it has been questioned whether they are offering anything new theoretically. Richards (1999) contends that the relational school has constructed a false dichotomy between drive theory and relational theory, and points out that Freud recognized that patients' problematic relational histories created patterns of relating that tended to be repeated in later life and caused most of their difficulties. Freud developed the concepts of internalization, relational templates, transference, countertransference, and the Oedipus complex, all of which indicated his interest in relatedness. As Freud suggested:

> rarely and under certain exceptional conditions is individual psychology in a position to disregard relations of this individual to others. In the individual's mental life someone else is invariably involved . . . so from the very first individual psychology . . . is at the same time social psychology.

> (Freud, 1921, p. 69)

Mills (2005) suggests that the most important contribution from the "relational turn" in psychoanalysis is clinical rather than theoretical; relational therapists offer a more flexible treatment frame, demonstrate less adherence to dogma, and, most importantly, have abandoned the role of the "prototypic solemn analyst who is fundamentally removed from relating as one human being to another" (Mills, 2005, p. 36). Relational theorists advocate (as did Ferenczi, Sullivan, Jung, and Kohut before them) a more spontaneous, humane, and genuine manner towards the client; it is this change in clinical attitude coupled with a constructivist epistemology that has shifted the therapeutic endeavour away from the classical goals of interpretation and insight to a focus on therapy as a relational process.

CLINICAL EXAMPLE

Linda, a 44-year-old civil servant, presented for counselling complaining of exhaustion and depression; previous medical examinations had ruled out a physical cause. When I began working with Linda she had been on the clinic's waiting list for 12 months but she expressed no irritation or protest about this when questioned, just passive acceptance. Linda clearly struggled with self-assertion and self-esteem but what unfolded over the course of our work together was a repetitive pattern of self-sabotage in all areas of her life, particularly in her relationships with others.

Linda's domineering, ambitious mother appeared to have been determined that her daughter would fulfil her own frustrated academic and career ambitions. Linda had not done so and consequently felt herself to be a failure. Linda described her father as a remote figure who had spent most of his time away from the family home, leaving Linda feeling responsible for her chronically dissatisfied mother and younger brother. Linda's brother, more oppositional in childhood, had achieved a degree of autonomy and had moved to Australia while Linda remained enmeshed with her mother. She recalled being absorbed by her mother's anxieties and her attempts to relieve them from an early age; she had made a conscious effort to be "good" and comply with her mother's wishes, mainly by limiting self-expression, yet ultimately had succeeded in thwarting her mother's attempts at total domination.

Having had an early experience of submission to a dominant Other, Linda's *relational templates* ensured that she re-enacted her pattern of servile and submissive behaviour with others. She seemed to choose critical and controlling partners and friends who would do all her complaining for her, protest being something that Linda struggled with. I hypothesized to myself that Linda would unconsciously *transfer* onto me an expectation that I would be critical and controlling (as well as an unconscious invocation to behave in this way), and that *countertransferentially* I may therefore be drawn into an *enactment* whereby I became the controlling/ambitious/frustrated mother. Within the psychodynamic framework enactments are considered to be inevitable expressions of transference/countertransference dynamics that reveal largely unconscious patterns of relating to self and others in both client and therapist.

Our early work together appeared to go well and Linda seemed, on the surface at least, to be engaged, insightful, and reflective. I had made some tentative links, or *trial interpretations*, between her present situation and her early experiences which she had seemed willing to reflect on, in session at least. (On reflection, I wondered if this initial compliance may have been more to do with her desire for my approval but at the time I neglected to consider this.) However, just at the point where hope seemed to be activated Linda applied the brakes and became increasingly resistant to further exploration; our work stalled and our pattern of relating became entrenched. Rather than bringing any new associations or observations for us to explore together, Linda now spent each

session expressing hopelessness and asserting the absolute impossibility of change in any aspect of her life: the job that she disliked, the relationship that undermined her, her lack of a social life, her depression. Our sessions became increasingly similar, or, to be more precise, identical. I wondered if Linda was defending herself against the anxiety that the prospect of change may have evoked. But it was the repetition of Linda's relational templates and my role in the enactment that I had predicted that ultimately led to therapeutic stalemate.

Following Linda's retreat I noticed that I was becoming increasingly active in our sessions; Linda appeared to be "communicating by impact" (Casement, 1985); that is, she would induce in me an unbearable sense of being defeated which was so powerful that I fought to keep it at bay by becoming preoccupied by solutions and challenging her when she reproached herself, rather than sitting back and reflecting on what was being evoked in me by her projections. Heimann (1950) suggests that the role of the psychoanalyst/psychodynamic therapist is to endure the feelings that are stirred up in him or her, rather than dismissing or repressing them as the client has learned to do (or acting them out as I was clearly doing); only then can their meaning be analysed in the service of the client. However, I was increasingly being drawn into a directive way of working that felt uncharacteristic and uncomfortable for me; the psychodynamic therapist neither advises nor directs but rather attempts to offer a nonjudgemental environment wherein the client can speak freely about whatever comes to mind. Working within a two-person intersubjective framework it was essential that I used my countertransferential response to acknowledge and make sense of what was being created between us.

I reflected back to Linda my observation that she seemed to defend herself against feeling hopeful and appeared anxious to convince both of us that nothing could or would change. Without stopping to reflect on this Linda countered that she had already tried everything to remedy her situation, which was why she knew that change was not possible. Fighting a rising urge to challenge this point and engage in a battle of wills I tried to reflect instead on what was being induced in me; I was feeling increasingly determined to take responsibility for Linda's progress in a way that seemed to recreate patterns from childhood—both Linda's and my own.

Through the use of supervision (both internal and actual) I came to a clearer understanding of my countertransferential responses. I realized that I was feeling solely responsible for the outcome and acting this out, and that my therapeutic optimism and desire to enliven Linda derived from a pattern of my own: I couldn't bear her hopelessness and my inability to do anything about it. Prior to catching this enactment and reflecting on my directiveness I unconsciously acted out these feelings, which served only to entrench Linda's pessimism and led us into interminable rounds of "why don't you/yes but" (Berne, 1964). However, Linda was an old hand at that game and I lost every round—to her obvious satisfaction.

My reflections on this enactment were also helped by a dream I had about Linda: I was busily tidying her kitchen while she remained passively staring out of a window doing nothing to help. But equally I was making no effort to engage her—just taking over and infantilizing her in much the same way as her mother had done. However, while I was becoming increasingly alert to the fact that I was being pulled into the role of ambitious and controlling mother (i.e., determined that Linda would do well and make progress), the inducement was often so powerful that it was often difficult for me to sit back and reflect on it rather than acting it out in session.

The construct of "moral masochism"—the tendency to engage in self-defeating behaviours (Freud, 1924a) was helpful to me both in terms of conceptualizing Linda's interpersonal difficulties as well as my response to this pattern. Freud observed that a masochistic pattern of self-defeat indicates that the child's will has been crushed; the pattern involves re-enacting this struggle by defeating both self and other in areas such as work, education, or relationships while ensuring a pyrrhic victory by preserving a sense of will. In "failing" to fulfil her mother's ambitions Linda hadn't achieved her own potential but she was not subjugated and retained a faint sense of an independent (albeit enfeebled) self—and a will of her own. Fairbairn suggests that re-enacting the pattern also allows the individual to preserve their emotional link with the "bad object" and that it is this desire to retain contact with these reassuringly familiar internalizations, no matter how painful, that makes dysfunctional patterns so resistant to change (Fairbairn, 1974).

In our therapeutic relationship, therefore, it was important for me to resist being pulled into a battle of wills with Linda, while owning and using my countertransference response of frustration and helplessness to understand Linda's pattern of relating to self and to others; important too that I remained hopeful (rather than defensively optimistic) and did not allow myself to be defeated by Linda's projected sense of despair and pessimism or provoked into retaliation by her passive aggressive behaviours. Understanding my countertransference response from a two-person perspective enabled me to use this enactment to develop a more empathic awareness of Linda's interpersonal world as well as an improved understanding of my own. Only then was I able to relinquish my intrusive sense of responsibility, detach from my engagement in the outcome, and enable Linda to begin her journey towards autonomy.

FUTURE ORIENTATIONS

In his 1895 *Project for a Scientific Psychology* (published posthumously in 1950) Freud attempted to develop a neural model of the mind, but later abandoned this project anticipating that an attempt to integrate his understanding about neurological mechanisms with his psychoanalytic thinking were premature (Kouvelas, 2012). From this point onwards Freud vowed to focus on psychoanalytic theorizing and to, "carefully avoid the temptation to determine psychological locality in any anatomical fashion. I shall remain upon psychological ground . . ." (Freud, 1900, p. 536). However, Schore (1997) proposes that the time is now right for a rapprochement between psychoanalysis and neuroscience, arguing that recent developments in the field of neuroanalysis have provided support for many of Freud's psychoanalytic concepts. (For a detailed account of these developments in neuroanalysis, the interested reader is referred to Schore, 1994, 1997.).

Research evidence is also accumulating to support the efficacy of psychodynamic practice, particularly for depression, anxiety, panic, somatoform disorders, eating disorders, substance-related disorders, and personality disorders (Bateman and Fonagy, 2008; Blatt & Ford, 1994; Crits-Christoph & Connolly, 1998; Fonagy, 2015; Leichsenring, 2005; Leichsenring and Rabung (2008); Milrod et al., 2007). Not only has psychodynamic therapy been found to be as effective as other empirically supported therapies, but the effects have been shown to last long after treatment has terminated—the so called "incubator effect" (Shedler, 2010).

However, while few would dispute that practice should be informed by research, just as research should be informed by practice, a constructivist perspective entails a critique of the *underlying* presuppositions of empirical research. For relational therapists, adopting a critical constructivist position towards the "expert" objective analyst while uncritically accepting the positivist findings of empirical research leads to epistemological incoherence; a postmodern approach to research acknowledges that reality is socially constructed, rather than discovered. Hoffman (2009) argues that the "privileged status" accorded to research and neuroscience (rather than in-depth case studies) is unwarranted and potentially damaging—both to developing understanding of the therapeutic process and ultimately to the quality of clinical work. He does not suggest that these forms of research are of *no* value; his concerns are about the conceding of "superordinate status" to objectivist knowledge. In any case, most of the central theoretical and clinical concepts in psychoanalysis have been developed on the basis of clinical observations and the debates and discussions these have stimulated, rather than on the findings of systematic research (Hoffman, 2009; Seth Warren, 2012).

Strupp (2001) contests that "Given the uniqueness of every therapeutic dyad and the multitude of relevant interacting variables influencing the course of treatment, the 'empirical validation' of any therapy is utterly illusory" (p. 613). Much of the available psychotherapy research investigates short-term, problem focused treatment using randomized controlled trials (RCTs) and treatment manuals, and hence are not representative of mainstream psychodynamic work; that is, they lack external validity. Therefore, it is important, as Vivona (2012) suggests, for therapists to develop research methods that assess treatment appropriately and guard against "an uncritical attitude about research findings, including the common tendency to downplay the limitations inherent in all systematic study. We must not compromise our openness to uncertainty in the wake of efforts to know" (p. 128)

CONCLUSION

Therapists tend to gravitate towards theories and methods that suit their own personality, epistemology, values, clinical experience, relational style, cultural background, and so on, as well as being influenced by the theoretical orientation of supervisors and therapists and those theorists with whom they feel an affinity (Lenthall, 1995). Arthur (2001) suggests that those who are attracted to the psychodynamic model tend to be more subjective than objective and more interested in the intrapsychic and the metaphorical than the measurable and the rational. He advises that orientation "fit" may take some time to develop during training, but suggests that an awareness of one's own epistemology and personality style can help direct therapists towards a theoretical model that resonates with them, thereby preventing dissonance in the clinical situation.

A coherent framework, both theoretical and supervisory, is invaluable in enabling the therapist to "think under fire" (Bion, 1959) while in session, to help make sense of complex processes and to provide conceptual direction for clinical interventions. As such it can help to contain intolerable anxiety in the face of risk and uncertainty, thereby enabling practitioners to withstand the pressures inherent in the work. However, theory can also be used defensively during those times when anxieties, stimulated by clinical work and by the training process itself, threaten to overwhelm the practitioner. Consequently, it is important that the therapist seeks regular psychodynamic supervision, remains open and curious, learns to tolerate "not knowing," and ensures that theoretical models and constructs don't obstruct the therapeutic relationship. As Jung (1928) stressed, it is the personality of the therapist that is primary rather than his or her technique, and he cautioned trainee therapists as follows: "learn your theories as well as you can, but put them aside when you touch the miracle of the living soul. Not theories, but your own creative individuality must decide" (pp. 361).

SUGGESTED FURTHER READING

Borden, W. (2009). *Contemporary psychodynamic theory and practice*. Chicago, IL: Lyceum Books, Inc.

Kahn, M. (1991). *Between therapist and client: The new relationship* (revised ed.). New York: W. H. Freeman & Co.

Wachtel, P. L. (2008) *Relational theory and the practice of psychotherapy* London: The Guilford Press.

REFERENCES

Aron, L. (1991 [1999]). The patient's experience of the analyst's subjectivity. In S. Mitchell & L. Aron (Eds.), *Relational psychoanalysis: The emergence of a tradition* (pp. 243–268). Hillsdale, NJ: Analytic Press.

Aron, L. (1996). *A Meeting of Minds: Mutuality in Psychoanalysis*. Hove: Analytic Press.

Arthur, A. R. (2001). Personality, epistemology and psychotherapists' choice of theoretical model: A review and analysis. *European Journal of Psychotherapy, Counselling and Health*, *4*(1), 45–64.

Bateman, A., & Fonagy, P. (2008). 8-year follow-up of patients treated for borderline personality disorder: Mentalization-based treatment versus treatment as usual. *American Journal of Psychiatry*, *165*, 631–638. DOI: 10.1176/appi.ajp.2007.07040636.

Berne, E. (1964). *The games people play: The psychology of human relationship*. New York: Ballantine Books.

Bion, W. R. (1959). Attack on linking. *International Journal of Psychoanalysis*, *40*, 308–315.

Blatt, S. J., & Ford, R. Q. (1994). *Therapeutic change*. New York: Plenum Press.

Borden, W. (2009). *Contemporary psychodynamic theory and practice*. Chicago, IL: Lyceum Books, Inc.

Bornstein, R. F. (1988). Psychoanalysis in the undergraduate curriculum: The treatment of psychoanalytic theory in abnormal psychology texts. *Psychoanalytic Psychology*, *5*, 83–93. DOI: 10.1037/h0085122.

Bowlby, J. (1979). *The making and breaking of affectional bonds*. London: Tavistock Publications Ltd.

Casement, P. (1985). *On learning from the patient*. London: Tavistock Publications.

Cooper, S. H. (1998). Changing notions of defense within psychoanalytic theory. *Journal of Personality*, *66*(6), 947–964.

Crits-Christoph, P., & Connolly, M. B. (1998). Empirical basis of supportive-expressive psychodynamic psychotherapy. In R. F. Bornstein & J. M. Masling (Eds.), *Empirical studies of the therapeutic hour* (pp. 109–151). Washington, DC: American Psychological Association.

Fairbairn, R. D. (1974). *Psychoanalytic studies of the personality*. New York: Routledge, Chapman & Hall.

Ferenczi, S. (1933 [1980]). The confusion of tongues between adults and the child: The language of tenderness and passion. In M. Balint (Ed.) & E. Mosbacher et al. (Trans.), *Final contributions to the problems and methods of psyho-analysis* (pp. 156–167). London: Karnac Books.

Fonagy, P. (2015). The effectiveness of psychodynamic therapies: An update. *World Psychiatry*, *14*, 137–150.

Freud, S. All references are to *The standard edition of the complete psychological works of Sigmund Freud*, volumes 1–24. London: Hogarth Press, 1953–1974. (*SE*)

    1895a. *Project for a scientific psychology. SE, 1*, 283–387.

    1900. *The interpretation of dreams. SE, 4* and *5*.

    1910d. *Five lectures on psycho-analysis. SE, 11*, 7–55.

    1921. *Group psychology and the analysis of the ego. SE, 18*, 65–143.

    1923a. *The ego and the id. SE, 19*, 1–66.

    1924a. *The economic problem of masochism. SE, 19*, 155–170.

    1926c. *Psycho-analysis. SE, 20*, 259–270.

    1937. *Analysis terminable and interminable. SE, 23*, 209–253.

Fromm, E. (1962). *Beyond the chains of illusion*. New York: Simon and Schuster.

Gergen, K. J. (1991). *The saturated self: Dilemmas of identity in contemporary life*. New York: Basic Books.

Greenberg, J. (1996). Psychoanalytic words and psychoanalytic acts—a brief history *Contemporary Psychoanalysis, 32*, 195.

Greenberg, J., & Mitchell, S. (1983). *Object relations in psychoanalytic theory*. Cambridge, MA: Harvard University Press.

Guntrip, H. (1971). *Psychoanalytic theory, therapy and the self*. New York: Basic Books.

Hansen, J. (2006). Counseling theories within a postmodernist epistemology: New roles for theories in counseling practice. *Journal of Counseling and Development, 8*, 291–297.

Heimann, P. (1950). On countertransference. *International Journal of Psychoanalysis, 31*, 81–84.

Hoffman, I. L. (2009). Double thinking our way to "scientific" legitimacy: The desiccation of human experience. *Journal of the American Psychoanalytic Association, 57*, 1043–1069.

Horney, K. (1950). *Neurosis and human growth: The struggle toward self-realisation*. New York: Norton.

Jacobs, M. (1988). *Psychodynamic counselling in action*. London: Sage.

Jung, C. G. (1928). Analytical psychotherapy and education. In H. G. Baynes & F.C. Baynes (Trans.), *Contributions to analytical psychology* (pp. 313–382). London: Trench Trubner.

Jung, C. G. (1929 [1966]). Problems of modern psychotherapy. In *CW: The Practice of Psychotherapy* (Vol. 16).

Kahn, M. (1991). *Between therapist and client: The new relationship* (revised ed.). New York: W. H. Freeman & Co.

Klein, M. (1946). Notes on some schizoid mechanisms. *Envy and gratitude and other works*. New York: Delacotte Press.

Kohut, H. (1977). *The restoration of the self*. New York: International Universities Press.

Kouvelas, E. D. (2012). Unconscious and plasticity: Bridges between psychoanalysis and neuroscience. *International Forum of Psychoanalysis, 21*, 214–217.

Leary, K. (1994). Psychoanalytic "problems" and postmodern "solutions."*Psychoanalytic Quarterly, 63*, 433–465.

Leichsenring, F. (2005). Are psychodynamic and psychoanalytic therapies effective? *International Journal of Psychoanalysis, 86*, 841–868.

Leichsenring, F., & Rabung, S. (2008). Effectiveness of long-term psychodynamic psychotherapy. *Journal of the American Medical Association, 300*, 1551–1565.

Lenthall, A. (1995). On counsellors' investment in theory. *Psychodynamic Practice, 1*(3), 437–448.

Loewald, H. (1970 [1980]). Psychanalytic theory and the psychoanalytic process. In *Papers on Psychanalysis* (pp. 277–301). New Haven, CT: Yale University Press.

Masson, J. M. (1984). *The Assault on truth: Freud's suppression of the seduction theory*. New York: Farrar, Straus and Giroux.

McNamee, S., & Gergen, K. J. (Eds.) (1992). *Therapy as social construction*. London: Sage.

Mills, J. (2005). A critique of relational psychoanalysis. *Psychoanalytic Psychology, 22*(2), 155–188.

Milrod, B., Leon, A. C., Busch, F., Rudden, M., Schwalberg, M., Clarkin, J., . . . & Shear, M. K. (2007). A randomized control trial of psychoanalytic psychotherapy for panic disorder. *American Journal of Psychiatry, 164*, 265–272.

Mitchell, S. (1988). *Relational concepts in psychoanalysis*. Cambridge, MA: Harvard University Press.

Mitchell, S. (2000). Relationality: From attachment to intersubjectivity. Hillsdale, NJ: Analytic Press.

Mitchell, S., & Aron, L. (1999). Preface. In S. Mitchell & L. Aron (Eds.), *Relational psychoanalysis: The emergence of a tradition* (pp. ix–xx). Hillsdale, NJ: Analytic Press.

Richards, A. D. (1999). Book Review of *Ritual and spontaneity in the psychoanalytic process: A dialectical constructivist point of view. Psychoanalytic Psychology, 16*(2), 288–302.

Robinson, P. (1993). *Freud and his critics*. Berkeley, CA: University of California Press.

Sandler, J. (1976). Countertransference and role-responsiveness. *International Review of Psycho-Analysis, 3*, 43–47.

Schore, A. N. (1994). *Affect regulation and the origin of the self: The neurobiology of emotional development*. Hillsdale, NJ: Lawrence Erlbaum.

Schore, A. N. (1997). A century after Freud's project: Is a rapprochement between psychoanalysis and neurobiology at hand? *Journal of the American Psychoanalytic Association, 45*, 807–840.

Seth Warren. C. (2012). Faustian science and the future of psychoanalysis. *Journal of the American Psychoanalytic Association, 60*, 131–144.

Shedler, J. (2010). The efficacy of psychodynamic psychotherapy. *American Psychologist, 65*, 98–109.

Strupp, H. H. (2001). Implications of the empirically supported treatment movement for psychoanalysis. *Psychoanalytic Dialogues, 11*(4), 605–619.

Sullivan, H. S. (1940). *Conceptions of modern psychiatry*. New York: Norton.

Sullivan, H. S. (1953). *The interpersonal theory of psychiatry*. New York: Norton.

Vivona, J. M. (2012). Between a rock and a hard science: How should psychoanalysis respond to pressures for quantitative evidence of effectiveness? *Journal of the American Psychoanalytic Association, 60*, 121–129.

Wachtel, P. (2008). *Relational theory and the practice of psychotherapy*. New York: Guildford Press.

Winnicott, D. W. (1960). Ego distortion in terms of true and false self. *The maturational process and the facilitating environment* (pp. 140–152). New York: International Universities Press.

Winnicott, D. W. (1965). The maturational process and the facilitating environment. *International Psycho-Analysis Library, 64*, 1–276.

8 Cognitive-Behavioural Counselling Psychology

WINDY DRYDEN

CHAPTER OUTLINE

INTRODUCTION 105

ONTOLOGICAL ASSUMPTIONS: IMAGE OF THE PERSON 105

EPISTEMOLOGIES: THE WAYS OF KNOWING 106

GUIDING PRINCIPLES: CORE THEORETICAL ASSUMPTIONS 107

NATURE AND UNDERSTANDING OF PSYCHOLOGICAL DISTRESS 108

THE ROLE AND PLACE OF THE THERAPEUTIC RELATIONSHIP 110

THERAPIST, CLIENT, AND RELATIONAL CONTRIBUTIONS TO EFFECTIVE COGNITIVE-BEHAVIOURAL THERAPY 111

CONTEMPORARY ADAPTATIONS, DEVELOPMENTS, EXTENSIONS 113

FUTURE ORIENTATIONS 116

CONCLUSION 117

Counselling Psychology: A Textbook for Study and Practice, First Edition. Edited by David Murphy.
© 2017 John Wiley & Sons Ltd. Published 2017 by John Wiley & Sons Ltd.

LEARNING OUTCOMES

BY THE END OF THIS CHAPTER YOU SHOULD BE ABLE TO ANSWER THE FOLLOWING KEY QUESTIONS:

1. What are the main philosophical and theoretical ideas underpinning the cognitive-behavioural approach to counselling psychology?

2. In what ways does cognitive-behavioural counselling psychology differ from other approaches?

3. What are the main issues for practice in the area of cognitive-behavioural counselling psychology?

INTRODUCTION

This chapter looks at the cognitive-behavioural tradition within counselling psychology. Strictly speaking it does not make sense to speak of *the* cognitive-behavioural approach to counselling psychology as there is no one single cognitive-behavioural approach. Rather, there can be said to be a cognitive-behavioural *tradition* comprising a number of related cognitive-behavioural approaches, all of which have distinctive features as I will elaborate on later.[1]

ONTOLOGICAL ASSUMPTIONS: IMAGE OF THE PERSON

While cognitive-behavioural counselling psychology, by its very nature, sees humans as thinking and behaviourally based organisms, the approaches that comprise the CBT tradition all tend to adhere to the principle of psychological interactionism. This argues that "cognition, emotion and behaviour are not separate psychological systems, rather, they are overlapping processes and that when we think in terms of cognition, for example, we should also think of the affective (emotional) and behavioural (actual behaviours or action tendencies) components of these cognitions" (Dryden, 2015, p. 9). However, context influences what the person feels-thinks-acts, not only in the proximal sense of the immediate environment the person finds themselves in, but also in the distal sense of the past environments that exert an ongoing influence on present functioning. The more behavioural approaches within cognitive-behavioural

---

[1] My own approach to CBT is known as Rational Emotive Behaviour Therapy (REBT). While I will write the chapter from a broad perspective, at times I will show how REBT differs from the CBT mainstream.

therapy (CBT) also argue that people are not only influenced by the actual and perceived stimuli that they face, but also by the reinforcements they experience when they respond to these stimuli.

Not all CBT approaches privilege social learning in explaining present functioning however. For example, Rational Emotive Behaviour Therapy (REBT) argues that humans are not only influenced to think "irrationally" by the social messages to which they are exposed, but also and perhaps more profoundly by their biologically based tendency to think irrationally, particularly when their strong desires are thwarted. Ellis (1976) in this respect, argued that humans have two major biologically based tendencies—to think irrationally and to respond to this thinking with the tools of empiricism, logic, and pragmatism, thereby developing rational beliefs strengthened by repeated cognitive-behavioural rehearsal of these new beliefs. Paul Gilbert in developing compassion-focused therapy (CFT) drew upon both social contextualism and evolutionary psychology in outlining CFT's image of the person. Thus, Gilbert and Irons (2014, p. 302) say that "our sense of self is created from a combination of genes we inherit plus the social circumstances that choreographed and shaped our minds."

Other approaches within the CBT tradition emphasize that how people think and act need to be understood within a transcultural context, and that CBT techniques need to be applied with the person's cultural context in mind (Hays & Iwamasa, 2006), and counselling psychologists have been urged to be mindful of their clients' spiritual beliefs in designing a CBT treatment programme (e.g. Waller, Trepka, Collerton, & Hawkins, 2010).

EPISTEMOLOGIES: THE WAYS OF KNOWING

As mentioned above, cognitive-behavioural counselling psychology is a tradition and not *an* approach and thus different approaches within this tradition stress different ways of knowing within the therapeutic relationship.

One of the leading approaches within the CBT tradition—Aaron T. Beck's cognitive therapy—emphasizes the development of what has been termed "collaborative empiricism" (e.g., J. Beck, 2011). Here the therapist and client are active participants in collaborating to investigate the *validity* of the client's interpretations and beliefs. To this central ingredient of Beck's cognitive approach might be added the development of what might be called "collaborative pragmatism," where the therapist and client actively collaborate to investigate the *pragmatic* nature of the client's cognitions.

REBT also uses these empirical and pragmatic criteria (and adds the criterion of logic) in the investigation of the client's beliefs, but tends not to apply these three criteria to the client's interpretations until irrational beliefs have been identified, examined, and changed. Thus, when a client says: "my girlfriend lied to me," a therapist cannot know for certain if this is the case. However, while the cognitive therapist might ask for empirical evidence for and against this interpretation, the REBT therapist is likely to encourage the client to assume temporarily that their interpretation was true, as a way of identifying their underlying beliefs. Also REBT would argue that until the underlying beliefs are dealt with the client's disturbed feelings about their interpretation will colour any investigation of the empirical status of that interpretation. Here, psychological disturbance is deemed to influence interpretational knowledge. This latter point shows that REBT, in part, supports the epistemology of constructivism—that humans construct their own realities. Ellis (1994) argued that humans construct rigid ideas and are not just influenced to think rigidly by their proximal and distal environments. In constructing these rigid ideas, humans also construct the psychological disturbance underpinned by these ideas and that understanding such disturbance from an REBT perspective needs to take into account these constructivistic processes.

Newer approaches to CBT (e.g., mindfulness-based CBT and acceptance and commitment therapy [ACT]) are more sceptical about targeting the client's thinking as a way of knowing about and tackling the client's problems. Indeed, ACT therapists, in particular, consider that getting caught up in the business of examining the validity of so-called distorted thinking parallels the very process that explains why the person developed problems in the first. Practitioners of these newer approaches are thus more likely to encourage the client to accept the existence of such thinking and thence to get on with the process of value-based living as the most pragmatic approach to their problems.

In summary, cognitive-behavioural counselling psychology uses different epistemologies according to the assumptions made about the best way of helping people address their problems—empirical, pragmatic, logical, and constructivistic ways of knowing can all be found in the CBT tradition.

GUIDING PRINCIPLES: CORE THEORETICAL ASSUMPTIONS

Westbrook, Kennerley, and Kirk (2011) offer a useful review of the core theoretical assumptions of cognitive-behavioural counselling psychology.

1) *The cognitive principle*. Our emotional and behavioural responses to events depend, in large part, on how we cognitively process what happens to us. This is not a novel idea as it can be traced back to the Greek Stoic philosopher, Epictetus, who maintained that "people are not disturbed by things, but by the view they take of them."

2) *The behavioural principle*: This principle points to the importance of behaviour and the powerful influence that it exerts on our thoughts and emotions. For this reason I am discussing "cognitive-*behavioural* counselling psychology" rather than "cognitive counselling psychology." Let me share a personal example to show the importance of behaviour. I have a stammer, which was much worse in my late teens to the extent that I avoided talking in public whenever I could because I was anxious about stammering. My anxiety was based on

the rigid belief that I must not stammer and it would be terrible if I did. My behavioural avoidance kept me safe, but reinforced this belief. I overcame my anxiety by (a) developing a more flexible belief (i.e., "I don't want to stammer, but that does not mean that I must not do so and it would be unfortunate, but not terrible if I did"), and (b) by acting on this belief by taking every opportunity to speak in public. It was this cognitively mediated behavioural practice that helped me. Without this behavioural emphasis, I would not have changed my belief and I would have remained anxious about speaking in public. In CBT, an important distinction is made between overt behaviour and action tendencies. In the former the person converts the latter into some kind of action. An important task of the cognitive-behavioural counselling psychologist is to encourage clients to identify and accept their action tendencies and instead of acting on them to initiate a more healthy cognitive-behavioural process.

3) *The here-and-now principle*. While CBT therapists recognize that people are influenced by their past experiences, we also argue that it is what people take from these experiences and maintain in the present that is more relevant to here-and-now problems and thus it is usually more fruitful to focus on current cognitive-behavioural processes rather than what happened in the past. Having said this, some CBT approaches (e.g., schema therapy) place more emphasis on past experiences than do others (e.g., REBT).

4) *The interacting-systems principle*. As already mentioned, while cognitive-behavioural counselling psychologists may talk about emotions, cognitions, behaviour, and physiology separately, CBT as a psychotherapeutic tradition adheres to the interacting systems principle and its practitioners look at client problems as interactions between thoughts, emotions, behaviour, and physiology, and the environment in which the person operates.

5) *The empirical principle*. Cognitive-behavioural counselling psychologists operate on the principle that it is important to evaluate both our theories and our therapy empirically—using quantitative and qualitative procedures. Indeed, seeking ongoing client feedback is a feature of the CBT tradition.

NATURE AND UNDERSTANDING OF PSYCHOLOGICAL DISTRESS

The stance that cognitive-behavioural counselling psychologists tend to take on the issue of psychological distress is basically a functional one. Thus, it is not the fact that a person may experience anxiety that points to psychological distress, but the impact that this anxiety has on their life. Thus, some individuals accept that they are anxious and get on with the business of pursuing valued goals, while others who may experience the same level of anxiety are less accepting of their feelings and stop pursuing their goals. When it is clear that a person experiences dysfunctional psychological distress in the sense that it has a deleterious impact on one or more areas of their life, CBT therapists conceptualize this in two main ways—treating the dysfunctional distress as (a) a response and (b) a stimulus.

When treating the distress as a response, the therapist looks for the presence of problematic cognitive-behavioural processes that occasion this distress. Cognitively, the focus may be on negative automatic thoughts, dysfunctional assumptions, or rigidly held schemas or irrational beliefs about something that the person is distressed about (henceforth referred to as an adversity). Behaviourally, the emphasis may be on avoidance, the implementation of safety-seeking strategies, or the use of overcompensatory strategies to deal with the adversity being faced. This conceptualization suggests suitable treatment strategies to help the person deal with the adversity in more functional ways.

When treating the distress as a stimulus, the CBT practitioner considers how the person responds to the distress, both cognitively and behaviourally. When looking at the emotional components of dysfunctional distress the therapist may look for the meaning that the person puts on that distress that may, paradoxically, deepen their distress. Thus, a person may consider that they are a weak person for feeling depressed and this may serve to perpetuate and deepen their depressed feelings. When looking at the cognitive components of dysfunctional distress, the therapist may look for how the person responds to their own thoughts (see Fisher & Wells, 2009). The presence of worry and rumination, for example, points to failed attempts that the person may have made to control their thoughts and may point to positive ideas that the person may have about these cognitive processes (e.g., "Worry is a way of being prepared to handle future threat"). A more recent emphasis in CBT has been on the role that intolerance of negative affective states has on the deepening of dysfunctional distress. Such intolerance leads the person to avoid both troublesome feelings and the adversities that frame the presence of these emotions. As you can see from this example, it is not easy to see the boundary between conceptualizing dysfunctional distress as a response or as a stimulus. When looking at the behavioural components of dysfunctional distress, it is also clear that people hold ideas about what they should do when they are distressed, which again often serves to deepen the distress. Thus, people often think that behavioural avoidance and verbally disavowing the experience of distress are good ways of handling their distressed feelings when, in fact, the opposite is the case (see Leahy, 2015). Robert Leahy's (2015) book on emotional schema therapy, an approach to treatment based on understanding and responding to people's idiosyncratic ideas about their emotions and how to best regulate them, crystallizes this focus on distress as a stimulus rather than as a response.

The view that psychological distress is a fact of human life and that it is our attempts to deal with this distress rather than the distress itself that is the problem is a strong feature of ACT (e.g., Flaxman, Blackledge, & Bond, 2010), and this approach is outspoken in its approach to understanding and dealing with distress as stimulus rather than response.

THE ROLE AND PLACE OF THE THERAPEUTIC RELATIONSHIP

Murphy (this volume) has outlined the person-centred experiential position on the therapeutic relationship in that tradition. It is one that specifies the necessity and sufficiency of certain experienced therapeutic conditions. In CBT, we have a somewhat different perspective. This position was stated clearly by Beck, Rush, Shaw, and Emery (1979) in their seminal book *Cognitive Therapy of Depression*. They began by outlining three desirable characteristics for the cognitive therapist and in doing so acknowledged their debt to Rogers (1957). These characteristics are: warmth, accurate empathy, and genuineness. They continued by arguing that effective cognitive therapists develop and maintain a basic sense of trust in the therapeutic relationship and create rapport with the client. Then, they stressed the importance of engaging the client in what they call a "therapeutic alliance of collaboration" (Beck et al., 1979, p. 54). This sense of collaboration is linked to the basic tasks of the therapeutic dyad, which are to co-investigate the empirical status of the patient's cognitions as they are manifest in his depressive reactions. This linkage between style of relating and therapeutic tasks came to be known as "collaborative empiricism" and has been a cornerstone of Beck's cognitive therapy ever since. Perhaps typically, Albert Ellis (1959) was more forthright in making clear that, in his view, the core conditions as outlined by Rogers were desirable, but neither necessary nor sufficient for therapeutic change to occur. While CBT therapists might quibble about the necessity vs. desirability of the presence of certain therapist conditions with respect to therapeutic change, most would agree that these conditions are rarely sufficient for such change to be maintained.

Drawing on and extending working alliance theory, which was first put forward by Ed Bordin (1979), I have argued that the therapeutic relationship in CBT can be viewed in four domains (Dryden, 2011). In the first, the *bond* domain, which points to the interpersonal connectedness between therapist and client and in which the above discussion on the role of therapist conditions can be located, additional issues become salient. For example, from an alliance perspective, it is important to consider the interpersonal styles of both client and therapist, and the fact that the therapy bond can be enhanced when the "fit" between the interpersonal styles of therapist and client is good and threatened when such a fit is poor. In Beck's cognitive therapy the preferred style, as we have seen, is where the two participants are actively collaborating in working with the cognitive-behavioural elements of the client's problems. However, not all clients can collaborate with the therapist in the way preferred by Beck and thus the CBT therapist needs to be flexible and open to the use of other styles, for example, being more didactic, more humorous, and more self-disclosing with some clients than with others. Lazarus (1993) argued that effective therapists need to be authentic chameleons, changing their style to meet the needs of clients, but doing so authentically.

Space restrictions mean that I can only briefly mention the three other domains of the working alliance in CBT. Effective CBT tends to take place when therapist and clients: (a) share common *views* on the nature of the client's psychological distress and how this can best be addressed; (b) agree on what the client's *goals* are; and (c) understand and agree to implement a set of *tasks* that will not only help the client achieve their goals, but can be effectively implemented by both parties and which have sufficient potency to effect change.

THERAPIST, CLIENT, AND RELATIONAL CONTRIBUTIONS TO EFFECTIVE COGNITIVE-BEHAVIOURAL THERAPY

While CBT is often seen as a highly technical approach to therapy, like other therapies, it is based on a relationship between therapist and client, which makes a difference to outcome. This relationship may not be regarded as all important in CBT, but it is important enough for its practitioners to ensure that they develop and maintain a good working alliance with their clients. Indeed, this ability to form and sustain such an alliance and to deal effectively with actual and potential threats to this alliance is an important therapist competency in CBT. The manual of the revised Cognitive Therapy Scale (CTS-R),[2] widely used in the training of CBT therapists and in research on CBT outlines other therapist competencies (James, Blackburn, & Reichelt, 2001).

Competent CBT therapists do the following:

- Establish an *agenda* for each therapy session jointly with the client to review the previous week's homework assignment, to focus on one item for the session and to negotiate suitable homework for the following week and to adhere to this agenda.
- Provide and elicit *feedback* to ensure client comprehension and that the two have a shared understanding of the client's issues and how these may be fruitfully addressed.
- Initiate and maintain a productive *collaboration* with the client to ensure that the latter is actively involved in CBT.

- *Utilize time effectively* in sessions and *pace* sessions according to the client's ability to focus and learn.
- Elicit the *appropriate expression of emotions* in the client bearing in mind that emotional levels that are too high or too low are likely to interfere with therapy.
- Help the client gain access to his/her *cognitions* (thoughts, assumptions, and beliefs) and to understand the relationship between these and their distressing emotions.
- Help the client understand the role that their *behaviour* plays in maintaining their problems.
- Engage the client in a process of *guided discovery* whereby the person is helped

---

[2] While the CTS-R was developed specifically with Beck's cognitive therapy in mind, it does have wider applicability.

to develop hypotheses regarding their current situation and to generate potential solutions for themselves.
- Work with the client to develop a full *conceptualization* of the client's problems, understanding how they fit together and how the person unwittingly maintains them.

- Use skilfully, and help the patient to use, appropriate cognitive and behavioural *techniques* in line with the conceptualization.
- Negotiate with the client suitable *homework assignments* that flow from the work done in the session and review these in the following session.

While much of the CBT literature has focused on techniques and methods and the contribution of therapists, it must not be forgotten that clients also make an important contribution to the process. Twenty-five years ago, Safran and Segal (1990) developed an interview and rating schedule to assess clients' suitability for short-term CBT (SSCT). They put forward 10 such suitability criteria:

- Being able to access automatic thoughts.
- Being aware of and able to differentiate emotional states.
- Accepting personal responsibility for change.
- Understanding and accepting a cognitive-behavioural conceptualization of psychological distress.
- Having good potential to form a therapeutic alliance within therapy.
- Having good potential to form a therapeutic alliance outside therapy.
- Having problems that are acute rather than chronic.
- Being able to explore problems in therapy without the use of security operations.
- Being able to focus on issues in therapy.
- Being optimistic about therapy.

Renaud, Russell, and Myhr (2014) did a factor analysis of the SSCT, which yielded two factors: (a) capacity for participation in the CBT process, and (b) having attitudes relevant to the CBT process. They found that the first factor uniquely predicted improvement at the end of therapy. It seems, then, that being able to engage in CBT is more important than being well disposed towards it. This is also shown in the literature on homework in CBT, which clearly shows that gains are more likely to be experienced by clients who regularly carry out homework tasks than by clients who don't (e.g., Kazantzis, Deane, & Ronan, 2000).

As I mentioned earlier, while CBT is a technical approach to therapy, relational factors also play an important part in determining therapeutic outcome. Andrusyna et al. (2001) argued that it is important to distinguish between two factors of the working alliance between therapist and client in CBT and that these should be independently measured. The first factor considers the client's agreement with the therapist on goals and tasks, and the bond issue of having confidence in the therapist, while the second considers other bond issues such as mutual liking, being appreciated by the therapist, and experiencing trust in the therapist. Research has yet to study fully the comparative impact of technical and relational issues on outcome in CBT.

CONTEMPORARY ADAPTATIONS, DEVELOPMENTS, EXTENSIONS

Hayes (2004) argued that the development of behaviour therapy can be categorized into three generations or "waves."[3] He noted that the "[E]arly behavior therapists[4] believed that theories should be built upon the bedrock of scientifically well-established basic principles, and that applied technologies should be well-specified and rigorously tested" (Hayes, 2004, p. 640). Given this emphasis, the focus was on the observable, problematic behaviour that was linked to distressed emotion based on conditioning and associative principles. As cognition was deemed to be unobservable and thus not amenable to scientific study, it did not feature in behaviour therapy of the first wave.

In the 1960s, based on a frustration with what were seen as the limits of conditioning and associative learning principles in the understanding of psychological distress and its treatment and on a growing interest in cognitive mediational models in psychology, second wave behaviour therapy developed. Key theorists like Ellis (1962), Beck (1976), Mahoney (1974), and Meichenbaum (1977) focused on identifying, assessing, and modifying problematic cognitions and faulty cognitive processes that were increasingly seen as playing a central role in the acquisition and perpetuation of the emotional disorders. These and other key theorists were, however, keen to point out that an understanding of behaviour was still key, and ground-breaking work was being done in the late 1960s into the 1970s on the interplay of cognitive and behavioural factors. This field became known as "cognitive-behaviour therapy."

As mentioned above, second wave CBT is distinguished by its focus on identifying, responding to, and changing problematic cognition and dysfunctional behaviour, and helping the person to think and act in more healthy ways. Its emphasis is largely, although not exclusively, on psychological distress as response (as opposed to as stimulus). Increasingly, CBT therapists began to be aware that direct modification of cognitive factors in particular was problematic. As some clients strove to identify and respond to problematic cognitions, they tended to get caught up with doing so and began to get embroiled in ruminative-based thinking, for example. In particular, attempts to get rid of problematic cognitions either by avoidance, suppression, or by responding to them "rationally" until they were either gone or lost their power to disturb, had counterproductive effects in the sense that they increased rather

---

[3] As CBT theorists and therapists have tended to use the term "waves" rather than "generations," I will use this terminology in this chapter.

[4] That is, in the first "wave."

than decreased. Some theorists and practitioners began to question the call to modify problematic cognitions that were a feature of second wave CBT. As a result, and given the increasing flexibility of the field (in contrast to the more restrictive nature of first wave behaviour therapy), there was an increasing emphasis on a different approach to facilitating psychological change. Consequently, third wave CBT therapists make much use of strategies that encourage clients to take an approach to their distress and associative features based on acceptance and mindfulness rather than on direct attempts to modify them. There is some research to support the differences in practice between second and third wave CBT therapists. In an American study, Brown, Gaudiano, and Miller (2011) found these therapists in these two groups differed at the level of technique. Third wave practitioners reported greater use of mindfulness/acceptance techniques and, interestingly, greater use of exposure techniques, while second wave practitioners reported greater use of cognitive restructuring and relaxation techniques. Perhaps in line with the wider theoretical base that underpins third wave approaches, practitioners identifying with this wave were more eclectic at the technique level, and demonstrated significantly greater use of family systems techniques, existential/humanistic techniques, and the total number of techniques used then second wave therapists.

The emphasis of acceptance and mindfulness-based procedures demonstrates an openness of CBT therapists to theories and practices outside mainstream psychology. In particular, Buddhist psychology has had a decided influence on third wave CBT, and this is also shown in the work of Paul Gilbert, who established "compassion focused therapy," which can be seen as an important third wave approach (see Gilbert & Irons, 2014).

CLINICAL EXAMPLE

Farah, a 19-year-old woman of Middle Eastern origin, and living and studying in England, consulted me for help with examination anxiety. She had to retake her first year at university because she had a panic attack in her first examination and refused to sit her other papers. Her initially stated goal was to sit her examinations without anxiety. On assessment, it emerged that when she was anxious, Farah experienced both proximal (i.e., immediate) threat and distal (i.e., more general, less immediate) threat. Her major proximal threat was going blank in the exam room and she had two distal threats: (a) that she would fail her degree, and (b) that her parents would disapprove of her if she failed her degree. Farah and I decided to tackle her anxiety about her proximal threat first. Using REBT's

Situational ABC framework, I helped her to see that she was anxious about going blank in her exam because she held a rigid and an extreme belief about going blank. Thus:

Situation = In the examination room

"A" (Adversity) = My mind will go blank

"B" (Rigid belief) = My mind must not go blank
(Extreme belief) = It would be terrible if my mind went blank

"C" (Emotional consequence) = Anxiety
(Behavioural consequence) = Rushing out of the exam room
(Thinking consequence) = If my mind goes blank I will not get my degree
= If I do not get my degree, my parents will disapprove of me

You can see from this assessment that Farah's rigid and extreme beliefs about going blank in the exam room (i.e., her proximal threat) led her to "construct" her distal threats (i.e., failing her degree and her parents disapproving of her as a result). Based on this assessment Farah and I developed a more healthy way of dealing with her proximal threat based on alternative flexible and nonextreme beliefs. Namely:

Situation = In the examination room

"A" (Adversity) = My mind will go blank

"B" (Flexible belief) = I don't want my mind to go blank, but that does not mean that it must not do so

(Non-extreme belief) = It would be bad if my mind went blank, but not terrible

"C" (Emotional consequence) = Concern

(Behavioural consequence) = Staying in the exam room and starting a different question

(Thinking consequence) = If my mind goes blank, it does not mean that I will not get my degree

= If I do not get my degree, my parents would be disappointed, but they probably would not disapprove of me

---

My next task was to encourage Farah to digest and internalize these new flexible and nonextreme beliefs. I did this in several ways. Thus, I:

- Engaged Farah in a Socratic dialogue concerning the empirical, logical, and pragmatic status of her rigid vs. flexible beliefs and her extreme vs. nonextreme beliefs.
- Encouraged her to strengthen her flexible and nonextreme beliefs by attacking them and persuasively responding to these attacks.
- Suggested that she rehearsed her developing flexible and nonextreme beliefs in imagery and before she sat timed practice examinations kindly organized by her university department.

In addition, I helped her develop some practical ways of responding should her mind actually go blank in the examination situation.

As a result of these and other cognitive-behavioural interventions (e.g., controlled breathing techniques), Farah came to be concerned, but not anxious about her mind going blank in the exam room.[5] She was able to sit her end-of-year examinations, which she passed with good grades. By agreement, we did not tackle Farah's anxiety about her distal threats of failing her degree and her parents' disapproval, because she thought that these threats were now unlikely to occur.

Nine months later, Farah made an appointment to see me again. She had started dating someone of whom her father disapproved. He gave Farah an ultimatum that he would disown her if she did not end her relationship with this man. Farah became very anxious about the possibility of being disowned, but she refused to give up her boyfriend. The distal threat of her parents' disapproval as it related to her mind going blank in the exam room had become a proximal reality over the issue of her boyfriend. Using a range of cognitive techniques, I helped Farah develop a set of flexible and nonextreme beliefs about

---

[5] You will note that initially Farah stated that her goal was to sit her exams without anxiety. This goal related to the situation and not the adversity ("mind going blank") and can be regarded as a pre-assessment goal. As a result of the work that we did, her new goal was to be concerned, but not anxious about this adversity. This can be regarded as a post-assessment goal.

not only being disapproved of by her parents, but by being disowned by them. She could see that it was only by dealing with these issues that she could make a clearly thought out decision about her boyfriend. Once Farah strengthened her belief that it would be a personal tragedy to be disowned by her parents, but that this would not be the end of the world and that she could accept herself in the face of being disowned, she was able to do a clearly thought out cost–benefit analysis of her decision about her boyfriend. She decided that her life was her own and not her parents' and that, despite the risk of being disowned, she was not going to stop seeing her boyfriend, whom she loved. Consequently, her father refused to see her anymore, but her mother defied her father and stayed in contact with her, as did her two older sisters.

A year later, Farah wrote to me that she had just gotten engaged and that her family situation had not changed. She said that she was tremendously sad about losing contact with her father, but that she was sure that she had done the right thing.

FUTURE ORIENTATIONS

Engaging in speculation about the future developments of CBT is problematic. Who could have foreseen the current focus on acceptance, mindfulness, and compassion, for example, 25 years ago? As such, I prefer to focus on the future challenges for this field rather than on making predictions. This is also the approach adopted by Mansell (2008), who identified seven challenges for CBT, which in my view are still relevant:

1) *The clarity challenge.* While there is general agreement on the characteristics of CBT, there needs to be greater clarity as to its distinctive features that would identify it and distinguish it from other therapies.

2) *The coherence challenge.* At present, Mansell (2008) argues that CBT lacks coherence and recommends greater collaboration among the different CBT approaches to identify and strengthen areas of commonality.

3) *The cohesive challenge.* Here there is a need for CBT practitioners from the different professions to set aside their professional differences and to respect different ways of working within CBT.

4) *The competence challenge.* Here there is a need to establish not that CBT is effective, but that therapists practise it effectively (both during and after training) and can make a significant difference with their clients.

5) *The convenience challenge.* This centres on the challenge to make CBT more widely accessible without diluting its therapeutic potency.

6) *The comprehensiveness challenge.* This points to the importance of providing comprehensive services, not only across the entire range of client problems but across the country (i.e., UK) as well. Mansell (2008) noted that the presence of resistant attitudes towards CBT may be a barrier here and needs to be addressed.

7) *The connectivity challenge.* This points to the need to improve the connections between CBT and other therapeutic approaches and associated professional disciplines. Mansell (2008) argues that CBT therapists and theorists need to use the language of others to demonstrate such connections rather than expect these others to understand and connect with CBT terminology.

It will be interesting to see how the field of CBT has responded to these challenges when future editions of this work have been published!

CONCLUSION

I was one of the first British counselling psychologists to undergo an extensive training in CBT, beginning my training in 1978 with Albert Ellis, and continuing it in the 1980s with Aaron Beck and Arnold Lazarus. At that time it was quite a lonely experience working as a CBT therapist, while the vast majority of my colleagues were practising humanistic and psychodynamic approaches. Almost half a century later, the situation has changed unrecognizably. Rightly or wrongly CBT is the predominant therapeutic approach in the NHS and is accepted as an empirically supported treatment for an increasing number of psychological problems. Like it or loathe it, counselling psychologists ignore CBT at their peril. It is now an established therapeutic tradition that continues to grow and develop, sometimes in unpredictable ways. However, given that counselling psychology is a pluralistic discipline, CBT-oriented counselling psychologists cannot afford to become insular and ignore developments in other branches of our field. To the extent that CBT becomes a part of this pluralistic movement, then, in my view, it will influence and be influenced by this wider zeitgeist and that is healthy for the continued growth of counselling psychology.

SUGGESTED FURTHER READING

Bennett-Levy, J., Thwaites, R., Haarhoff, B., & Perry, H. (2015). *Experiencing CBT from the inside out: A self-practice/self-reflection workbook for therapists.* New York: Guilford Press.
This well-structured workbook is a good way for non-CBT counselling psychologists to get a "feel" for what it is likely to experience CBT, both as therapist and client.

Dryden, W. (Ed.) (2012). *Cognitive behaviour therapies.* London: Sage.
Once the development of CBT in Britain has been charted, 11 exponents of major CBT approaches working in Britain outline the distinctive features of their approach. A common chapter structure facilitates comparative analysis.

Hoffman, S. G. (2012). *An introduction to modern CBT: Psychological solutions to mental health problems.* Chichester: Wiley-Blackwell.
Hoffman shows how CBT can be applied to a range of common emotional and behavioural problems. Clinical examples are used liberally to bring the text alive.

REFERENCES

Andrusyna, T. P., Tang, T. Z., DeRubeis, R. J., & Luborsky, L. (2001). The factor structure of the working alliance inventory in cognitive-behavioral therapy. *Journal of Psychotherapy Practice and Research, 10*, 173–178.

Beck, A. T. (1976). *Cognitive therapy and the emotional disorders.* New York: International Universities Press.

Beck, A. T., Rush, A. J., Shaw, B. F., & Emery, G. (1979). *Cognitive therapy of depression.* New York: Guilford Press.

Beck, J. S. (2011). *Cognitive behaviour therapy: Basics and beyond* (2nd ed.). New York: Guilford Press.

Bordin, E. S. (1979). The generalizability of the psychoanalytic concept of the working alliance. *Psychotherapy: Theory, Research and Practice, 16*, 252–260.

Brown, L. A., Gaudiano, B. A., & Miller, I. W. (2011). Investigating the similarities and differences between practitioners of second- and third-wave cognitive-behavioral therapies. *Behavior Modification, 35*, 187–200.

Dryden, W. (2011). *Counselling in a nutshell* (2nd ed.). London: Sage.

Dryden, W. (2015). *Rational emotive behaviour therapy: Distinctive features* (2nd ed.). Hove: Routledge.

Ellis, A. (1959). Requisite conditions for basic personality change. *Journal of Consulting Psychology, 23*, 538–540.

Ellis, A. (1962). *Reason and emotion in psychotherapy.* Secaucus, NJ: Citadel.

Ellis, A. (1976). The biological basis of human irrationality. *Journal of Individual Psychology, 32*, 145–168.

Ellis, A. (1994). *Reason and emotion in psychotherapy* (revised and updated ed.) New York: Birch Lane Press.

Fisher, P., & Wells, A. (2009). *Metacognitive therapy: Distinctive features.* Hove: Routledge.

Flaxman, P. E., Blackledge, J. T., & Bond, F. W. (2010). *Acceptance and commitment therapy: Distinctive features.* Hove: Routledge.

Gilbert, P., & Irons, C. (2014). Compassion-focused therapy. In W. Dryden & A. Reeves (Eds.), *The handbook of individual therapy* (pp. 301–328). London: Sage.

Hayes, S. C. (2004). Acceptance and commitment therapy: Relational frame theory, and the third wave of behavioural and cognitive therapies. *Behavior Therapy, 35*, 639–665.

Hays, P. A., & Iwamasa, G. Y. (Eds.) (2006). *Culturally responsive cognitive-behavioral therapy: Assessment, practice, and supervision.* Washington, DC: American Psychological Association.

James, I. A., Blackburn, I.-M., & Reichelt, F. K. (2001). *Manual of the revised cognitive therapy scale (CTS-R).* Newcastle: Tyne & Wear NHS Trust.

Kazantzis, N., Deane, F. P., & Ronan, K. R. (2000). Homework assignments in cognitive and behavioral therapy: A meta-analysis. *Clinical Psychology: Science and Practice, 7*, 189–202.

Lazarus, A. A. (1993). Tailoring the therapeutic relationship, or being an authentic chameleon. *Psychotherapy: Theory, Research, Practice, Training, 30*, 404–407.

Leahy, R. L. (2015). *Emotional schema therapy.* New York: Guilford Press.

Mahoney, M. J. (1974). *Cognition and behaviour modification.* Cambridge, MA: Ballinger.

Mansell, W. (2008). The seven C's of CBT: A consideration of the future challenges for cognitive behaviour therapy. *Behavioural and Cognitive Psychotherapy, 36*, 641–649.

Meichenaum, D. (1977). *Cognitive-behaviour modification.* New York: Plenum.

Renaud, J., Russell, J. J., & Myhr, G. (2014). Predicting who benefits most from cognitive-behavioral therapy for anxiety and depression. *Journal of Clinical Psychology, 70,* 924–932.

Rogers, C. R. (1957). The necessary and sufficient conditions of therapeutic personality change. *Journal of Consulting Psychology, 21,* 95–103.

Safran, J. D., & Segal, Z. V. (1990). *Interpersonal process in cognitive therapy.* New York: Basic Books.

Waller, R., Trepka, C., Collerton, D., & Hawkins, J. (2010). Addressing spirituality in CBT. *The Cognitive Behaviour Therapist, 3,* 95–106.

Westbrook, D., Kennerley, H., & Kirk, J. (2011). *An introduction to cognitive behaviour Therapy* (2nd ed.). London: Sage.

Counselling Psychology

JOHN ROWAN

CHAPTER OUTLINE

INTRODUCTION 121

ONTOLOGICAL ASSUMPTIONS: IMAGE
OF THE PERSON 121

EPISTEMOLOGIES: WAYS OF KNOWING
IN TRANSPERSONAL COUNSELLING
PSYCHOLOGY 122

GUIDING PRINCIPLES AND CORE
THEORETICAL ASSUMPTIONS 123

NATURE AND UNDERSTANDING
OF PSYCHOLOGICAL DISTRESS 124

THE ROLE AND PLACE OF THE THERAPEUTIC
RELATIONSHIP 125

THERAPIST, CLIENT, AND RELATIONAL
CONTRIBUTIONS TO EFFECTIVE
TRANSPERSONAL COUNSELLING
PSYCHOLOGY 127

CONTEMPORARY ADAPTATIONS,
DEVELOPMENTS, EXTENSIONS 129

FUTURE ORIENTATIONS 131

CONCLUSION 131

LEARNING OUTCOMES

BY THE END OF THIS CHAPTER YOU SHOULD
BE ABLE TO ANSWER THE FOLLOWING KEY
QUESTIONS:

1. What are the main philosophical and theoretical ideas underpinning transpersonal
   counselling psychology?

2. In what ways does transpersonal counselling psychology differ from other
   approaches?

3. What are the main issues for practice in
   the area of transpersonal counselling
   psychology?

Counselling Psychology: A Textbook for Study and Practice, First Edition. Edited by David Murphy.
© 2017 John Wiley & Sons Ltd. Published 2017 by John Wiley & Sons Ltd.

INTRODUCTION

Counselling psychology is an important strand in the current psychological scene, having quite a different approach to clinical psychology, which is more identified with the idea of mental health. Counselling psychology does not see itself as being about mental health or the NHS, but rather as meeting and dealing with the whole person. Consequently, it does not deal with the question of fixing people, or solving problems, but is more interested in the I-Thou, as described by Martin Buber. As a result, its approach to transpersonal psychology is not something that would fit well with a medical orientation.

ONTOLOGICAL ASSUMPTIONS: IMAGE OF THE PERSON

The transpersonal approach assumes that the person is infinite. The person is a soul and a spirit, not just a perambulating bunch of matter with a brain. People have a deeper and richer internal life than they imagine at first and have more inner resources than they think. Problems are small things compared to the immensity within. By pretending that we are small and helpless, we reduce ourselves to a fragment of what we really are. As Walt Whitman said: "I am large: I contain multitudes." People have within them many unrealized potentialities, some of which are suppressed or repressed through hate and fear. They can all be actualized and integrated. In order to develop and move on, we have to let go of what is holding us back. Often this is revenge, envy, resentment, or judgementalism. We may have to let go of all that we take for granted. The reason why the telephone box that is a whole spaceship inside (the TARDIS in the Doctor Who series) is such an acceptable and immediately understandable image is because it is an image of the human mind—flesh and bone on the outside and infinity inside.

This is perhaps too abrupt an account of the basic assumptions of the transpersonal approach, but it is one I would want to defend. Since the founding of the *Journal of Transpersonal Psychology* in 1969, and the formation of the Association for Transpersonal Psychology (ATP) in 1972, the transpersonal has been studied scientifically, and in 1996 the British Psychological Society (BPS) founded the Transpersonal Psychology Section, which publishes the peer reviewed *Transpersonal Psychology Review*. This and the publication of a variety of books (e.g., Cortright, 1997; Ferrer, 2002; Rowan, 2005; West, 2000; Wilber, 2000), have made the subject respectable and well-based. One of the best recent accounts of transpersonal psychology is to be found in Stan Grof's sparkling essay in the *Wiley-Blackwell Handbook of Transpersonal Psychology* (2013).

This is of course a radical view of the human being, which goes against much of the current thinking in the field. But if there is any validity in it at all, it must be seen as an important and challenging addition to our thoughts on the whole field of counselling psychology, and indeed therapy and counselling in general.

EPISTEMOLOGIES: WAYS OF KNOWING IN TRANSPERSONAL COUNSELLING PSYCHOLOGY

The main way of knowing in this realm is through intuition. There is such an identification with intuition that at this stage the person may say, perhaps: "I am intuition. Intuition has overcome the me-ness of me. I'm not interested in solving problems—I can't even see any problems." This could be described as illumination, or transcendence. This is quite clearly transpersonal, and explicitly mentioned by people like Mark Epstein (1996) and David Brazier (1995). It is an interesting exercise, however, to try approaching any problem in the spirit of seeing that there is no problem. This may enable us sometimes to see the whole thing quite differently and act more constructively.

David Brazier (1995, p. 205) puts it like this:

> The best therapy is completely empty (*shunya*). Empty of what? Empty of ego. Shunyata (emptiness) means the therapist is wholly there for the client, the other. As therapy proceeds, the client also becomes shunya. Then they can examine their life without ego getting in the way.

The right mental attitude is well summed up in the phrase of John Keats—"negative capability"—which means the ability to do without factual answers and tangible footholds. The way of knowing here is not necessarily knowing anything at all, but rather being and remaining open to what may come. When the therapist needs to know something, he or she has to go into a place of nonknowing, and wait. This is the openness that is valued here.

Knowing is now not seen as something that one does, but rather as something one allows. Instead of claiming ownership for one's knowing, one surrenders to what comes. Instead of looking for answers, one awaits them by staying open to them. This is again a radical view of the field, which goes against any instrumental version of the matter, looking for answers, solutions, or cures.

In a way, I don't know anything. This is okay, because I don't need to know anything. Indeed, holding on tight to what we think we know can be a serious fault and quite dangerous. It can get in the way of our direct experience of the client, which is the source of our counselling relationship. Both Carl Jung and Carl Rogers warned against bringing our theories into the consulting room, which we now see as the *temenos*, the sacred space in which wonderful things can happen.

GUIDING PRINCIPLES AND CORE THEORETICAL ASSUMPTIONS

One of the main insights of the transpersonal approach is that there are a number of levels of consciousness. These have been labelled and described by a number of people, but I have found the simplest and most effective version for the purpose of counselling psychology is the account offered by Ken Wilber (2000).

In all of Wilber's work, the transpersonal includes two important (but very different) levels of consciousness: the subtle and the causal. The subtle, which I have also called Transpersonal 1, because it is the most used in psychotherapy, is the realm of archetypes, deities, nature spirits, symbols and images, dreams, fairy tales, visions—all the usual concrete representations of the divine. It is the level of soul. It entails the therapist admitting that he or she is a spiritual being. Now some people do not like the term "soul," and so it is useful to offer them some synonyms that may be more acceptable. Here is an incomplete list of such, which can be offered as substitutes:

- higher self
- inner teacher
- deep self
- heart (Sufi usage)
- transpersonal self (1)
  - genius (Latin)
  - daimon (Greek)
  - guidance self
  - higher intuitive self
  - archetype of the self (Jung)
  - guardian angel (golden dawn)
  - wise being
  - bliss self
  - savikalpa (Buddhism)
  - luminosity
- psychic centre
  - antaratman (aurobindo)

By using such synonyms, we may get over the problem of owning the word "soul." Jung (2009) and Assagioli (1975) are the great pioneers of working at this level in psychotherapy, but we should also include the extensive work of

Stanislav Grof (Grof & Grof, 1990), who has taken it so much further. Also in this field we should mention the important contribution from women such as Jean Houston (1996) and Marie-Louise von Franz (1977). We all have a soul, or as some would say, we are all souls. The latter is really preferable, because to admit identity is more productive than to admit ownership. Dreams all come from the soul, as Hillman (1979) has well argued, and so we all have direct experience of the soul, because we all have dreams—the scientific experts say about five times a night in most cases.

If we want to go to the heartland of the transpersonal as it reveals itself in therapy, we have to enter the subtle level. It is here that we find the phenomena that truly go beyond the personal. It is here we find what Henri Corbin (1969) has called the "imaginal world," what Schwartz-Salant (1986) has called "the subtle body," what Whitmont (1987) has called "the guidance self," what Assagioli (1975) has called "the higher self," what Hillman (1997) has called "the soul," what Jung (1968) has called "the high archetypes," what Buddhists (Govinda, 1973) have called "the sambhogakaya," and so forth. We all have access to this level, the level of the subtle self, if only we will engage in the practices that can make it real for us. Brant Cortright has laid out this field with a masterly and comprehensive conspectus. He says: "A transpersonal orientation implies an openness to transpersonal content when it arises in the course of psychotherapy" (Cortright, 1997, p. 237). He also says, quite unequivocally, that "Transpersonal psychotherapy is heart-centred" (p. 239). Compassion is very important at this level, and it is a kind of juicy compassion, not like the earnest compassion of the Centaur or the calm unwavering compassion of the causal.

The causal, which I have also called Transpersonal 2, is the deep ocean of spirituality, often labelled as mysticism, where there are no symbols, no images, no signposts, no landmarks, no boundaries. and no words. It can be conceptualized as the One, the All, or the None, and it does not matter which of these terms we use. In philosophy it is often called the Absolute—it is the level at which mystics say that Everything is One. In therapy, we cannot use this very much, because it is too far away from the experience of our clients, so it is the subtle that is called into use most often. But if the counselling psychologist is familiar with this level of consciousness, it can be offered to the client as an option in case of need, and I have in fact done this on occasion, with exciting results.

NATURE AND UNDERSTANDING OF PSYCHOLOGICAL DISTRESS

We see psychological distress as something that people do, rather than as something that happens to them. People entertain problems, or create problems, which they then cling to as if they came from elsewhere. These fictions are then used to make them miserable or pained. It is not necessary to do this, but thousands of people do it, and we obviously have to deal with it in some way. The main way to deal with it is to recognize it for what it is—fiction and make-believe.

Then, having identified it, the next task is to drop it. Ultimately, this is what all transpersonal therapy is really about—dropping false assumptions.

False assumptions are not only the secret of transpersonal psychotherapy and counselling, but also of spiritual growth and development. The more false assumptions we can drop, the more whole we shall be. Spiritual development is of course much more rigorous than counselling, but the principle is the same.

One of the main illusions, which has to be faced and dealt with, is the false belief that we are determined by our previous experiences. The word that is unfortunately too often used for this is "conditioning," and this is believed in as a real entity with its own fixed laws. From a transpersonal point of view, conditioning may well apply to rats and other organisms, but not to the human soul, which is unconditioned. This is certainly so at the level we have called Transpersonal 1, where we are more inclined to say that "Wounds are for healing." James Hillman (1975) has been particularly keen to emphasize this aspect of the matter, and it is interesting that he refuses to talk about Transpersonal 2, and sticks firmly to Transpersonal 1.

This approach may well seem unsympathetic, but the harsh rigour of the basic statement covers a deep compassion that is rich and juicy. We as transpersonal therapists have no sympathy with the creation and nurturing of problems, but we still care for the person who is doing this. It is just a question of enabling and encouraging the client to drop the so-called problems rather than indulging them.

THE ROLE AND PLACE OF THE THERAPEUTIC RELATIONSHIP

This is really the key thing in transpersonal counselling. Somehow the counsellor has to set up a relationship of trust and mutual understanding. This is doubly difficult for the transpersonal counselling psychologist, who is continually challenging the client's way of seeing the world. One thing that may help here is prayer. Through prayer to a deity of some kind, counsellor and client may achieve a new level of consciousness where the normal laws of thought do not operate. Instead of seeing the person as a poor suffering wreck with a load of problems, a new way of seeing may open up the doors of perception, showing the possibility of an infinite consciousness. From a transpersonal point of view, the role of the counselling psychologist is that of a companion along the way. There is no assumption of expertise, or leadership, or superiority in any way. It is more like a wise companion on a journey, who does not argue about the way, does not criticize any mistakes, encourages the weary, witnesses the struggles, does not really offer anything but a presence that is nourishing and warm and open.

The relationship is undemanding, supportive, realistic, truthful, observant, and continually offering to go into different dimensions with the client. Many people today say that "the power of a strong collaborative relationship cannot be underestimated," but the transpersonal relationship goes further than that—it opens up a space in which both client and coach can coexist, in a deeply spiritual way. The counselling psychologist may say "Here is a soul who has challenges and obstacles to overcome on her journey through the university of life. This is another such learning opportunity."

The therapeutic room becomes the *temenos*—the sacred space where real transformation can happen. This is a Jungian idea, but it fits very well with our stance here.

It is these other dimensions that make the difference between a transpersonal counselling psychologist and some other kind. This counselling psychologist might say: "What does your soul say about this?" This would be an invitation to enter the subtle realm (Transpersonal 1), as might be the simple question: "What image does that bring to mind?" Even a basic question like: "Who would know the answer to that? Fact or fiction, past or present?" would be likely to take the client into the subtle realm. The subtle realm allows for the possibility that the answer to a problem might lie outside a person, rather than inside them. It allows for the possibility of inspiration. There is actually a standard exercise in psychosynthesis (Brown, 2004) that allows for communication with one's very own Wise Person.

And when we come to Transpersonal 2 (if we ever do) all the symbols and images and archetypes disappear, and we are left with no signposts and no hand-rails and no landmarks. This can sometimes be accessed by such a simple question as: "What would an impersonal witness say about this?" More commonly, the invitation would be to go to a place where there are no problems, and look at the issues from there. Suppose we dropped all the labels such as: "This is a problem." "This is not the way it should be." "This is hurtful." What if the situation just *Is*? From the phrase "This is wrong," we simply drop the word "wrong." This is a different dimension, and not every client is ready for this. But with the right person, at the right moment, it can hit a unique button not accessible by other means. This is quite different from the subtle, although both are within the transpersonal.

The transpersonal counselling psychologist is both a rock and a serpent. At the subtle level, he/she is a serpent, wriggling round obstacles and not being stuck with a rigid answer to anything—a "feminine" presence that encourages the client to work round so-called problems and not take anything for granted. At this level nothing is absolutely true, so it is easy to see other possibilities than the ones first presented. At the causal level the transpersonal counselling psychologist is like a rock, with an unswerving solidity that makes the client feel supported in an unwavering way, with a steady compassion that does not fall short.

To understand the rock better, consider the Christian hymn that goes— "Rock of Ages, cleft for me, let me hide myself in thee." At the subtle level this is the ability to use the counselling psychologist as a resource, to take advantage of the deep solidity offered. At the causal level it becomes the ability to become the rock oneself. Instead of depending on the rock, one may turn into the rock. We can now see both possibilities, and not be stuck with just one of them.

The main goal here is to enable clients to disengage from whatever beliefs are holding them back from their higher or deeper possibilities. In the transpersonal approach, the human mind is seen as infinite, and the human soul is divine, but clients may or may not be open to this perspective.

The task is to enable clients to work at the level most appropriate for them. It is said in therapy that some clients need glue, while others need solvent. Some clients need help in consolidating their previous gains and finding more applications for what they know already. Other clients need help in getting rid of false assumptions and false trails, and finding new directions. Some clients need a combination of both—discovering, for example, the best ideas on negotiation, so as to yield the optimal result for all the parties involved. From a transpersonal perspective, everyone is right, and the trick is to enable the client to discover that, and to use such insights productively. Unlike New Age approaches, transpersonal coaching has a place for the negative, and recognizes that destruction has a value alongside creation, and is indeed part of the same process.

In fact, the kind of thinking found at the transpersonal level of functioning is very interesting in itself. It operates according to the laws of what Wilber calls vision-logic, and what others have called dialectical logic. Instead of using the logical starting-point of "A is A" (which is true of formal or Aristotelian logic) we start with the standpoint of "A is not simply A." We can see straight away how this makes a difference in counselling psychology: if a client comes into the room and we say "Anna is Anna," this is quite uninspiring and gives us no clue as to what happens next. However, if instead we say "Anna is not simply Anna," this immediately gives us an opening through which we can start moving.

THERAPIST, CLIENT, AND RELATIONAL CONTRIBUTIONS TO EFFECTIVE TRANSPERSONAL COUNSELLING PSYCHOLOGY

Some people are very reluctant to admit that they have a soul. There are many ways to get round this. One is simply to rename it: such terms as "higher self," "inner teacher," "wise being," "psychic centre" or even just "heart" may be enough to make this acceptable. (We have given a list of such terms above.) Another way is to use the concept from transactional analysis of the "nurturing parent": it is not often realized that this concept contains most of the elements necessary to the soul. Like the soul, it is often neglected, and only needs to be brought into action by paying attention to it. Another way is to ask the client to think of someone they would really trust to have the answer or give understanding: I have had Sir Alex Ferguson, Sherlock Holmes, Aldous Huxley, and many others standing in for this role. Simpler still is to ask the client to think of a stranger from another land who has been everywhere and seen everything, and has become very wise. What would this character say about the question? The psychosynthesis people have developed this idea under such headings as the Wise Being, as we have mentioned already.

Another technique is to ask the client to imagine something ideal and removed from the current scene. This has been called "stepping into the future," and others have called it "what makes your heart sing?" The client is asked to bring this to life as if it is happening now. When this has been done, the client is asked "What year, what month is it now?" When this has been answered convincingly, the next question is "What happened in the previous year to make that possible?" And so we go backwards until the present is reached, whereupon the client is asked to take the first step forward and see what that feels like. The key thing is to undermine the common assumptions that are often made, such as that the client is a victim, or that the client is powerless.

However, the main tools of the transpersonal counselling psychologist are intuition and imagery. At the level of Transpersonal 1, intuition has become the main way of thinking, the main platform for interacting with the client, and imagery is our main tool. Instead of saying "What happened in that meeting with your boss?" we might say "When you imagine that meeting with your boss, what is the image that comes to mind?" And we then allow that answer to sink in to our consciousness and evoke a response in us. We enter into the imaginal world using our intuition.

Again, if a client has a problem with something or somebody, we can ask "If that . . . turned into an animal, what would that animal be?" And if the person answers "A rat," the next question is "How do you feel about rats?" This often leads to more insight into the nature of the problem. If the client produces an image spontaneously, we might become interested in what archetype it represented: at this level archetypes become very real. The anima and the animus, for example, can be very much worthwhile exploring, as strongly affecting perception of a person or event (Woolger, 1990).

Imagery is one of the most useful entries into the world of the transpersonal, because it is so flexible. People like Dina Glouberman (1995) have shown that imagery covers a wide range of possibilities. One of the earliest books to appear is still one of the best (Stevens & Lampert, 2007), and it has been kept in print. It gives a wealth of examples of how to use imagery and awareness as useful methods of working in this. Jean Houston is a mistress of the art of dealing with imagery, and her books (1982, 1987) give all the details of how she uses it to address the transpersonal. The book by her follower Jay Earley (1990) is also excellent.

Obviously imagery is not necessarily transpersonal. It can be prepersonal, personal, or transpersonal, but it does offer, just as do dreams, an opening that sometimes leads to the transpersonal. The thing to remember is that subtle consciousness is immensely and continuously creative, because it offers no barriers to inspiration and intuition, and hence new techniques may be invented in every session—often involving imagery in some form. For example, in working with resistance, it is often useful to personify the resistance, dialogue respectfully with it, and then ask the client to visualize it transforming in some way. The theory of the dialogical-self offers many useful hints on using this kind of approach (Rowan, 2010).

Dreams are not often mentioned in relation to counselling psychology, but at this level dreams can be very useful in throwing light on everyday issues. The point of this is to undermine the client's taken-for-granted way of seeing the world, and question radically the assumptions that are holding them back. This questioning also affects the issue of goals. Sometimes the client's goals are just as dubious as any of the other assumptions that may be holding them back.

This does not mean, of course, that we can downplay the importance of the relationship between client and counsellor. The importance of intersubjectivity cannot be overstated. The psychologist is genuinely present with the client, and this co-presence is central to all that we do.

CONTEMPORARY ADAPTATIONS, DEVELOPMENTS, EXTENSIONS

There is now a great deal of cross-cultural work involving discarnate entities of one kind or another, ranging from gods and goddesses to demons and devils, and from loas, orishas, and zar to ghosts and witches. A great deal of fear may be aroused by such material for the client, and may be picked up by a therapist who is not well versed in this area. The transpersonal therapist is of course much better able to handle this material than other therapists, because their experience of the subtle realms, and the transformations of consciousness, will stand them in good stead (See Wilber, Engler, & Brown, 1986). Also the whole idea of the pre/trans fallacy may be important in placing the phenomenon into the right place.

Here is an example, taken from an interview with a patient in a mental hospital detailed by Eugenie Georgaca, which goes like this:

INTERVIEWER: *So did, did something specific happen yesterday that made you feel so bad?*

PATIENT: *Yeah.*

INTERVIEWER: *What was it?*

PATIENT: *Those spirits. Spirits have been following me, spirits that, you know, they are coming up, they are coming out.*

INTERVIEWER: *Yeah. So what type, I mean, what type of spirit is it?*

PATIENT: *I would say a mind spirit.*

INTERVIEWER: *Yeah, yeah, I mean, obviously that's, I mean, you haven't seen it or heard it or anything, you just . . .*

PATIENT: *I feel it.*

INTERVIEWER: *Yeah, you're just feeling it. So how do you know it's a spirit then?*

PATIENT: *The world made up of, the world made up of body I just think it's spirit.*

INTERVIEWER: *Hmmmm, but it doesn't do anything else to you, does it?*

PATIENT: *That it makes me sick, it makes me sick.*

(Georgaca, 2000, p. 233)

The interviewer goes on to avoid all the issues raised by this conversation, and to retreat to a rational form of dismissal of the experience as delusional. The first questions a transpersonal counselling psychologist might ask could be: "Does this spirit have a name?" "Does it have a personality?" "What does it want?" Because the interviewer had no understanding of the mind-set of the patient, such a question could not be asked. But it is a well-known fact amongst people who believe in spirits that once you know the name of a spirit it gives you much more control of them. It makes it much easier to talk to the spirit and have a dialogue with it. This means that the transpersonal approach can be particularly valuable in cross-cultural work where the culture of origin of the client is very different from the host culture. Until recently, this was an uncharted area, but now the excellent book by Fukuyama and Sevig (1999) is available to help us with a multitude of research studies and a great deal of insight.

It may be worthwhile to comment on the important contribution that the transpersonal approach has made towards working with diversity. Transpersonal therapy is particularly well suited to work in the field of diversity, because of its open acceptance of the spiritual, which is so important in some cultures. Fukuyama and Sevig (1999) have written well about this, and Kate Maguire (2001) has written very movingly about one particular aspect. She draws attention to the importance of metaphor in working with clients from other cultures. Of course different cultures have different labels for the levels of consciousness that we have outlined here. In yoga, for example, what we have called the subtle corresponds quite well with what they call the Bhakti approach; while what we have called the causal corresponds well with what they call the Jnana approach. But many other cultures recognize the levels that have been outlined here, and it just needs the practitioner to use the language understood by the client.

Similarly, many cultures do not accept the individualism that is so characteristic of what we have called the Centaur level of consciousness. They have a more communal view of self and society, but this is highly compatible with the higher levels, of subtle and causal, which we have concentrated on here. In fact, these ideas often came in the first case from Eastern cultures, which are also compatible with Jewish culture as found, for example, in the Kabbalah.

CLINICAL EXAMPLE

An example of the kind of work we do at this level comes in the shape of work with a dream. The client was a young man whose main presenting problem was a compulsion to expose himself in difficult and unsuitable situations. In the dream he was walking along a familiar street, when all at once appeared a large number of black puppies. As they moved along and as the numbers proliferated, he noticed that some of them were distorted out of shape, and appeared to be suffering from some pain or disability: they became quite ugly and threatening, as if they could do him some harm. More and more of them appeared and took up the whole field of view. The dream then came to an end. I entered into the subtle field of consciousness, and went into the dream with him. I immediately became aware of a distinctive colour—a sort of aura that covered the whole scene—and saw that this colour was what the puppies were following. They were trying to get more into the colour somehow. I could then see that the puppies represented the client's temptation to expose himself, and that the whole effort was really to be seen in a certain light. But this desire to be seen was offset by the ugliness of the whole scene—these puppies were ugly and diseased, not normal, not healthy.

When we came out of the scene together, the client expressed amazement at the deep insight offered by the dream. Although he felt the need to expose himself, he now became much more aware of the opposite need: to hide and to feel shame at any exposure. It became clear to him that he had been hiding from himself the sheer ugliness of the exposure, and the way in which it was compulsive rather than chosen. He had been attracted by the light, and unaware of the darkness surrounding it, and the ugliness of the vision. When we met later, he revealed that he had now given up self-exposure as much too ambiguous and complex, revealing far too much about how he had been deceiving himself about it and treating it as quite trivial, when it was really anything but.

FUTURE ORIENTATIONS

It seems that the future of the transpersonal approach is assured. The recent book by Nigel Hamilton (2014) shows how the work is still developing and growing. Even more impressively, the compendious *Wiley-Blackwell Handbook of Transpersonal Psychology* (Friedman & Hartelius, 2013) with its 38 chapters by prestigious authors gives an even stronger hint that doors are opening.

I have myself written on transformational research (Rowan, 1998), which is the kind of research that can take us forward in this area: "It is a form of research which goes beyond being non-alienating and thinks in terms of genuine transformation. Not so much involving the people being studied, but more like *being* the people studied. The barrier between researcher and subject, which had been eroded a good deal in collaborative research, disappears altogether at times" (p. 158). See also the extensive material in Anderson and Braud (2011).

These books, and others like them, show that research is going on and that new ground is being broken in this area. For example, the chapter by Roberts and Winkelman in the Handbook just mentioned updates the situation on psychedelic drugs, which were off the approved list for a number of years. More and more attention is being given to this area now, and we may confidently suppose that much useful data will emerge.

CONCLUSION

It seems that the transpersonal approach is growing in popularity, and several recent edited volumes have contained useful chapters on it (Rowan, 2014). Today there is far more interest in spirituality, as witness the recent work of Len Sperry (2012), although some of the expressions of it are quite dubious and lacking in authenticity. The work of David Matteson (2008), however, shows how the transpersonal approach can offer a critique of religious prejudice in the area of homosexuality, which is much more sophisticated and well-argued than most other approaches in this field.

SUGGESTED FURTHER READING

Grof, C., & Grof, S. (1990). *The stormy search for the self*. Los Angeles: Tarcher.
This book is about spiritual emergencies.

Rowan, J. (2005). *The transpersonal: Spirituality in counselling and psychotherapy* (2nd ed.). Hove: Routledge.
A general overview covering a wide range of issues for transpersonal counselling psychology.

Fukuyama, M. A., & Sevig, T. D. (1999). *Integrating spirituality into multicultural counselling*. London: Sage.
Essential reading for transpersonal counselling psychologists working with people from different cultures.

REFERENCES

Anderson, R., & Braud, W. (2011). *Transforming self and others through research: Transpersonal research methods and skills for the human sciences*. Albany, NY: SUNY Press.

Assagioli, R. (1975). *Psychosynthesis*. London: Watkins.

Brazier, D. (1995). *Zen therapy*. London: Constable.

Brown, M. Y. (2004). *Unfolding self: The practice of psychosynthesis*. New York: Helios Press.

Corbin, H. (1969). *Creative imagination in the Sufism of Ibn 'Arabi*. Princeton, NJ: Princeton University Press.

Cortright, B. (1997). *Psychotherapy and spirit: Theory and practice in transpersonal psychotherapy*. Albany, NY: SUNY Press.

Earley, J. (1990). *Inner journeys: A guide to personal and social transformations*. Newburyport, MA: Red Wheel Weiser.

Epstein, M. (1996). *Thoughts without a thinker*. London: Duckworth.

Ferrer, J. (2002). *Revisioning transpersonal theory: A participatory vision of human spirituality*. Albany, NY: SUNY Press.

Friedman, H. L., & Hartelius, G. (Eds.) (2013). *The Wiley-Blackwell handbook of transpersonal psychology*. Chichester: Wiley.

Fukuyama, M. A., & Sevig, T. D. (1999). *Integrating spirituality into multicultural counselling*. London: Sage.

Georgaca, E. (2000). Reality and discourse: A critical analysis of the category of "delusions." *British Journal of Medical Psychology, 73*, 227–242.

Glouberman, D. (1995). *Life chances, life changes*. Shanklin: Skyros Books.

Govinda, L. (1973). *Foundations of Tibetan mysticism*. New York: Weiser.

Grof, C., & Grof, S. (1990). *The stormy search for the self*. Los Angeles, CA: Tarcher.

Grof, S. (2013). Revision and re-enchantment of psychology: Legacy from half a century of consciousness research. In H. L. Friedman & G. Hartelius (Eds.), *The Wiley-Blackwell handbook of transpersonal psychology*. Chichester: Wiley-Blackwell.

Hamilton, N. (2014). *Awakening through dreams: The journey through the inner landscape.* London: Karnac Books.

Hillman, J. (1975). *Re-visioning psychology.* London: Harper Colophon.

Hillman, J. (1979). *The dream and the underworld.* San Francisco, CA: Harper & Row.

Hillman, J. (1997). *The soul's code.* New York: Bantam.

Houston, J. (1982). *The possible human.* Los Angeles, CA: Tarcher.

Houston, J. (1987). *The search for the beloved: Journeys in sacred psychology.* Los Angeles, CA: Tarcher.

Houston, J. (1996). *A mythic life: Learning to live our greater story.* San Francisco, CA: Harper.

Jung, C. G. (1968). *The archetypes and the collective unconscious.* Collected Works, Vol. 9, Part 1 (2nd ed.). London: Routledge.

Jung, C. G. (2009). *The red book.* London: Watkins.

Maguire, K. (2001). Working with survivors of torture and extreme experiences. In S. King-Spooner & C. Newnes (Eds.), *Spirituality and psychotherapy.* Ross-on-Wye: PCCS Books.

Matteson, D. R. (2008). *Exploring the spiritual: Paths for counsellors and psychotherapists.* Hove: Routledge.

Rowan, J. (1998). Transformational research. In P. Clarkson (Ed.), *Counselling psychology: Integrating theory, research and supervised practice.* Hove: Routledge.

Rowan, J. (2003). Counselling psychology practice: A transpersonal perspective. In R. Woolfe, W. Dryden, & S. Strawbridge (Eds.), *Handbook of Counselling Psychology* (2nd ed., pp. 221–240). London: Sage.

Rowan, J. (2005). *The transpersonal: Spirituality in counselling and psychotherapy* (2nd ed.). Hove: Routledge.

Rowan, J. (2010). *Personification. Using the dialogical self in psychotherapy and counselling.* London: Routledge.

Rowan, J. (2014). The transpersonal in individual therapy. In W. Dryden & A. Reeves (Eds.), *The handbook of individual therapy* (6th ed.). London: Sage.

Schwartz-Salant, N. (1986). On the subtle-body concept in clinical practice. In N. Schwartz-Salant & M. Stein (Eds.), *The body in analysis.* Wilmette, IL: Chiron.

Sperry, L. (2012). *Spirituality in clinical practice: Theory and practice of spiritually oriented psychotherapy* (2nd ed.). Hove: Routledge.

Stevens, J. O., & Lampert, R. (2007). *Awareness: Exploring, experimenting, experiencing.* Gouldsboro: The Gestalt Journal Press.

von Franz, M.-L. (1977). *Individuation in fairy tales.* Zurich: Spring.

West, W. (2000). *Psychotherapy and spirituality.* London: Sage.

Whitmont, E. (1987). Archetypal and personal interaction in the clinical process. In N. Schwartz-Salant & M. Stein (Eds.), *Archetypal processes in psychotherapy.* Wilmette, IL: Chiron.

Wilber, K. (2000). *Integral psychology.* Boston, MA: Shambhala.

Wilber, K., Engler, J., & Brown, D. (1986). *Transformations of consciousness.* Boston, MA and London: Shambhala.

Woolger, R. J. (1990). *Other lives, other selves: A Jungian psychotherapist discovers past lives.* Wellingborough: Crucible.

Psychology

TERRY HANLEY, LAURA ANNE WINTER, JOHN McLEOD, AND MICK COOPER

CHAPTER OUTLINE

INTRODUCTION 135

ONTOLOGICAL ASSUMPTIONS: IMAGE
OF THE PERSON 136

EPISTEMOLOGIES: WAYS
OF KNOWING 136

GUIDING PRINCIPLES: CORE THEORETICAL
ASSUMPTIONS 137

NATURE AND UNDERSTANDING
OF PSYCHOLOGICAL DISTRESS 138

THE ROLE AND PLACE OF THE THERAPEUTIC
RELATIONSHIP 139

THERAPIST, CLIENT, AND RELATIONAL
CONTRIBUTIONS TO EFFECTIVE PLURALISTIC
COUNSELLING PSYCHOLOGY 140
    Therapeutic Goals 140
    Therapeutic Tasks 141
    Therapeutic Methods 141

CONTEMPORARY ADAPTATIONS,
DEVELOPMENTS, EXTENSIONS 141

FUTURE ORIENTATIONS 145

CONCLUSION 146

LEARNING OUTCOMES

BY THE END OF THIS CHAPTER YOU SHOULD BE ABLE TO ANSWER THE FOLLOWING KEY QUESTIONS:

1. What are the main philosophical and theoretical ideas underpinning pluralistic counselling psychology?

2. In what ways does pluralistic counselling psychology differ from other approaches?

3. What are the main issues for practice in the area of pluralistic counselling psychology?

INTRODUCTION

This chapter provides an introduction to pluralistic counselling psychology. Working pluralistically emphasizes a number of equally plausible and potentially successful responses to the issues that individuals present within therapy. A pluralistic approach is closely tied to the practice and values of counselling psychology (Cooper, 2009; McAteer, 2010). As part of this, it overlaps considerably with the integrative and eclectic therapies (see Chapter 11 this volume; McLeod, 2013). However, because the pluralistic approach is grounded in a particular set of values—humanistic, existential, and postmodern—it is somewhat distinct from an integrative approach, per se. A first important difference is that the pluralistic approach is a framework for thinking about therapeutic practice as a whole, and can be embracing of single orientation—as well as multiple orientation—practices. Second, and closely related to this, while some integrative therapists advocate a particular "brand" of multi-orientation therapy, a pluralistic framework advocates an openness towards, and appreciation of, the widest possible range of therapeutic understandings and methods. Third, a pluralistic approach places particular emphasis on shared decision making and tailoring the therapy to the individual client. This is also true of many integrative practices, but is not inherent to this approach. Hence, while a pluralistic therapeutic practice can be considered synonymous with a collaborative integrative approach, it is possible to hold a pluralistic viewpoint without practising in an integrative way, and there are forms of integrative and eclectic practice that can be considered outside of a pluralistic value base.

A pluralistic approach, by definition, may take on many forms. This chapter aims to reflect primarily upon contemporary developments in pluralistic thinking and practice. In recent years, many of the debates and dialogues that have surrounded pluralistic therapy have been harnessed into a practical framework by Cooper and McLeod (2007, 2011) that highlights the importance of a collaborative therapeutic relationship and therapeutic *goals*, *tasks*, and *methods* within the work of counselling psychologists. In this chapter we will introduce the key elements to pluralistic counselling psychology and provide examples from therapeutic practice to illustrate these concepts in action.

ONTOLOGICAL ASSUMPTIONS: IMAGE OF THE PERSON

Pluralism starts from the assumption that there is a great deal of diversity across human being. That is, people differ in such fundamental characteristics as their values, life goals, and ways of experiencing the world, and that we can never reduce human being to a single set of characteristics, laws, or mechanisms. Such an ontology is rooted in the existential and humanistic emphasis on the uniqueness and irreducibility of human being (e.g., Buber, 1958). In addition, drawing from contemporary postmodern and postexistential thinking (e.g., Derrida, 1974; Levinas, 1969), pluralism holds a reflexive, critical lens to this, and any other, set of assumptions—including pluralistic ones—themselves. An important aspect of a pluralistic worldview is that it challenges the notion that practice can be grounded in a single ontological position. There are two facets of this challenge. First, a pluralistic perspective holds that ontology rests on a deeper set of principles: ethics. From a pluralistic standpoint, what is truly fundamental is not how we *conceptualize* each other, but how we *treat* each other. Second, a pluralistic stance is associated with an acceptance that we exist in a world characterized by multiple plausible ontologies, including realist, constructivist, and transcendental/spiritual. An effective pluralistic practitioner needs to be open to appreciating the diversity of worldviews espoused by different clients. While each of us, as psychologists, may operate from a preferred ontological position, a commitment to pluralism requires a capacity to be open to respectful dialogue with colleagues and service users who see the world differently from us.

EPISTEMOLOGIES: WAYS OF KNOWING

Pluralism is aligned to the writings of phenomenological philosophers and psychologists (Husserl, 1913 [1962]), which view people as intentional in nature (i.e., they strive towards particular goals) and value the importance of understanding a person's experience from his or her own viewpoint. Further, phenomenological enquiry suggests that personal worlds exist within an intersubjective field: people are viewed as social/relational beings who make meaning through dialogue with others.

A pluralistic position to therapy assumes that there are likely to be multiple useful ways of knowing in relation to any complex presenting issue (Bergner, 2006). For example, within the ongoing flow of a therapy session, a clinician may at various points draw on personal, cultural, practical, theoretical, and research-based knowledge (McLeod, 2016). Similarly, a client may need to reconcile the tension between the evidence of their own personal experience, and the recommendations made by authority figures in their life. A pluralistic position adopts a pragmatic standpoint and assumes that some ways of knowing will be more useful in some circumstances and less helpful in other situations, or more/less consistent with ethical and moral considerations (Scott, 2013). Epistemological pragmatism and diversity play a central role in pluralistic practice, with clients being encouraged to use different strategies for exploring and conveying what it is that they know, such as talking, writing, drawing, and filling in measures.

GUIDING PRINCIPLES: CORE THEORETICAL ASSUMPTIONS

The guiding principles that inform the work of pluralistic counselling psychologists can be understood at two levels. First, there are principles that refer to the overarching metatheoretical perspective adopted by pluralistic practitioners. Second, there are principles that are grounded in the specific concepts and methods that are drawn upon by the client and the therapist in the context of each case.

As a philosophical construct, the concept of pluralism operates at a metatheoretical level in relation to theories of counselling psychology. Reflection on the meaning and implications of the concept of pluralism leads to a set of general principles that can be used to inform the conduct of therapy:

- There is no single or unitary truth: any activity or practice can be therapeutic or non-therapeutic.
- A commitment to pluralism leads to an appreciation that differences in beliefs about the best, or true course of action cannot usually be resolved through the adoption of one position and rejection of the opposing stance. Instead, an appreciation of the meaning of pluralism inevitably leads in the direction of recognizing the centrality of dialogue within effective and constructive human action.
- A consistently enacted therapist position of deep respect for the strengths, knowledge, and capabilities of the client is necessary to overcome the power imbalance that exists in professional relationships and may impede authentic dialogue.
- The use of "both/and" thinking and problem-solving is more productive than the adoption of an "either/or" stance.

In practice, pluralistic therapists make use of concepts and methods from a range of therapy approaches, such as psychodynamic, cognitive-behavioural therapy (CBT) and person-centred. This occurs through a collaborative process, in which the therapist may consult the client on what they believe would be most helpful, or the therapist explains or demonstrates ideas and methods, and checks out whether the client sees them as useful. In these situations, it is essential for therapists to possess an understanding of what they are offering, and be able to explain this to the client, at the level of the therapeutic principles that justify the use of the concept or method. If the therapist has developed only a superficial understanding of the concepts and methods they are using, there is a risk that the client may experience the therapist as inauthentic or confused.

Pluralistic therapy is part of a trend within the world of counselling psychology and psychotherapy, in the direction of therapy integration. Proponents of therapy integration (see Chapter 11) believe that while many therapy theories are useful, none of them is sufficient in itself. Several different styles of therapy integration have been developed, including eclecticism, theoretical integration, assimilative integration, and the common factors model. As a relatively recent entrant to the field of therapy integration, the pluralistic framework for practice has been able to incorporate the most useful features of all of the existing integrative frameworks, while (hopefully) avoiding their drawbacks (McLeod and Sundet, 2016). The distinctive features of pluralistic therapy, as an integrative orientation, lie in its collaborative and dialogical stance, and its open-ness to the potential value of any idea or method in the context of a specific case.

NATURE AND UNDERSTANDING OF PSYCHOLOGICAL DISTRESS

A commitment to dialogical, collaborative working means that pluralistic counselling psychologists need to be aware of their own assumptions about the nature of psychological distress, and at the same time sensitive to the possible ideas and assumptions that might be espoused by their clients. This means that it is helpful for pluralistic practitioners to be aware of sociological and social anthropological research into the ways in which ordinary people, within the cultural settings represented in their client population, make sense of problems in living.

From a pluralistic perspective, it is not assumed that everyone enters therapy in order to alleviate psychological distress. Within the pluralistic therapy literature, the term "problems in living" is used to denote a broader understanding of the difficulties that might be resolvable through talking to a therapist. In this respect, pluralistic therapy is closely aligned with the social justice orientation that informs much recent practice in counselling psychology: distress is often the result of oppression, exclusion, and deprivation.

The practice of pluralistic counselling psychology requires a capacity to conceptualize the distress and goals of the client from different perspectives. It is assumed that both client and therapist have their own perspectives and understandings around the nature of psychological distress, and that each is able to contribute to the creation of a shared space within which the client can explore, choose, and find meaning that will guide action. In addition, when making sense of the problems being presented by the client, a practitioner needs to be able to achieve an appropriate level of both separation and connection between the legitimate aims of the service within which he or she is employed (e.g., to deliver counselling for depression) and the goals of the client (e.g., to explore their sexuality).

THE ROLE AND PLACE OF THE THERAPEUTIC RELATIONSHIP

The client–therapist relationship tends to be central to pluralistic practice. However, it is not assumed that any one mode of relationship will be appropriate to all clients, or to the same client at different times, or that all clients need a particular kind of relationship to the same extent. For example, a distressed client at an early stage of therapy may find it helpful to receive a psychodynamic "holding" relationship, and then at a later stage benefit from a "coaching" style as they try new coping skills in everyday situations. In making sense of these shifts, it is useful for pluralistic therapists to develop a broad understanding of the diversity of forms of human relationship that are possible (Josselson, 1996). Underpinning this flexibility is a process of dialogue between the therapist and client: "a mutual, equal, active collaboration between two intelligences in which two streams of expertise enrich one another and blend" (Bohart & Tallman, 1999, p. 224).

Within the field of pluralistic therapy, effective dialogue is promoted through regular *metatherapeutic communication* (Cooper, 2016). This is an extension of Rennie's (1998) concept of "metacommunication," and can be defined as "the process of talking to clients about what they want from therapy, and how they think they may be most likely to achieve it" (Cooper & McLeod, 2012, p. 7). Metatherapeutic communication is dialogue about the therapeutic process itself and has many parallels with the concept of *shared decision making*, which has been widely adopted within the wider health care field (The Health Foundation, 2014). Shared decision making is a process by which clinicians and patients work together to identify the most suitable treatments, tests, and procedures for the patient, and has been shown to increase levels of patient satisfaction and involvement with care, as well as reducing drop out (The Health Foundation, 2014).

Research suggests that metatherapeutic communication can be conceptualized in terms of three dimensions (Cooper, Dryden, Martin, & Papayianni, 2016). The first dimension is *when* it takes place. In many instances, this is in a first assessment session, but it might also be at the beginning of sessions, during review sessions, or even before therapy has taken place. The second dimension is *what* the subject matter of the metatherapeutic communication is. In many cases, it is about the goals or methods of therapy, but it may also be about the content to be discussed, an understanding of how the client's problems arose, or the client's experiences in therapy. The third dimension is the temporal focus of the metatherapeutic communication. For instance, is it about what takes place in the current session, what has taken place, or what therapist and client should do for the therapeutic work as a whole?

Based on the available evidence and clinical experience, Cooper et al. (2016) suggest to therapists nine basic principles for effective metatherapeutic communication:

1. Address metatherapeutic issues from the start of therapy.
2. Actively invite clients to share their views.
3. See metatherapeutic communication as an ongoing process, rather than a one-off event.
4. Use your own sense of uncertainty about what to do with a client as an indicator of when metatherapeutic communication may be helpful.
5. Be actively involved in the dialogue.
6. Describe to clients what the options might be.
7. Consider using process and outcome measures.
8. Tailor levels of metatherapeutic communication to the preferences of the particular client.
9. If you are working in a service, implement the principles of shared decision making across the service as a whole—not just in individual therapy.

Given this emphasis on collaboration, a pluralistic approach puts the therapeutic relationship right at the heart of pluralistic practice. Moreover, given the strength of the evidence associating relationship factors to outcomes (Norcross, 2011), a pluralistic approach assumes that, for many clients, such relational factors as empathy and unconditional acceptance will be essential to good outcomes. However, from a pluralistic standpoint, it is also important to acknowledge that, for some clients at some points in time, relational factors may be less central to their process of change. And research shows that guided self-help programmes can be of considerable value (see Cooper, 2008). In fact, as research in the shared decision making field shows (The Health Foundation, 2014), service users vary even in how much shared decision making they want. Consistent with its ethics and ontology, then, a pluralistic approach tries to avoid any rigid assumptions about the role and the place of the therapeutic relationship.

THERAPIST, CLIENT, AND RELATIONAL CONTRIBUTIONS TO EFFECTIVE PLURALISTIC COUNSELLING PSYCHOLOGY

The process engaged in by therapist and client can prove incredibly varied in its form. One means of reflecting upon this diversity is to break the activities into three components: (a) therapeutic goals, (b) therapeutic tasks, and (c) therapeutic methods. These are discussed in turn below:

Therapeutic Goals

When clients arrive at therapy they have a goal to the meetings in which they are engaging. This might not be easily identified (or be viewed using the language of goals), however pluralistic therapists work with the view that clients do have a purpose for entering therapy and that part of the therapist's role is to support the client in articulating this (see Hanley, Sefi, & Ersahin, 2016, for more discussion around goal articulation). It is important to recognize here that it is the client's ideas about what they want from therapy that are fundamental to pluralistic practice not, for example, what a referrer suggests might be useful for that particular client.

Therapeutic Tasks

Once a therapy goal has been identified, a pluralistic therapist will then try to work with the client to identify an appropriate way of working. For instance, a therapy goal of trying to make sense of life after being bereaved by a partner might consist of numerous tasks. These could include ones that are very broad and existential in nature (e.g., taking stock of what life means to the individual); or ones that are equally as important but more practical in nature (e.g., having space to reflect upon more day-to-day occurrences such as cooking or managing bank accounts without their partner). From a pluralistic perspective, working out which tasks are most appropriate for the client to work on will be collaborative in nature, with both the therapist and client being actively involved in deciding upon the direction of therapy.

Therapeutic Methods

The methods that are adopted in pluralistic therapy are drawn from numerous sources. These might be techniques or strategies that are used in different therapeutic models; for example, making use of behavioural experiments from a cognitive-behavioural model, or two-chair work from Gestalt therapy (for a fuller overview of therapeutic methods that different approaches might contribute here, see Cooper & Dryden, 2016). Furthermore, because of the collaborative and individualized approach to therapy (i.e., the methods used in therapy are not simply "prescribed" by the therapist), methods might come from the client or therapist's personal knowledge or experience, or their culture. For example, therapeutic methods might also include the client engaging in sporting/creative activities or involvement in community groups or political campaigns.

In bringing together these three concepts the analogy of a journey is commonly utilized to describe the process. Here the *goal* might be viewed as the destination, the *task* the route that the therapist and client might take (of which there can be many), and the *method* the vehicle that they might travel in.

CONTEMPORARY ADAPTATIONS, DEVELOPMENTS, EXTENSIONS

Despite being a relatively new addition to the therapeutic literature, the pluralistic framework in counselling and psychotherapy has already been developed substantially since its initial presentation by Cooper and McLeod (2007).

By definition, given the pluralistic underpinnings discussed above, the approach welcomes challenges and revisions, and aims to function as a fluid set of practices rather than something quite rigid. Therefore, as opposed to having a monolithic set of fixed beliefs determined by one or two "leaders," the approach hopes to continually develop, change, and adapt. Further, it is hoped that this development emerges from a community of individuals that includes both academics and practitioners alike.

As has been indicated above, developments to pluralistic practice include contributions from numerous therapeutic approaches. These include contributions from humanistic, cognitive-behavioural, psychodynamic, existential, narrative, and integrative perspectives. Additionally, authors have considered the implication of working therapeutically with different client goals, including improving relationships, addressing grief, and overcoming addictions (Cooper & Dryden, 2016). When considering both the therapeutic orientation and the client goal, individuals are encouraged to hold the theoretical and research knowledge lightly and consider it alongside other factors when making decisions in therapeutic practice (see Hanley, Cutts, Gordon, & Scott, 2013). For example, in discussing what *tasks* and *methods* might be useful with particular goals, pluralistic practitioners are cautious about moving away from the pluralistic roots and towards a "one size fits all" approach.

The pluralistic framework prizes and centres upon a commitment to diversity and difference but may be critiqued for focusing upon the needs of the individual. Winter, Guo, Wilk, and Hanley (2016) present a diversity perspective to the pluralistic framework and reflect on the importance of group differences, power, and oppression. Such an approach calls on the pluralistic therapist to acknowledge and address issues of diversity and social justice in their work as therapists, both inside and outside of the therapy room. Similarly, Hanley, Sefi, and Williams (2013) reflect upon some of the nuances of developing a "youth friendly" therapeutic service. Here they apply the pluralistic framework to therapeutic work with young people/young adults and highlight the importance of being flexible and responsive in such work.

Another area in which the pluralistic approach is developing is in relation to research. For example, Hanley and Winter (2016) discuss the connections between the framework and research, and an agenda for research related to the pluralistic framework is put forward. This encourages individuals to be both strategic (e.g., being strategic as a group of interested researchers to create more impactful projects and emphasizing a research-informed approach over a research-driven one) and to work in a way that is in keeping with the value base of a pluralistic stance (e.g., actively collaborating with stakeholders in research, emphasizing trustworthiness in research and disseminating findings to a range of stakeholders in and outside of academia). Furthermore, research designs such as rich case study designs have been suggested to more fully reflect upon and evaluate pluralistic practices (see McLeod & Cooper, 2011), and tools that are pluralistic in focus and straddle both the practice and research worlds have begun to be developed e.g., the Cooper-Norcross Inventory of Preferences (Cooper & Norcross, 2015).

CLINICAL EXAMPLE

Context

Jenny was a 32-year-old woman who had been referred to meet with a counselling psychologist by her doctor. In recent months Jenny had felt increasingly anxious about her work and had been constantly fatigued. Although Jenny identified herself as "a bit of a worrier" and "overly anxious at times," things had been exacerbated following the recent separation from her partner. Jenny went to her doctors as she felt she was no longer coping well at work, with the combination of new demands meaning that she was "increasingly behind with everything." She went to the doctors primarily due to the physiological side of things (feeling increasingly tired), however, her doctor felt that psychological input might be helpful at this stage alongside some medication to help with Jenny's sleeping.

The counselling psychology service Jenny was attending was linked to her doctor's surgery. It offered individuals between 6 and 12 meetings following an initial assessment meeting. The therapy was pluralistic in nature and focused around the issues that the client wished to work on. The counselling psychologist Jenny met with, Kavita, initially trained on a programme that focused upon the person-centred and cognitive-behavioural approaches of therapy. It harnessed these approaches with discussions around the pluralistic framework. Following on from this core training, Kavita completed numerous additional brief training programmes, for example, a short course on emotion focused therapy and a day input on working with different presenting issues.

Beginning

Jenny and Kavita met for an assessment session about a week after Jenny's appointment with her doctor. During this appointment Kavita initially went through the information about the counselling psychology service and explained the way that she worked as a psychologist. In going through this information, Kavita hoped to provide Jenny with information that would help her to gain a greater sense of what therapy with her may be like and to actively take part in the therapeutic process. Kavita explained her training briefly and described the collaborative nature of the way she worked with clients. An information sheet about the service was also given to Jenny at the end of the session.

In addition to providing information about the service Kavita asked Jenny to complete a number of questionnaires related to their work together. These included information related to demographic details, risk assessment, and general well-being (CORE-OM). Although these identified that Jenny was struggling from high levels of anxiety, no imminent safety risks were identified. The final questionnaire that Kavita presented was a Goals Form (see www.pluralistictherapy.com). This form asked Jenny to write down what goals she might wish to work on within their meetings together. To start with, Jenny was not sure what to write down and so Kavita facilitated a conversation around this.

KAVITA: *Sometimes it can be difficult pinning down what you might want to work on. Some people find it helpful to think about how they hope things might look differently at the end of therapy. Do you have any ideas around that?*

JENNY: *I guess the main thing is that I want to feel more in control of my life. Everything feels a bit all over the place at present.*

KAVITA: *Okay that's helpful to hear. Shall we write that down as our goal for now? [Jenny nods and Kavita writes down*

"I want to feel more in control of my life" on the form]

KAVITA: *So, if you were more in control, what sorts of things might change?*

JENNY: *Well . . . [pause] I'd have less panic attacks [Kavita: Okay—and writes "have less panic attacks" on a small wipe board on the desk]. I also hope that I might want to get back into dating again. I'm not getting any younger [Jenny—writes "get back into dating again"].*

KAVITA: *Okay. Well, we have two areas we could focus in upon there for sure. Do you have a sense of which one of those might be most important for you?*

JENNY: *To be honest, it's the second of those at the moment.*

KAVITA: *So spending some time working on getting back into dating would come first.*

JENNY: *Yes.*

At this stage, Kavita and Jenny have identified a primary therapy goal to work on and two related therapy tasks. Once these have been identified, Kavita moves to consider with Jenny what methods might be best suited to her needs.

KAVITA: *As I mentioned earlier, counselling can take all manner of forms. It can be quite open, with me mainly listening, or I could get more involved as we talked about earlier. I wonder if you have had any ideas about what might be good for you?*

JENNY: *I'm not sure. I just want to get stuff off my chest at the moment. You mentioned that stuff with the two chairs before. I don't mind giving it a go, but I think I just want to talk and offload. The doctor mentioned cognitive-behaviour something for the panic*

attacks, but I don't really know what that means. What do you think?

KAVITA: *Well, from what you've said, maybe having a space to talk through things and get things off your chest might be a good starting point. Cognitive-behavioural therapy is . . . [Kavita provides a brief definition of this approach and provides a weblink for further information]. This can be a good way of working with anxiety and panic attacks.*

JENNY: *Okay. Thanks. Yes, then. Let's be a bit more open to start with. I'll look at the CBT stuff and maybe we can do that another time?*

Overview of the Therapeutic Work

Jenny and Kavita agreed to meet for 6 weeks initially prior to scheduling a review session for the work. Kavita primarily utilized a person-centred approach to therapy, initially helping facilitate Jenny to talk and experience her feelings related to the recent separation (method). These conversations took a more existential turn as Jenny reflected upon her desire to have children and considered how she perceived the purpose of her life if she did not end up having children.

During the time Kavita and Jenny were working together, Jenny had several panic attacks when she encountered stressful events (e.g., attending a friend's wedding as a bridesmaid). Three weeks into the meetings it was negotiated that Kavita would actively teach Jenny some relaxation techniques at the end of each session (method), thus attending more explicitly to the second task identified within the first session. Specifically, Kavita supported Jenny in undertaking a number of breathing exercises that she could utilize on her own if a stressful event was to occur. Both agreed that allocating 10 min at the end of each session for the relaxation activities would be sufficient for the time being, with Kavita taking responsibility to manage the time between the two methods.

Reviewing the Therapeutic Work

An important part of working pluralistically is the need to remain mindful of the client's perspective on the therapeutic work. Kavita encouraged Jenny to provide feedback throughout the meetings by using meta-therapeutic communication. Specifically, Kavita utilized two main strategies here: (a) encouraging facilitative conversations within the therapeutic meetings (e.g., Kavita: *Okay. So that's how the relaxation activities might go. So we can get a sense of whether that's something we should do again, I wonder if you could say a bit about how that was for you?*), and (b) using formal review techniques—here Kavita utilized the Session Rating Scale (a brief sessional measure to help raise the conversation

if therapy was heading in the right direction for Jenny) and scheduled some review time on the sixth session to discuss the work so far.

During the review meeting, Jenny reflected that things seemed to be getting better for her over the past few weeks. Having the space to talk had been "helping to get things off her chest" and she had been actively using the relaxation exercises in her day-to-day activities. Kavita asked Jenny to rate how much of her initial goal of "I want to feel in more control of my life" had been achieved. They revisited the Goals Form and Jenny circled a 5 out of 7 on the form (7 indicating the goal is completely achieved). This proved a positive marker for the therapy, however, Jenny also noted that she felt that further support would be helpful. At this stage, Kavita revisited the Goals Form with Jenny with a view to working with her to decide the direction that the future meetings might take.

FUTURE ORIENTATIONS

Despite the apparent popularity of single school therapy that can be manualized and offered to a large number of individuals, the demand for more responsive interventions remains. The acknowledgement of the need for psychologists to engage with the complexity of psychological distress/problems of living, and not to wield themselves as blunt unbending tools, is becoming increasingly commonplace (e.g., discussions around therapeutic common factors (Sparks, Duncan, & Miller, 2008)) or transdiagnostic ways of working (e.g., Mansell, Carey, & Tai, 2102). Additionally, there are increasing numbers of empirical studies reflecting upon the potential benefits for a pluralistic attitude towards therapy for client groups (e.g., Omylinska-Thurston & Cooper, 2014) and, as a consequence of such a move towards pluralistic thinking, the challenges of individuals training in and working with such frameworks (e.g., Scott & Hanley, 2012; Tilley, McLeod, & McLeod, 2015, respectively). Thus, developments in this area are moving at a relatively fast pace. In doing so, however, challenges inevitably appear for the pluralistic framework discussed here. For instance, in contrast to many of the theoretical developments and refinements that are being engaged with by academics and practitioners, the engagement with research remains relatively limited. To date, there are limited examples of empirical research exploring the framework being utilized in practice. Two examples of such work are:

- Cooper et al. (2015) Practice based evidence

This practice-based research study explored the impact that pluralistic therapists have upon individuals experiencing moderate to high levels of depression. Of 39 individuals who completed two or more sessions, 28 (71.8%) of the clients showed reliable improvement and 17 (43.6%) of clients showed reliable recovery. The effect sizes for the interventions proved large: 1.83 for symptoms of depression and 1.16 for symptoms of anxiety.

- Ward and Hogan (2015) Pragmatic case study

This pragmatic case study explored the impact of a pluralistic approach to therapy upon a client experiencing emotional disruption and who had been affected by long-standing executive difficulties due to a head injury sustained at work. Qualitative and quantitative information indicated that the client's well-being had improved during the course of therapy.

Such developments prove positive. However, a clear future agenda for pluralistic working is to continue to investigate the impact of this way of working, as well as the pathways through which practice can be most effective.

CONCLUSION

The pluralistic approach is not proposed as a "shiny new" form of therapy, but as an articulation of how many therapists—particularly, perhaps, counselling psychologists—have thought and practised for many years. The value of such an articulation, however, is that it forms a basis for more focused development and research.

This chapter has outlined how pluralistic counselling psychology is underpinned by existential and humanistic thinking. It adopts a position that is welcoming of the diversity of others and prizes their uniqueness. With this in mind, it holds that a "one size fits all" attitude towards therapeutic work proves counterintuitive and potentially misses much of the richness of human experience that therapists engage with. The pluralistic therapist believes that any activity has the potential to be therapeutic (or nontherapeutic); holds a commitment to collaborative engagement between those involved in therapy; and values the strengths, knowledge, and capabilities of the client. Further, it does not automatically assume that clients attend therapy to reduce psychological distress, and emphasizes the importance of dialogue between therapist and client to understand and direct the therapeutic work.

At the core of pluralistic work is the relationship between the therapist and the client, an alliance that provides the foundation for any work that follows. Therapeutic work is broken down into "goals," "tasks," and "methods." Goals reflect the purpose of the therapy for the client. Tasks reflect the different components that can be identified to address the goals that have been articulated. Methods are the specific way in which the therapy will unfold to address the task being worked upon. This framework can provide scaffolding for considering the amalgamation of methods from different therapeutic orientations. Despite the developing theoretical background to the pluralistic framework, there is presently only a limited empirical base for this way of working. Therefore, alongside the continuation of theoretical developments (unpacking new challenges such as engaging with difference and diversity in therapy), future developments need to focus upon understanding the outcomes of this approach, and mechanisms through which clients can change and grow.

SUGGESTED FURTHER READING

Cooper, M., & McLeod, J. (2011). *Pluralistic counselling and psychotherapy*. London: Sage.
This book provides a comprehensive introduction to the position presented in this chapter.

Cooper, M., & Dryden, W. (Eds.) (2016). *Handbook of pluralistic counselling and psychotherapy*. London: Sage.
This edited text provides a substantial development from Cooper and McLeod's initial book. It includes chapters outlining how numerous therapeutic approaches and issues might be viewed from a pluralistic standpoint.

Hanley, T., Humphrey, N., & Lennie, C. (Eds.) (2013). *Adolescent counselling psychology: Theory, research and practice*. London: Routledge.
This book introduces how a pluralistic position might be adopted for working with young people and young adults.

REFERENCES

Bergner, R. M. (2006). Many secure knowledge bases of psychotherapy. *American Journal of Psychotherapy, 60*, 215–231.

Bohart, A. C., & Tallman, K. (1999). *How clients make therapy work: The process of active self-healing*. Washington, DC: American Psychological Association.

Buber, M. (1958). *I and Thou* (R. G. Smith, Trans., 2nd ed.). Edinburgh: T & T Clark Ltd.

Cooper, M. (2008). *Essential research findings in counselling and psychotherapy: The facts are friendly*. London: Sage.

Cooper, M. (2009). Welcoming the Other: Actualising the humanistic ethic at the core of counselling psychology practice. *Counselling Psychology Review, 24*(3&4), 119–129.

Cooper, M., Dryden, W., Martin, K., & Papayianni, F. (2016). Metatherapeutic communication and shared decision-making. In M. Cooper & W. Dryden (Eds.), *Handbook of pluralistic counselling and psychotherapy* (pp. 42–54). London: Sage.

Cooper, M., & McLeod, J. (2007). A pluralistic framework for counselling and psychotherapy: Implications for research. *Counselling and Psychotherapy Research, 7*(3), 135–143.

Cooper, M., & McLeod, J. (2011). *Pluralistic counselling and psychotherapy*. London: Sage.

Cooper, M., & Norcross, J. C. (2015). A brief, multidimensional measure of clients' therapy preferences: The Cooper-Norcross Inventory of Preferences (C-NIP). *International Journal of Clinical and Health Psychology, 16*(1), 87–98. doi: 10.1016/j.ijchp.2015.08.003

Cooper, M., Wild, C., Rijn, B. v., Ward, T., McLeod, J., Cassar, S., . . . & Sreenath, S. (2015). Pluralistic therapy for depression: Acceptability, outcomes and helpful aspects in a multi-site study. *Counselling Psychology Review, 30*(1), 6–20.

Derrida, J. (1974). *Of grammatology* (G. C. Spivak, Trans.). Baltimore, MD: The John Hopkins University Press.

Hanley, T., Cutts, L., Gordon, R., & Scott, A. (2013). A research informed approach to counselling psychology. In G. Davey. (Ed.). *Applied Psychology* (pp. 1–23). London: BPS Wiley-Blackwell.

Hanley, T., Scott, A., & Winter, L. (2016). Humanistic approaches and pluralism. In M. Cooper & W. Dryden. (Eds.). *Handbook of pluralistic counselling and psychotherapy* (pp. 95–108). London: Sage

Hanley, T., Williams, G., & Sefi, A. (2013). Pluralistic counselling for young people. In T. Hanley, N. Humphrey, & C. Lennie (Eds.). *Adolescent counselling psychology: Theory, research and practice* (pp. 133–156). London: Routledge

Hanley, T., & Winter, L. (2016). Research and pluralism. In M. Cooper & W. Dryden. (Eds.). *Handbook of pluralistic counselling and psychotherapy* (pp. 337–349). London: Sage.

Husserl, E. (1913 [1962]). *Ideas: General introduction to pure phenomenology* (W. R. Boyce Gibson, Trans.). London, New York: Collier, Macmillan.

Josselson, R. (1996). *The space between us: Exploring the dimensions of human relationships.* Thousand Oaks, CA: Sage.

Levinas, E. (1969). *Totality and infinity: An essay on exteriority* (A. Lingis, Trans.). Pittsburgh, PA: Duquesne University Press.

Mansell, W., Carey, T. A., & Tai, S. J. (2012). *A transdiagnostic CBT using method of levels therapy.* London: Routledge.

McAteer, D. (2010). Philosophical pluralism: Navigating the sea of diversity in psychotherapeutic and counselling psychology practice. In M. Milton (Ed.), *Therapy and beyond: Counselling psychology contributions to therapeutic and social issues* (pp. 5–20). Chichester: Wiley-Blackwell.

McLeod, J. (2013). *An Introduction to Counselling* (5th ed.). Maidenhead: Open University Press.

McLeod, J. (2016). *Using research in counselling and psychotherapy.* London: Sage.

McLeod, J., & Cooper, M. (2011). A protocol for systematic case study research in pluralistic counselling and psychotherapy. *Counselling Psychology Review, 26*(4), 47–58.

McLeod, J., & Sundet, R. (2016). Integrative and eclectic approaches and pluralism. In M. Cooper & W. Dryden (Eds.), *Handbook of pluralistic counselling and psychotherapy.* London: Sage.

Norcross, J. C. (Ed.) (2011). *Psychotherapy relationships that work: Evidence based responsiveness* (2nd ed.). New York: Oxford University Press.

Omylinska-Thurston, J., & Cooper, M. (2014). Helpful processes in psychological therapy for patients with primary cancers: A qualitative interview study. *Counselling and Psychotherapy Research, 14*(2), 84–92.

Rennie, D. L. (1998) *Person-centred counselling: An experiential approach.* London: Sage.

Scott, A. J. (2014). How to skin a cat: A case for and against the use of mindfulness-based cognitive therapy in pluralistic therapy. *Counselling Psychology Review, 28*(1), 81–90.

Scott, A. J., & Hanley, T. (2012). On becoming a pluralistic therapist: A case study of a student's reflexive journal. *Counselling Psychology Review, 27*(4), 29.

Sparks, J., Duncan, B., & Miller, S. (2008). Common factor in psychotherapy: Common means to uncommon outcomes. In J. Lebow (Ed.), *21st century psychotherapies* (pp. 453–498). New York: John Wiley & Sons.

The Health Foundation. (2014). Person-centred care: From ideas to action. London: The Health Foundation.

Tilley, E., McLeod, J., & McLeod, J. (2015). An exploratory qualitative study of values issues associated with training and practice in pluralistic counseling. *Counselling and Psychotherapy Research, 15*(3), 180–187.

Ward, T., & Hogan, K. (2015) Using client-centered psychotherapy embedded within a pluralistic integrative approach to help a client with executive dysfunction: The case of "Judith," *Pragmatic Case Studies in Psychotherapy, 11*(1), 1–20.

Winter, L., Wilk, K., Hanley, T., & Guo, D. (2016). Difference and diversity in pluralistic therapy. In M. Cooper & W. Dryden (Eds). *Handbook of pluralistic counselling and psychotherapy* (pp. 275–287). London: Sage.

11 Psychotherapy Integration for Counselling Psychology

MICHAEL J. LAMBERT AND JOHN C. NORCROSS

CHAPTER OUTLINE

INTRODUCTION 151

VARIETIES OF INTEGRATION 152
   Technical Eclecticism 152
   Theoretical Integration 153
   Common Factors 154
   Assimilative Integration 154

ONTOLOGICAL ASSUMPTIONS: IMAGE
OF THE PERSON 155

EPISTEMOLOGIES: WAYS
OF KNOWING 155

GUIDING PRINCIPLES AND CORE
THEORETICAL ASSUMPTIONS 156

NATURE AND UNDERSTANDING
OF PSYCHOLOGICAL DISTRESS 158

THE ROLE AND PLACE OF THE THERAPEUTIC
RELATIONSHIP 159

THERAPIST, CLIENT, AND RELATIONAL
CONTRIBUTIONS TO EFFECTIVE
COUNSELLING PSYCHOLOGY 161

CONTEMPORARY ADAPTATIONS,
DEVELOPMENTS, EXTENSIONS 162

CONCLUSIONS AND FUTURE
DIRECTIONS 164

LEARNING OUTCOMES

BY THE END OF THIS CHAPTER YOU SHOULD BE ABLE TO ANSWER THE FOLLOWING KEY QUESTIONS:

1. Can you distinguish between variations of integration: technical eclecticism, assimilative integration, common factors, and theoretical integration?

2. How do the majority of integrationists view the role played by the therapeutic relationship in psychotherapy?

3. What role is psychotherapy integration likely to play in the future practice of counselling and psychotherapy practice?

INTRODUCTION

Conventional "brand name" therapies are part and parcel of the integration movement and are highly important to the integration movement. In fact, integration could not occur without the constituent elements provided by the respective therapies—their theoretical systems and clinical methods (Norcross, 2005). Single-school theories add to our therapeutic armamentarium, enrich our understanding of the clinical process, and produce the process and outcome research from which integration heavily draws. One cannot integrate what one does not know.

The vast majority of psychotherapists rarely identify solely with a single orientation. In large studies conducted in the USA (Cook, Biyanova, Elhia, Schnurr, & Coyne, 2010) and in the UK (Hollanders & McLeod, 1999), only 2 to 12% of therapists take a pure-form approach to psychotherapy. While not all of the remaining would describe themselves as integrative, many would. Indeed, *eclecticism* or the increasingly popular term *integrative* is usually the modal theoretical orientation of mental health professionals in developed countries (Norcross, 2005).

Psychotherapy integration is defined by both dissatisfaction with single-system approaches and a concomitant desire to look across school boundaries to incorporate other ways of conducting and conceptualizing therapy. The ultimate aim of doing so is more effective and efficient treatment that fits the individual client and the singular situation.

The multiple indices of integration fuel debate on whether certain brand-name therapies can be rightfully called integrative. For example, cognitive-behavioural therapy (CBT) is explicitly a hybrid of two approaches, but not all would characterize it as integrative. If one adds acceptance and mindfulness approaches to CBT, such as in dialectical behaviour therapy or acceptance and commitment therapy, then the boundary into integration seems to have been crossed.

The clinical reality is that most theories inevitably represent assimilation of previous theories. Emotion-focused couples therapy is a case in point: it proclaims itself an amalgam of experiential, systemic, person-centred, relational, and attachment theories (Greenberg & Johnson, 2010). Although integration's boundary permeability may occasionally prove confusing, it does illustrate the inevitable thrust toward sophisticated integration.

Compounding the definitional confusion is the issue of what is to be integrated. One routinely encounters references in the literature and in the classroom to integrating therapy formats/modalities (individual, couples, family, group), combining psychotherapy and pharmacotherapy (typically termed *combination treatment*), blending self-help and psychotherapy, integrating research and practice, synthesizing Western and Eastern perspectives, integrating social advocacy with psychotherapy, and so on. Two recent recommendations are to infuse multicultural theory and spirituality/religion into clinical practice. All are indeed laudable pursuits deserving of clinical consideration, but we restrict ourselves in this chapter to the traditional meaning of integration as the blending of diverse theoretical orientations.

VARIETIES OF INTEGRATION

A nagging problem in describing psychotherapy integration (or any psychotherapy system, for that matter) is that it does not represent a single monolith but multiple varieties. At least four recognizable variations or subtypes among integrative psychotherapies exist that counselling psychologists might adopt.

Technical Eclecticism

Eclecticism seeks to improve the ability to select the best treatment for the person and the problem. The search for the optimal client–treatment match is guided primarily by research on what has worked best in the past for others with similar problems and similar characteristics. Eclecticism emphasizes predicting for whom interventions will work—the foundation is actuarial rather than theoretical. The eclectic mandate is embodied in Gordon Paul's (1967) famous question: *What* treatment, by *whom*, is most effective for *this* individual with *that* specific problem and under *which* set of circumstances? But of course that dictum implies that there is just one problem rather than a set of diverse problems that need to be addressed—a situation that often prompts eclectic practice.

Proponents of technical eclecticism use procedures drawn from different sources without necessarily subscribing to the theories from which they originated. For technical eclectics, no necessary connection exists between meta-beliefs and techniques. As Arnold Lazarus described it, "To attempt a theoretical rapprochement is as futile as trying to picture the edge of the universe. But to read through the vast amount of literature on psychotherapy, *in search of techniques*, can be clinically enriching and therapeutically rewarding" (Lazarus, 1967, p. 416).

The term *eclectic* has acquired an emotionally ambivalent (if not negative) connotation for some clinicians because of its allegedly disorganized and indecisive nature. Indeed, it is surprising that so many clinicians admit to being eclectic in their work, given the negative valence the term has acquired (Garfield, 1980). But accusations of being "wishy-washy" should be properly redirected to *syncretism*—uncritical and unsystematic combinations. Such haphazard "eclecticism" is primarily an outgrowth of pet techniques and inadequate training, which by default produce an arbitrary, if not capricious, blend of methods (Eysenck, 1970). Such a muddle of idiosyncratic clinical creations might be the opposite of effective psychotherapy, which in its best form is the product of years of painstaking clinical research and experience.

Here it can be stated that both authors of this chapter favour technical eclecticism and more relational approaches (to life and therapy). In addition to our respective approaches and Lazarus' *multimodal therapy*, Larry Beutler's (Beutler & Clarkin, 1990) *systematic treatment selection* exemplifies the evidence-based selection of particular methods and techniques for particular patients and problems.

Theoretical Integration

The most popular approach to integration blends or bridges two or more psychotherapy systems in the hope that the result will be better than the component therapies alone. It goes beyond mixing and matching techniques from various theories; as the name implies, there is an emphasis on integrating the underlying *theories* of psychotherapy along with the techniques from each. It seeks a theory that is more than the sum of its parts and that leads to new directions for practice and research. Theoretical integration represents the most popular variant of integration among clinical and counselling psychologists in the United States (Lichtenberg, Goodyear, Overland, Hutman, & Norcross, 2015).

Paul Wachtel's (1977, 1987) influential efforts to bridge psychoanalytical, behavioural, and interpersonal theories illustrate this direction, as do efforts to blend cognitive and psychoanalytic therapies, notably Anthony Ryle's (1990) cognitive-analytic therapy. Grander schemes have been advanced to meld most of the major systems of psychotherapy, for example, the *transtheoretical approach* (involving the stages of change) of James Prochaska and Carlo DiClemente (1984; Prochaska & Norcross, 2013). All of these stop short, however, of a grand unifying theory of psychotherapy (Magnavita & Anchin, 2014), which may or may not eventually prove possible.

Psychotherapists combine multiple theories in creating their integrative hybrids. When 187 self-identified integrative psychologists rated their use of six major theories (behavioural, cognitive, humanistic, interpersonal, psychoanalytic, systems), the resulting 15 dyads were each selected by at least one therapist (Norcross, Karpiak, & Lister, 2005). The most common dyads endorsed in the mid-1970s was psychoanalytic-behavioural (Garfield & Kurtz, 1977); in the mid-1980s, the three most popular hybrids all involved cognitive therapy (Norcross & Prochaska, 1988); and in the early 2000s, cognitive therapy dominated the list of combinations. Cognitive therapy accounted for 42% of the hybrid combinations in the US; less so in other countries.

Common Factors

The common factors approach is at once a variety of psychotherapy integration and a scientific position predicated on the cumulative body of psychotherapy research. As a subtype of integration, it seeks to identify core ingredients shared by different therapies with the eventual goal of creating more parsimonious and efficacious treatments based on those commonalities. This search is predicated on the belief that commonalities are more important in accounting for therapy success than the unique factors that differentiate among them. The research-informed models of Jerome Frank (Frank & Frank, 1973) and Bruce Wampold (2014) exemplify the common factors route.

Literature reviews have discovered that the most consensual commonalities across theories are the development of a therapeutic alliance, opportunity for catharsis, acquisition and practice of new behaviours, and clients' positive expectancies (Grencavage & Norcross, 1990).

Marvin Goldfried (1980), a leader of the integration movement, argued,

> [to] the extent that clinicians of varying orientations are able to arrive at a common set of strategies, it is likely that what emerges will consist of robust phenomena, as they have managed to survive the distortions imposed by the therapists' varying theoretical biases.

> (p. 996)

In specifying what is common across orientations, we may also be selecting what works best among them.

Assimilative Integration

The fourth variant of integration entails a firm grounding in one system of psychotherapy, with a willingness to selectively incorporate (assimilate) practices and views from other systems (Messer, 1992). In doing so, assimilative integration combines the advantages of a single, coherent theoretical system with the flexibility of a broader range of techniques from multiple systems. A behaviour therapist, for example, might use the Gestalt two-chair dialogue in an otherwise behavioural course of treatment. In addition to Stanley Messer's (1992, 2001) original explication of it, exemplars of assimilative integration are George Stricker and Jerold Gold's (1996) assimilative psychodynamic therapy, and Louis Castonguay and associates' (2004) cognitive-behavioural assimilative therapy.

To its proponents, assimilative integration is a realistic way station to a sophisticated integration; to its detractors, it is more of a waste station of people unwilling to commit to an evidence-based integration or monotherapy. Both sides agree that assimilation is a partial step towards full integration; most therapists have been and continue to be trained in a single approach, and most gradually incorporate parts and methods of other approaches once they discover the limitations of their original approach.

The personal journeys of seasoned psychotherapists (e.g., Goldfried, 2001; Dryden & Spurling, 1989) suggest that this is how therapists actually modify their clinical practices and expand their repertoires. Therapists do not discard original ideas and practices, but rework them, add to them, and cast them in new forms. They gradually, inevitably assimilate new methods into their home theory (and life experiences) to formulate an effective treatment plan.

ONTOLOGICAL ASSUMPTIONS: IMAGE OF THE PERSON

In the context of discovery, psychotherapy integration (and an emphasis on relationship factors) relies on pluralism and pragmatism. *Pluralism* denotes a diversity of perspectives and methods rather than a single theory or technique. One size does not fit all. A cardinal presumption of integrative work is that people suffer from a multitude of problems within a unique personality situated in a particular sociohistorical context. Psychotherapy, similarly, should tailor itself to the multiverse of each individual and culture. That is why integration is so compatible with, and embraced by, many multicultural, systemic, person-centred, experiential, and humanistic therapies.

As a philosophical tradition that began in the United States, *pragmatism* eschews abstract theorizing about reality and instead emphasizes practical uses and successes. Integration's raison d'etre is improved client outcomes, not simply its intellectual appeal. That is why integration is so compatible with, and embraced by, many cognitive, behavioural, exposure, and solution-oriented therapies.

In the context of justification, any therapy requires some empirical support, so there is empiricism as well. *Empiricism* in this context refers to validating the efficacy and safety of any psychological treatment by means of scientific research. In this way, psychotherapy integration is simpatico with narrowing the pernicious practice–research gap and infusing counselling psychology with the best available research evidence.

There is no a priori view of human nature. Integration allows for and indeed encourages diverse views on whether a person is inherently evil, good, or *tabula rasa*. Whether nature, nurture, or their bidirectional interaction primarily drives mental disorders. Indeed, a narrow, either/or perspective is a core limitation of single-theory approaches that try to squeeze their clients into pre-formulated notions.

EPISTEMOLOGIES: WAYS OF KNOWING

Consistent with pluralism, integration prizes multiple ways of knowing in psychotherapy practice, research, and education. Not a single epistemology but multiple epistemologies; in the (impractical) extreme, as many as there are individual clients and therapists.

At the same time, a guiding principle of integrative psychotherapy is the therapist's experience and assessment of the patient. Clinical experience and research evidence alike enjoin the therapist to attend closely to the patient's response to the therapeutic relationship and treatment methods. Here we can speak of a primary interest in the patient's emotional and behavioural reactions to psychotherapy within the session as well as between sessions over the course of treatment.

This "way of knowing" makes it easy for many integrative clinicians to incorporate formal methods to track client treatment response. Such systematic outcomes-monitoring demonstrably improves therapy outcomes in routine care (Lambert, 2010). Client-reported mental health vital signs are monitored weekly on several scales, and predictive algorithms are applied to see if clients are responding to therapy as expected (the way most clients do), and, more importantly, if they are predicted to have a negative outcome. Client treatment response and algorithms are supplied to therapists and clients in graphic form, with alerts indicating predicted treatment failure. Such feedback facilitates discussion, problem-solving, and treatment modifications when appropriate. Thus, many integrative therapists integrate advances in clinical science, including assessment, advanced statistics, and information technology, with their subjective experience.

GUIDING PRINCIPLES AND CORE THEORETICAL ASSUMPTIONS

As psychotherapy has matured over the past century, the theoretical substrate of each system has undergone intensive reappraisal, as psychotherapists acknowledge the inadequacies of any one system and the potential value of others. Psychotherapy integration is characterized by a desire to look beyond the confines of single-school approaches to see what can be learned and how clients can benefit from other approaches. Although integration goes by different terms (eclecticism, rapprochement, assimilation, etc.), its objective is the same: to enhance the effectiveness and efficiency of psychotherapy by tailoring it to the unique needs and singular contexts of the client.

A guiding principle is not so much theoretical as it is empirical. Integrative therapists are confident that enough evidence exists about effective change processes, therapeutic relationships, and treatment methods to adapt them systematically to individual clients and that doing so improves patient success. As we shall see, this principle is rarely supported if one only tailors therapy methods to particular behavioural disorders, but it is strongly supported if one takes a broader view and systematically adapts both therapy relationships and treatment methods to the transdiagnostic features of the entire client. That is, treatment method $\times$ diagnostic condition matching is weak, but relationship and method $\times$ entire patient is strong.

The vast majority of psychotherapy outcome research suggests that few differences in efficacy have arisen between name-brand psychotherapies over the past 50 years (Lambert, 2013). We know that clients benefit from treatment more than they do from the mere passage of time and that psychotherapies are more effective than psychological and medication placebos. Still, there are very few replicated studies that show impressive differences between different bona fide therapies (including any advantage for integrative psychotherapies). Eclectic therapists have many choices when selecting add on techniques because there are so many therapies that have been shown to work, but there is little consensus on what must be integrated.

In contrast to the weak evidence for matching a particular treatment method to a particular diagnostic condition, there is compelling evidence for matching the therapy relationship and method to transdiagnostic features of the whole patient (Norcross, 2011). Consider these thumbnail research summaries of tailoring therapy to the client's reactance level, stage of change, preferences, and culture; we illustrate their respective uses later in our case study.

Research confirms what one would expect: high patient reactance or resistance is consistently associated with poorer therapy outcomes (in 82% of studies). But matching therapist directiveness to client reactance mightily improves therapy outcome. Specifically, clients presenting with high reactance benefited more from self-control methods, minimal therapist directiveness, and paradoxical interventions. By contrast, clients with low reactance benefited more from therapist directiveness and explicit guidance. This consistent finding can be expressed as a large effect size (d) of 0.76 (Beutler, Harwood, Michelson, Song, & Holman, 2011).

The amount of progress clients make in psychotherapy tends to be a direct function of their pretreatment stage of change—precontemplation, contemplation, preparation, action, and maintenance (Norcross, Krebs, & Prochaska, 2011). More importantly, research in behavioural medicine and psychotherapy converges in showing that different processes of change are differentially effective in certain stages of change. A meta-analysis (Rosen, 2000) of 47 studies examining relationships among the stages and the processes of change showed large effect sizes ($d = 0.70$ and 0.80). That is, adapting therapy to the client's stage of change significantly improves outcome across disorders (Prochaska & Norcross, 2013).

These client features provide prescriptive as well as proscriptive guidance to the therapist. In reactance, the prescriptive implication is to match the therapist's amount of directiveness to the patient's reactance, and the proscriptive implication is to avoid meeting high client reactance with high therapist direction. In stages of change, action-oriented therapies are quite effective with individuals who are in the preparation or action stages. However, these same therapies tend to be less effective or even detrimental with individuals in the precontemplation and contemplation stages.

Likewise, client preferences are frequently direct indicators of the best therapeutic method and healing relationship for that person. Decades of empirical evidence attest to the benefit of seriously considering, and at least beginning with, the relational preferences and treatment goals of the client. A meta-analysis of 35 studies compared the treatment outcomes of clients matched to their preferred treatment to outcomes of clients not matched to their preference. The findings indicated a medium positive effect ($d = 0.31$) in favour of clients matched to preferences. Clients who were matched to their preference were one-third less likely to drop out of psychotherapy—a powerful effect indeed (Swift, Callahan, & Vollmer, 2011).

As a final exemplar, a meta-analysis of 65 studies, encompassing 8,620 clients, evaluated the effectiveness of culturally adapted therapies versus traditional, nonadapted therapies. The most frequent methods of adaptation in the studies involved incorporating cultural content and values, using the client's preferred language, and matching therapists of similar ethnicity. The results revealed a positive effect ($d = 0.46$) in favour of clients receiving culturally adapted treatments (Smith, Rodriguez, & Bernal, 2011). Cultural "fit" works, not only as an ethical commitment but also as an evidence-based practice.

NATURE AND UNDERSTANDING OF PSYCHOLOGICAL DISTRESS

Most integrative theories emphasize the process of change, not the content of change. Integration is directly focused on the selection of therapy methods and relationships, rather than theoretical constructs of how people and psychopathology develop. Most integrative conceptualization makes no specific assumptions about how personality and psychopathology occur.

To the extent that there is an integrative theory of personality, it is predictably broad and inclusive. Humans are the products of a complex interplay of genetic endowment, learning history, socio-cultural context, and physical environment. By the same token, integrative conceptualizations of mental disorders are that they result from numerous, biopsychosocial influences.

A few integrative theorists have attempted to explain how ostensibly contradictory theories of psychopathology are in fact complementary. An exemplar in this regard is Wachtel's notion of *cyclical psychodynamics*, which builds a conceptual bridge between psychoanalysis and behaviourism. Conflicts that dominate a person's life can be understood as following from, as well as causing, the way he or she lives. Intrapsychic conflicts create problematic behaviour; problematic behaviour creates intrapsychic conflicts. A person's meek and self-denigrating lifestyle, for instance, may be caused by repressed rage. But a meek and self-denigrating lifestyle may also generate rage. It's a vicious, self-perpetuating cycle. The client's current way of living both stems from and simultaneously perpetuates his or her problems. Defeating this vicious cycle probably requires both insight and action strategies, both psychodynamic and behavioural methods.

To say that integrative theories do not rely on a theory of personality is not to say that they pay no heed to personality characteristics. Indeed they do. But it is not in how personality per se develops or runs pathological; it concerns the patient's personality as a key determinant in integrative therapy, as are the therapist's personality and their mutual match. Personality characteristics are not separated into a broader theory of human development and motivation. Like other patient characteristics in most integrative therapies, personality traits are incorporated to the extent that the research evidence demonstrated that identifying them contributes to effective treatment.

Assimilative integrationists with an abiding home theory will undoubtedly favour that theory's view of personality and psychopathology, but most integrative psychologists maintain that we do not need to know how a problem developed in order to solve it. Instead, when therapists encounter particular behaviour patterns or environmental characteristics, it is more important to know what treatment is likely to promote change. For example, a patient's coping style is critical to decisions regarding insight-oriented or symptom-change methods (Beutler, Harwood, Kimpara, Verdirame, & Blau, 2011). Coping style is a trait that describes an individual's response to stressful experiences.

THE ROLE AND PLACE OF THE THERAPEUTIC RELATIONSHIP

Psychotherapy is, at root, a relationship. Decades of psychological science have demonstrated that the relationship generally accounts for more of psychotherapy success (and failure) than the particular treatment method (Norcross & Lambert, 2014), and multiple meta-analyses have identified many of the relational behaviours that contribute to and predict successful psychotherapy (Norcross, 2011). In fact, *evidence-based therapy relationships* have been highlighted on the National Registry of Evidence-Based Programs and Practices (NREPP; www.nrepp.samhsa.gov/norcross.aspx). In Table 11.1 below we summarize some of the variables just discussed as well as the most frequently studied relationship variables and their correlation with measures of therapy outcomes.

- *The therapeutic alliance.* The alliance is an emergent quality of partnership between therapist and client, built principally on a positive emotional bond between therapist and client, and their ability to agree on the goals of treatment and to reach a mutual consensus on the tasks.

- *Empathic understanding.* Much of the research continues to follow Carl Rogers' (1957) definition of empathic understanding as the therapist's sensitive ability to understand the client's thoughts, feelings, and struggles from the client's point of view and accurately communicate that understanding to the client. Empathy predicted treatment outcome consistently across different theoretical orientations (e.g., cognitive-behavioural, psychodynamic, humanistic).

- *Goal consensus and collaboration.* Agreement about the nature of the problem for which the client is seeking help, goals for treatment, and the way that the two parties work together to achieve these goals are the essence of goal consensus. As with goal consensus, this result suggests that patient well-being is considerably enhanced with a better collaborative relationship.

Table 11.1 *Relationship behaviours and their association/prediction with psychotherapy outcomes.*

Author	Construct	Effect size (r)	Effect size (d)	% of variance in outcome
Horvath, Del Re, Flückiger, & Symonds, 2011	Therapeutic alliance (adult)	.28	.58	8%
Shirk and Karver, 2011	Therapeutic alliance (child/adolescent)	.19	.39	4%
Friedlander, Escudero, Heatherington, & Diamond, 2011	Therapeutic alliance (couple/family)	.26	.53	7%
Burlingame, McClendon, & Alonso, 2011	Cohesion in group therapy	.25	.51	6%
Elliott, Bohart, Watson, & Greenberg, 2011	Empathy	.30	.62	9%
Tryon & Winograd, 2011	Goal consensus and collaboration	.34	.72	12%
Farber & Doolin, 2011	Positive regard and affirmation	.27	.56	7%
Kolden, Klein, Wang, & Austin, 2011.	Congruence and genuineness	.24	.49	6%
Lambert & Shimokawa, 2011	Collecting client feedback	.25	.51	6%
Safran, Muran, & Eubanks-Carter, 2011	Repairing alliance ruptures	.24	.49	6%
Hayes, Gelso, & Hummel, 2011	Managing countertransference	−.16	.32	3%

Note: The number of studies considered in each meta-analysis ranges from 9 to 57. Effect size is reported as *d*, where 0 indicates no effect; 0.20 represents a small effect; 0.50 represents a medium effect; and 0.80 and above, a large effect (Cohen, 1988). To put the strength of relationship variables in context, in a majority of studies the percentage of outcome accounted for by specific techniques approached zero. Original meta-analyses published in Norcross (2011).

- *Affirmation/positive regard.* The degree to which therapists are rated as prizing clients can be measured and shows a moderate relationship with outcome.
- *Collecting client feedback.* In this relational behaviour, the therapist systematically monitors a client's mental health through the use of standardized scales and deviations from an expected treatment response. Clients are better off when practitioners routinely monitor

their ongoing mental health functioning and examine alarm signals and problem-solving tools. Such monitoring leads to increased opportunities to repair alliance ruptures, enhance motivation, and reduce premature termination. Systematic feedback is especially useful in helping clinicians identify the possible failure of ongoing treatment and collaborate with the client in enhancing positive outcomes.

- *Rupture repair*. Virtually all courses of psychotherapy contain ruptures between the therapist and client. Fortunately, research demonstrates effective ways to train the therapist in recognizing and repairing these problems in the relationship that naturally arise.
- *Managing countertransference*. Counsellors can and do, by virtue of their own relationship histories, have unique relationship problems that can be addressed to the benefit of treatment success.

The attentive reader will be able to observe that researchers cannot study all of these relationship behaviours simultaneously, and there is considerable overlap in these constructs. At the same time, it is demonstrably true that these relationship behaviours and attitudes are important predictors and contributors to psychotherapy success that can be learned and, in most cases, taught. While none of these relationship variables is unique to integrative approaches, they are heavily emphasized in most integrative approaches, especially the relational psychotherapies.

THERAPIST, CLIENT, AND RELATIONAL CONTRIBUTIONS TO EFFECTIVE COUNSELLING PSYCHOLOGY

Integration is the first step: the clinician opens to the full menu of evidence-based psychotherapy methods, relationships, and formats, pragmatically using what works regardless of its theoretical parentage. The second step is to adapt or tailor those interventions to particular people and problems. Specifically match to the individual case and context.

From there, the different forms or varieties of integrative practice diverge, so it is difficult to pinpoint key strategies. Nonetheless, certain principles guide virtually all integrative therapists.

Certainly they do not feel constrained to limit strategies, or to hesitate shifting strategies based on the evolving needs of clients. It would be typical to formulate and prioritize treatment goals in collaboration with the client while being sensitive to the fact that goals often change and new goals arise during the course of treatment. Early sessions are characterized by constructing a strong therapeutic alliance and by encouraging expression of feelings and experiences without the use of too many specific questions or requests for details. This will often be followed by requesting specific information from the client to identity treatment goals and to guide selection of the particular methods. Frequently, out-of-session (homework) assignments will be agreed upon and executed by the client. The flexibility to incorporate diverse styles in being maximally responsive to the client is an attractive feature to client and clinician alike.

CONTEMPORARY ADAPTATIONS, DEVELOPMENTS, EXTENSIONS

The early forms of eclecticism or integration endeavoured to select a particular treatment method for a particular mental disorder. What is the technique or theory of choice for, say, depression, eating disorder, or substance abuse? However, this pursuit has been gradually abandoned in light of the repeated finding that various forms of bona fide psychotherapy work equally well for most conditions. "All have won and everyone must have prizes," as the Dodo Bird announced in Alice in Wonderland (Luborsky, Singer, & Luborsky, 1975). The contemporary development is to match both treatment method and therapeutic relationships to the entire patient—not only diagnosis but to the *transdiagnostic characteristics* of the patient. Meta-analytic research has found six demonstrably effective transdiagnostic client features that guide such adaptations: reactance level, stages of change, preferences, culture, coping style, and religion/spirituality (Norcross, 2011). Two other client markers—expectations and attachment style—are promising in this respect. As Sir William Osler (1906), father of modern medicine, wrote: "It is much more important to know what sort of a patient has a disease than what sort of disease a patient has."

CLINICAL EXAMPLE

"Jan" was a 23-year-old woman who had recently graduated from college and requested counselling after spending months unsuccessfully looking for work despite having a near-perfect grade point average. The client can best be described as depressed, demoralized, anxious, and lost. She denied suicidal intention. She was questioning her assumptions about how the world operated, including her religious faith. In addition, she was losing her friends as they graduated from college themselves. Her financial situation was poor and worsening. She was overweight, had difficulty falling asleep, and experienced occasional thoughts of ending her life.

She had a conflicted relationship with her parents, who lived far away and could offer her little support. Her mother had been recently diagnosed with multiple sclerosis. Jan rarely dated and had been recently rejected by a man in whom she was interested. She lived in an apartment with roommates, but the relationships were poor and she wanted to move.

The client's psychiatric history did not include prior use of medications or psychotherapy. She described her mother as depressed and her father as mean, judgemental, and rigid. Her brother was abusing drugs and alcohol. As a child she had many phobias and continued to be particularly bothered by a phobia of birds (ornithophobia), which kept her from outdoor activities, including exercise.

She met diagnostic criteria for multiple disorders (depression, anxiety, relationship conflicts, phobias) was at a low in her life, and had many practical problems, and poor social supports.

As a relational integrative psychotherapist, "B" blended an assortment of therapy relationship stances and treatment methods, tailored to Jan's problems, personality, and preferences. The therapist concentrated on providing a safe environment characterized by high levels of congruent empathy and nonpossessive warmth (Rogers, 1957). The early sessions focused on emotion, felt meaning of experience, sorting out and clarifying what was happening within her, and what she needed to do to restore the meaning of life. B employed these and other emotion-focused methods (Elliott, Watson, Goldman, & Greenberg, 2004), especially the empty chair technique to help resolve Jan's ambivalence about religious beliefs as well as taking care of unfinished business with her father. Cognitive therapy methods, like decisional balance and Socratic questioning, were used in reaching important life-altering decisions. The therapist made every attempt to work through the emotions and symptoms that brought her to therapy and she became more aware of and honest with herself.

At the inception of therapy, Jan scored a 78 (T score of 66) and was at the 95th percentile of the normative population on the Outcome Questionnaire-45 (OQ-45). She was tracked at each therapy session, made steady progress, and comparisons with the progress of other clients who entered treatment at the same level of disturbance were heartening.

After several months of weekly psychotherapy and many life improvements, Jan came back to her bird phobia and its degree of life impairment. At this juncture, the therapist provided psychoeducational material on phobias and a behavioural explanation of their origins and maintenance. Jan agreed to collaborate in exposure-based treatment based on imaginary exposure. The transition to this well-known behaviour therapy appeared rather seamless, and Jan was fully cooperative with homework and in-session exposure trials, even though they were difficult.

After 17 sessions of psychotherapy, Jan's OQ-45 score was 55 (T = 56; 73rd percentile). This score placed her functioning within the functional range (cut-off of 63). She had a steady relationship, had taken leave from church activity, found a better job, and was more optimistic, although not completely satisfied that she had found an occupation. Her relationship with her parents had improved but was not healed.

This case demonstrates the fluid, continuous integration of evidence-based therapy methods hailing from diverse theoretical traditions (e.g., person-centred, emotion-focused, cognitive, behavioural) matched to the client's multiple problems within a strong therapeutic alliance. The integrative therapy initially prioritized the more painful and confusing aspects of Jan's existence (contemplation stage) and ended with more specific therapist-directed treatment of her phobia (action stage). The seamless blend of method and relationship, secular and religious, practice and science, flexibly and effectively responded to Jan's unique needs. Research-infused therapy frequently requires the use of disparate relationships and methods that prove not contradictory, but complementary.

CONCLUSIONS AND FUTURE DIRECTIONS

Integrative psychotherapies are intellectually vibrant, clinically popular, and demonstrably effective. Transtheoretical dialogue and cross-fertilization fostered by the integrative spirit have produced new ways of thinking about psychotherapy and researching behaviour change. Integration converges with the *evidence-based practice* (EBP) movement in emphasizing that different people and problems frequently require different solutions, and that these solutions increasingly can be selected on the basis of outcome research. Integrative therapies offer the research and responsiveness to meet the needs of individual patients and their unique cultures.

For these reasons, integration in its several variations will assuredly be a therapeutic mainstay of the 21st century. Indeed, a dispassionate panel of psychotherapy experts portended its escalating popularity in the coming decade (Norcross, Pfund, & Prochaska, 2013). This closing section outlines probable directions of integrative therapy in training, research, and practice.

Training in integrative work will assuredly continue in the future, but this could prove a mixed blessing. On the one hand, integrative training addresses the daily needs of clinical practice, satisfies the intellectual quest for an informed pluralism, and responds to the research evidence that different patients prosper under different treatments and relationships. On the other hand, integrative training increases the pressure for students to obtain clinical competence in multiple methods and formats and, in addition, challenges the faculty to create a coordinated training enterprise (Norcross & Halgin, 2005). Although exposure to multiple theories occurs in virtually all training programmes in psychology, social work, and counselling, ensuring student competence and mastery in multiple theories and interventions has occurred almost nowhere. It represents an unprecedented task in the history of psychotherapy. Which training path to integration will prove best for which students still needs to be determined.

What we can hope for, however, is that the overreliance on theories to guide psychological therapy will eventually give way to research evidence, a goal long sought by many integrationists over the years (e.g., Thorne, 1967; Garfield, 1980; Beutler, 1989). We immodestly predict that the chronic gap between research evidence and clinical practice will narrow. We also predict that greater consensus will emerge about what and how to integrate in psychotherapy.

SUGGESTED FURTHER READING

More extensive coverage of integration is available in the following books:

Lambert, M. J. (Ed.). (2013). *Bergin and Garfield's handbook of psychotherapy and behavior change* (6th ed.). Hoboken, NJ: Wiley.

Norcross, J. C. (Ed.). (2011). *Psychotherapy relationships that work* (2nd ed.). New York: Oxford University Press.

Norcross, J. C., & M. R. Goldfried (Eds.). (2018). *Handbook of psychotherapy integration* (3rd ed.). New York: Oxford University Press.

REFERENCES

Beutler, L. E. (1989). The misplaced role of theory in psychotherapy integration. *Journal of Integrative and Eclectic Psychotherapy, 8*, 17–22.

Beutler, L. E., & Clarkin, J. (1990). *Systematic treatment selection: Toward targeted therapeutic interventions*. New York: Brunner/Mazel.

Beutler, L. E., Harwood, T. M., Kimpara, S., Verdirame, D., & Blau, K. (2011). Coping style. In J. C. Norcross (Ed.), *Psychotherapy relationships that work* (2nd ed., pp. 336–353). New York: Oxford University Press.

Beutler, L. E., Harwood, T. M., Michelson, A., Song, X., & Holman, J. (2011). Reactance/resistance. In J. C. Norcross (Ed.), *Psychotherapy relationships that work* (2nd ed., pp. 261–278). New York: Oxford University Press.

Burlingame, G., McClendon, D. T., Alonso, J. (2011). Group cohesion. In J. C. Norcross (Ed.), *Psychotherapy relationships that work* (2nd ed., pp. 110–131). New York: Oxford University Press.

Castonguay, L. G., Schut, A. J., Aikins, D. E., Constantino, M. J., Laurenceau, J. P., Bologh, L., . . . & Burns, D. (2004). Integrative cognitive therapy for depression: A preliminary investigation. *Journal of Psychotherapy Integration, 14*, 4–20.

Cohen, J. (1988). *Statistical power analysis for the behavioral sciences* (2nd ed.). Hillsdale, NJ: Erlbaum.

Cook, J. M., Biyanova, T., Elhai, J., Schnurr, P. P., & Coyne, J. C. (2010). What do psychotherapists really do in practice? An internet study of over 2,000 practitioners. *Psychotherapy, 47*, 260–267.

Dryden, W., & Spurling, L. (1989). *On becoming a therapist*. London: Routledge.

Elliott, R., Bohart, A.C., Watson, J. C., & Greenberg, L. S. (2011). Empathy. In J. C. Norcross (Ed.), *Psychotherapy relationships that work* (2nd ed., pp. 132–152). New York: Oxford University Press.

Elliott, R., Watson, J. C., Goldman, R. N., & Greenberg, L. S. (2004). *Learning emotion-focused psychotherapy: The process-experiential approach to change*. Washington, DC: American Psychological Association.

Eysenck, H. J. (1970). A mish-mash of theories. *International Journal of Psychiatry, 9*, 140–146.

Farber, B. A., & Doolin, E. M. (2011). Positive regard. In J. C. Norcross (Ed.), *Psychotherapy relationships that work* (2nd ed., pp. 168–186). New York: Oxford University Press.

Frank, J. D., & Frank, J. B. (1973). *Persuasion and healing: A comparative study of psychotherapy*. Baltimore, MD: Johns Hopkins Press.

Friedlander, M. L., Escudero, V., Heatherington, L., & Diamond, G. M. (2011). Alliance in couple and family therapy. In J. C. Norcross (Ed.), *Psychotherapy relationships that work* (2nd ed., pp. 92–109). New York: Oxford University Press.

Garfield, S. L. (1980). *Psychotherapy: An eclectic approach*. New York: Wiley.

Garfield, S. L., & Kurtz, R. (1977). A study of eclectic views. *Journal of Clinical and Consulting Psychology, 45*, 78–83.

Goldfried, M. R. (1980). Toward the delineation of therapeutic change principles. *American Psychologist, 35*, 991–999.

Goldfried, M. R. (Ed.). (2001). *How therapists change: Personal and professional reflections*. Washington, DC: American Psychological Association.

Greenberg, L.S., & Johnson, S.S. (2010). *Emotionally focused therapy for couples*. New York: Guilford.

Grencavage, L. M., & Norcross, J. C. (1990). Where are the commonalities among the therapeutic common factors? *Professional Psychology: Research and Practice, 21*, 372–378.

Hayes, J. A., Gelso, C. J., & Hummel, A. M. (2011). Managing countertransference. In J. C. Norcross (Ed.), *Psychotherapy relationships that work* (2nd ed., pp. 239–258). New York: Oxford University Press.

Hollanders, H., & McLeod, J. (1999). Theoretical orientation and reported practice: A survey of eclecticism among counsellors in Britain. *British Journal of Guidance and Counselling, 27*, 405–414.

Horvath, A. O., Del Re, A., Flückiger, C., & Symonds, D. (2011). Alliance in individual psychotherapy. In J. C. Norcross (Ed.), *Psychotherapy relationships that work* (2nd ed., pp. 25–69). New York: Oxford University Press.

Kolden, G. G., Klein, M. H., Wang, C. C., & Austin, S. B. (2011). Congruence/genuineness. In J. C. Norcross (Ed.), *Psychotherapy relationships that work* (2nd ed., pp. 187–202). New York: Oxford University Press.

Lambert, M. J. (2010). *Prevention of treatment failure: The use of measuring, monitoring, and feedback in clinical practice*. Washington, DC: American Psychological Association.

Lambert, M. J. (2013). The efficacy and effectiveness of psychotherapy. In M. J. Lambert (Ed.) *Bergin and Garfield's Handbook of Psychotherapy and Behavior Change* (6th ed., pp. 169–218). New York: John Wiley & Sons.

Lambert, M. J., & Shimokawa, K. (2011). Collecting client feedback. In J. C. Norcross (Ed.), *Psychotherapy relationships that work* (2nd ed., pp. 203–223). New York: Oxford University Press.

Lazarus, A. A. (1967). In support of technical eclecticism. *Psychological Reports, 21*, 415–416.

Lichtenberg, J. W., Goodyear, R. K., Overland, E., Hutman, H., & Norcross, J. C. (2016). *Portrait of a speciality: Counseling psychology in the U.S. in relation to clinical psychology and to itself across three decades*. Manuscript under review.

Luborsky, L., Singer, B., & Luborsky, L. (1975). Comparative studies of psychotherapies: Is it true that "everybody has won and all must have prizes?" *Archives of General Psychiatry, 32*, 995–1008.

Magnavita, J. J., & Anchin, J. C. (2014). *Unifying psychotherapy: Principles, methods, and evidence from clinical science*. New York: Springer.

Messer, S. B. (1992). A critical examination of belief structures in integrative and eclectic psychotherapy. In J. C. Norcross & M. R. Goldfried (Eds.), *Handbook of psychotherapy integration* (pp. 130–168). New York: Basic Books.

Messer, S. B. (2001). Introduction to the special issue on assimilative integration. *Journal of Psychotherapy Integration, 11*, 1–19.

Norcross, J. C. (2005). A primer on psychotherapy integration. In J. C. Norcross & M. R. Goldfried (Eds.). *Handbook of psychotherapy integration* (2nd ed., pp. 3–23). New York: Oxford University Press.

Norcross, J. C. (Ed.). (2011). *Psychotherapy relationships that work* (2nd ed.). New York: Oxford University Press.

Norcross, J. C., & Halgin, R. P. (2005). Training in psychotherapy integration. In J. C. Norcross and M. R. Goldfried (Eds.), *Handbook of psychotherapy integration* (2nd ed., pp. 439–458). New York: Oxford University Press.

Norcross, J. C., Karpiak, C. P., & Lister, K. M. (2005). What's an integrationist? A study of self-identified integrative and (occasionally) eclectic psychologists. *Journal of Clinical Psychology, 61*, 1587–1594.

Norcross, J. C., Krebs, P. M., & Prochaska, J. O. (2011). Stages of change. In J. C. Norcross (Ed.), *Psychotherapy relationships that work* (2nd ed, pp. 279–300). New York: Oxford University Press.

Norcross, J. C., & Lambert, M. J. (2014). Relationship science and practice in psychotherapy: Closing commentary. *Psychotherapy, 51*, 398–403.

Norcross, J. C., Pfund, R. A., & Prochaska, J. O. (2013). Psychotherapy in 2022: A Delphi poll on its future. *Professional Psychology: Research and Practice, 44*, 363–370.

Norcross, J. C., & Prochaska, J. O. (1988). A study of eclectic (and integrative) views revisited. *Professional Psychology: Research and Practice, 19*, 170–174.

Osler, W. (1906). *Aequanimatas*. New York: McGraw-Hill.

Paul, G. L. (1967). Strategy of outcome research in psychotherapy. *Journal of Consulting Psychology, 31*, 109–118.

Prochaska, J. O., & DiClemente, C. C. (1984). *The transtheoretical approach: Crossing the traditional boundaries of therapy*. Homewood, IL: Dow Jones-Irwin.

Prochaska, J.O., & Norcross, J.C. (2013). *Systems of psychotherapy: A transtheoretical analysis* (8th ed.). Pacific Grove, CA: Brooks/Cole.

Rogers, C. R. (1957). The necessary and sufficient conditions of therapeutic personality change. *Journal of Consulting Psychology, 21*, 95–103.

Rosen, C. S. (2000). Is the sequencing of change processes by stage consistent across health problems? A meta-analysis. *Health Psychology, 19*, 593–604.

Ryle, A. (1990). *Cognitive-analytic therapy: Active participation in change*. Chichester: Wiley.

Safran, J. D., Muran, J. C., & Eubanks-Carter, C. (2011). Repairing alliance ruptures. In J. C. Norcross (Ed.), *Psychotherapy relationships that work* (2nd ed., pp. 224–238). New York: Oxford University Press.

Shirk, S. R., & Karver, M. (2011). Alliance in child and adolescent therapy. In J. C. Norcross (Ed.), *Psychotherapy relationships that work* (2nd ed., pp. 70–91). New York: Oxford University Press.

Smith, T. B., Rodriguez, M. D., & Bernal, G. (2011). Culture. In J. C. Norcross (Ed.), *Psychotherapy relationships that work* (2nd ed., pp. 316–335). New York: Oxford University Press.

Stricker, G., & Gold, J. (1996) An assimilative model of psychodynamically oriented integrative psychotherapy. *Clinical Psychology: Science and Practice, 3*, 47–58.

Swift, J. K., Callahan, J. L., & Vollmer, B. M. (2011). Preferences. In J. C. Norcross (Ed.), *Psychotherapy relationships that work* (2nd ed., pp. 301–315). New York: Oxford University Press.

Thorne, F. C. (1967). The structure of integrative psychology. *Journal of Clinical Psychology, 23*, 3–11.

Tryon, G. S., & Winograd, G. (2011). Goal consensus and collaboration. In J. C. Norcross (Ed.), *Psychotherapy relationships that work* (2nd ed., pp. 153–167). New York: Oxford University Press.

Wachtel, P. L. (1977). *Psychoanalysis and behavior therapy: Toward an integration*. New York: Basic Books.

Wachtel, P. L. (1987). *Action and insight*. New York: Guilford Press.

Wampold, B. E. (2014, August). *Evidence for a humanistic understanding of psychology*. Presentation at the American Psychological Association Annual Convention, Washington, DC.

PART 3 Working with Client Groups

12 Counselling Psychology for Children and Young People

TERRY HANLEY, JASMINA FRZINA, AND NAFEESA NIZAMI

CHAPTER OUTLINE

INTRODUCTION 172

BACKGROUND AND SCOPE OF WORK FOR COUNSELLING PSYCHOLOGISTS WORKING WITH CHILDREN AND YOUNG PEOPLE 172

GUIDING PRINCIPLES FOR PRACTITIONERS 174
   The Source of the Referral Needs to Be Considered Carefully 174
   The Need for Services to Be Youth Friendly and Accessible 174
   The Therapeutic Relationship Needs to Be Cautiously Navigated 175
   The Need to Be Responsive to the Person and the Presenting Issues 175

CONCEPTUALIZING DISTRESS FOR THIS GROUP 176
   Developmental Stages 176
   Social Factors 177

COMMON ISSUES 177

REVIEW OF EVIDENCE-BASED METHODS 178

LEGAL AND ETHICAL ISSUES AND RELEVANT FRAMEWORKS FOR REFERENCE 179

CONCLUSION 182

LEARNING OUTCOMES

BY THE END OF THIS CHAPTER YOU SHOULD BE ABLE TO ANSWER THE FOLLOWING KEY QUESTIONS:

1. What are the main theoretical ideas underpinning counselling psychology for children and young people?

2. In what ways does counselling psychology for children and young people differ from work with older populations?

3. What are the main issues for practice for counselling psychologists working with children and young people?

INTRODUCTION

This chapter introduces the work that counselling psychologists undertake with children and young people (CYP). It begins by providing an overview of some of the important issues that counselling psychologists encounter when working with this client group. Specifically, we address issues of terminology when describing different age groups, the prevalence of mental health issues, and the types of settings in which professionals work with CYP. Following this, a number of important guiding principles related to practice with CYP are introduced. These focus upon the different phases of therapeutic work and are considered alongside research findings based on the views of CYP. Additionally, common conceptualizations of distress (developmental and social factors) are introduced and are accompanied by a brief overview of the literature concerning the effectiveness of therapeutic work with CYP. Finally, we reflect upon specific legal and ethical issues that are essential to consider. To bring the content to life, a case example is presented to reflect upon and highlight the issues that will be discussed in this chapter.

BACKGROUND AND SCOPE OF WORK FOR COUNSELLING PSYCHOLOGISTS WORKING WITH CHILDREN AND YOUNG PEOPLE

To start it is necessary to acknowledge some of the complexity inherent in using the terms "children" and "young people." These are terms that are used in a wide variety of ways and commonly used interchangeably (whilst simultaneously conveying very different messages). For instance, we might consider whether it would seem adequate to describe a 10-year-old as a child or a young person? In attempting to answer this question, context becomes incredibly important and we would encourage people not to take on board an overly simplistic definition—with the biological, psychological, and social circumstances of each 10-year-old being likely to vary greatly. Despite this complexity, for ease of reference here, when referring to therapeutic work with those aged 10 and below we will use the term "children" and those 11–18, the term "young people." This division, although inherent in difficulties, commonly reflects the transition from primary to secondary schooling in the UK and thus becomes a useful marker. Further, although many services and public policy work with age groups up to 25, we do not consider work with this group here. These are often viewed as young adults and thus guidance related to older individuals might be more transferable to this group.

There are numerous studies that reflect the high prevalence of distress within the population of CYP in the UK. Surveys conclude that approximately 10% of 5- to 15-year-olds experience mental health problems (equating to three individuals on average in each classroom in the state school education system) (Green, McGinnity, Meltzer, Ford, & Goodman, 2005) and it is believed that 50% of all of mental ill health in adult life is thought to start before the age of 15, and 75% by the age of 18 (Murphy & Fonagy, 2012). These findings prove worrying, and economists highlight the large costs associated with supporting individuals with mental health difficulties throughout later life stages (Suhrcke, Pillas, & Selai, 2008).

Many of the debates around the purpose and processes of education question whether the process of learning should emphasize the development of a person's intellectual or social and emotional capacity (e.g., Pring, 2010). Historically, however, these two activities have commonly run side by side and been addressed in social (e.g., family and friendship groups) and educational settings. It is only within more recent decades that the distinct act of offering therapy to CYP has become increasingly prevalent. For instance, in the UK, school-based counselling is still embedding itself into typical school structures (Hanley, Noble, & Toor, 2017). School-based services vary greatly in delivery and commonly focus upon the individual's growth as a person, rather than adopting a more systemic role. Such a position contrasts with other countries where services have been statutory in nature for a long time, commonly include the delivery of systemic/group interventions, and are more aligned to the academic attainment of students (Harris, 2013).

The settings in which counselling psychology services for this age group exist are wide and varied. Historically, therapeutic interventions have typically been associated with health care and thus developed in these settings (often being referred to as child and adolescent mental health services and ranging from outpatient to inpatient care). As demand has increased for services to be more responsive to the needs and wants of young service users, alternative settings for accessing support are now commonplace. As mentioned above, school-based counselling has become a major area of development, and schools are increasingly being viewed as forums to provide support for emotional well-being (Department of Health, 2015). In addition to this, services have developed online and in community settings. The wide variety of settings in which services have been developed reflects the diversity of avenues through which CYP are seeking out support (Rickwood, Deane, & Wilson, 2007).

GUIDING PRINCIPLES FOR PRACTITIONERS

Below are a number of interrelated guiding principles that we recommend for working with CYP. These are (a) the source of the referral needs to be considered carefully, (b) the need for services to be youth friendly and accessible, (c) the therapeutic relationship needs to be cautiously navigated, and (d) the need to be responsive to the person and presenting needs.

The Source of the Referral Needs to Be Considered Carefully

"When I first went, I didn't really spill everything out. . . . I just got to know her and said 'hi' and told her a little bit about myself. Just not about problems or anything. Just saying hi and that kind of stuff" (Gibson & Cartwright, 2013, p. 344).

There are a number of differences between therapeutic work with adults and CYP clients. A major difference is that CYP are typically referred to therapeutic services by adult caregivers (parents, teachers, guardians, and other professionals). This may mean they are yet to fully consider their motivation to engage in therapy, and their commitment to change is likely to vary greatly as a consequence. There is also the potential that a referral may reflect a more systemic issue in which the young person is unhelpfully considered the source of the difficulty leading to the referral.

There are important issues to consider when a child or young person is referred from one agency to another in order to receive therapy. For example, there might be differing views about the issue to be considered or the goals of therapy. This may result in an understandable reluctance to engage in therapy. Practitioners might therefore be faced with complex dynamics in which long silences or nondescriptive responses such as "not sure" and "I don't know" have to be navigated carefully. Such dynamics emphasize the need for careful consideration of some of the issues noted below, or raise the question of whether therapy is the most helpful response at this point in time.

The Need for Services to Be Youth Friendly and Accessible

JELLYKID3:   oh yea part my life would never been discussed if was not for online work

JELLYKID3:   words you can't always say face-face to people

JOHN: that makes sense do you find you talk about different stuff online to face-to-face

JELLYKID3:   i cried online before better noone can see you

JELLYKID3:   noone needs to know your crying and don't know unless you say

(Hanley, 2012, p. 40)

There are numerous settings in which therapy is offered to CYP. The above quote refers to an online counselling setting. Such practice may prove challenging for some therapists; however, meeting younger clients in settings of their choice can help to develop a level(or more level) playing field. Further, the different contexts have implications for a number of therapeutic decisions that are made. Considerations include, but are not limited to, the therapeutic approach (person-centred, humanistic, cognitive-behavioural, integrative, etc.), the modalities of working (one-to-one, group work, or working with families), and logistical issues (e.g., how will a young client get to the centre and where do services set their limits regarding disclosure of harm). Therapists might also use more expressive approaches and have equipment such as pens and paints or toys to hand. Services can vary greatly, but are commonly encouraged to be accessible and relevantly framed for young people (e.g., Hanley, Williams, & Sefi, 2013). Such a position helps to challenge some of the stigma that can be associated with counselling psychology services (e.g., Prior, 2012) and reminds us that developing accessible services is essential.

The Therapeutic Relationship Needs to Be Cautiously Navigated

"Before I started, I pictured those movies where you see the person lying down on a leather little recliner thing and the psychologist is sitting there and they're not really paying attention to them and the person is just blabbing and blabbing" (Everall & Paulson, 2002, p. 81).

As with therapeutic work with adults, the therapeutic relationship is viewed as a vitally important factor in successful therapy with CYP (Hanley, Williams, et al., 2013). The emphasis on developing a safe, trusting, and stable relationship is commonly considered the bedrock of successful therapeutic work. Forming a positive relationship can, however, be a challenging task (e.g., Binder, Holgersen, & Nielsen, 2008) and there can be numerous pitfalls (with some being highlighted above). Consequently, although at times it can be difficult, we argue that CYP need to be at the centre of any psychological assessment and subsequent decision making related to their future therapy. This leads us directly to our next point.

The Need to Be Responsive to the Person and the Presenting Issues

"Yeah how do you say to an [adult] 'Hey by the way, I don't think that's quite right'? Yeah sometimes you should. But I've not got the courage to" (Gibson & Cartwright, 2013, p. 349).

For any therapeutic encounter to be successful, the wishes and needs expressed by the client should be taken seriously and carefully amalgamated into the work. Further, promoting the client's agency within therapeutic work is particularly important due to a number of the aforementioned potential blockages to a meaningful therapeutic encounter (e.g., encountering an unwelcoming referral point). Sensitivity to issues around power, involvement in decision making, and the desire for an equal relationship have featured highly in research on the views from young people who have accessed counselling (Everall & Paulson, 2002; Gibson & Cartwright, 2013). Counselling psychologists are therefore encouraged to pay particular attention to these issues in their work.

Counselling psychologists should be dynamic and responsive in the way that they work. Robinson (2001), when discussing education, describes the need to find the right media for helping people to realize their creative potential. In a similar way, counselling psychologists might think creatively about how they engage with CYP. For instance, where a young person's vocabulary skills may be limited, a therapist might try to communicate using an approach that does not solely focus upon language. Developing artwork or bringing technology into the therapy room might therefore prove to be more successful in engaging the individual.

CONCEPTUALIZING DISTRESS FOR THIS GROUP

There are numerous ways of conceptualizing the distress that CYP encounter in their lives. As a consequence, professionals might utilize a multitude of therapeutic approaches, with many of these being discussed elsewhere in this book (e.g., different psychological therapeutic approaches). There are, however, distinct elements associated with working with this client group to consider. These include the biological and psychological developmental stages that CYP go through, and the relatively distinct influence of social factors that they encounter.

Developmental Stages

CYP experience more rapid changes than at any other life stage. The various biological and psychological changes that occur during this period of life ultimately represent a passage from childhood to adulthood (Brown & Larson, 2002). Common milestones that are often referred to include physical developments such as puberty and sexual maturation, changes in thinking and reasoning capacities, and consolidation of individual personal identity (e.g., Coleman, 2011).

When working with this age group, the intense change and growth can be categorized into two groups: intrapersonal (e.g., information processing skills, self-reflection, abstract thinking, emotional awareness, and regulation and problem solving) and interpersonal (e.g., peer relationships, group identity, and seeking autonomy from parental control). The experience of distress may also be conceptualized as either internally focused distress (e.g., low self-worth) or externally focused distress (e.g., aggressiveness towards others). Dependent on the severity of difficulties, and at times the setting, the distress experienced may be accompanied by a formal diagnosis, defined by instruments such as the Diagnostic and Statistical Manual of Mental Disorders 5 (DSM-5) (American Psychiatric Association, 2013) and the International Classification of Diseases 10 (ICD-10) (World Health Organization, 2010). The issue of diagnosis is rooted in a medical model understanding of distress and counselling psychologists might find themselves being pressured by such thinking, but they are not to be completely guided by it (see Chapter 3, this volume). Diagnosis raises much debate within the field of counselling psychology and, in many ways, proves even more controversial with younger people.

Social Factors

Linked with the developmental stages discussed above, childhood and adolescence are periods of life where individuals' understanding of "self" constantly evolve. Due to the proximity and reliance upon others, the self-identity might be most helpfully conceptualized as forming within a network of relationships (e.g., Bronfenbrenner, 1979). Thus, theories support the notion of self-identity being relative to the adolescents' micro- (e.g., immediate and wider family, other adults, and peers) and macro-environments (e.g., society, community, and culture). The impact on the developing self-identity, and the subsequent difficulties, are more apparent when considering that young people are commonly unable to transcend their environment. Consequently, it is not surprising that the most commonly identified difficulties identified by young clients are associated with family relationships (Cooper, 2013).

Emphasis on the biological and psychological stages alone neglects the fact that each young person is part of a complex social system. For instance, it is inevitable that the physiological changes and the continuous redefining of self-identity of a young person will feed into the social relationships that they have (e.g., with friends or parents). As such, all of these elements interact with one another and thus complicate our notion of distress for this age group.

COMMON ISSUES

In a recent review of school-based counselling (Cooper, 2013) the following issues were identified as central to therapeutic work. The primary reason that young people attended therapy was to discuss family issues. Issues related to anger, talking about significant bereavements, managing behaviour, coping with bullying, addressing issues of self-worth, and those that focus upon relationships in general, followed this. It is notable that the identification of these issues came from the therapists working with young people; however, the breadth of the issues may not come as a surprise to those who work in this field. Where young people have been asked to provide goals for therapy (Rupani et al., 2013), the most common concern was to "increase self-confidence and self-acceptance." This was followed by "controlling or reducing anger," "improving relationships with family," "increasing happiness / reducing upset," and "reducing anxiety/worry." Although there is utility in both viewpoints, being aware of the emphasis the different perspectives provide can prove helpful and thought provoking.

REVIEW OF EVIDENCE-BASED METHODS

The issues related to what therapeutic approaches work for CYP echo those with adult populations. There are numerous possible approaches that can be adopted. Kazdin (2000) actively counted 551 types of interventions at the turn of the century and there have been at least 1,500 clinical trials examining therapeutic work in this area (Durlak, Wells, Cotten, & Johnson, 1995; Kazdin, 2000).

Meta-analyses of controlled trials conclude that young people who access therapy are likely to show more improvements in well-being than those who do not (Weisz, Sandler, Durlak, & Anton, 2005). Such findings, although not representative of all therapeutic approaches (there being a skew towards more cognitive and behavioural approaches), clearly indicate promise for the positive impact that therapy can have upon the well-being of CYP (see also Hanley & Noble, 2017). When looking further to include studies from real-world settings, a similar picture emerges. For example, two systematic reviews commissioned by the British Association of Counselling and Psychotherapy, which compared findings from studies examining cognitive-behavioural, psychoanalytic, humanistic, and creative therapies, concluded that all approaches appear to be effective for a broad range of issues (McLaughlin, Holliday, Clarke, & Ilie, 2013; Pattison & Harris, 2006).

So what approaches should individuals use in their counselling psychology practice with CYP? As indicated above there are a wide variety of ways of working. These can include approaches that focus upon the individual, families, or even communities (in the case of whole school social and emotional learning interventions). In accounting for the findings prevalent within the outcome study literature and the qualitative research noted in previous sections, it is recommended that counselling psychologists remain cautious in adopting fixed ways of working with CYP. Practitioners are encouraged to utilize research *informed* approaches, rather than research *directed* ones, that are responsive to the particular needs of the individuals that they meet (Hanley, Sefi, Cutts, & Pattison, 2013). To support such a process, individuals need to be mindful of walking the tightrope between scientist-practitioner and reflexive-practitioner. Furthermore, practitioners might consider using client-centred approaches that pro-actively solicit feedback from individuals to help direct the work and keep it targeted towards the needs and wants of the client. Although such approaches will not work for everyone, where they have been explored in real-world practice positive effects have been observed (Cooper, Stewart, Sparks, & Bunting, 2013).

LEGAL AND ETHICAL ISSUES AND RELEVANT FRAMEWORKS FOR REFERENCE

When working with CYP it is important to understand the legal challenges that may face counselling psychologists. The British Psychological Society's (BPS) stance on working with CYP draws upon the United Nations' *Convention on the Rights of the Child* (UNICEF, 1989) as well as *Working Together to Safeguard Children* guidance (Her Majesty's Government, 2015). The BPS state that

> all professionals, including psychologists, have a clear legal duty to consider the welfare of the child as paramount. "Safeguarding children" remains the most fundamental responsibility of all psychologists whose work impinges on the lives of children either directly or indirectly.
>
> (British Psychological Society, 2014, p. 4)

There is no single piece of legislation that covers child protection in the UK, and psychologists need to keep themselves informed about new developments. The BPS provide guidance within the document *Safeguarding and Promoting the Welfare of Children* (British Psychological Society, 2014), and further up-to-date guidance can be sought from organizations such as the Children's Legal Centre. These organizations provide overviews of key legislation and guidance documents that are helpful for applied psychologists to consider.

One of the most important concepts in UK law, in regards to working with CYP, is that of Gillick competence (*Gillick v. West Norfolk*, 1985, see Jenkins, 2007 for more information). Under Gillick, the law allows children under the age of 16 a right to consent to, and to receive, confidential treatment if they are deemed to be competent to make this decision. In the instance that an individual is viewed as competent to make the decision to enter into therapy, it is believed that without confidentiality, consent would be infringed. Such a principle therefore has implications for the need to solicit permission from another (e.g., parental consent) prior to commencing therapy, and the confidentiality agreement with the individual. Many organizations will have their own specific guidelines and policies related to working with this issue.

The legal situation in regard to children, young people, and mental health in psychiatric settings is particularly complex. There is no minimum age set for admission to hospital, and each case should be assessed on a specific individual basis (for more information, see Mitchels, 2015). The general key principles are, however: young people should be kept fully informed about their treatment, individuals should generally be regarded as capable to make their own decision regarding health care, and any intervention made should be the least restrictive possible (Jenkins, 2007).

The professional systems in place to support ethical practice when working as a counselling psychologist are those of contracting and clinical supervision (see Chapters 20 and 23 for developing personal ethics and ethical decision making, respectively). The BPS outlines, in its Professional Practice Guidelines (Division of Counselling Psychology, 2005, 2007), the importance of both of these activities. In relation to contracts, counselling psychologists need to be responsible for making contracts that are clear and explicit and to inform clients of issues of confidentiality, including those pertaining to record keeping, supervision, research, and continuing professional development, during the contracting process. Further, contracts must be subject to regular review. Thus, when considering the contracting process with CYP, it is important that terms such as *confidentiality* are explained in an age appropriate manner (and that any limits to the confidential nature of the work are appropriately outlined, i.e., safeguarding concerns).

Supervision is a requirement of ethical practice as a counselling psychologist. It is outlined by the BPS (Division of Counselling Psychology, 2005) as follows:

> Supervision support is a contractually negotiated relationship between practitioners for the purpose of supporting, evaluating and developing professional practice. There is an ethical requirement for every practitioner to have regular supervision support from a chartered counselling psychologist, or where more appropriate, from another suitably accredited or experienced supervisor. . . . The basic requirement for individual supervision is 1.5 hours per month for a minimal caseload, increasing proportionally with the case load.

(p.5)

When working with CYP there may be times when serious concerns around the individual's safety, or the safety of someone else, may be raised. In these cases it is important to remember that, although in the UK reporting child abuse is not a legal requirement at this time, professionals may have an obligation to act on concerns under the terms of their employment or professional code of ethics (Daniels & Jenkins, 2010). Thus, it is important to refer to the organizational policy of the place in which the work with CYP is taking place in order to establish what the responsibilities of individual counselling psychologists are in regards to reporting concerns. It is recommended that any concerns around the safety of a child or young person should be reported and discussed in supervision.

SAMPLE CASE EXAMPLE

Charlotte is an 11-year-old who recently moved from primary school to secondary school. Charlotte's teacher noticed that she had been finding it difficult to settle in at her new school, and that she had become increasingly withdrawn from activities and from her friendship group. When asked about how she is settling in, Charlotte told the teacher that her parents had recently separated. As a result Charlotte's teacher has recommended that she talk to the counselling psychologist (Nadim) in the school. Charlotte agreed that meeting Nadim "might be of help" but was concerned that she might be viewed by her friends as "a little bit mad." Nadim came into the school 1 day a week whilst working for an outside agency. He received the referral from Charlotte's teacher and was able to meet with her during the subsequent week. During the first meeting he explained what counselling might be like:

NADIM: *Counselling can be quite different to other relationships with adults. A lot of the time you might find that I don't talk that much and mainly I will just listen to what you are telling me. A lot of people believe that having a safe space to talk and get things off your chest can help work things out.*

CHARLOTTE: *Okay. It sounds a bit weird.*

NADIM: *[smiles] Would you be willing to give it a go and see how you find it?*

During the meetings Charlotte slowly told Nadim about the situations in which she was finding herself. Although both knew the referral from the teacher had mentioned Charlotte's parents' separation, this was not explicitly discussed in the first two sessions. Charlotte talked primarily about the difficulties she was having with her peers at school and the challenge of finding her way around a much larger school than she was used to. Although Nadim felt the separation was causing Charlotte significant distress, he decided not to explicitly raise this himself while the therapeutic relationship developed. In the fourth session Charlotte moved to talk about her parents:

CHARLOTTE: *You remember that Miss said my parents had split up?*

NADIM *Yes, I remember.*

CHARLOTTE: *Well my dad's gone all funny recently. I think he's seeing someone else and I hardly get to see him now.*

NADIM: *And, it sounds like you miss seeing him?*

CHARLOTTE: *Yes. I used to do everything with him. But now he doesn't have the time. Before he left he gave me this [gets out phone and shows Nadim a picture of necklace]. It was his mum's ...*

Charlotte and Nadim met for a further 6 weeks. The sessions primarily focused upon Charlotte's changing relationship with her father. At times this returned to the difficulties with peers; however, this became a more secondary focus of the work.

Reviewing the Therapeutic Work

The service that Nadim works for asks clients to complete the young persons' CORE outcome measure (YP-CORE) at the start and end of therapy. Additionally Nadim factored in several review periods within the sessions to check that Charlotte felt that she was finding the sessions helpful. The CORE-YP reflected that Charlotte felt things had improved during the time she met with Nadim. During the review periods Charlotte explained that she found it useful to talk through the things that were in her head. Knowing that Nadim wouldn't feedback to her parents or the teachers proved a vitally important part of the therapy for Charlotte.

Nadim found it particularly useful to make use of supervision during the meetings. As he had a young daughter of a similar age it was helpful to discuss how this relationship impacted upon the way he interacted with Charlotte. In particular, he noticed that he responded in a more parental role when Charlotte's behaviours were similar to those of his daughter. Although he felt this aided the development of the relationship, he was also mindful of not slipping too far into this more paternal role whilst working with Charlotte.

CONCLUSION

As society becomes sensitized to the potential benefits associated with therapeutic work with CYP, the work of counselling psychologists in this area is on the increase. In response, there is a growing body of research that focuses upon therapeutic work with this age group. Primarily such work demonstrates that individuals benefit from these relationships. It also, provides an important reflection into how young clients experience working with adult practitioners.

A key thread that runs throughout the literature in this area (theoretical and empirical) is the need to be responsive to the young people who are encountered. This may take place at an organizational level, with services being designed for this age group, and on an individual level with practitioners adapting their style and interventions. In considering this, although numerous therapeutic approaches are used to work with CYP, psychologists should not assume that they are automatically transferable. As is discussed above, issues such as the referral pathway and the youth friendly nature of the service can play significant roles in the development of a successful service/therapeutic relationship. Further, as childhood and adolescence are far from static periods in individuals' lives, practitioners should also familiarize themselves with the developmental literature in this area. The different life stages that CYP go through pose important challenges and, accompanying these, practitioners need to be aware of specific legal and ethical issues that they may encounter as a consequence.

SUGGESTED FURTHER READING

Hanley, T., Humphrey, N., & Lennie, C. (Eds.) (2013). *Adolescent counselling psychology: Theory, research and practice.* London: Routledge.
This is a textbook that provides an overview of the theory, research, and practice related to working with young people and young adults. It advocates a research informed pluralistic approach to therapy.

Pattison, S., Robson, M., & Benyon, A. (Eds.) (2015). *The SAGE handbook for counselling children and young people.* London: Sage.
This is a comprehensive edited text that provides an abundance of useful information and resources related to working with CYP.

The MindEd website: https://www.minded.org.uk
This is a free educational resource focusing upon CYP's mental health. It includes a specific section for counsellors wanting to work with younger clients.

REFERENCES

American Psychiatric Association. (2013). *Diagnostic and statistical manual of mental disorders: DSM-V. American Psychiatric Association* (5th ed.). Washington, DC: American Psychiatric Association.

Binder, P.-E., Holgersen, H., & Nielsen, G. H. Ø. (2008). Establishing a bond that works: A qualitative study of how psychotherapists make contact with adolescent patients. *European Journal of Psychotherapy and Counselling, 10*(1), 55–69. http://doi.org/10.1080/13642530701869730

British Psychological Society. (2014). *Safeguarding and promoting the welfare of children; position paper* (2nd ed). Leicester: BPS.

Bronfenbrenner, U. (1979). *The ecology of human development: Experiments by nature and design.* Cambridge, MA: Harvard University Press.

Brown, B., & Larson, R. W. (2002). The kaleidoscope of adolescence: Experiences of the world's youth at the beginning of the 21st Century. In B. Brown, R. Larson, & T. Saraswathi (Eds.), *The world's youth: Adolescence in eight regions of the globe* (pp. 1–20). New York: Cambridge University Press.

Coleman, J. C. (2011). *The nature of adolescence* (4th ed). London: Routledge.

Cooper, M. (2013). *School-based counselling in UK secondary schools: A review and critical evaluation.* Glasgow: University of Strathclyde.

Cooper, M., Stewart, D., Sparks, J., & Bunting, L. (2013). School-based counseling using systematic feedback: A cohort study evaluating outcomes and predictors of change. *Psychotherapy Research : Journal of the Society for Psychotherapy Research, 23*(4), 474–488. http://doi.org/10.1080/10503307.2012.735777

Daniels, D., & Jenkins, P. (2010). *Therapy with children: Children's rights, confidentiality and the law* (2nd ed.). London: Sage.

Department of Health. (2015). *Future in mind: Promoting, protecting and improving our children and young people's mental health and wellbeing.* London: NHS England.

Division of Counselling Psychology. (2005). *Professional practice guidelines, Leicester: BPS.* Leicester: British Psychological Society.

Division of Counselling Psychology. (2007). *Guidelines for supervision.* Leicester: British Psychological Society.

Durlak, J. A., Wells, A. M., Cotten, J. K., & Johnson, S. (1995). Analysis of selected methodological issues in child psychotherapy research. *Journal of Clinical Child Psychology, 24*(2), 141–148. http://doi.org/10.1207/s15374424jccp2402_2

Everall, R. D., & Paulson, B. L. (2002). The therapeutic alliance: Adolescent perspectives. *Counselling and Psychotherapy Research, 2*(2), 78–87. http://doi.org/10.1080/14733140212331384857

Gibson, K., & Cartwright, C. (2013). Agency in young clients' narratives of counseling: "It's whatever you want to make of it". *Journal of Counseling Psychology, 60*(3), 340–352. http://doi.org/10.1037/a0033110

Green, H., McGinnity, A., Meltzer, H., Ford, T., & Goodman, R. (2005). *Mental health of children and young people in Great Britain 2004.* London: Palgrave.

Hanley, T. (2012). Understanding the online therapeutic alliance through the eyes of adolescent service users. *Counselling and Psychotherapy Research, 12*(1), 35–43. http://doi.org/10.1080/14733145.2011.560273

Hanley, T., & Noble, J. (2017). Therapy outcomes: Is child and adolescent counselling and therapy effective? In N. Midgley, M. Cooper, & J. Hayes (Eds.), *Essential research findings in child and adolescent counselling and psychotherapy: The facts are friendly* (pp.59–68). London: Sage.

Hanley, T., Noble, J., & Toor, N. (2017). Policy, policy research on school-based counseling in the United Kingdom. In J. Carey, B. Harris, S. M. Lee, & J. Mushaandja (Eds.), *International handbook for policy research in school-based counseling.* Cham, Switzerland: Springer.

Hanley, T., Sefi, A., Cutts, L., & Pattison, S. (2013). Research into youth counselling: A rationale for research-informed pluralistic practice. In T. Hanley, N. Humphrey, & C. Lennie (Eds.), *Adolescent counselling psychology* (pp. 88–108). London: Routledge.

Hanley, T., Williams, G., & Sefi, A. (2013). Pluralistic counselling for young people. In T. Hanley, N. Humphrey, & C. Lennie (Eds.), *Adolescent Counselling Psychology* (pp. 133–156). London: Routledge.

Harris, B. (2013). *International school-based counselling*. Lutterworth: BACP.

Her Majesty's Government. (2015). *Working together to safeguard children: a guide to interagency working to safeguard and promote the welfare of children*. London: Department for Education.

Jenkins, P. (2007). *Counselling, psychotherapy and the law* (2nd ed.). London: Sage.

Kazdin, A. (2000). *Psychotherapy for children and adolescents: Directions for research and practice*. Oxford: Oxford University Press.

McLaughlin, C., Holliday, C., Clarke, B., & Ilie, S. (2013). *Research on counselling and psychotherapy with children and young people: A systematic scoping review of the evidence for its effectiveness from 2003–2011*. Lutterworth: BACP.

Mitchels, B. (2015). *Legal issues and resources for counselling children and young people in England, Northern Ireland and Wales in school contexts*. Lutterworth: BACP.

Murphy, M., & Fonagy, P. (2012). Mental health problems in children and young people. *In Annual Report of the Chief Medical Officer 2012*. London: Department of Health.

Pattison, S., & Harris, B. (2006). Counselling children and young people: A review of the evidence for its effectiveness. *Counselling and Psychotherapy Research, 6*(4), 233–237. http://doi.org/10.1080/14733140601022659

Pring, R. (2010). The philosophy of education and educational practice. In R. Bailey, R. Barrow, D. Carr, & C. McCarthy (Eds.), *The SAGE handbook of philosophy of education* (pp. 55–66). London: Sage.

Prior, S. (2012). Overcoming stigma: How young people position themselves as counselling service users. *Sociology of Health and Illness, 34*(5), 697–713. http://doi.org/10.1111/j.1467-9566.2011.01430.x

Rickwood, D. J., Deane, F. P., & Wilson, C. J. (2007). *When and how do young people seek professional help for mental health problems? The Medical Journal of Australia, 187*(7), 35–39. http://doi.org/ric10279_fm [pii]

Robinson, K. (2001). *Out of our minds*. Chichester: Capstone.

Rupani, P., Cooper, M., McArthur, K., Pybis, J., Cromarty, K., Hill, A., . . . Turner, N. (2013). The goals of young people in school-based counselling and their achievement of these goals. *Counselling and Psychotherapy Research, 14*(4), 306–314. http://doi.org/10.1080/14733145.2013.816758

Suhrcke, M., Pillas, D., & Selai, C. (2008). *Economic aspects of mental health in children and adolescents. Social cohesion for mental wellbeing among adolescents*. Copenhagen: WHO Regional Office for Europe.

UNICEF (The United Nations Children's Fund) (1989). *Convention on the Rights of the Child*. London: Office of the United Nations High Commissioner for Human Rights.

Weisz, J. R., Sandler, I. N., Durlak, J. A, & Anton, B. S. (2005). Promoting and protecting youth mental health through evidence-based prevention and treatment. *The American Psychologist, 60*(6), 628–648. http://doi.org/10.1037/0003-066X.60.6.628

World Health Organization. (2010). *International classification of diseases* (10th Ed.). Geneva: WHO.

13 Counselling Psychologists Working with People with Special Needs and Disabilities

ANNE EMERSON

CHAPTER OUTLINE

INTRODUCTION 186

MODELS OF DISABILITY 187

GUIDING PRINCIPLES FOR
PRACTITIONERS 187
  Attitudes Towards, and Perceptions of, People
  with Special Needs and Disabilities 187
  Power of Attitudes and Expectations 190

CONCEPTUALIZING DISTRESS 191
  Risks to Emotional Well-being 191
  The Effects of Special Needs on Well-being 192

Lack of Opportunities 193
Risk of Abuse and Violence 193

COUNSELLING PSYCHOLOGY APPROACHES
FOR SND 194

CONCLUSION 196

Counselling Psychology: A Textbook for Study and Practice, First Edition. Edited by David Murphy.
© 2017 John Wiley & Sons Ltd. Published 2017 by John Wiley & Sons Ltd.

LEARNING OUTCOMES

BY THE END OF THIS CHAPTER YOU SHOULD BE ABLE TO ANSWER THE FOLLOWING KEY QUESTIONS:

1. What are the particular risks to emotional well-being experienced by people with special needs and disabilities?

2. In what ways do our perceptions of people with special needs and disabilities impact on our relationships with them?

3. In what ways can people be supported when they are not effectively verbal?

INTRODUCTION

People with disabilities are as, if not more, prone to mental health difficulties as the rest of the population (Buckles, Luckasson, & Keefe, 2013). Their needs might stem specifically from their impairment, or more probably, from society's reaction to it. People can acquire disability through illness or physical injury; the acquisition of disability can lead to depression, anxiety, and a need for support through a period of grief and adjustment to altered roles and relationships (Dorstyn, Mathias, & Denson, 2011). Disability can also be congenital and across the world societies do not see the birth of a child with disabilities positively; in the UK expectant parents are offered screening for conditions such as Down's syndrome and spina bifida. When a child is born with an evident disability this tends to be treated as a tragic event, affecting the usual birth celebrations and the child's welcome to the world (Mason, 2008). The ongoing well-being of people with disabilities, as with other marginalized groups, can be affected by the attitudes of health professionals, educationalists, and society in general (Morin, Rivard, Crocker, Boursier, & Caron, 2013). In this chapter the additional risks to mental health and well-being that accrue from special needs and disabilities (SND) for the individual and their family will be considered, and the role that counselling psychologists can have in the lives of people with SND will be explored.

This chapter, therefore, aims to inform those with an interest in counselling psychology about some of the specific needs of people with disabilities and their families. There is relatively little focus in counselling psychology journals on the needs of people with SND. Foley-Nicpon and Lee (2012) see this as "at worst an exclusionary atmosphere toward people with disabilities and at best limited awareness about empirically based practices for assessment and intervention" (p. 393). Kelsey and Smart (2012) similarly state "by not acknowledging the social injustices faced by many people with disabilities, rehabilitation counselors and general counselors may fail to provide the services that could benefit people with disabilities the most" (p. 230). As with any other area of counselling psychology clients with disabilities are people first and therefore heterogeneous; however, there are a set of considerations that may apply to someone with a disability, which are less likely to apply to the general population. In this chapter the reasons for some of these differences are outlined and suggestions made about ways in which counselling psychologists may adapt their practice to accommodate the additional needs of some clients. For example people who are described as having "learning disabilities" or "intellectual impairment" may need specific adaptations to overcome their difficulties with understanding and communication. Many counselling psychologists may hesitate about accepting a client with learning disabilities, particularly because they fear that they will not have sufficient skill to support them (Kelsey & Smart, 2012). However, the needs of this group of people are at least as great, if not greater, than others, and people with learning disabilities can benefit greatly from counselling psychology.

MODELS OF DISABILITY

The predominant way of viewing people with disabilities in the past was grounded in the medical model, which saw the person as having an impairment, which needed to be cured or to which they needed to adjust (Shakespeare, 2006). Kelsey and Smart (2012, p. 234) suggest that "counseling undertaken with the assumptions of the medical model are considered socially unjust." Disabled people led the move to a new construction of disabilities, the social model, which suggests that it is not the actual impairments that someone has that disables them but society's lack of adaption. An integrated model has more recently been suggested (Shakespeare, 2006) that combines an understanding of the impact of impairment with an additional focus on societal adaptation.

GUIDING PRINCIPLES FOR PRACTITIONERS

Attitudes Towards, and Perceptions of, People with SND

People who have visible disabilities often provoke a range of reactions from the general public. Action by disabled people against their portrayal as the "poor unfortunate" or "victim" has impacted on fundraisers, who now tend to focus on strengths and overcoming adversity. Media coverage of the Paralympics in 2012 and the BBC programme *The Last Leg* have helped to make disability something that could be talked and even laughed about. Many common myths about disabled people, such as that they were to be pitied, were challenged through a model of capacity and empowerment.

People who have hidden disabilities have a different set of challenges: they can be met by a lack of recognition or disbelief that they actually require any accommodation. Since many people with disabilities are strong and powerful, and can advocate for themselves, this section will consider those who tend to be the least understood and the most disadvantaged.

The definition of people with a learning disability (intellectual impairment) is those who fall below a certain score on an IQ test. These tests were originally devised by Binet in 1904 (Boake, 2002) to uncover a person's profile of scores across a range of areas of development, looking for areas of strength as well as weakness. However, throughout their history IQ tests have tended to be used to apply blanket categories that determined where someone would go to school and what expectations could be held of them. IQ was originally conceptualized as movable, but has come to be seen as a fixed state. The developmental model underpins all special education, that is, children with learning difficulties will proceed through the same steps as all children although at a different pace. From this comes the notion of "arrested" development where someone can have a different "mental age" from their chronological one (e.g., see Klintwall, Eldevik, & Eikeseth, 2015). Piaget's theory of cognitive development proceeding through a series of stages contributes to this view, whereas Vygotsky's Zone of Proximal Development suggests a different view of someone with learning difficulty by suggesting that developmental level is not an absolute and can be affected by support and education.

As an alternative to the developmental model (Carnaby, 2007), which can, at its worst, lead to people attempting the same tasks over many years as they are unable to reach the threshold for progress, is neuroconstructivism (Thelen & Smith, 1994). The neuroconstructivist model suggests that genes, brain, cognition, and environment interact multidirectionally and that processing deficits may affect several domains but to differing degrees and at different developmental times. The brain is seen as self-structuring, dynamic, changing over time, and influenced by multiple interactions at multiple levels. It is by considering the interaction of these multiple systems that disabilities can be best understood, "not so much how the whole can be understood as a function of the pieces, but how the pieces can come together to produce the whole" (Thelen & Smith, 1994, p. xviii). Neuroplasticity (Cramer, Sur, Dobkin, O'Brien, Sanger, et al., 2011) is a term that refers to the way in which the brain is able to reorganize itself, throughout the life span, by forming new neural connections. Neuroplasticity allows the brain to respond to new situations and environments as well as to compensate for injury and disease (Cramer et al., 2011; Iuculano et al., 2015).

What is important about neuroconstructivist theory is the understanding that having a disability that is present from birth, or in the early years, can affect all learning in all domains. However, it will not be possible to ascertain anyone's capacity without detailed and ongoing assessment on multiple levels considering all aspects of functioning. The "least dangerous assumption" (Donnellan, 1984) is to presume competence and understanding in the person with disabilities, unless it is clear that someone needs help and support and, importantly, to recognize that the ability to learn can change over time. Another important aspect of this theory is that once someone has a difficulty in one sphere it will impact on most others, and people are unlikely to present in typical ways. Counselling psychologists need to suspend judgement about outside appearances, which are governed by motor skills, coordination, and muscle tone as well as emotion. Instead, when counselling psychologists consider therapeutic work they need to hold a holistic view of people's functioning, capacities, and potentials.

Counselling psychologists may also be interested in Gardner's (2011) work on Multiple Intelligences, which despite lacking a well-developed evidence base, has become popular across the globe. The theory of Multiple Intelligences encourages people to be viewed as having strengths in a range of areas as well as weaknesses. There is also a focus on considering emotional intelligence (Goleman, 1997), which recognizes that someone can develop differently in different spheres of life. This would suggest that even if someone is not literate beyond a basic level they can still have an emotional maturity that is comparable with their adult peers. This links, too, to the concept of "twice exceptionality," where someone can have learning disabilities as well as particular gifts (Assouline, Nicpon, & Huber, 2006). It is not, therefore, appropriate for a counselling psychologist to treat an adult with learning disabilities like a child, particularly when it comes to their emotions, or to refer to them as having a "mental age" that is less than their chronological age as if this negates their awareness and sensitivities. There was until relatively recently a perception that people with a measured IQ that put them in the severe intellectual impairment category were not aware that they had a disability. It was considered desirable to protect them and keep them happy, rather than to have any expectations of involvement in society. This thinking went along with the move to place people with disabilities in long-stay hospitals outside communities. It was seen as being for "their own good," but Mason (2000) argues that it was more about protecting the rest of society from the reality of disability.

One of the main problems with how people with learning disabilities have traditionally been viewed is that they have been seen as lacking insight into their difficulties and therefore beyond help or even beyond the need of emotional support. In the notes accompanying a video about autism (*A is for Autism*, 1992) which was created by people with autism to explain how they view the world, Jordan (1992) suggests that although what people have to say about autism is interesting it cannot be taken as serious insight because of their difficulty with introspection. This attitude has changed greatly in recent years, many people with autism have written about the condition from inside and their insights have led to many changes. The Diagnostic and Statistical Manual of Mental Disorders 5 (DSM-5) (American Psychiatric Association, 2013) has included sensory differences as a feature of autism for the first time in recognition of many self-reports. Counselling psychologists can learn from researchers who have recognized that people with learning disabilities are able to express emotions, concerns, and anxieties (van Nijnatten & Heestermans, 2012). Most importantly though counselling psychologists need to listen to their clients and aim to understand them and their experiences. An issue of particular relevance to counselling psychologists is the way that people with some disabilities present themselves and how this is perceived and interpreted. Differences in ways of moving, body structure, and difficulties with movement control lead to many people with disabilities having altered behaviour and appearance. Some people have low muscle tone, which leads to lack of accuracy in movement and increased tiredness, and can also contribute to having a lack of facial expression. Alongside this people can quickly move from no animation to what can look like a high level of arousal. Until a counselling psychologist is familiar with the person and their movements it is important not to make assumptions based on the counselling psychologist's internal frame of reference as to what is "normal" bodily movement, facial expressing, and behaviour (see Vignette on Pablo).

In some people with learning disabilities what would be read as lack of interest in someone with typical development may not signal this at all. We tend to rely on eye contact to know that the person we are talking to is aware of us and interested; however, some people with autism particularly say that they can only listen if they are not looking (Williams, 2002). In summary counselling psychologists should not assume the meaning of any nonverbal behaviour and should check their perceptions and interpretations before coming to any firm conclusions as to how their client is feeling.

Power of Attitudes and Expectations

It has long been thought that the expectation a teacher has for their pupils has an impact on the child's ultimate achievement (Rist, 2000). People with all disabilities and learning disabilities in particular, are at risk from the expectations of those around them. Parents can limit their children through overprotection and reducing risk taking, or reassure them that they do not need to achieve academically in order to help them to feel less pressure. In their study of physically disabled high achievers, Shah, Travers, and Arnold (2004) identified that people with disabilities need a mix of challenge and support in order to succeed.

It is important, therefore, that counselling psychologists develop a set of beneficial attitudes to support and empower their clients. First, is to trust in the belief that the client would like to be in relationship with you if you can provide the optimum conditions. These conditions include going at the client's pace, even if this might seem very slow, and being open to the potential of leaving long silences (van Nijnatten & Heestermans, 2012). Not expecting direct eye contact, and thinking out loud to check hypotheses; for example, suggesting an explanation for a particular response or behaviour that is framed as a query ("I wonder if you were thinking . . ." or "I noticed that you looked quite sad when I said . . .") rather than direct questions, but to which there may be a nonverbal response. These are what person-centred experiential therapists do a lot of, and it is suggested that all therapists need to develop these empathic and accepting attitudes. This approach goes along with a view that the client is always doing their best, and if the counselling is not going well adjustments need to be made by the counselling psychologist. Overall the counselling psychologist needs to believe that their client can and will benefit from their help if supported in the right way and the right relational environmental conditions can be created.

A particular challenge to counselling psychologists are clients who have minimal or no speech. The work of Rosemary Crossley (1999) emphasizes that just because someone cannot speak does not mean that they have nothing to say. People who are nonverbal will be prone to all emotional difficulties and may have higher rates of frustration and anxiety than many other clients. When working with someone with minimal verbal skills the counselling psychologist will need to increase their reliance on visual supports. In fact using a range of visual aids can enhance the understanding and expression of all clients with learning disabilities (see the box on "Specific Approaches" below).

Another important point that counselling psychologists need to consider is that anxiety may be high in many people with disabilities. Since their experience tells them that they are likely to find many situations throughout their day challenging, they can live in a permanent state of heightened alert. This can be particularly the case for people with autism, who experience pain and discomfort from sensory input, and for people with Down's syndrome, who often struggle to understand what is expected of them.

CONCEPTUALIZING DISTRESS

Risks to Emotional Well-being

It is not inevitable that someone with a special need or disability will have less mental well-being than nondisabled people. However, and principally due to societal influences, many people struggle to fit in to the fast-paced and competitive contemporary world. In fact Mason (2000) reminds us that one of the gifts that people with disabilities bring is the reminder to slow down. The move to inclusive education is generally welcomed by disabled people (ALLFIE, n.d.) as the main way to bring about an inclusive society. However, this can come at a cost for many young people and their families. Despite the right to attend a mainstream school being enshrined in UK law, and included in the United Nations Convention on the Rights of the Child, many families find that this is still something that they have to fight for, and even when a place is won there is no guarantee that their child will be welcomed and supported in the best way. There is still a stigma in many schools, particularly at secondary level, about any form of difference, which leads, for example, to children refusing to wear the hearing aids that they need to benefit from the lesson. Children are generally aware of how they are achieving in relation to their peers and may be under increased stress due to difficulties with keeping up with class work, worrying about being asked to read in class, feeling anxious about trying to speak in front of others, or attracting unwelcome attention. The demands of school social life are even greater, particularly as children get older. Many children do not want to be seen being friends with someone with a disability and children with special needs frequently experience isolation. In many schools those with special needs will retreat to the safety of their special unit to avoid the potential embarrassment and humiliation of the school playground. These occurrences are evidently not only experienced by those with special needs but their risk tends to be much higher, and as with other marginalized groups the impact can be life-long. Counselling psychologists working in schools or other settings with young people will be wise to be attuned to these potential risks to well-being.

Adults with special needs are at high risk of isolation (Contact a Family, 2011), unemployment, poverty, and hate crime (DWP, 2013). Many people with Down's syndrome avoid being in public at times when children are going to and from school because of the name calling and taunting they experience. This has a knock-on effect on their chances of employment. Being aware of the kinds of risks that people with Down's syndrome face is an important aspect of a counselling psychologist's responsibilities in being prepared to engage in the work with this client group.

The Effects of Special Needs on Well-being

Understanding the impact of special needs and disability on clients and their families is helpful for counselling psychologists. Being open to and receptive to the range of difficulties and challenges that are faced is evidence of a counselling psychologist's commitment to their client and the possible sources of their distress. It can be very difficult for a child with special needs to grow up valuing themselves and with high self-worth. The threat to this starts from birth with the before-mentioned lack of welcome by society and even family members, which can affect parental attachment (Janssen, Schuengel, & Stolk, 2002; Mason, 2000).

Mothers tend to socialize less when they have a child with special needs to avoid questions and comments, and many children with significant disabilities attend special school from the age of 2, which may require a long journey and breaks contacts with the local community (Mason, 2000). Once children are at school they may begin to compare themselves less favourably with their peers, and a common response is to avoid anything that they know they will find difficult. This can apply to academic, sporting, or social aspects of school life. For some children this desire to stay in their comfort zone can develop into learned helplessness (Peterson, Maier, & Seligman, 1993), when they will no longer try to accomplish anything. This can have a lasting impact, even when the problem that caused the initial difficulties has disappeared; for example, in the case of a hearing impairment from glue ear, or early literacy difficulties. In other children the manifestation of a fear of not succeeding can be frustration, anger, disruptive behaviours as a form of avoidance, and even challenging behaviour. These set up a cycle of the young person having low self-confidence and a view of themselves as a failure, which reduces their resilience and thwarts self-determination. This, in turn, can lead to developing behaviours that lead others to have poor perception and prognosis for the student. Statistics released by the English Department for Education (2015) indicate that 70% of permanent exclusions from schools in the UK are children who have recognized special needs, and they are also at higher risk of fixed term exclusions than other children.

Many of these issues are particularly evident in young people who have speech, language, and communication problems. Recent research has indicated that in some urban areas of the UK 50% of children in primary classes have communication skills that are inappropriate for their age (Locke, Ginsborg, & Peers, 2002), but school staff significantly under-identify these children (Gascoigne, 2014). Since these children are receiving no support they struggle with all school work and hence start the downwards spiral towards helplessness or recklessness. This then makes sense of the statistic that 60–90% of people in young offenders' institutions and prisons are found to have communication impairments (Bryan, Freer, & Furlong, 2007).The difficulties faced by young people with special needs, some of which are outlined above, are frequently compounded by the lack of understanding they encounter from those around them. Adults including parents, teachers, psychologists, and medical experts, as well as peers, can all, mostly inadvertently, contribute to a young person's lack of self-esteem and their reduced sense of agency and autonomy. Research indicates that from 40–100% of children with disabilities have been the victims of bullying (NSPCC, 2014), which can lead to school refusal and truanting and leave life-long emotional scars. Being given a label or diagnosis can benefit a young person by helping them to understand themselves and gain access to helpful resources. However, labels can also have negative impacts such as a lack of expectations and aspirations, and a focus on education or intervention delivered to address the label rather than discovering what is right for the individual.

Conversely, unrecognized difficulties can lead to an inaccurate interpretation of the actions and difficulties of the young person. People, even those with significant disabilities, can be referred to as "lazy" or "not trying" because of a lack of adult understanding. This, in turn, can become a self-fulfilling prophecy; that is, people who are seen negatively by others will come to see themselves negatively and thus behave in ways consistent with this self-image.

Lack of Opportunities

As already outlined a lack of expectations of the abilities of people with SND can lead to a lack of opportunity to show what they are capable of. People with SND often have a reduced ability to advocate for themselves and therefore a greater reliance on others to create opportunities for them along with the right support to facilitate success. Many parents, and sectors of society, can have "paternalistic" attitudes of protection and/or overassistance. Even where people are initially required to do something for themselves their slower operating speed can lead to others stepping in to "help" them. In our generally quite risk-averse society people with SND are more prone to be held back to avoid hurting themselves, being disappointed, or being taken advantage of or abused by others.

Risk of Abuse and Violence

There are many indications that people with SND, and most particularly those with behaviour/conduct disorders, severe intellectual impairment, and communication impairments, are vulnerable to violence, abuse, and exploitation. A review of the records of over 50,000 children in a US city indicated that children with disabilities were 3.4 times more likely to be abused or neglected than nondisabled children (Sullivan & Knutson, 2000) equating to the abuse of 31% of disabled children as opposed to 9% of the nondisabled child population. Their findings also indicated that children with disabilities were more likely to be abused more often and for longer. The United Nations Children's Fund (UNICEF) (2013) state that children with disabilities in high-income countries across the world are 3 to 4 times more likely to be victims of violence than their non-disabled peers. "Children with mental or intellectual disabilities were found to be 4.6 times more likely to be victims of sexual violence than peers without disabilities" (UNICEF, 2013, p. 12). It is believed that children with disabilities are at higher risk of violence from caregivers due to their high care needs or because they are placed in residential care and because they may not have the verbal ability to report the abuse (NSPCC, 2014). There are also myths about sexual abuse of children with disabilities that can hinder protection, such as refusing to believe that it happens, believing that it is less harmful than in a typical child, or thinking that children with disabilities are more likely to lie (NSPCC, 2014). Abuse can last into adulthood: a report by Mencap (2001) suggested reasons that adults with learning disabilities are vulnerable to abuse include low self-esteem and therefore lack of power, lack of social awareness, a difficulty challenging others, not recognizing that abuse has taken place, or being afraid to report it.

COUNSELLING PSYCHOLOGY APPROACHES FOR SND

It is likely that clients with SND will benefit from a range of different therapeutic approaches depending on the nature of their difficulty. The integrative approaches that tailor the therapy to each individual client are likely to be effective. There is some consensus that counselling psychologists need to view their work with people with SND through the lens of social justice in order to appreciate the sorts of stresses that people experience in their everyday lives and avoid inappropriate treatments (Kelsey & Smart, 2012). People with SND are often oppressed by those with greater advantage in life and this disadvantage can cause distress, "[A] social justice perspective recognizes that unequal power, unearned privilege and oppression can be the cause of psychological stress and disorder; thereby, acknowledging that an individual's presenting problem may originate from factors outside of the individual (Alston, Harley, & Middleton, 2006)" (Kelsey & Smart, 2012, p. 233). Counselling psychologists need to establish those aspects of difficulties experienced by an individual that stem from intrapsychic difficulties and those stemming from lack of social justice; it is also important to consider the intersection of these potential sources of distress in order to progress the counselling.

Foley-Nicpon and Lee (2012) suggested that little is known about specific effective models for counselling children and adults with disabilities and suggested counsellors need to apply models developed for typical adults (such as person-centred play therapy and cognitive-behavioural therapy (CBT). It is, however, evident that there needs to be a focus on the relationship between counselling psychologist and client as there is in all therapy (Jones, 2013). There is recognition that a focus on strengths in order to build resilience rather than examining what someone cannot do, is more likely to "lead to empowerment and change in a counseling relationship" (Foley-Nicpon & Lee, 2012, p. 396). Smyth (2013) advocates pre-therapy (Prouty, 1990) and focusing (Gendlin, 1978)—both approaches fall in the person-centred experiential counselling psychology, for working with people with severe intellectual impairment as an effective way of building a therapeutic relationship. A case study used a form of child-centred play therapy with the rationale that although the two adults involved were in their 20s their developmental stage was like a child (Demanchick, Cochran, & Cochran, 2003). As discussed above, the assumption that an adult showing an interest in toys may be emotionally like a child could be a dangerous one to make. However, there may be elements of play therapy that could be utilized appropriately with adults. The participants' enhanced mood and reductions in self-injury were attributed to the person-centred approach adopted by the play therapist. Bereavement counselling was found to be effective in a study of adults with intellectual impairment (Dowling, Hubert, White, & Hollins, 2006).

SPECIFIC APPROACHES

Behaviourist approaches for problems that seem to have been learnt and might respond well to positive reinforcements, for example selective mutism.

Person-centred experiential counselling psychology for developing a deeper understanding of the nature of a client's difficulties as they are experienced by the client themselves.

Cognitive-behavioural counselling psychology for help with specific problems such as anxiety or phobia.

- How can counselling psychologists support someone when they are not effectively verbal?
  - *Visual supports.* Visual aids may be pictures depicting actions or emotions, they might be symbols that the person is used to using for emotional expression (Makaton). Some clients may benefit from a written approach, perhaps including comic strip stories (Gray, 1994) to remind them of an expected response or way of coping.
  - *Play.* As with young children, some people with learning disabilities may benefit from play based approaches, although these should be adapted to their chronological age.
  - *Engagement.* The intensive interaction approach builds relationships with children and adults with severe disabilities by joining them in their activities and behaviours (Nind, 1996).
- What alternatives are there that counselling psychologists can employ to allow people to express themselves?
  - art
  - movement
  - play.

Legal and ethical issues and relevant frameworks for reference:

The Human Rights Act 1998
Carers and Disabled Children Act 2000
The Mental Capacity Act 2005

United Nations (UN) Convention on the Rights of Persons with Disabilities 2008
The Equality Act 2010
Health and Social Care Act 2012
Valuing People 2001 and Valuing People Now 2009 (White Papers)

SAMPLE CASE VIGNETTES

Michael has no official diagnosis but is generally considered to be on the autistic spectrum. In his primary school he had a circle of friends who invited him to their homes, played with him in the playground when he wanted to join them, enjoyed his sense of humour, supported him with his work, and protected him from making inadvertent errors. Michael's classmates learnt that loud noises upset him, that he struggled to understand some instructions, that he was not very good at concentrating, that he was terrified of being told off, and that they could help him with all of these things. Michael's teacher found that in helping Michael his classmates improved their own work, behaviour, and social skills.

When he made the transition from primary to secondary school Michael's parents provided a clear description of his needs, which, other than academic skills, mainly focused on reducing anxiety by making everything predictable or warning Michael of anything out of the ordinary. Within one term of his attendance at the secondary school Michael was experiencing such high anxiety on a daily basis that he was not eating or sleeping. The school had not been able to meet his needs, he was constantly on high alert for the next frightening and unexpected occurrence, and when they occurred he broke the school rules by running out of class and thereby encountered the additional damaging reaction of being disciplined. Michael needed the support of a counselling psychologist to help him to reduce his anxiety. He learned relaxation and breathing techniques to apply in high stress situations. He learned cognitive strategies to cope when encountering situations he found frightening. By talking about his fears he was able to gain insight into his reactions and reduce his anxiety.

Pablo is a young adult with mild physical impairment, learning disabilities, and limited communication. He lives in a group home with a small group of other disabled people and a team of staff who provide support around the clock. Pablo was prone to extreme violent behaviour towards staff several times a day that led to him being placed in a padded seclusion room where it would take him some time to calm down. In order to try to understand this problem the regular sequence of events that led to these outbursts were examined under the supervision of a psychiatrist. Pablo would be in his room engaging with his belongings. He would appear in the common area and approach staff with a smile on his face and ask for something such as a balloon—one of a number of "favourite" items that appeared to be related to his youth and living with his family. Some staff members were wary of Pablo and would provide minimal response. Other staff members took pride in being kind to him, would find him the desired item, or tell him that it was not available. From this point Pablo would become more and more demanding of the item verbally, even when he was given it, and this would escalate to violent behaviour. As part of communication therapy Pablo practised answering "yes" and "no" questions by pointing to the words. When asked by the counselling psychologist if he liked balloons and all the other items that he would regularly request he pointed emphatically to "no". Under supervision of the counselling psychologist those caring for Pablo altered their response to his smiles and animation. When these actions were seen as being a sign of agitation and distress, and when staff offered verbal reassurance and distraction in the form of exercise or other activity, Pablo returned to his typical calm state.

CONCLUSION

People with disabilities and special needs should have access to counselling psychology and when this is delivered in a person-centred way there are likely to be significant benefits. The counselling psychologist needs to take time to get to know their client and build a relationship. From this point they need to be open to a wide range of interpretations of behaviour, which can be checked using verbal and nonverbal means.

SUGGESTED FURTHER READING

Mason M. (2000). *Incurably human*. London: Working Press.
Micheline Mason is a woman with disabilities, an author, and disability activist. In this book she highlights issues of social understanding of disability.

Sinason, V. (2010). *Mental handicap and the human condition: An analytic approach to intellectual disability*. London: Free Association Books.
Valerie Sinason is a child psychotherapist and adult psychoanalyst. This book includes case studies of her work with people with a range of disabilities, including those who are nonverbal.

Webb J. (2013) *A guide to psychological understanding of people with learning disabilities: Eight domains and three stories*. London: Routledge.
Jenny Webb writes about understanding from her perspective as a practising clinical psychologist.

REFERENCES

ALLFIE (n.d.). *Alliance for Inclusive Education*. (online) Retrieved from http://www.allfie.org.uk (accessed March 8, 2017).

American Psychiatric Association (2013). *Diagnostic and statistical manual of mental disorders* (5th ed.). Arlington, VA: American Psychiatric Association.

Assouline, S. G., Nicpon, M., & Huber D. H. (2006). The impact of vulnerabilities and strengths on the academic experiences of twice-exceptional students: A message to school counsellors. *Professional School Counseling, 10*(1), 14–24.

Boake, C. (2002). From the Binet-Simon to the Wechsler-Bellevue: Tracing the history of intelligence testing. *Journal of Clinical and Experimental Neuropsychology, 24* (3), 38–405.

Bryan, K., Freer, J., & Furlong, C. (2007). Language and communication difficulties in juvenile offenders. *International Journal of Language and Communication Disorders, 42*(5), 505–520.

Buckles, J., Luckasson, R., & Keefe, E. (2013). A systematic review of the prevalence of psychiatric disorders in adults with intellectual disability, 2003–2010. *Journal of Mental Health Research in Intellectual Disabilities, 6*(3), 181–207.

Carnaby, S. (2007). Developing good practice in the clinical assessment of people with profound intellectual disabilities and multiple impairment. *Journal of Policy and Practice in Intellectual Disabilities, 4*(2), 88–96.

Contact a Family (2011). *Forgotten families: The impact of isolation on families with disabled children across the UK*. London: Contact a Family.

Cramer, S. C., Sur, M., Dobkin, B. H., O'Brien, C., Sanger, T. D., Trojanowski, J. Q., . . . & Vinogradov, S. (2011). Harnessing neuroplasticity for clinical applications. *Brain, 134*, 1591–1609.

Crossley, R. (1999). *Speechless: Facilitating communication for people without voices*. New York: Dutton.

Demanchick, S. P., Cochran, N. H., & Cochran, J. L. (2003). Person-centred play therapy for adults with developmental disabilities. *International Journal of Play Therapy, 12*(1), 47–65.

Department for Education (2015). National statistics permanent and fixed-period exclusions in England: 2013 to 2014. Retrieved from https://www.gov.uk/government/statistics/permanent-and-fixed-period-exclusions-in-england-2013-to-2014 (accessed March 8, 2017).

Donnellan, A. (1984). The criterion of the least dangerous assumption. *Behavior Disorders, 9,* 141–150.

Dorstyn, D. S., Mathias, J. L., & Denson, L. A. (2011). Psychosocial outcomes of telephone-based counseling for adults with an acquired physical disability: A meta-analysis. *Rehabilitation Psychology, 56*(1), 1–14.

Dowling, S., Hubert, J., White, S., & Hollins, S. (2006). Bereaved adults with intellectual disabilities: A combined randomized controlled trial and qualitative study of two community-based interventions. *Journal of Intellectual Disability Research, 50*(4), 277–287.

DWP (Department for Work and Pensions) (2013). *Fulfilling potential: Building a deeper understanding of disability in the UK today.* London: Crown.

Department for Education (2015). *Collection: Statistics—exclusions* (online). Retrieved from https://www.gov.uk/government/collections/statistics-exclusions (accessed March 8, 2017).

Foley-Nicpon, M., & Lee, S. (2012). Disability research in counseling psychology journals: A 20-year content analysis. *Journal of Counseling Psychology, 59*(3), 392–398.

Gardner, H. (2011). *Frames of mind: The theory of multiple intelligences.* New York: Basic Books.

Gascoigne, M. (2014). *Implementing the SEND reforms: Joint commissioning for children and young people with speech, language and communication needs (SLCN).* Retrieved from www.thecommunicationtrust.org.uk/slcncommissioningreport (accessed March 8, 2017).

Gendlin, E. (1978). *Focusing.* New York: Everest House.

Goleman, D. (1997). *Emotional intelligence.* New York: Bantam.

Gray, C. (1994). *Comic strip conversations: Illustrated interactions that teach conversation skills to students with autism and related disorders.* Arlington, TX: Future Horizons.

Iuculano, T., Rosenberg-Lee, M., Richardson, J., Tenison, C., Fuchs, L., Supekar, K., & Meno, V. (2015). Cognitive tutoring induces widespread neuroplasticity and remediates brain function in children with mathematical learning disabilities. *Nature Communications, 6,* 8453. DOI: 10.1038/ncomms9453

Janssen, C. G. C., Schuengel, C., & Stolk, J. (2002). Understanding challenging behaviour in people with severe and profound intellectual disability: A stress-attachment model. *Journal of Intellectual Disability Research, 46*(6), 445–453.

Jones, R. A. (2013). Therapeutic relationships with individuals with learning disabilities: A qualitative study of the counselling psychologists' experience. *British Journal of Learning Disabilities, 42,* 193–203.

Jordan, R. (1992). *Notes for the video 'A is for Autism'.* Channel 4.

Kelsey, D., & Smart, J. F. (2012). Social justice, disability, and rehabilitation education. *Rehabilitation Education, 26*(2&3), 229–240.

Klintwall, L., Eldevik, S., & Eikeseth, S. (2015). Narrowing the gap: Effects of intervention on developmental trajectories in autism. *Autism, 19*(1), 53–63.

Locke, A., Ginsborg, J., & Peers, I. (2002). Development and disadvantage: Implications for early years. *International Journal of Language and Communication Disorders, 27*(1), 3–15.

Mason, M. (2000). *Incurably human.* London: Working Press.

Mason, M. (2008). *Dear parents . . .* Nottingham: Inclusive Solutions.

Mencap (2001). *Behind closed doors: Preventing sexual abuse against adults with a learning disability.* London: Mencap.

Morin, D., Rivard, M., Crocker, A. G., Boursier, C. P., & Caron, J. (2013). Public attitudes towards intellectual disability: A multidimensional perspective. *Journal of Intellectual Disability Research, 57*(3), 279–292.

Nind, M. (1996). Efficacy of intensive interaction: developing sociability and communication in people with severe and complex learning difficulties using an approach based on caregiver-infant interaction. *European Journal of Special Needs Education, 11*(1), 48–66.

NSPCC (2014). *"We have the right to be safe": Protecting disabled children from abuse.* London: NSPCC.

Peterson, C., Maier, S. F., & Seligman, M. E. P. (1993). *Learned helplessness: A theory for the age of personal control.* Oxford: Oxford University Press.

Prouty, G. E. (1990). Pre-therapy: A theoretical evolution in the person-centered/experiential psychotherapy of schizophrenia and retardation. In G. Lietaer, J. Rombauts, & R. Van Balen (Eds.), *Client-centered and experiential psychotherapy in the nineties* (pp. 645–658). Leuven: University of Leuven Press.

Rist, R. C. (2000). HER classic: Student social class and teacher expectations: The self-fulfilling prophecy in ghetto education. *Harvard Educational Review, 70,* 257–301.

Shah, S., Travers, C., & Arnold, J. (2004). Disabled and successful: Education in the life stories of disabled high achievers. *Journal of Research in Special Educational Needs, 4*(3), 122–132.

Shakespeare, T. (2006). *Disability rights and wrongs.* Abingdon: Routledge.

Smyth, D. (2013). *Person-centred therapy with children and young people.* London: Sage.

Sullivan P. M., & Knutson J. F. (2000) Maltreatment and disabilities: A population based epidemiological study. *Child Abuse and Neglect, 24*(10), 1257–1273.

Thelen, E., & Smith, L. B. (1994). *A dynamic system approach to the development of cognition and action.* Cambridge, MA: MIT Press.

UNICEF (United Nations Children's Fund) (2013). The state of the world's children 2013: Children with disabilities. New York: UNICEF.

van Nijnatten, C., & Heestermans, M. (2012). Communicative empowerment of people with intellectual disability. *Journal of Intellectual and Developmental Disability, 37*(2), 100–111.

Williams, D. (2002). *Exposure anxiety—the invisible cage: An exploration of self-protection responses in the autism spectrum.* London: Jessica Kingsley.

14 Counselling Psychology for Clients with Asperger Syndrome

ANJA RUTTEN

CHAPTER OUTLINE

INTRODUCTION 201

AUTISM AND ASPERGER SYNDROME 201

DIAGNOSTIC LABELS 202

CONSIDERING AUTISM AS COUNSELLING PSYCHOLOGISTS 202

IS AUTISM A DISABILITY? 203

PERSON-FIRST LANGUAGE OR NOT? 204

AUTISTIC PEOPLE'S DISTRESS 204

THERAPEUTIC WORK WITH CLIENTS WITH ASPERGER SYNDROME 205

EXPERIENCES OF THERAPY 207

CONCLUSION 209

LEARNING OUTCOMES

BY THE END OF THIS CHAPTER YOU SHOULD BE ABLE TO ANSWER THE FOLLOWING KEY QUESTIONS:

1. What is your understanding of autism?
2. In your view, is autism a disability? What do you base this view on?
3. What are some of the key issues in offering therapy to clients on the autism spectrum?

Counselling Psychology: A Textbook for Study and Practice, First Edition. Edited by David Murphy.
© 2017 John Wiley & Sons Ltd. Published 2017 by John Wiley & Sons Ltd.

INTRODUCTION

Autism and Asperger Syndrome are now more in people's awareness than ever before. We have wider representation of autistic people in popular media, with programmes such as *The Undateables*, *The Autistic Gardener*, *Born Naughty*, and *Young Autistic and Stagestruck* offering some, inevitably highly edited, glimpses of what life as a person with autism can be like. Some of these programmes are more positive and respectful portrayals than others, but it is now at least possible to encounter images of successful and independent autistic adults, such as the lead character Saga Norén in the Scandinavian crime drama *The Bridge*.

Awareness, however, is not the same as knowledge and understanding, and whilst the *Rainman* stereotype is now no longer the only image of autism, lack of acceptance and understanding from a predominantly neurotypical (nonautistic) society remains an obstacle for many individuals with autism (Parsons, 2015). In the previous chapter Anne Emerson considered work generically with special needs and disabilities, in this chapter we will look more deeply at the work of counselling psychologists with people identified as being on the autism spectrum. It is important for helpers, including counselling psychologists, to have a deeper understanding of autism itself, the range of issues that can face this client group, as well as building specific knowledge about the client over the course of therapy. Whilst the latter depends on the client and the therapeutic relationship, other aspects can be addressed through various other channels, including this book chapter.

AUTISM AND ASPERGER SYNDROME

Autism is a rather diffuse concept. The terms *autism spectrum disorder/condition* or *autism* are generally used to describe and label people whose way of processing experiences of themselves, others, and the world is not *neurotypical* or conforming to the *predominant neurotype* (Chown, 2013). Autism is described as a spectrum (Wing & Attwood, 1987), to explain variability in presentation of impairments. Autism also intersects with a spectrum of intellectual ability: a significant proportion of autistic people are considered to have a learning disability (defined as IQ <70), ranging from 25% (Bowler, 2007) to 50% (NICE, 2011).

Autism affects the social domains of interaction, communication, and imagination, often termed the "Triad of Impairment" (Wing, 1996). In addition, people can have a narrow range of interests and differences in sensory experiencing. A large corpus of psychological publications attempts to explain what causes these differences (commonly framed as deficits), and their impact. In this literature, there is now acceptance that no one theory has the power to explain autism completely (Happé, Ronald, & Plomin, 2006) and in addition, that none is exclusive to autism (Bowler, 2007; Vanegas & Davidson, 2015).

Autism affects about 1% of the population, although estimates vary and have increased over recent years, probably due to changes in diagnostic practices

(Dhaval & Fernandez, 2015; Hansen, Schendel, & Parner, 2015). Autism is considered to be at least in part genetic, although there is no consensus over its aetiology (Kim & Leventhal, 2015). The current gender ratio stands at 4 males to 1 female (Halladay et al., 2015), due to genetic factors making autism more likely in males (Mottron et al., 2015), or the underidentification of females (Dworzynski, Ronald, Bolton, & Happé, 2012).

DIAGNOSTIC LABELS

The term *autism spectrum disorder/condition* is generally used to describe a *pervasive developmental disorder*, meaning that development and functioning are affected in multiple areas of daily life in a way that is not typical in the population as a whole. *Autism* is used as an umbrella term to describe this, but this term also doubles up as a descriptor of autistic people who have additional learning disabilities (IQ <70). This group of people is also described as having *classic autism* or *Kanner's autism*. *Asperger syndrome* and *high-functioning autism* are generally used for autistic people who have (above) average intelligence (IQ ≥70).

The fifth edition of the Diagnostic Statistical Manual of Mental Disorders (DSM-5) (American Psychiatric Association, 2013) has imposed a simplification in terminology, at least for new diagnoses: it simply refers to all variations of autism as *autism spectrum disorder* and classifies different elements of the diagnostic category in terms of level of support required. By all accounts this happened without much consultation with the autism community, or regard for the fact that some autistic people prefer the Asperger description and have heavily invested in this identity (Spillers, Sensui, & Linton, 2014).

Concern about different autism-related terms and diagnostic criteria also exists in professional circles (Wing, Gould, & Gillberg, 2011), quite apart from the increasing principled disquiet many professionals have around concepts such as "diagnosis" and "disorder" (Milton, 2012; Moloney, 2010). Current diagnostic procedures are diverse (Falkmer, Anderson, Falkmer, & Horlin, 2013) and neither terminology nor criteria are uniform (Sharma, Woolfson, & Hunter, 2012). In any event, as *Asperger syndrome* and *high-functioning autism* are still in existence in other diagnostic systems, have been widely used in the literature, and form part of people's identities, it is likely that these terms will be around for the foreseeable future.

CONSIDERING AUTISM AS COUNSELLING PSYCHOLOGISTS

Counselling psychology's humanistic value base and emphasis on subjective client experience make its relationship with social constructs such as *disorder* and *diagnosis* complex (Cooper, 2009; Moloney, 2013; Walsh & Frankland, 2009) (or so it should!). Academic discourse tends to take a deficit-based view of autism and the use of medicalized language still prevails (Leatherland & Chown, 2015). Words like *deficit* and *abnormal* suggest that there is something "wrong" with autistic people, and lead to the idea that "treatment" is necessary, if not of autism itself, then at least of its "comorbidities" (common difficulties associated with autism). People with autism themselves are questioning the dominance of the neurotypical (i.e., nonautistic) way of conceptualizing autism, and offer alternatives in the form of a discourse of difference (e.g., Chown, 2013). Counselling psychology is in a unique position to support this move away from pathologizing and increasingly questions the validity of diagnosis as the vehicle for understanding difference, whether resulting from physical impairment, emotional distress (Johnstone & Dallos, 2006), or autism (Timimi, Gardner, & McCabe, 2010). Formulation of problems in lived experience, rather than labelling people as disordered, offers a less stigmatizing and more even-handed way of understanding people in both their difficulties and areas of strength. Therapy can help people come to terms with distress, but it should not take the place of social change or be "prescribed" instead of righting societal wrongs (Moloney, 2013). Neither should counselling psychology be limited to the removal of "dysfunction," a bringing up to a minimal "normal functioning." Instead it can (and ought to) be a catalyst for development, growth, and flourishing (Joseph, 2015). There are significant tensions between medical and social constructions of autism (Cascio, 2015) and although it is not this chapter's remit to give a full exploration, some attention to this debate is useful.

IS AUTISM A DISABILITY?

In Chapter 13 we learnt there are several conceptualizations of disability and impairment (Brownlee & Cureton, 2009), including the medical model and social model. In a medical model of disability, impairment leads to, or is equal to, disability, and disability is therefore situated in the individual. The social model of disability sees this rather differently: impairment and disability are not causally linked and disability only happens if people with impairments experience societal barriers (Middleton, 2015; Oliver, 1990, 1996). Disability is therefore located in society, not individuals. It is society's responsibility to include all its citizens, not an individual's responsibility to overcome disability that has been imposed on them. The Equality Act 2010 enshrines the right of *all* people to participate in society and requires *reasonable adjustments* to be made to ensure this is possible.

For people with invisible impairments, the situation is complex. In the absence of visual clues, many people will assume the other person does not have impairments. The result can be (although this is not inevitable) that pressure is put upon people to conform to societal norms and this may result in disabled people being *ontologically invalidated* (Hughes, 2012). *Ableism*, as the disability movement describes it, enables this oppression of people with impairments. This is slowly changing for those who, for example, experience chronic emotional distress, where society's attitude is showing signs of shifting from "pull your socks up" to one of inclusion, at least in principle.

For people with autism to be fully included in society there is a long way to go. Autistic people experience themselves, other people, and the world in a way that is *qualitatively* different, and therefore reasonable adjustments may need to be *qualitatively* different from those required by others with impairments. For example, it is now commonplace for organizations to have invested in hearing loops, and so a deaf client is able to participate in therapy because that reasonable adjustment has been made. The needs of a client with Asperger syndrome may be very different: for example, they may need eye contact to be disregarded as an indicator of ability to engage in therapeutic contact. These adjustments can appear problematic as they require a qualitative shift on the part of the counselling psychologist, who may filter their impressions through a neuronormative lens. This, however, is not the client's problem.

There are examples of societal attitude shifts towards groups of people who until fairly recently were considered "deviant" or "disordered." Whilst we're still not there yet with our attitudes towards people's sexualities or skin colour, the situation for left-handers appears improved. So what is "normal" really depends on how that is constructed. The question of whether an autistic person is disabled can therefore often be answered by "yes," though this is not identical to autism being a disability. In other words, whilst autism is not a disability, disablement of autistic people is common.

PERSON-FIRST LANGUAGE OR NOT?

A recent online survey (Kenny et al., 2015) highlighted the multitudes of terms to describe autistic people. With increasing understanding of the role of language in shaping experience and ultimately society (the so-called Sapir–Whorf Hypothesis) (O'Neill, 2015) and the efforts of the disability movement, the 1980s and 1990s saw a change in the use of language around diversity. Where disabled people were often referred to by impairment (e.g., a "spastic"), emphasis shifted to *person-first language* (a "person with cerebral palsy"), to emphasize the person rather than just their impairment. The term *person with autism* is therefore used widely, particularly by professionals. However, many autistic people are rejecting person-first language on the basis that autism is very much part of their identity (Sinclair, 1999), and not "bolted on"." They therefore prefer the term "autistic person" to reflect this.

As will have become obvious, in this chapter, I use the terms *autistic person* and *person with autism* or *person with Asperger syndrome* interchangeably.

AUTISTIC PEOPLE'S DISTRESS

Distress and its enduring effects on well-being are common, with approximately a quarter of the UK population experiencing "some kind of mental health problem in the course of a year" (Mental Health Foundation, 2015). Some therapeutic literature frames this in medical model discourse, and people are said to "suffer from," for example, "mood disorders" or "anxiety disorders," though when "disorders" affect a quarter of the population they seem fairly "normal" to me.

This conceptualization of emotional distress is problematic as it does not pay attention to what causes distress and is used as a political device separating people into categories of dubious scientific status (Moncrieff, 2010). Taking a social model approach, a number of factors are known to influence mental health in a profoundly negative way, including poverty and a wide societal gap between rich and poor (Pickett & Wilkinson, 2015), in addition to absence of meaningful occupation (Bartley, Sacker, & Clarke, 2004) and social isolation (Rohde, D'Ambrosio, Tang, & Rao, 2016). Whilst therapy has an important role to play in helping people cope with and work through distress, social justice needs to be at the heart of the agenda of counselling psychologists in order to effect change in society, rather than risking people simply resigning themselves to their fate. The statement that *the personal is political* (Hanisch, 1969) still holds.

This argument is relevant for people with autism, who are reported to have high levels of emotional distress significantly exceeding population averages (Deudney & Shah, 2001; Hirvikoski & Blomqvist, 2015). Ritualized thoughts and behaviours, anxiety, chronic stress, and low mood are common experiences (Gillott, Furniss, & Walter, 2001; Howlin, 1997a, b; Moss, Howlin, Savage, Bolton, & Rutter, 2015; Tantam, 2000). Sensory integration difficulties, highly accurate but slower processing styles, and attentional differences leading to difficulties in letting go, can all be part of an autistic process. Interactions with other people may be unsatisfactory or misunderstood, and cause distress. Difficulties with anticipation or transitions between environments may leave people in a constant state of anxiety about change without notice. All of these things can be the case, *and* people with Asperger syndrome often are disadvantaged by society. Only 16% of the autistic population is in full-time employment (National Autistic Society, 2015). This means that the majority of adults with autism, after they leaving school or university, do not have the prestructured work experience that for many of us is a gateway into social opportunities and a decent income. Life on benefits is difficult for many, but combined with lack of social opportunities and low expectations of change, it is unsurprising that many people with autism are distressed.

THERAPEUTIC WORK WITH CLIENTS WITH ASPERGER SYNDROME

Counselling, psychotherapy and counselling psychology are common ways of helping people in distress with an excellent evidence base (Cooper, 2008). Relationship factors continue to be seen as highly pertinent to good therapy outcomes (Norcross, 2011), and differences between therapy modalities are marginal at best (King, Marston, & Bower, 2014). Matching client choice of therapist and length of therapy (Seligman, 1996) is important in predicting outcome. This is at odds with the current provision of therapy via the NHS, where short-term cognitive-behavioural approaches dominate and client choice appears limited, though choices are starting to widen and seem better in the voluntary and private sectors. Clients with Asperger syndrome, like clients of other minority backgrounds (Loewenthal, 2015) are underrepresented in accessing mainstream, funded, counselling services, and report difficulties in getting their needs met. In addition, the evidence base for therapy with clients with Asperger syndrome is still developing and there are significant gaps in the literature. For example, more research with adults and longer term follow up of outcome studies are required. Autistic people with learning disabilities are mostly excluded, and older adults are remarkably absent. Studies of therapy with clients in modalities other than cognitive-behavioural therapy are needed, as is research into how gains in therapy are generalized to life outside of therapy. Above all, there is currently no research representing client voices and experiences and therefore, therapy is based on neuronormative assumptions of "what works." Whilst it may well be the case that therapeutic work is useful for clients with autism, we are not currently able to state with confidence that positive outcomes are due to therapy, or despite therapy.

Early in the history of documenting therapy with autistic clients, publications often focused on psychodynamic work, difficulties in therapeutic relationships, and interpretations of this, arising out of the client's Asperger syndrome (e.g., Mero, 2002; Topel & Lachmann, 2011). Given the interest in development of personality in the psychodynamic approach, this was initially a natural path to take. Increased clarity that parenting does not cause autism appears to have reduced this line of enquiry considerably. From a contemporary psychodynamic point of view, mentalizing (the ability to be aware of and respond to our own and others' mental states) and difficulties surrounding this (Allen, Fonagy, & Bateman, 2008) is seen as important in therapy with people with autism (Cohler & Weiner, 2011).

From a cognitive-behavioural perspective, there is increasing evidence that therapy with people with autism is effective (e.g., Selles et al., 2015; Storch et al., 2015). In addition, mindfulness reports good outcomes (e.g., Kiep, Spek, & Hoeben, 2015). Studies from this paradigm initially focused mostly on children with high-functioning autism and on group-based intervention, though increasingly research now also includes adults.

Outcome studies from a person-centred perspective are not yet included in the literature, though there are now publications addressing therapy with people with autism from a person-centred perspective (Knibbs & Moran, 2005; Rutten, 2014; Stinckens & Becaus, 2008; Vuijk, 2013). Regardless of the approach, it needs to be clear that counselling psychology does not (and should not) intend to "treat" or change a client's autism. Its aim is to help people make sense of and come to terms with experiences they've had, as would happen for neurotypical clients. What may change is the client's perspective on their own experience, their relationships with others, the way they manage anxiety, how they feel, and how they act in the world, but this will not change the client's autism. In addition, therapeutic work should not take the place of societal changes required to ensure inclusion and fairness for those who are disadvantaged (Moloney, 2013).

EXPERIENCES OF THERAPY[1]

The way clients with Asperger syndrome use counselling psychology, psycho-therapy, or counselling may be *qualitatively* different to neurotypical ways. The best way to find out what works for autistic clients would of course be to seek their views, but there are no known academic publications that report on autis-tic clients' experiences of therapy. Whilst outcome literature suggests that ther-apy works with autistic clients, many adults with Asperger syndrome report that they often do not find counselling useful. Some say their experiences have been very positive, or even life-changing, but I have also received comments in personal conversations and through my research (Rutten, 2015a, 2015b) about the lack of understanding autistic people face from our profession. In addition, some say they are (illegally) denied access to mental health services on the basis of their autism.

As Hodge (2013) points out, ableist ways of working impact on the experi-ence and expression of counsellor empathy. This is similar to working cross-culturally, or with other client groups who present as different to self. Whilst counselling psychologists are often not able to change their lived experience of belonging to a specific minority, they can work on their understanding of diver-sity by accessing training and supervision that deproblematizes or depathol-ogizes clients to build affirmative practice. Understanding of clients who are qualitatively different may be helped by counselling psychologists increas-ing knowledge and understanding, as a stepping stone to advancing empathy (Stinckens & Becaus, 2008). Whatever modality counselling psychologists are working from, making reasonable adjustments, being able to relate to clients, and being able to enter their world are facilitated by understanding some of the differences in client experiences, and the implications of this. The case study below illustrates this.

CLINICAL EXAMPLE

Claire is a 40-year-old woman with Asperger syndrome. She is single, lives in an apartment near her parents, and works part-time. Claire feels low and anxious and has had some counselling sessions on the NHS. Because of her high level of distress, Claire was referred to the psychiatric team, but did not feel this was the best help for her. She wanted regu-lar appointments and not to be rushed in and out of the service. Claire decided to find a private counsellor on her GP's advice, and picked Beth because Beth's private practice was near her work.

This is Claire's perspective of the first session:

> She said to make myself comfortable so I moved the chair and I moved the plant from the table onto the window sill. I felt a bit more comfortable then, but I didn't really find Beth very helpful because she seemed to twiddle her thumbs a lot and that was all I could see. I'll go back because it took me a while to get used to

---

[1] The example is a composite vignette made up of a mix of experiences to protect client anonymity.

my previous therapist, but I am worried that I am going to be sent away.

Beth is a counselling psychologist with 7 years' postqualifying experience. She describes her practice as integrative. She works 2 days per week for a voluntary sector agency working with children, and has started a private practice alongside this. She has never worked with an adult with Asperger syndrome before, although she had heard and read about it.

This is Beth's perspective of the first session:

> When Claire arrived, she seemed so anxious, so I told her to make herself comfortable. I was completely thrown when Claire started to rearrange furniture and I started to worry about who I had taken on as a client. I couldn't get a word in and she seemed all over the place. I felt out of my depth. I just wanted the session to end because I had no idea how to respond. I hope I haven't scared Claire off, but I am also concerned I might not be the therapist for her.

This type of scenario is unfortunately not uncommon, but it is not inevitable. The counselling psychologist's response to Claire in her second session is highly likely to determine whether Claire feels helped and "met" more fully.

Potentially, therapy could end badly. In between sessions, Beth has been to see her supervisor, and together they have discussed Claire's lack of understanding of boundaries. Beth has decided that she needs to be firm with Claire and address the issue head-on before focusing on the presenting problem, Claire's anxiety.

BETH: *Claire, I wonder how last week was for you?*

CLAIRE: *You were twiddling your thumbs a lot and I was worried you were bored.*

BETH: *No I wasn't bored but I think we need to talk about why you moved the furniture last week.*

CLAIRE: *You told me to make myself comfortable, and so that's what I did. Did I do wrong? I'm sorry I'm not trying to get it wrong. See this is what happens all the time.*

BETH: *It was just a figure of speech. I don't think moving furniture is the main priority here, so now we've cleared that up, let's move on to talk about your anxiety.*

Claire now feels confused about whether moving the furniture is okay or not, insecure about her relationship with Beth, and more worried about whether therapy will work. The trust she wanted to have in Beth has reduced even more, and her anxiety has skyrocketed.

A more positive Session 2 could lead to Claire feeling accepted more fully, and better able to use therapy to process some of the anxiety and low moods she is experiencing. In an alternative scenario, Beth consulted her supervisor and talked to a colleague with good knowledge of autism. They pointed out to her that her statement might have been taken literally, and that Beth needs to own her part in the misunderstanding. Then Beth will need to think together with Claire about how they will communicate.

BETH: *Claire, I wonder how last week was for you?*

CLAIRE: *You were twiddling your thumbs a lot and I was worried you were bored.*

BETH: *I'm sorry, Claire. I wasn't bored but you're right I wasn't paying attention to you all the time. I felt a bit taken aback when you moved the furniture and I got distracted by that because that was unexpected. I wonder if we can talk about this a bit more?*

CLAIRE: *You told me to make myself comfortable, so that's what I did. Did I do wrong? I'm sorry I'm not trying to get it wrong. See this is what happens all the time.*

BETH: *I think we may have had a misunderstanding in our communication, and I think that happened because I was not clear. When I said "make yourself comfortable" I meant it in a nonliteral way, it's something I say that helps people take a bit of time to relax when they arrive. I guess you took it literally because what I meant and what I said were not the same. So it's not your fault, and perhaps we* *can talk a bit about how I need to communicate more clearly. I can understand how things like this make you feel stressed, especially when you are worried about not getting it right.*

CLAIRE [SIGHS WITH [RELIEF]: *I'd like that, because this happens all the time and it makes me really anxious.*

The empathic response from Beth, with the clear explanation of what was happening for her, helped Claire express her fear about doing things wrong, and enabled her to accept Beth's help. Claire now feels heard, her anxiety reduces, and she and Beth can get to work.

CONCLUSION

Learning about diverse client groups, for example, in relation to race, class, sexuality, and gender is considered essential as a first step towards working ethically and safely, with due regard for the power invested in the role of those providing psychological services. Counselling psychology's humanistic underpinning forms the best possible foundation for respectful, sensitive, and useful work with autistic clients.

Autism is an issue of difference and diversity, not pathology and therefore requires no "treatment." The experiences of minority client groups are often qualitatively different and this can be misunderstood. Being part of a minority group can also bring additional stresses due to others' lack of acceptance and experiences of discrimination or exclusion—and this does need to change for our clients with autism.

SUGGESTED FURTHER READING

The books below give different views: the first one is an excellent overview, the second a fascinating critical take, the third one a brilliant collection of writing by people with Asperger syndrome.

Attwood, T. (2008). *The complete guide to Asperger's syndrome* (revised ed.). London: Jessica Kingsley.

Timimi, S., Gardner, N., & McCabe, B. (2011). *The myth of autism: Medicalising men's and boys' social and emotional competence.* London: Palgrave McMillan.

Worton, D., & Beardon, L. (Eds.) (2011). *Aspies and mental health: Speaking for ourselves.* London: Jessica Kingsley.

REFERENCES

Allen, J.G., Fonagy, P., & Bateman, A.W. (2008) *Mentalizing in clinical practice*. Washington, DC: American Psychiatric Publishing.

American Psychiatric Association (2013). *American Psychiatric Association: Diagnostic and statistical manual of mental disorders* (5th ed.). Arlington, VA: American Psychiatric Association.

Bartley, M., Sacker, A., & Clarke, P. (2004). Employment status, employment conditions, and limiting illness: Prospective evidence from the British household panel survey 1991–2001. *Journal of Epidemiology and Community Health, 58*, 501–506. DOI:10.1136/jech.2003.009878

Bowler, D. (2007). *Autism spectrum disorders: Psychological theory and research*. Chichester: John Wiley & Sons.

Brownlee, K., & Cureton, A. (Eds.) (2009). *Disability and disadvantage*. Oxford: Oxford University Press.

Cascio, M. A. (2015). Cross-cultural autism studies, neurodiversity, and conceptualizations of autism. *Culture, Medicine and Psychiatry, 39*, 207–212. DOI: 10.007/s/11013-015-9450-y

Chown, N. (2013). The mismeasure of autism: A challenge to orthodox autism theory. *Autonomy, the Critical Journal of Interdisciplinary Autism Studies, 1*(2), 1–10.

Cohler, B. J., & Weiner, T. (2011). The inner fortress: Symptom and meaning in Asperger's. *Psychoanalytic Inquiry, 31*, 208–221. DOI: 10.1080/07351690.2010.513592

Cooper, M. (2008). *Essential research findings in counselling and psychotherapy: The facts are friendly*. London: Sage.

Cooper, M. (2009). Welcoming the other: Actualising the humanistic ethic at the core of counselling psychology practice. *Counselling Psychology Review, 24*(3), 119–129.

Deudney, C., & Shah, A. (2001). *Mental health and Asperger syndrome: Information sheet*. London: The National Autistic Society.

Dhaval, D.M., & Fernandez, J.M. (2015). Rising autism prevalence: Real or displacing other mental disorders? Evidence from demand for auxiliary healthcare workers in California. *Economic Inquiry, 53*(1), 448–468.

Dworzynski, K., Ronald, A., Bolton, P., & Happé, F. (2012). How different are girls and boys above and below the diagnostic threshold for autism spectrum disorders. *Journal of the American Academy of Child and Adolescent Psychiatry, 51*(8), 788–797.

Falkmer, T., Anderson, K. Falkmer, M., & Horlin, C. (2013). Diagnostic procedures in autism spectrum disorders: A systematic literature review. *European Child and Adolescent Psychiatry, 22*(6), 329–240.

Gillott, A., Furniss, F., & Walter, A. (2001). Anxiety in high-functioning children with autism. *Autism, 5*(3), 277–286.

Halladay, A. K, Bishop, S., Constantino, J. N., Daniels, A. M., Koenig, K., Palmer, K., . . . Szatmari, P. (2015). Sex and gender differences in autism spectrum disorder: Summarizing evidence gaps and identifying emerging areas of priority. *Molecular Autism, 6*(36), 1–5. DOI: 10.1186/s13229-015-0019-y

Hanisch, C. (1969). *The personal is political*. Retrieved from http://www.carolhanisch.org/CHwritings/PIP.html (accessed August 25, 2015).

Hansen, S. N., Schendel, D. E., & Parner, E. T. (2015). Explaining the increase in the prevalence of autism spectrum disorders: The proportion attributable to changes in reporting practices. *JAMA Pediatrics, 169*(1), 56–62.

Happé, F., Ronald, A., & Plomin, R. (2006). Time to give up on a single explanation for autism. *Nature and Neuroscience, 10*(9), 1218–1220.

Hirvikoski, T., & Blomqvist, M. (2015). High self-perceived stress and poor coping in intellectually able adults with autism spectrum disorder. *Autism, 19*(6), 752–757. DOI: 10.1177/1362361314543530

Hodge, N. (2013). Counselling, autism and the problem of empathy. *British Journal of Guidance and Counselling, 41*(2), 105–116.

Howlin, P. (1997a). *Autism: Preparing for adulthood*. London: Routledge.

Howlin, P. (1997b). Psychiatric disturbances in adulthood. In P Howlin (Ed.), *Autism: Preparing for adulthood* (pp. 216–235). London: Routledge.

Hughes, B. (2012). Civilising modernity and the ontological invalidation of disabled people. In D. Goodley, B. Hughes, & L. Davis (Eds.), *Disability and social theory: New developments and directions* (pp. 17–32). London: Palgrave MacMillan.

Johnstone, L., & Dallos, R. (2006). *Formulation in psychology and psychotherapy: Making sense of people's problems*. Hove: Routledge.

Joseph, S. (2015). *Positive therapy: Building bridges between positive psychology and person-centred psychotherapy* (2nd ed.). Hove: Routledge.

Kenny, L., Hattersley, C., Molins, B., Buckley, C., Povey, C., & Pellicano, L. (2015). Which terms should be used to describe autism? Perspectives from the UK autism community. *Autism, 20*(4), 442–462. DOI: 10.1177/1362361315588200

Kiep, M., Spek, A. A., & Hoeben, L. (2015). Mindfulness-based therapy in adults with an autism spectrum disorder: Do treatment effects last? *Mindfulness, 6,* 637–644. DOI: 10.1007/s12671-014-0299-x

Kim, Y. S., & Leventhal, B. L. (2015). Genetic epidemiology and insights into interactive genetic and environmental effects in autism spectrum disorders. *Biological Psychiatry, 77*(1), 66–74.

King, M., Marston, L., & Bower, P. (2014). Comparison of non-directive counselling and cognitive behaviour therapy for patients presenting in general practice with an ICD-10 depressive episode: A randomized control trial. *Psychological Medicine, 44*(9), 1835–1844. DOI: 10.1017/S0033291713002377.

Knibbs, J., & Moran, H. (2005). Autism and asperger syndrome: Person-centred approaches. In S. Joseph, & R. Worsley (Eds.), *Person-centred psychopathology* (pp. 260–275). Ross-on-Wye: PCCS Books.

Leatherland, J., & Chown, N. (2015). What is autism? A content analysis of online autism information. *Good Autism Practice,16*(1), 27–41.

Loewenthal, D. (Ed.) (2015). *Critical psychotherapy, psychoanalysis and counselling: Implications for practice*. London: Palgrave Macmillan.

Mental Health Foundation (2015). *Mental health statistics*. Retrieved from www.mentalhealth. org.uk (accessed March 8, 2017).

Mero, M.-M. (2002). Asperger syndrome with comorbid emotional disorder—treatment with psychoanalytic psychotherapy. *International Journal of Circumpolar Health, 61*(Suppl 2), 80–89.

Middleton, H. (2015). The medical model: What is it, where did it come from and how long has it got? In D. Loewenthal (Ed.), *Critical psychotherapy, psychoanalysis and counselling* (pp. 29–40). London: Palgrave Macmillan.

Milton, M. (Ed.) (2012). *Diagnosis and beyond: Counselling psychology contributions to understanding human distress*. Ross-on-Wye: PCCS Books.

Moloney, P. (2010). "How can a chord be weird if it expresses your soul?" Some critical reflections on the diagnosis of Asperger syndrome. *Disability and Society, 25*(2), 135–148. DOI: 10.1080/0968750903534254

Moloney, P. (2013). *The therapy industry: The irresistible rise of the talking cure and why it doesn't work*. London: Pluto Press.

Moncrieff, J. (2010). Psychiatric diagnosis as a political device. *Social Theory and Health, 8*(4), 370–382.

Moss, P., Howlin, P., Savage, S., Bolton, P., & Rutter, M. (2015). Self and informant reports of mental health difficulties among adults with autism findings from a long-term follow-up study. *Autism, 19*(7), 832–841. DOI: 10.1177/1362361315585916

Mottron, L., Duret, P., Mueller, S., Moore, R. D., Forgeot d'Arc, B., Jacquemont, S., & Xiong, L. (2015). Sex differences in brain plasticity: A new hypothesis for sex ratio bias in autism. *Molecular Autism, 6,* 33.

National Autistic Society (2015). *The undiscovered workforce campaign.* Retrieved from http://www.autism.org.uk/about/what-is/myths-facts-stats.aspx (accessed March 8, 2017).

NICE (National Institute for Health and Care Excellence) (2011). *Autism: Recognition, referral and diagnosis of children and young people on the autism spectrum, CG128.* London: NICE.

Norcross, J. C. (Ed.) (2011). *Psychotherapy relationships that work* (2nd ed.). New York: Oxford University Press.

Oliver, M. (1990). *The politics of disablement.* Basingstoke: Macmillan.

Oliver, M. (1996). *Understanding disability: From theory to practice.* Basingstoke: Macmillan.

O'Neill, S. P. (2015). Sapir–Whorf hypothesis. *The International Encyclopedia of Language and Social Interaction,* 1–10. DOI: 10.1002/9781118611463.wbielsi086

Parsons, S. (2015). "Why are we an ignored group?" Mainstream educational experiences and current life satisfaction of adults on the autism spectrum from an online survey. *International Journal of Inclusive Education, 19*(4), 397–421.

Pickett, K. E., & Wilkinson, R. G. (2015). Income inequality and health: A causal review. *Social Science and Medicine, 128,* 316–326.

Rohde, N., D'Ambrosio, C., Tang, K. K., & Rao, P. (2016). Estimating the mental health effects of social isolation. *Applied Research in Quality of Life, 11*(3), 853–869. DOI: 10.1007/s11482-015-9401-3

Rutten, A. (2014). A person-centred approach to counselling clients with autistic process. In P. Pearce, & L. Sommerbeck (Eds.), *Person-centred work at the difficult edge* (pp. 74–87). Ross-on-Wye: PCCS Books.

Rutten, A. (2015a). *"If you don't get me, I don't need you to": What clients with Asperger syndrome say about making therapy work.* Paper presented at the meeting of the British Association for Counselling and Psychotherapy Research Conference, Nottingham.

Rutten, A. (2015b). *What clients with Asperger syndrome say about making therapy work: A grounded theory exploration.* Paper presented at the meeting of the British Psychological Society Division of Counselling Psychology Research Conference, Harrogate.

Seligman, M. E. P. (1995). The effectiveness of psychotherapy: The consumer reports study. *American Psychologist, 50*(12), 965–974.

Selles, R. R., Arnold, E. B., Phares, V., Lewin, A. B., Murphy, T. K., & Storch, E.A. (2015). Cognitive-behavioral therapy for anxiety in youth with an autism spectrum disorder: A follow-up study. *Autism, 19*(5), 613–621. DOI: 10.1177/1362361314537912

Sharma, S., Woolfson, L. M., & Hunter, S.C. (2012). Confusion and inconsistency in diagnosis of Asperger syndrome: A review of studies from 1981 to 2010. *Autism, 16*(5), 465–486.

Sinclair, J. (1999). Why I dislike "person-first" language. Retrieved from http://autismmythbusters.com/ (accessed March 8, 2017).

Spillers, J. L., Sensui, L. M., & Linton, K. F. (2014). Concerns about identity and services among people with autism and Asperger's regarding DSM-5 changes. *Journal of Social Work, Disability and Rehabilitation, 13*(3), 247–260.

Stinckens, N., & Becaus, L. (2008) Opereren op vreemd grondgebied. Kennis als toegangspoort tot contact bij de stoornis van Asperger. *Tijdschrift Cliëntgerichte Psychotherapie, 46*(1), 17–37.

Storch, E. A., Lewin, A. B., Collier, A. B., Arnold, E., De Nadai, A. S., Dane, B. F., Nadeau, J. M., Mutch, P. J., & Murphy, T. K. (2015). A randomized controlled trial of cognitive-behavioral therapy versus treatment as usual for adolescents with autism spectrum disorders and comorbid anxiety. *Depression and Anxiety, 32*(3), 174–181.

Tantam, D. (2012). *Autism spectrum disorders through the life span.* London: Jessica Kingsley.

Timimi, S., Gardner, N., & McCabe, B. (2010). *The myth of autism: Medicalising men's and boys' social and emotional competence.* Basingstoke: Palgrave Macmillan.

Topel, E.-M., & Lachmann, F. M. (2011). Connecting with two Asperger's syndrome patients—with the help of some ants. *Psychoanalytic Enquiry, 31,* 303–319. DOI: 10.1080/07351690.2010.513669

Vanegas, S.B., & Davidson, D. (2015). Investigating distinct and related contributions of weak central coherence, executive dysfunction, and systemizing theories to the cognitive profiles of children with autism spectrum disorders and typically developing children. *Research in Autism Spectrum Disorders, 11,* 77–92.

Vuijk, R. (2013). Procesgerichte gesprekstherapie: enige gedachten over een procesbehan-deling van normaal intelligente volwassenen met autismespectrumstoornissen (ASS). *Tijdschrift Cliëntgerichte Psychotherapie, 51*(2), 120–127.

Walsh, Y., & Frankland, A. (2009). The next 10 years: Some reflections on earlier predictions for counselling psychology. *Counselling Psychology Review, 24*(1), 38–43.

Wing, L. (1996). *The autistic spectrum.* London: Constable & Robinson.

Wing, L., & Attwood, A. (1987). Syndromes of autism and atypical development. In D. Cohen, & A. Donnellan (Eds.), *Handbook of pervasive developmental disorders* (pp. 3–19). New York: John Wiley & Sons.

Wing, L., Gould, J., & Gillberg, C. (2011). Autism spectrum disorders in the DSM-V: Better or worse than the DSM-IV? *Research in Developmental Disabilities, 32*(2), 768–773.

15 Counselling Psychology for Trauma in Emergency Services Occupations

NOREEN TEHRANI

CHAPTER OUTLINE

INTRODUCTION 215

THE NATURE OF TRAUMATIC EXPOSURE IN ORGANIZATIONS 215

THE IMPACT OF TRAUMA ON EMERGENCY SERVICE PERSONNEL 217

HIGH RISK ROLES AND DUTY OF CARE 218

EARLY TRAUMA INTERVENTIONS 220

TRAUMA THERAPY 222

CONCLUSION 226

LEARNING OUTCOMES

BY THE END OF THIS CHAPTER YOU SHOULD BE ABLE TO ANSWER THE FOLLOWING KEY QUESTIONS:

1. What kinds of events are most likely to cause emergency service workers to experience posttraumatic stress?

2. Why is it important to emergency services to provide support for their workers?

3. What are the essential skills counselling psychologists need to develop for being effective when working in organizational settings?

Counselling Psychology: A Textbook for Study and Practice, First Edition. Edited by David Murphy.
© 2017 John Wiley & Sons Ltd. Published 2017 by John Wiley & Sons Ltd.

INTRODUCTION

Emergency service personnel (ESP) face difficult, demanding, and traumatic situations as part of their everyday work. They become skilled at knowing what to do when others may panic or become overwhelmed with grief. The public rely on fire fighters, police officers, and paramedics to be available to calm, control, comfort, and contain disasters and crisis situations. These activities are not without cost to the ESP in terms of their physical and emotional health and well-being.

This chapter will look at the way in which counselling psychology can be used to support these professional workers to maintain their psychological health and well-being through a systematic approach involving a *control cycle* where psychological screening, surveillance, education, interventions, and monitoring are integrated into the way that the organizations undertake their activities.

The chapter addresses six main sections examining: the nature of traumatic exposure in organizations, the impact of trauma on ESP, high risk roles, and duty of care, the need for early interventions, a trauma therapy programme for ESP, and the role of the counselling psychologist in organizations. It is hoped that the reader will be able to identify the importance of working in a way that meets the needs of organizations and how meeting the needs of the organization through its employees makes good business sense.

Emergency service organizations (ESOs) are under significant pressure to operate within restricted public finances, increase efficiency, and yet deal with some of the most difficult and demanding tasks imaginable. When providing services as a counselling psychologist within an organization it is important to be aware not only of the needs and issues of the employee but also the stresses and strains being experienced by the organization.

This chapter considers a model for support provided for some police, fire and rescue, and ambulance services in the UK. It is not possible within a single chapter to provide in-depth descriptions of all the systems or interventions used, but wherever possible there are references provided that signpost some important information. In this chapter I have concentrated on dealing with traumatic stress; however, ESP have many other counselling needs that are not discussed. At the end of each of the six sections there is a set of reflections that might help the counselling psychologist interested to move into this area of work.

THE NATURE OF TRAUMATIC EXPOSURE IN ORGANIZATIONS

Although ESP expect to deal with death, injury, disasters, and crisis as an everyday part of their role it is important to remember that these men and woman are not very different to the rest of the population. ESP learn how to increase their resilience during training and a probationary period. They pick up and use a range of coping skills to help them deal with the range of incidents that they meet during the course of their work. ESP will almost immediately be expected to respond to traumatic events on a daily basis and most of the time they can cope with this, however, even the most experienced ESP may find themselves getting caught out by a particular event or circumstance. Unexpected events where there is no time for mental preparation create particular difficulty for ESP; for example, investigating a complaint of noise in an expensive block of flats and finding a brutal multiple murder, or being off duty and witnessing someone jump under a train is shocking, leaving no time to mentally prepare and create a professional emotional barrier. ESP can also be upset by circumstances or features of a traumatic event that includes features they can identify with, for example, if the name of a victim is the same or similar to one of their family members or a close friend. This can create an empathic link causing the trauma to feel more meaningful due to the personal connection. ESP may be mentally prepared but become shocked by something strange or unexpected; for example, a paramedic being called to a suicide found that the children of the young woman who had hanged herself were still in the house and as she arrived they were looking at their mother's body.

Sometimes the work activities themselves are risky, involving dealing with major fires or floods, which put the lives of the ESP in danger. When an ESP is killed or severely injured carrying out their duties, other colleagues will experience heightened distress. In these incidents the shift colleagues and others may be left with feelings of responsibility and guilt for not having been able to foresee or prevent the death or injury. This guilt and shame has the potential to complicate the trauma symptoms. Working as a counselling psychologist within emergency services requires being empathetic to victims and bereaved families without becoming entangled and caught up in the emotion; these skills are easier for some people than others, but if they are not developed can cause high levels of stress, potential burnout, and even secondary trauma (Salston & Figley, 2003).

Often a forgotten group in organizations is the professionals who are rather more distant from the traumatic event. This group includes occupational roles where there is a need to investigate or explore what happened in the traumatic event. Investigations in such detail mean that workers recreate in their minds the images and other sensations that accompany the traumatic narrative. These constructed trauma memories can create the full range of trauma responses. This phenomenon has been recognized in the latest version of the Diagnostic and Statistical Manual of Mental Disorders (DSM-5) (American Psychiatric Association, 2013, p. 271–274).

The impact of a traumatic event may involve a complex combination of factors including the nature and meaning of the traumatic event, the experience and training of the employee, and their skills in managing empathetic attunement. It is always important to take a full personal history of an ESP, to understand the nature of the role undertaken and the significance or meaning of the event to them.

THE IMPACT OF TRAUMA ON EMERGENCY SERVICE PERSONNEL

Exposure to one or more traumatic events can lead to a number of responses; these include, amongst others, major depression, anxiety, and posttraumatic stress. However, even the most traumatic events do not automatically lead to the development of a psychiatric condition and a formal diagnosis. In a longitudinal study of posttraumatic stress disorders (PTSDs) Shalev and Yehuda (1998) found that of 211 civilian trauma survivors, 141 showed no symptoms, 16 had pure PTSD, 19 pure anxiety, 11 pure major depression, and the remaining 24 had a mixture of symptoms. DSM-5 (American Psychiatric Association, 2013) has revised the diagnostic criteria for assessing the effects of trauma with the requirement of a tangible precipitating event such as a direct experience, or witnessing or learning about a traumatic incident from others. The symptoms required for making the diagnosis have been revised so that now in addition to the three previous symptoms of hyperarousal, avoidance, and re-experiencing there is an additional symptom of negative alterations in cognitions and mood, which includes the inability to remember aspects of the trauma, negative personal beliefs or expectations, distorted thinking including the apportioning of blame to self or others, a loss of interest in activities, and feelings of detachment. For counselling psychologists working with trauma a useful tool has been developed (Tehrani, 2012) to help identify types of trauma; these begin with a simple traumatic exposure to complex trauma caused by more than one traumatic agent (see Table 15.1).

As the level of complexity in trauma increases, the skills required to work with the client are also greater. Complex cases of traumatic stress where a client has been exposed to relational or developmental trauma require the counselling psychologist to have specialist trauma training.

Table 15.1 *Four Types of Traumatic Exposures*

Simple	Trauma related to a physical event, e.g., earthquake, car crash, accidental injury
Relational	Trauma involving the perceived intentional behaviour of another person(s), e.g., kidnap, rape, bullying, robbery
Developmental	Trauma that occurred at a time in life when the individual had not achieved the capacity to deal with it, e.g., child bereavement, loss of parent, child accident
Complex	a) Trauma related to a combination of two or more of the above, e.g., a car crash where the other driver was drunk, child sex abuse, school bullying. b) A series of traumatic events that are connected by a repetition of one or more traumatic feature

Counselling psychologists need to be confident in their use of psychometric tools and to be able to undertake a full assessment or formulation with their client. Trauma counselling is a specialist area that requires training and experience; it is important to make referrals if the nature of the traumatic exposure is outside the level of competence.

HIGH RISK ROLES AND DUTY OF CARE

For ESP there are a number of risk factors that will increase the occurrence of posttraumatic stress if not handled appropriately at the time of the traumatic exposure. Counselling psychologists working in emergency services need to be active in identifying these risk factors and, where possible, mitigate them through supporting or coordinating an appropriate organizational approach. It is important to manage the various stages of response to the traumatic event, and important to ensure that prior to deployment into known high risk roles (including body recovery, child abuse investigations, and undercover work; Paton & Burke, 2007), ESP are not already experiencing high levels of anxiety, depression, or burnout. They need to have the necessary training, experience, and support to carry out their tasks and should not be currently experiencing posttraumatic stress symptoms related to previous exposure to a trauma event. Exposure to a traumatic event will create a greater impact where (a) it involves significant loss of life, (b) ESP remain at the scene for more than 8 hr, (c) there is intense exposure to horrific sights, or (d) the incident has a special personal meaning, such as the death of a colleague (Tehrani, 2011).

The most appropriate framework to use to manage a traumatic event is based on the Health and Safety Executive (HSE) risk assessment-risk management approach (HSE, 2014). In emergency services there is a known high level of risk of psychological trauma; therefore, a control cycle that deals with all major requirements of the HSE has been adopted in some organizations (Tehrani, 2011, chapter 14) (Figure 15.1).

The trauma control cycle requires an organization being supported by a counselling psychologist to undertake role risk assessments in order to identify the magnitude of risk of trauma involved in all of the ESP roles. ESP should then be screened using reliable and valid screening questionnaires (Tehrani, 2014). There should be a tailored psychoeducation programme and, where necessary, early trauma interventions including trauma-focused therapy. There is also a need for within-post screening surveillance to ensure that the well-being of all the ESP is constantly monitored. Pre-employment screening and ongoing screening is essential in high risk roles where there is a high level of traumatic exposure. Psychological screening can be undertaken online and there are a number of organizations providing these services to organizations. When choosing a provider it is important to ensure that the questionnaires being used are validated through published peer-reviewed journal reports and show good

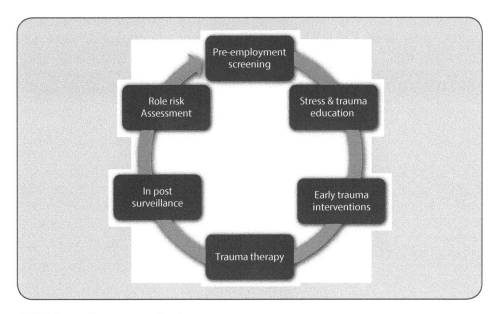

FIGURE 15.1 *Trauma control cycle.*

Source: Tehrani, 2011.

reliability. It is also important to be clear that their use has been authorized by the publishers. There is also a need to check the quality of the data protection to ensure that none of the data can be accessed by unauthorized people.

In the model illustrated in Figure 15.2 the screening data will be guided by inbuilt cut-off points that indicate whether an individual is clearly fit for their role or requires a structured interview to further assess their fitness. The structured interview is typically undertaken by an occupational health nurse or counsellor. Where there are clear indications that the ESP is showing signs of

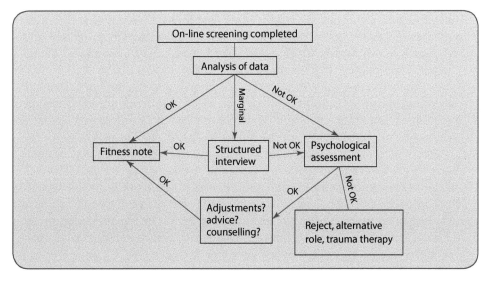

FIGURE 15.2 *Screening and surveillance model.*

significant clinical symptoms, a psychological assessment would be undertaken by a counselling or clinical psychologist. To take part in this programme the occupational health advisors and counsellors will need training in structured interviewing; counselling and clinical psychologists would also be given training to conduct formal structured psychological assessments. These two assessments are critical to identifying what actions need to be taken to safeguard the health of the worker and to help the organization meet its duty of care.

Working in organizations requires the counselling psychologist to understand and respond to the systemic needs of the organization. Counselling is not a neutral process; it needs to be embedded within an organizational system if it is to be successful.

Counselling psychologists may need to develop a range of other skills such as undertaking risk assessments, engaging with rehabilitation planning, and being a witness in court if things go wrong.

EARLY TRAUMA INTERVENTIONS

There are two main types of early interventions following trauma: debriefing and psychological first aid. Although on the surface these appear similar, the origin of the models is different. Debriefing originated in the military and involves a trauma-focused approach. Marshall (1947) identified that, following a battle, military personnel brought together to review or debrief events were able to overcome their fears and gain some sense of mastery over the stressful event. Critical to this debriefing process is the sharing of experiences with colleagues or peers present at the time of the trauma. Debriefing was introduced into emergency services in the early 1980s, with one of the most popular models being critical incident stress debriefing (Mitchell, 1983). Debriefing has been found to significantly reduce distress and increase cohesion within military groups (Shalev, 2000), reduce symptoms of traumatic stress, anxiety, and depression in prison staff (Ruck, Bowes, & Tehrani, 2013), and reduce alcohol use and improve quality of life in fire fighters (Tuckey & Scott, 2013).

Psychological first aid (PFA) has evolved from a model of support originally developed to help civilians involved in a major fire (Lindermann, 1944). Unlike the military and emergency services where the traumatic exposure involves a working team of people briefed and trained in dealing with crises and disasters, members of the public caught up in a disaster are typically unprepared and inexperienced in responding to the demands of the traumatic event. The lack of trauma awareness in the general public makes it difficult to apply the debriefing approach. This is the case apart from in trauma exposed groups that have achieved a high level of social cohesion brought about by regular engagement. This can be found in other working groups such as miners, transport engineers, retailers, bank clerks, or prison staff.

With PFA group members only need to have shared the same traumatic event or experience to benefit from the process. PFA is a resilience building approach where the goal is to instil a sense of safety, calmness, self- and community efficacy, connectedness, and hope (Hobfall, Watson, Bell, Bryant, & Brymer, 2007). There are a number of variants of PFA that have been widely adopted in humanitarian organizations; however, as with debriefing, the evidence of effectiveness is not strong (Deiltjens et al., 2014).

Traumatic incidents can have an immediate impact on ESP and, despite the knowledge that traumatic exposure can cause serious psychological injury, many ESOs are not confident in knowing the best way to respond. Part of the reason for the lack of robust research into early interventions has been the National Institute for Clinical Excellence (NICE) guidance for posttraumatic stress disorder (NICE, 2005), which suggested that psychological debriefing could be harmful. In many ESOs this guidance put a stop to programmes of support that had previously assisted ESP during the first month following a traumatic exposure. However, concern over the quality of the research that underpins the NICE guidance prompted the British Psychological Society's (BPS) Crisis, Disaster and Trauma section to organize two symposia to examine the evidence for and against debriefing and other early interventions (BPS, 2015).

The symposia demonstrated that the evidence for calling for a cessation on the use debriefing was weak. More concerning was the influence that the guidance had on restricting essential research into early interventions, and depriving the ESP of the support that had previously been available to them. To some extent this situation was temporarily addressed by the development of quasi debriefing models. The trauma risk management (TRiM) protocol was developed in the Marines and involves peer support wherein the participants are taken through the traumatic event looking at what happened before, during, and after the trauma exposure, exploring facts, feelings, and the future. The protocol involves assessing 10 risk factors (Jones, Roberts, & Greenberg, 2003).

Support Post Trauma (SPoT) was developed in the Post Office and is a form of debriefing delivered by managers that focuses on exploring the traumatic exposure, identifying sensory experiences, and then providing information and support (Rick, O'Regan, & Kinder, 2006). Following the presentation of the BPS report the NICE guidance executive group has recognized these concerns and thus opened opportunities to researchers to undertake important research that can evaluate the full range of early intervention models (NICE, 2015).

Despite the lack of conclusive evidence for any particular early intervention model, emergency services need to develop a programme of trauma support programmes, which should include three main stages. The first stage is to manage the disaster and its immediate aftermath (Tehrani, 2004). Typically this will involve an assessment of the magnitude of the incident and the impact on all the ESP who may become involved; this should include everyone from the call centre staff receiving the initial calls, the front line professionals dealing with the incident, to the other ESP who may become involved in a postincident supporting or investigatory role. In this stage the responsibility for the well-being of the employees rests with the line manager, who should provide immediate practical, social, and emotional support. The line manager should also provide information on further support and, where necessary, make a referral for an additional intervention within the occupational health section. In emergency services the debriefing approach is the most appropriate, with group debriefing providing the best opportunity for the creation of social support and an opportunity to create a trauma narrative. This can help in reprocessing a fragmented trauma memory into one that can facilitate enhanced understanding and resilience. In some organizations the debriefing is undertaken by trained peers, whilst in other organizations the debriefing will be undertaken by occupational health practitioners, counsellors, and counselling psychologists.

TRAUMA THERAPY

The final stage of the trauma support programme involves a referral for trauma therapy for ESP who find that the posttraumatic stress symptoms continue to disrupt their personal and working life. Although most counselling will involve some difficult and distressing experience, such as bereavement, relationship breakdowns, and redundancy, where the client is suffering from posttraumatic stress symptoms it is important that the counselling psychologist has had the appropriate training in an effective therapeutic model. There are numerous models of trauma therapy; however, only two have been recommended by NICE (NICE, 2005, pp. 52–65). The recommended trauma interventions are Eye Movement Desensitization and Reprocessing (EMDR) (Shapiro, 2001) and trauma-focused cognitive-behavioural therapy (TF-CBT) (Ehlers et al., 2005).

CASE STUDY: TRAUMA THERAPY PROGRAMME FOR EMERGENCY SERVICE PERSONNEL

The following case study details a trauma therapy programme developed for use with ESP. Currently the programme is being delivered within five police forces in the UK, two ambulance, and two fire and rescue services. The ESP referred to the programme have all been identified by the screening and surveillance programme or referred directly by an occupational health professional. This programme is only used when the traumatic exposure has been work-related. The case study presents the trauma therapy programme conducted between 2013 and 2015 in which time there were 60 referrals. In the first year all referrals were from the police; however, in the second year there were also referrals from two ambulance and a fire and rescue service. Of the 60 referrals, 58% were women and 42% men, 17 of the cases were

still open at the time of writing this chapter, and 43 cases have been completed. Of the 43 completed cases 60% were completed within six sessions; the remaining 40% took an additional two sessions with each of these extensions being supported by a written request from the counsellor together with a justification, treatment plan, and treatment objectives.

The background and approach adopted by the trauma counsellors is critical to the success of the programme. Counsellors are all trained and experienced in working within organizations and in providing a service that recognizes the needs of the organization as well as those of the client. Each of the counsellors is supervised by the programme's managing psychologist, and the delivery of interventions is closely monitored and evaluated to ensure the quality and effectiveness of interventions. The counselling adopted an approach involving either TF-CBT or EMDR as the core intervention. The counsellors are all accredited counsellors and trauma psychologists qualified in one or both of these trauma interventions.

The treatment programme involves a clinical screening and referral for between six and eight 1 hr 30 min therapy sessions. The programme's managing psychologist maintains contact with the occupational health service and the trauma therapists throughout the therapy, resolving any issues that arise for the counsellor or the organization. As referrals to the programme were only for work-related trauma, other difficulties are signposted to general workplace counsellors. The work-related traumatic events included (a) primary traumas involving a threat to life, the death of a colleague, or being subject to a violent attack, and (b) secondary trauma, such as dealing with images of child abuse or working with the victims of grooming or sexual abuse. Many of the ESP had experienced childhood traumas that had been reactivated by aspects of the work trauma. Figure 15.3 shows the number of ESP by type experiencing childhood trauma. The results show that ESP described experiencing a trauma incident including sexual, physical, or emotional abuse. Relationship difficulties included the death of a parent, separation, or a parent being sent to prison. Some ESP reported they had been raped during childhood.

The personal and working lives of ESP can often interact with each other, with personal problems reducing resilience and creating difficulties with partners (Hall, Dollard, Tuckey, Winefield, & Thompson, 2010). The screening identified that many of the ESP were coping with a range of difficulties in their personal lives that contributed to their high level of clinical scores. In Figure 15.4 the rates of different personal problems are reported. These included ESP exposure to relationship problems, often marital breakdown or traumatic bereavements, rape—in some cases this was by a colleague, which added to their distress—and problems with alcohol.

The ESP were often exposed to primary trauma in which their own lives were in danger, or they had been involved in the recovery of a body or in rescuing someone seriously injured. ESP could also experience secondary trauma through indirect exposure to traumatic images of child abuse, testimony of victims, or examining evidence related to traumatic events. Figure 15.5 shows the various sources of trauma for ESP.

Therapeutic work planning the ending involved identifying options and strategies to support the ESP in re-engaging with their work role, with colleagues, and, when necessary, looking for alternative roles or employment. The counsellor's suggestions were communicated to the managing

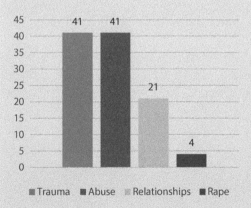

FIGURE 15.3 *Levels of childhood trauma found in ESP (n = 60).*

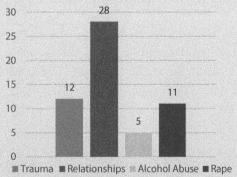

FIGURE 15.4 *Levels of personal trauma found in ESP (n = 60).*

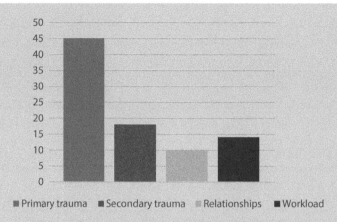

FIGURE 15.5 *Levels of work-related trauma found in ESP (n = 60).*

psychologist, who checked that they were practical and reasonable in terms of the operational constrains of the role. The responsible occupational health advisor and the managing psychologist would then identify reasonable adjustments and rehabilitation plans that will assist a return to work. This advice was communicated to line management and human resources so that the practical implications of the rehabilitation plan could be organized with any changes to shifts, additional support, or temporary or permanent adjustments to the role implemented.

During the final therapy session, a feedback and assessment form is completed by the client. This assesses any changes in clinical symptoms, improvements in functioning, and levels of satisfaction with the programme. The feedback showed that the ESP were broadly satisfied with the services (Figure 15.6).

Clinical scores were assessed using the Goldberg Anxiety/Depression Scale. The results in Figure 15.7 showed a large reduction in mean score for anxiety and depression.

The greatest clinical change was found in the trauma symptoms as measured by the Impact of Events Scale—Revised (Tehrani, Cox, & Cox, 2002), with a mean score of 64 before the trauma counselling and a mean score of 14.1 at the end of the counselling (Figure 15.8).

The sense of coherence questionnaire (Antonovsky, 1979) measures levels of resilience. When employees feel able to find meaning in their work, understand what is expected of them, and are able to manage the nature of the work and the workload, they

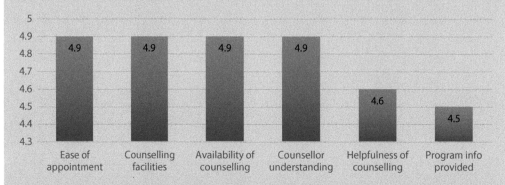

FIGURE 15.6 *Satisfaction with trauma counselling.*

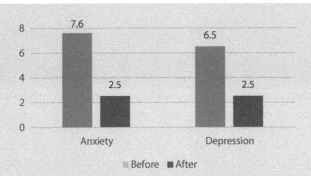

FIGURE 15.7 *Levels of anxiety and depression before and after counselling.*

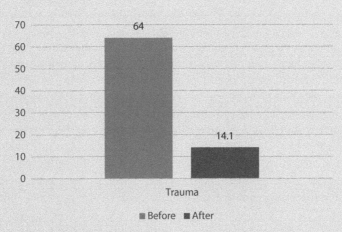

FIGURE 15.8 *Trauma scores.*

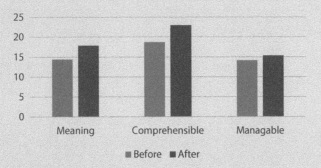

FIGURE 15.9 *Sense of coherence scores.*

are much more likely to be able to deal with trauma, stress, and burnout (Figure 15.9).

These are not particularly good scores, although there have been some improvements. These results can be used to inform the counselling psychologist that when these employees return to work they will need additional support to help them engage with the work more closely, to be better informed on how their role fits into a larger picture, and that they have reasonable workloads and there are reasonable expectations made of them.

CONCLUSION

I have worked as a counselling psychologist in the workplace for over 25 years. I have been given opportunities to work with some incredibly interesting and diverse organizations, and faced many trials and challenges along the way. What I have learned is that to be successful one has to have respect for the organization and a desire to help them become efficient, effective, and responsive to the aspirations and needs of their workers. It is my view that to become an effective organizational counselling psychologist it is essential to gain experience of working in a noncounselling psychology role within an organization where you are faced with problems of managing profits and productivity, facing impossible targets, and working to deadlines. Having access to the language of business, being able to talk about profit and loss accounts, and being interested in the process of re-engineering and marketing not only creates a shared language but also adds to your counselling toolbox. One of the major problems with psychology is our inability or unwillingness to market our products to the real customers. We find comfort in talking about our "wares" in a language that we understand, and provide products and services that are designed to suit us rather than suit our clients and customers. I spend much of my time protecting the health and well-being of organizations, and helping them to become more successful. Working as a counselling psychologist to an organization is not easy, and with some of our individual clients there are times when you have to be courageous in pointing out what you see in their behaviour that may be getting in the way of development and growth.

SUGGESTED FURTHER READING

Tehrani, N. (2004). *Workplace trauma—concepts, assessments and interventions*. London: Taylor & Francis.

Tehrani, N. (2010). *Managing trauma in the workplace: Supporting workers and organisations*. London: Routledge.

REFERENCES

American Psychiatric Association (2013). *Diagnostic and statistical manual of mental disorders (DSM-5)*. Arlington, VA: American Psychiatric Association.

Antonovsky, A. (1979). *Health, stress and coping*. San Francisco, CA and London: Jossey-Bass.

BPS (British Psychological Society) (2015). *Early interventions for trauma*. Leicester: BPS.

Ehlers, A., Clark, D. M., Hackman, A., McManus, F., & Fennell, M. (2005). Cognitive therapy for posttraumatic stress disorder: development and evaluation, *Behaviour, Research and Therapy, 43*(4), 413–431.

Hall, G. H., Dollared, M. F., Tuckey, M. R., Winefield, A. H., & Thompson, B. M. (2010). Job demands, work-family conflict and emotional exhaustion: A longitudinal test of competing theories. *Journal of Occupational and Organizational Psychology, 83*, 237–250.

Hobfall, S. E., Watson, P., Bell C. C., Bryant, R. A., & Brymer, M. J. (2007). Five essential elements of immediate and mid-term mass trauma intervention: Empirical evidence. *Psychiatry, 70*, 283–315.

HSE (2014). Risk assessment: A brief guide to controlling risks in the workplace. Retrieved from http://www.hse.gov.uk/pubns/indg163.pdf (accessed March 9, 2017).

Jones, N., Roberts, P., & Greenberg, N. (2003). Peer group risk assessment: A post-trauma management strategy for hierarchical organisations. *Occupational Medicine, 53*, 469–475.

Lindermann, E. (1944). Symptomatology and management of acute grief. *American Journal of Psychiatry, 101*, 141–149.

Marshall, S. L. A. (1947). *Men under fire: The problem of battle command in future war.* New York: William Morrow.

Mitchell, J. T. (1983). When disaster strikes . . . The critical incident stress debriefing. *Journal of Emergency Medical Services, 13*(11), 49–52.

NICE (National Institute for Clinical Excellence) (2005). *Post-traumatic stress disorder: The management of PTSD in adults and children in primary and secondary care.* London: Gaskell & Leicester, BPS.

NICE (National Institute for Clinical Excellence) (2015). CG26—PTSD, surveillance proposal GE document, 16 June 2015. Retrieved from https://www.nice.org.uk/guidance/cg26/evidence/surveillance-review-decision-2015-546162877 (accessed March 24, 2017).

Paton, D., & Burke, K. J. (2007). Personal and organisational predictors of posttraumatic adaptation and growth in police officers. *Australian Journal of Disasters and Trauma Studies, 1*, 1–16.

Rick, J., O'Regan, S., & Kinder, A. (2006). *Early intervention following trauma: A controlled longitudinal study at Royal Mail Group.* Brighton: IES.

Ruck, S., Bowes, N., & Tehrani, N. (2013). Evaluating trauma debriefing within the UK prison service. *Journal of Forensic Practice, 15*(4), 281–290.

Salston, M. D., & Figley, S. R. (2003). Secondary traumatic stress effects of working with survivors of criminal victimisation. *Journal of Traumatic Stress, 16*(2), 167–174.

Shalev, A. Y. (2000). Stress management and debriefing: historical concepts and present patterns. In B. Raphael, & J. P. Wilson (Eds.), *Psychological debriefing: Theory, practice and evidence* (pp. 17–31). New York, Cambridge University Press.

Shalev, A. Y., & Yehuda, R. (1998). Longitudinal development of traumatic stress disorders. In R. Yehuda (Ed.), *Psychological trauma.* Washington, DC: American Psychiatric Press.

Shapiro, F. (2001). *Eye movement desensitization: Basic principles, protocols and procedures* (2nd ed.). New York: Guildford Press.

Tehrani, N. (2004). *Workplace trauma: concepts, assessment and interventions.* Hove: Routledge.

Tehrani, N. (2011). Supporting employees at risk of developing secondary trauma and burnout. In N. Tehrani (Ed.), *Managing trauma in the workplace: Supporting workers and organisations.* Hove: Routledge.

Tehrani, N. (2012). Bullying and post-traumatic stress. In *Workplace bullying: Symptoms and solutions.* Hove: Routledge.

Tehrani, N. (2014). Psychological screening and surveillance in the workplace. *Occupational Health, November*, 27–29.

Tehrani, N., Cox, T., & Cox, S. (2002). Assessing the impact of traumatic stress incidents: The development of an extended impact of events scale. *Counselling Psychology Quarterly, 9*, 29–36.

Tuckey, M. R., & Scott, J. E. (2013). Group critical incident stress debriefing with emergency services personnel: A randomised controlled trial. *Anxiety, Stress and Coping, 27*, 38–54.

16 Sexualities in Counselling Psychology

ERIC E. ARNOLD AND MELANIE E. BREWSTER

CHAPTER OUTLINE

INTRODUCTION 232

DIVERSE SEXUAL PRACTICES 232

UNPACKING THE ALPHABET SOUP: LGB
IDENTITIES 233

IDENTITY INTERSECTIONALITY
IN A MULTICULTURAL WORLD 235
  Racial/Ethnic Minority Communities 236
  Religiosity 236
  Socioeconomic Status 237
  Level of Urbanity 237

MINORITY STRESS AND
MARGINALIZATION 238

IDENTITY DEVELOPMENT 238

EXPERIENCES IN SCHOOL AND WORK 239

INTIMACY AND FAMILIES 240

PHYSICAL HEALTH IN LGB COMMUNITIES 241

MENTAL HEALTH 242

LEARNING OUTCOMES

BY THE END OF THIS CHAPTER YOU SHOULD
BE ABLE TO ANSWER THE FOLLOWING KEY
QUESTIONS:

1. How has counselling psychology addressed issues of sexuality
   and sexual orientation?

2. What are the ways in which broader
   multicultural issues intersect with diverse
   sexualities?

3. What are the main issues for therapeutic practice regarding sexualities in
   counselling psychology?

Counselling Psychology: A Textbook for Study and Practice, First Edition. Edited by David Murphy.
© 2017 John Wiley & Sons Ltd. Published 2017 by John Wiley & Sons Ltd.

INTRODUCTION

Counselling psychologists' conceptualizations of sexuality and sexual orientation have become increasingly complex and affirming. While the field's treatment of individuals who engage in diverse sexual practices has evolved, members from these communities continue to experience discrimination that impacts their mental health (Bezreh, Weinberg, & Edgar, 2012; Meyer, 2003). This chapter is an overview of stressors uniquely experienced by those who identify as a sexual minority and/or engage in diverse sexual behaviour, protective strategies employed by members of these communities to cope with these stressors, and an examination of a case to illustrate how counselling psychologists can support clients struggling to manage issues around sexuality.

DIVERSE SEXUAL PRACTICES

Despite being difficult to codify, many scholars have attempted to define sexuality parsimoniously (Soble, 2002). For example, theologian Gilbert Meilaender (1987) stated that vaginal penetrative sex between a man and a woman is "the act in which human beings are present most fully and give themselves totally to each other" (p. 47). This myopic perspective of sexuality suggests that straight identified individuals can only be "present most fully" if engaging in vaginal intercourse and simultaneously invalidates those who do not express their sexuality in this way. While narrow in scope, this and similar definitions of sexuality have been widely applied throughout history to restrict what is considered *normal* or *healthy* sexuality (Ullerstam, 1966). Fortunately, the World Health Organization (WHO) (2002) provides a more comprehensive definition of sexuality: the WHO defines sexuality as significant to the human experience and posits that sexuality "encompasses sex, gender identities and roles, sexual orientation, eroticism, pleasure, intimacy and reproduction" (WHO, 2002, p. 5). This definition challenges the oft-held belief that sexuality is static. Rather, sexuality—much like sexual orientation—is fluid and can be conceptualized as existing on a continuum of behaviours, feelings, and beliefs.

Across cultures, sexual and romantic desires are assumed to be both normative and ubiquitous aspects of the human experience (Scherrer, 2008). Considering the assumed universality of sexual drives, those who do not experience such sensations may be made to feel aberrant or marginal to the broader "sexual" society. However, roughly 1% of the population identifies as asexual—a group characterized by a lack of attraction towards or desire for sexual activity with other people (Bogaert, 2004). A growing body of scholarship suggests that there may be notable diversity among individuals who identify with asexual communities. For example, some asexual people may still desire romantic relationships (with or without physical expressions of intimacy), some may regularly masturbate, and some may express no sexual or romantic interest; despite their general lack of interest in sex, most asexual people still report having a clear sexual orientation towards other genders (Brotto, Knudson, Inskip, Rhodes, & Erskine, 2010; Scherrer, 2008).

Those who are interested in sex but prefer sexual experiences that involve various fetishes (e.g., leather, domination, feet, transvestism) may identify as kinky. *Kink* is an identity that is as salient as sexual orientation, race, or gender for some individuals. Many in the kink community have taken steps to ensure that their sexual expression is practised ethically; credos like "safe, sane, and consensual" and the practice of "risk aware consensual kink" guide individuals in their sexual exploration (Stein, 2002; Switch, 2001). Unfortunately, despite taking such precautions to ensure safe sexual play, many perceive variations of sexual behaviour like bondage, dominance, and sadomasochism (BDSM) as deviant and pathological (Nichols, 2006). However, empirical evidence suggests that individuals in the BDSM community are psychologically and socially well-adjusted, are better educated, and earn higher incomes than those who engage in conventional sexual practices (Moser & Levitt, 1987).

Both the Diagnostic and Statistical Manual of Mental Disorders Fifth Edition (DSM-5) and the International Statistical Classification of Diseases and Related Health Problems Tenth Revision (ICD-10) include sexual variations in their lists of mental disorders, the inclusion of which can serve to stigmatize individuals who engage in these behaviours. The DSM-5 has attempted to reduce stigma by only including sexual behaviours that are performed with nonconsenting partners and/or sexual behaviours that cause impairment to daily interpersonal and occupational functioning. Fortunately, some practitioners have recognized the deleterious effects of espousing a narrow definition of sexuality and as a result have adopted a sex positive clinical orientation. Sex positivity is guided by the simple principle that "sex is good" (Glickman, 2000).

In addition to the various expressions of sexuality, there is also variety in terms of how individuals organize their romantic relationships. Monogamy is often used as the template for how romantic relationships are cultivated. However, findings indicate that this is an erroneous assumption. A study of more than 3,500 families in the United States found that 15–28% of the sample was in a nonmonogamous relationship (Weitzman, 2006). Some define these relationships as polyamorous. Graham (2014) defines polyamory as "'many' and 'love,' [and as] . . . the philosophy or state of being in love or romantically involved with more than one person at the same time" (p. 1031). Clinicians should attend to hidden biases about polyamory; even a well-intentioned couple therapist can further stigmatize people who are polyamorous if they are unaware of their internalization of monogamy as the norm for conceptualizing relationships.

UNPACKING THE ALPHABET SOUP: LGB IDENTITIES

The past two decades have yielded unprecedented progress in rights movements for LGB communities across the world. From marriage equality legislation, to employment discrimination protection, to increased protection against hate crimes, campaigns for civil liberties moved from grassroots platforms to the topics of popular young adult television shows. Yet, despite these changes in social and political climates, deeper public knowledge regarding the lived experiences of LGB people remains limited. The same news and media outlets that have helped spread awareness about civil rights issues often also paint the LGB community as a monolithic group, with members sharing the same needs, values, and characteristics.

Use of the phrase *sexual minorities* to describe "LGBT"—the 'T' signifying transgender—people is one clear indication of monolithic grouping. Aptly stated by Fassinger and Arsenau (2007, p. 19), "the increasingly frequent addition of 'T' to 'LGB' speaks to the public—and professional—conflation of all sexual minority concerns under a shared umbrella of invisibility, isolation, and discrimination." A more accurate snapshot of human sexuality would be a series of spectra, wherein sex, gender, attraction, and behaviours were each flexible and independent from one another, rather than dichotomous and inter-dependent classifiers. For example, someone whose biological sex is male is assumed to identify his gender as "man," be attracted to individuals who iden-tify as women, and only engage in sexual behaviours with people whose biological sex is female.

Increasingly, sexual identity is discussed as a multidimensional construct, capturing—but not limited to—attraction, sexual behaviours, emotional con-nections, social preferences, lifestyle desires, societal gender roles, erotic fantasies, and gender identity (Peplau & Garnets, 2000). Considering this multi-dimensionality, the same person from the previous example may have had their sex assigned "male" at birth, but identify their gender as androgynous and their sexual orientation as queer; they may choose to have close emotional partner-ships with women, but sexual encounters with transgender men. Clearly, sexu-alities are rarely one size fits all. Even within the confines of labels that most people are familiar with—such as "lesbian"—there may be notable within-group variations and within-person variations in attraction levels, behaviours, and self-identity (Diamond, 2008). Thus, the following definitions should be read critically, knowing that they may not fully capture the lived experiences of all sexual minorities who claim these terms as their own.

Sex refers to biological markers of male-ness (e.g., XY chromosomes, androgens, male genitalia, secondary sex characteristics such as an Adam's apple) and female-ness (e.g., XX chromosomes, female genitalia, secondary sex characteristics), typically noted and formally assigned by a doctor at birth. Most often, doctors assign sex at birth by visual inspection of a baby—not by examining chromosomes or hormones. While people often assume that bio-logical sex yields only two options (male or female), such an assumption overlooks the realities of biology. Individuals may also be born *intersex*, gener-ally described as someone whose anatomy does not clearly fit all the markers of male or female. Sometimes these differences are notable at birth, some-times they are only detected later in life during an attempt to have a child, and sometimes they are not detected at all. And of course, even among individuals of the same sex who are not intersex, genitalia can look dramatically different person by person.

Sexual orientation is defined as a sense of to whom one feels attracted sexually, emotionally, and/or relationally—generally, we think of sexual orientations as including identities such as heterosexual, gay, lesbian, and bisexual. *Heterosexual* people typically desire to have romantic and/or sexual encounters with people of another gender. Individuals who are transgender may also identify as heterosexual (i.e., a transgender woman who is in a relationship with a man), which is why it is inappropriate to assume that transgender people are by default LGB or "sexual minorities."

Gay used to be used as a broader term to capture anyone who was attracted to people of their own gender; currently, the term gay is primarily used for men who are attracted to other men. The term "homosexual" is typically not preferred among LGB people as it is considered antiquated and reminiscent of a medical model that pathologized same-sex attraction (for more, see Herek, 2010). Complementary to gay, *lesbian* refers to women who are attracted to other women. *Bisexual* people are individuals who have the capacity to be erotically and/or relationally attracted to women and men. In more recent years, other sexual orientations such as *pansexual* or *omnisexual* have emerged to challenge labels tending to discuss attraction on a gender binary (woman/man). Someone who is pansexual, for example, might state that they are attracted to "the person" and do not care what their gender identity or presentation is. Other identities such as *demisexual* and *sapiosexual* have also arisen in response to views that LGB orientations position physical appearance-based attraction over other dimensions of attraction (e.g., intelligence). Finally, *pomosexual* (short for postmodern) and *queer* are both identities that individuals may use when they do not want their sexualities to be defined or constrained by traditional sexual orientation labels. Of course, transgender people (see Chapter 19) may claim any of the sexual orientations described above.

Importantly, sexual orientation and gender diversity are always framed by culture, experience, and worldview. Much of the earliest framing of LGB experiences was laden with white/European values and biases, and negated cross-cultural differences in identities. Thus, attending to the many ways in which race/ethnicity, religiosity, socioeconomic status, and level of urbanity interact with identity is crucial.

IDENTITY INTERSECTIONALITY IN A MULTICULTURAL WORLD

The *intersectionality model* (Cole, 2009) purports that identification with more than one minority group (e.g., race, social class, sexual orientation) constructs a novel experience that is nonadditive and not divisible into individual and isolated identities. For instance, a person may be both a Thai immigrant and a lesbian woman, but the intersectionality model contends that each identity's meaning and associated experience can only be fully understood within the context of the other social identities with which they coexist (Diamond & Butterworth, 2008). Illustratively, in some studies about prejudice, researchers note that participants have difficulty determining the social identity that elicited the discrimination experiences they described (Yoder & McDonald, 1998). Rather than attributing their discrimination experiences to being a *lesbian*, *woman*, or *Thai*, they stated that their experiences were due to their being a *Thai lesbian woman*, a unique social identity intersection not reducible to any one identity alone.

Racial/Ethnic Minority Communities

Compared to scholarship from white/European framing, little research and practice has attended to the experiences of LGB people from diverse racial and ethnic backgrounds (e.g., Huang et al., 2010). In addition, some of the literature that has begun to address these communities has been littered with limitations (DeBlaere, Brewster, Sarkess, & Moradi, 2010). The use of culturally aware and inclusive terminology continues to be problematic, as many racial/ethnic minority people do not identify as LGB; terms such as *same-gender loving* or *Fa'fafine* may be used commonly within cultural communities, but be unknown to scholars and clinicians (DeBlaere et al., 2010).

Given the significant immigration histories of Asian populations in the UK, level of acculturation and enculturation and associated traditionality of family values are important to consider when conceptualizing the identity development and experience of Asian LGB people. Lower levels of acculturation and more traditional family values may be linked to lower tolerance towards LGB people within families; moreover, values common among many Asian cultures such as respect, deference to elders, interdependence, *ishin-denshin* (communicating without words), conformity, and maintenance of traditional gender roles may contribute to explicitly coming out being viewed as threatening, disrespectful, and/or a disobedient act towards the family and a rejection of traditional cultural values (Akerlund & Cheung, 2000). Consequently, some LGB Asian individuals may fear coming out because they believe that they will bring shame to their families, be shunned by their community, or have their identity negated/denied.

Similarly, while closeness of family can provide a source of support for LGB youth, it may also foster a need to remain secretive about sexual orientation identity if youth believe that their identity will not be accepted. Further, close-knit family structures in some cultures often come with the expectation that youth will live with their parents until they are married: an arrangement that is understandably problematic for an LGB or a gender diverse person who is not out to their family (Akerlund & Cheung, 2000). To evade heterosexist stigma and in-group discrimination, some LGB people may engage in unsafe same-gender sex on the "down low"—a practice that is linked with sexually transmitted infections (Wolitski, Jones, Wasserman, & Smith, 2006).

Religiosity

Religious affiliations often provide support systems for their congregations—and for many people, strong faith is linked to psychological well-being and physical health (Steger & Frazier, 2005). However, this link is muddier for LGB individuals when "religions in general, and Christianity in particular, are often perceived as anathema" to LGB identity (O'Brien, 2004, p. 180). Copious research documents the persistence of heterosexist attitudes and policies within religious groups; for example, one woman in a qualitative study reflected upon growing up as a lesbian youth in the Pentecostal church and stated when it came to LGB issues, the preacher would "always group us in with the so-called perverts, you know, like child molesters and just awful people" (Barton, 2010, p. 472). Traumatizing early experiences such as these are depicted commonly in research with religious LGB people (Gold, 2008). It is important to note, however, that a growing body of research finds that many LGB people are able to make peace with their beliefs and sexuality, overcome guilt and feelings of betrayal, and find affirming spiritual groups and religious communities with whom they can connect (Halderman, 2004). Finally, some people may decide that they can be fulfilled without formal ties to a belief system—compared with heterosexual people, LGB people are about 30% more likely to identify as atheist (Brewster, 2013).

Socioeconomic Status

Consistent with an intersectionality perspective, socioeconomic status (SES) must be considered within the context of its complex interactions with other salient identities—as evidence points to strong links between poverty and psychological distress (Smith, 2005). Classist attitudes and actions enable those of more privileged social classes to discriminate, exclude, and disempower the poor. Among the most poor, homelessness rates are rising, with LGB youth being among some of the most vulnerable to homelessness (Reck, 2009). While not necessarily a product of childhood poverty, LGB youth may be kicked out of their homes and lose the economic support of their families because of their sexual orientations or gender identities. In these circumstances, LGB individuals may be forced to employ more extreme strategies (e.g., dealing drugs or sex work) to obtain money for food and shelter (Reck, 2009). Considering the bleak protections for sexual orientation and gender-based workplace discrimination in some countries (discussed later), finding a safe and steady job may be challenging for some LGB people (Brewster et al., 2014).

Level of Urbanity

To date, most scholarship on LGB issues has focused on the experiences of people who live in large cities and metropolitan regions as they tend to be easier to sample (Huang et al., 2010). Because of the emphasis on urban LGB people, much less is known about the development of LGB youth and families in suburban or rural areas—however, some limited data suggest that LGB people may opt to often remain invisible due to overarching fear and discomfort in rural areas (D'Augelli & Hart, 1987). Oswald and Culton (2003) discuss the prevailing attitude that "rural" and "gay" are incompatible terms. This perceived incompatibility may be compounded by influential community leaders (e.g., church leaders, city officials) if they do not acknowledge LGB individuals or espouse gay affirming attitudes.

Additionally, rural communities often have fewer resources for LGB issues. Parents of LGB youth in these regions may have nowhere to go for support, no models for how to cope with their children's coming out, and no help from organizations such as "Parents and Friends of Lesbians and Gays" (PFLAG;

Oswald & Culton, 2003). While support structures are readily available in metropolitan regions, they may be viewed as too controversial for more rural and religiously conservative villages and townships. For adults, some of the most accessible gay social opportunities may be gay bars. However, most of these venues are not accessible to underage youth; as such, LGB people may rely heavily on the internet—social media such as Facebook, Twitter, and Tumblr, or sex/dating apps like Grindr—for their community support (Oswald & Culton, 2003).

MINORITY STRESS AND MARGINALIZATION

Exposure to heterosexism, transphobia, and other societal views that marginalize people with diverse sexual orientations and gender identities may create a chronically stressful environment. Grounded in the work of pioneering scholars in the area of psychological stress who theorized that disproportionate stress due to minority status may be linked to higher rates of psychological distress among minority populations (e.g., Allport, 1954), research specific to marginalized groups highlights that such stressors may be related to poor psychological outcomes for some individuals. The Pew Research Center (2013a) found higher numbers of LGB victims of sexual and physical violence compared with heterosexuals. This report also found that two-thirds of LGB adults had experienced some form of discrimination because of their sexual orientation, while 30% of respondents reported having been physically threatened or attacked. For LGB persons, it is important for clinicians to acknowledge that experiences of specific stressors (e.g., heterosexist prejudice and violence) may translate to psychological distress, discussed further later. Thus, scholars and clinicians should be aware of how minority stressors may pervade and interact with other dimensions of life (e.g., forming relationships, school, work) for LGB people.

IDENTITY DEVELOPMENT

"Coming out" as LGB involves disclosure of one's same-gender attraction to other people. One's degree of "outness," or conversely the decision to conceal one's sexual orientation, depends on a number of factors; for example, concealment of same-gender attraction may serve to protect an individual from discrimination or harm in a situations in which anti-LGB sentiment is explicit. On the other hand, as Shilo and Savaya (2011) found in their study of youths in Tel Aviv, peer and familial support foster positive coming out experiences. The researchers discovered most individuals in their sample expressed same-gender attraction by age 16. The coming out process begins with self-acceptance prior to external disclosures. This process has formally been described using stage models.

Stage models are widely cited in psychological literature on the development of sexual orientations. Cass' (1979) six-stage identity formation model conceptualizes the process through which gay and lesbian individuals progress towards developing an integrated and positive same-gender orientation. Cass' model posits that same-gender attraction begins in a stage of identity confusion and—through the successful resolution of various internal and external conflicts—arrives at the most "actualized" stage, identity synthesis. While Cass' and similar stage models provide a rough framework for understanding lesbian and gay identity, many researchers believe that stage models are limited in their ability to effectively capture the nuances of *coming out*—for instance, these models fail to adequately address gender, fluidity of sexuality/same-gender sexual orientation, bisexual identity development, race, culture, ethnicity, and the experiences of youth (Reynolds & Hanjorgiris, 2000).

Few studies have focused explicitly on the identity development of bisexual or sexually fluid individuals; however, recent work has highlighted the tendency of bisexual youth to embrace sexual fluidity and express "a reluctance to label their sexuality" (Entrup & Firestein, 2007, p. 89). Unfortunately, bisexual men and women can experience invalidation from heterosexual men and women, gay men, and lesbian women; bisexual men and women may wrongly be accused of being confused or presumed to occupy a bisexual identity until they fully accept their gay/lesbian or heterosexual sexual orientation. Not only must bisexual individuals create, accept, and maintain their sexual orientation, but they must do so despite "encounters with cultural bias, denial, and personal invalidation, which [all] carry constant threats of isolation and invisibility" (Bradford, 2004, p. 19).

The roles of race, culture, and ethnicity must be considered as factors that may affect LGB identity development. For example, the Stonewall Report on Ethnicity and Health (2012) found that black men in the UK are twice as likely to describe themselves as bisexual compared with white men. One could argue that racial identity may impact black men's decision to come out as gay. On the other hand, this finding may also suggest that black men are more affirming of a bisexual identity. Other studies in the United States have found that Latino youths report earlier awareness of a sexual minority identity compared with their black and white cohorts, and that Asian American youths tend to engage in same-sex sexual behaviour only after identifying as gay or bisexual (Dubé & Savin-Williams, 1999).

EXPERIENCES IN SCHOOL AND WORK

In the summer of 2014, school boards across British Columbia passed formal policies to protect the rights of LGB and gender diverse students (Loutzenheiser, 2015). Such actions in Canada are representative of larger movements to acknowledge that children and teens often experience homophobic and transphobic bullying in schools. Peer victimization has strong links to mental health and educational outcomes: LGB students who were bullied have lower grades, higher truancy, greater expectations that they will not finish school, and lower expectations that they will attend university (Aragon, Poteat, Espelange, & Koenig, 2014). While many of the harmful actions perpetrated in schools are from peers, reports often indicate that teachers and administrators may also intentionally or inadvertently contribute to an unsafe environment for their LGB students. The National School Climate Survey from the United States reported that almost 64% of LGB students sampled report feeling unsafe at school because of their sexual orientation (Kosciw, Greytak, & Diaz, 2009). Another large-scale study from the United States found that nearly 34% of youth who reported a homophobic bullying experience to a teacher or professional at school said nothing was done in response to help them (Kosciw et al., 2010). Such patterns of feeling marginalized within the primary context of one's daily life may continue as LGB individuals leave school and enter the workforce.

Studies have explored the links of factors such as workplace climate, experiences of discrimination, and identity management with health and vocational outcomes for LGB people (e.g., Brewster, Velez, DeBlaere, & Moradi, 2012; Hufmann, Watrous-Rodriguez, & King, 2008). When LGB employees face "chilly" climates at their workplaces, they report lower job satisfaction, less productivity, and higher intention to quit; by contrast, working in an environment that affirms LGB identities promotes job satisfaction and broader psychological health (Waldo, 1999). Such outcomes must be considered in the legal climate of certain countries (i.e., the United States) where there may not be national laws prohibiting employment discrimination based on sexual orientation or gender identity.

Scott Button (2004) discussed the use of "identity management strategies" at work. Such strategies refer to opting to disclose or conceal one's LGB identity at work. These approaches may arise in the use of different techniques such as being explicitly out (e.g., talking about being gay with your colleagues), being implicitly out (e.g., having a picture of your same-gender partner on your desk at work, but not necessarily talking about them), passing (e.g., letting people assume that you are heterosexual), or covering one's sexual orientation (e.g., denying going to gay bars or changing the gender pronoun when talking about a partner). The success of identity management strategies is partially dependent on perceived climate of the organization and personal comfort level. For some individuals, being more "in the closet" at work may actually be safer (if they are in an unaffirming workplace), while for others concealing a large part of who you are at work may be very stressful and hinder forging genuine connection with coworkers. Before advising an LGB client to "come out" at work, it is important to assess the climate of their workplace and whether they would have support from supervisors and colleagues.

INTIMACY AND FAMILIES

Recent data suggest that people in many countries throughout Europe believe that LGB individuals should be accepted by society (Pew Research Center, 2013b). This global shift in views about LGB individuals is forcing people to confront antiquated stereotypes about same-gender relationships and simultaneously redefine what is considered a "normal" relationship. Comparisons between heterosexual and same-gender couples reveal more within- than between-group differences. In fact, Green (2012) found that longevity in heterosexual and same-gender couples were predicted by similar variables. However, studies do indicate that same-gender couples and heterosexual couples differ across a number of domains. For example, Gotta and colleagues (2011) found that same-gender couples tend to divide household labour and decision making more equally than heterosexual couples, noting that same-gender couples cannot rely upon stereotypic gender norms to dictate roles or authority. Thus, they are forced to define household rules and tasks based on skill and preference versus what is assumed to be the job of a man or woman. Research has also indicated that when conflict does arise within same-gender couples—compared with heterosexual couples—"softer initiation" of confrontation and more humour is used to avoid escalating tension (Green, 2012). Lastly, same-gender relationships tend to not last as long as heterosexual relationships. Research suggests that same-gender couples may not be as likely to "tough it out" as heterosexual couples because same-gender couples are less likely to have children (Green, 2012).

Another between-group difference is that coupled gay men tend to have higher rates of nonmonogamous agreements than heterosexual couples (Gotta et al., 2011). Researchers posit that this is likely the result of men being more likely than women to engage in nonmonogamy or because gay men may be more willing than heterosexual men and woman to admit to nonmonogamous behaviour. Relatedly, Weitzman (2006) noted that a growing number of LGB people are forming polyamorous relationships. While prevalence rates vary, some studies have noted that anywhere from 33–65% of LGB people may be in consensually nonmonogamous relationships (Blumstein & Schwartz, 1983; Page, 2004).

With respect to child rearing, same-gender couples are less likely to become parents than heterosexual couples. While there may be a number of reasons for this, some may include the cost prohibitive nature of adoption, insemination, and gestational carrier/surrogacy fees. The process requires intensive planning and a level of organization that may be beyond the capabilities of many couples.

PHYSICAL HEALTH IN LGB COMMUNITIES

Research indicates that LGB individuals are at increased risk for a variety of physical and sexual health concerns. The vulnerability of these groups to various health issues underscores how important it is for health care systems to remove any barriers preventing sexual minority and gender diverse individuals from accessing necessary treatment.

Lesbians and bisexual women are overrepresented in modifiable risk factors that cause heart disease and—compared with heterosexual women—they have higher rates of obesity, alcohol and tobacco use, and stress (Cochran, 2009; Diamant, Wold, Spitzer, & Gelberg, 2000). Sexual minority women may also be at higher risk for breast, endometrial, and ovarian cancer. While few studies have focused on sexually transmitted infection (STI) transmission among women who have sex with women (WSW), Diamant and colleagues (2000) found that lesbian women may be at risk for certain STIs. A study conducted by Stevens and Hall (2001) found that 56% of WSW engaged in sexual risk behaviours such as having unprotected oral sex and sharing unsterilized sex toys. One explanation for this finding was that WSW had a lack of knowledge about risk behaviour and disease transmission that occluded them from taking the necessary steps to protect themselves from STIs.

Heart disease has also been found to be a concern for sexual minority men, with studies finding a higher prevalence of modifiable risk factors like smoking among gay and bisexual men compared with heterosexual men (Ryan, Wortley, Easton, Pederson, & Greenwood, 2000). Men who have sex with men (MSM) are at increased risk of developing anal cancer from human papillomavirus (HPV), which can be transmitted through anal sex (Ryan, Compton, & Mayer, 2000). However, one of the most glaring risks to the health of MSM continues to be HIV. Illustratively, a report by Public Health England estimated that 1 in 20 MSM was HIV-positive (Skingsley, 2015). Fortunately, treatment as prevention interventions such as post-exposure prophylaxis (PEP: antiretroviral medication taken by HIV-negative individuals 24–72 hr after HIV exposure) and pre-exposure prophylaxis (PrEP: antiretroviral medication taken daily by HIV-negative individuals to reduce the likelihood of seroconversion if exposure to HIV occurs) have yielded promising results regarding HIV prevention, and have the potential to reduce the number of new HIV infections among MSM (Baeten et al., 2015).

Systemically, discrimination creates barriers for LGB people who attempt to access health care. One study found that 98% of individuals surveyed believed it was important to come out to service providers, yet 64% also believed that this disclosure would have negative consequences regarding their care (Shatz & O'Hanlan, 1994). Patients may experience increased anxiety when deciding if they should disclose their sexual orientation to care providers. As a protective strategy to guard against discrimination, patients may not disclose their sexual orientation and thus foreclose the possibility of getting the most accurate and effective care.

MENTAL HEALTH

Turning towards mental health, while attitudes about LGB issues are rapidly changing, there is a legacy of mistreatment of this population that continues to impact their mental health. As previously discussed, minority stress (e.g., stigma and discrimination) is now posited to be at the heart of discrepant rates of mental health concerns for LGB people compared with heterosexual people. Specifically, within LGB groups, minority stressors have been found to be related to a number of psychological distress indicators including high risk sexual behaviours, anxiety, depression, substance abuse, eating disorders, self-harm, and suicidal ideation (Meyer, 2003; Szymanski, Kashbubeck-West,

& Meyer, 2008). King and colleagues (2008) reported that LGB individuals have a risk of depression and anxiety that is 1.5 times higher than heterosexual individuals. Studies reveal that the risk of suicide attempts for lesbian, gay, and bisexuals is approximately twice as great as the risk for heterosexuals (Institute of Medicine, 2011).

The literature reveals a need for culturally competent mental health care for LGB individuals. Unfortunately, barriers often stand in the way of LGB individuals accessing the support they need. These barriers include a lack of health insurance, fear of discrimination, dissatisfaction with services, and lack of sensitivity to LGB issues on the part of providers (Heck, Sell, & Gorin, 2006). The following case example illustrates the importance of multicultural therapy when working with a client in a clinical setting.

PRESENTING CONCERNS

Darren is a 20-year-old black male living in New York. Darren presented to treatment with depressive symptoms related to the end of his relationship—he has not been eating regularly, his sleep is restless, and he has lost interest in his school work. Darren reported that he has been using crystal methamphetamine ("Tina"). When he uses Tina he logs on to Grindr to find sex partners to engage in anonymous, unprotected sex. Darren revealed that his ex-boyfriend, Jason, ended their relationship because the client refused to disclose his sexual orientation to his friends and family.

Client Background

Darren is an only child and of black-English and Jamaican heritage. He was raised in a rural town in northern England. Regarding his family life, Darren reported having supportive parents; they affirmed his unique heritages and made sure Darren was equipped to combat racism. Darren recalled, however, that his parents held anti-LGB beliefs. Darren has always been attracted to men and women, but because of his parents' negative attitudes about LGB individuals he never explored his attraction to men.

Darren met Jason at a party during his freshman year. After a night of drinking, Jason confessed his attraction to Darren. Darren reported being repelled by the disclosure initially, however, a week later Darren expressed that the feeling was mutual and they began a clandestine relationship. Darren did not feel comfortable being affectionate with Jason unless they were using Tina. Darren's ex-partner is the only person who knows Darren identifies as bisexual.

Treatment

Multicultural counselling requires that the therapist conceptualize the client's distress in the context of larger sociopolitical issues that may contribute to how the client presents. Multicultural counselling also requires the therapist to have an awareness of their own social location and how this positionality may impact treatment. This is particularly relevant for this case. A therapist working with Darren should explore their own identity development across race, sexual orientation, and gender. For example, a therapist who is unaware of the importance of racial identity may erroneously assume that Darren's parents' anti-LGB beliefs discredit them from being a source of support for him. In fact, not only has Darren received love and support from his parents, but they have also been instrumental in helping Darren develop protective factors to combat individual and systemic racism. A therapist working with Darren must be able to hold the complexity of his relationship with his parents; to assume that foreclosure of this relationship is the best course of action is shortsighted and neglects the importance of Darren's race and cultural identities. Additionally, this could rupture one of the few remaining support systems in Darren's life and ultimately exacerbate the client's depressive symptoms. However, the therapist must also be willing to challenge anti-LGB sentiments that Darren's parents and society have and support the client as he explores how his bisexual identity development has been impacted by these negative beliefs.

Early treatment should also focus on building rapport with the client. This is especially relevant considering that the only person who affirmed Darren as an integrated whole (Jason) is no longer in his life. Early treatment should focus on creating a healthy, supportive, and affirming therapeutic relationship. As treatment progresses, it may be useful to begin to use interventions to help Darren process his feelings about the end of his relationship. Within the context of a multicultural therapeutic alliance, the therapist may use Gestalt interventions to help Darren become more aware of his emotional experience. The therapist can work with Darren in the treatment room to identify how sadness is manifested physiologically (e.g., heaviness in chest, slumping shoulders, unable to smile). The therapist and Darren can then begin to use here-and-now interventions to help the client express this emotion in treatment. Once this foundational therapeutic work has been established, the therapist and client can then explore Darren's history and identify situations that have caused him to feel similarly (e.g., when he heard his parents make anti-LGB statements). Finally, the client and therapist can develop concrete strategies for managing sadness moving forward (e.g., physiological awareness, going to the gym, calling a friend, journalling).

Multicultural counsellors need to act as liaisons between clients and support systems. A therapist working with Darren should consult with local organizations to identify groups that may be appropriate for Darren (e.g., support groups for depression, substance use, bisexuality).

This case exemplifies the necessity of counselling psychologists to be aware of and sensitive to multicultural issues. Darren has few outlets where he is able to understand himself as an integrated being—creating a space for him to do so will improve the therapist's ability to help Darren manage depressive symptoms related to his recent break up.

SUGGESTED FURTHER READING

Bieschke, K. J., Perez, R. M., & DeBord, K. A. (Eds.) (2007). *Handbook of counseling and psychotherapy with lesbian, gay, bisexual, and transgender clients* (2nd ed., pp. 19–49). Washington, DC: American Psychological Association.

Huang, Y., Brewster, M. E., Moradi, B., Goodman, M., Wiseman, M., & Martin, A. (2010). Content analysis of literature about LGB people of color: 1998–2007. *The Counseling Psychologist, 38,* 363–396. DOI: 10.1177/0011000009335255

REFERENCES

Akerlund, M., & Cheung, M. (2000). Teaching beyond the deficit model: Gay and lesbian issues among African Americans, Latinos, and Asian Americans. *Journal of Social Work Education, 36,* 279–292.

Allport, G. W. (1954). *The nature of prejudice*. Cambridge, MA: Perseus Books.

Aragon, S. R., Poteat, V. P., Espelange, D. L., & Koenig, B. W. (2014). The influence of peer victimization on educational outcomes for LGBTQ and non-LGBTQ high school students. *Journal of LGBT Youth, 11*, 1–19.

Baeten, J., Heffron, R., Kidoguchi, L., Mugo, N., Katabira, E., Bukusi, E., . . . & Celum, C. (2015). *Near elimination of HIV transmission in a demonstration project of PrEP and ART*. Abstract number 24: Preventing HIV and HSV-2: What will it take? Seattle, Wa.

Barton, B. (2010). "Abomination"—Life as a bible belt gay. *Journal of Homosexuality, 57*, 465–484. DOI: 10.1080/00918361003608558

Bezreh, T., Weinberg, T.S., & Edgar, T. (2012). BDSM disclosure and stigma management: Identifying opportunities for sex education. *American Journal of Sexuality Education, 7*(1), 37–61.

Blumstein, P., & Schwartz, P. (1983). *American couples: Money, work, sex*. New York: Morrow.

Bogaert, A. F. (2004). Asexuality: Prevalence and associated factors in a national probability sample. *Journal of Sex Research, 41*, 279–287. DOI: 10.1080/00224490409552235

Bradford, M. (2004). The bisexual experience. *Journal of Bisexuality, 4*(1–2), 7–23.

Brewster M. E. (2013). Atheism, gender, and sexuality. In S. Bullivant, M. Ruse M. (Eds.), *The Oxford handbook of atheism* (pp. 511–524). Oxford: Oxford University Press.

Brewster, M. E., Velez, B. L., DeBlaere, C., & Moradi, B. (2012). Transgender individuals' workplace experiences: The applicability of sexual minority measures and models. *Journal of Counseling Psychology, 59*, 60–70.

Brewster, M. E., Velez, B. L., Mennicke, A., & Tebbe, E. (2014). Voices from beyond: A thematic content analysis of transgender employees' workplace experiences. *Psychology of Sexual Orientation and Gender Diversity, 1*, 159–169.

Brotto, L. A., Knudson, G., Inskip, J., Rhodes, K., & Erskine, Y. (2010). Asexuality: A mixed-methods approach. *Archives of Sexual Behavior, 39*, 599–618. DOI: 10.1007/s10508-008-9434-x

Button, S. (2004). Identity management strategies utilized by lesbian and gay employees: A quantitative investigation. *Group and Organization Management, 29*, 470–494.

Cass, V. C. (1979). Homosexual identity formation: A theoretical model. *Journal of Homosexuality, 4*(3), 219–235.

Cochran, S. D. (2009). *Review of lesbian and bisexual health FAQ*. Washington, DC: United States Department of Health and Human Services Office on Women's Health of the Council of Representatives. *American Psychologist, 30*, 620–651.

Cole, E. R. (2009). Intersectionality and research in psychology. *American Psychologist, 64*, 170–180. DOI: 10.1037/a0014564

D'Augelli, A. R., & Hart, M. M. (1987). Gay women, men, and families in rural settings: Toward the development of helping communities. *American Journal of Community Psychology, 15*, 79–93.

DeBlaere, C., Brewster, M. E., Sarkess, A., & Moradi, B. (2010). Conducting research with LGB people of color: Methodological challenges and strategies. *The Counseling Psychologist, 38*, 331–362. DOI: 10.1177/0011000009335257

Diamond, L. M. (2008). Female bisexuality from adolescence to adulthood: Results from a 10-year longitudinal study. *Developmental Psychology, 44*(1), 5–14.

Diamond, L. M., & Butterworth, M. (2008). Questioning gender and sexual identity: Dynamic links over time. *Sex Roles, 59*, 365–376. DOI: 10.1007/s11199-008-9425-3

Diamant, A. L., Wold, C., Spitzer, K., & Gelberg, L. (2000). Health behaviors, health status, and access to and use of health care: A population-based study of lesbian, bisexual, and heterosexual women. *Archives of Family Medicine, 9*(10), 1043–1051.

Dubé, E. M., & Savin-Williams, R. C. (1999). Sexual identity development among ethnic sexual minority male youths. *Developmental Psychology, 35*, 1389–1398.

Entrup, L., & Firestein, B. A. (2007). Developmental and spiritual issues of young people and bisexuals of the next generation. In B. A. Firestein (Ed.), *Becoming visible: Counseling bisexuals across the lifespan* (pp. 89–107). New York: Columbia University Press.

Fassinger, R. E., & Arseneau, J. R. (2007). "I'd rather get wet than be under that umbrella": Differentiating the experiences and identities of lesbian, gay, bisexual, and transgender people. In K. J. Bieschke, Perez, R. M., & DeBord, K. A. (Eds.), *Handbook of counseling and psychotherapy with lesbian, gay, bisexual, and transgender clients* (2nd ed., pp. 19–49). Washington, DC: American Psychological Association.

Glickman, C. (2000). The language of sex-positivity. *Electronic Journal of Human Sexuality, 3*. Retrieved from: http://www.ejhs.org/volume3/sexpositive.htm (accessed March 10, 2017).

Gold, M. (2008). *Crisis: 40 stories revealing the personal, social, and religious pain and trauma of growing up gay in America*. Austin, TX: Greenleaf Book Group Press.

Gotta, G., Green, R.-J., Rothblum, E., Solomon, S., Balsam, K., & Schwartz, P. (2011). Lesbian, gay male, and heterosexual relationships: A comparison of couples in 1975 and 2000. *Family Process, 50*, 353–376.

Graham, N. (2014). Polyamory: A call for increased mental health professional awareness. *Archives of Sexual Behavior, 43*(6), 1031–1034.

Green, R. J. (2012). Gay and lesbian family life: Risk, resilience, and rising expectations. In F. Walsh (Ed.), *Normal family processes* (4th ed., pp. 172–195). New York: Guilford.

Halderman, D. W. (2004). When sexual and religious orientations collide: Considerations in working with conflicted same-sex attracted male clients. *The Counseling Psychologist, 32*, 691–715. DOI: 10.1177/0011000004267560

Heck, J. E., Sell, R. L., & Gorin, S. S. (2006). Health care access among individuals involved in same-sex relationships. *American Journal of Public Health, 96*(6), 1111–1118.

Herek, G. M. (2010). Sexual orientation differences as deficits: Science and stigma in the history of American psychology. *Perspectives on Psychological Science, 5*, 693–699.

Huang, Y., Brewster, M. E., Moradi, B., Goodman, M., Wiseman, M., & Martin, A. (2010). Content analysis of literature about LGB people of color: 1998–2007. *The Counseling Psychologist, 38*, 363–396. DOI: 10.1177/0011000009335255

Huffman, A. H., Watrous-Rodriguez, K. M., & King, E. B. (2008). Supporting a diverse workforce: What type of support is most meaningful for lesbian and gay employees? *Human Resource Management, 47*, 237–253. DOI: 10.1002/hrm.20210

Institute of Medicine. (2011). *The health of lesbian, gay, bisexual, and transgender people: Building a foundation for better understanding*. Washington, DC: National Academies Press.

King, M., Semlyen, J., See Tai, S., Killaspy, H., Osborn, D., Popelyuk, D., & Nazareth, I. (2008). A systematic review of mental disorder, suicide and deliberate self-harm in lesbian, gay and bisexual people. *BMC Psychiatry, 8*. DOI: 10.1186/1471-244X-8-70

Kosciw, J. G., Greytak, E. A., & Diaz, E. M. (2010). *The 2009 National School Climate Survey: The experiences of lesbian, gay, bisexual and transgender youth in our nation's schools*. New York: Gay, Lesbian and Straight Education Network.

Loutzenheiser, L. W. (2015). "Who are you calling a problem?": Addressing transphobia and homophobia through school policy. *Critical Studies in Education, 56*, 99–115.

Meilaender, G. (1987). *The limits of love: Some theological explorations*. University Park, PA: Pennsylvania State University Press.

Meyer, I. H. (2003). Prejudice, social stress, and mental health in lesbian, gay and bisexual populations: Conceptual issues and research evidence. *Psychological Bulletin, 129*, 674–697. DOI: 10.1037/0033-2909.129.5.674

Moser, C., & Levitt, E. E. (1987). An exploratory-descriptive study of a sadomasochistically oriented sample. *The Journal of Sex Research, 23*(3), 322–337.

Nichols, M. (2006). Psychotherapeutic issues with "kinky" clients: Clinical problems, yours and theirs. *Journal of Homosexuality, 50*(2–3), 281–300.

O'Brien, J. (2004). Wrestling the angel of contradiction: Queer Christian identities. *Culture and Religion, 5*(2), 179–202. DOI: 10.1080/143830042000225420

Oswald, R. F., & Culton, L. S. (2003). Under the rainbow: Rural gay life and its relevance for family providers. *Family Relations, 52*, 72–81. DOI: 10.1111/j.1741-3729.2003.00072.x

Page, E. (2004). Mental health services experiences of bisexual women and bisexual men: An empirical study. *Journal of Bisexuality, 3*(3/4), 137–160.

Peplau, A. L., & Garnets, L. D. (2000). A new paradigm for understanding women's sexuality and sexual attraction. *Journal of Social Issues, 56*, 330–350.

Pew Research Center (2013a). *LGBT in changing times: Attitudes, experiences and growing acceptance.* Washington, DC: Pew Research Center.

Pew Research Center (2013b). *The global divide on homosexuality: Greater acceptance in more secular and affluent countries.* Washington, DC: Pew Research Center.

Reck, J. (2009). Homeless gay and transgender youth of color in San Francisco: "No one likes street kids"—even in the Castro. *Journal of LGBT Youth, 6*, 223–242. DOI: 10.1080/19361650903013519

Reynolds, A. L., & Hanjorgiris, W. F. (2000). Coming out: Lesbian, gay, and bisexual identity development. In W. F. Perez, K. A. DeBord, & K. J. Bieschke (Eds.), *Handbook of counseling and psychotherapy with lesbian, gay, and bisexual clients* (pp. 35–55). Washington, DC: American Psychological Association.

Ryan, D. P., Compton, C. C., & Mayer, R. J. (2000). Carcinoma of the anal canal. *New England Journal of Medicine, 342*(11), 792–800.

Ryan, H., Wortley, P. M., Easton, A., Pederson, L., & Greenwood, G. (2000). Smoking among lesbians, gays, and bisexuals: A review of the literature. *American Journal of Preventive Medicine, 21*(2), 142–149.

Scherrer, K. S. (2008). Coming to an asexual identity: Negotiating identity, negotiating desire. *Sexualities, 11*(5), 621–641.

Shilo, G., & Savaya, R. (2012). Mental health of lesbian, gay, and bisexual youth and young adults: Differential effects of age, gender, religiosity, and sexual orientation. *Journal of Research on Adolescence, 22*, 310–325.

Skingsley, A., Yin, Z., Kirwan, P., Croxford, S., Chau, C., & Delpech, V. C. (2015). HIV in the UK—situation report 2015. London: Public Health England.

Smith, L. (2005). Psychotherapy, classism, and the poor: Conspicuous by their absence. *American Psychologist, 60*, 687–696. DOI: 10.1037/0003-066X.60.7.687

Soble, A. (Ed.). (2002). *The philosophy of sex: Contemporary readings* (4th ed.). Lanham, MD: Rowman & Littlefield.

Steger, M. F., & Frazier, P. (2005). Meaning in life: One link in the chain from religiousness to well-being. *Journal of Counseling Psychology, 52*, 574–582.

Stein, D. (2002). Safe sane consensual: The making of a shibboleth. [Online editorial]. Retrieved from http://www.boybear.us/ssc.pdf (accessed March 24, 2017).

Stevens, P., & Hall, J. (2001). Sexuality and safer sex: The issues for lesbians and bisexual women. *Journal of Obstetric, Gynecologic, and Neonatal Nursing, 30*(4), 439–447.

Stonewall Report (2012). *Ethnicity – Stonewall health briefing.* Retrieved from https://www.stonewall.org.uk/resources/ethnicity-%E2%80%93-stonewall-health-briefing-2012 (accessed March 24, 2017).

Switch, G. (2001). *Origin of RACK; RACK vs. SSC.* Retrieved from http://www.leathernroses.com/generalbdsm/garyswitchrack.htm (accessed April 24, 2016).Szymanski, D. M.,

Kashubeck-West, S., & Meyer, J. (2008). Internalized heterosexism: Measurement, psychosocial correlates, and research directions. *The Counseling Psychologist, 36,* 525–574. DOI: 10.1177/0011000007309489

Ullerstam, L. (1966). *A Sexual bill of rights for the erotic minorities.* Gothenburg: Zindermans.

Waldo, C. R. (1999). Working in a majority context: A structural model of heterosexism as minority stress in the workplace. *Journal of Counseling Psychology, 46,* 218–232.

Weitzman, G. (2006). Therapy with clients who are bisexual and polyamorous. *Journal of Bisexuality, 6*(1/2), 137–164.

WHO (World Health Organization) (2002). *Defining sexual health: Report of a technical consultation on sexual health.* Geneva: WHO.

Wolitski, R. J., Jones, K. T., Wasserman, J. L., & Jones, J. C. (2006). Self-identification as "down-low" among men who have sex with men (MSM) from 12 US cities. *AIDS and Behavior, 10,* 519–529.

Yoder, J. D., & McDonald, T. W. (1998). Measuring sexist discrimination in the workplace: Support for the validity of the Schedule of Sexist Events. *Psychology of Women Quarterly, 22,* 487–491. DOI: 10.1111/j.1471-6402.1998.tb00170.x

Counselling Psychology

WILLIAM MING LIU AND ALEX J. COLBOW

CHAPTER OUTLINE

INTRODUCTION 250

SOCIAL CLASS AND PSYCHOLOGICAL
DISTRESS 251
    Classism 251
    Health Outcomes 252
    Stereotype Threat 253

COUNSELLING PSYCHOLOGY AS A
TRANSMITTER OF CLASSISM 253
    Comfort with Social Class 255

WHAT STUDENTS AND CLINICIANS
CAN DO 256

UPWARD MOBILITY BIAS 258

CONCLUSION 260

LEARNING OUTCOMES

BY THE END OF THIS CHAPTER YOU SHOULD BE ABLE TO ANSWER THE FOLLOWING KEY QUESTIONS:

1. How have social class concepts been integrated into multicultural competencies?

2. In what ways does classism affect a person's psychological and physical health?

3. What are the ways in which classism is communicated in mental health practice?

Counselling Psychology: A Textbook for Study and Practice, First Edition. Edited by David Murphy.
© 2017 John Wiley & Sons Ltd. Published 2017 by John Wiley & Sons Ltd.

INTRODUCTION

For some time in psychology and counselling, it was unclear how social class, classism, and economic inequality became meaningful in a person's life. That is, how does social class get "under one's skin" (Lupie, King, Meaney, & McEwen, 2001)? Describing the context of poverty and inequality helped psychologists and counsellors to contextualize the life of people but did little to explain how these contextual (societal) factors impact the day-to-day life and life-course of individuals in these situations. Researchers were able to finally identify the mechanisms by which these social factors became consequential in people's lives. The hypothalamic-pituitary-adrenocortical axis (HPA) was implicated as the pathway by which environmental stressors (e.g., chronic poverty) disrupted hormonal regulation and the person's psychological functioning and physical health (Miller, Chen, & Zhou, 2007).

For some racial ethnic minority men like African Americans, these stressors alongside experiences of racism create chromosomal changes (shortening telomere length) that reduce the overall lifespan of the men (Chae et al., 2014). These findings were important for psychologists because now chronic stress was the mechanism that could trigger and exacerbate physical and mental health conditions. And much of the stress could be associated with environmental conditions (e.g., poverty) and deleterious interpersonal interactions (e.g., racism).

Counselling psychologists, counsellors, and other mental health care providers can understand the importance of integrating social class and classism into their clinical work. Increasing the well-being, both physically and psychologically, of the clients means addressing these contextual factors that have seemingly invisible links to the clients' lives. But this also begs larger questions for mental health care providers: What does it mean to integrate an understanding of social class and classism into their work? How might this understanding transform their approach and work with clients? And, how do mental health care providers perpetuate inequality?

Social class is a relatively new multicultural concept for psychologists to integrate into their clinical work. For many years, social class was viewed narrowly as a person's income, education, and occupation. These concepts were useful in the sociological literature, but less so in understanding an individual's psychology (Liu, 2011, 2012). Psychology researchers often found themselves importing sociological constructs and theories to parse some understanding of social class at the individual level. Previous research conflated terms and constructs like social class and socioeconomic status, and tended to leave off any mention of classism (Liu, 2013). Furthermore, psychology researchers were fixed on the idea of finding the exact objective indicators (e.g., income, and educational level) that would place a person into a certain social class group or level even though there was little evidence that this form of grouping would work methodologically and empirically (Brown, Fukunaga, Umemoto, & Wicker, 1996).

Even though social class and classism were important, psychology researchers largely ignored the constructs. Liu (2013) suggested that social class could only be understood as a co-construct with classism, much like race and racism or gender and sexism. Social class and classism had to be used as associated terms that implicated one's perception but also experiences and actions/behaviours. Similar to race and racism, especially racial identity, these associated terms allowed psychologists to understand better how one may perceive him/herself racially, how experiences with race and racism were internalized, but also what types of behaviours may be manifest (e.g., withdrawal). Liu (2013) maintained that using these terms and moving away from social class groups as well as objective indicators allowed psychology research and clinicians to better focus on the subjective and phenomenological experiences of the person.

Increasingly, psychologists are more aware of the role social class, specifically subjective social class and classism, plays in people's lives. The term subjective social class used here includes individuals' attitudes, preferences, values, skills, social networks, physical and mental attributes, and behaviours associated with various social class cultures. Subjective social class is important to study, understand, and integrate into clinical work because it is a better predictor of mental and physical health outcomes (Aries & Seider, 2005; Daly, Boyce, & Wood, 2014; Elbogen, Johnson, Wagner, Newton, & Beckham, 2012), rates of college retention (Joo, Durband, & Grable, 2009), and self-esteem (Bui, 2002; Covarrubias, Romero, & Trivelli, 2014), when compared with objective indicators. In the sections below we review how social class relates to psychological distress, the ways counselling psychology is a transmitter of classism, and actions students and clinicians can undertake to identify and curtail the effects of classist attitudes and behaviours.

SOCIAL CLASS AND PSYCHOLOGICAL DISTRESS

As we build an understanding of the various factors contributing to the experiences of social class and classism and what may lead to psychological distress, we will focus on several areas with empirical research such as classism, health outcomes, and stereotype threat.

Classism

From an ecological framework, classism may be best exemplified as exposure to toxins and violence wherein people who are poor are at a greater risk of both (APA, 2015). Women from poorer households and youth from low-income neighbourhoods are more likely to experience and witness acts of violence compared with other groups (Browne, Salomon, & Bassuk, 1999; Buka, Stichick, Birdthistle, & Earls, 2001). Classism and inequality are starkly illustrated here as biological and physiological risks to the well-being of those who are poor.

People's experiences of classism can be detrimental to their mental health and well-being (Thompson & Subich, 2013). Classism has parallels to other prejudices such as sexism, racism, or homophobia. Like these other prejudices, several forms have been identified in the literature. These include institutional/systemic, citational, and interpersonal (Thompson & Subich, 2013). Institutional/ systemic classism occurs when organizational structures are in place which favour particular groups over others (Langhout, Rosselli, & Feinstein, 2007). Citational classism is when people tell disparaging jokes or make stereotypic comments about people from lower socioeconomic status (Langhout, Drake, & Rosselli, 2009). Interpersonal classism transpires when individuals are purposely excluded or avoided based on their social class (Langhout et al., 2007). Individuals who experience various forms of classism are also more likely to report increased depression, anxiety, stress, lower self-esteem, and lower psychological wellness (Thompson & Subich, 2013).

Classism, the experience of and actions of persons, may come in the form of upward, downward, and lateral classism, as well as experiences of internalized classism. Downward classism is the derogation of those perceived to be in lower social classes. For example, there may be a perception that people in lower social class communities lack the interest or ability to move upward. Yet research shows that low-income parents hold the same attitudes about education as their wealthier counterparts. However, parents who are poor are more likely to work multiple jobs, work evenings, have jobs without paid leave, and have fewer resources for transportation, which relate to reductions in attendance of school functions (Gorski, 2008).

Upward classism is negative sentiments directed to those perceived to be in a higher social class than the individual's current social class. Lateral classism is the experience of "keeping up with the Jones" that may come from those in a similar social class group reminding a person that they need to upgrade their car, computer, or home, for example, to maintain their social standing with everyone around them. Internalized classism may be construed as the feelings of anxiety, depression, or even despondency coming from one's failure to stay within one's social class. For instance, losing a job, investment, or social network causes a person to lose their ability to maintain a social class position and they do not believe they have the opportunity, time, or capital. Liu (2002) speculated that for some men who lose a job, anger and rage may come from their loss of social class status and their identity as the "breadwinner." For these men, aggression, fighting, or abuse may be behaviours related to internalized classism.

Health Outcomes

Coming from a lower subjective social status is related to worse mental and physical health outcomes. Specifically, people's perceived social class position relative to others is a better predictor of physical health outcomes compared with objective indicators of socioeconomic status (Daly et al., 2014; Singh-Manoux, Marmot, & Adler, 2005). These physical health outcomes include heart rate, sleep, body fat distribution, and cortisol responses (Adler, Epel, Castellazzo, & Ickovics, 2000). Looking at mental health, when people transition into new social class environments and interact with individuals from higher perceived social standing, this can lead to feelings of intimidation, discomfort, inadequacy, exclusion, and powerlessness (Aries & Seider, 2005). Individuals from a lower social class background are more likely to explain social and personal outcomes in terms of contextual or external influences rather than internal influences.

This external locus of control is also tied to feelings of helplessness in various contexts. (Kraus, Piff, & Keltner, 2009).

Stereotype Threat

Stereotypes about people who are poor include portrayals of being stupid, drinking beer all day, shooting guns (in the USA), having many children, being dirty, violent, inbred, lazy, unkempt, having low ambition, and being less moral (Spencer & Castano, 2007). When confronted with the possibility of confirming stereotypes about one's group, this apprehension, termed "stereotype threat," impairs performance on challenging tasks (Steele, 1997). Most research completed on this phenomenon has focused on racial or gender stereotype threats (Walton & Spencer, 2009). However, researchers have also demonstrated that stereotype threat applies to social class (Harrison, Stevens, Monty, & Coakley, 2006; Spencer & Castano, 2007). Researchers found that even a simple demographic item asking for household and individual income is sufficient to elicit stereotype threat for students who come from poor backgrounds. This elicitation created a cognitive load related to these stereotypes that in turn depressed their performance on innocuous test items. For students at universities, eliciting social class stereotype threat results in reduced academic performance on standardized tests (Spencer & Castano, 2007; Walton & Spencer, 2009).

COUNSELLING PSYCHOLOGY AS A TRANSMITTER OF CLASSISM

Conducting research while not correctly integrating social class as a variable may transmit inaccurate information about the role of social class and classism in people's lives (Liu et al., 2004; Smith, 2005). When the sole focus of research is on objective indicators of social class rather than attitudes, beliefs, values, and experiences, this gives only a partial explanation of what is occurring. An overreliance on objective indicators misses people's interpretations and understanding of their relative position in relation to others, how people make sense of this, and their evaluations of themselves based on these judgements. It informs people where they fit and how to act towards others. Moreover, psychologists' reliance on samples derived from university/college students reduces the variance and usefulness of the data collected, particularly when studying social class. Generally, university/college students are a unique population given their geographic locations, level of education, and willingness to engage in a system of higher education.

Even in the study of university/college students, the culture in which students are immersed is not measured or integrated into the study. University cultures emphasize individuality (Stephens, Fryberg, Markus, Johnson, & Covarrubias, 2012; Stephens, Townsend, Markus, & Phillips, 2012). This is often reflected in values around expanding one's knowledge of the world, being an independent thinker, and exploring personal interests (Harackiewicz et al., 2014).

This counters more collectivistic values such as helping family, being a community role model, giving back to community, and providing a better life for one's children (Harackiewicz et al., 2014). Tying in literature on person–environment fit, people who can buy in or acclimate to a particular context are more likely to be successful in that context (Holland, 1997; Kieffer, Schinka, & Curtiss, 2004). It has also been found that people will adopt the values of their surroundings (Sagiv & Schwartz, 2000; Schwartz & Bardi, 1997). These ideas apply to student psychologists in university settings. Even if a student is from a low income background or is a first-generation student, if s/he is successful in higher education, it is likely that they successfully adopted many of the beliefs and values associated with institutions of higher education, and may inadvertently propagate these attitudes and values in their work.

Counselling psychologists and trainees may push clients to focus on more individualistic goals such as the attainment of a degree or other personal interests at the cost of not being able to help one's family financially by bringing in income from working more hours, or spending less time in one's community. This may run counter to family and community values some clients have grown up in. They may direct clients to focus less on student loan debt or having a financial safety net, which may be critical for an individual whose families may not have the means to support them financially. While these issues may be less important to individuals whose families are financially stable, individuals who come from a lower socioeconomic status may face severe consequences for coming out of college with a bachelor's degree and $100,000 in debt.

Holding upper or middle class values may lead to the devaluing of a lower class individual's situations, experiences, and needs. Suggesting activities that patients cannot afford, not appreciating financial burdens, assuming someone can afford things (e.g., transportation, going out with peers, vacations) when they are unable, can all induce shame or embarrassment on the client's part. Placing one's own values of independence or just world beliefs on clients may be detrimental to clients' health and well-being. This cultural norm mismatch between higher education and individuals from low income backgrounds leads to higher rates of dropout as well as psychological distress (Aries & Seider, 2005; Finlan, 2013; Hsu & Ketchen, 2013; Lehmann, 2009; Stephens, Fryberg, et al., 2012; Stephens, Townsend, et al., 2012).

Many counselling psychologists receive their training in university settings and are frequently employed in college counselling centres (Michalski, Kohout, Wicherski, & Hart, 2011). Of counselling psychologists surveyed in 2009, 58% of them were employed in university settings as counsellors, professors, or in other capacities (Michalski et al., 2011). This is a large portion of counselling psychologists who do not go into community mental health, veteran affairs, hospitals, or other institutions that serve a more diverse clientele. Moreover, in higher education, psychologists tend to encounter a population that is relatively restricted in terms of social class diversity. Due to counselling psychologists being employed in this type of setting, they are less likely to encounter individuals coming from working class or blue collar backgrounds in their training (Bui, 2002; McCarron & Inkelas, 2006). This is especially important as increasing numbers of nontraditional students (e.g., first generation, veterans, working adults) are entering higher education. These nontraditional student have unique demands placed upon them beyond those of traditional students, which include: work and family obligations (Shields, 2002), working more hours (Pascarella, Pierson, Wolniak, & Terenzini, 2004; Terenzini, Pascarella, & Blimling, 1996), less financial support (Engle, 2007), and they are more likely to live off campus and miss out on interactions with other students (Pascarella et al., 2004).

Another problem encountered that hides social class is students' ability to take out student loans to attend university/college. Moreover, access to credit and student loans blurs the lines of social class salience as individuals can use credit to compensate for their financial standing. Furthermore, psychologists and counsellors in university and college counselling services may not address social class issues since students in economic and financial distress, especially those who cannot afford to stay in education, are not going to be clients. Therefore, social class, classism, and inequality issues may remain relatively invisible to clinicians in these settings.

For psychologists and counsellors in training, education for psychologists has been growing, which extends the amount of time and debt students take on to complete degrees (De Vaney Olvey, Hogg, & Counts, 2002). The requirement for up to 7 years of graduate training as well as the associated debt may lead psychologists into areas of work removed from the least and most wealthy groups of people. De Vaney Olvey et al. (2002) found that psychologist licensure requirements in the USA are disproportionate relative to other professions (e.g., dentistry, medicine, social work). Their research suggests that psychologists take 3 years longer on average to get licensure compared with medical doctors, veterinarians, podiatrists, and dentists. This extended time to licensure is due to the education and training requirements set out by licensing boards. This may result in reduced desire to enter careers/employment settings that serve low socioeconomic status individuals in need of psychological services. Moreover, individuals in greater debt report increased psychological distress (Brown, Taylor, & Wheatley Price, 2005; Cooke, Barkham, Audin, Bradley, & Davy, 2004; Ross, Cleland, & Macleod, 2006). For psychologists who do enter employment in areas helping underserved populations where they may receive lower pay, this could result in increased distress for clinicians and reduced quality of service provided to clients.

Comfort with Social Class

In counselling, psychologists do not usually address the role of social class as they would with other diversity issues such as race or sex (Liu et al., 2004; Smith, 2005). This is partly due to the discussion of finances being relatively taboo (Liu, 2011). As people do not grow up talking about social class, they do not have a framework for communicating ideas about social class, and are reluctant to discuss these topics. As a result, most people's views on social class are limited to rich versus poor and judgements on how people manage money.

KNOWLEDGE OF SOCIAL CLASS, CLASSISM, AND PERSONAL BIAS

Misperceptions about the realities of social class may also play a role in the perpetuation of classism.

- The UK and the US (Chetty, Hendren, Kline, & Saez, 2014) have a far less mobile society than those of many industrialized nations.
  - Consequence in therapy: overestimating people's potential for social class mobility—they may assume clients' life circumstances are due to traits inherent to the individuals. This may lead to class-based microaggressions towards clients of working class or blue collar backgrounds.
- Individuals from different social class backgrounds encounter and cope with different events and stressors (Lott, 2012).
  - Consequence: recognizing the reality of these differences is critical to psychologists' work with clients.
- Individuals who are poor are typically viewed as lacking warmth, trustworthiness, and competence. They are stereotyped as lazy, stupid, dishonest, uncivilized, and blamed for their social class positions (Tablante & Fiske, 2015).
  - Therapists should be aware that research indicates that poor working adults work more hours each week than their wealthy counterparts (Gorski, 2008). Moreover, poor adults are more likely to work more than one job (Gorski, 2008).
- Piff, Stancato, Côté, Mendoza-Denton, and Keltner (2012) found that upper class individuals are more likely to break traffic laws, exhibit unethical decision making, take goods from others, lie, cheat, and behave unethically at work when compared with lower class individuals.
  - Therapists should know when unethical behaviour is self-beneficial; social class positively predicts unethical behaviour in wealthier groups, while negatively predicting it in low wealth groups (Dubois et al., 2015).
- Individuals who are poor tend to spend more money on others rather than themselves (Rucker, Dubois, & Galinsky, 2011), on social activities (Banerjee & Duflo, 2007), and charity (Piff, Kraus, Côté, Cheng, & Keltner, 2010).
  - Therapists should know researchers have found that feelings of powerlessness tend to be associated with greater spending on status enhancing items (Rucker & Galinsky, 2008). People will often try and compensate for their lower status by purchasing goods that will enhance others' perceptions of them.

WHAT STUDENTS AND CLINICIANS CAN DO

What does it mean for psychologists to integrate an understanding of social class and classism into their clinical work? Similar to the way in which the chapter began, how might these situational, contextual, and societal factors change the way in which clinical practice is conducted? Students, psychologists, and teachers may find benefit in reflecting on the following social class topics (see text box):

1. Consider family social class environment and the associated values. How have your values changed as you transitioned through your education?
2. What were you taught about what money means and what you deem worthy to spend it on?
3. What are your beliefs about work ethic and leisure?
4. What are your beliefs about material wealth and displaying wealth? How do you display it in your own life and career?
5. What are your beliefs about justice and fairness in the world?
6. What do you think it takes to be successful in the world?
7. How do you define success?
8. Include subjective measures of social class in research. Incorporate social class appropriately into psychological research (materialism, classism, Protestant work ethic, etc.).
9. Write about personal values.
10. Talk about social class with clients.

There is research suggesting that minority and first-generation students who are given opportunities to affirm their values through writing (e.g., writing about their most important values) can reestablish perceptions of personal integrity and worth, which bolsters them against challenges and stress (Harackiewicz et al., 2014). This simple intervention was found to augment first generation student grades not only in the class where it was completed, but also in other classes the individual took that semester (Harackiewicz et al., 2014). Similar interventions including writing about the utility of a course to one's personal life and goals have demonstrated similar results for first generation and minority students (Canning & Harackiewicz, 2015; Harackiewicz, Canning, Tibbetts, Priniski, & Hyde, 2015).

Similar to those who may be living in poverty, near-poverty, or in situations of economic inequality, it is insufficient to merely address and recognize these contextual factors in a person's life. Clinicians need to transform how their work is conducted. More effort, attention, and advocacy are needed at the lower economic stratum. That would require clinicians to reconsider number of clinical sessions for a client, the length of time for the standard session, and extra-therapeutic advocacy work with the client (e.g., looking up information on the computer, calling hospitals). The beginning stages are the most critical and likely most unstable. But once the client is able to gain momentum, the work with the client can be renegotiated.

Take, for instance, the standard question of income that one might encounter on a survey. The question of income assumes that the person knows their month-to-month and annual income, and those who might be best able to report this number are those who receive a standard salary. For those who live on an hourly wage and tips, this income amount may vary from week to week and so asking for a yearly salary figure may not be accurate. Furthermore, asking students or children to report a parent's yearly income is notoriously inaccurate (Liu, 2012, 2013). Income as a term is problematic for those in wealth and affluence who may derive their monies from investments and inheritances. Income may be zero for these individuals so this metric may not capture the impact of wealth in their lives.

Also, wealth and poverty have differential effects at varying times in a person's life. For racial ethnic minority families, contact with law enforcement, in particular incarceration rates, is more pronounced for them than their white counterparts (Zaw, Hamilton, & Darity, 2016). Regardless of wealth, African Americans are more likely to be incarcerated in the USA than whites (even poor whites) (Zaw et al., 2016). Additionally, the long-term consequences of incarceration are more detrimental for racial ethnic minorities than whites (Zaw et al., 2016). Thus, research into social class and classism has to focus on the intersections of multiple factors like race, age, and gender, and our theories of social class and classism have to take into account these factors rather than a uniform theory that assumes everyone has equal opportunities and access for upward mobility.

UPWARD MOBILITY BIAS

A principal tenet in multicultural competency literature, research, and practice is the importance of self-awareness especially in areas of bias. This may be especially true for clinicians in terms of how societal assumptions about social class may be translated to the client, sometimes unintentionally (Liu, Corkery, & Thome, 2010). One of the more subtle and sometime pernicious expectations is the upward mobility bias (UMB) (Liu, Corkery, & Thome, 2010). The UMB is centred on the idea that people are expected to want to move upward in social status. What comes from this expectation is the assumption that people are seeking opportunities for advancement in work and school, that people are continually in an effort of self-development especially as it is tied to upward social mobility, and that people may eschew those who are stagnant in their upward mobility.

The clinician may negatively describe or attribute poorer prognosis to those individuals who may not subscribe to upward mobility, status seeking, high materialistic values, or extending one's social networks. The UMB provides a rationale (a cultural ideology) for the clinician to describe this person as deviant from the normal expectations of society. While the clinician may not specifically identify the UMB as an aspect in the description, diagnosis, or prognosis of the individual, other descriptive terms may be used such as poor self-esteem, lack of self-efficacy, poor interpersonal skills, or lacks initiative. In this way, we suspect that the practice of psychology, counselling, and mental health may have been complicit in perpetuating classism by providing poorer prognoses for individuals in poverty, more severe diagnoses for these same individuals, and less effort in clinical work with clients. The UMB becomes a catalyst for magnifying life stressors that may lead to poorer clinical activity and work for those people in poverty.

But the UMB does not appear magically. These biases and worldviews are socialized and cultivated by friends, families, and peers (Liu, 2014). As Liu posited, these socialized worldviews and values about social class are not only lenses through which the person views the world and interpersonal relationships, but also important ways in which the individual being socialized remains connected to the family of origin, friends, and peers. Thus, learning to change this language and worldview is not isolated to the individual but also implicates larger networks of relationships. In other words, becoming aware of one's UMB and changing it means changing how one relates to family, parents, peers, and friends who helped socialize the person into the worldview. The UMB, like any other entrenched worldview, has deeper connections and emotions tied to it than simply the explicit cognitions and perceptions.

The UMB also focuses clinical and research attention on those in poverty or who are poor without much critical attention on those who are in wealth and affluence. We might assume that the more wealth you have the happier you will be. However, there is literature suggesting some discrepancies in this assumption. Kushlev, Dunn, and Lucas (2015) found that greater wealth is associated with less sadness but not more happiness. People who are wealthy have the ability to take care of basic needs and are less concerned about feeding and sheltering their families, but they encounter other concerns such as the maintenance of wealth, pressures to continue to succeed, and the need to keep up with others in their social groups. Wealth has also been shown to negatively influence people's ability to savour experiences (Quoidbach, Dunn, Petrides, & Mikolajczak, 2010). This appears to be related to reduced enjoyment of small pleasures associated with having constant access to the best things in life. If one has the means to partake in the best activities or have the best material goods, there is less need to appreciate or savour the moment, an activity, or a new object.

Certainly it is accurate to say that those who have poorer access to health care and who suffer from the detrimental effects of poverty will likely have mental health concerns (Hopps & Liu, 2006) and so it is appropriate to focus attention on these communities. However, as Luthar and her colleagues have found, incidences of substance use among wealthy adolescents are either higher or equal to those adolescents from lower social class environments. It seems that, in general, young adults from higher social class families are more likely to use alcohol and marijuana (Patrick, Wightman, Schoeni, & Schulenberg, 2012). Upper class children demonstrate elevated rates of anxiety, depression, and substance use related to excessive pressure to achieve, and physical and emotional isolation from parents (Luthar, 2003; Luthar & Latendresse, 2005). It is a misconception that individuals from poorer backgrounds are more likely to abuse alcohol and drugs (Gorski, 2008).

Similarly, Levine (2006) found in her exploration of affluent and wealthy adolescents that they also suffered from anxiety related to perfectionism as well as problems with negative feedback such as a poor grade. What she found was that many of these adolescents and young adults were raised in environments where they were considered outstanding and their parents focused exclusively on achievements and being competitive, which sometimes led to children believing their self-worth was tied to external achievements. As role models, parents were often unavailable because of work and travel, and the child's care was left to nannies and other caretakers (Shafran, 1992). Sometimes parents believed that self-sufficiency and autonomy were better fostered by their absence (Hochschild, 1997). Hence, mental health issues do appear, potentially, across the economic spectrum from low to high, but there may be differential causes and presentations depending on the economic context. It is important for clinicians to understand and remember that economic means and affluence are not necessarily protective factors against mental health problems and that it is imperative to explore the phenomenological worldview of the person.

CONCLUSION

Counselling psychologists have a challenge ahead of them if they are to be multiculturally competent around social class and classism. Not only is this a burgeoning area of research and scholarship in professional psychology and counselling, there is little from which to draw to integrate into practice with a client and little guidance about how to understand one's own biases. This chapter focused on those current limitations in the literature and was meant to provide some guidance for counselling practice but also self-awareness. The focus of the chapter was to provide a survey of the current empirical literature on aspects related to social class and classism, and to help synthesize the findings for practitioners. In research, there is still much to do with respect to theory development and empirical (qualitative and quantitative) research.

In clinical practice, we offer the metaphor of the rocket launch to illustrate what we believe it means to help someone build momentum in his/her life as a means towards upward mobility. At the same time, it is important that practitioners be aware of how their own UMB may distort how they interact with clients, as well as how diagnoses and prognoses are reported. The UMB also focuses attention on those in the lower social class groups without equal attention to and critique of those in higher social class groups. Mental health concerns exist across the economic spectrum but the causes, manifest symptoms, and treatment may have to be culturally adapted.

SUGGESTED FURTHER READING

Liu, W. M. (Eds.) (2013). *The Oxford handbook of social class in counseling.* Oxford University Press.

REFERENCES

Adler, N., Epel, E. S., Castellazzo, G., & Ickovics, J. R. (2000). Relationship of subjective and objective social status with psychological and physiological functioning: Preliminary data in healthy white women. *Health Psychology, 19*(6), 586–592.

American Psychological Association (2015). Violence and socioeconomic status. Retrieved from http://www.apa.org/pi/ses/resources/publications/factsheet-violence.aspx (accessed December 15, 2015).

Aries, E., & Seider, M. (2005). The interactive relationship between class identity and the college experience: The case of lower income students. *Qualitative Sociology, 28*(4), 419–443. DOI: 10.1007/s11133-005-8366-1

Banerjee, A. V., & Duflo, E. (2007). The economic lives of the poor. *The Journal of Economic Perspectives, 21*, 141–167. https://doi.org/10.1257/jep.21.1.141

Brown, M. T., Fukunaga, C., Umemoto, D., & Wicker, L. (1996). Annual review, 1990–1996: Social class, work and retirement behavior. *Journal of Vocational Behavior, 49*(2), 159–189.

Brown, S., Taylor, K., & Wheatley Price, S. (2005). Debt and distress: Evaluating the psychological cost of credit. *Journal of Economic Psychology, 26*(5), 642–663. DOI: 10.1016/j.joep.2005.01.002

Browne, A., Salomon, A., & Bassuk, S. S. (1999). The impact of recent partner violence on poor women's capacity to maintain work. *Violence Against Women, 5*(4), 393–426. DOI: 10.1177/10778019922181284

Bui, K. V. T. (2002). First-generation college students at a four-year university: Background characteristics, reasons for pursuing higher education, and first-year experiences. *College Student Journal, 36*(1), 3–11.

Buka, S. L., Stichick, T. L., Birdthistle, I., & Earls, F. J. (2001). Youth exposure to violence: Prevalence, risks, and consequences. *American Journal of Orthopsychiatry, 71*(3), 298–310. DOI: 10.1037/0002-9432.71.3.298

Canning, E. A., & Harackiewicz, J. M. (2015). Teach it, don't preach it: The differential effects of directly-communicated and self-generated utility-value information. *Motivation Science, 1*(1), 47–71. DOI: 10.1037/mot0000015

Chae, D. H., Nuru-Jeter, A. M., Brody, G. H., Lin, J., Blackburn, E. H., & Epel, E. S. (2014). Discrimination, racial bias, and telomere length in African-American men. *American Journal of Preventive Medicine, 46*(2), 103–111.

Chetty, R., Hendren, N., Kline, P., & Saez, E. (2014). Where is the land of opportunity? The geography of intergenerational mobility in the U.S. NBER Working Paper No. 19843. Cambridge, MA: NBER.

Cooke, R., Barkham, M., Audin, K., Bradley, M., & Davy, J. (2004). Student debt and its relation to student mental health. *Journal of Further and Higher Education, 28*(1), 53–66. DOI: 10.1080/0309877032000161814

Covarrubias, R., Romero, A., & Trivelli, M. (2014). Family achievement guilt and mental well-being of college students. *Journal of Child and Family Studies, 24*(7), 2031–2037. DOI: 10.1007/s10826-014-0003-8

Daly, M., Boyce, C., & Wood, A. (2014). A social rank explanation of how money influences health. *Health Psychology, 34*(3), 222–230. DOI: 10.1037/hea0000098

De Vaney Olvey, C., Hogg, A., & Counts, W. (2002). Licensure requirements: Have we raised the bar too far? *Professional Psychology: Research and Practice, 33*(3), 323–329. DOI: 10.1037/0735-7028.33.3.323

Dubois, D., Rucker, D. D., & Galinsky, A. D. (2015, January 26). Social class, power, and selfishness: When and why upper and lower class individuals behave unethically. *Journal of Personality and Social Psychology.* Advance online publication. https://doi.org/10.1037/pspi0000008

Elbogen, E. B., Johnson, S. C., Wagner, H. R., Newton, V. M., & Beckham, J. C. (2012). Financial well-being and postdeployment adjustment among Iraq and Afghanistan war veterans. *Military Medicine, 177*(6), 669–675. DOI: 10.7205/MILMED-D-11-00388

Engle, J. (2007). Postsecondary access and success for first-generation college students. *American Academic*, 25–48.

Finlan, A. (2013). *Contemporary military cultura and strategic studies: US and UK armed forces in the 21st century.* New York: Routledge.

Gorski, P. (2008). The myth of the "culture of poverty'." *Educational Leadership, 65*(7), 32.

Harackiewicz, J. M., Canning, E. A., Tibbetts, Y., Giffen, C. J., Blair, S. S., Rouse, D. I., & Hyde, J. S. (2014). Closing the social class achievement gap for first-generation students in undergraduate biology. *Journal of Educational Psychology, 106*(2), 375–389. DOI: 10.1037/a0034679

Harackiewicz, J. M., Canning, E. A., Tibbetts, Y., Priniski, S. J., & Hyde, J. S. (2015). Closing achievement gaps with a utility-value intervention: Disentangling race and social class. *Journal of Personality and Social Psychology,111*(5), 745–765. DOI: 10.1037/pspp0000075

Harrison, L. A., Stevens, C. M., Monty, A. N., & Coakley, C. A. (2006). The consequences of stereotype threat on the academic performance of white and non-white lower income college students. *Social Psychology of Education, 9*(3), 341–357. DOI: 10.1007/s11218-005-5456-6

Hochshild, A. R. (1997). *The time bind: When work becomes home and home becomes work.* New York: Metropolitan/Holt.

Holland, J. L. (1997). *Making vocational choices: A theory of vocational personalities and work environment* (3rd ed.). Odessa, FL: Psychological Assessment Resources.

Hopps, J. A., & Liu, W. M. (2006). Working for social justice from within the health care system: The role of social class in psychology. In R. L. Toporek, L. H. Gerstein, N. A. Fouad, G. Roysircar, & T. Israel (Eds.), *Handbook for social justice in counseling psychology: Leadership, vision, and action* (pp. 318–337). Thousand Oaks, CA: Sage Publications.

Hsu, J., & Ketchen, B. (2013). Working with veterans, social class, and counseling: understanding the veteran population and implications for treatment. In W. M. Liu (Ed.), *The Oxford handbook of social class in counselling.* Oxford: Oxford University Press.

Joo, S., Durband, D. B., & Grable, J. (2009). The academic impact of financial stress on college students. *Journal of College Student Retention: Research, Theory and Practice, 10*(3), 287–305.

Kieffer, K. M., Schinka, J. A., & Curtiss, G. (2004). Person-environment congruence and personality domains in the prediction of job performance and work quality. *Journal of Counselling Psychology, 51*(2), 168–177. DOI: 10.1037/0022-0167.51.2.168

Kraus, M. W., Piff, P. K., & Keltner, D. (2009). Social class, sense of control, and social explanation. *Journal of Personality and Social Psychology, 97*(6), 992–1004. DOI: 10.1037/a0016357

Kushlev, K., Dunn, E. W., & Lucas, R. E. (2015). Higher income is associated with less daily sadness but not more daily happiness. *Social Psychological and Personality Science, 6*(5), 483–489. DOI: 10.1177/1948550614568161

Langhout, R. D., Drake, P., & Rosselli, F. (2009). Classism in the university setting: Examining student antecedents and outcomes. *Journal of Diversity in Higher Education, 2*(3), 166–181. DOI: 10.1037/a0016209

Langhout, R. D., Rosselli, F., & Feinstein, J. (2007). Assessing classism in academic settings. *Review of Higher Education: Journal of the Association for the Study of Higher Education, 30*(2), 145–184. DOI: 10.1353/rhe.2006.0073

Lehmann, W. (2009). Becoming middle class: How working-class university students draw and transgress moral class boundaries. *Sociology—the Journal of the British Sociological Association, 43*(4), 631–647. DOI: 10.1177/0038038509105412

Levine, R. (Ed.) (2006). *Social class and stratification: Classic statements and heoretical debates* (2nd ed.). Oxford: Rowman & Littlefield Publishers Inc.

Liu, W. M. (2002). A new framework to understand social class in counselling: The social class worldview model and modern classism theory. *Journal of Multicultural Counseling and Development, 32*, 95–122.

Liu, W. M. (2011). *Social class and classism in the helping professions.* Thousand Oaks, CA: Sage.

Liu, W. M. (2012). Developing a social class and classism consciousness: Implications for research and practice. In E. Altmaier & J. I. Hansen (Eds.), *Handbook of counseling psychology* (pp. 326–345). New York: Oxford University Press.

Liu, W. M. (2013). Future directions for scholarship in social class and classism in psychology. In W. M. Liu (Ed.), *The Oxford handbook of social class in counseling*. Oxford: Oxford University Press.

Liu, W. M., Ali, S. R., Soleck, G., Hopps, J., Dunston, K., & Pickett, T. (2004). Using social class in counseling psychology research. *Journal of Counselling Psychology, 51*(1), 3–18. DOI: 10.1037/0022-0167.15.1.3

Liu, W. M., Corkery, J., & Thome, J. (2010). Developing competency in social class and classism in counseling and psychotherapy. In J. A. Erickson Cornish, B. A. Schreier, L. I. Nadkarni, L. H. Metzger, & E. R. Rodolfa (Eds.), *Handbook of multicultural counseling competencies* (pp. 358–371). Hoboken, NJ: Wiley.

Lott, B. (2012). The social psychology of class and classism. *American Psychologist, 67*, 650–658. DOI: 10.1037/a0029369

Lupie, S. J., King, S., Meaney, M. J., & McEwen, B. S. (2001). Can poverty get under your skin? Basal cortisol levels and cognitive function in children from low and high socioeconomic status. *Developmental Psychopathology, 13*(3), 653–676.

Luthar, S. S. (2003). The culture of affluence: Psychological costs of material wealth. *Child Development, 74*(6), 1581–1593.

Luthar, S. S., & Latendresse, S. J. (2005). Children of the affluent: Challenges to well-being. *Current Directions in Psychological Science, 14*(1), 49–53. DOI: 10.1111/j.0963-7214.2005.00333.x

McCarron, G. P., & Inkelas, K. K. (2006). The gap between educational aspirations and attainment for first-generation college students and the role of parental involvement. *Journal of College Student Development, 47*(5), 534–549. DOI: 10.1353/csd.2006.0059

Michalski, D., Kohout, J., Wicherski, M., & Hart, B. (2011). 2009 doctorate employment survey. Center for Workforce Studies: American Psychological Association.

Miller, G. E., Chen, E., & Zhou, E. S. (2007). If it goes up, must it come down? Chronic stress and the hypothalamic pituarty-adrenocortical axis in humans. *Psychological Bulletin, 133*(1), 25–45.

Pascarella, E. T., Pierson, C. T., Wolniak, G. C., & Terenzini, P. T. (2004). First-generation college students: Additional evidence on college experiences and outcomes. *The Journal of Higher Education, 75*(3), 249–284. DOI: 10.1353/jhe.2004.0016

Patrick, M. E., Wightman, P., Schoeni, R. F., & Schulenberg, J. E. (2012). Socioeconomic status and substance use among young adults: A comparison across constructs and drugs. *Journal of Studies on Alcohol and Drugs, 73*(5), 772–782.

Piff, P. K., Kraus, M. W., Côté, S., Cheng, B. H., & Keltner, D. (2010). Having less, giving more: The influence of social class on prosocial behavior. *Journal of Personality and Social Psychology, 99*, 771–784. https://doi.org/10.1037/a0020092

Piff, P. K., Stancato, D. M., Côté, S., Mendoza-Denton, R., & Keltner, D. (2012). Higher social class predicts increased unethical behaviour. *Proceedings of the National Academy of Science USA, 109*(11), 4086–4091.

Quoidbach, J., Dunn, E. W., Petrides, K. V., & Mikolajczak, M. (2010). Money giveth, money taketh away: The dual effect of wealth on happiness. *Psychological Science, 21*(6), 759–763. DOI: 10.1177/0956797610371963

Ross, S., Cleland, J., & Macleod, M. J. (2006). Stress, debt and undergraduate medical student performance. *Medical Education, 40*(6), 584–589. DOI: 10.1111/j.1365-2929.2006.02448.x

Rucker, D. D., Dubois, D., & Galinsky, A. D. (2011). Generous paupers and stingy princes: Power drives consumer spending on self versus others. *Journal of Consumer Research, 37,* 1015–1029. 10.1086/657162

Rucker, D. D., & Galinsky, A. D. (2008). Desire to acquire: Powerlessness and compensatory consumption. *Journal of Consumer Research, 35,* 257–267. https://doi.org/10.1086/588569

Sagiv, L., & Schwartz, S. H. (2000). Value priorities and subjective well-being: Direct relations and congruity effects. *European Journal of Social Psychology, 30*(2), 177–198. DOI: 10.1002/(SICI)1099-0992(200003/04)30:2<177::AID-EJSP982>3.0.CO;2-Z

Schwartz, S. H., & Bardi, A. (1997). Influences of adaptation to communist rule on value priorities in eastern Europe. *Political Psychology, 18*(2), 385–410. DOI: 10.1111/0162-895x.00062

Shafran, R. B. (1992). Children of affluent parents. In J. D. O'Brien, & D. J. Pilowsky (Eds.), *Psychotherapies with children and adolescents: Adapting the psychodynamic process* (pp. 269–288). Washington, DC: American Psychiatric Association.

Shields, N. (2002). Anticipatory socialization, adjustment to university life, and perceived stress: Generational and sibling effects. *Social Psychology of Education, 5*(4), 365–392. DOI: 10.1023/a:1020929822361

Singh-Manoux, A., Marmot, M. G., & Adler, N. E. (2005). Does subjective social status predict health and change in health status better than objective status? *Psychosomatic Medicine, 67*(6), 855–861. DOI: 10.1097/01.psy.0000188434.52941.a0

Smith, L. (2005). Psychotherapy, classism, and the poor: Conspicuous by their absence. *American Psychologist, 60*(7), 687–696. DOI: 10.1037/0003-066X.60.7.687

Spencer, B., & Castano, E. (2007). Social class is dead. Long live social class! Stereotype threat among low socioeconomic status individuals. *Social Justice Research, 20*(4), 418–432. DOI: 10.1007/s11211-007-0047-7

Steele, C. M. (1997). A threat in the air: How stereotypes shape intellectual identity and performance. *American Psychologist, 52*(6), 613–629. DOI: 10.1037/0003-066X.52.6.613

Stephens, N. M., Fryberg, S., Markus, H., Johnson, C., & Covarrubias, R. (2012). Unseen disadvantage: How American universities' focus on independence undermines the academic performance of first-generation college students. *Journal of Personality and Social Psychology, 102*(6), 1178–1197. DOI: 10.1037/a0027143

Stephens, N. M., Townsend, S. S. M., Markus, H. R., & Phillips, L. T. (2012). A cultural mismatch: Independent cultural norms produce greater increases in cortisol and more negative emotions among first-generation college students. *Journal of Experimental Social Psychology, 48*(6), 1389–1393. DOI: 10.1016/j.jesp.2012.07.008

Tablante, C. B., & Fiske, S. T. (2015). Teaching social class. *Teaching Psychology, 42*(2), 184–190.

Terenzini, P. T., Pascarella, E. T., & Blimling, G. S. (1996). Students' out-of-class experiences and their influence on learning and cognitive development: A literature review. *Journal of College Student Development, 37*(2), 149–162.

Thompson, M. N., & Subich, L. M. (2013). Development and exploration of the experiences with classism scale. *Journal of Career Assessment, 21*(1), 139–158. DOI: 10.1177/1069072712450494

Walton, G. M., & Spencer, S. J. (2009). Latent ability: Grades and test scores systematically underestimate the intellectual ability of negatively stereotyped students. *Psychological Science, 20*(9), 1132–1139. DOI: 10.1111/j.1467-9280.2009.02417.x

Zaw, K., Hamilton, D., & Darity Jr, W. (2016). Race, wealth and incarceration: Results from the National Longitudinal Survey of Youth. *Race and Social Problems, 8*(1), 103–115.

18 Issues of Race and Ethnicity in Counselling Psychology

OHEMAA NKANSA-DWAMENA

CHAPTER OUTLINE

INTRODUCTION 266

DIALOGUE AND NARRATIVE: HOW DOES
COUNSELLING PSYCHOLOGY THINK ABOUT
RACE AND ETHNICITY? 267

PRIVILEGE, PREJUDICE, BIAS,
AND RACE 269

CHALLENGING STEREOTYPES 270

CLINICAL PRACTICE: HOW DO WE ENGAGE
WITH RACE AND ETHNICITY? 271
  Therapist Matching 271
  Claire 272

WORKING ACROSS THE LIFESPAN: HISTORY IN
RACE AND ETHNICITY 274
  Maxwell 276

CONCLUSION 278

LEARNING OUTCOMES

BY THE END OF THIS CHAPTER YOU SHOULD
BE ABLE TO ANSWER THE FOLLOWING KEY
QUESTIONS:

1. What are the important aspects to
consider when working with black and
minority clients in a therapeutic setting?

2. In what ways do positions of privilege
impact practice?

3. How can the concept of intersectionality
help us to better understand the experiences of black and minority ethnic clients?

Counselling Psychology: A Textbook for Study and Practice, First Edition. Edited by David Murphy.
© 2017 John Wiley & Sons Ltd. Published 2017 by John Wiley & Sons Ltd.

INTRODUCTION

The demographic landscape of the UK reveals a society rich in multicultural backgrounds. In the UK there is continued evolution of communities made up of different cultures, ethnicities, races, religions, and sexualities. However, as a professional community, we may not always acknowledge or incorporate these elements of difference and diversity when therapeutic services are developed. The people this is most likely to affect are those from black minority ethnic (BME) groups. A consequence of culturally insensitive service design of psychological therapies is that people from BME groups are more likely to have difficulty accessing services for counselling (Murphy & Godbehere, 2015).

When considering the lived experiences of BME people, it is imperative to consider the intersectionality of identity and understand how race and ethnicity interact with other aspects of identity, including, for example, sexuality, gender, and social class. Taking an intersectional approach tells us much more about the individual, how they perceive themselves, and any threats there might be to identity negotiation. Crenshaw (2012) has written extensively on intersectionality and suggests that it is improbable to view the experiences of black individuals through a singular lens, and to do so minimizes our understanding of the multiple levels of oppression and discrimination that black people may experience. For example, when considering issues of advancement in the workplace for women, a black woman might have to contend with both racial and gender discrimination. To view her experiences purely through the lens of her gender identity alters and minimizes her experiences as a black woman and does not take into full account the various social inequities she may have to contend with in regard to the combination of racial and gender discrimination. As such, it is important that counselling psychologists approach their work from an intersectional positioning, understanding how race and ethnicity, or sexuality and social class, or age and gender, or any combination of such variables will intersect and have an impact on the client's narratives and experiences.

Ethically, counselling psychologists have a responsibility to learn, practice, and dialogue in a way that is understanding of issues concerning diversity and inclusion. This awareness is imperative to the counselling psychology profession, especially because the historical development of most therapeutic frameworks has been attributed to white men from Western cultures. Until recently, aspects of race and ethnicity were not widely considered in therapeutic applications. This is despite research that suggests an overrepresentation of black service users in secondary care services, and the uptake of therapeutic care services by ethnic minority individuals remaining low (Institute of Race Relations, n.d.). This low take-up of services is linked to several factors, including limited cultural awareness in some service provisions; therapeutic frameworks that do not lend themselves wholly to inclusivity; and a limited dialogue in the therapeutic field around race, ethnicity, and culture, and the interplay between these and other identity components as well as mental health and well-being (Codner, 2015; Lowe, 2013).

In this chapter I will explore issues of race, ethnicity, and counselling psychology using case vignettes to highlight two main areas:

- Dialogue and narrative: how can counselling psychology think about race and ethnicity?
- Clinical practice: how do we engage with race and ethnicity? The development of awareness and application to therapeutic practice.

DIALOGUE AND NARRATIVE: HOW DOES COUNSELLING PSYCHOLOGY THINK ABOUT RACE AND ETHNICITY?

The terms race and ethnicity are often used interchangeably. Historically, race has referred to physical and biological constructs; ethnicity on the other hand is also defined by physical characteristics but also refers to historical and cultural patterns and collective identities shared by groups from specific geographic regions of the world (Cabral & Smith, 2011). Whilst race and ethnicity have significant overlap, they are in fact different constructs. Fernando (2002) captured this in his description of the two: race is largely about physical features and is socially (not genetically) constructed, and ethnicity is psychological because of its reliance on the identity of the person.

Issues of race and ethnicity are highly politically, emotionally, and psychologically charged. The issue is complex and rooted in historical processes such as slavery and colonization, which still have an impact today on the individual psyche, group processes, and interpersonal dynamics. The effects can be seen in racial discrimination and the oppression of ethnic minority individuals. For example, the struggle with social oppression did not end with slavery but continues through racial discrimination targeting immigrants to the UK. A consequence of racism for immigrants coming to the UK has been an identity conflict. As people strove to establish a black British identity they did so in the face of racism deeply rooted in a history of slavery and colonization (Fryer, 1993).

More covert forms of discrimination also exist and are also rooted in these historical processes. Micro-aggressions and unconscious bias are examples of covert and subtle racism that can emerge in the therapeutic setting and in the field of counselling psychology (Fakhry-Davids, 2011). For some ethnic minority people, a common experience is a sense of "otherness" and a pronounced experience of feeling different, not belonging, and not being really seen or heard. Additionally, current narratives surrounding race and ethnicity continue to be highly relevant and visible today in the form of recent injustices such as police shootings, deaths in custody, and overtly racist political narratives. The rise of social media has provided a platform for speaking out about such difficulties and injustices. However, race remains a complex and difficult issue to speak about and it is often met with fear, silence, and avoidance.

Limiting engagement with issues of race contributes to and extends existing inequalities on social, political, educational, and economic grounds. Oppression due to race leads to overrepresentation of ethnic minority individuals entering the probation and prison systems, and can add to discrimination in higher education with regard to both acceptance and completion rates (Weale, 2016). According to Fitzpatrick, Kumar, Nkansa-Dwamena, and Thorne (2014) clients frequently experience repeat instances of racism in therapy. This is due to a lack of therapist knowledge and competence. Such a gap in knowledge can prompt inappropriate questioning and underpin assumptions, disacknowledgement of clients' multiple identities, misdiagnosis or overdiagnosis of individuals, and minimization of their experiences and identities. Clearly there is a lot of work to do for counselling psychologists to become aware of and better informed about narratives around race and ethnicity.

Having an open dialogue in the field of counselling psychology about race and ethnicity is certainly an effective way for therapists to incorporate these issues into their work. Being open and willing to engage in client narratives around race and ethnicity can support the therapeutic process and the development of trust, connection, and respect. Being understanding with an active enquiry and exploration of race and race-related issues can have a positive impact. This can support clients from BME groups to access services and prevent early termination of therapy.

Some practitioners may attempt to engage on a more superficial level; engaging in tick box exercises, such as attending a short talk on diversity and doing the bare minimum to understand issues of race and diversity. This might be due to cursory reading around the issues, rather than engaging in a deeper, more self-reflective consideration. Engagement at a deeper level can include respectful enquiry and being curious about one's own position in relation to others, and checking one's own biases and privilege. Additionally, it is not uncommon for practitioners to struggle in knowing how to initiate conversations around race and ethnicity: whether to wait and engage with these only when a client raises these issues, or to only attend to issues of race if it happens to be brought up in a supervisory context. In other words, some practitioners might avoid or disacknowledge that which may not be part of their lived experience or hold the same relevance to them (Lago, 2011).

REFLECTION POINTS

- What are the most important aspects to consider when working with BME clients in a therapeutic setting?
- How do you consider your impact in the practice room and wider therapeutic community?
- How does the concept of intersectionality help us to better engage and understand therapeutic explorations with BME clients?

All too often it falls to clients to bring up race. However, clients often don't broach this area if they have doubts about the practitioner's competence to speak about race and ethnicity. A cycle can then be repeated, wherein BME clients are silenced and thereby their identity and core sense of self are impacted. This might reinforce prior experiences of invisibility and minimization, and have an adverse impact on their self-esteem and psychological well-being.

It is likely that today's practitioners have developed at least an intellectual appreciation of race and ethnicity in the therapeutic context and are striving to be sensitive to these in practice. However, it is not enough to have knowledge and sensitivity alone; counselling psychologists must also have the skill and the competency to know how to incorporate these into their practice. This point is summed up well by Cardemil and Battle (2003), who suggest many therapists

> may agree that it is important to examine one's personal assumptions and recognise the value of cultural beliefs and traditions other than those embraced by the dominant culture . . . many therapists do not know how to incorporate their appreciation of racial and ethnic diversity into therapy in a tangible way. (p. 278)

PRIVILEGE, PREJUDICE, BIAS, AND RACE

The inherent privilege of the majority race has not been explored in depth in the field of counselling psychology, even though, as noted above, the pervasiveness of it underlies therapeutic systems and relationships. Ancis and Sysmanzki (2001) write of the various ways in which privilege is interwoven into societal systems, including work and education settings, housing, and in the legal system. Effectively, the presence of privilege "perpetuates inequities for some and unearned advantages and opportunities for others" (Ancis & Sysmanzki, 2001, p. 548). Privilege can facilitate unearned benefits and disacknowledge and ignore race discrimination, and often privileges associated with a majority race are unexamined and unarticulated by those who benefit. In the UK the majority race is white, which suggests that counselling psychologists who are white have an ethical duty to explore in depth what can be termed as "white privilege."

Even though the awareness of therapist bias and knowledge about race and ethnicity are encouraged in some trainings, and are important components of cultural competence as a practitioner, only limited attention is paid to naming, exploring, and fostering therapists' racial and ethnic self-awareness. It is important to consider both the conscious and subconscious ways this might impede the therapeutic process and therapist self-development (Alleyne, 2011).

It is imperative that therapists acknowledge their own positions of privilege and power. This requires therapists to consider and reflect upon aspects of their selves and experiences they may not have previously considered. In their qualitative study examining counsellor privilege and bias, Ancis and Szymanski (2001) qualitatively analysed responses to described experiences of privilege developed by Peggy McIntosh (1988). Their study revealed a varied level of awareness of privilege ranging from no awareness to demonstrated awareness, from unwillingness to engage in pro-action to a more pronounced awareness of privilege and efforts to attempt to eradicate this. It can be helpful to encourage counselling psychologists in training to complete an experiential exercise in which they consider their various positions of privilege and, in relation to race, think about what gains they receive from this position, but also what it might be like to be in the converse position.

Reflective exercise: below are a sample of indicators of privilege as identified by Peggy McIntosh (1988). Consider how many of these you recognize or identify with:

- I can go shopping alone most of the time, pretty well assured that I will not be followed or harassed.
- I can turn on the television or look at the front page of the paper and see people of my race widely represented.
- I can be sure that my children will be given curricular materials that testify to the existence of their race.
- I can be pretty sure of having my voice heard in a group in which I am the only member of my race.
- I can do well in a challenging situation without being called a credit to my race.
- I can criticize our government and talk about how much I fear its policies and behaviour without being seen as a cultural outsider.
- I can be pretty sure that if I ask to talk to the "person in charge," I will be facing a person of my race.

Another theme connected to the consideration of privilege is colour blindness. Some therapists adopt this stance of colour blindness and might say "I don't see race" or "I don't see colour." Whilst "we are all equal" may seem plausible in theory, in a very real and practical sense, denying aspects of a person's identity adds to and creates inequity, rather than addressing issues of discrimination and racism (Ade-Serrano & Nkansa-Dwamena, 2016). The danger of colour-blindness is that it impacts counselling psychologists' ability to engage in dialogue about race and can be a barrier to hearing about experiences of race and discrimination.

CHALLENGING STEREOTYPES

Eleftheriadou (2010) suggests that another way to consider issues of race and ethnicity in counselling psychology is to challenge and be aware of stereotyping individuals from minority backgrounds. This is linked directly to privilege and bias as it is possible that it is from privileged and biased positions that negative stereotypes develop. Stereotypes can perpetuate separation and segregation by referring to ethnic minorities as "them" or "they." Eleftheriadou (2010) also suggests challenging the negative images people might have of ethnic minorities that stem from the media and evoke people's fears about difference. In relation to therapeutic interventions and engagement it is important not to see clients as representatives of their ethnic groups, or dismiss them as unsuitable for therapy because their narratives do not "fit" with Eurocentric frameworks and approaches. This also connects to the concept of viewing clients through an intersectional lens that takes into account the multiple facets of their identities and narratives, and is not based on assumptions or fixed notions of race and ethnicity.

Reflection point: the use of pronouns such as "their" or "they" might be considered appropriate when referring to people who actively request to be referred to in this way. One example might be where a person's gender identity does not match with more frequently used personal pronouns such as "he/she." In this instance it can be preferable to use this term not because it is used to describe a group but because it is used in respect of an individual preference. How might you feel using these pronouns in different contexts with different people depending on your own personal background and experiences? What things come to mind?

CLINICAL PRACTICE: HOW DO WE ENGAGE WITH RACE AND ETHNICITY?

Therapist Matching

Some research suggests that clients should be matched with therapists who are similar in race and ethnicity (Burkard & Knox, 2004; Cabral & Smith, 2011). It is proposed that being racially and ethnically similar might facilitate comfort and trust in the therapeutic relationship. Whilst research (e.g., Gray-Little & Kaplan, 2000) does not consistently support sameness as a necessary element of the therapeutic relationship, what is important is that there are particular elements of a therapeutic relationship that will support therapeutic progress. This includes openness of the therapist, willingness to explore the whole of the client, and competency to hear and engage with the narratives around race, ethnicity, racism, and discrimination.

It is not as helpful if a counselling psychologist ignores or circumvents the issue of race. To ignore the racial aspect of someone's experiences is to cut off part of their self and identity. Instances where therapists have felt uncomfortable talking about race, or empathiing with the "whole of the client's world," which means to consider their history, their (racial)identity, can have a negative effect on the therapeutic relationship. This can also reinforce negative experiences or beliefs that the client may have in relation to their race. It is helpful when issues arise related to sameness, difference, and race, if counselling psychologists openly address these with the client.

The issue of matching client and therapist is not, however, straightforward. Below is a case vignette that demonstrates an instance of therapist and client matching that prompted difficulty in the therapeutic relationship, and how a failure to explore this led the client to withdraw from therapy.

Claire

Background Context

Claire was a black woman who was referred by her GP for short term psychological therapy. Claire had been in an abusive relationship and had taken steps to divorce her partner. Making the transition from wife and mother to a single woman and single mother was difficult and triggered a depressive episode. The referral stated that Claire had been feeling low, emotionally labile, and was experiencing a lack of energy.

Claire was seen for four sessions of cognitive-behavioural therapy for treatment of symptoms of depression. Her therapeutic goals included processing her history of abuse, supporting strengths, and development of a positive and constructive way forward and modification of unhelpful thoughts and beliefs. Claire was briefed on the boundaries of confidentiality.

Presenting Issues

At assessment, Claire reported that her daily functioning was much better than it had been at the point of referral. She was feeling more optimistic and stronger than she had felt in a long time. She had a good support network in the form of friends and family. She had reached a point where she could let go of her anger towards her ex-husband and her anger about being abused both physically and mentally. Despite these positive feelings, when the divorce was first finalized she stopped eating, overworked herself, and stopped taking care of herself. Her ex-husband continued to taunt her; he often sent abusive texts and messages through other people. She reported that she had been having negative thoughts regarding her self-perception and her ability to function. She felt tired and demotivated, even though she had taken steps to move on from the relationship and rebuild her life.

Initial Meeting

When I first met Claire, she had already been assessed by my supervisor, who was white. Claire was visibly uncomfortable in the first few sessions with me; her body language was quite closed. She protested against my note taking and said "I don't want you writing things about me, everybody will know about me." In the session, Claire spoke of the shame she felt because she was divorcing her husband and everybody was talking about her in the community. She felt she had violated her religious beliefs by seeking a divorce. Her religion helped her to navigate the abusive relationship; she said it kept her sane and was the constant she could rely on. She was ashamed and angry that she had stayed in the relationship for so long. She described her fear that I thought she was a coward, and stupid for conceding to her husband and for subjecting her children to a hostile environment? Surely I didn't respect her because I was a black woman? These were not my feelings at all, in fact I admired Claire for her courage and strength, and so I wondered what it was about me that might relay the messages to her and trigger these fears in her.

Content and Process of Sessions

In subsequent sessions, Claire's discomfort with our similarities also revealed itself in her constant questioning of my religious and cultural background. With Claire, any displayed or suggested similarity posed a problem. When she posed questions about my religious and cultural background, experience taught me that it would be helpful to explore the reasoning behind her line of questioning. I gently pointed out to her that this was her time and her space to explore, evolve, and address issues important to her. I was curious as to why she wanted information about my background, and why she thought it might be useful to her progress in therapy. She thought about this for a while, before revealing that if I practised the same religion, she would feel judged, because that was the attitude previously displayed by her community. The same sentiment was applicable to my cultural background. If I turned out to be similar, I would think she was weak for staying in such an abusive situation. The fact that I was visibly black and female was difficult for her to deal with. However, I chose not to disclose my cultural background, as I wanted to keep the focus on Claire and her problems. I tried to reassure her that I was her therapist first and foremost, and one of the most important aspects of my job was to make sure that our work existed in a nonjudgemental therapeutic environment. Second, it was important that we explored the underlying issue with regards to her distrust of me: it seemed that the reactions that she had experienced from her community had caused her much hurt and pain, and she had projected these feelings onto me. I had become a part of the fabric, a part of the meshed group of people who had criticized her for leaving her marriage and had not fully supported her decision to divorce. To an extent, there was a larger issue at play. Claire's self-esteem and confidence had slowly been eroded during the course of her relationship, and an exploration of her thoughts revealed that she had a very low opinion of herself and a negative self-perception. Real and imagined criticism had an adverse effect on her. Coming to therapy was an admission that she could not cope; therefore, she interpreted this as she was weak and added weight to the critical statements that others had made to her. Our similarities were a stark reminder of her perceived failure as a black woman, and of every comment that had been made about her as a wife and as a black person.

Outcome

My attempt to reassure Claire of the safety of the therapeutic relationship did not have a positive effect on the therapeutic encounter. Claire repeatedly cancelled her appointments and, when she did attend, she seemed to be detached: it was as if she had not fully engaged in therapy. My attempts to help her challenge her negative thoughts and modify her dysfunctional beliefs proved unsuccessful. In one session she brought her child along. I interpreted that this action was a defence mechanism. By having her child in the room, Claire might feel protected and would be less likely to reveal anything that might require proper exploration. Of course, I did not get the chance to explore this with her in the session, and I made a mental note to address this in her next session. She never came back to therapy after that, and my attempts to contact her failed. I was always slightly concerned about the effect my race, gender, religious affinity, and culture had on our therapeutic relationship. The experience prompted a long period of self-reflection for me. One of the most prominent issues that seemed to re-emerge was the role of the "therapist self" in therapy. I often wondered if her experience might have been different if she had seen a therapist of a different race, or one from a different background. I also reflected on the assumed "sameness" between Claire and me. Although we were both black and female, her cultural and religious background differentiated her from me, and I failed to acknowledge this.

This case was complicated because it was the first time my "sameness and difference" to a client played such a significantly negative role in the outcome of therapy. Our racial, gender, and religious similarities and differences affected therapy to such an extent that this client terminated therapy after attending only sporadically.

Thompson, Kent, and Smith (2002) challenge the belief that clients should prefer ethnically matched therapists; their research found that utilization of mental health services by African American individuals was low because they perceived African American therapists to be elitist, judgemental, or detached. This was very much the case with Claire, even though it was not my intention to cause this discomfort within her.

WORKING ACROSS THE LIFESPAN: HISTORY IN RACE AND ETHNICITY

Considering issues of race and ethnicity in an assessment should include an exploration of a client's cultural context. This can help to develop an understanding of different worldviews. Individuals from ethnic minority groups have their own unique sense of life stage expectations, which will be informed by social structures, including their family and community history and their environmental contexts. This may be directly linked to experiences of their racial and ethnic identities and the ways they have been perceived by mainstream society at various stages in their lives. It will also be informed by the messages they received within their family and community about race, racial issues, ethnicity, and intersecting identities. An example of this may include what it means to be a black girl transitioning into womanhood, from a working class background, and the challenges this might raise.

In clinical practice, when working with issues of race and ethnicity, counselling psychologists must also have an understanding of and be able to acknowledge the historical impact of racism and other forms of racial oppression on clients' construction of self. This is an area that often either goes unnoticed or is minimized. Although historical events will differ across ethnic minority groups, a way of understanding this notion better is to consider the impact of historical slavery and marginalization for black people. McKenzie-Mavinga (2011) speaks powerfully about this in her work, where she draws a link between slavery and historical trauma and the ways in which this can filter into many aspects of black people's lives, including their identity development, the way in which they relate to others, and their mental health.

It is not being suggested here that individuals from majority groups will not have relevant markers for their life stage experiences, but for individuals for whom issues of race and ethnicity form a part of their everyday narrative, this is an added layer of identity formation that may feature within their therapy narratives. As such, it is important that counselling psychologists are cognizant of this potential. Additionally, when working across the life span, counselling psychologists can respectfully enquire into cultural norms and influences, taking the time to step away from racial stereotypes and perceptions to which the client may have already been subjected. Bypassing this maintains an unhealthy pattern of not fully acknowledging the race and ethnicity of the client, and the therapeutic encounter can become yet another hostile space in which clients from ethnic minority backgrounds are not fully seen or heard.

ISSUES OF RACE AND ETHNICITY IN PRACTICE: A REVIEW

Several authors have developed helpful frameworks and recommendations to help therapists integrate factors concerning race, ethnicity, and multicultural issues into their practice. In their development of a more practical way to apply knowledge and reflection around race and ethnicity, Cardemil and Battle (2003, pp. 279–282) identified some crucial elements to aid this process. They suggest that therapists should employ the following:

- Suspend preconceptions.
- Understand differences in conceptualization of mental health.
- Understand and explore differences in communication.
- Err on the side of discussion and take risks in exploring issues pertaining to race and ethnicity.

- Keep on updating knowledge and understanding processes related to race and ethnicity.

This is echoed by Alleyne (2011, p. 127), who, in addition to the above, suggests that therapists:

- Acknowledge and actively deal with racism operating at these levels; namely, individual, institutional, intentional, and unintentional.
- Become aware of hidden feelings and subtle expressions of indifference, not caring, not being concerned or interested in the concerns of the racial "other."
- Recognize the influence of the community.
- Redefine and work appropriately with Eurocentric concepts of mental health.
- Reappraise what psychological yardsticks are culturally relevant in determining psychic equilibrium and "cure."

Farooq and Abbas' (2013, pp. 660–663) article, which was published in the *Psychologist*, entitled "No Voice, No Choice," expands on "cultural competency tips" and builds yet further on Alleyne's suggestions with the following:

- Understanding and acknowledging how individual groups and universal features of being human affect the client.
- Having an awareness of values and customs of the client's culture.
- Managing self-disclosure.
- Adapting assessment, intervention, and research methods in line with the client's cultural background.
- Having knowledge of the client's language and the pragmatics of its use.
- Identifying and challenging own assumptions and stereotypes.
- Understanding your own cultural background and how it influences your work.

A model by Hays (2009, pp. 356–358) also offers some insight into how therapists can apply their awareness and engage with issues pertaining to race, ethnicity, and culture by suggesting:

- Identification of culturally related strengths and supports.
- For environmentally based problems, focus on helping the client to make changes that minimize stressors, increase personal strengths and supports, and build skills for interacting more effectively with the social and physical environment.
- Validation of clients' self-reported experiences of oppression.
- Emphasis of collaboration over confrontation, with attention to client–therapist differences.

The following case vignette attempts to illustrate how a therapist may apply some of these competences.

Maxwell

Brief Context/Biography

Maxwell was a black woman of African descent. She worked part time and was also a student. She self-referred to the psychological therapy service following a depressive episode, ongoing anxiety, and struggles with low self-esteem. Her referral stated that she had been experiencing persistent low mood, with alternating periods of high-level anxiety and panic. She had begun to isolate herself, and struggled to engage with her work. She worried that her performance was not reflective of her intellect and effort, and this had shaken her confidence.

Maxwell was seen for brief cognitive-behavioural therapy for the treatment of symptoms of depression and anxiety and low self-esteem. Her therapeutic goals included managing her mood, developing healthier coping strategies, and improvement of self-esteem. She also wanted to work on building a healthier narrative about her capabilities as an ethnic minority individual in a predominantly white setting.

Presenting Issues

On the surface, this case could have been a very straightforward presentation of depression and anxiety that could be managed and addressed within a short-term context. However, Maxwell's presentation was underlined by racial, ethnic, and cultural complexities, which intertwined with her sense of self and her self-esteem, affecting her beliefs and thoughts about herself.

When she came for assessment, Maxwell felt she had emerged from a very difficult period where she experienced thoughts of not wanting to exist, and did not want to alert her family and friends to the confusion, frustration, and helplessness she felt. She was cautiously optimistic about how therapy might help her, but admitted she was someone who did not like to reveal when she was struggling. However, she had a good support network in the form of friends and family. She had been having negative thoughts regarding her self-perception and her ability to function. She felt tired and demotivated, even though she felt her worst period had passed.

Initial Meeting

When I first met Maxwell she appeared to be quite shy and introverted, she responded to my questions with succinct and clear answers. Her body language suggested a protectiveness of herself from the environment and the process. As the session continued, she relaxed slightly, which may have been prompted by my gentle enquiry, and my attempts to build trust and containment within the room.

I attempted to build a bigger picture of who Maxwell is and what may have been contributing to her current difficulties. She spoke of existing in an academic environment where her sense of "otherness" was made very apparent to her, through overt and subtle comments and interactions. This had prompted memories from her younger years where she experienced bullying and discrimination due to her race and her religion. She held multiple identities in terms of race, culture, religion, and gender, and the intersection of these was a process she was still trying to figure out. While initially it was put to her that her discomfort and low self-esteem were due to her difficulty adapting to a new environment, further exploration showed the situation to be much more complex. I purposely made sure to explore all parts of her, and not be purely guided by the obvious symptoms or the initial referral.

Content and Process of Sessions

In attempting to improve Maxwell's self-esteem and mood, it was important for us to explore her intersectionality and the ways in which she perceived herself. I learned from her that her family had been subjected to racism and discrimination, which had impacted on her ownership of her racial identity. She stated she oscillated between not quite knowing where she belonged and trying to embrace and have pride in her racial, cultural, and ethnic background. She also noticed that as she became more aware of her identity, her self-esteem started to suffer, and this was further compounded when she was bullied during her early secondary school years. She had previously tried to build a protective barrier to manage the anxieties she felt coming to a new environment. However, as she struggled to find her place, and experience a sense of belonging, she questioned her academic skills and abilities, and found herself slipping into a place of "darkness." She also felt she could not speak to anyone about this as she feared they would either dismiss her concerns, or not understand her experience, especially as she was trying to make sense of this herself.

Outcome

Maxwell gradually began to build confidence and appreciate herself as she used the space in therapy to consider her intersecting identities, and examine her relationship with the different aspects of herself. We had explored her relationship to her environment and her sense of belonging, paying particular attention to her own self-perceptions, and the systemic issues that may have been further influencing her negative beliefs about herself. We took the time to process some of her past experiences and examine the discrimination she and her family had been subjected to, and the ways in which she had internalized certain messages. Despite this she had been able to make great gains academically and in her connections with other people. She attempted to test her fears by speaking out more, by trying not to minimize herself so persistently, and by developing a healthier narrative around who she was as a person—taking into consideration that she had many different unique parts to her. This was not a way to disacknowledge the difficulties and realities pertaining to race and ethnicity, but instead it was an attempt to address these and construct an alternative dialogue. Maxwell commented that in some ways, she has never really had the chance to consider her whole self in this manner, and further understand how her distress had been connected to underlying and historical issues.

CONCLUSION

In this chapter we have considered how reflecting on issues of race and ethnicity in counselling psychology allows practitioners, students, and trainees to explore the intersectionality of identities of ethnic minority individuals. Additionally, several important competencies have been presented that help highlight a number of different areas of practice and potential blind spots for therapists to be aware of, and the need to consider the multiple levels of engagement when working with race and ethnicity.

To fully engage with race and ethnicity in counselling psychology is to have a better understanding of how these present in practice, and to understand what we each bring to our work as counselling psychologists by how we individually conceptualize issues of race and ethnicity. Counselling psychology is an opportunity to acknowledge and work with the impact that privilege and bias can have on engagement with racial and ethnic diversity, and to learn and apply an intersectional view that will better prepare us to work with issues of race and ethnicity in the many forms they may be present.

SUGGESTED FURTHER READING

Lowe, F. (Ed.). (2013). *Thinking space: Promoting thinking about race, culture and diversity in psychotherapy and beyond.* London: Karnac Books.
A book of essays on race, culture, and diversity as they pertains to psychotherapy and other contexts.

Cardemil, E. V., & Battle, C. L. (2003). Guess who's coming to therapy? Getting comfortable with conversations about race and ethnicity in psychotherapy. *Professional Psychology: Research and Practice, 34*(3), 278–286.
A journal article that challenges readers to think extensively about how they may actually engage with race and ethnicity in practice.

REFERENCES

Ade-Serrano, Y., & Nkansa-Dwamena, O. (2016). Voicing the uncomfortable: How can we talk about race? *Counselling Psychology Review, 31*(2), 5–9.

Alleyne, A. (2011). Overcoming racism, discrimination and oppression in psychotherapy. In Colin Lago (Ed.), *The Handbook of Transcultural Counselling and Psychotherapy* (pp. 117–129). London: McGraw-Hill Education.

Ancis, J. R., & Szymanski, D. M. (2001). Awareness of white privilege among white counselling trainees. *The Counselling Psychologist, 29*(4), 548–569.

Burkard, A. W., & Knox, S. (2004). Effect of therapist colour-blindness on empathy and attributions in cross-cultural counselling. *Journal of Counselling Psychology, 51*(4), 387–397.

Cabral, R. R., & Smith, T. B. (2011). Racial/ethnic matching of clients and therapists in mental health services: A meta-analytic review of preferences, perceptions, and outcomes. *Journal of Counselling Psychology, 58* (4), 537–554.

Cardemil, E. V., & Battle, C. L. (2003). Guess who's coming to therapy? Getting comfortable with conversations about race and ethnicity in psychotherapy. *Professional Psychology: Research and Practice, 34*(3), 278–286.

Codner, N. (2015). Mixed race identity and counselling. *Therapy Today, 26*(10), 16–20.

Crenshaw, K. (2012). *On intersectionality: The essential writings of Kimberlé Crenshaw.* New York: New Press

Eleftheriadou, Z. (2010). *Psychotherapy and culture: Weaving inner and outer worlds.* London: Karnac Books.

Fakhry-Davids, M. (2011). *Internal racism: A psychoanalytical approach to difference.* Basingstoke: Palgrave Macmillan.

Farooq, R., & Abbas, I. (2013). No voice, no choice. *The Psychologist, September 26*, 660–663.

Fernando, S. (2002). *Mental health, race and culture.* Basingstoke: Palgrave.

Fitzpatrick, R., Kumar, S., Nkansa-Dwamena, O. & Thorne, L. (2014). *Ethnic inequalities in mental health.* Retrieved from https://lankellychase.org.uk/wp-content/uploads/2015/07/Ethnic-Inequality-in-Mental-Health-Confluence-Full-Report-March2014.pdf (accessed March 13, 2017).

Fryer, P. (1993). *Aspects of black British history.* London: Index Books Ltd.

Gray-Little, B., & Kaplan, D. (2000). Race and ethnicity and psychotherapy research. In C. R. Snyder and R. E. Ingram (Eds.), *Handbook of psychological change: Psychotherapy processes and practices for the 21st century* (pp. 591–613). New York: Wiley.

Hays, P. A. (2009). Integrating evidence-based practice, CBT, and multicultural therapy: Ten steps for culturally competent practice. *Professional Psychology: Research and Practice, 40,* 354–360.

Institute of Race Relations (nd). Health and mental health statistics. Retrieved from http://www.irr.org.uk/research/statistics/health/ (accessed March 13, 2017).

Lago, C. (Ed.). (2011). *The handbook of transcultural counselling and psychotherapy.* London: McGraw-Hill Education.

Lowe, F. (Ed.). (2013). *Thinking space: Promoting thinking about race, culture and diversity in psychotherapy and beyond.* London: Karnac Books.

McIntosh, P. (1988). White privilege: Unpacking the invisible knapsack. *Race, class, and gender in the United States: An integrated study, 4,* 165–169.

McKenzie-Mavinga, I. (2011). Training for multicultural therapy: The course curriculum. In Lago, C. (Ed.), *The handbook of transcultural counselling and psychotherapy* (pp. 30–42). London: McGraw-Hill Education.

Murphy, D., & Godbehere, N. (2015). Improving the equity of access to psychological therapies: A study of factors affecting the equity of access to primary care psychological therapies. University of Nottingham. Unpublished report to Nottingham City Care.

Thompson, A. R., Kent, G., & Smith, J. A. (2002). Living with vitiligo: Dealing with difference. *British Journal of Health Psychology, 7,* 213–225.

Weale, S. (2016, February 11). Universities told to raise numbers of working class and black students. *The Guardian.* Retrieved from https://www.theguardian.com/education/2016/feb/11/universities-told-to-raise-numbers-of-working-class-and-black-students (accessed March 13, 2017).

Psychology

MEG-JOHN BARKER AND CHRISTINA RICHARDS

CHAPTER OUTLINE

INTRODUCTION 282

UNDERSTANDING GENDER 283
Dominant Cultural Understandings
of Gender 283
A More Complex and Diverse Psychological
Understanding of Gender 284
Implications of a Simple Fixed Binary Model in
a Complex Nonbinary Fluid World 286

COUNSELLING PSYCHOLOGY WITH
CISGENDER WOMEN AND MEN 286

COUNSELLING PSYCHOLOGY WITH TRANS
MEN AND WOMEN 288

COUNSELLING PSYCHOLOGY WITH
NONBINARY PEOPLE 290

CONCLUSION 293

LEARNING OUTCOMES

BY THE END OF THIS CHAPTER YOU SHOULD
BE ABLE TO ANSWER THE FOLLOWING KEY
QUESTIONS:

1. Why should counselling psychologists
   be intersectionally aware, and explicitly
   consider issues around gender?

2. How is gender commonly understood, and
   why is this problematic from a counselling
   psychology perspective?

3. How can counselling psychologists best
   work with cisgender men and women,
   trans women and men, and nonbinary people?

Counselling Psychology: A Textbook for Study and Practice, First Edition. Edited by David Murphy.
© 2017 John Wiley & Sons Ltd. Published 2017 by John Wiley & Sons Ltd.

INTRODUCTION

Due to its focus on individual human experience, psychology has historically tended to neglect features of a person's social context such as their gender, race, class, sexuality, disability, and so on (Barker, 2010), with such elements often being regarded as the domain of sociology rather than psychology. Where they are considered in psychology this is often in a rather universalized way strips them from their social embeddedness, or individualizes them (e.g., in the unconsidered question "How do men and women differ?"), rather than paying attention to the ways in which each person's identity is uniquely situated within multiple intersecting axes of societal position (e.g., "What forms of femininity are available to this particular person in this specific time and place? Why? And what are the implications of this?") (Barker, 2015).

Similarly with counselling and psychotherapy, which often draw on psychology, there are similar issues with a predominant focus on internal, individual experiences (Gergen, 2000). Indeed, few programmes that we are aware of include in-depth training on gender, race, class, sexuality, or disability (to name but a few areas), and many do not even include single sessions on these topics (Davies & Barker, 2015). It could be argued that such areas are vital for therapists and other mental health professionals to be mindful of—given that they have a huge impact upon whether a person will experience distress and be diagnosed with a psychiatric disorder, and consequently what treatment that they will receive. For example, research repeatedly finds higher levels of anxiety and depression amongst women, trans people, lesbian gay and bisexual people, and people of colour than amongst men, cisgender people (who remain the gender they were assigned at birth), heterosexual people, and white people (Barker, 2010; Semlyen, King, Varney, & Hagger-Johnson, 2016).

Additionally, gender, sexuality, race, class, and so on all have a powerful influence on how a person experiences and expresses their emotions, which possibilities are available to them in life and which are not, how they engage in relationships, and pretty much every topic that is commonly discussed in the encounter between a mental health professional and client. These aspects are therefore not just relevant to those who are obviously marginalized or discriminated against, but rather to everyone a mental health professional may see.

With its commitment to ethical, socially, and politically conscious practice (BPS, 2009), counselling psychology is the obvious discipline to lead the way—both for psychology and for therapeutic practice—in ensuring that all practice is intersectionally aware practice, and that professionals are mindful of the ways in which gender and other intersectional identities inflect and infuse the experiences of *all* clients (not just women, for example, or trans people).

In this chapter we first briefly set out what we currently know about gender from psychological and related literature, particularly in relation to mental health. We then go on to consider how counselling psychologists can work with cisgender women and men, with trans men and women, and with nonbinary people, ending each section with a case study for readers to consider how they might work with a client from these groups. We conclude the chapter with general good practice for counselling psychologists around gender.

UNDERSTANDING GENDER

Dominant Cultural Understandings of Gender

All clients, whatever their gender, will be influenced by the wider dominant understandings of gender in the world around them. Therefore, it is helpful for counselling psychologists to have a good awareness of what this is, as well as a reflexive sense of how it influences their own gender and gendered assumptions, as well as the lived experiences of diverse clients.

The current dominant understanding of the high gross domestic product (GDP) global West is that people are born either male or female (their "biological sex"), and that males naturally become masculine in appearance and behaviour (their gender as men) and females naturally become feminine (their gender as women) (see Barker & Scheele, 2016). If you have a moment at this point you might like to pause to reflect on what currently constitutes masculinity and femininity in the world around you, perhaps thinking about how men and women are commonly portrayed in mainstream movies, television, magazines, news, advertising, etc. (Barker, 2013).

Such a reflection demonstrates that the masculinity/femininity binary is grounded on many further binaries: rational/emotional, active/passive, dominant/submissive, delicate/tough, independent/dependent, concerned with practical matters/appearance and frivolity, etc. Like masculinity/femininity, most of these binaries are hierarchical (with the "masculine" side frequently privileged culturally over the "feminine" side). The gender binary is also interconnected with sexuality in the ways in which masculinity and femininity are frequently demonstrated through sexual attraction to the "opposite" sex in a straight/gay binary (with "straight" also privileged over "gay," see Chapter 16).

Psychological research demonstrates how strongly people adhere to these gendered assumptions. For example, the classic—and often replicated—"baby X" study presented adults with the same baby wearing either blue or pink clothing (Seavey, Katz, & Rosenberg Zalk, 1975). People play with the baby wearing blue more roughly than the one wearing pink, give them "boys toys" or "girls toys," and see them as "angry" or "fearful," respectively, if they show distress. Social psychological research on media representations also finds that men and women are treated very differently according to gender stereotypes, as well as being regarded as having contrasting interests, attitudes, and behaviours (Gill, 2006).

Expanding on such work, Fine's important (2010) book summarizes the neuroscientific, cognitive, and developmental psychological evidence that constant exposure to gender stereotypes shapes neural connections and pushes cognition and behaviour in gender stereotyped directions. For example, if you prime young people to think about gender—even just by ticking a gender box on a form—they become more confident, interested, and able in gender stereotyped subjects (e.g., maths for boys, arts for girls), and less so in subjects that go against gender stereotypes (cf. Chatard, Guimon, & Selimbegovic, 2007; McGlone & Aronson, 2006; Sinclair, Hardin, & Lowery, 2006). Given that clothing, toys, advertising, stories, and television programmes are strongly gender segregated from an early age, children are constantly primed regarding such stereotypes. As they learn gender labels and identities they shift into gender stereotyped play and begin to police their own behaviours and that of one another (Zosuls et al., 2009), thus channelling towards conventionally gendered interests (Francis, 2010). However, if you counter-stereotype toys, stories, and so on, gender stereotyped behaviour becomes less pronounced (Green, Bigler, & Catherwood, 2004).

A More Complex and Diverse Psychological Understanding of Gender

Thinking back to the masculinity/femininity binary that we considered before, a moment's thought raises problems with the binary way of understanding gender that is prevalent. Even without engaging in more sustained feminist critique, anybody presented with such a list of masculine and feminine features will readily be able to point to ways in which they personally don't fit either side of the binary perfectly, and will probably be able to point to men or women whom they know who fit the "opposite" side better than their "own" side.

Another useful thought experiment to do at this point is to consider how you know that you are the gender that you are. What are the features that "make" a person a man or a woman? Again, for each of these can you think of exceptions?

We can see that there are problems with every aspect of the conventional understanding of gender that we presented above. Significantly:

- neither sex nor gender is binary;
- we cannot simply distinguish biological sex from social gender;
- sex/gender is not necessarily fixed but frequently shifts over time;
- what we *mean* by gender is multiple and complex—intersecting with all other aspects of our identities.

First of all it is important to recognize that at all biological, psychological, and social levels sex and gender are not binary. Whether we're considering chromosomal constellations, hormonal milieu, primary or secondary sex characteristics, neural configurations, or gender roles and experiences, there is diversity rather than any kind of simple binary division. As geneticist Fausto-Sterling (1999, p. 31) puts it: "while male and female stand on the extreme ends of a biological continuum, there are many bodies . . . that evidently mix together anatomical components conventionally attributed to both males and females." Historically, intersex people whose bodies at birth do not clearly meet the expectations of "a boy" or "a girl" have been given unnecessary surgeries in order to assign them as male or female, although thankfully this is slowly changing (see Roen, 2015—an in-depth consideration of intersex is beyond the scope of this chapter). Recent research by Joel and colleagues (2015) found that only a tiny proportion of the population have what was once regarded as a "male" or "female" brain. The vast majority of us combine features of both. At a cultural level, many societies globally have more or less than two gender categories (Herdt, 1993).

Related to this is the fact that it is not really possible to tease apart biological sex from psychological gender, or either of these from the social understandings in which we are embedded. For this reason Fausto-Sterling (2012) and others often refer to sex/gender rather than distinguishing between the two. The word "biopsychosocial" is a useful one for capturing the ways in which gender—like many of the other aspects of identity mentioned earlier—is a complex combination of our biological bodies and brains, our psychological background and experience, and our social and cultural context, with all of these elements constantly influencing each other in a hugely complex network of feedback loops. For example, it is clear from the Baby X studies that a baby's genitals have a major impact on the way they are treated (the biological influencing psychological), but research by Fine (2010) and others makes it clear that being treated in gender stereotyped (or counter-stereotyped) ways impacts our brains and bodies through neuroplasticity (the psychological influencing the biological). And, of course, social assumptions about gender influence what the prevailing stereotypes are, and how we treat people based on these (the social influencing the psychological), but these also alter over time, as a result of activism, for example, (the psychological influencing the social).

This also reminds us that gender is not necessarily fixed on any level, but can also shift and change. For example it is clear that social understandings of gender have altered as a result of each wave of feminism. Additionally, an individual's way of expressing their gender can shift markedly over the course of their lives (think about how a man might embody his masculinity at 5, 15, 45, and 65, for example). Also, due to the impact of our behaviour on bodies and brains, gender is not static at the biological level either. Importantly, the degree to which gender is experienced as fixed or fluid, and congruent or incongruent with birth-assigned gender, varies markedly from person to person—whether they have an identity term that reflects this or not—and it is vital to practice in a way that affirms this rather than trying to impose fixity on fluidity, or vice versa (Richards & Barker, 2013).

Finally, what we *mean* by gender is multiple and complex, intersecting with all other aspects of our identities. Going back to lists of what is understood by masculinity and femininity, each individual would see themselves as more or less masculine/feminine depending on which meaning they were focusing on. For example, we might places ourselves at the "feminine" end of a nurturing/distant continuum, but at the "masculine" end of a delicate/tough continuum, and somewhere in the middle of a creative/technical continuum (Barker, 2013). Social psychological research has challenged the notion of one dominant masculinity and one dominant femininity. For example, one study by Wetherell and Edley (1999) found that some men did present themselves with a stereotypical hard, strong, "real men" persona. However, others presented much more of an "everyday bloke" kind of masculinity, perhaps like Homer Simpson, and others presented more of an "alternative" masculinity, which included emotional expression and care about appearance. Many drew upon different masculinities to varying degrees at different times. Such multiplicity often reflects the ways in which gender intersects with class, race, sexuality, and other features of our background and identity. For example, psychological research has found physical aggression—often regarded as masculine—to be part of some white, working class, heterosexual femininities (Day, Gough, & McFadden, 2003).

Implications of a Simple Fixed Binary Model in a Complex Nonbinary Fluid World

The divergence between the dominant cultural understanding of gender and the diverse ways in which many people actually *experience* their genders has important implications for all of us, particularly in relation to mental health.

Since the 1970s it has been recognized that people who are able to flexibly adopt both culturally "masculine" and "feminine" traits are more psychologically healthy than those who stick rigidly to prescribed gender roles (Bem & Lewis, 1975). Also recent research finds that over a third of people experience themselves as being to some extent the "other" gender, "both genders" and/or "neither gender" (Joel et al., 2014). However, at the same time, the hierarchical binary opposite model of gender is strongly policed—with those who do not fit frequently being bullied and discriminated against (Rivers, 2011), and particularly high—even homicidal—sanctions against those who attempt to transition from the gender that they were assigned at birth (see Murjan & Bouman, 2015).

Where this leaves us is in a place where everyone's mental health suffers from cultural assumptions about gender (Richards & Barker, 2013). Those who do attempt to fit in with the social norms of what it means to be a man or a woman often suffer due to the pressures of attempting to adopt and express the rigid rules involved, and those who attempt to shift to a gender expression that feels more comfortable to them face prejudice, discrimination, and even violence. In the following sections we will unpack the implications of this for cisgender women and men, for trans men and women, and for nonbinary people.

COUNSELLING PSYCHOLOGY WITH CISGENDER WOMEN AND MEN

Cisgender women and men are women and men who were respectively assigned female or male at birth and who have remained in that gender throughout their lives (McGeeney & Harvey, 2015). Many of the issues that relate to gender roles which cisgender women and men face will be similar to those faced by trans women and men, given that they are all intelligible within a binary gender system and we will consider these below. However, there are naturally some specific issues that impact trans people differently, related to having shifted from the gender that was assigned at birth. It is worth bearing in mind that cisgender people are generally less likely than trans people to have reflected on their gender, or to have *deliberately* taken on certain elements of it, and these things therefore bear consideration in the therapy room (Richards & Barker, 2013).

For this reason, probably the most common ways in which cisgender women's and men's genders are linked to their mental health relate to an often unquestioning acceptance of wider gender expectations, to the point where these become constraining. This may bring them to the attention of a counselling psychologist if some aspect of their experience is making them concerned that they may not be "normal," if rigid adherence to gender norms is interfering with their lives, or if some change in their lives means that they cannot conform to gender ideals as well as they used to (e.g., retirement meaning that a man struggles to demonstrate his ambition and breadwinner status, or changes in appearance over time meaning a woman struggles to demonstrate conventionally attractive femininity) (Richards & Barker, 2013).

In general, cisgender women are diagnosed with common mental health problems such as anxiety and depression far more than cisgender men are. They also express distress in different ways, with bodily practices such as control over eating and self-harming being particularly prevalent. This has been linked to the social pressure on women to have "attractive" bodies and to measure their worth in relation to narrow ideals of feminine desirability and beauty (BMA, 2000). Women's high rates of mental health problems have also been linked to their identities being bound up in relationships with others (Barker, 2011), meaning that they can be particularly concerned with how others see them and struggle to find a sense of themselves. Middle-aged mothers have been found to be at particularly high risk of depression, for example, related to the loss of their identity as a nurturer and carer when children leave home (Johnstone, 2000). Competing demands on women to meet earlier ideals of femininity at the same time as meeting newer pressures to excel in work and to be assertive can also create a set of contradictions that many struggle to balance or resolve (McGeeney & Harvey, 2015). Women are also at greater risk than men of some key situations that are linked to emotional struggles, such as domestic violence and sexual abuse.

Cisgender men, however, do not escape mental health difficulties. Rather, they experience and express these in different ways, which can often mean that they are criminalized rather than pathologized (Harrower, 1998). For example, strong cultural messages that "real men" are rational and strong make expressions of fear and sadness difficult. Thus, men are more likely to express pain through alcoholism and drug addiction and to be diagnosed with "disorders" relating to aggression and antisocial behaviour (Johnstone, 2000). The tendency of men to be seen as "bad" rather than "mad" relates to a wider culture of men being regarded as more responsible and autonomous than women are, which is detrimental to both: it can disempower women, keeping them in "victim" roles, whilst putting huge pressures on men, considering them culpable for actions that may be equally grounded in distress (Vossler, Havard, Pike, Barker, & Rabbe, 2017). Men who do experience traumas such as sexual or domestic violence often feel unable to speak about it. The "crisis of masculinity" refers to the persistence of stereotypes of strong, hard men despite a decline in traditional male jobs and roles (Gauntlett, 2008). This has been linked to high rates of suicide in men (75% of all suicides; Mind, 2007).

Consider the following case study to think about the ways in which gender may play a part in the issues faced by a cisgender client, how these may intersect with other aspects of a person's identity, what assumptions you might hold based on wider cultural understandings of gender, and how you might work with a client in a gender-aware way.

CASE STUDY: PAUL

Paul is a middle class, white, heterosexual, cisgender man in his mid-30s. He presents to you concerned that he is not sleeping properly. He says that he is dissatisfied with a number of areas of his life that he finds himself mulling over in the early hours. He explains that he had always wished that he could be a cabinet maker but had found himself employed as a clerk in an office, which he finds unsatisfactory. He continues that much of his life is like this, as he had had a series of unsatisfying relationships with women who seemed "on paper" to be the perfect partner but whom he found he had little in common with after the initial sexual frisson had declined, particularly in relation to their goals of marriage, home-making, and children and his desire to spend a lot of time with his group of male friends.

Two key arenas for Paul are work and relationships. It would be useful to start by examining your own assumptions about masculinity in these areas. For example, men are often expected to be providers and to earn money, which may prevent a leap into a potentially risky new occupation. However, there may also be expectations around being a success and leaving a mark on the world that may lead to dissatisfaction in a less obviously meaningful job. Similarly, Paul may retain an older set of values about the need to settle down with a female partner and start a family, at the same time as questioning these to some extent, but perhaps not enough to seek out partners who hold different views about relationships and who may therefore possibly sit outside of conventional cisgender femininity in other ways.

Becoming stuck within shifting societal gender norms is not uncommon for cisgender people, and may be particularly prevalent at the moment given radical shifts in work, family, and relationship roles in recent years. As a counselling psychologist it may be useful to help cisgender clients like Paul to clearly see the tensions that they are negotiating, normalizing the fact that this can be challenging, and illuminating the kinds of losses and gains that will come from choosing in either direction.

COUNSELLING PSYCHOLOGY WITH TRANS MEN AND WOMEN

As with cisgender people above, trans people may struggle with the restrictions and limitations of societal gender norms—albeit that these are not the gender norms that are associated with their birth assigned gender, but rather those of their experienced gender. Trans people, however, may have the added difficulty of facing opprobrium both if they adhere to societal norms (not really being themselves—just "pretending" by sticking to the rules) *and* if they transgress the rules (not "really" being a woman or a man because they are doing something atypical). Naturally, being in such a no-win position by trying to be authentic, and to fit in to the extent that life is liveable, can put stress on people's psychological functioning (Claes et al., 2015).

As seen above, trans people may also experience stress due to prejudice (McNeil, Bailey, Ellis, Morton, & Regan, 2012), which can, in turn, lead to psychological problems. Note that there is no evidence that trans people are mentally ill in and of themselves (Hoshiai et al., 2010), rather that those people who experience prejudice—whether explicit or implicit—may become anxious or depressed and so have secondary psychopathology. This process is called *minority stress* or *marginalization stress* (cf. Meyer, 1995) and it makes clear that the pathology lies in the society and the perpetrators of the prejudice, rather than the recipients.

While prejudice towards some trans people is lessening in some areas of the world, there are still significant barriers faced by many trans people, including such everyday things as which toilets they are allowed to use. These barriers and negative societal discourses can lead trans people to struggle with coming out due to fears about people's reactions (which may be unfounded), and also internalized transphobia where the trans person has internalized these negative messages about being trans (Richards & Barker, 2013). Trans people may also be worried about the continuation of their occupation, intimate relationships, families, and so on, all of which can put psychological strain on people.

Consequently, some trans people may seek the services of a counselling psychologist to assist with sorting through these matters, as well as for the non-trans-related matters that cisgender people may seek assistance with. When the matter is not related to the person's trans status, unnecessary questions should not be asked about their gender, and certainly not about their genitals or any medical interventions they may or may not have undergone. Naturally their trans status should be borne in mind—as with all other demographic details such as age, ethnicity, sexuality, and so on, but that should not form the basis of the intervention. Only when the trans person's gender status is pertinent to the presentation should it be the focus of enquiry; for example, if they wish to have assistance with the process of transitioning from their birth-assigned gender.

Unfortunately trans people have not been well served by the "psy" professions in the past and indeed have been subjected to aversion "therapies" such as electroshock "treatment" and emetics (cf. Dickinson, Cook, Playle, & Hallett, 2012). More recently, trans people have not been accepted as their gender and have been pathologized and marginalized (Richards & Barker, 2015). For this reason many trans people are understandably wary of psychologists and it behoves us to build the bridge that our predecessors burned with such abandon. There may, therefore, be more work in building rapport with trans people before therapy can start, but we as a profession (if not individually) arguably have only ourselves to blame (cf. Benson, 2013; Kidd, Veltman, Gately, Chan, & Cohen, 2011). One way of building rapport is to have a good awareness of the client group we are seeing such that we can know where any stumbling blocks may lie, and also to avoid further marginalizing our clients by asking about very simple elements of their lives, which may make them feel like they are so incomprehensible that even the most basic information is alien.

Taking all these elements into account now, consider how you might work with the client in the following case study. How might their trans status be irrelevant? How might it be pertinent? How might it intersect with other aspects of their identity? What assumptions are you making? Where might you have overlooked something?

CASE STUDY: CHARLOTTE

Charlotte is a 46-year-old person, who was assigned male at birth. She manages a small engineering company and comes from a white English background. She married a woman at 24 and has two children from that relationship. Now that her children have gone to university she has decided that she would like to transition and start living in a female role full time—instead of some weekends and evenings when her wife and children have gone out. She comes to you explaining that she has been suffering with dysthymia for some years, although she is unsure why. She is concerned that if she does transition she will lose her wife, her children, and her business.

In considering a client like Charlotte it is important to take a positive view about trans in general to balance again the common negative societal view, and to recognize that transition for many people leads to very positive outcomes. It is also important to think alongside Charlotte about what a transition would mean *for her specifically*—whether there would be losses or gains (or likely both) and if she has any cognitive distortions in her way of thinking about this (note this is the *way* of thinking, not the content, which cannot be fully known by the counselling psychologist). Giving space to think the matters through may also be helpful, as will considering if the dysthymia is related or unrelated to her gender status.

Charlotte may offload worries onto her wife or children, or work—saying that she would transition if not for them and it can be useful to unpick which parts of that are about them and which are her own concerns. It can also be useful to work through what those concerns are and how they may be addressed. While it would be nice to have certain answers, these things can inevitably have a high degree of uncertainty and it will be important to consider how she, as a person, wishes to live in the world—both in her immediate social situation and the wider culture—and the potential difficulties, and joys, associated with that (see Richards, 2011).

COUNSELLING PSYCHOLOGY WITH NONBINARY PEOPLE

Earlier in the chapter we mentioned that many cultures worldwide do not understand gender in binary ways, meaning that this will certainly be the cultural backdrop of some of our clients. Indeed, even within a Western context over a third of people do not *experience* themselves simply as men or as women, although until recently it has been relatively uncommon to *identify* as nonbinary in terms of gender. More recently, however, it has been estimated that between a quarter and a third of trans people identify in some way outside the gender binary—putting the proportion of the population who identify as outside the male/female binary at around 0.4% (Titman, 2014). The existence of nonbinary people and communities received public attention when social media site Facebook opened up gender options to include over 70 gender categories, and a gender neutral pronoun (they) (Barker & Richards, 2015).

The umbrella terms "nonbinary" and "genderqueer" encompass a range of gender identities, experiences, and expressions including those who experience themselves: as both male and female; as neither or as having no gender; as between the two; as a further separate gender; and as beyond the gender binary entirely. As with cisgender men and women, and trans men and women, some nonbinary people experience their gender as relatively fixed, and others as changing over time. Some experience their gender as something they naturally *are*, others as something more socially constituted, developed over time, or personally chosen.

The evidence so far strongly suggests that those who identify as nonbinary have worse mental health than the general population (Barker & Richards, 2015). For example, McNeil et al. (2012) found that those who identify as nonbinary, and/or express themselves in ways that explicitly challenge binary gender, face similarly high levels of mental health difficulties to those of trans people more generally. Harrison, Grant, and Herman (2012) found that over 40% of nonbinary people had attempted suicide at some point, a third had experienced physical assault, and a sixth sexual assault based on their gender—experiences that we know are strongly related to psychological distress. These rates were even higher than for trans men and women.

Regarding the likely explanations for these disturbing findings, we might look to the wider literatures on trans and on bisexuality. As we've seen, for trans people generally, poor mental health is strongly linked to explicit and implicit transphobia, and to pressure to conform to cisgenderist, binary views of gender. Whilst cisgender bisexual people do not share the gender experiences of nonbinary people, they do share the experience of falling outside of widespread binary understandings. The evidence is overwhelming that bisexual people experience worse mental health than either heterosexual or lesbian/gay people, probably due to the biphobia, erasure, and invisibility they experience for falling outside of the sexuality binary (Barker et al., 2012). It is likely that this is similarly true for nonbinary people: falling outside the gender binary means that they experience erasure and invisibility (people rarely recognizing or validating their gender), and discrimination on the basis of not fitting either side of the binary (particularly if they are visibly nonbinary in any way). Many nonbinary people therefore face the challenging aspects of being both trans and outside the cultural binary way of seeing gender/sexuality (Barker & Scheele, 2016). Navigating nonbinary experience within a binary world is therefore a key issue for many nonbinary people, with people making different decisions depending on their work situation, wider community, and levels of safety, for example.

Until very recently there was little provision for nonbinary genders within gender services. However, nonbinary experiences are now included within the

American Psychiatric Association Diagnostic and Statistical Manual's conceptualization of gender dysphoria, and within the World Professional Association for Transgender Health Standards of Care for trans people. Gender specialist clinicians of all kinds are increasingly offering a range of psychological and medical services to suit nonbinary experience to those who require it (see Richards, Bouman, & Barker, 2017).

For the nonspecialist counselling psychologist who finds themselves working with a nonbinary client, as with other trans clients, it is worth reflecting on whether you have the necessary expertise to undertake such work, especially if the client is presenting specifically to talk about their gender. Referring on is always acceptable if not, and it is important that you don't continue working with them if you have not undergone training in this area and/or would require them to educate you in order to understand where they were coming from.

However, as with the other genders considered in this chapter, in many cases the trans or nonbinary status of a client will not be highly relevant to the issues they want to discuss, and in such cases it is important not to unnecessarily refer them on as being too "specialist" when in fact they are not. It would be sufficient to have engaged in some reading around the topic (such as this chapter and perhaps Richards & Barker, 2013), to the extent to which you're familiar with how to use gender-neutral pronouns (if relevant), for example, and that you've engaged reflexively in considering wider social gender norms and your own place within these.

Consider the following case study to think about the ways in which gender may play a part in the issues faced by a nonbinary client, how these may intersect with other aspects of their identity, what assumptions you might hold based on wider cultural understandings of gender, and how you might work with the client in a gender-aware way.

CASE STUDY: RIVER

River is a queer student in their early 20s from a South Asian background, who comes to you for some support around relationships. They are single at the moment but would like to get into a relationship. However, they want to reflect upon how they go about it because they have found themselves "rushing into things" in the past, meaning that relationships became intense very quickly, and then ended painfully. On the paperwork for your service they ticked the gender box "other" and wrote that their pronouns are "they."

In this kind of situation where a client presents with a general issue such as relationships, work stress, or bereavement, there is no reason to think that gender will be any more relevant than it would be to any other client. Given that River will likely have experienced professionals interrogating their gender in the past, and may well fear being pathologized or discriminated again here, it would be particularly important to communicate that you take their gender at face value by using the correct name and pronouns, and not asking unnecessary questions about their gender.

However, of course, as we have seen elsewhere in the chapter, our own— and others'—expectations around gender do influence how we experience relationships, emotions, and other aspects of life. Therefore, it would be useful to include discussion of gender, alongside other intersecting aspects of River's identity, once rapport has been established, but being very clear why this is relevant. For example, it could be that relationships are seen as desirable due to a connection with femininity, because past experience of transphobia leaves River desperate for a place of relative safety, and/or because in a binary world they long for just one relationship where a person sees them in the nonbinary way in which they experience themselves. It would equally be worth exploring the overlapping cultures of South Asian communities, higher education, and queer communities, which River occupies—all of which may well influence what ways of doing relationships are available to them, and/or feel required in some way (Choudrey, 2016).

CONCLUSION

To conclude, we would like to reinforce the fact that gender is relevant to all clients. A biopsychosocial, intersectional, multidimensional approach is helpful, taking account of where each unique client is in relation to the multiple interconnected aspects of identity.

The following are general good practice points to keep in mind in this area:

- Reflexively engage with your own assumptions about gender (and encourage all staff within your service to do the same).
- Ensure that you are well educated on trans and nonbinary issues, and comfortable with relevant terminology and options available, or be prepared to refer trans and nonbinary clients on if you are not (do not expect clients to educate you).
- Be careful not to assume the gender or trans/cisgender status of any client, ensure that forms and paperwork are inclusive of all possible options, and do not disclose a client's trans or nonbinary status to others without their express permission to do so.
- Be aware of cultural norms around gender, and recognize the variety of possibilities rather than perpetuating a fixed notion of what men, women, or nonbinary people should be like. Normalize trans and nonbinary genders for clients who are unfamiliar with these.
- Encourage client awareness about the expectations and assumptions that they have around gender, and where these come from, but do not overly focus on gender where it is not relevant to the presenting issue.
- Be aware of intersections—acknowledging the differences in how gender is experienced across race, culture, class, sexuality, disability, age, generation, body type, and so on.
- Ensure that images, materials, and resources present in your service reflect gender diversity and create a space that is comfortable and inclusive of all genders.

SUGGESTED FURTHER READING

Fine, C. (2010). *Delusions of gender: The real science behind sex differences*. London: Icon Books.

Richards, C., & Barker, M. (2013). *Sexuality and gender for mental health professionals: A practical guide*. London: Sage.

Richards, C., & Barker, M. J. (Eds.) (2015). *Handbook of the psychology of sexuality and gender*. Basingstoke: Palgrave Macmillan.

Richards, C., Bouman, W., & Barker, M. J. (Eds.) (2017). *Genderqueer and non-binary genders*. Basingstoke: Palgrave Macmillan.

REFERENCES

Barker, M. (2010). Sociocultural issues. In M. Barker, A. Vossler, & D. Langdridge, (Eds.), *Understanding counselling and psychotherapy* (pp. 211–233). London: Sage.

Barker, M. (2011). De Beauvoir, Bridget Jones' pants and vaginismus. *Existential Analysis, 22*(2), 203–216.

Barker, M. (2013). *Rewriting the rules: An integrative guide to love, sex and relationships*. London: Routledge.

Barker, M.-J. (2016). *Social mindfulness*. Retrieved from http://rewriting-the-rules.com/zines/#1473331637426-0bbbbd47-fd7f (accessed March 27, 2017).

Barker, M. J., & Richards, C. (2016). Further genders. In C. Richards & M. J. Barker (Eds.), *Handbook of the psychology of sexuality and gender* (pp. 166–182.) Basingstoke: Palgrave Macmillan.

Barker, M., Richards, C., Jones, R., Bowes-Catton, H., & Plowman, T. (2012). *The bisexuality report: Bisexual inclusion in LGBT equality and diversity*. Milton Keynes: The Open University, Centre for Citizenship, Identity and Governance.

Barker, M.-J., & Scheele, J. (2016). *Queer: A graphic history*. London: Icon Books.

Bem, S. L., & Lewis, S. A. (1975). Sex role adaptability: One consequence of psychological androgyny. *Journal of Personality and Social Psychology, 31*(4), 634–643.

Benson, K. E. (2013). Seeking support: Transgender client experiences with mental health services. *Journal of Feminist Family Therapy, 25*(1), 17–40.

BMA (British Medical Association) (2000). *Eating disorders, body image and the media*. London: BMA Board of Science and Education.

BPS (British Psychological Society) (2009). *Code of ethics and conduct*. Leicester: British Psychological Society.

Chatard, A., Guimond, S., & Selimbegovic, L. (2007). "How good are you in math?" The effect of gender stereotypes on students' recollections of their school marks. *Journal of Experimental Social Psychology, 43*(6), 1017–1024.

Choudrey, S. (2016). *Inclusivity: Supporting BAME trans people*. Retrieved from www.gires.org.uk/assets/Support-Assets/BAME_Inclusivity.pdf (accessed March 27, 2017).

Claes, L., Bouman, W. P., Witcomb, G., Thurston, M., Fernandez-Aranda, F., & Arcelus, J. (2015). Non-suicidal self-injury in trans people: Associations with psychological symptoms, victimization, interpersonal functioning, and perceived social support. *The Journal of Sexual Medicine, 12*(1), 168–179.

Davies, D., & Barker, M. J. (2015). How GSD is your therapy training? *The Psychotherapist, 61*, 8–10.

Day, K., Gough, B., & McFadden, M. (2003). Women who drink and fight: A discourse analysis of working-class women's talk. *Feminism and Psychology, 13*(2), 141–158.

Dickinson, T., Cook, M., Playle, J., & Hallett, C (2012). "Queer" treatments: Giving a voice to former patients who received treatments for their "sexual deviations." *Journal of Clinical Nursing, 21*(9–10), 1345–1354.

Fausto-Sterling, A. (1999). *Sexing the body.* New York: Basic Books.

Fausto-Sterling, A. (2012). *Sex/gender: Biology in a social world.* London: Routledge.

Fine, C. (2010). *Delusions of gender: The real science behind sex differences.* London: Icon Books.

Francis, B. (2010). Gender, toys and learning. *Oxford Review of Education, 36*(3), 325–344.

Gauntlett, D. (2008). *Media, gender and identity: An introduction.* London: Routledge.

Gergen, K. J. (2000). *The saturated self.* New York: Basic Books.

Gill, R. (2006). *Gender and the media.* London: Polity Press.

Green, V. A., Bigler, R., & Catherwood, D. (2004). The variability and flexibility of gender-typed toy play: A close look at children's behavioural responses to countersterotypic models. *Sex Roles, 51*(7/8), 371–386.

Harrison, J., Grant, J., & Herman, J. L. (2012). *A gender not listed here: Genderqueers, gender rebels, and otherwise in the National Transgender Discrimination Survey.* Los Angeles, CA: eScholarship, University of California.

Harrower, J. (1998). *Applying psychology to crime.* London: Hodder & Stoughton.

Herdt, G. H. (1993). *Third sex, third gender: Beyond sexual dimorphism in culture and history.* New York: Zone Books.

Hoshiai, M., Matsumoto, Y., Sato, T., Ohnishi, M., Okabe, N., Kishimoto, Y., Terada, S., & Kuroda, S. (2010). Psychiatric comorbidity among patients with gender identity disorder. *Psychiatry and Clinical Neurosciences, 64*, 514–519.

Joel, D., Tarrasch, R., Berman, Z., Mukamel, M., & Ziv, E. (2014). Queering gender: Studying gender identity in "normative" individuals. *Psychology and Sexuality, 5*(4), 291–321.

Joel, D., Berman, Z., Tavor, I., Wexler, N., Gaber, O., Stein, Y., . . . & Liem, F. (2015). Sex beyond the genitalia: The human brain mosaic. *Proceedings of the National Academy of Sciences USA, 112*(50), 15468–15473.

Johnstone, L. (2000). *Users and abusers of psychiatry.* London: Routledge.

Kidd, S. A., Veltman, A., Gately, C., Chan, K. J., & Cohen, J. N. (2011). Lesbian, gay, and transgender persons with severe mental illness: Negotiating wellness in the context of multiple sources of stigma. *American Journal of Psychiatric Rehabilitation, 14*(1), 13–39.

McGeeney, E., & Harvey, L. (2015). Cisgender—Living in the Gender Assigned at Birth. In C. Richards, & M. J. Barker (Eds.), *Handbook of the psychology of sexuality and gender* (pp. 149–165). Basingstoke: Palgrave Macmillan.

McGlone, M. S., & Aronson, J. (2006). Stereotype threat, identity salience, and spatial reasoning. *Journal of Applied Developmental Psychology, 27*(5), 486–493.

McNeil, J., Bailey, L., Ellis, S., Morton, J., & Regan, M. (2012). *Trans mental health study 2012.* Retrieved from www.scottishtrans.org (accessed March 27, 2017).

Meyer, I. H. (1995). Minority stress and mental health in gay men. *Journal of Health and Social Behavior, 36*, 38–56.

Mind (2007). *Suicide rates, risks and prevention strategies.* Retrieved from www.mind.org.uk/Information/Factsheets/Suicide/#Men (accessed March 27, 2017).

Murjan, S., & Bouman, W. P. (2015). In C. Richards, & M. J. Barker (Eds.), *Handbook of the psychology of sexuality and gender* (pp. 198–215). Basingstoke: Palgrave Macmillan.

Richards, C. (2011). Transsexualism and existentialism. *Existential Analysis, 22*(2), 272–279.

Richards, C., & Barker, M. (2013). *Sexuality and gender for mental health professionals: A practical guide.* London: Sage.

Richards, C., & Barker, M. J. (Eds.) (2015). *Handbook of the psychology of sexuality and gender*. Basingstoke: Palgrave Macmillan.

Richards, C., Bouman, W., & Barker, M. J. (Eds.) (2016). *Genderqueer and non-binary genders*. Basingstoke: Palgrave Macmillan.

Rivers, I. (2011). *Homophobic bullying: Research and theoretical perspectives*. Oxford: Oxford University Press.

Roen, K. (2015). Intersex. In C. Richards, & M. J. Barker (Eds.), *Handbook of the psychology of sexuality and gender* (pp. 183–197). Basingstoke: Palgrave Macmillan.

Seavey, C. A., Katz, P. A., & Rosenberg Zalk, S. (1975). Baby X: The effect of gender labels on adult responses to infants. *Sex Roles, 1*(2), 103–109.

Semlyen, J., King, M., Varney, J., & Hagger-Johnson, G. (2016). Sexual orientation and symptoms of common mental disorder or low wellbeing: Combined meta-analysis of 12 UK population health surveys. *BMC Psychiatry, 16*(1), 1.

Sinclair, S., Hardin, C. S., & Lowery, B. S. (2006). Self-stereotyping in the context of multiple social identities. *Journal of Personality and Social Psychology, 90*(4), 529–542.

Titman, N. (2014). *How many people in the United Kingdom are nonbinary?* Retrieved from www.practicalandrogyny.com (accessed March 27, 2017).

Vossler, A., Havard, C., Pike, G., Barker, M. J., & Rabbe, B. (Eds.) (2017). *Mad or bad? A critical approach to counselling and forensic psychology*. London: Sage.

Wetherell, M., & Edley, N. (1999). Negotiating hegemonic masculinity: Imagery positions and psycho-discursive practices. *Feminism and Psychology, 9*(3), 335–356.

Zosuls, K. M., Ruble, D. N., Tamis-Le Monda, C. S., Shrout, P. E., Bornstein, M. H., & Greulick, F. K. (2009). The acquisition of gender labels in infancy: Implications for sex-typed play. *Developmental Psychology, 45*(3), 688–701.

20 Developing Ethical Awareness Whilst Training to Be a Counselling Psychologist

PAM JAMES

CHAPTER OUTLINE

INTRODUCTION 300

QUESTION 1: WHAT IS WORKING ETHICALLY? 300

QUESTION 2: WHY IS IT NECESSARY TO HAVE CODES OF PRACTICE AND WHAT ARE THEY? 302

QUESTION 3: WHAT IS THE SPECIFIC NATURE OF COUNSELLING PSYCHOLOGY TRAINING? 304

QUESTION 4: DOES THE WAY OF WORKING ETHICALLY CHANGE FROM PRE- TO POSTQUALIFICATION? 306
    In Training to Be a Counselling Psychologist as Psychotherapist 307

In Training Whilst on Placement 308
In Training as a Researcher (*and When Qualified*) 308
The Qualified Counselling Psychologist as Psychotherapist 309
The Qualified Counselling Psychologist as Supervisor and Manager 309
    As a Supervisee When Qualified 310
    As a Manager When Qualified 310
    The Experienced Counselling Psychologist 311

GENERAL LEARNING POINTS FOR THE DEVELOPMENT OF A PERSONAL ETHICAL AWARENESS 312

CONCLUSION 312

Counselling Psychology: A Textbook for Study and Practice, First Edition. Edited by David Murphy.
© 2017 John Wiley & Sons Ltd. Published 2017 by John Wiley & Sons Ltd.

LEARNING OUTCOMES

BY THE END OF THIS CHAPTER YOU SHOULD BE ABLE TO ANSWER THE FOLLOWING KEY QUESTIONS:

1. What does developing a sense of personal ethical awareness mean for your practice?

2. In what ways do ethical codes act as a guide to practice?

3. To what extent does overall ethical awareness change during training and after becoming a qualified counselling psychologist?

INTRODUCTION

In this chapter the development of ethical awareness in counselling psychologists' training will be considered. Three questions are posed below that are concerned with ethics and the context in which training occurs. A fourth question holds a particular focus as it invites the reader to consider the concept of a "personal ethics." There is a need to consider not only the individuality of the trainee, but also the training context and ethical codes. In this chapter you will consider whether, during the training process, a sense of *personal ethics* develops and strengthens? If this is the desired process and product of training, this *personal ethical awareness* requires discussion in supervision and a readiness to visit and revisit guidelines as different ethical situations arise. This focus now supports the model of reflective practice, which includes not only a personal ethics, but also willingness and responsibility to share and discuss with colleagues as appropriate.

Throughout the four questions posed below, the reader is asked to keep the concept of personal ethics in mind.

1. What is "working ethically"?
2. Why is it necessary to have codes of practice and what are they?
3. What is the specific nature of counselling psychology training?
4. Does the way of working ethically change from pre- to postqualification?

QUESTION 1: WHAT IS WORKING ETHICALLY?

What is ethics? The word ethics comes from the Greek language and its translation is habit or custom. Ethics is a branch of moral philosophy that concerns a consideration of right and wrong. For example, Kitchener (1996) links ethics with moral philosophy. Working ethically involves the relationship between an action and a behaviour that is associated with a belief.

Actions are not always congruent with beliefs, as discussed by Carlson and Erikson (1999). For example, a person may value freedom of speech, yet find their own ability to express what they wish does not follow. There are usually intervening factors that assist in explaining why this might be. This is a factor for reflection that may be appropriate to consider in the development of this chapter.

> Can you think of a time or situation where you felt unable to speak out even though you knew it was the right thing to do? What were the circumstances? What were the implications of either speaking out or not speaking out? Were there particular emotions involved that prevented you from acting on what you thought was the right thing to do?

Questions of whether all cultures follow the same ethical code and whether there is such a concept as "universal ethics" also arise. Gauthier (2004) considers a universal declaration of ethical principles for psychologists. Mele and Sanchez-Runde (2013) write about universality in a business context; one of the comments from their article points out that whilst cultures may be neighbours with each other, they are not necessarily brothers and there needs to be a fostering of relationships in the "global human family." Turning to the concepts of universal values begins to provide the background for the content of ethical thinking and the development of ethical codes.

It is important to note that the concept of values is not synonymous with the concept of ethics. It is helpful to see if there are universal values and, if so, might there then also be a satisfactory universal ethical code? Schwartz and Bilsky (1990) have researched cross-culturally, mainly in Australia, Finland, Hong Kong, Spain, and the United States, and outline the universal values of achievement, enjoyment, maturity, prosocial, restricting conformity, security, and self-direction. Rokeach (2008) wrote about the nature of human values (individual and societal), largely drawing on the American culture. The types of values in this study reflect those associated with love, beauty, security, and peace. Comparing these two sources suggests that there is a lack of agreement in the nature of values emerging.

Most usually, it is underlying belief and value systems that form the basis for resulting behaviours and action. Paprocki (2014) has also noted that in some situations there may be a lack of agreement between resulting actions and underpinning value systems. It is in the search and sometimes struggle for consistency that the nature of ethical practice is formed, first as a generic concept and then in codes of specific ethical practice as relevant to the counselling psychologist. The person who decides to train as a counselling psychologist enters this position as a person who already has a personally considered value-base. Although there is no research evidence to support this statement it is likely to be true, and of note to this chapter's emphasis when considering the development of working ethically. What is being proposed here is that the trainee already has a personal awareness of values; it is the training process itself that provides the arena for the development of ethical practice.

Ethical codes have existed for hundreds of years; for example, Hammurabi's (a Babylonian King 2,500 years ago) Code of Laws and the Law of Moses (Millard, 1997). They are based on providing sets of laws for people to co-exist fairly and to regulate society ensuring equity and peace. However, currently and professionally based, there are various codes of practice to guide working professionally as a counselling psychologist in the British Psychological Society.

QUESTION 2: WHY IS IT NECESSARY TO HAVE CODES OF PRACTICE AND WHAT ARE THEY?

If codes of practice exist they can function as a statement of values and a reference point for decision making in professional situations. They also uphold an agreed standard and can function both as a training guide and a reference point to see if an action or particular practice is ethically appropriate and acceptable. Working within an ethical framework acts as a guide to keep the person themselves and the other people that they work with from situations that may cause harm, including damage to interpersonal relationships.

The British Psychological Society (BPS) provides helpful guidelines for researchers, teachers, and practitioners. These include the Code of Ethics and Conduct (BPS, 2009a), for example. The Code is based on four ethical principles of respect, competence, responsibility, and integrity, which should be considered when faced with ethical issues. Also included is the Code of Human Research Ethics (BPS, 2014), including: respect for the autonomy, privacy, and dignity of individuals and communities; scientific integrity; social responsibility; maximizing benefit; and minimizing harm.

In addition, the Division of Counselling Psychology has the following: The Guidelines for Professional Practice in Counselling Psychology, which emphasize and outline ethical aspects: to self and to clients; to self and to colleagues; to self and to society. These are supplementary to the Society's Code of Conduct, Ethical Principles and Guidelines, which sets a *minimum* standard below which behaviour should not fall. Breaches of the Society's Code, when identified, may be subject to disciplinary procedures. However, since 2009, practitioner psychologists have been regulated by the Health and Care Professions Council (HCPC), which is concerned with the protection of the public. Counselling psychologists must abide by both the Society's Code of Ethics and the HCPC's (2008) Standards of Conduct and Performance.

Codes of ethics operate at all stages of the counselling psychologist's practice, in research, teaching and when working with colleagues, clients, and supervisees. The counselling psychologist in training is in the environment of the university doctoral programme or is working towards the Qualification in Counselling Psychology (QCoP). Their introduction to the Society's Code of

Ethics and to the Division's Guidelines for Professional Practice will probably be either a lecture in this area, or in reading material. Practical involvements with ethical issues may occur in training exercises, often initially in the classroom and before beginning supervised practice with clients. This anecdote shows how ethical matters can arise:

> A trainee (Marie) heard from a fellow trainee (Liz) that one of the course participants (Fiona) had experienced a recent bereavement. Marie wondered whether she should approach Fiona to offer her condolences. Marie reflected and decided that she would not approach Fiona. Marie felt uncomfortable as she knew that she wanted to speak with Fiona, but she didn't want to speak about the bereavement as she hadn't heard directly from her. Eventually, Fiona told Marie about her loss.

Ethical comment: Marie didn't have a designated other to discuss this issue with, that is, if it had involved a client, then supervision could have been an appropriate venue. However, Marie did respond to her own incongruence. This means that she had a sense of knowing and feeling that something wasn't comfortable, that is, it wasn't congruent (in agreement) with her personal ethical base. She consulted her Division Guidelines for Professional Practice regarding self and colleagues. She noted that confidentiality and respect were the principles involved. She also thought about the alternative outcome that could have occurred if she had spoken to Fiona. This could have betrayed a confidence that Fiona had shared with Liz, and possibly disrupted their relationship. Thinking about different possible outcomes of actions can assist in working through ethical decision making. Although reading ethical codes is necessary in training, being in actual situations has experiential impact that aids learning and builds experience.

Learning point: be aware of feelings that may be generated by the event; think before you act; consider if there is any written guideline or code to assist, and colleagues to discuss the matter with if appropriate; reflect and take the position of the other; come to a conclusion. Thinking about a situation from the perspective of the other (using the application of the Theory of Mind) can be a helpful guide when considering the ethical nature of an issue.

When in training, ethical issues can arise in connection with colleagues, on placement working with clients, and carrying out research. Once supervision has been established, this is the place where questions can be discussed and guided by codes of ethics. When becoming qualified the counselling psychologist is likely to expand the number of interpersonal situations to include working with colleagues on committees and taking supervisees. This increase in complexity of professional personal encounters expands as the counselling psychologist becomes more experienced; some of these involve management of colleagues as well as individual and group therapy, supervision training, and committee work.

One situation that can present for the counselling psychologist at any point in their professional life is a conflict of interests. Consider this anecdote where personal gain came into conflict with a client's best outcomes:

> John had been referred by his GP to see a counselling psychologist, who worked as an independent practitioner. John was experiencing stress in his workplace and found that his usual coping mechanisms were not helping. In therapy he explored underlying factors that were making his life more difficult and had contracted to work for six sessions. After these were completed, John said that his anxiety was reducing and he felt more able to cope again; however, he wanted to continue his sessions.
>
> The counselling psychologist (Sheila) was aware that there was financial benefit to herself from John remaining in therapy, whilst hearing from John that he was now more able to cope. Sheila was reminded of an earlier situation when she had needed more practice hours to complete her training log, yet the client she was working with was ready to leave therapy.
>
> Helped by the supervision she had received in training, Sheila recognized that this present situation was one that needed exploration.
>
> Sheila was able to work through her incongruence in supervision, guided by the ethical code that upheld the client's autonomy, in preference to the tension caused by needing to satisfy her own needs.

Ethical comment: the learning experience whilst training had transferability to the situation encountered when qualified. The personal tension that presented in feeling uncomfortable and considering what this was about resulted in exploration in supervision guided by ethical principles.

Learning point: recognizing the tension expressed in feelings and thoughts was learnt whilst in training, together with the response to discuss this in supervision. Whether it becomes possible for a more experienced practitioner to think through such tensions produced by their own reflection (i.e., not necessarily in supervision) is perhaps a matter of individual difference or preference, and may depend on the extent of the tension produced. What is clear though, is that the Codes of Ethics from both HCPC and the BPS are frameworks and guides that function as a continuous "handrail" at all stages of professional life, keeping both other and self held in a respectful manner and supporting a duty of care.

QUESTION 3: WHAT IS THE SPECIFIC NATURE OF COUNSELLING PSYCHOLOGY TRAINING?

Further deliberation opens to the third question: is there anything particular about working ethically as a counselling psychologist, when compared with other applied psychologists or counsellors and psychotherapists?

Reflections would suggest that the answer to this question is no, as all involve working with people and there is a commonality of respect for the other person as a human being with their own thoughts, feelings, and dignity. Counselling psychologists work from an underlying philosophy that includes a humanistic-valuing base (see Chapter 2 and Chapter 3, this volume; or Cooper, 2009). The values of counselling psychology are intrinsically mindful of other people as well as the self. Consequently, ethical principles are to the forefront of thinking, as they are in the professions of counselling and psychotherapy. Enlarging from this humanistic-valuing base to the principles of human rights and ways of working with people, all other professions that have an interpersonal element also strive to respect the other person as well as themselves.

Those ethical values of respecting the other person are particularly present when working with people in a way that involves them speaking about their inner feelings, which involve many personal reflections, hopes, and fears. It is in the opening up of one's inner experiences that human vulnerability occurs and particular care and vigilance are necessary.

There are similar aspects of the training in each of the above therapeutic professions. For example, the concepts of congruence from person-centred theory and counter-transference from psychodynamic approaches both necessitate the therapist being open to and aware of their own thoughts and feelings. Training and supervision explain how to process these feeling reactions whether they originate from the intra- or the interpersonal milieu. The ability to process in this way is part of the emergent values and ethical awareness of the counselling psychologist. The climate of training, which encourages discussion amongst peers within appropriate boundaries and where supervision is mandatory, provides the context in which it is expected that ethical matters can be discussed. This is facilitated through the development of experiential learning within the training programme.

As trainee and qualified counselling psychologists are legally bound by the HCPC Standards of Proficiency, this code of ethics is relevant to that profession. Further ethical codes from the BPS provide helpful guidelines for researchers, teachers and practitioners, namely the Code of Ethics and Conduct (BPS, 2009a) (at the time of writing, this Code is being updated); the Code of Human Research Ethics (BPS, 2014); plus the Guidelines for Professional Practice in Counselling Psychology (BPS, 2009b) and the Society's Professional Practice Guidelines (also being updated at the time of writing). In addition, many counselling psychologists are dual qualified. Amongst others, there are three professional bodies most commonly noted, namely the British Association for Counselling and Psychotherapy (BACP), the British Association of Behavioural and Cognitive Psychotherapy (BABCP) and the United Kingdom Counselling and Psychotherapy (UKCP).

For example, BACP has recently published its new *Ethical Framework for the Counselling Professions* (BACP, 2016), which replaced the existing Framework in July 2016. Looking at other organizations can be a helpful process as it can be seen which new areas are receiving a focus of attention.

There may be possible advantages for counselling psychologists having dual accreditation in their enhanced ethical awareness to different areas of practice. It is unlikely that having different ethical codes to underpin practice could result in confusion as all codes, HCPC, BPS, BACP, and BABCP alike, are based on common values. In fact, inspection of the codes of ethics of these professional bodies shows considerable overlap: the pillars of respect, competence, integrity, and responsibility being paramount. Any revisions of these codes show a further emphasis to detail, for example, the attention to awareness of cultural diversity is represented by all professional bodies; a Commitment to Candour (BACP, 2016) is also included in HCPC's revised Standards (2016).

QUESTION 4: DOES THE WAY OF WORKING ETHICALLY CHANGE FROM PRE- TO POSTQUALIFICATION?

The fourth question is considered tracing the passage from pretraining through to being an experienced practitioner. When starting to train as a counselling psychologist, it is the beginning of working with people in situations where one is privy to the personal life experience of another person, whether this is a fellow trainee or a client. It could be considered that if a trainee has grown up in a life situation where there is respect for others and themselves, the concept of ethics is not new. Growing up in families or other child-rearing situations is the initial arena where relationships are formed. This interpersonal milieu widens with the beginning of school life and other social situations. Much is learnt in the tangled web of personal relationships. Most theories of development recognize the impact of interpersonal learning in relationships, some preferring modelling; others refer to a process called introjection whereby values and behaviours are taken in almost unknowingly in the developmental and later years. Newns, Paul and Creedy (2015) look at the learning process using "action method techniques" when raising awareness of ethical practice. So what is transferred into training?

Answers to this question could include: respect for another person and their situation; some sense of a need to keep another person's information confidential; and a sense of care to look after another person and protect them from harm/facilitating the other person to be aware of the need to take care of themselves. The aim is to do the best possible for another and not exploit them by using the power of knowledge or role, so that they are in some way disadvantaged. These principles become formalized into codes of practice.

These points are very much a set of standards and a code for living, however their universality is questionable. Without having any empirical studies to underpin the above, the best we can do at this point is refer to anecdotal evidence. Some people do grow up in living situations where their identity is not respected, where their personal thoughts and feelings are ridiculed, their belongings disregarded, and only their "usefulness" is considered. It is a point of reflection as to whether on entering training to be a counselling psychologist, there is a need for personal therapy as a reflective space to consider the impact of some of these possible earlier experiences. Again anecdotally, when people entering training begin to be aware of their own development years, they can need reflective and therapeutic time. Each person has their own experience and each attempts to address these accordingly. At this point it is only possible to recognize that trainees, as all people, have individual and different developmental lives. Perhaps the training genre can endeavour to foster an environment where trainees can reflect on such personal matters, so that they will not be "acted out" in the inter-personal working environment (see Chapter 7 for a discussion on in therapy enactments). These tensions are part of the training process.

The trainee's developing professional life emerges and in doing so is in parallel with their existing personal relationships. The personal and professional are frequently a matter of reflection whilst in training, and particularly so whilst striving for and working within ethical codes. As a trainee counselling psychologist, there are different roles that are part of the training programme. These include: a colleague or peers, whilst practising counselling skills in the university or college training environment; a member of personal development groups, whilst on placement; a researcher.

In Training to Be a Counselling Psychologist as Psychotherapist

Awareness of ethical boundaries and principles is critical in training when counselling skills are practised with peers in a college or university setting. Appropriate boundaries of confidentiality are agreed; similarly in any self-awareness groups. The BPS Codes of Practice (2009) and the HCPC Code for Trainees both apply in the training context. A duty of care to oneself is also important ethically; for example, not working having had a very distressing bereavement, or when excessively tired.

Students in a university setting were involved in a counselling psychology programme. Part of the training involved learning counselling skills, during which trainees were asked to bring small cameos from their life experience to speak about in training sessions. Without due attention to ethical principles, this setting has the possibility of breaks of confidentiality and the experiencing of distress by the participants. Clear boundaries set out in advance of agreeing to enter training prepare the trainee for what is expected. Ethical principles of respect prepare the student to know that they will be speaking about personal material, and that they hold the control and choice over what they are prepared to discuss. There also needs to be a "safety net" of a counselling service available that is freely available for students to approach if personal issues emerge which they feel require further exploration or support.

A developing awareness of the need to respect the other in establishing appropriate boundaries is also demonstrated when the trainee is part of an experiential personal development group. Not only is personal material shared in such groups, but also the processes between and amongst participants is part of the learning experience. Here trainees are challenged by the need to keep appropriate confidentiality boundaries, and also to address group members respectfully. Situations in this kind of groupwork also carry training responsibilities for the trainer, who is supported by supervision. There are interpersonal styles of dialogue that assist in such learning, for example:

> Consider the situation in a personal development group where one trainee experienced feeling bullied by another. She was facilitated (by the group conductor) to express this as "When you speak to me like that, I feel bullied." This was in contrast to "You're bullying me." It's clear that in the first statement, the trainee was taking personal ownership of her experience, rather than criticizing another.

In Training Whilst on Placement

A counselling psychologist will have a placement in more than one setting during training. Here, the trainee's developing *professional* role now enters the *professional* setting. The HCPC Ethical Codes function for the protection of the public; BPS Codes of Practice and Guidelines function to protect the public and the trainee. Consider this anecdote:

> John had been on placement in an NHS adult mental health service and was assigned a supervisor in the department. Meetings were timetabled into the diary. However, John's supervisor never arrived on time, cancelled, and postponed the meetings. Although John was striving to observe ethical working with his clients, he was not receiving such attention himself. Fortunately, there had been a contract of working and the trainee knew he could raise the matter with his university tutor. John did have some personal reflections as to whether he should first of all let his supervisor know. Although this was a difficult conversation for John, he decided that he would let his supervisor know first. This would most probably have been a difficult conversation because John may have feared that his supervisor would have rejected him as a supervisee, made things difficult in the placement environment, or even terminated the placement.

Ethical comment: did ethical awareness help John in deciding what to do? Yes, because he had a duty to protect the public; and supervision supported his clients' casework and himself. Yes, as he was guided by consideration of respect for himself.

Learning point: John learnt that striving for an acknowledgement of such practice involved care in interpersonal relationships that sometimes meant tension and difficulty, and that support would be necessary.

In Training as a Researcher (and When Qualified)

Again ethical aspects are important and many of the points focus around the need for respect of the other, and not to use the unequal relationship in a way that might exploit research participants. Some research designs speak of co-researchers, to illustrate the shared relationship in the construction of knowledge. The application for ethical consent for the project itself turns around these two points and includes: voluntary consent to be a participant; accurate details about what the participant needs to do; anonymity and confidentiality; right to withdraw; right to know the outcome of the research; knowledge about the storage of the data; and duty of care to provide some care if the participant is upset. The personal safety of the researcher is also a consideration.

The above is necessary for both trainees and qualified counselling psychologists carrying out research, and research projects need the scrutiny of ethics committees to make sure that all considerations have been met. The principle of respect for the participant is guiding here, so that no person becomes the object of another's endeavour without knowing that they are taking part. Ethical principles ensure a duty of care to researchers and to their participants.

Consider a situation where a researcher whilst in training wanted to go out to visit clients in their homes to interview them about a particular experience, for example, being in an abusive relationship. Ethical considerations would attend to the researcher in terms of his or her safety when on a home visit. Ethics committees are unlikely to approve of projects where the researcher is in a potentially risky situation that may result in their harm whilst in the home of the participant. It would be risky as the environment cannot be confirmed as safe. The project's approval would most likely have the condition that participants must enter an organizational setting to conduct the research.

The Qualified Counselling Psychologist as Psychotherapist

When the trainee becomes qualified, and is working as a psychotherapist, they should not know the client in a social capacity, or be working with anyone else in the client's family. Qualified counselling psychologists will have experienced their role as therapist whilst on placements; working as a therapist may involve becoming an employee and, in that capacity, conforming to the codes of that organization.

Confidentiality boundaries need to be clearly understood so that these can be commonly observed and the client can be made aware of what these are. In the NHS or any organization where there are multidisciplinary meetings, clients need to be aware that their personal information may be discussed with other colleagues to facilitate the client's best care. Letting the client know in advance that their personal information may be shared with other professionals respects the person and allows trust to be maintained in the therapeutic relationship.

The Qualified Counselling Psychologist as Supervisor and Manager

These roles must also be carried out ethically. With qualification comes the enlargement of roles and responsibilities. The recent revision of the training syllabus BPS (2015) now includes competences that prepare counselling psychologists for this role enlargement. These roles belong to the qualified counselling psychologist. As a supervisor there is much to observe; models of supervision are helpful here—the principle in operation is that the supervisor is supporting the therapist whilst working with the client. There is a duty of care to both client and supervisee. The supervisor carries clinical responsibility for their supervisees' clients' well-being.

All interactions with the supervisee must support the therapist to support the client. This relationship has been described by Hawkins and Shohet (2012) as a "nursing triad." It is probably the most helpful aspect of supervision: where the supervisory relationship must be so that it helps the supervisee. Many points follow from that, namely a shared theoretical understanding, and a carefully observed set of ethical boundaries.

As a Supervisee When Qualified

Counselling psychologists have an ongoing requirement to attend supervision for their work once qualified. The supervisory relationship provides a valuable space for reflecting on the therapeutic work being conducted with clients, for the training, management, or supervision that they are involved with. All aspects of a counselling psychologist's work will be considered in supervision. The minimum requirement for qualified counselling psychologists' supervision is to attend for monthly supervision meetings. However, ideally, supervision will take place fortnightly.

With regard to the development and maintenance of ethical practice, supervision plays a vital role. As a reflective space it ensures that the work being conducted by the counselling psychologist is kept to a good standard. It ensures the well-being of the counselling psychologist and, most importantly, it ensures that the work with clients is also being carried out ethically. This investment in supervision for the benefit of their clients can also provide new learning and insights into the therapeutic relationships being developed with clients. The same ethical standards that apply to therapeutic work with clients are also relevant to the supervisory process. Consider the following.

A newly qualified counselling psychologist, Caroline, was working in a small department in an organization where the start time of supervision was not observed punctually and the members of the small peer group arrived consistently late. Although Caroline was only a junior member of the department, she aimed to model the starting and ending time boundaries and make sure that the supervisory room was available. This resulted in raising awareness and a new adherence to boundaries that respected the clients being discussed, the professionals involved, and the process itself.

As a Manager When Qualified

Counselling psychologists that are also managers of teams can face particularly challenging ethical issues. A situation presented itself when an NHS department lost a contract, which meant that it was taken over by another trust. Some of the people working with clients had to close their caseloads.

Immediately a situation presented itself that was required to be discussed in supervision. All clients' contracts were considered and the length of time before closure of their cases was reviewed. Each client was told that due to a service reorganization their number of sessions had to be renegotiated. Adequate time was provided in the therapy sessions to renegotiate the number of sessions remaining and to consider ongoing referrals, should these be necessary.

The same department had to redeploy staff. This time the duty of care was from the manager to the employees. To show respect, the management needed to explain the overall organization situation, make the employment choices clearly known, and ensure the availability of help from the human resources department. The employees present were able to have adequate time to discuss their position in a face-to-face meeting with their line manager. This showed respect for them as people and, although some disruption occurred both practically and emotionally, respect was shown for everyone concerned. This resulted in the maintenance of good relationships and avoided mistrust and anger.

Anecdotal information was given by other colleagues who experienced change differently, where there were no clear outlines of what was occurring regarding their new roles. A lack of respect for employees and colleagues can lead to an atmosphere of basic mistrust, anger, and, in some cases, absenteeism. The ethical principle of respect for others was not observed.

Ethical comment: when counselling psychologists hold multiple roles, it is necessary to use the supervision opportunity to be aware that consideration of others is always necessary. As a manager, some of the "demands of the job" to meet deadlines and also to make economic decisions may result in overlooking the effect of some changes on other people. This "splitting" of ethical actions may happen below the level of awareness.

The newly qualified counselling psychologist will gradually be acquiring experience in a range of employment situations. The underpinning to training holds a philosophical position that supports the enhancement and attention to the perceptions of the other person as experienced in context.

Consider a situation where a counselling psychologist takes employment that requires the utilization of a therapy delivered from a manual. Here, procedures and processes must be followed. The conflation of information includes that the therapy itself is evidence-based, whilst the client's subjective and contextual perspectives may be less able to be appreciated. Anecdotally, counselling psychologists have reported ways of working which reflect that the *manner* in which the content of the therapy is transmitted can begin to deal with any lack of congruence between directive and nondirective therapies. Again, anecdotally, some employment contexts have been so concerned with the quantitative outcomes that show clients' improvement in therapy, that the need to also consider the views of the staff has been overlooked.

The Experienced Counselling Psychologist

Over time, the counselling psychologist will most probably have an increase in and expansion of roles. Ethical awareness proceeds in parallel. It is not uncommon to find that a number of roles and employments are being concurrently held.

For example, a counselling psychologist could work for 2 days in an employed setting, 2 days as a self-employed psychologist seeing clients and supervisees privately, have a position as an online tutor for trainees, and be a member of various committees in the professional body. As in any capacity there is an ethical need for self-care and to be mindful of role conflict. There may be more than one supervisory relationship to support such a portfolio. In an employment market where jobs may become more scarce, competition will naturally occur. There is a responsibility to maintain ethical awareness in a climate that could become overshadowed by the need to meet targets, obtain employment, and see only the perspective of *self* and ignore the *other*.

GENERAL LEARNING POINTS FOR THE DEVELOPMENT OF A PERSONAL ETHICAL AWARENESS

A number of different scenarios have been presented as examples occurring during the training process, through to postqualification. These can be synthesized to create a simplified process involving a number of stages.

- Notice your own thoughts and feelings that arise in response to a particular situation.
- Reflect on these as a matter of priority. It is recognized that this process may happen alone if no other colleagues are there. For example, a child safeguarding issue could occur "out of the blue" in a client session, and a response to the client may be needed immediately.
- As soon as possible, follow up the necessary reflection with colleagues and with your supervisor; look at the codes of ethics; maybe refer to ethics committees.
- Decide whether there is a need for an active response or a "watchful wait," or even no action.

Engaging with these steps is part of an ongoing professional learning process. It is not a critical check up to see if you have behaved "correctly." Of course, it is reasonable to note that if you were not to observe these steps repeatedly, then there would be a need to look more closely at why this might be occurring. This sense of personal ethical thinking and compliance has been thoughtfully reflected in an article by Dalal (2014).

CONCLUSION

This chapter initially posed four questions; the answers to these sought to show the progression of the development of a personal ethical awareness for counselling psychologists. Some examples have shown the variety of situations that may present. The content and role of the ethical codes are paramount as an embodiment of the underpinning values of the profession. Counselling psychologists will be supervised for their professional activities; this is one important part of the ethical process, and perhaps the main opportunity to reflect on ethical issues and ensure their ethical compass is in good working order. Dilemmas and difficult decisions may be encountered; these themes are the focus of another part of this book (see Chapter 21, this volume).

SUGGESTED FURTHER READING

Rokeach, M. (2008). *Understanding human values*. New York: Simon and Schuster.

REFERENCES

BACP (British Association of Counselling and Psychotherapy) (2015). *New ethical framework*. Retrieved from https://www.bacp.co.uk/ethical_framework/ (accessed March 22, 2017). Lutterworth: BACP

BPS (British Psychological Society) (2014). *Code of human research ethics*. Retrieved from http://www.bps.org.uk/system/files/Public%20files/code_of_human_research_ethics_dec_2014_inf180_web.pdf (accessed March 22, 2017). Leicester: British Psychological Society.

BPS (British Psychological Society) (2009a). *Code of human research ethics and conduct*. Retrieved from www.bps.org.uk/sites/default/files/documents/code_of_human_research_ethics.pdf (accessed March 22, 2017). Leicester: British Psychological Society.

BPS (British Psychological Society) (2009b). *Guidelines for professional practice in counselling psychology*. Retrieved from http://shop.bps.org.uk/division-of-counselling-psychology-professional-practice-guidelines.html (accessed March 22, 2017). Leicester: British Psychological Society.

BPS (British Psychological Society) (2015). *Standards of accreditation and training in counselling psychology*. Leicester: British Psychological Society.

Carlson, T. D., & Erikson, M. J. (1999). Recapturing the person in the therapist: An exploration of personal values, commitments and beliefs. *Contemporary Family Therapy: An International Journal, 21*(1), 57–76.

Cooper, M. (2009). Welcoming the other: Actualising the humanistic ethic at the core of counselling psychology practice. *Counselling Psychology Review, 24*(3/4), 119–129.

Dalal, F. (2014). Ethics versus compliance. The institution, ethical psychotherapy practice (and me). *Journal of Group Analysis, 47*(1), 62–81.

Gauthier, J. (2004). Towards a universal declaration of ethical principles for psychologists. *Applied Psychology: An International Review Supplement, 53*, 10–19.

Hawkins, P., & Shohet, R. (2012). *Supervision in the helping professions* (4th ed.). Maidenhead: McGraw Hill.

Health and Care Professions Council (2008). *Standards of conduct and performance*. Retrieved from http://www.hpc-uk.org/aboutregistration/standards/standardsofconductperformanceandethics/ (accessed March 22, 2017).

Kitchener, K. S. (1996). Professional codes in ethics and on-going moral problems in psychology. In W. O'Donohue and R. F. Kitchener (Eds.), *The philosophy of psychology* (pp. 361–370). London: Sage.

Mele, D., & Sanchez-Runde, C. (2013). Cultural diversity and universal ethics in a global world. *Journal of Business Ethics, 116*(4), 681–687.

Millard, A. (1997). *Discoveries from Bible times*. Oxford: Lion Publishing.

Newns, K., Paul, M., & Creedy, K. (2015). Action ethics: Using action method techniques to facilitate training on ethical practice. *Journal of Family Therapy, 37*(2), 246–258.

Paprocki, C. M. (2014). When personal and professional values conflict: Trainee Perspectives on tensions between religious beliefs and affirming treatment of LGBT Clients. *Ethics and Behavior, 24*(4), 279–292.

Rokeach, M. (2008). *Understanding human values*. New York: Simon and Schuster.

Schwartz, S., & Bilsky, W. (1990). Toward a theory of the universal content and structure of values: Extensions and cross-cultural replications. *Journal of Personality and Social Psychology, 58*(5), 878–891.

Counselling Psychology

DEE DANCHEV

CHAPTER OUTLINE

INTRODUCTION 316

TRUST 316

CODES, PRINCIPLES, AND VIRTUES 317

DILEMMAS AND STRUCTURES FOR SOLVING
DILEMMAS 318

ARE THERE ETHICAL DIFFERENCES AMONG
THERAPEUTIC ORIENTATIONS? 322

RESPONSIBILITY 322

ONLINE COUNSELLING 323

WHAT ARE UNETHICAL ACTIONS? 325

PRACTICE SUPERVISION 325

LEARNING OUTCOMES

BY THE END OF THIS CHAPTER YOU SHOULD
BE ABLE TO ANSWER THE FOLLOWING KEY
QUESTIONS:

1. What are the main ethical factors
   associated with establishing a strong
   therapeutic alliance?

2. What kinds of structures might be useful
   to aid the resolution of ethical dilemmas?

3. Why is supervision necessary for
   ethical practice?

Counselling Psychology: A Textbook for Study and Practice, First Edition. Edited by David Murphy.
© 2017 John Wiley & Sons Ltd. Published 2017 by John Wiley & Sons Ltd.

INTRODUCTION

Ethical practice is fundamental to the formation and development of the therapeutic relationship, and research shows that the quality of the therapeutic relationship is closely linked to a successful therapeutic outcome (Clarkson, 2003; Horvath and Symonds, 1991). In this chapter I begin by focusing on trust and the ethical underpinnings of trust, which I will argue are key factors in the formation of an effective ethical working relationship with clients. I then discuss the ethical principles and virtues and their role in solving ethical dilemmas. Following this, two structures to aid ethical problem-solving in practice are suggested. The degree of responsibility that we should hold in relation to our clients is discussed with particular reference to the work of Emmanuel Levinas and Petrushka Clarkson. The emergence of online counselling has opened up a series of new challenges for the application of existing ethical norms. Current thinking in this area is discussed and some suggestions for ethical practice are given. In order to encourage counselling psychologists to review their ethical practice, different types of unethical behaviour are outlined. Finally, I consider the factors involved in supporting and maintaining ethical practice, and focus on the role of supervision. Some ideas for items to be included in a supervision contract are given and the supervisory relationship is discussed.

My aim is that this chapter will stimulate counselling psychologists to think more deeply about the ethical basis of their practice and enable them to feel more confident when dealing with ethical practice issues.

TRUST

Trust is a key factor in all relationships. As Fukuyama (1995) and Gambetta (1988) note, society could not function without it. It facilitates social cohesion. Trust is established between people by means of rational decision making and it has to be built (Reemtsma, 2012). Counselling psychologists need to convey that they are trustworthy in order to facilitate a therapeutic relationship with their clients. Reemtsma (2012, p. 14) defines trustworthiness in the following way:

> What does it mean to be trustworthy? We are trustworthy when we keep our promises, the implicit as well as the explicit. But this is only half the story. We wouldn't call someone trustworthy who threatens to hurt us and then makes good on it. Reliability alone does not make a person trustworthy. Being trustworthy is not only about keeping promises; it means refraining from saying and doing things. No less than knowing what to expect from a person is knowing what not to expect.

Counselling psychologists are in a privileged position in relation to trust. Giddens (1990) says that institutions that have reputations for fair practice are considered to be trustworthy. As members of trustworthy institutions with high ethical standards, such as professional bodies, therapeutic organizations and universities, counselling psychologists do not begin their therapeutic relationship with zero trust. It can be argued that as professionals linked to and accredited by these institutions they already have a form of trust "capital."

It has been asserted that ruptures and repairs are a feature of a successful therapeutic relationship (Safran, Muran, & Eubanks-Carter, 2011). By rupture Safran et al. mean some form of breakdown in the therapeutic relationship. This may be caused by such things as a misunderstanding or a premature challenge on the part of the therapist. In all usual circumstances these ruptures should not be generated by a lack of trust. It is difficult to imagine a circumstance where a rupture of trust on the part of a counselling psychologist is justifiable. If thorough verbal and written contracting is undertaken at the start of the relationship then trust issues are unlikely to arise. For example, if the bounds of confidentiality and process of disclosure to third parties are clearly discussed and stated in the contract, then although difficult for all parties involved, trust is not necessarily damaged if a situation arises in which a breach of confidentiality is necessary. Pettit (1995) says that "Trust materializes reliably among people to the extent that they have beliefs about one another that make trust a sensible attitude to adopt. And trust reliably survives among people to the extent that those beliefs prove to be correct" (p. 202).

Pettit's (1995) use of the word "materializes" in the above definition draws attention to the fragility of trust. It is easily broken and once broken it is hard to regain fully. It is especially difficult to regain trust when the practitioner is an accredited professional. The trust "capital" means that more is lost than just trust in the individual. It reflects on the whole profession.

Trust can be transitive. Existing trust can be transferred to others. By this I mean that if a counselling psychologist is trusted by a client and they are then referred to another person by that counselling psychologist, the client may assume that the recommended person is trustworthy. This calls for care in making referrals to ensure within reason that the person taking our client is trustworthy.

Trust is not of itself an ethic. It is generated by ethical practice (Danchev & Ross, 2014). For counselling psychologists ethical practice is defined by a code of ethics and conduct, which is discussed briefly below (BPS, 2009).

CODES, PRINCIPLES, AND VIRTUES

Codes of ethics and conduct that outline ethical behaviour for psychologists are mostly based on principle ethics (Beauchamp & Childress, 2001). These principles, derived from bioethics, are beneficence (do good), nonmaleficence (do no evil), justice (fairness), and autonomy (respect for self-determination). Further principles have been included for counselling psychology. Shillito-Clarke (1996) adds Kitchener's (1984) principle of fidelity (faithfulness), and Meara, Schmidt, and Day (1996) have included veracity (truthfulness). Principle ethics, as will be shown, can be a useful means by which to explore the underlying concerns of ethical dilemmas. However, they have been widely criticized. The most frequently discussed criticism is that they are derived from Western individualistic values (Pederson, 1989;) and therefore do not represent the ethics of more family and community-focused societies where group needs may be prioritized over individual needs. Another well-argued criticism comes from feminists (Rave & Larsen, 1995), who assert that the feeling-intuitive dimension is underemphasized.

In a ground-breaking paper, Meara et al. (1996) suggest that counselling psychologists should focus on virtue ethics rather than principle ethics as a basis for their practice. They argue that ethical practice is generated by who we are rather than by a set of principles or rules. As Kitchener (1996) says, no set of rules can make an individual practice ethically. Gordon's (1999, pp. 35–36) view of codes of conduct and ethical principles is similar:

> [T]hey do little or nothing to protect the public. They tell us nothing, surely, that we do not accept for ourselves as a result of how we understand the process of psychotherapy. As a psychotherapist I do not need a code of ethics to tell me not to exploit someone. . . . I do not do this because of my own personal ethics and because of my understanding of transference and of the power relationship between therapist and patient.

As James says in Chapter 20, in order to practise ethically we have to work on developing our own ethical capacity and especially on developing virtues such as prudence, fortitude, and integrity (Meara et al., 1996). Shillito-Clarke (2010) encourages psychologists to develop ethical mindfulness in relation to all aspects of their work. Ethical mindfulness involves asking moral questions of ourselves, our practice, and our professional relationships as routine (Shillito-Clarke, 2010). "It is a sort of ethical minesweeping of our actions. . . . Rather than a set of skills to be learned [ethical practice] is a state of being that needs continuous attention" (Danchev & Ross, 2014, p. 16).

Professional ethical practice is not only present in the counselling room, it pervades the whole of our lives (Danchev, 2006). Codes of conduct and principle ethics cannot produce ethical practitioners, but they can act as guides and are useful tools when ethical dilemmas are encountered.

DILEMMAS AND STRUCTURES FOR SOLVING DILEMMAS

Ethical dilemmas occur when there are two equally valid options to solve a problem and neither is ideal. It takes courage to deal with a dilemma as dilemmas come freighted with complexity. The pros and cons of each aspect of the issue have to be weighed carefully. Such situations generate anxiety, and a structure for approaching and resolving dilemmas can be helpful, but it should be borne in mind that the ethical application of any structure is closely related to the degree of ethical development of the person using it. Several types of structure have been suggested. Two that counselling psychologists have found useful are described below, but first we will examine a dilemma using the ethical principles as a guide (see text box).

THE RECORD KEEPING DILEMMA

Sarah, a counselling psychologist, works as a counsellor for a public body. She has a first counselling session with James. James holds a very senior position within the organization and serves on high profile government committees. He is very anxious and has become entangled in a situation that could harm his reputation. He admits that at times he has felt suicidal. The organization that Sarah works for is security conscious. It has strict rules relating to confidentiality. It also insists on full records being kept. The records are written by hand and are stored in locked cabinets in a secure building. Sarah's manager, who is not a psychologist, nor a member of a counselling organization, has duplicate keys to these cabinets. Sarah does not think that her written records have ever been viewed by the manager or by a third party. However, she recognizes that this could occur.

Sarah underlines that James should seek medical help if his suicidal feelings persist. When she explains about the bounds of confidentiality and record keeping James says that he cannot engage in counselling with her if she writes anything down about his situation. But he says he does trust her and he particularly wants to see someone whom he trusts and who understands the organization in depth. He is frightened of seeing an external person as his situation concerns an unwise relationship and could be of interest to the press. Sarah is unsure how to proceed. Both her professional organization and her work setting require her to keep notes. Additionally, she is used to keeping notes and worries that she may not perform to her usual standard without the reflective aid of her note keeping.

Ideally Sarah would discuss her dilemma with her manager, but she is concerned that this may draw unwanted attention to her client. She will discuss this dilemma with her supervisor but first she decides to work through the issues involved. If she applies the ethical principles to this situation the following might reflect her thoughts on the matter:

Beneficence (To Do Good)

James is clearly in need of counselling. He is highly anxious and at times feels suicidal—he needs immediate attention and anchorage. He trusts me and I feel that we already have the beginnings of a strong therapeutic alliance.

Nonmaleficence (Do No Harm)

To refuse to see him would risk James being without support.

He is suicidal and very anxious.

His emotional state is very likely to worsen if I refuse to see him.

Referring him to an external counsellor might feel like I was abandoning him and he says he is afraid of disclosing his situation to others.

If I do not keep records I might not work as well as usual.

Autonomy (Self-Determination)

This raises an interesting issue that I have not really thought about in depth before. Now I'm thinking that clients should be able to choose whether detailed information is written about them and how these records are stored. I don't think that either my professional body or my organization have prioritized client rights in this respect.

Justice (Fairness)

Fairness means he should have help. His work and role mean that he is vulnerable to press intrusion and he does not have the same level of freedom and privacy as other members of the public. In other circumstances a client would be able to discuss his type of issue freely without fear of external consequences.

Fidelity (Faithfulness)

If I see him I feel that I will be being faithful to my client and to myself. I don't think that I will be being faithful to my organization in relation to record keeping. I'm not sure how this plays out in relation to my professional organization. I hope I am being a faithful professional in that I'm striving to do my best in difficult circumstances.

Veracity (Truthfulness)

This one is very difficult. I'm okay with veracity in relation to my client. I will be open and truthful with my supervisor. But I'm feeling that I can't tell my organization if I do decide not to keep notes. This involves lying by omission rather than commission, but both are

equally bad I think. I'm also feeling that I'm not going to highlight this specific instance with my professional organization. However, I could take this up as a general issue with my professional organization in the future.

There is no ideal outcome to this issue and different practitioners may well arrive at a different decision. Having looked at the principles, Sarah is drawn towards agreeing not to keep records but alerting her client to the fact that she may not work as effectively as she might without notes. She does not think she will tell either her organization or her professional body. She discusses the situation with her supervisor. They both feel that James should have an opportunity to receive counselling. They are hopeful that if their professional organization became involved there would be an understanding of the particular circumstances. Sarah is not so sure about her work organization but she decides that she must prioritize her client over any future risk of sanctions against herself.

There are a variety of more structured means of exploring ethical dilemmas. Psychologists have found the following two to be useful. The first is called the "clarify, consult, consider, choose, and check model" (see box below). It was devised by Bond (1996) and then modified by Shilito-Clarke (1996) for use by counselling psychologists.

THE CLARIFY, CONSULT, CONSIDER, CHOOSE, AND CHECK MODEL

Clarify

- Describe the issue as clearly as possible.
- Identify the elements involved.
- Imagine the perspective of each person who may be involved.
- Produce a list of evidence for and against a particular action (at this point you could run through the ethical principle analysis described above).

Consult

- Read the BPS code of ethics and conduct, and the codes of any relevant professional body or organization. Consult any people who might be helpful (bearing in mind client confidentiality). These might include the managers of any organizations involved or participant representatives.
- Could there be any legal implications of your actions? If so consult your organization, professional body,

insurer, or a legally qualified person as appropriate.

Consider

- Discuss the issue with your practice supervisor and any suitably qualified and experienced peers. Ensure that you are maintaining appropriate confidentiality.
- Keep notes of these consultations.

Choose

- Select the best action and provide further space for review before action.

Check

- Reflect on the outcome and whether this was the best option.
- What is there to be learned about this situation and yourself?

The second scheme is suggested by Dubois (2008). It is known as "So Far No Objections" (SFNO). Similar frameworks have been devised by Thomasma, Marshall, and Kondratowicz (1995) and Jennings, Kahn, Mastroianni, and Parker (2003). Dubois (2008) argues that dilemmas arise from three types of circumstances. These are:

1) Different people are involved who have competing interests.
2) Uncertainty or disagreement exists about relevant facts.
3) Uncertainty, conflict, or disagreement exist regarding ethical norms.

Dubois (2008, p. 49)

When a dilemma occurs Dubois recommends that the following information is collected. The acronym SFNO is used as a memory aid and can be summarized as follows:

S—Stakeholders: who will be significantly affected by the decision made? First, consider whether reasons exist for giving priority to the interests of one party over another. Second, identify who is invested with decision-making authority.

F—Facts: what issues might generate disagreement?

N—Norms: what ethical principles, norms, or values are at stake? Which are relevant and which generate disagreement?

O—Options: what actions or policies deserve serious consideration? If the ethical ideal is not possible what compromises can be made?

It is important to bear in mind that ethical practice is not a static enterprise. Actions that are considered to be ethical in one decade may change in the next decade. Mostly these changes are subtle. Being an active member of your professional bodies and ensuring that your continuing professional development is up to date helps with staying in touch with the latest cultural and professional norms.

ARE THERE ETHICAL DIFFERENCES AMONG THERAPEUTIC ORIENTATIONS?

A more complex ethical practice issue that has not been thoroughly researched is: are there subtle differences in ethical practice standards among the different theoretical orientations? Are there circumstances, for example, in which a psychoanalytic practitioner might consider self-disclosure unethical, whereas a person-centred practitioner in similar circumstances would regard such a disclosure to be both ethically and therapeutically necessary? These kinds of questions are ripe for research and also remind us that to practise ethically we should have a sound knowledge of our theoretical orientation and use this knowledge to underpin our therapeutic interventions.

RESPONSIBILITY

What should our degree of responsibility for our clients be? The word responsibility tends to induce anxiety as it can imply a burden which may not always be welcome. Within counselling and psychotherapy there is a frequently held view that we have responsibilities *towards* our clients but that we are not responsible *for* them. But can we avoid feelings of responsibility *for* our clients? Emmanuel Levinas, a French philosopher, said that we cannot. Levinas (1990) talks about "the face." He says that once you have gazed into the face of another you are captive to them: you become their hostage. The face "in a certain way, in its silence, it calls you. Your reaction to the face is a response. Not just a response but a responsibility" (Wright, Hughes, & Ainley, 1988). When Levinas talks about "the face" he does not necessarily mean the face as such. It can mean a hunched shoulder or some other indication from a person that conveys distress or need. Many counselling psychologists will recognize this feeling of responsibility. When we see distress or need in another some part of us becomes almost compelled to respond to it. An awareness of this form of responsibility can help to maintain the balance between providing adequate support and embarking on the negative path of undermining the client's self-confidence and autonomy.

Clarkson (2003) is concerned that responsibility is not sidestepped. She has warned practitioners against becoming bystanders: passive observers of distress and need. When at risk of becoming a therapeutic bystander she advocates moving to the ethical position of *standing by* the client. Standing by can involve some form of external action in addition to therapeutic support. If, for example, a form of injustice becomes evident then it would be ethically appropriate and possibly even ethically necessary to be part of some form of intervention, within the context of individual client confidentiality. This could involve supporting the client with reports for legal or medical action and/or alerting authorities or pressure groups to that particular form of injustice. It can be argued that to take an inactive position is unethical. At times the only ethical action is to stand up and be counted—uncomfortable though that may be.

ONLINE COUNSELLING

The application of ethics to practice is currently meeting its greatest challenge in relation to online counselling psychology. Communication with clients by online means is a feature of modern practice. In face-to-face counselling psychology practice this is mostly limited to the use of email and text messaging to make and confirm appointments. However, many counselling and psychology services now also provide a means of online counselling contact. In some services it is a means to maintain contact with clients when they are temporarily at a distance from their counsellors or because illness or disability prevents attendance. In other services online counselling is offered as a client choice.

The first ethical question to ask in relation to online counselling is "does it work?" Questions have been raised as to whether it is possible to achieve the intensity of contact that is necessary for good practice. For example, nonverbal behaviour cannot be monitored via nonvisual means, and the quality of visual media often makes it difficult to observe subtle changes in clients. Although reservations have been expressed (Kraus, Stricker, & Speyer, 2011), there is evidence from research that it can be a valuable means of contact for clients and especially for those who are geographically distant from help, have mobility problems, or find it difficult to discuss their emotional issues in a face-to-face setting (Callahan & Inckle, 2012; Osenbach, O'Brien, Mishkind, & Smolenski, 2013). Additionally, Simpson and Reid (2014) have found that there is no sign of difference in the quality of the therapeutic alliance between face-to-face psychotherapy and an online means of providing therapy.

Essentially the underlying ethical principles of online counselling psychology are exactly the same as for any other form of client work. The ethical challenge with online counselling psychology is applying the ethical standards to these modes of communication.

> [I]t seems that no fundamentally new ethical territory has been created by the advent of online counselling; there is, rather, merely new technological territory which challenges us to grasp its ramifications for normative principles.
>
> (Mulhauser, 2005)

Ethical questions relating to competence are an especially important area for online counselling psychologists. To practise online counselling psychology it is reasonable to argue that practice competence should also embrace technical mastery of the medium that is being used. This view is particularly relevant in the area of client confidentiality. These days we are only too aware that online means of communication are not completely secure. This calls for an ability to understand the technology and issues relating to online security including the use of and limits of encryption. Ethical contracting with clients requires openness about the limits of online confidentiality and agreement about safe-guards such as the use of pseudonyms, and so on. Ingenuity and forethought are often necessary to maximize security. To guard against the possibility of third parties misrepresenting themselves as the client in nonvisual contact, the inclusion of a previously agreed word or phrase in each message can help to confirm identity.

Ethical contracting with online clients would include clarity about the amount of contact. If an asynchronous medium such as email is used then defining the timing of replies, the number of emails that can be sent per week, and the length of emails that is acceptable is an important part of the contract.

For practitioners used to working in a verbal face-to-face mode, where thera-pist responses can also be conveyed nonverbally and paraverbally, it is not always easy to change to an online written means of communication (e.g., instant mes-saging). Mulhauser (2005) finds that empathy is especially difficult to convey in a written form and to do it well requires the ability to capture and express feelings in writing, which not all psychologists may possess.

Another area of ethical concern is the suitability of working online with suicidal people or clients who have a form of severe pathology (Haberstroh, Parr, Bradley, Morgan-Fleming, & Gee, 2008; Lovejoy, Demireva, Grayson, & McNamara, 2009). There are concerns that it may not be possible to provide help quickly in an emergency situation. Several studies have found that online support is of benefit to those feeling suicidal or in a crisis. The identification of how emergency help can be mobilized can be included in the initial contract. If asynchronous contact is used then it must be made clear that emergency help is unlikely to be provided in a timely fashion (Callahan & Inckle, 2012; Gros, Veronee, Strachan, Ruggiero, & Acierno, 2011). Luxton, O'Brien, Pruitt, Johnson, and Kramer (2014) have described their experience of managing sui-cide risk in online work with suicidal US veterans who have posttraumatic stress disorder. Their procedures for managing suicide risk are useful for online work with all types of client issues.

Some interesting research relating to online counselling has been carried out by Perle et al. (2013). They looked at psychologists' attitudes to the use of online media and found that practitioners whose theoretical orientations were cognitive, behavioural, cognitive-behavioural, or systemic were more accepting of the use of online therapy than dynamic, analytical, or existential practition-ers. It is worth reflecting on whether our own theoretical orientation is reason-ably or unreasonably biased against online therapy. More research is needed on the outcomes of therapy conducted online by practitioners from different orientations. However, if there is an evidence base that demonstrates success-ful outcomes for a wide range of theoretical orientations it would be wrong to restrict practice to face-to-face means if there are clients who would benefit from this resource.

Several online practitioners, and online counselling and psychotherapy codes of conduct, contain warnings about working online with people from other regions and countries. These concerns mainly relate to the boundaries of prac-titioner insurance, legality, and ethical recourse if a client wishes to complain.

Technology is advancing rapidly and there is a sense of practitioners and their professional organizations having to work hard to keep up with the latest developments. A range of recent (2013–2015) informative guidelines and research papers on online mental health support can be accessed at http://kspope.com/telepsychology.php.

WHAT ARE UNETHICAL ACTIONS?

In order to review the ethical nature of practice, it is worth considering the different degrees of unethical action as they can stimulate reflection and discussion.

The most common form of behaviour that can result in an unethical action is mistakes. Everyone makes mistakes from time to time even though they may strive to minimize errors. Popper (1996), the philosopher, agrees that mistakes are unavoidable. He says that we only move into the unethical realm when we try to hide our mistakes. He argues that we must be open about them and ensure that we learn from them. We must also take remedial action to redress any wrongs that may have occurred.

Unethical behaviour may also result from a fear of failure or a fantasy of rejection. This can manifest itself through a reluctance to ask for help and guidance when it is needed.

Palmer Barnes (1998) identifies three additional forms of unethical action. These are poor practice, negligence, and malpractice. Poor practice can result from actions such as misrepresenting our skills and training, failing to contract effectively, being unreliable in relation to clients and colleagues, or cancelling sessions without good reason.

Negligence is about failing to ensure that no harm comes to others, either through ignorance or from other motivations. Actions such as not liaising with the appropriate services about at risk clients would come into this category. Other examples are failing to act to prevent serious physical or mental harm to a third party or failing to ensure that confidential data are securely kept.

Malpractice involves committing active misdemeanours such as entering into exploitative sexual or financial relationships with clients. Sometimes malpractice can result from external pressures to produce results and individual career motivations.

Fortunately, serious malpractice is relatively rare.

PRACTICE SUPERVISION

In Chapter 20 James writes about the development and maintenance of the ethical counselling psychologist. An important aspect of ethical practice is personal and professional self-care. A crucial means of support in the development and maintenance of ethical practice is the effective use of supervision. Ideally, the counselling psychologist and practice supervisor are freely chosen and care is taken to maximize the type of supervisory relationship that will be most beneficial for the counselling psychologist's practice and development. In many ways the supervisory relationship mirrors the therapeutic relationship but it includes one important additional factor: the main responsibility of the supervisor is not to the supervisee, it is to the client. For trainees the supervisor is also reporting on the quality of their practice, and trainees are dependent on obtaining a positive report to gain their qualification. These factors can result in defensive practice within supervision where mistakes and anxieties are concealed by the trainee. Refocusing on the primary aim to prioritize the client and to maximize the developmental and supportive benefits of supervision it is necessary to be open about anxieties, about feelings of hopelessness, about being ineffective, and actively disclosing mistakes. Being open about these things risks feelings of shame and humiliation. Trust, as in client work, is a huge factor in a successful supervisory relationship. The ideal situation is for trainees and supervisors to be free to choose whom they enter into a supervisory relationship with. However, during training this may not be possible. Placements in organizations often come with in-house supervision and choice is not a factor on either side. In order to get the most out of any supervisory relationship openness and a clear contract are necessary ingredients.

A clear contract will usually include the following elements:

- Meeting times and location(s);
- Frequency;
- Client/supervision ratio;
- Theoretical orientation(s);
- Payment;
- Ethical standards to be worked to;
- Organizational standards and requirements;
- University/training organization requirements;
- Nonattendance procedure;
- The process for arbitration if a rupture or breakdown occurs in the supervisory relationship.

Areas of discussion for a first supervision meeting (ideally this is a discussion between two people and not just with the emphasis on the trainee/supervisee):

- Training history.
- Identification by both people of any issues that may influence practice such as factors in personal history.
- A discussion of theoretical approach(es).
- Modes of presentation of client work.
- Any health issues that may influence practice.
- The power dynamics in the supervisory relationship.
- Identification of factors that may get in the way of openness in the supervisory relationship.
- The contract.

A contract is usually drafted either during the session or just after and then rediscussed and signed at the next meeting.

Most counselling psychologists find supervision to be supportive and an effective means of developing and maintaining their best practice. Watkins (1996) has described the supervisory relationship as a means to remoralize the counsellor. This formulation not only embraces the means of keeping the supervisee on the ethical straight and narrow, but it also underlines that good supervision serves to raise their morale. It gives us what we all need: the courage and skills to stay with painful and complex work.

Ethics underpin all the aspects of our practice and ethical dilemmas inevitably arise. Sometimes the right course of action is clear, but often the complexity of our clients' issues and the constraints of our work settings leave us unsure of the best course of action when a decision is necessary. I hope that this chapter has provided some assistance in helping you to think through your ethical dilemmas. We are fortunate in working in a profession that requires practice supervision and enables us to have a network of colleagues who understand the stresses and strains of our work and the bounds of confidentiality. Supervisors and colleagues are great resources for ethical consultation and discussion; they are often our best form of support.

SUGGESTED FURTHER READING

Gabriel, L., & Casemore, R. (Eds.) (2009). *Relational ethics in practice: Narratives from counselling and psychotherapy*. Hove: Routledge.

Gordon, P. (1999). *Face to face: Therapy as ethics*. London: Constable.

Tjeltveit, A. C. (1999). *Ethics and values in psychotherapy*. London: Routledge.

REFERENCES

Beauchamp, T.L., & Childress, J. F. (2001). *Principles of biomedical ethics* (5th ed.). New York: Oxford University Press.

Bond, T. (1996). Counselling-supervision—ethical issues. In S. Palmer, S. Dainow, & P. Milner (Eds.), *The BAC counselling reader* (pp. 430–439). London: Sage.

BPS (British Psychological Society) (2009). *The code of ethics and conduct*. Leicester: British Psychological Society.

Callahan, A., & Inckle, K. (2012). Cybertherapy or psychobabble? A mixed methods study of online emotional support. *British Journal of Guidance and Counselling*, 40(3), 261–278.

Clarkson, P. (2003). *The therapeutic relationship*. London: Whurr.

Danchev, D. (2006). *Counselling psychologists' perspectives on professionalism*. Unpublished D.Psych. thesis. London: City University.

Danchev, D., & Ross, A. (2014). *Research ethics for counsellors, nurses and social workers*. London: Sage.

Dubois, J. M. (2008). *Ethics in mental health research*. New York: Oxford University Press.

Fukuyama, F. (1995). *Trust. The social virtues and the creation of prosperity*. New York: Basic Books.

Gambetta, D. (1988). Can we trust? In D. Gambetta (Ed.), *Trust: Making and breaking cooperative relations*. Oxford: Blackwell.

Giddens, A. (1990). *The consequences of modernity*. Oxford: Polity Press.

Gordon, P. (1999). *Face to face: Therapy as ethics*. London: Constable

Gros, D. F., Veronee, K., Strachan, M., Ruggiero, K. J., & Acierno, R. (2011). Managing suicidality in home-based telehealth. *Journal of Telemedicine and Telecare, 17*, 332–335.

Haberstroh, S., Parr, G., Bradley, L., Morgan-Fleming, B., & Gee, R. (2008). Facilitating online counselling: Perspectives from counsellors in training. *Journal of Counselling and Development, 86*(4), 460–470.

Horvath, A. O., & Symonds, B. D. (1991). The relationship between the working alliance and outcome in psychotherapy: A meta-analysis. *Journal of Counselling Psychology, 38*(2), 139–149.

Jennings, B., Kahn, J., Mastroianni, A., & Parker, L. S. (2003). *Ethics and public health: Model curriculum*. Yale School of Public Health. Retrieved from: http://www.aspph.org/wp-content/uploads/2014/02/EthicsCurriculum.pdf (accessed June 21, 2015).

Kitchener, K. S. (1984). Intuition, critical evaluation and ethical principles: The foundation for ethical decisions in counseling psychology. *The Counseling Psychologist, 12*(3), 43–55.

Kitchener, K. S. (1996). Professional codes of ethics and on-going moral problems in psychology. In W. O'Donohue, & R. F. Kitchener (Eds.), *The philosophy of psychology* (pp. 361–380). London: Sage.

Kraus, R., Stricker, G., & Speyer, C. (2011). *Online counselling: A handbook for mental health professionals* (2nd ed.). San Diego, CA: Elsevier Academic Press.

Levinas, E. (1963, 1990). *Difficult freedom: Essays on Judaism* (transl. S. Hand). Baltimore, MD: The Johns Hopkins University Press.

Lovejoy, T., Demireva, P., Grayson, J., & McNamara, J. (2009). Advancing the practice of online psychotherapy: An application of Rogers' diffusion of innovations theory. *Psychotherapy: Theory, Research, Practice, Training, 46*, 112–124.

Luxton, D. D., O'Brien, K., Pruitt, L. D., Johnson, K., & Kramer, G. (2014). Suicide risk management during clinical telepractice. *International Journal of Psychiatry in Medicine, 48*(1), 19–31.

Meara, N. M., Schmidt, L. D., & Day, J. D. (1996). Principles and virtues: A foundation for ethical decisions, policies and character. *The Counselling Psychologist, 24*(1), 4–77.

Mulhauser, G. R. (2005). 9 observations about the practice and process of online therapy using email. Retrieved from http://counsellingresource.com/papers/online-practice/ (accessed on May 15, 2015).

Osenbach, J. E., O'Brien, K. M., Mishkind, M., & Smolenski, D. J. (2013). Synchronous telehealth technologies in psychotherapy for depression: A metaanalysis. *Depression and Anxiety, 30*(11), 1058–1067.

Palmer Barnes, F. (1998). *Complaints and grievances in psychotherapy: A handbook of ethical practice*. London: Routledge.

Pederson. P. (1989). Developing multicultural ethical guidelines for psychology. *International Journal of Psychology, 24*, 643–652.

Perle, J. G., Langsam, L. C., Randel, A., Lutchman, S., Levine, A., B., Odland, A. P., Nierenberg, B., & Marker, C. D. (2013). Attitudes toward psychological telehealth: current and future clinical psychologists' opinions of internet-based interventions. *Journal of Clinical Psychology, 69*(1), 100–113.

Pettit, P. (1995). The cunning of trust. *Philosophy and Public Affairs, 24*(3), 202–225.

Popper, K. (1996). *Toleration and intellectual responsibility. In search of a better world: Lectures and essays from thirty years*. Laura J. Bennett (Trans.). London: Routledge.

Rave, E. J., & Larsen, C. C. (1995). *Ethical decision making in therapy: Feminist perspectives*. New York: Guilford Press.

Reemtsma, J. P. (2012). *Trust and violence*. Princeton, NJ: Princeton University Press.

Safran, J. D., Muran, J. C., & Eubanks-Carter, C. (2011). Repairing alliance ruptures. *Psychotherapy, 48*(1), 80–87.

Shillito-Clarke, C. (1996). Ethical issues in counselling psychology. In R. Woolfe and W. Dryden (Eds.), *The handbook of counselling psychology*. London: Sage.

Shillito-Clarke. C. (2010). Ethical issues in counselling psychology. In R. Woolfe, S. Strawbridge, B. Douglas, & W. Dryden (Eds.), *Handbook of counselling psychology* (pp. 507–528). London: Sage.

Simpson, S. G., & Reid, C. L. (2014). Therapeutic alliance in videoconferencing psychotherapy: A review. *Australian Journal of Rural Health, 22*(6), 280–299.

Thomasma, D. C., Marshall, P. A., & Kondratowicz, D. (1995). *Clinical medical ethics: Casees and Readings: Loyola University of Chicago, Stritch School of Medicine, Medical Humanities Program*. Lanham, MD: University Press of America.

Watkins, C. E. (1996). On demoralization and awe in psychotherapy supervision. *The Clinical Supervisor, 14*(1), 139–148.

Wright, T., Hughes, P., & Ainley, A. (1988). The paradox of morality: An interview with Emmanuel Levinas. In R. Bernasconi and D. Wood (Eds.), *The provocation of Levinas* (pp. 160–180). London: Routledge.

Counselling Psychology

COLIN FELTHAM AND RICHARD HOUSE

CHAPTER OUTLINE

INTRODUCTION 331

POLITICS AND COUNSELLING
PSYCHOLOGISTS 331

ALIGNMENT WITH MARGINALIZED
AND OPPRESSED GROUPS 334

PROFESSIONAL POLITICS 336

WIDER APPLICATIONS OF
COUNSELLING PSYCHOLOGY THEORY,
AND CROSSOVERS 339

CONCLUSION 341

LEARNING OUTCOMES

BY THE END OF THIS CHAPTER YOU SHOULD
BE ABLE TO ANSWER THE FOLLOWING KEY
QUESTIONS:

1. In what ways can counselling psychology
   be considered political?

2. Does counselling psychology inevitably
   entail left wing commitments and biases?
3. Which political, economic, and social
   policy issues are most closely associated
   with, and relevant to, the mental health
   professions?

Counselling Psychology: A Textbook for Study and Practice, First Edition. Edited by David Murphy.
© 2017 John Wiley & Sons Ltd. Published 2017 by John Wiley & Sons Ltd.

INTRODUCTION

Counselling psychology is a political activity. In this chapter we present four broad foci as the basis for structural analysis: (a) conventional/formal political affiliation (left/right wing); (b) politics as personal and mental health specific—for example, identity politics, social justice, or cultural Marxism; (c) intra-professional politics (a profession's internal tactics/goals); and (d) wider sociopolitical applications of counselling psychology theory. We write mainly about the British context, and aspire to an even-handed, critical thinking ethos, but our partialities and prejudices may show, as no-one can completely escape from complexity, bias, and ignorance. This vast subject is unavoidably condensed, and fuller contributions are available, for example, in Kovel (1988), Parker (2007), Samuels (1993), and Totton (2000, 2006); and in journals such as *Psychotherapy and Politics International*.

POLITICS AND COUNSELLING PSYCHOLOGISTS

Most counselling and psychotherapy have traditionally been presented as apolitical, undisclosed in the practice setting, and neutral in publications. Yet the helping/caring professions and associated academia are predominantly left-leaning. Related professions (in the NHS, education, social work) have high female staffing levels. Most caring professions have voluntary sector roots, with staff motivated by compassion. Counselling psychology retains disproportionately high levels of female trainees and practitioners, with trainers likely being left-leaning (Williams, 2014). Their interest in inner experience and the therapeutic relationship is mirrored in clients' profiles, likely more female than male, who are willing to work through personal issues. Right wing sympathizers are traditionally more likely to be "stiff upper lipped" or psychologically defensive, to support stoicism, suppression of feelings, and distraction (e.g., Dalrymple, 2003). Academically anecdotal, such speculations are unavoidable as these issues are barely raised.

We cannot know how counselling psychologists vote, but our experience-based impression is that the majority is probably on the centre-left. The British Association for Counselling and Psychotherapy (BACP) (2015) outlined five party-political mental health policies before the 2015 general election, but remained neutral. Most counselling psychologists appear broadly middle class, and affluent enough to fund expensive training, a trend exacerbated by demands for doctoral qualifications. There is little if any data on clients' class and income levels or political affiliations, though at a guess they might be more left than right wing. Someone could also vote right wing, but encounter personal difficulties and warm to counselling through effective help, though not necessarily changing political affiliation. It is of course possible that some counselling psychologists vote Conservative without sharing this with colleagues (the "shy Conservative" syndrome). Warm personal feelings for others and emotional intelligence are not an exclusive preserve of the political left.

Critical psychologists, especially those of a social-materialist orientation (Moloney, 2013; Smail, 2005), challenge the low profile given to analysing living conditions, and make links between social power relations and psychological problems (see also Berardi, 2015; Verhaeghe, 2014). Some go further leftwards still, embracing variations of (post-)Marxist analysis, even referring to "Marxist psychology" (Bosteels, 2012; Parker, 2007). Some "critical psychologists" would also identify strongly with poststructuralist or transpersonal worldviews (e.g., Henriques, Hollway, Urwin, Venn, & Walkerdine, 1998).

Critical psychology appears to challenge the counselling psychologist's traditional political neutrality, at least among practitioners if not within practice itself (Loewenthal, 2015). But how many counselling psychologists work privately and/or in statutory positions, espousing radical/left wing politics whilst enjoying a relatively high income? Indeed, is it credible to practise in one-to-one professional systems when socialism suggests *community*, not individualism, to be healing? Money has also not received the attention we might expect (but see Murdin, 2012; Tudor, 1998).

The traditional political right favours free markets with few welfare safeguards; opposes a large state and significant social interventions; is ambivalent about structural "equal opportunities"; typically favours punitive criminal justice; endorses national identity, opposing significant immigration; and believes in a competitive, self-regarding, and kin-favouring culture, as opposed to a pro-social, cooperative ethos. Counselling psychologists will likely doubt the benefits of competitive schools and workplaces, working directly with systems' casualties (e.g., Duffell, 2014). They help offenders understand the familial/societal causes of offending, tend towards multicultural awareness, and typically embrace humanistic psychology principles (e.g., human goodness, resourcefulness, and potential). Counselling psychology theory considers parent–child relationships, the importance of early nurture, and freedom from conditions of worth. Counselling psychology practice privileges the centrality of trusting therapeutic relationships as a healing factor (Knox & Cooper, 2015).

Halmos (1966) argued that counselling arose in the 1950s, as politics and religion in the UK were losing credibility. Others have pointed to the influence of "Jewish psychological evangelism" (Heinze, 2004), with many founders of psychological therapies being Jewish. The perceived rise in the West of the autonomous, hedonistically driven individual appeared to favour counselling's focus on inner and interpersonal above sociopolitical and metaphysical interests (but see Proctor, Cooper, Sanders, & Malcolm, 2006). Counselling psychology tacitly benefits from the commodification of human distress, but also suffers from neglecting underpinning social dynamics. The growth of the humanistic therapies, counter-cultural encounter groups, Red Therapy, the "barefoot psychoanalyst," co-counselling, cooperative enquiry, social therapy, soma (anarchist) therapy, *The Radical Therapist* journal, and Marxist-informed psychoanalysis have all in their distinct ways challenged the status quo. But in moving towards endorsement by the NHS and mainstream societal institutions, counselling psychology is arguably losing much of its critical potency.

The current paradigm is dominated by cognitive-behaviour therapy (CBT), focusing on individual rationality, and its evidence-based, short-term, manualized, government-funded, and Improving Access to Psychological Therapies (IAPT)-boosted therapy of choice fits well the technical-rational-bureaucratic social norm prevalent in late capitalist technocratic societies. British CBT has many ironic features. Professor Lord Richard Layard, a CBT champion, had a psychoanalyst father, and is an affluent Old Etonian and a Labour peer sitting in the House of Lords. As a health economist, he has argued for a focus on happiness and well-being as key to success, protesting with David Clark that mental health is neglected compared with physical health (Layard & Clark, 2014). Layard's "science of happiness" includes both recommending CBT, and attention to happiness research arguing for greater socioeconomic equality. Radical CBT requires no social equality for personal equanimity (Ellis, 2006), yet an ostensibly left wing academic-politician is calling for both personal stoicism (which CBT represents) and, simultaneously, greater economic equality. At best this depicts unintentionally muddled thinking. CBT's sibling, positive psychology, is now in some of its formats big business, with many thriving proponents. In the USA, Martin Seligman reportedly commands fees of $30,000–50,000 per engagement (Anthony, 2014).

Oliver James, the media-oriented clinical psychologist whose parents were psychoanalysts, argues against "affluenza" and "selfish capitalism" (James, 2008) as well as against CBT. Sue Gerhardt (2010), a psychoanalytic psychotherapist, criticizes the "selfish society," calling attention to babies' needs for extensive maternal care, which remains problematic for many feminists. Celebrated left wing social epidemiologists Wilkinson and Pickett (2010) claim their "evidence-based politics" demonstrate inequality causing mental distress, reportedly finding less in more equal societies. Their thesis, and selective evidence, is however disputed (Snowdon, 2010).

When well-intentioned left wing therapists and academics engage in mental health battles, we see some mixed motivations, confused thinking, and personal biases. While left wing politics is more concerned with these matters than the *laissez-faire* right wing, the left can also be misinformed or overambitious. Many counselling psychologists argue that counselling should be freely and universally available, without realistic concern for macro-economics, while the "stiff upper lip" anticounselling right wing mistrusts the profession addressing psychological distress with talking therapy, regarding it as a luxury. Layard and others emphasize selective *evidence* but tend to ignore inconvenient data and conflicting accounts.

Psychotherapy critic Epstein (1995) argues from an American social work perspective that the poorest citizens require far more attention and expenditure than they need psychotherapy (see also Smail, 2005). Denmark is a comparatively equal society economically, commonly ranked the world's happiest country, yet it is also socially homogeneous, with high rates of antidepressant and alcohol consumption, smoking, and domestic violence, and little free counselling. Mother-provided infant childcare might be best developmentally, but sits uneasily with feminist agendas of state-provided childcare and equal career status.

Proponents of greater equality and less capitalist selfishness are themselves usually relatively affluent. The nonacquisitive and anticommodity-fetishism ideals of Thoreau, Marx, Gandhi, and others are reflected in Fromm's writings (2013) on the pernicious effects of materialistic lifestyles (cf. Verhaeghe, 2014). In Western politics, few socialists match Uruguayan President José Mujica's integrity, giving 90% of his salary to charity.

Regarding anarchism, few if any counselling psychologists are likely to be authentic, active anarchists. Some may have "old hippie" or voluntarily low income lifestyles, and a few may style themselves "barefoot analysts" or similar. Certainly some, including ourselves, may sympathize with anticapitalist protests and entertain armchair revolutionary fantasies. Most anarchist sympathizers, like many Marxists, tend to regard individualized psychotherapy with suspicion or disdain, believing the aetiology of personal distress to have civilizational roots, with remedies residing wholly in sociopolitical upheaval (e.g., Invisible Committee, 2009; Jensen & Keith, 2012; Zerzan, 2002). Certainly, few on the extreme right, made up of sub-fascist groups, will have sympathy with or expressed desire for therapy.

ALIGNMENT WITH MARGINALIZED AND OPPRESSED GROUPS

Counselling psychology has always privileged confidentiality, and emphasized ethical oversight. With good reason, writers of the ethical codes and frameworks have agonized over professional boundaries, including clients offering gifts, seeking friendship, and so on. Professional bodies are clearly more comfortable with decontextualized professional micro-ethics than with social macro-ethics and politics. Counselling psychology programmes, accused of sociopolitical naivety, often respond by building in "social contexts" modules to address Foucauldian themes of power—bolt-on, token responses, perhaps?

Counselling psychology developed when many "isms" were being forcefully challenged, guided by *"the personal is the political"* slogan. Counselling psychology programmes emphasize such sociopolitical awareness, and it has always been natural for counsellors to underline women's position in society, since so many *are* women. Original Freudian theory distorted analysis of female psychology and female patients' reports of sexual abuse (Masson, 1992), but thankfully this has changed. The rise of feminist therapy, incorporating consciousness-raising groups (Ernst & Goodison, 1981), challenged the solely individual focus and politically neutral texture of counselling and psychotherapy. While not a social minority, women remain underrepresented in positions of power, are on average paid significantly less across a lifetime, and do more domestic work, childrearing, and elder care. Women's position means they value family life, more likely voting for parties with family-friendly policies—that is, the left (Poole, 2014). The value of unconditional positive regard starkly contrasts with attitudes of racism and insensitivity/prejudice towards people different from most counsellors, for example, those with disabilities, LGBT identities, working/under-class origins, religious affiliations, and the aged and mentally ill. Counselling psychologists are certainly not exclusively white, able-bodied, heterosexual, middle class, and free from mental health problems (but see below), but attitudinal bias exists among trainees, practitioners, and academics. Accordingly, training courses have long emphasized the importance of antidiscriminatory practice (Lago & Smith, 2010). Professional bodies have strongly challenged right wing religious groups commending gay conversion therapy (e.g., Anon, 2012; UKCP, 2013).

But antidiscriminatory sensitivity has an unrecognized downside. Groups mentioned above are probably not statistically representative (Feltham, 2014). At least 85% of the UK population is white, 70% is reportedly Christian, 8% is above the age of 75, and around 96% is heterosexual. West (2015) argues that the multicultural social model itself creates social problems, including unrecognized mental health problems for many minorities. Preaching to the converted on the left may not present a rounded picture of counselling psychology's politics.

The unemployed, low-paid, and "precariat" (on insecure, zero-hours contracts) and the elderly are probably underrepresented in caseloads, and certainly underrepresented in publications. Practitioners are increasingly younger and better paid than most clients. *Starting* salary for a trainee counselling psychologist is slightly above the *average* UK wage. Trainings address only part of this mismatch. The field has shifted from its former preference for the "psychologically minded," and the YAVIS group (young, attractive, verbal, intelligent, and successful), but might still be accused of tacit gerontophobia and aversion to low-paid, poorly educated clients, who may anyway regard counselling as irrelevant. Well-meaning proselytizers have also inadvertently exported Western (largely American) models of counselling/therapy to countries, such as Kenya, where it has little natural fit, believing these models to be culturally neutral. Fanon (2001), however, famously warned against such colonialist moves decades ago, and Watters (2011) challenges the US tendency to export psychodiagnostic categories and alleged cures worldwide.

One current hot political "psy" issue is the disparity between physical and mental health provisions. In line with Layard and Clark (2014), BACP (2014) and the British Psychological Society (BPS) are pushing for greater commitment to addressing mental health problems. It appears scandalous that mental health receives far less funding, with the perception that psychological suffering is less significant. People with mental health problems constitute a sizeable group (perhaps around 25% of the population across the lifespan), and we are all potentially susceptible. The 2014 BACP document, while recommending choice of evidence-based treatments, fails to question the notion of "evidence" itself amid the proliferation of psychotherapeutic models; to address realistically the cost of increasing services (physical illnesses *are* often more life-threatening); and to note the inevitable downside of statutory regulation/control that changes might demand (e.g., Mowbray, 1995). While favouring addressing the age-old mind–body nexus, far greater changes would likely be required than those suggested.

PROFESSIONAL POLITICS

Most original therapy models were initiated by single prominent figureheads (mostly white and male) and immediate supporters. Freud has been criticized for putting self-advancement above clients' welfare (Borch-Jacobsen & Shamdasani, 2012), but fought to have psychoanalysis distinct from medicine, and open to lay analysts. Similarly, Carl Rogers took on US psychiatry's forbidding him the title "psychotherapist," popularizing the terms "counselling" and "client" instead of "patient." From the beginning counselling and psychotherapy were in tension with psychiatry and psychology. Pre-1970 developments were characterized by grassroots movements, the voluntary sector and humanistic values, left wing alignments, and revolutionary visions. Meanwhile, psychoanalytic practitioners quietly built private practices and established professional societies; behaviour therapists and clinical psychologists worked in and through universities; the BPS boosted their scientific credentials; and humanistic practitioners ran workshops and private practices, slowly raising their profile in BACP, the Association for Humanistic Psychology (AHP), and the Independent Practitioners Network (IPN) (the latter group being the most counter-cultural; House, 2004). And far from "antipsychiatry" having been silenced by the return of biomedical power, it had a significant influence via critical and liberatory psychiatry (Cohen & Timimi, 2008; Moncrieff, Rapley, & Speed, 2014) and the antipharmaceutical lobby (Moncrieff, 2013).

Statutory regulation has been a highly contentious issue, splitting the "Psy" field over several decades. Notable is the extent to which any coherent case for regulation has been comprehensively swamped by a vast literature challenging the appropriateness of the state regulation of the psychological therapies (e.g., House, 1996; House & Totton, 1997 [2011]; Mowbray, 1995). Some key landmarks on the unfolding Psy regulatory landscape were the Foster report of 1971, the Sieghart Report of 1978, the launch of the United Kingdom Council for Psychotherapy (UKCP) in 1993, the advent of statutory regulation for psychologists in 2009, and the government's unexpected withdrawal of plans to statutorily regulate counselling and psychotherapy in 2010. Scientology became a major media concern in 1966, when a national daily newspaper reported on "The Case of the Processed Woman" (Foster, 1971). When Scientology was investigated, their practices of "auditing" and "processing" were seen as so dangerous that the statutory regulation of psychotherapy was called for. Following the subsequent Sieghart Report of 1978, some 12 years of deliberations led to the UKCP launching a national register of psychotherapists in 1993. And following a number of therapy scandals in the 1990s, the British Labour government decided to widen statutory regulation, to include psychologists—including, of course, counselling psychologists.

While the BPS favoured statutory regulation, it opposed having the then Health Professions Council as regulator, preferring a new "Psychological Professions Council" that would map on to its particular responsibilities. However, the HPC won the day, and in June 2009, under the Health Care and Associated Professions (Miscellaneous Amendments) Order, regulation of most of the psychology professions was passed over to the HPC, subsequently renamed the

Health and Care Professions Council (HCPC). Following this came a further government intention to statutorily regulate counselling and psychotherapy, but a powerful rear-guard action led by the Alliance for Counselling and Psychotherapy (Postle & House, 2009), culminating in a famous judicial review court victory and humiliating defeat for the HPC, led to the new government dropping these plans in 2010, replacing the statutory plans with a voluntary register under the Council for Healthcare Regulatory Excellence (CHRE) (see Bilton, 2012).

Though some still canvass for statutory regulation, the counselling and psychotherapy field is currently regulated voluntarily via the Professional Standards Authority, and this means that there exists a significant "accountability split" within the psy field, between counselling (and clinical) psychologists, who are HCPC-regulated, and counsellors and psychotherapists, who are voluntarily regulated. This merely contributes to the "status wars" and power struggles over professional titles to which the field is inevitably subject. We should also mention the important UK campaigning organization, Psychotherapists and Counsellors for Social Responsibility (PCSR), which, *inter alia*, explicitly recognizes the impact of the political dimension on the client–practitioner relationship, seeks to integrate social, political, environmental, and cultural issues into theory and practice, and offers psychological perspectives on debates regarding current social, cultural, environmental, and political issues. The Alliance for Counselling and Psychotherapy and the PCSR, along with Psychologists for Social Change, give activist-inclined counselling psychologists every opportunity to engage fully with the politics of psy work.

Counselling was formally recognized by BPS counselling psychology members in 1982. Although perhaps beneficently motivated, the BPS Counselling Psychology Division has more recently made professionalizing moves, with lengthy doctoral training now routine in counselling psychology, and endorsement by the HCPC, with implications for the employment market and private fees. No evidence exists that lengthy academic (or even psychological) training makes for better practitioners (House, 1996), but the production of doctoral mental health professionals erroneously implies that this is the only legitimate route to professional competence. The BPS reports that in 2008, counselling psychologist members charged private fees of at least £80 an hour (Porter, 2010), with fees of counsellors and psychotherapists typically only half that. Although no counselling psychologists presumably claim twice the effectiveness of mental health practitioners who are lower in the "pecking order," a market forces assumption underpins such fee levels: many clients believe that "you get what you pay for," and therefore are advised to pay more for "properly qualified" practitioners. Little wonder that, whatever the evidence, such professionalizing assumptions are rarely questioned from within the profession, for to do so would risk undermining the hard-fought-for professional foundation of much therapy work.

The (inevitable?) turf wars and primitive pecking orders that exist across the "psy" world need to be named and critically considered, but seldom are in any honest analysis of the field. Thus, counselling psychologists compete with clinical psychologists not only in terms of clinical epistemology but also, crucially, regarding status, pay, and employment opportunities. Private health practice is arguably antithetical to NHS principles, and discriminates against the poor

(Pilgrim, 2012). Some counselling psychologists do reserve part of their caseload for a sliding scale accessible to poorer clients (see Free Psychotherapy Network, n.d.), but some practitioners deliberately rent rooms in London's prestigious Harley Street (or regional equivalents), demanding high hourly rates. In contrast with doctoral upscaling many foundation counselling degrees are much shorter than counselling psychology courses, recruiting far more working class/nontraditional students, with much lower status and employment prospects.

Reticence prevails in the personal income realm, yet what arguably lies beneath any "politics of envy" is a chasm of unexamined (and often unjustified) inequalities. At "the bottom" are qualified counsellors working voluntarily (unpaid), often towards the 450 hrs required for accreditation. At "the top" are university professors of counselling psychology, NHS consultant counselling psychologists, workplace counselling organization executives, BACP/BPS chief executive officers, and executives of international publishing companies publishing counselling-related texts. (Rarely mentioned is the academic publishing industry's reliance on the unremunerated or very low-paid labour of "psy" writers.) The material quality of life of these high earners typically vastly exceeds that of those at the bottom. Moreover, trainees, private clients, taxpayers, and charity donors unwittingly support this pyramid of inequality. A "politics of naivety" may feed the lack of awareness of these discrepancies—inequalities routinely exploited by those at the top. Salaries do give some indication of perceived social worth, with low incomes associated with poor mental and physical health (Santiago, Kaltman, & Miranda, 2013).

We now ask whether any concealed "politics" exist here. Specifically, are the principles of psychodynamic, humanistic and cognitive-behavioural, and other therapies in any sense political, rather than politically neutral? In the psychotherapy of Nathaniel Branden, for example, his former close association with Ayn Rand, the fiercely pro-capitalist writer, likely influenced his therapy model and psychology of self-esteem (Branden, 2001). Thomas Szasz, the psychiatrist who vociferously critiqued psychotherapy, was a right wing libertarian. In contrast, Wilhelm Reich explicitly championed a Marxist position (Reich, 1997). An interesting comparison of the politics of R. D. Laing and Szasz is found in Itten and Roberts (2006). It is easy enough, too, to see that "Big Pharma," the pharmaceutical industry, has a strong vested interest in protecting its commercial interests by prioritizing profit over human welfare (Cohen & Timimi, 2008; Itten & Roberts, 2014).

It is much more contentious to argue that CBT is inherently right wing. Almost all therapies emphasize individual autonomy, pursuing one's goals and meeting one's needs, with some feminist therapy constituting one major exception (Robb, 2007). Does a therapy emphasizing thinking and behaviour, rather than feeling, necessarily incline towards the political right? Probably not, but CBT does arguably reinforce a stoical, "grin and bear it" mentality. It would certainly be interesting to research the varying political allegiances of therapists working in different modalities. An argument can be made that "government-approved" CBT, in its underwriting of a "back to work/off benefits" strategy, is a reactionary form of therapy (Guilfoyle, 2008). It is also difficult to separate today's CBT entirely from the 1950s when Hans Eysenck was promoting clinical psychology, denigrating psychoanalytic therapy while approving behaviour therapy, and being associated with views on intelligence perceived as racist (Buchanan, 2010).

Though occasional exceptions exist, therapeutic models emphasizing strong feelings and awareness of environments that suppress feelings—that is, humanistic therapies—tend to be left wing in their leaning. Carl Rogers' person-centred approach is sometimes referred to as "a gentle revolution," being *person*-centred, not institution-centred, and aiming at personal empowerment that impacts wider social environments (Kearney, 1996; Proctor et al., 2006; Rogers, 1978). Re-evaluation co-counselling explicitly recommends the discharge of distress patterns associated with racism, sexism, classism, and so on. Janov (1973), however, argued that those re-experiencing strong early feelings in therapy would become oriented to real inner needs rather than false social systems or symbolic political struggles, and would be unlikely to have any political involvement.

Does psychodynamic counselling psychology possess any political bias? Freud regarded psychoanalysis as a scientific endeavour altogether above politics. Yet Reich, Roheim, Adorno, Fromm, Marcuse, Lacan, Althusser, Žižek, Parker, and others have attempted to create Freudo-Marxist forms of analysis and societal critique—though these remain more relevant to academics than to ordinary people (Stavrakakis, 2007). Karen Horney's work is also important as a pioneering "feminist psychology" and her engagement with cultural differences, as well as intra-psychic ones.

Of those favouring Lacanian social analyses, and citing the psychoanalytically oriented Oliver James and Lacanian-enamoured Slavoj Žižek, Fisher writes: "We must convert widespread mental health problems from medicalized conditions into effective antagonisms. Affective disorders are captured discontent; this disaffection can and must be channelled outwards, directed towards its real cause, Capital" (2009, p. 80). Anticapitalist rhetoric of this kind certainly has emotional pull, but perhaps offers little if any practical way forward to those suffering most. The gaps between intellectualization, politico-emotional rhetoric, and practical solutions remain intact, and problematic.

WIDER APPLICATIONS OF COUNSELLING PSYCHOLOGY THEORY, AND CROSSOVERS

As well as individual-level work, psychological therapy is also provided to couples, families, and in groups, and its associated theory and skills have been used in organizational consulting, for example, by London's Tavistock Institute; and systemic and social constructionist therapies (e.g., McNamee & Gergen, 1992) have attempted to widen the parameters of theory and practice. So what are the politically relevant theoretical and practical applications of psychologists' and therapists' work in wider society? Freud, however apolitical, famously viewed modern civilization as repressive (Freud, 1930 [2002]). Alfred Adler was always concerned with "social interest and community feeling" (Adler & Brett, 2009).

Reich pioneered bringing psychotherapy and politics together. B. F. Skinner (1948) wrote a utopian novel based on behavioural principles. Abraham Maslow promoted a vision of a future "eupsychia," where self-actualizing individuals come together synergistically. As Milton (2002) pointed out, however, Esalen in California was a mixed testimony to Maslovian aspirations. Carl Rogers ran encounter groups around the world, including Northern Ireland, attempting to increase understanding and promote peace (Rogers & Russell, 2002). Erich Fromm campaigned tirelessly for the importance of psychological insights towards a more humane society (Ortmeyer, 1998). Hans Eysenck, typically remembered negatively, contributed significant views on personality and choice of political affiliation (Eysenck, 1998). Aaron Beck (1999) wrote about social hate and violence from a cognitive-behavioural perspective. Mark Bracher (2009), among many, applies psychoanalytic concepts to sociopolitical problems. In 2001 Andrew Samuels, Susie Orbach, and others launched Antidote, a campaign to promote emotional literacy (Orbach, 2003). Digby Tantam (2014) writes engagingly about the politics of well-being. Sally Weintrobe (2013) has brought psychoanalytic theory into interdisciplinary dialogue on the problems of climate change. Nick Totton founded the journal *Psychotherapy and Politics International*, now edited by Keith Tudor and in its 13th volume, showcasing incisive writing at the politics/therapy interface. And the journal *Self and Society: International Journal for Humanistic Psychology* has similarly published articles at the self/society interface since 1973. This is merely a suggestive selection of relevant contributions.

Politicians are very occasionally informed by psychoanalytic theory. For example, Leo Abse (2003) and David Owen (2007) offer informed analyses of the psychopathology of political leadership styles; and see also the study of how political affiliations are formed developmentally or transmitted within families (Sears & Brown, 2013). Lord John Alderdice, a Northern Ireland politician with a parallel profession as psychiatric consultant in psychotherapy, brought an (ultimately unsuccessful) psychotherapy bill to the House of Lords in 2000. Nessa Childers, an Irish Member of the European Parliament, was a psychoanalyst before entering politics. Brad Blanton, an American Gestalt therapist, was a candidate for the US House of Representatives, attempting—unsuccessfully—to bring "radical honesty" into mainstream politics. Influential therapists like Andrew Samuels also discreetly consult with prominent political leaders (Samuels, 2004).

There are also some important negative dimensions. Psychiatry and psychology were severely abused in the USSR in the mid-20th century, with political dissidents hospitalized on false grounds (van Voren, 2010). In the USA, "Big Pharma" and the *Diagnostic and Statistical Manual of Mental Disorders* (DSM) have profited enormously from false medicalization (Frances, 2014). Infamously, Edward Bernays, Freud's nephew, used psychoanalytic knowledge to glamorize cigarette smoking among women in the 1920s. Regarded as a hero of American capitalism, today we would likely condemn his cynical and deadly exploits. Troubling in a different way is Carl Rogers' arguably naive 1950s acceptance of Central Intelligence Agency (CIA) research funds under cover of the Society for

THE POLITICS OF COUNSELLING PSYCHOLOGY

the Investigation of Human Ecology (Demanchick & Kirschenbaum, 2008). No dishonesty has been proven, but suspicions of disingenuousness and opportunism remain. Such cases add to doubts about whether counselling psychology and related "psy" practices can ever claim to be apolitical.

In spite of IAPT's rise in Britain, HCPC advances in overseeing the psychological therapies, greater recent public acceptance of counselling, and positive psychology's prominence in social policy initiatives, counselling psychology is surely little more than a minority priority compared with more traditional political concerns. A leading critical clinical psychologist, David Smail (2011), pointed out that in Marxist historian Eric Hobsbawm's commentary on 20th-century history, no mention whatsoever was made of Freud or the psychological therapies. The relative insignificance of any group beyond its own parochial concerns can be sobering. Counselling is an experience-near or proximal concern, and politics often appears distal. An ironic Foucauldian counterpoint is provided by Madsen (2014), Rose (1999), and others, for whom psychology generally has served neoliberal politics as "governance from a distance"—with citizens "persuaded" to take on a primarily psychological identity, to look inwards rather than to think or act politically.

CONCLUSION

Counselling psychologists commonly come into the profession for the best of motives, oriented to helping others with personal problems, but also need to secure their own livelihood. Counselling psychology represents a combination of perceived altruism and above-average salary. We have not analysed this here, but it is occasionally argued that counselling psychologists *should* be highly remunerated and that their profession is legitimately solely *clinical*, not political. This chapter has foregrounded *some* political issues relating to counselling psychology, hopefully enabling readers to reflect on relevant mainstream, antidiscriminatory and intra-professional politics. Greater attention needs to be paid to whether counselling psychology enriches political awareness more than it compensates for socioeconomic casualties, and to whether therapy empowers more than it undermines (Furedi, 2003).

Politics itself is acknowledged to involve "noble lies" and "dirty hands," yet massively idealized, utopian phantasies are easily projected on to it. Nonetheless, we hope that in the changing political landscape of post class-based politics, counselling psychologists will more explicitly address the relationship between their profession and wider society. We also await an updating of counselling theory—most of it originally rooted in, and culturally relative to, the early and mid-20th century—so it reflects better the cultural and political norms of 2017 and beyond, characterized by fundamentalist free market economics, geopolitical instability, religious conflict, vast wealth inequalities, government austerity policies, new migrational patterns, climate change, and other macro-threats (Walker, 2007).

SUGGESTED FURTHER READING

House, R., & Totton, N. (Eds.) (1997). *Implausible professions: Arguments for pluralism and autonomy in psychotherapy and counselling*. Ross-on-Wye: PCCS Books.

Loewenthal, D. (Ed.) (2015). *Critical psychotherapy, psychoanalysis and counselling*. London: Palgrave Macmillan.

REFERENCES

Abse, L. (2003). *Tony Blair: The man who lost his smile*. London: Robson.

Adler, A., & Brett (2009). *Social interest: Adler's key to the meaning of life*. London: Oneworld Publications.

Anon (2012). UK: BACP warns against gay conversion therapy. *Pink News*, October 2.

Anthony, A. (2014). The British amateur who debunked the mathematics of happiness. *The Observer*, January 19.

BACP (2014). *Psychological therapies and parity of esteem: From commitment to reality*. Lutterworth: British Association for Counselling and Psychotherapy.

BACP (2015). Which party gets your vote? *Therapy Today*, 26(3), 8–9.

Beck, A. T. (1999). *Prisoners of hate: The cognitive basis of anger, hostility, and violence*. New York: Harper Collins.

Berardi, F. (2015). *Heroes: Mass murder and suicide*. London: Verso Books.

Bilton, D. (2012). Setting up an accreditation scheme for voluntary register. *Self and Society*, 39(4), 6–10.

Borch-Jacobsen, M., & Shamdasani, S. (2012). *The Freud files: An inquiry into the history of psychoanalysis*. Cambridge: Cambridge University Press.

Bosteels, B. (2012). *Marx and Freud in Latin America*. London: Verso.

Bracher, M. (2009). *Social symptoms of identity needs*. London: Karnac.

Branden, N. (2001). *The psychology of self-esteem: A revolutionary approach to self-understanding*. New York: Jossey-Bass.

Buchanan, R. D. (2010). *Playing with fire: The controversial career of Hans J. Eysenck*. Oxford: Oxford University Press.

Cohen, C. I., & Timimi, S. (Eds.) (2008). *Liberatory psychiatry: Philosophy, politics and mental health*. Cambridge: Cambridge University Press.

Dalrymple, T. (2003). We need to pull ourselves together. *Daily Telegraph*, November 2.

Demanchick, S. P., & Kirschenbaum, H. (2008). Carl Rogers and the CIA. *Journal of Humanistic Psychology*, 48(1): 631.

Duffell, N. (2014). *Wounded leaders: British elitism and the entitlement illusion—a psychohistory*. Bridport: Lone Arrow Press.

Ellis, A. (2006). *How to stubbornly refuse to make yourself miserable about anything—yes, anything!* New York: Citadel.

Epstein, W. M. (1995). *The illusion of psychotherapy*. New York: Transaction.

Ernst, S., & Goodison, L. (1981). *In our own hands: Book of self-help therapy*. London: The Women's Press.

Eysenck, H. J. (1998). *The psychology of politics*. London: Transaction.

Fanon, F. (2001). *The wretched of the earth*. London: Penguin.

Feltham, C. (2014). If merely more words, what is the point? A critical response. *European Journal of Psychotherapy and Counselling*, 16(4), 376–387.

Fisher, M. (2009). *Capitalist realism: Is there no alternative?* Winchester: Zero Books.

Foster, J. G. (1971). *Enquiry into the practice and effects of scientology.* House of Commons Report 52, December. London: HMSO.

Frances, A. (2014). *Saving normal: An Insider's revolt against out-of-control psychiatric diagnosis.* . . . New York: Harper Collins.

Free Psychotherapy Network (n.d.) The free psychotherapy network. Retrieved from http://freepsychotherapynetwork.com (accessed April 22, 2015).

Freud, S. (1930 [2002]). *Civilization and its discontents.* London: Penguin.

Fromm, E. (2013). *To have or to be.* London: Bloomsbury.

Furedi, F. (2003). *Therapy culture: Cultivating vulnerability in an uncertain age.* London: Routledge.

Gerhardt, S. (2010). *The selfish society: How we all forgot to love one another and made money instead.* London: Simon & Schuster.

Guilfoyle, M. (2008). CBT's integration into social networks of power. In R. House, & D. Loewenthal (Eds.), *Against and for CBT: Towards a constructive dialogue?* Ross-on-Wye: PCCS.

Halmos, P. (1966). *The faith of the counsellors.* New York: Schocken.

Heinze, A. R. (2004). *Jews and the American soul: Human nature in the 20th century.* Princeton, NJ: Princeton University Press.

Henriques, J., Hollway, W., Urwin, C., Venn, C., & Walkerdine, V. (1998). *Changing the Subject: Psychology, social regulation and subjectivity* (2nd ed.). London: Routledge.

House, R. (1996). The professionalization of counselling: a coherent "case against"? *Counselling Psychology Quarterly, 9*(4), 343–358.

House, R. (2004). An unqualified good: The IPN as a path through and beyond professionalisation. *Self and Society, 32*(4), 14–22.

House, R., & Totton, N. (Eds.) (1997). *Implausible professions: Arguments for pluralism and autonomy in psychotherapy and counselling.* Ross-on-Wye: PCCS Books.

Itten, T., & Roberts, R. (2006). Laing and Szasz: Anti-psychiatry, capitalism, and therapy. *Psychoanalytic Review, 93*(5), 781–799.

Itten, T., & Roberts, R. (2014). *The new politics of experience and the bitter herbs.* Ross-on-Wye: PCCS Books.

James, O. (2008). *The selfish capitalist: Origins of affluenza.* London: Vermilion.

Janov, A. (1973). *The primal revolution.* New York: Simon & Schuster.

Jensen, D., & Keith, L. (2012). *The Derrick Jensen reader.* New York: Seven Stories Press.

Kearney, A. (1996). *Counselling, class and politics: Undeclared influences in therapy.* Ross-on-Wye: PCCS.

Knox, R., & Cooper, M. (2015). *The therapeutic relationship in counselling and psychotherapy.* London: Sage.

Kovel, J. (1988). *The radical spirit: Essays on psychoanalysis and society.* London: Free Association Books.

Lago, C., & Smith, B. (2010). *Antidiscriminatory practice in counselling and psychotherapy.* London: Sage.

Layard, R., & Clark, D. M. (2014). *Thrive: The power of evidence-based psychological therapies.* London: Allen Lane.

Loewenthal, D. (Ed.) (2015). *Critical psychotherapy, psychoanalysis and counselling.* London: Palgrave Macmillan.

Madsen, O. J. (2014). *The therapeutic turn: How psychology altered western culture.* Hove: Routledge.

Masson, J. M. (1992). *The assault on truth: Freud and child sexual abuse.* London: Flamingo.

McNamee, S., & Gergen, K. J. (Eds.) (1992). *Therapy as social construction.* London: Sage.

Milton, J. (2002). *The road to Malpsychia: Humanistic psychology and our discontents.* San Francisco, CA: Encounter Books.

Moloney, P. (2013). *The therapy industry: The irresistible rise of the talking cure, and why it doesn't work.* London: Pluto.

Moncrieff, J. (2013). *The bitterest pills: The troubling story of anti-psychotic drugs.* Houndmills: Palgrave.

Moncrieff, J., Rapley, M., & Speed, E. (Eds.) (2014). *Demedicalising misery II: Society, politics and the mental health industry.* London: Palgrave.

Mowbray, R. (1995). *The case against psychotherapy registration.* London: Trans Marginal Press.

Murdin, L. (2012). *How money talks.* London: Karnac.

Orbach, S. (2003). Therapy from the left: Interview with Susie Orbach. *European Journal of Psychotherapy and Counselling, 6,* 75–85.

Ortmeyer, D. H. (1998). Revisiting Erich Fromm. *International Forum of Psychoanalysis, 7,* 25–33.

Owen, D. (2007). *The Hubris syndrome: Bush, Blair and the intoxication of power.* London: Politico's.

Parker, I. (2007). *Revolution in psychology: Alienation to emancipation.* London: Pluto.

Pilgrim, D. (2012). Social class. In C. Feltham, & I. Horton (Eds.), *The Sage handbook of counselling and psychotherapy* (3rd ed.). London: Sage.

Poole, G. (2014). Eight reasons British woman are more left wing. *Inside Man,* October 17.

Porter, J. (2010). Working in private practice. In R. Woolfe, S. Strawbridge, B. Douglas, & W. Dryden (Eds). *Handbook of counselling psychology* (3rd ed.). London: Sage.

Postle, D., & House, R. (Eds.) (2009). *Compliance? Ambivalence? Rejection?—Nine papers challenging HPC regulation.* London: Wentworth Learning Resources.

Proctor, G., Cooper, M., Sanders, P., & Malcolm, B. (Eds.) (2006). *Politicising the person-centred approach: An agenda for social change.* Ross-on-Wye: PCCS.

Reich, W. (1997). *The mass psychology of fascism.* New York: Souvenir.

Robb, C. (2007). *This changes everything: The relational revolution in psychology.* New York: Picador.

Rogers, C. (1978). *On personal power: Inner strength and its revolutionary impact.* London: Constable.

Rogers, R., & Russell, D. E. (2002). *The quiet revolutionary: An oral history.* Roseville, CA: Penmarin Books.

Rose, N. (1999). *Governing the soul: Shaping of the self.* London: Free Association Books.

Samuels, A. (1993). *The political psyche.* London: Routledge.

Samuels, A. (2004). Politics and/of/in/for psychoanalysis. *Psychoanalytic Perspectives, 2,* 39–47.

Santiago, C. D., Kaltman, S., & Miranda, J. (2013). Poverty and mental health: How do low-income adults and children fare in psychotherapy? *Journal of Clinical Psychology, 69*(2), 115–126.

Sears, D. O., & Brown, C. (2013). Childhood and adult political development. In L. Huddy, D. O. Sears, & J. S. Levy (Eds.), *The Oxford handbook of political psychology.* Oxford: Oxford University Press.

Sieghart, P. (1978). *Statutory registration of psychotherapists: The report of a profession's joint working party.* London: Tavistock.

Skinner, B. F. (1948). *Walden two.* New York: Hackett.

Smail, D. (2005). *Power, interest and psychology: Elements of a social materialist understanding of distress.* Ross-on-Wye: PCCS.

Smail, D. (2011). Psychotherapy: Illusion with no future? In M. Rapley, J. Moncrieff, & J. Dillon (Eds.), *De-medicalizing misery I: Psychiatry, psychology and the human condition.* Houndmills: Palgrave.

Snowdon, C. (2010). *The spirit level delusion: Fact-checking the left's new theory of everything.* Ripon: Little Dice.

Stavrakakis, Y. (2007). *The Lacanian left: Psychoanalysis, theory, politics.* Albany, NY: State University of New York Press.

Tantam, D. (2014). *Emotional well-being and mental health: A guide for counsellors and psychotherapists.* London: Sage.

The Invisible Committee (2009). *The coming insurrection.* Los Angeles, CA: Semiotext(e).

Totton, N. (2000). *Psychotherapy and politics.* London: Sage.

Totton, N. (Ed.) (2006). *The politics of psychotherapy: New perspectives.* Maidenhead: Open University Press.

Tudor, K. (1998). Value for money?: Issues of fees in counselling and psychotherapy. *British Journal of Guidance and Counselling, 26*(4), 477–493.

UKCP (2013). Gay conversion or "reparative" therapy. Retrieved fromhttp://www.psychotherapy.org.uk/about-us/public-policy/gay-conversion-or-reparative-therapy (accessed April 22, 2015).

van Voren, R. (2010). Political abuse of psychiatry: An historical overview. *Schizophrenia Bulletin, 36*, 33–35.

Verhaeghe, P. (2014). *What about Me? The struggle for identity in a market-based society.* London: Scribe.

Walker, C. (2007). *Depression and globalization: The politics of mental health in the 21st century.* New York: Springer.

Watters, E. (2011). *Crazy like us: The globalization of the western mind.* New York: Robinson.

Weintrobe, S. (Ed.) (2013). *Engaging with climate change: Psychoanalytic and interdisciplinary perspectives.* Hove: Routledge.

West, E. (2015). *The diversity illusion: What we got wrong about immigration.* London: Gibson Square Books.

Wilkinson, R., & Pickett, K. (2010). *The spirit level: Why equality is better for everyone* (revised ed.). London: Penguin.

Williams, J. (2014). Teaching students not to think. *Spiked*, January 6.

Zerzan, J. (2002). *Running on emptiness: The pathology of civilization.* Los Angeles, CA: Feral House.

Counselling Psychology

MARY CREANER AND LADISLAV TIMULAK

CHAPTER OUTLINE

INTRODUCTION 347

DEFINING SUPERVISION IN COUNSELLING PSYCHOLOGY 347

THE RELATIONSHIP IN COUNSELLING PSYCHOLOGY SUPERVISION 349

MODELS OF SUPERVISION IN COUNSELLING PSYCHOLOGY 351

SUPERVISION COMPETENCIES 352

SUPERVISION TRAINING FOR COUNSELLING PSYCHOLOGISTS 353

MULTICULTURAL AND DIVERSITY ISSUES IN SUPERVISION 354

POSTTRAINING SUPERVISION IN COUNSELLING PSYCHOLOGY 354

FUTURE DIRECTIONS FOR SUPERVISION IN COUNSELLING PSYCHOLOGY 355

LEARNING OUTCOMES

BY THE END OF THIS CHAPTER YOU SHOULD BE ABLE TO ANSWER THE FOLLOWING KEY QUESTIONS:

1. What are the key elements of good supervision in counselling psychology?

2. How does the supervision relationship differ from a therapy relationship?

3. What are the key considerations for the future development of supervision in counselling psychology?

Counselling Psychology: A Textbook for Study and Practice, First Edition. Edited by David Murphy.
© 2017 John Wiley & Sons Ltd. Published 2017 by John Wiley & Sons Ltd.

INTRODUCTION

Supervision forms a significant part of the training of counselling psychologists (Bernard & Goodyear, 2014). It is well acknowledged that trainees frequently ascribe much of their professional development to clinical supervision (along with skills training, personal therapy, etc.) (e.g., Hill & Knox, 2013) and hence, supervisees invest considerable resources in their professional development through supervision. Career-long participation in supervision is also a professional requirement for counselling psychologists in the UK (BPS, 2007). Furthermore, providing supervision has been recognized as a core competency in professional psychology (Falender et al., 2004) and an anticipated professional activity for counselling psychologists throughout their career.

Any consideration of supervision needs to accommodate the complex system in which it occurs with reference to the supervisor–supervisee system, the supervisee–client system, and the broader context of the work (Hawkins & Shohet, 2012). By the same token, the values inherent in counselling psychology practice also need to inform supervision across the scope of that practice. Inherent in these principles are the values of relationship, equality, awareness, and respect for different worldviews and perceptions of reality, empowerment, inclusivity, and autonomy (BPS, 2005). Along with awareness of the contexts in which practice occurs, both in supervision and in therapy, supervisors also need to be cognizant of the art and science required for that practice. Supervision provides a formal setting in which the supervisor ideally creates a collaborative and strengths-based learning environment defined by these principles and values in the provision of supervision and also in the promotion and overseeing of this philosophical stance in the supervisee's professional practice.

DEFINING SUPERVISION IN COUNSELLING PSYCHOLOGY

Within the range of definitions available, there is general agreement that supervision is a professional activity in which the supervisor and supervisee actively engage in the supervision process for the professional development and well-being of the supervisee and ultimately for the benefit of the supervisee's clients (Bernard & Goodyear, 2014). Proctor (1987) has articulated the functions of supervision as normative (e.g., facilitating and monitoring best professional ethical practice and standards), formative (e.g., facilitating supervisee learning and competency development), and restorative (e.g., promoting supervisee well-being). Building on both of these definitions, Milne (2007) also stresses that supervision is relationship-based learning. The emphasis on the relational aspect of supervision points to the fact that supervision occurs in a relationship and this emphasis is most congruent with the relational approach of counselling psychology in all its areas of involvement. These definitions and descriptions provide an accessible framework that may be easily adapted for conceptualizing supervision throughout the career life span in counselling psychology.

As an educative endeavour, the "formative" dimension of clinical supervision draws on learning theory with a view to facilitating supervisee learning in a variety of counselling psychology learning domains (e.g., therapeutic skills, case conceptualization, case management, assessment, etc.) and with the goal of enhancing the artful application of science to ethical and best practice (Creaner, 2014). Supervision may be considered as the "crucible" in which the requisite forms of propositional, professional, and personal knowledge (Eraut, 1994) may be coherently brought together to further professional development (Bernard & Goodyear, 2014, p. 4) and critical reflection in that regard (Schön, 1983). Drawing on supervision praxis, this integrative learning may be facilitated through a variety of methods and interventions (e.g., experiential learning, teaching, providing feedback, reviewing audio recordings of sessions, goal-setting, role-play, discussion, and so forth; see Milne, Aylott, Fitzpatrick, & Ellis, 2008). Optimally, the choice of method will be decided in consultation with the supervisee with respect to their learning needs, though not at the cost of avoiding interventions that have been demonstrated to facilitate learning (i.e., reviewing recorded client sessions) (Creaner & Timulak, 2016).

The "normative" function of supervision speaks to ethical practice, quality control, accountability, professionalism, gatekeeping, and the monitoring of standards of the counselling psychology profession and best practice principles in the supervisee's work. In the training context, and referred to as the "defining aspect of supervision," evaluation is an integral part of the gatekeeping role (Bernard & Goodyear, 2014, p. 204). Such monitoring and evaluation can be challenging for trainees in particular. Concerns about evaluation and the power differential that can become even more explicit in this circumstance, may have a negative impact on trainee engagement (e.g., supervisee nondisclosure of pertinent information) in the supervision process, particularly if a poor supervisory relationship is concurrently experienced (Sweeney & Creaner, 2014).

Moreover, much variation appears to exist in how evaluation is conducted in training supervision, and the challenges of evaluation may be further compounded by the lack of training in this task, inconsistency in assessment, gender and rating biases, and the lack of psychometrically robust measures (Bernard & Goodyear, 2014; Gonsalvez & Crowe, 2014). Although trainees acknowledge the importance and necessity of training programmes implementing gatekeeping procedures, it is also essential for these procedures to be explicit from the outset and implemented with regard to due process (Foster, Leppma, & Hutchinson, 2014). In their recent edition of the *Fundamentals of Clinical Supervision*, Bernard and Goodyear (2014), highlight that gatekeeping is an ongoing consideration in supervision, not only at the entry level. Hence, the gatekeeping role and the monitoring task (Holloway, 1995) with reference to fitness to practise considerations are integral to supervision and no matter what the developmental stage of the supervisee across the career lifespan, there is always an evaluative element present in supervision (Creaner, 2014).

As the remit of supervision in counselling psychology relates to all aspects of the psychologist's role including the evaluation of supervisee ongoing professional development, as mentioned, outcomes in psychological therapy and assessment as well as outcomes in supervision also need to be monitored and evaluated. Of course, we also need to establish a firm research base in all of these areas. In a systematic review of the impact of supervision on supervisees and their clients, Wheeler and Richards (2007) concluded that supervision had a constructive impact on supervisee self-awareness, skills development, self-efficacy beliefs, and theoretical orientation and on feeling supported. In terms of the impact of supervision on client outcomes, few conclusions could be drawn from the studies reviewed. In a more recent review, Watkins (2011) also concluded that while there are provisional findings in this regard (see Bambling, King, Raue, Schweitzer, & Lambert, 2006), further research is clearly indicated.

It is well documented that training in counselling psychology can be very challenging and stressful, particularly for beginning trainees (e.g., Folkes-Skinner, Elliott, & Wheeler, 2010; Kumary & Baker, 2008; Orlinsky & Rønnestad, 2005) and, consequently, the restorative or supportive function of supervision can help ameliorate these stresses and normalize supervisee experiences (Worthen & McNeill, 1996). While individual differences are of note, beginning supervisees appear to value "supervisor care and concern" together with supervisor experience and expertise, both as a supervisor and as a practitioner (Jordan, 2007, p. 43); experience reduced anxiety with role induction to supervision (Ellis, Hutman, & Chapin, 2015); and appreciate clarity regarding therapy theory and application of theory to their practice (Haugaard Jacobsen, & Tanggaard, 2009). Within and posttraining, clinical supervision has also been reported to mitigate potential burnout and vicarious trauma among practitioners (Vec, Vec, & Zorga, 2014). Whether in training or at qualified status, the "ethical imperative" of self-care is ever-present (Norcross & Guy, 2007, p. 5), and good supervision can help support supervisee well-being, resourcefulness, and resilience in the work (Hawkins & Shohet, 2012).

THE RELATIONSHIP IN COUNSELLING PSYCHOLOGY SUPERVISION

The concept of the working alliance (Bordin, 1979) has a strong tradition in therapy and has been demonstrated to be a good predictor of outcomes in this context (Norcross & Wampold, 2011). In relation to supervision, the working alliance is characterized by an emotional bond, and involves the agreement of goals and tasks between the supervisor and supervisee. According to Bordin (1983, pp. 37–38), the goals of supervision provide a clear supervision agenda. In summary, these goals refer to facilitating the supervisee's self, other and process awareness, knowledge and skills development, and the ability to apply their competency in the best service of the client.

The tasks of supervision in this context refer to how these specific goals may be achieved (i.e., though direct observation of or listening to a session with a client; supervisee selection of issues to bring to supervision, etc.). The emphasis on mutual agreement (across goals and tasks) is an opportunity to personalize the supervisory experience (Wallace & Cooper, 2015), which requires a clear contract between the supervisor and supervisee, irrespective of the supervision format (e.g., individual or group). The main functions of a contract or supervision learning agreement is, then, to explicate the expectations, practicalities, learning needs, evaluation criteria, and so forth (Creaner, 2014). The supervisory agreement also helps to establish the professional boundaries of this professional activity (BPS, 2007). Within this framework, there is also a focus on supervision as a stimulus for research or practice informed by research. Indeed, supervision provides rich opportunities wherein a research attitude can be fostered and reinforced with supervisees (Creaner & Timulak, 2016), and an orientation to evidence-based and research-informed counselling psychology practice can be facilitated. Watkins (2014) suggests the concept of the working alliance, while the form and structure may vary across theoretical approaches, is widely accepted to form the basis for good supervision. Ironically, or perhaps equally, the alliance may be the ground on which supervision can perish, and poor supervisory relationships and alliances have been implicated in poor outcomes (Ladany, 2014). For instance, in their qualitative meta-synthesis of trainees' experiences of supervision, Wilson, Davies, and Weatherhead (2015) found that supervision may potentially be experienced as stressful and undermining of self-efficacy. To that end, and in acknowledgement of the intrinsic power imbalance, the authors recommend that evaluation of supervisors and the supervision experience should be a feature of good supervision.

Furthermore, a number of supervision studies have elucidated the negative and potentially harmful experiences in supervision (e.g., Ellis et al., 2014). For instance, a recent comparative study (Ellis, Creaner, Hutman, & Timulak, 2015) of supervisees in the US and the Republic of Ireland found that experiences of inadequate and harmful supervision were not uncommon in either country. Considering that harmful supervision may have impacts on supervisees comparable to harmful therapy effects on clients, there is a need to educate and empower supervisees, particularly trainees, to voice these issues (Ellis et al., 2014). Similarly, in noting the prevalence of inadequate and harmful supervision, there is also a need for training courses to routinely monitor the quality of supervision provided to trainees (Ellis, Creaner, Hutman & Timulak, 2015; Wilson et al., 2015; see Bernard & Goodyear, 2014; Wheeler, Aveline, & Barkham, 2011, for recommended supervision measures).

Finally, while we wanted to stress the importance of Bordin's (1983) concept of the alliance in supervision, it is also important to mention the distinction pertaining to the alliance in the context of supervision in comparison to therapy. Although Bordin refers to the differential in status between the supervisor and supervisee and the challenges that reality may present, one criticism of this model is that it does not adequately address such issues in relation to the roles of gatekeeper and evaluator held by supervisors, which clearly impact the goals and tasks of supervision as well as the bond between the supervisee and the supervisor (Falender, Ellis, & Burnes, 2012).

MODELS OF SUPERVISION IN COUNSELLING PSYCHOLOGY

In the therapy context, supervision has existed since the beginning of therapy training and owes much of its subsequent development, in particular, to counselling psychology (Carroll, 2007; Ladany & Inman, 2012). Originally, the approach to supervision was positioned firmly within the therapeutic model being taught, with the principles being applied to therapy being transferred to the supervisory process (Carroll, 2007; Holloway, 2014). Nonetheless, as well articulated by Ladany (2014), it is something of an assumption that therapy models can be easily translated to the supervisory context wherein the supervisory endeavour, in contrast to therapy, is frequently "involuntary, didactic in purpose, and evaluative" (p. 1099).

As supervision conceptualization began to move away from counselling-bound models and was distinguished as a "distinct professional activity" and an educational endeavour (Falender & Shafranske, 2004, p. 3) several supervision-specific models have emerged. These range from conceptual and experiential frameworks to research- and theory-informed models (e.g., the Process Model, Hawkins & Shohet, 2012; System Approach to Supervision (SAS) model, Holloway, 1995; Generic Integrative Model, Carroll, 1996; Integrated Developmental Model (IDM), Stoltenberg, McNeill, & Delworth, 1998; Best Evidence Synthesis (BES) model, Milne et al., 2008). A number of these models are rather generic and pan-theoretical frameworks focusing on the roles of the supervisor; for example, teacher, consultant, mentor, and so forth (Bernard & Goodyear, 2014) and supervision tasks (e.g., creating a learning environment, teaching, monitoring ethical practice, evaluation of outcomes, promoting emotional awareness). Whilst many of these conceptual supervision frameworks can be useful to guide supervision experientially, they are on tenuous ground in terms of an evidence base or their predictive power. Problems abound with reference to supervision models in that few have been established from empirical supervision literature, few have been empirically tested (Milne et al., 2008), and few capture the intricacies of the supervision process (Ellis, 2010). Additionally, few provide methodologies for the implementation of supervision (Bernard, 2014) or sufficiently take into account the "complex social networks" in which supervision occurs (Falender et al., 2004, p. 779). Clearly, much work remains in this area to establish empirically robust supervision models.

REFLECTIVE QUESTIONS

For supervisees: As you reflect on your current experience of supervision, consider the following reflective questions:

1. What do you identify as the key components of a good supervision relationship?

2. How would you describe your working alliance (i.e., goals, tasks, bond) with your supervisor?

3. What factors have contributed to how this supervision relationship has developed?

4. How do you articulate your formative, normative, and restorative needs in supervision?

5. How do you evaluate your supervision experience with your supervisor?
6. How does supervision contribute to your professional development and outcomes for your clients?

For supervisors: As you reflect on your current provision of supervision, consider the following reflective questions:

1. What do you identify as the key components of a good supervision relationship?
2. How would you describe your working alliance (i.e., goals, tasks, bond) with your supervisee?

3. How do you facilitate your supervisee's formative, normative, and restorative needs in supervision?
4. How does your supervisee's developmental level influence how you work?
5. Which models or frameworks of supervision are congruent for you and how do they guide your work?
6. How do you monitor and evaluate supervision outcomes for your supervisee? For their clients?

SUPERVISION COMPETENCIES

The move away from counselling bound models of supervision also signalled a paradigm shift in understanding supervision as requiring distinct professional competencies (Falender & Shafranske, 2004). One of the seminal events in this regard was the conference "Competencies 2002: Future Directions in Education and Credentialing in Professional Psychology" convened in Arizona, USA, which included a working group on supervision (Falender et al., 2004). What resulted from this working group was a consensus regarding a Supervision Competencies Framework, which delineated the requisite knowledge, skills, and values in supervision along with acknowledgement of the social context of supervision and with recommendations for supervision training and assessment. Subsequently, a new wave of competency-based supervision models and frameworks emerged (e.g., Falender & Shafranske, 2004) and have been adopted and implemented by some professional organizations (see for example, the *Guidelines for Clinical Supervision in Health Service Psychology*; American Psychological Association, 2014).

Within the NHS in the UK, the Improving Access to Psychological Therapies (IAPT) (Department of Health, 2007) initiative also consolidated competency-based supervision to support the implementation of the National Institute for Health and Care Excellence (NICE) guidelines for anxiety and depression. IAPT assigns much responsibility to supervision when they state that "supervision is a key activity which will determine the success of the IAPT programme" (IAPT, 2011a, p. 2). To support this endeavour and standardize supervision provision, IAPT provides a supervision competency framework denoting general, specialist, and metacompetencies for supervisors across therapy modalities (see Roth & Pilling, 2009); a *Supervision Guidance* document indicating the forms, purpose, and requirements of supervision for qualified staff and trainees working at different levels within IAPT (see IAPT, 2011a), and *Guidance for Commissioning IAPT Supervisor Training* (see IAPT, 2011b). More generally, the Health and Care Professions Council (HCPC, 2015) *Standards of Proficiency for Practitioner Psychologists* broadly refer to supervision competency in requiring that psychologists:

1.6   Understand the importance of participation in training, supervision and mentoring.

11.4   Understand models of supervision and their contribution to practice.

SUPERVISION TRAINING FOR COUNSELLING PSYCHOLOGISTS

In terms of the provision of supervision to trainees, the BPS (2015) accreditation criteria for counselling psychology programmes specify that "All supervisors are expected to have completed training in supervision as recognised by the Society or provided by the education provider" (p. 27). The BPS (2011) maintains a *Register of Applied Psychology Practice Supervisors* (RAPPS) to recognize expertise in supervision practice, and offers a series of supervision skills workshops to facilitate supervisor competency development. Organized by the BPS Professional Development Centre, these workshops comprise 4 days of sequenced training covering the theory and practice of supervision. BPS (2014) also provides a register of additional approved supervision training courses. Chartered members, who have undertaken BPS approved supervision training, are eligible to apply and become registered as supervisors.

A relatively recent development in counselling psychology training has been the introduction of supervision training for doctoral trainees, which has now become a requirement in BPS (2015) accreditation criteria, wherein trainees are required to "understand the main principles of and approaches to supervision and have knowledge of how to apply these at an appropriate level within their own sphere of competence" (para. 4.13). Similarly, in the Republic of Ireland, the Psychological Society of Ireland (PSI, 2013) accreditation for counselling psychology states that "in the final year of their training, doctoral level students develop clinical supervision core competencies in dedicated supervision training" (para. 3.2.8). As a relatively new requirement, and as supervision training has not, as yet, been standardized, a curious anomaly may arise wherein a trainee who is undergoing supervision may be supervised by a supervisor who has not had the same level of dedicated supervision training.

Undertaking supervision training on a doctoral counselling psychology course can be challenging for trainees. A study by Gazzola, De Stefano, Thériault, and Audet (2013) qualitatively explored these challenges with 10 counselling psychology first year doctoral students, who, under supervision, provided individual and group supervision to masters level counselling students. The authors identified the key challenges, which related to holding the gatekeeping role, managing multiple processes, and establishing a supervisory stance. Furthermore, developing a supervisor identity at a time when other aspects of a trainee's professional identity are at a formative stage can lead to role confusion and self-doubt. Considering the impact on trainees and the other demands of their training, the question is raised of the optimal time to introduce supervision training and how best to assess this training.

In the absence of an empirical base for the provision of supervision training, it is challenging to assess the quality of such training. As with supervision models, and as mentioned above, the lack of theory-driven models of training is problematic (Barker & Hunsley, 2013) despite the concerted call in the field for supervision training. However, unless training curricula are systematic, defined by clear learning outcomes and assessment procedures, it is unlikely to have a modifying effect on supervisor behaviour. On the positive side, there are a number of resources available for supervisor training (systematic reviews, e.g., Milne, Sheikh, Pattison, Wilkinson, 2011; best practice training principles, e.g., Borders, 2010; models of supervisor development, e.g., Hess, 1986, Watkins, 1993; and training curricula, e.g., Borders et al., 1991), all of which provide a firm foundation on which to build.

MULTICULTURAL AND DIVERSITY ISSUES IN SUPERVISION

Over the past decades, the focus on cultural awareness and multiculturalism in therapy has also become evident in the supervision literature (e.g., Soheilian, Inman, Klinger, Isenberg, & Kulp, 2014). Competence in clinical supervision encompasses the "ability to work with difference" (Roth & Pilling, 2009, p. 11) wherein the supervisor is cognizant of and has developed the ability to discuss and address issues of diversity both in supervision and in their supervisee's provision of therapy. It has been argued that "all supervision is multicultural" (Chopra, 2013, p. 336), hence, every encounter with a supervisee is a unique and multicultural experience. Each supervisor and supervisee brings their demographic position, worldview, and preconceptions to supervision, and each supervisee also brings their clients' diversity to the same frame. Within that frame, the supervisor not only needs to hold a heightened awareness of multicultural issues and issues of diversity, but also to enact that awareness within the supervisory relationship to best provide for supervisee development and client welfare.

POSTTRAINING SUPERVISION IN COUNSELLING PSYCHOLOGY

As posttraining supervision (as distinct from consultation) has not been the norm in the US, from where a good portion of supervision research has emanated (Ellis, Creaner, Hutman, & Timulak, 2015), much of our knowledge of supervision is situated at the trainee developmental level. In addition, whereas most counsellors and therapists have a relatively long tradition of mandated career-long supervision, this requirement has had a comparatively shorter history in professional counselling psychology. Indeed, considering the lack of empirical support for supervision at this developmental level, the question of compulsory supervision posttraining received critical comment in the literature in terms of qualified practitioner autonomy and potential for engendering "the dynamics of the mandatory" in the helping profession (Feltham, 2000, p. 9). Nevertheless, counselling psychologists in the UK are required to engage in supervision across their career lifespan (Orlans & Van Scoyoc, 2009). As stated by the British Psychological Society (2007) Division of Counselling Psychology "supervision is a cornerstone of Counselling Psychology training and practice and a requirement of every practitioner, however senior, throughout their working life" (p. 3). Moreover, experienced supervisees appear to value supervision and report its benefits, as noted below.

For instance, in a recent study conducted in the Irish context, McMahon and Errity (2014) surveyed qualified professional psychologists working in a variety of practice settings (e.g., health service; private practice, etc.) regarding their experiences in supervision. Of the participants surveyed, a large majority reported that they currently participated in either clinical supervision or line management supervision, mostly on a monthly basis, and endorsed supervision as a necessary support for their work. However, there was an expressed need to have supervision prioritized in the workplace, and a need for clinical supervision and line management supervision to be separate professional activities, referring to concerns about psychological safety and power relations with one's manager in the role of supervisor.

From the few studies that exist in the area of posttraining supervision for qualified practitioners and similar to findings in supervision research with trainees, the supervisory alliance is also identified as a key variable in good supervision (McMahon & Errity, 2014) with, for instance, good supervisory alliances facilitating collegiality and egalitarianism (Weaks, 2002). In addition, a number of benefits have been reported across disciplines; for example, in school counselling, decreased isolation, feeling supported (e.g., less stress, burnout) personal and professional development, increased accountability, an opportunity to debrief, and perceived benefits with regard to client outcomes were noted (McMahon & Patton, 2000). In career counselling, support and debriefing were also noted along with receiving feedback and the acquisition of new strategies for the work (McMahon, 2003).

FUTURE DIRECTIONS FOR SUPERVISION IN COUNSELLING PSYCHOLOGY

Although much has been achieved in recognizing supervision as a professional activity that is distinct in its own right (Falender & Shafranske, 2004) much work remains in establishing an evidence base for supervision practice and the training of supervisors. By way of conclusion, we offer the following as potential direction points for the ongoing development of supervision research, practice and training in counselling psychology:

1) The need to identify the key components of effective supervision (Hill & Knox, 2013)

2) The need to routinely monitor supervision outcomes and supervisee outcomes with their clients and establish the impact of supervision on client outcomes (Watkins, 2011; Wheeler & Richards, 2007).

3) The need to examine change processes in supervisee learning and professional development, in training, and posttraining (Folkes-Skinner et al., 2010).

4) The need to establish the variables associated with inadequate and harmful supervision (Ellis, Creaner, Hutman, & Timulak, 2015).

5) The need to establish empirically supported models of supervision training and assessment (Barker & Hunsley, 2013; Ladany, 2014).

6) The need to develop theory-driven supervision research wherein designs are methodologically robust and constructs are clear (Milne et al., 2008).

SUGGESTED FURTHER READING

Bernard, J. M., & Goodyear, R. K. (2014). *Fundamentals of clinical supervision* (5th ed.). Boston, MA: Pearson.

Creaner, M. (2014). *Getting the best out of supervision in counselling and psychotherapy: A guide for the supervisee*. London: Sage.

Watkins, C. E., Jr., & Milne, D. L. (Eds.) (2014). *The Wiley international handbook of clinical supervision*. Chichester: Wiley.

REFERENCES

American Psychological Association (2014). *Guidelines for clinical supervision in health service psychology*. Washington, DC: Author. Retrieved from http://www.apa.org/about/policy/guidelines-supervision.pdf (accessed March 23, 2017).

Bambling, M., King, R., Raue, P., Schweitzer, R., & Lambert, W. (2006). Clinical supervision: Its influence on client-rated working alliance and client symptom reduction in the brief treatment of major depression. *Psychotherapy Research, 16*, 317–331.

Barker, K. K., & Hunsley, J. (2013). The use of theoretical models in psychology supervisor development research from 1994 to 2010: A systematic review. *Canadian Psychology/Psychologie Canadienne, 54*(3), 176–185.

Bernard, J. (2014). The use of supervision notes as a targeted training strategy. *American Journal of Psychotherapy, 68*(2), 195–212.

Bernard, J. M., & Goodyear, R. K. (2014). *Fundamentals of clinical supervision* (5th ed.). Boston, MA: Allyn & Bacon.

Borders, L. D. (2010). Principles of best practice for clinical supervisor training programs. In J. R. Culbreth, & L. L. Brown (Eds.), *State of the art in clinical supervision* (pp. 127–150). London: Routledge.

Borders, L. D., Bernard, J. M., Dye, H. A., Fong, M. L., Henderson, P., & Nance, D. W. (1991). Curriculum guide for training counseling supervisors: Rationale, development, and implementation. *Counselor Education and Supervision, 31*, 58–80. DOI: 10.1002/j.1556-6978.1991.tb00371.x

Bordin, E. S. (1979). The generalizability of the psychoanalytic concept of the working alliance. *Psychotherapy: Theory, Research, and Practice, 16*, 252–260.

Bordin, E. S. (1983). A working alliance model of supervision. *The Counseling Psychologist, 11*(1), 35–42.

BPS (British Psychological Society) (2005). *Division of Counselling Psychology: Professional practice guidelines*. Retrieved from http://www.bps.org.uk/sites/default/files/documents/professional_practice_guidelines_-_division_of_counselling_psychology.pdf (accessed March 23, 2017).

BPS (British Psychological Society) (2007). *Division of Counselling Psychology: Guidelines for supervision*. Retrieved from http://www.bps.org.uk/system/files/images/guidelines_for_supervision.pdf (accessed March 23, 2017).

BPS (British Psychological Society) (2011). *Register of applied psychology practice supervisors (RAPPS)*. Retrieved from http://www.bps.org.uk/what-we-do/developing-profession/register-applied-psychology-practice-supervisors-rapps/register-applied-psychology-practice-supervisors-rapps (accessed March 27, 2017).

BPS (British Psychological Society) (2014). *Register of applied psychology practice supervisors (RAPPS): Society approved training courses*. Retrieved from http://www.bps.org.uk/what-we-do/developing-profession/register-applied-psychology-practice-supervisors-rapps/register-applied-psychology-practice-supervisors-rapps (accessed March 27, 2017).

BPS (British Psychological Society) (2015). *Standards for the accreditation of doctoral programmes in Counselling Psychology*. Retrieved from http://www.bps.org.uk/system/files/Public%20files/PaCT/counselling_accreditation_2015_web.pdf (accessed March 23, 2017).

Carroll, M. (1996). *Counselling supervision: Theory, skills and practice*. London: Cassell.

Carroll, M. (2007). One more time: What is supervision? *Psychotherapy in Australia, 13*(3), 34–40.

Chopra, T. (2013). All supervision is multicultural: A review of literature on the need for multicultural supervision in counseling. *Psychological Study, 58*(3), 335–338. DOI: 10.1007/s12646-013-0206-x

Creaner, M. (2014). *Getting the best out of supervision in counselling and psychotherapy: A guide for the supervisee*. London: Sage.

Creaner, M., & Timulak, L. (2016). Supervision in pluralistic counselling and psychotherapy. In: M. Cooper & W. Dryden (Eds.), *The handbook of pluralistic counselling and psychotherapy* (pp. 314–325). London: Sage.

Department of Health (2007). *Improving access to psychological therapies (IAPT): A practical approach to workforce development*. London: Department of Health.

Ellis, M. V., Berger, L., Hanus, A. E., Ayala, E. E., Swords, B. A., & Siembor, M. (2014). Inadequate and harmful clinical supervision: Testing a revised framework and assessing occurrence. *The Counseling Psychologist, 42*, 434–472. DOI: 10.1177/0011000013508656

Ellis, M. V., Creaner, M., Hutman, H., & Timulak, L. (2015). A comparative study of clinical supervision in the Republic of Ireland and the US. *Journal of Counseling Psychology, 62*(4), 621–631. DOI: 10.1037/cou0000110

Ellis, M. V., Hutman, H., & Chapin, J. (2015). Reducing supervisee anxiety: Effects of a role induction intervention for clinical supervision. *Journal of Counseling Psychology, 62*(4), 608–620. DOI: 10.1037/cou0000099

Eraut, M. (1994). *Developing professional knowledge and competence.* London: Falmer Press.

Falender, C. A., & Shafranske, E. P. (2004). *Clinical supervision: A competency-based approach.* Washington, DC: American Psychological Association.

Falender, C. A., Cornish, J. A. E., Goodyear, R., Hatcher, R., Kaslow, N. J., Leventhal, G . . . Grus, C. (2004). Defining competencies in psychology supervision: A consensus statement. *Journal of Clinical Psychology, 80,* 771–786.

Falender, C. A., Ellis, M. V., & Burnes, T. R. (2013). Response to reactions to major contribution: Multicultural clinical supervision and benchmarks. *The Counseling Psychologist, 41,* 140–151. DOI: 10.1177/0011000012464061

Feltham, C. (2000). Counselling supervision: Baselines, problems and possibilities. In B. Lawton, & C. Feltham (Eds.), *Taking supervision forward* (pp. 5–24). London: Sage.

Folkes-Skinner, J., Elliott, R., & Wheeler, S. (2010). "A baptism of fire": A qualitative investigation of a trainee counsellor's experience at the start of training. *Counselling and Psychotherapy Research, 10*(2), 83–92. DOI: 10.1080/14733141003750509

Foster, J. M., Leppma, M., & Hutchinson, T. S. (2014). Students' perspectives on gatekeeping in counselor education: A case study. *Counselor Education and Supervision, 53*(3), 190–203. DOI: 10.1002/j.1556-6978.2014.00057.x

Gazzola, N., De Stefano, J., Thériault, A., & Audet, C. T. (2013). Learning to be supervisors: A qualitative investigation of difficulties experienced by supervisors-in-training. *The Clinical Supervisor, 32*(1), 15–39. DOI: 0.1080/07325223.2013.778678

Gonsalvez, C. C., & Crowe, T. P. (2014). Evaluation of psychology practitioner competence in clinical supervision. *American Journal of Psychotherapy, 68*(2), 177–193.

Haugaard Jacobsen, C., & Tanggaard, L. (2009). Beginning therapists' experiences of what constitutes good and bad psychotherapy supervision with a special focus on individual differences. *Nordic Psychology, 61*(4), 59–84.

Hawkins, P., & Shohet, R. (2012). *Supervision in the helping professions* (4th ed.). Maidenhead: Open University Press.

Health and Care Professions Council (HCPC) (2015). *Standards of proficiency: Practitioner psychologists.* Retrieved from http://www.hpc-uk.org/assets/documents/10002963sop_practitioner_psychologists.pdf (accessed March 23, 2017).

Hess, A. K. (1986). Growth in supervision: Stages of supervisee and supervisor development. *The Clinical Supervisor, 4*(1–2), 51–67.

Hill, C. E., & Knox, S. (2013). Training and supervision in psychotherapy. In M. J. Lambert (Ed.), *Garfield and Bergin's handbook of psychotherapy and behavior change* (6th ed., pp. 775–812). Hoboken, NJ: Wiley.

Holloway, E. L. (1995). *Clinical supervision: A systems approach.* Thousand Oaks, CA: Sage.

Holloway, E. L. (2014). Supervisory roles within systems of practice. In C. E. Watkins, Jr., & D. L. Milne (Eds.) *The Wiley international handbook of clinical supervision* (pp. 598–621). Chichester: Wiley.

IAPT (2011a). *Supervision guidance.* Retrieved from http://webarchive.nationalarchives.gov.uk/20160302154833/http://www.iapt.nhs.uk/workforce/supervisors/ (accessed March 23, 2017).

IAPT (2011b). *Guidance for commissioning IAPT supervisor training.* Retrieved from http://webarchive.nationalarchives.gov.uk/20160302154833/http://www.iapt.nhs.uk/workforce/supervisors/ (accessed March 23, 2017).

Jordan, K. (2007). Beginning supervisees' identity: The importance of relationship variables and experience versus gender matches in the supervisee/supervisor interplay. *The Clinical Supervisor, 25*(1–2), 43–51. DOI: 10.1300/J001v25n01_04

Kumary, A., & Baker, M. (2008). Stresses reported by UK trainee counselling psychologists. *Counselling Psychology Quarterly, 21*(1), 19–28. DOI: 10.1080/09515070801895626

Ladany, L. (2014). The ingredients of supervisor failure. *Journal of Clinical Psychology: In Session, 70*(11), 1094–1103. DOI: 10.1002/jclp.22130

Ladany, N., & Inman, A. G. (2012). Training and supervision. In E. M. Altmaier, & J. C. Hansen (Eds.), *The Oxford handbook of counseling psychology* (pp. 179–207). New York: Oxford University Press.

McMahon, A., & Errity, D. (2014). From new vistas to life lines: Psychologists' satisfaction with supervision and confidence in supervising. *Clinical Psychology and Psychotherapy, 21*, 264–275. DOI: 10.1002/cpp.1835

McMahon, M. (2003). Supervision and career counsellors: A little explored practice with an uncertain future. *British Journal of Guidance and Counselling, 31*(2), 177–189.

McMahon, M., & Patton, W. (2000). Conversations on clinical supervision: Benefits perceived by school counsellors. *British Journal of Guidance and Counselling, 28*(3), 339–351.

Milne, D. L. (2007). An empirical definition of clinical supervision. *British Journal of Clinical Psychology, 46*, 437–447. DOI: 10.1348/014466507X197415

Milne, D., Aylott, H., Fitzpatrick, H., & Ellis, M. V. (2008). How does clinical supervision work? Using a "best evidence synthesis" approach to construct a basic model of supervision. *The Clinical Supervisor, 27*(2), 170–190. DOI: 10.1080/07325220802487915

Milne, D. L., Sheikh, A. I., Pattison, S., & Wilkinson, A. (2011). Evidence-based training for clinical supervisors: A systematic review of 11 controlled studies. *The Clinical Supervisor, 30*(1), 53–71. DOI: 10.1080/07325223.2011.564955

Norcross, J. C., & Wampold, B. E. (2011). Evidence-based therapy relationships: Research conclusions and clinical practices. *Psychotherapy, 48*(1), 98–102. DOI: 10.1037/a0022161

Norcross, J. C., & Guy, Jr., J. D. (2007). *Leaving it at the office: A guide to psychotherapist self-care.* New York: Guilford Press.

Orlans, V., & Van Scoyoc, S. (2009). *A short introduction to counselling psychology.* London: Sage.

Orlinsky, D. E., & Rønnestad, M. H. (2005). *How psychotherapists develop.* Washington, DC: American Psychological Association.

Proctor, B. (1987) Supervision: A co-operative exercise in accountability. In M. Marken, & M. Payne (Eds.), *Enabling and ensuring: Supervision in practice* (pp. 21–34). Leicester: National Youth Bureau, Council for Education and Training in Youth and Community Work.

Psychological Society of Ireland (PSI) (2013). *Guidelines for the assessment of postgraduate professional programmes in counselling psychology.* Retrieved from http://www.psihq.ie/accreditation (accessed March 23, 2017).

Roth, A. D., & Pilling, S. (2009). *A competence framework for the supervision of psychological therapies.* Retrieved from https://www.ucl.ac.uk/pals/research/cehp/research-groups/core/pdfs/Supervision_of_Psychological_Therapies/background-supervision-competences (accessed March 23, 2017).

Schön, D. (1983). *The reflective practitioner: How professionals think in action.* New York: Basic Books.

Soheilian, S., Inman, A. G., Klinger, R., Isenberg, D., & Kulp, L. (2014). Multicultural supervision: Supervisees' reflections on culturally competent supervision. *Counselling Psychology Quarterly, 27*(4), 379–392. DOI: 10.1080/09515070.2014.961408

Stoltenberg, C. D., McNeill, B. W., & Delworth, U. (1998). *IDM supervision: An integrated developmental model for supervising counselors and therapists*. San Francisco, CA: Jossey-Bass.

Sweeney, J., & Creaner, M. (2014). What's not being said? Recollections of nondisclosure in clinical supervision while in training. *British Journal of Guidance and Counselling, 42*, 211–224. DOI: 10.1080/03069885.2013.872223

Vec, T., Vec, T. R., & Zorga, S. (2014). Understanding how supervision works and what it can achieve. In C. E. Watkins, Jr., & D.L. Milne (Eds.), *The Wiley international handbook of clinical supervision* (pp. 110–127). Chichester: Wiley.

Wallace, K., & Cooper, M. (2015). Development of supervision personalisation forms: A qualitative study of the dimensions along which supervisors' practices vary. *Counselling and Psychotherapy Research, 15*(1), 31–40.

Watkins, C. E., Jr. (1993). Development of the psychotherapy supervisor: Concepts, assumptions, and hypotheses of the supervisor complexity model. *American Journal of Psychotherapy, 47*, 58–74.

Watkins, C. E., Jr. (2011). Does psychotherapy supervision contribute to patient outcomes? Considering thirty years of research. *The Clinical Supervisor, 30*, 235–256. DOI: 10.1080/07325223.2011.619417

Watkins, C. E., Jr. (2014). The supervisory alliance: A half century of theory, practice, and research in critical perspective. *American Journal of Psychotherapy, 68*, 19–55.

Weaks, D, (2002). Unlocking the secrets of "good supervision": A phenomenological exploration of experienced counsellors' perceptions of good supervision. *Counselling and Psychotherapy Research, 2*(1), 33–39. DOI: 10.1080/14733140212331384968

Wheeler, S., Aveline, M., & Barkham, M. (2011). Practice-based supervision research: A network of researchers using a common toolkit. *Counselling and Psychotherapy Research, 11*, 88–96. DOI:10.1080/14733145.2011.562982

Wheeler, S., & Richards, K. (2007). The impact of clinical supervision on counsellors and therapists, their practice and their clients: A systematic review of the literature. *Counselling and Psychotherapy Research, 7*(1), 54–65.

Wilson, H. N., Davies, J. S., & Weatherhead, S. (2015). Trainee therapists' experiences of supervision during training: A meta-synthesis. *Clinical Psychology and Psychotherapy, 23*, 340–351. DOI: 10.1002/cpp.1957

Worthen, V., & McNeill, B. W. (1996). A phenomenological investigation of "good" supervision events. *Journal of Counseling Psychology, 43*(1), 25–34. DOI: 10.1037/0022-0167.43.1.25

Psychology

EWAN GILLON, LADISLAV TIMULAK, AND MARY CREANER

CHAPTER OUTLINE

INTRODUCTION 362

THE STRUCTURE OF COUNSELLING PSYCHOLOGY TRAINING IN THE UK 362

THE ORGANIZATION OF COUNSELLING PSYCHOLOGY TRAINING IN THE UK 364
   The Core Domains of Counselling Psychology Training 364

TRAINING STANDARDS IN COUNSELLING PSYCHOLOGY INTERNATIONALLY 369

DEVELOPING THE TRAINING AGENDA IN THE UK 372

CONCLUSION 373

LEARNING OUTCOMES

BY THE END OF THIS CHAPTER YOU SHOULD BE ABLE TO ANSWER THE FOLLOWING KEY QUESTIONS:

1. What are the main factors underpinning the development of counselling psychology in the UK and internationally?

2. In what ways do counselling psychology training programmes meet professional and regulatory requirements in the UK?

3. What are the key tensions and issues that may impact upon the development of counselling psychology training programmes in the future?

Counselling Psychology: A Textbook for Study and Practice, First Edition. Edited by David Murphy.
© 2017 John Wiley & Sons Ltd. Published 2017 by John Wiley & Sons Ltd.

INTRODUCTION

Counselling psychology is rooted firmly in a humanistic value system emphasizing human potential, experiencing, and the "centrality of relationship and the intersubjective nature of therapeutic processes" (Strawbridge & Woolfe, 2010, p. 10). It is also strongly influenced by the development of Western psychology and the ways in which much psychology research and practice, particularly that manifest within clinical settings, has been aligned with the medical model drawing on the natural science paradigm of research and emphasizing "doing" over "being" in the delivery of psychological interventions. Due to the tensions between these two forces, the practice of counselling psychology holds a variety of philosophical and practical contradictions that can blur, to those both within and without the profession, what it means to be a counselling psychologist and, of course, what kind of training should be involved in becoming one.

Training in counselling psychology involves two separate endeavours. It is both the cultivation or shaping of a *personal* commitment towards humanistic values in action (Cooper, 2009), and the acquisition of the broad range of competencies necessary for the effective delivery of context-relevant psychological interventions within a range of applied settings. In balancing learning in each of these domains, as well as the tensions between them, trainees are required to develop a capacity to work in a way that embraces uncertainty in the context of both personal and professional development. This is not a straightforward process and training in counselling psychology is thus a challenging endeavour in the psychological field.

In this chapter we consider the nature and basis of counselling psychology training. We start by providing a brief summary of the context within which training operates, particularly in terms of the standards set for it by the key stakeholders in the field, reflecting the humanistic value base of the profession as well as the practical skills and knowledge base of the profession. Following this we will consider some of the primary ways these standards are supported and assessed throughout the training process. We will contextualize this by moving towards a wider consideration of training standards in counselling psychology internationally before, finally, considering some contemporary debates and issues regarding the training process in the UK as it stands at present. These will allow us to summarize some of the key training issues we believe to be of importance for the development of the profession going forward.

THE STRUCTURE OF COUNSELLING PSYCHOLOGY TRAINING IN THE UK

Counselling psychology training in the UK is orientated around the standards for the profession as defined by two bodies. The first of these, the Health and Care Professions Council (HCPC) is the statutory regulator for counselling psychology in the UK, with which all qualified counselling psychologists in practice are legally required to be registered. The HCPC requires all education providers who offer an HCPC "approved" training in counselling psychology to ensure graduates meet the standards defined by them as necessary for proficient practice in counselling psychology. These standards are termed "Standards of Proficiency" (SOPS), and are the baselines for professional practice in counselling psychology in the UK. At the time of writing there are 15 broad domains within which standards are identified (see text box).

To be able to practise safely and effectively within their scope of practice; to be able to practise within the legal and ethical boundaries of their profession; to be able to maintain fitness to practise; to be able to practise as an autonomous professional, exercising their own professional judgement; to be aware of the impact of culture, equality, and diversity on practice; to be able to practise in a nondiscriminatory manner; to understand the importance of and be able to maintain confidentiality; to be able to communicate effectively; to be able to work appropriately with others; to be able to maintain records effectively; to be able to reflect on and review practice; to be able to assure the quality of their practice; to understand the key concepts of the knowledge base relevant to their profession; to be able to draw on appropriate knowledge and skills to inform practice; to understand the need to establish and maintain a safe practice environment (HCPC, 2015).

All training programmes are initially visited and then audited on a yearly basis to ensure they meet the "Standards of Education and Training" (SETS) required of an education provider, as well as continuing to deliver effective training with regards to the SOPS.

In addition to the HCPC, the British Psychological Society (BPS) plays a significant role in the UK to ensure the training provided to trainees in counselling psychology is appropriate and relevant to the needs of the discipline as it presently stands. As a professional body, the BPS has no formal role in the regulation (i.e., protecting the public) of counselling psychologists or those in training. However, its expertise and interest in counselling psychology ensure it takes an informed role in promoting good practice and ensuring training programmes maintain a synergy with the requirements of the profession as it evolves. In practice, this process is organized through the formal "accreditation" of programmes that have been deemed to meet the "Accreditation Standards for Doctoral Programmes in Counselling Psychology" (BPS, 2015). These standards, which are not the same as those of the HCPC, offer a nuanced and professionally detailed outline of the knowledge base, skills, and competencies that a trainee must be able to demonstrate upon completion of the programme, as well as promoting best practice in all relevant domains. Thus, they may be seen to add flesh to the bones of the standards (SOPS) identified by the HCPC, which are more general in form and designed as a baseline or threshold level for registration with them. In practice, both organizations work together in partnership to ensure counselling psychology training is of a standard to ensure the public are protected (the role of the HCPC) as well as to promote the highest possible standard for professional practice in the field (the main interest of the BPS).

Although the focus for both organizations is on the "outcomes" of the training process, the BPS takes a significant interest in the *process* of training, with the intention of fostering a supportive professional community through the sharing of best practice. Therefore, it takes a keen interest in ensuring counselling psychology training programmes reflect *both* the humanistic value base of the profession as well as the key competences necessary for effective psychological practice.

THE ORGANIZATION OF COUNSELLING PSYCHOLOGY TRAINING IN THE UK

There are two main training routes in the UK available to those wishing to qualify as a counselling psychologist. The first of these is a formal HCPC "approved" training programme within a university, or affiliated institution. Such programmes are invariably at doctorate level, and lead to the trainee becoming eligible (note: eligibility is not a guarantee of registration) for registration as a counselling psychologist with the HCPC. If the programme is also accredited by the BPS—and at the time of writing all HCPC-approved programmes in the UK also meet this criteria—the trainee will also become eligible to apply for Chartership in Counselling Psychology with the BPS. This is a marker of professional standing and remains attractive to many graduates who value being formally recognized by their professional body.

The second training route is provided by the BPS itself and is formally termed the Qualification in Counselling Psychology. This route offers trainees a flexible pathway towards eligibility for HCPC registration (it is an HCPC "approved" programme) and BPS chartered status. Trainees work independently (no formal training is provided by the BPS) to acquire and demonstrate the necessary competencies via an agreed plan of learning including a Master's level training in a core psychotherapeutic model, in addition to significant additional training and development in a range of areas. Whilst the flexibility of this approach is attractive to those who prefer not to undertake a formal training programme within a university or training setting, it is important to note that trainees who complete the Qualification in Counselling Psychology do not gain a doctorate, as the BPS do not presently have the educational authority to award doctorate degrees, despite the programme being assessed at doctoral level.

The Core Domains of Counselling Psychology Training

In order to meet the standards set out by the HCPC and BPS for the profession, training programmes in counselling psychology orientate around four main domains of activity. These are personal development, psychological theory, psychological research, and clinical skills. Although programmes differ in terms of how these domains are addressed as part of the training process, they are invariably seen as part of an integrated whole. Trainees will normally be expected to be able to draw on their learning in one domain to support their work in the others, and so on.

Personal Development

As may be expected from its underlying humanistic value base, counselling psychology places great emphasis on developing the personal experiencing of the practitioner, which is regarded as a vital element in cultivating a relational focus and intersubjective perspective. On a practical level, an understanding of "self" is seen as an important professional competence, guarding against therapeutic processes being unduly influenced by a practitioner's own unacknowledged needs and wishes, as well as enabling greater empathy with clients seeking help due to their own prior experience in receiving therapeutic support (Lewis, 2008). Counselling psychology programmes in the UK require trainees to undertake a minimum of 40 hr of personal therapy (alongside the programme), and undertake a range of personal development activities in relationship with others to ensure these requirements are addressed.

Although the emphasis on personal development differs significantly to other branches of applied psychology, such as clinical psychology, there are divergences within different training programmes relating to how personal development is embedded in the curriculum in addition to personal therapy, and what requirements are placed upon trainees to engage with those activities that do take place (Moller, Alilovic, & Mundra, 2008). Most programmes offer a "personal development group" within which trainees are able to explore their own reactions and experiences on the course in relation to other trainees, as well as more generally. There is a debate, however, as to the extent to which such groups help or hinder personal development as well as how best to structure them as a formal part of the training process (Galbraith & Hart, 2007).

Psychological Theory

One of the key components of any counselling psychology training is the depth and breadth of psychological theory embedded in the curriculum. Theoretical constructs, their underlying epistemology and ontology, as well as the insights they afford with regards to psychological practice, are seen as crucial components in providing a robust, coherent, and evidence-informed basis for counselling psychology interventions in a range of settings. It's important to appreciate that the theoretical contribution made to the counselling psychology curriculum is not limited to models of *counselling and psychotherapy*, although this is of course a fundamental element, but draws from a wide constituency of *psychological theory* including social and developmental psychology, community psychology, feminist/gender theory, theories of sexuality, neuropsychology and organizational psychology, as well as work in related areas such as medicine, social policy, philosophy, and life/health sciences. Of particular importance (cf. Sugarman, 2010) are theories around life stages, which are often seen as offering an integrating developmental framework for counselling psychology practice. Taken together, the range of theoretical constructs explored as part of the training process provides the trainee with a deep appreciation of counselling psychology interventions, their context, implications, and effects.

Counselling psychology training programmes encourage a highly critical and reflective stance in relation to theory as a result of the emphasis within the profession on social constructionist understandings of knowledge (cf. Burr, 2015), which propose there is no single "truth" or "right way" of conceptualizing any psychological phenomena. This perspective emphasizes a particular *relationship to psychological theory* that rejects a single irrefutable way of understanding and instead encourages a meta-theoretical perspective inviting critique, reflection, and contextual relevance over the deployment of unitary theories of psychological wellness and distress designed to both describe and explain "reality." Such a position may be applied in practice through the pluralistic framework in counselling and psychotherapy articulated by Cooper and McLeod (2011). This resonates with the pluralistic and/or integrative emphasis within counselling psychology, and proposes viewing therapy as a co-created process (i.e., one in which both client and therapist are seen as active agents in determining the form and process of the therapy). Accordingly, practitioners have available to them a range of therapeutic methods and approaches, and make use of these in discussion/negotiation with the client, and in terms of the client's own perceived needs, goals, and aspirations for the therapy.

While a pluralistic stance may link theory to practice in a philosophically congruent way, it presents some significant tensions for the counselling psychology training agenda, within which the mastery of a single therapeutic model for practice is emphasized (albeit within a context providing a working knowledge of one or more additional models). These tensions can invoke a highly unsettling and uncertain training experience, and present significant emotional difficulties for trainees (e.g., Rizq, 2006). However, counselling psychology training programmes are designed to support trainees to manage such tensions in the balancing of perspectives rather than the ultimate resolving of contradictions. Trainees are provided with diverse range of forums within which to undertake learning in this regard, and as such, their relation to psychological theory is encouraged to become both reflective and critical, as well as sufficiently schooled in the technical details necessary for practical application. As the current volume presents in Chapters 5–11 on approaches, pluralism is presented as *one of the many* approaches rather than *the* approach to counselling psychology.

Counselling Psychology Skills in Practice

One of the most important mechanisms for developing insight and understanding of psychological theory in counselling psychology is in the practical domain, within which trainees are expected to work for a significant portion of the training. Developing psychotherapeutic and psychological intervention skills is a core component of counselling psychology training and involves a range of different learning activities, most commonly practice development role plays with other trainees (which often will take place in groups of three, with two participants and one observer rotating), observation through audio and video recordings or *in vivo*, and of course in placement settings where trainees build experience in working with clients presenting with a range of difficulties, and also in organizations offering particular interventions.

Counselling psychology trainees in the UK are required to undertake a minimum 450 hr of clinical placement work with clients over the course of their training programme, and normally gain experience in a number of different settings. The range of contexts within which placements are undertaken enables a broad constituency of different experiences to be completed, although the bulk of UK counselling psychology trainees undertake one or more placements in an adult mental health NHS setting—a reflection of employment opportunities and career aspirations in this domain. There are various other placement settings available, including third sector services, primary care, child and adolescent services, organizational employee assistance programmes, schools and educational counselling services, and the independent sector. Unlike clinical psychology trainees (at the time of writing), counselling psychology trainees do not receive funding from the NHS, and placement opportunities are therefore contextually broader but often unpaid.

Placement learning is supported in a range of ways, most significantly through the practice of clinical supervision whereby trainees review their work with an experienced practitioner (typically, a counselling psychologist) on a regular basis. Supervision groups and a range of other methods may also be employed to ensure good practice is developed, and the trainee is enabled to learn in depth.

Research

Research plays a fundamental part of any counselling psychology training, with the trainee completing a significant empirical research study as a core part of their training. The emphasis on research in the UK has increased over the past decade as counselling psychology training has become benchmarked at doctoral level, which invariably requires the completion of a substantial independent research project that demonstrates both originality and makes a practical contribution to the field (Kaskett, 2012). Although there are differences as to the way the research is embedded in the training process, trainees are required to demonstrate a substantial and critical capability for independent research activity, something that can appear challenging to those drawn to counselling psychology primarily with an interest in clinical practice. It would be wrong, however, to view research and practice as separate domains. Each supports the other, and the precise relationship between them may be seen as a fundamental element of underlying structuring of the counselling psychology training process. Debates around this are often focused on the centrality and applicability of the scientist-practitioner model, which formulates a particular kind of relationship between the research and practice domains.

The scientist-practitioner model originated from the American Psychological Association (APA) Boulder Conference on Graduate Education in Clinical Psychology proceedings in 1949, and advocated training professional psychologists as both scientists and practitioners (Cautin & Baker, 2014). Its key focus is the integration of scientific research and clinical practice in all aspects of the psychologist's role (Nicholson & Madson, 2015), meaning that the values and constructs of "science" become prioritized as the dominant basis of clinical practice, and practitioners are seen as both active *producers* and *users* of psychological research to guide therapeutic activity. As may be expected, such an approach fits well within a psychology profession dedicated to empirical research and the acquisition of robust empirical data, and certainly both clinical and counselling psychology in the UK have orientated their professional identities around the scientist-practitioner construct.

The scientist-practitioner model has been identified as the model to which counselling psychology has predominately subscribed internationally and in the UK (Nicholson & Madson, 2015; Orlans & Van Scoyoc, 2009). With reference to the UK perspective, professional doctoral programmes at least formally aspire to this model, while also stressing that the practitioner should be reflective (see also below; BPS, 2015). Nonetheless, the model has not been without some controversy in terms of its "fit" for counselling psychology training, arising in particular from its emphasis on "scientific" knowledge and the tensions this presents in relation to the prioritizing of human experiencing/subjectivity (Lane & Corrie, 2006; Martin, 2010) within the counselling psychology domain.

Furthermore, there may be a question as to its applicability simply due to the observation that, in practice, most clinicians do not undertake empirical research on an ongoing basis, and therefore should not be considered as active producers of research. A number of alternative models of the relationship between science and practice have subsequently evolved, such as the practitioner-scholar model also known as the Vail model (Bell & Hausman, 2014), which advocates practitioners developing a strong ability to engage in and utilize empirical research, whilst not necessarily producing it. Of course, such a standpoint involves the framing of empirical research as an activity that is necessarily distinct from clinical practice, which has itself been challenged by the move towards "practice-based evidence" and the potential for scientific research to include observational data derived from clinical practice in a "bottom-up" sense.

Systematic case study methodologies, such as those described by McLeod and Elliott (2011) (See Chapters 28 and 29, this volume) are a good example of how practice-based approaches may be utilized by trainees to meet the research requirements of their programme whilst integrating clinical and research domains in a pragmatic way.

In addition to the debates around the scientist-practitioner model and its derivatives, some have argued that a different underpinning model should be utilized as the basis for professional practice in the psychological domain. Bell and Hausman (2014), for example, recommend that professional psychology needs to move beyond models emphasizing science as the basis of professional psychological practice. Woolfe (2012) agrees, proposing that a different conceptualization, namely, the reflective-practitioner model, may be a more relevant formulation, facilitating a bridge across the perceived gap between science and practice positions. The reflective-practitioner model, developed by Schön (1983), asserts that there are several knowledge domains and forms of evidence that may inform practice, in addition to those acquired by research or "scientific" means, and that all of these may be used in a critical, reflective way to ensure clinical practice is both effective and relevant to the context as well as the needs of the client. This approach resonates with some of the social constructionist and pluralistic ideas discussed previously, and may thus be considered a core notion in the counselling psychology training field. However, the profession retains its emphasis on research and the scientist-practitioner approach, and as such trainees must find a way of drawing on both reflective-practitioner and scientist-practitioner models in formulating a professional identity.

TRAINING STANDARDS IN COUNSELLING PSYCHOLOGY INTERNATIONALLY

As may be expected, many of the training standards and issues in the UK training agenda for counselling psychology resonate internationally. Indeed the birth of counselling psychology dates to the 1940s in the USA, where, due to the demand of care for World War II veterans, the US Veterans Administration (VA) expanded its psychological services. Alongside practising clinical psychologists, the VA introduced a new psychological specialty of "counseling psychologist" (Whiteley, 1980; Wrenn, 1966). The VA negotiated with the then existing APA Division 17 (formerly the Division of Personnel and Guidance; and renamed as Counseling Psychology in the 1950s) educational standards for counselling psychologists that closely followed established requirements for clinical psychology (i.e., a doctoral [PhD] level qualification accomplished within 4–6 years of training; 1-year-long full-time internship and a licence exam) (Munley, Duncan, McDonnell, & Sauer, 2004). These standards embraced the scientist-practitioner model, which was further expanded to include the practitioner-scholar model and a professional doctorate route (PsyD level).

The current version of the standards regulates all areas of professional psychology in the US (in particular clinical, counselling, and school psychology [US equivalent of educational psychology]) using the same standards. The standards (the Guidelines and Principles for Accreditation in Professional Psychology; APA, 2006—which are to be replaced by the Standards of Accreditation for Health Service Psychology, APA, 2015) regulate training curricula and clinical practical experience (an equivalent to UK placement experience). In addition, they offer specific regulations for full-time internships provided in an external service or agency independent of the training institution, and for which trainees from various programmes have to compete. The main services that provide internship experiences are psychology services, who in their mission, provide for the training of professional psychologists (the same internship placements host clinical and counselling psychology trainees) and offer their services to the public. Internships offering such services undergo an accreditation process that is not dissimilar from the accreditation process of the university-based training programmes. Finally, of interest is that the APA accreditation guidelines also incorporate regulations for postdoctoral residencies that offer an "avenue of preparation for practice at advanced levels of competency in a substantive traditional or specialty practice area of professional psychology" (APA, 2006, p. 9) and are intended for specialized training of already qualified psychologists, including counselling psychologists.

The APA accredited pre-qualification training programmes and internships aim at achieving learning outcomes that would lead to the development of foundational and functional competencies (that can be further broken up into required knowledge, skills, and desirable attitudes (Fouad et al., 2009; Fouad & Grus, 2014; Fuertes, Spokane, & Holloway, 2013)). The competency benchmark framework (Fouad et al., 2009) recognizes foundational competencies that include professionalism; practice demonstrating reflective practice, self-assessment, and self-care; scientific knowledge and knowledge of research methods; capability of relating meaningfully; awareness, sensitivity, and skills in addressing individual and cultural diversity; ethical and legal awareness and knowledge; and knowledge pertaining to related disciplines. Functional competencies (see Fouad et al., 2009) include a mastery of psychological assessment; mastery of psychological interventions; ability to provide consultations; capability to conduct research; capability to provide supervision; teaching skills; managerial and administrative skills; and, finally, skills required to fulfil advocacy roles expected of psychologists.

While delineation of foundational and functional competencies involves all psychological specialties, Fuertes et al. (2013) looked specifically at those competencies in the context of counselling psychology. They, in particular, highlighted counselling psychology competencies in the provision of counselling and psychological therapies as well as in assessment and case conceptualization. They further stressed the emphasis of counselling psychology on ethical practice fostering diversity and advocacy for vulnerable groups. In line with the developments in the UK, they stress the importance of specific counselling psychology competencies in the provision of supervision and consultancy. In contrast to the tradition in the UK, where it is not a part of the counselling psychology scope of practice, they provide extensive discussion of competencies in career and vocational psychology that is unique to counselling psychology amongst psychology specialties in the US. Currently, there are around 70 doctoral programmes providing training in counselling psychology in the US.

In Canada, similar to the US, the accreditation standards for professional courses in clinical, counselling, and school psychology are shared across the specialties, with the exception of clinical neuropsychology, which has its own specific standards (Canadian Psychological Association, 2011). Counselling psychology programmes have been regulated since 1989 by the same criteria as clinical psychology programmes. Traditionally, the criteria were almost identical to APA standards, and Canadian programmes usually had a dual CPA/APA accreditation (this practice is now being discontinued; cf. Canadian Psychological Association, 2011). There are currently five doctoral counselling psychology programmes in Canada.

Doctoral level standards for counselling psychology training are also present in the Republic of Ireland (with currently one counselling psychology programme running). In comparison to the UK, the standards are very similar, but have some differences; for instance, practical experience across the lifespan is an essential part of placement requirements. Counselling psychology exists as a specialty in other English-speaking countries such as South Africa and Australia. While, a Master's level qualification is a requirement for practising counselling psychology in those countries, doctoral level courses also exist in Australia. Master's level courses are also typical for other countries that recognize the specialty of counselling psychology (see, e.g., Goodyear et al., 2016).

In continental Europe, it is more common to have applied psychology without a formal (legal) differentiation amongst the psychology specialties. If a specialty with a specific regulation exists, then it is typically clinical psychology (cf. Germany). However, there are some exceptions; for instance, Slovakia, has legally regulated specialties, among them counselling psychology. Again, in continental Europe Master's level qualification is a common requirement for practice (Lunt, Job, Lecuyer, Peiro, & Gorbeña, 2009). If specialty training exists, it is often in the form of post-Master's specialty training (often work-based competency development).

The training standards in Europe are particularly relevant as European Union (EU) membership allows practising psychologists to move between countries to engage in the profession. Since psychology is not a profession automatically recognized by the EU, a migrating psychologist has to request recognition of their qualification from the country in which they wish to practice (Directive 2013/55/EU of the European Parliament and of the Council of November 20, 2013 amending Directive 2005/36/EC on the recognition of professional qualifications). The standards existing in that country then serve as a benchmark for the recognition of the qualification. The authority to assess foreign qualification typically rests with the country's variation of the department of health (or a psychologists' regulatory body such as HCPC in the UK). That authority either recognizes the qualification or offers a period of adaptation with prescribed courses/placements that the psychologist has to take to obtain an equivalence status. It is also possible that the authority does not validate the qualification, if the standards from the country where the training initially took place are significantly different. There is also a possibility of offering an aptitude test in instances where the psychology qualification and training of the applicant for recognition of qualification differ from the standards used in the country in which he or she wishes to practice. The European regulations in this area are evolving, with the goal of enabling free movement of professionals (in this case, psychologists) within the EU, while respecting the safety of services offered to public. Of course, since the British decision to leave the EU the picture is increasingly uncertain as to what this means for crossing national borders for the future.

Looking at the differences between the countries, it is important to realise that external factors such as local social, cultural, socioeconomic, and political factors, and so forth, have a direct influence on the scope of practice of counselling psychology and training paths leading to the acquirement of a qualification. It is important to be aware that it is the community of counselling psychologists in a given country and the overall international community of counselling psychologists who are primarily responsible for the development of the field and profession in those respective cultural contexts and jurisdictions. Therefore, it is important that counselling psychologists play an active role and make clear to various stakeholders the assets, resources, and expertise they bring to the society, so the society could avail itself of this expertise to its benefit.

DEVELOPING THE TRAINING AGENDA IN THE UK

Turning once again to the UK, the relationship between counselling psychology and the context within which the profession exists is a key issue for many within the profession. Many of the themes that we have seen impacting on counselling psychology training internationally are pertinent to the development of the training agenda in the UK, and there are some particularly vital issues currently at stake with regard to the training process generally. One of the key issues here is the relationship between the training standards as set for the profession by the BPS and HCPC, and the needs expressed by employers for counselling psychologists to be able to undertake particular activities as part of their employment contract. This is particularly the case in NHS settings, where it is argued that the counselling psychology training agenda needs to better reflect the perceived requirements for applied psychologists (James & Bellamy, 2010), which are often defined around the professional activities and concerns of clinical psychologists. In addition, things have changed in recent years as a broader range of psychological practitioners have become integrated into the NHS setting, primarily to deliver cognitive-behavioural therapy (CBT) at various levels of complexity. The agenda is strongly influenced towards evidence-based therapies, delivered in an instrumental way, and clinical psychology has been forced to emphasize both its depth and breadth to ensure its distinctiveness and maintain its standing. This trend is also reflected internationally in, for example, the establishment of the Academy of Psychological Clinical Science (APCS), a Northern American organization for selected doctoral and internship programmes in clinical psychology. The APCS endorses the clinical scientist model (a more recent articulation of the scientist-practitioner model), which emphasizes training professional psychologists as scientists who produce empirical research and adhere to an evidence base for clinical practice (Fowles, 2015). This Academy has developed its own accreditation system independent of the traditional accreditation provided by the APA. This process also parallels developments in the Association for Psychological Science (APS), which distinguishes itself from the APA by its stronger scientific focus (see, for instance, the APS journal—*Clinical Psychological Science*). For those in the counselling psychology field, there is currently considerable concern that unless the profession develops towards greater synergy with clinical psychology, it will become deskilled and devalued once again, which is something to be resisted.

In order to reflect these concerns, the BPS revised its accreditation standards in 2014 in a manner that quite explicitly placed what it termed "clinical pragmatism" (BPS, 2014) more fully at the heart of the training agenda, and emphasized both the range of NHS-relevant skills required of counselling psychologists, and the commonalities shared with clinical psychology. The counselling psychology training standards thus broadened to include a greater emphasis on psychometric testing, neuropsychology, child and families work, and leadership/management skills. It remains to be seen whether such development will be sufficient to enable counselling psychology to meet the employability agenda as set by the NHS and the forces working upon this, or if instead, further reworking of the nature and basis of counselling psychology will itself become necessary.

Linked to the issue of employability in the NHS, the profession also faces wider questions with regards to its ongoing relationship with clinical psychology, with some calling for a greater integration between the two. It is argued, from this perspective (e.g., Kinderman, 2010) that there is far more similarity than difference between these areas of psychological practice, and as such the professional infrastructure should evolve to reflect this in terms of either integrating counselling psychology into clinical psychology as a single area of professional activity or developing training models to reflect far more significantly the overlaps and similarities between the different areas of applied psychology. Although some in the counselling psychology field would appear to welcome such advances, others take a more circumspect view, highlighting the distinctiveness of the humanistic value base within counselling psychology and the potential loss of this should a more generic set of standards be developed. Such a view emphasizes the importance of the counselling tradition as a fundamental part of counselling psychology training, and argues that to lose this would fundamentally be at odds with the underlying philosophy and basis of the profession itself.

CONCLUSION

In this chapter we have considered the issues for training in counselling psychology. Standing back from the profession specific issues around counselling psychology training, it is also important to take note of developments within the education field itself that will likely have a bearing on how the training agenda in counselling psychology may evolve in coming years. One of these is the structure of doctoral work within the higher education setting, and the increasing recognition of the role of professional doctorates in the applied health care field (UK Council for Graduate Education, 2010). A greater synergy of training systems and processes at the doctoral level is likely, with an inevitable impact on how counselling psychology training is delivered within university and independent settings. The demand for doctorates from employers is also likely to mean routes such as the BPS Qualification, which do not make a doctorate award, will become increasingly difficult to sustain over time.

The impact of technology, too, is likely to have significant bearing on counselling psychology training in the future. With online and blended learning becoming such a fundamental part of the educational experience, it is highly likely that innovative programmes will evolve, enabling those studying counselling psychology to study remotely, including undertaking placements in settings that may be unthinkable at present. Such innovation will inevitably support an increased diversity, which will have an impact on the nature of programmes being made available, their training processes, and, of course, their cost.

SUGGESTED FURTHER READING

Johnson, W. B., & Kaslow, N. J. (2014). *The Oxford handbook of education and training in professional psychology*. New York: Oxford University Press.

REFERENCES

APA (American Psychological Association) (2006). *Guidelines and principles for accreditation of programs in professional psychology (G&P)*. Retrieved from http://www.apa.org/ed/accreditation/about/policies/guiding-principles.pdf (accessed March 23, 2017).

APA (American Psychological Association) (2015). *The standards of accreditation for health service psychology (SoA)*. Retrieved from: https://www.apa.org/ed/accreditation/about/policies/standards-of-accreditation.pdf (accessed March 23, 2017).

Bell, D. J., & Hausman, E. M. (2014). Training models in professional psychology doctoral programs. In W. B. Johnson, & N. J. Kaslow (Eds.), *The Oxford handbook of education and training in professional psychology* (pp. 33–51). New York: Oxford University Press.

BPS (British Psychological Society) (2014). *Key revisions to the society's accreditation standards for counselling psychology programmes introduced in 2014/15*. Leicester: Partnership and Accreditation Team The British Psychological Society.

BPS (British Psychological Society) (2015). *Standards for accreditation of counselling psychology programmes*. Leicester: Partnership and Accreditation Team The British Psychological Society.

Burr, V. (2015). *Social constructionism*. London: Sage.

Canadian Psychological Association (2011). *Accreditation standards and procedures for doctoral programmes and internships in professional psychology*. Retrieved from http://www.cpa.ca/docs/File/Accreditation/Accreditation_2011.pdf

Cautin, R. L., & Baker, D. B. (2014). A history of education and training in professional psychology. In W. B. Johnson, & N. J. Kaslow (Eds.), *The Oxford handbook of education and training in professional psychology* (pp. 17–32). New York: Oxford University Press.

Cooper, M. (2009). Welcoming the other: Actualising the humanistic ethic at the core of counselling psychology practice. *Counselling Psychology Review, 24*(3&4), 119–129.

Cooper, M., & McLeod, J. (2011). *Pluralistic counselling and psychotherapy*. London: Sage.

Fowles, D. C. (2015). Academy of psychological clinical science (APCS). In R. L. Cautin, & S. O. Lilienfeld (Eds.), *The encyclopaedia of clinical psychology* (pp. 1–10). Oxford, UK: Wiley-Blackwell. Retrieved from https://www.acadpsychclinicalscience.org/cmss_files/attachmentlibrary/APCS-2015.pdf (accessed March 23, 2017).

Fouad, N. A., & Grus, C. L. (2014). Competency-based education and training in professional psychology. In W. B. Johnson, & N. J. Kaslow (Eds.), *The Oxford handbook of education and training in professional psychology* (pp. 105–119). New York: Oxford University Press.

Fouad, N. A., Grus, C. L., Hatcher, R. L., Kaslow, N. J., Hutchings, P. S., Madson, M. B., . . . & Crossman, R. E. (2009). Competency benchmarks: A model for understanding and measuring competence in professional psychology across training levels. *Training and Education in Professional Psychology, 3*, S5–S29.

Fuertes, J. N., Spokane, A., & Holloway, E. (2013). *Specialty competencies in counseling psychology*. New York: Oxford University Press.

Goodyear, R., Lichtenberg, J., Hutman, H., Overland, E., Bedi, R., Christiani, K., & Young, C. (2016). A global portrait of counselling psychologists' characteristics, perspectives, and professional behaviors. *Counselling Psychology Quarterly, 29*(2), 115–138.

Galbraith, V. E., & Hart, N. M. (2007). Personal development groups in counselling psychology training: The case for further training. *Counselling Psychology Review, 22*(4), 49–57.

HCPC (Health and Care Professions Council) (2015). Standards of proficiency: Practitioner psychologists. London: HCPC.

James, P. E., & Bellamy, A. (2010). Counselling psychology in the NHS. In R. Woolfe., S. Strawbridge., B. Douglas, & W. Dryden (Eds.), *The handbook of counselling psychology* (pp. 397–415). London: Sage.

Kaskett, E. (2012). The counselling psychologist researcher. *Counselling Psychology Review, 27*(2), 64–73.

Kinderman, P. (2010). The future of counselling psychology: A view from outside. *Counselling Psychology Review, 24*(16–21), 119–129.

Lane, D. A., & Corrie, S. (2006). Counselling psychology: Its influences and future. *Counselling Psychology Review, 21*, 12–24.

Lewis Y. (2008). Counselling psychology training: implications for "Self." *Counselling Psychology Review, 23*(3), 63–69.

Lunt, I., Job, R., Lecuyer, R., Peiro, J. M., & Gorbeña, S. (2009). *Tuning-EuroPsy: Reference points for the design and delivery of degree programmes in psychology*. Bilbao: Tuning Project.

Martin, P. (2010). Training and professional development. In R. Woolfe., S. Strawbridge., B. Douglas. & W. Dryden (Eds.), *The handbook of counselling psychology* (pp. 547–568). London: Sage.

McLeod, J., & Elliott, R. (2011). Systematic case study research: A practice-orientated introduction toward building and evidence-base for counselling and psychotherapy. *Counselling and Psychotherapy Research, 11*, 1–10.

Moller, N., Alilovic, K., & Mundra, N. (2008). What do we do about personal development? PD training in Counselling Psychology programmes. *Counselling Psychology Review, 23*(3), 82–85.

Munley, P. H., Duncan, L. E., McDonnell, K. A., & Sauer, E. M. (2004). Counseling psychology in the United States of America. *Counselling Psychology Quarterly, 17*, 247–271. DOI: 10.1080/09515070412331317602

Nicholson, B. C., & Madson, M. B. (2015). Introduction to the special issue: Science-practice integration in counseling psychology training: Trends and models. *Counselling Psychology Quarterly, 28*(3), 215–219. DOI: 10.1080/09515070.2015.1060669

Orlans, V., & Van Scoyoc, S. (2009). *A short introduction to counselling psychology*. London: Sage.

Rizq, R. (2006). Training and disillusion in counselling psychology: A psychoanalytic perspective. *Psychology and Psychotherapy: Theory, Research and Practice, 79*(4), 613–627.

Schön, D. (1983). *The reflective practitioner*. New York: Basic Books.

Strawbridge, S., & Woolfe, R. (2010). Training and professional development. In R. Woolfe., S. Strawbridge., B. Douglas, & W. Dryden (Eds.), *The handbook of counselling psychology* (pp. 3–22). London: Sage.

Sugarman, L. (2010). The life course: A framework for the practice of counselling psychology. In R. Woolfe., S. Strawbridge., B. Douglas, & W. Dryden (Eds.), *The handbook of counselling psychology* (pp. 279–297). London: Sage.

UK Council for Graduate Education (2010). *Professional doctorate awards in the UK*. London: UK Council for Graduate Education.

Whiteley, J. M. (Ed.) (1980). *The history of counseling psychology*. Monterey, CA: Brooks/Cole Publishing Company.

Woolfe, R. (2012). Risorgimento: A history of counselling psychology in Britain. *Counselling Psychology Review, 27*(4), 72–78.

Wrenn, C. G. (1966). Birth and early childhood of a journal. *Journal of Counseling Psychology, 13*, 485–488.

PART 6 Research in Counselling Psychology

Counselling Psychology

DEE DANCHEV

CHAPTER OUTLINE

INTRODUCTION 380

HISTORICAL CONTEXT 380

THE ETHICS OF THE RESEARCHER AND THEIR POSITIONING 381

THE PARTICIPANT'S PERSPECTIVE 383

THE USE OF INCENTIVES 384

INFORMED CONSENT 385

DECEPTION 387

ANONYMITY 387

ONLINE RESEARCH 388

RESEARCH METHOD, ANALYSIS, AND REPORTING FINDINGS 388

AFTERCARE OF PARTICIPANTS 389

DISSEMINATION AND THE RESEARCH AFTERLIFE 389

RESEARCHER SELF-CARE 390

CONCLUSION 391

LEARNING OUTCOMES

BY THE END OF THIS CHAPTER YOU SHOULD BE ABLE TO ANSWER THE FOLLOWING KEY QUESTIONS:

1. How might your individual positioning impact on your research process?

2. How can researchers ensure that they have informed consent from their participants?

3. Are online research methods ethically sound?

INTRODUCTION

Research ethics are sometimes thought of as a cumbersome stage in the research process and, whether you are a student, advanced trainee, or qualified practitioner, one that is often freighted with anxiety. Gaining permission from an ethics committee is a hurdle that has to be negotiated. Complex forms need to be completed and it seems that all the minutiae of the research process have to be thought through before the researcher has even begun their project; and sometimes gaining ethical permission can be a long and frustrating process. In this chapter I want to refocus on research ethics not as a pass or fail process but to encourage researchers to view research ethics as an entity that permeates the whole of the research process and across all methods and types of research—quantitative and qualitative alike.

Approaching research with a curiosity about the ethics of each action can stimulate some fascinating discussions and provide a good deal of material to back up arguments to support ethics applications. In this short chapter it is not possible to cover all the aspects of research ethics so I have focused on the kinds of issues that frequently arise. Questions that are often asked are: How does the researcher's individual positioning impact on their choice of topic and their relationship with their participants? How do researchers deal with issues of participant vulnerability? Is it acceptable to use incentives to recruit participants? How can informed consent be ensured? Is deception ever permissible? Are online research methods ethically sound? How far do researchers' responsibilities extend beyond the ending of data collection? But first, let's reflect on why research ethics and ethical scrutiny of research projects are so important.

HISTORICAL CONTEXT

Research ethics underwent an intense period of development in the aftermath of World War II. The cruelty of the Nazi experiments on prisoners in concentration camps and hospital inmates alerted the medical and science community to the need for an explicit statement on research ethics. The outcome of this was the Nuremberg Code (1947). The code emphasizes three important aspects of research ethics: a basis in human rights and natural law; the central importance of participant consent; and the need for participant care

(Annas & Grodin, 2008). At first it was felt that the Nuremberg Code was sufficient to prevent a repeat of atrocities being committed in the name of research. However, the realization slowly dawned that serious breaches of research ethics occurred not only in totalitarian regimes but also in liberal democracies. This understanding gave rise to the Helsinki Declaration (World Medical Association, 1964). The Helsinki Declaration is regularly amended to keep pace with changing ethical standards and the rapid advancement of medical and scientific knowledge. It is now in its eighth (2013) incarnation (see World Medical Association, n.d.). Its main aim is to guide and inspire researchers and ethical committees though it is not without criticism. Ashcroft (2008) says that it is too focused on Western needs and argues that it does not cater adequately for situations found in the developing world. Ashcroft has also criticized it for a lack of precision. As research ethics have developed mainly from a biomedical model, there is some discussion amongst psychologists and social scientists as to whether their kinds of research should be held to the same level of scrutiny as medical science researchers. Is it reasonable, for example, for the same level of ethical requirements that are applied in the testing of new drugs on humans to be applied to a study that involves interviewing people who have been bullied? This issue is especially pertinent for counselling psychologists who want to research an aspect of counselling in a medical setting and find that the ethics process is so geared to medical research that it is difficult to negotiate.

Knowledge of the history of the development of research ethics helps us to understand why ethical scrutiny of research is important. The next section looks at how researchers can develop and increase their ethical mindedness.

THE ETHICS OF THE RESEARCHER AND THEIR POSITIONING

Self-reflection is a vital ingredient in counselling psychology practice and focusing on one's own ethical awareness is a good starting point for any research project. Reading the British Psychological Society (BPS) Code of Human Research Research Ethics and those of allied organizations can draw attention to issues that the researcher may not have fully considered. As has been underlined in Chapters 20 and 21 no code of ethics can produce an ethical researcher but it can offer guidance and alert researchers to areas of importance (see BPS, 2010).

Work on personal ethical development is as necessary for ethical research as it is for ethical practice. In particular it is important to be sensitized to the position of the participant in the particular study. This demands empathy: the ability to understand what it means to be a research participant in a particular research process. I am using the term participant for the purposes of this chapter as this is the term that most accurately describes the majority of current research relationships. The use of terms for people involved in research reveals the power relationship between the researcher and the participant. In the past research was carried out with "subjects'"—a term freighted with disempowerment. At the other end of the scale, in recent decades, steps have been taken in some research traditions to make participants full co-researchers. In the best examples of this type of research full equality is achieved between the researcher and participants about the choice of research topic, research design, data analysis, and the presentation of results. Admirable examples of this approach can be found in the studies carried out by feminist, participatory, and action researchers where the co-researchers have experienced growth and empowerment through their full engagement with the research process (Cahill, 2007; Dona, 2007; Nelson and Prilleltensky, 2010). Cahill's (2007) research provides a good example of the transformatory nature of these kinds of research. Cahill and her co-researchers, six young women from New York, designed and carried out a research project entitled "Makes Me Mad: Stereotypes of Young Urban Womyn of Colour." Through being involved in the choice and design of the research, and telling and analysing their own stories of discrimination and repression, the women experienced a new understanding of themselves and the issues that they faced in their lives. Sometimes research studies describe participants as co-researchers but the term has been used loosely and, on close reading, it is evident that full co-researcher status has not been achieved or possibly even intended.

There are further facets of the power dynamics of research that warrant exploration. It has, in the past, been the practice in psychology for the researcher to be unknown apart from their name and affiliation. We have known a lot about the lives, skills, and opinions of participants but remarkably little about the people conducting the research. In addition, the researcher has been assumed to be in a neutral position in relation to their research topic. It is now more clearly understood that researcher neutrality is a myth. Neutrality is ideal but all researchers start with some kind of positioning, whether this relates to their philosophy, methodological preferences, prior knowledge of the subject, and/or personal experiences. Researcher openness and self-awareness about their positioning is particularly relevant to the choice of a research topic and one that has ethical implications.

There are all kinds of motivations that lead researchers to focus on a particular subject, and a lack of awareness on behalf of the researcher can lead to bias. Some researchers choose to research a topic that relates to a personal experience that they have deep feelings about. Personal knowledge and experience can enrich a research project as the researcher knows the area experientially and often with deep understanding and knowledge. Personally meaningful research studies can be successful and ethically sound if the researcher has the ability to be highly self-reflective so that they do not unduly influence the research process. Researching personally meaningful topics can also come at an emotional cost for the researcher, and careful consideration of their capacity to cope with, and reflect on, the powerful feelings that may be evoked by the research process is necessary. Prior and concurrent counselling and/or extra research supervision can act as safeguards to ensure that the research is conducted in a balanced way. Tufford and Newman (2012) recommend keeping a reflexive research diary, discussing the research process and possible biases with a trusted person, and keeping memos of research-related thoughts as they occur. These kinds of actions help the researcher to keep their ethical balance. Ideally the researcher is transparent about their motivation and their connection to the research project in a reflexive account so that the reader of the research can review the results and discussion in the light of this knowledge.

Reflexive accounts are usually included by qualitative researchers when writing up their research. It can be argued that it is equally important for quantitative researchers to do this. When collecting and analysing quantitative data sets, decisions have to be made about how the data are to be obtained and interrogated. Biases may creep in in subtle ways. Openness about the researcher's starting position enables the reader of the research to review the results and make their own judgements about the conditions of the research. A reflexive account also maps the researcher's learning throughout the research process, and their changes in perspective on the research topic provide evidence that any initial biases have not prevailed.

A further aspect of the researcher's positioning is the need for transparency about the involvement of third parties in the decision to research a particular area. The research may have been commissioned or funded by an organization or institution. These kinds of details should be freely disclosed so that the research context is clearly available to all. The focus now turns from the researcher to the participants and the issues that researchers need to be aware of to ensure ethical research practice.

THE PARTICIPANT'S PERSPECTIVE

Some research topics are clearly more sensitive than others. Issues relating to forms of abuse, bereavement, or trauma may evoke painful memories in participants. However, it is difficult to anticipate all sensitivities and even an apparently innocuous subject may have particular meaning or connections for some people.

A useful starting point to sensitize oneself to the perspective of the participant is to consider why a participant might have agreed to take part in a particular research project. There could be a wide variety of reasons behind this decision. It may be a wish to share experience or expertise out of a commitment to do something that benefits others. It may be of benefit to the participant in aiding them to think through their position on a particular issue, or it may have a reparative effect in enabling them to tell a story or share experiences about a difficult situation or experience. It may give them a voice on an issue that they are concerned about. It may simply be a way of connecting with others to reduce feelings of loneliness and isolation.

In addition to these kinds of motivation a participant may be agreeing to participate because of some form of vulnerability. This could be due to their current physical state through age or illness, or ability to understand the issues involved. In these situations it is necessary to involve a carer or advocate to ensure that the participant is not being exploited in some way. Some people may not feel empowered enough to refuse to participate. Examples of people in this situation are students and counselling clients where an unequal power relationship exists between the researcher and the participant. Or there may be a fear of some kind of sanction if they do not agree; this may apply in the case of prisoners, people detained under the mental health act, or employees of the organizations who are commissioning the research. Obtaining valid consent from children requires particular care. Cameron (2005) gives a helpful account of ethical ways of researching with children including age-appropriate methods of communication. Through their work with children Christensen and Prout (2002) propose the establishment of "ethical symmetry":

> By this we mean that the researcher takes as his or her starting point the view that the ethical relationship between researcher and informant is the same whether he or she conducts research with adults or with children. This has a number of implications. The first is that the researcher employs the same ethical principles whether they are researching children or adults. Second, that each right and ethical consideration in relation to adults in the research process has its counterpart for children. Third, the symmetrical treatment of children in research means that any differences between carrying out research with children or with adults should be allowed to arise from this starting point, according to the concrete situation of children, rather than being assumed in advance.

> (Christensen and Prout, 2002, p. 482)

Although Christensen and Prout developed the concept of ethical symmetry for research with children, it can be equally applied to all populations where a form of vulnerability may be evident.

There is a further kind of vulnerability to which researchers need to be sensitive. Engaging some participants in research may endanger them. Fontes (2004) trenchantly highlights the risks for participants who are in a violent relationship. Discussing their experience of domestic violence may precipitate a reaction from the abusive family member if their participation becomes known. Especial care about anonymity and a safe location for the vulnerable person to participate are key factors in ensuring their safety.

Heightened sensitivity is often required but it is important that concerns about vulnerability do not prevent research from being carried out with vulnerable populations. Their voices need to be heard and it can be easy to fall into the trap of prioritizing participants' vulnerability rather than their abilities. Closely connected to the issue of vulnerability is the use of incentives to encourage participation.

THE USE OF INCENTIVES

It is not always easy to recruit participants and the question can arise as to whether it is ethical to provide incentives to aid recruitment. Some researchers offer to reimburse travel expenses and provide compensation for lost work time. These kinds of incentives are generally viewed as acceptable. An increasing number of researchers are using online methods for recruitment such as "the Mechanical Turk or MTurk" (Mechanical Turk, n.d.). These types of methods often involve payment and are ethically sound if the payment for participation is appropriate. However, concerns about the use of incentives have been raised. Grant and Sugarman (2004) warn that they may cause people who might otherwise decide not to participate to change their minds. They believe that the incentive unduly influences their judgement. People who are in poverty, for example, might be strongly influenced by the prospect of a monetary reward.

> Where participants are hard to recruit and there is thus the greatest need for incentives, one ought to be most reluctant to offer them. The need for large incentives can be a rough indicator that there may be an ethical concern that requires attention. We might say as a rule of thumb that, if you cannot secure participation without offering large incentives, people probably have strong aversions to the study.

> (Grant & Sugarman, 2004, p. 734)

An opposing view might be that Grant and Sugarman are not respecting the ability of participants to make their own decisions. However, incentives, as well as influencing the initial decision to participate, might also make it difficult for the participant to withdraw from a study at a later stage. Grant and Sugarman (2004) have devised a useful checklist that outlines the problematic areas associated with incentives.

INCENTIVES CHECKLIST

Incentives are problematic when:

- Ease of voluntary exit from the study is compromised.
- There is a dependency relationship with the researcher.
- There is a high level of risk to the participant.
- The research may be degrading or shaming.
- The incentive has to be large to overcome participants' aversion to the study.
- The aversion is based on participants' principles.
- The research may cause participants harm.

(Grant & Sugarman, 2004, p. 732)

If incentives are used in recruitment they should be clearly identified in research reports and papers so that the reader is aware of the full context of the research. The above sections on vulnerability and incentives are fundamentally connected to the issue of consent. How can we ensure that our participants are freely consenting to participate in a research project?

INFORMED CONSENT

Informed consent is especially relevant for counselling psychologists as they have an enhanced level of interpersonal skills. They are adept at creating safe and warm atmospheres. It may be possible that participants more readily agree to participate, disclose more data, or go more deeply into personal issues during interviews than they might otherwise with a researcher who does not possess these skills.

Understanding this factor and the variety of motivations and vulnerabilities of participants helps researchers to be more vigilant about the issue of informed consent. In the past consent has often simply involved the practice of giving information about the research project and then asking participants to sign a form. It has been very much a "one off" practice that may take place immediately before the data are gathered—a "hit and run" approach as West (2002, p. 264) describes it. Munhall (1988) proposed a different approach. She recommended process permission and this has been applied to counselling and psychotherapy research by Grafanaki (1996). In process permission the participant is consulted about their wish to participate at several points in the research process. Detailed information is given about the research process and then thinking time given. The box below details the kinds of information that should usually be given. It should be presented in a clear form and be easily understood. Participants should be given space to reflect and encouraged to ask questions.

INFORMATION ABOUT THE RESEARCH STUDY

- The purpose of the research and why it is being undertaken.
- What the research process will involve.
- Any positive aspects or benefits that may occur.
- Any risks, possible harm or discomfort involved.
- Clarity about the fact that it is research and not a form of therapy.
- The extent of confidentiality and anonymity, and the safeguards that will be in place to maintain them.
- Data storage precautions.
- The involvement of any third parties (e.g., supervisor, translators, transcribers, or data consultants).
- How and when the data will be destroyed.
- The level of contact with the researcher.
- The support that will be available.
- The right to refuse to answer questions.
- The right to withdraw participation.
- The means of distributing the findings to participants.
- The contact details of the institution, researcher, and their supervisor.
- The complaints procedure.

(Danchev & Ross, 2014, p. 66)

Ideally the participant is given adequate time to digest the information, and best practice is to give information in advance of the time when the first request for permission is made and a form signed. The permission form itself usually includes a statement of the obligations of the researcher and would, of course, also include the right to withdraw up to the time of submission of the research for examination or publication. Second and third checks for permission are often made before and after the experiment, procedure, questionnaire, or interview. If the research method involves sending the participant the data to review (e.g., an interview transcript) further confirmation of permission should be sought at that time.

The permission form should be specific about for what permission is being given. Is it just for this piece of research and its allied papers or dissertation, and so on, or might there be further dissemination of the material? In particular it would be important to be clear about any possible media involvement. Misleading information or a lack of clarity amounts to deception.

DECEPTION

Deception associated with research can occur in two ways. It can be a matter of commission where full information is deliberately withheld. This would almost always be considered unethical but occasionally there are research studies where it is felt necessary to withhold some information about the research from participants in order to achieve a valid and reliable result. For example, if a researcher were interested in the frequency and use of metaphor by counsellors during therapy sessions, they might only disclose that they were interested in the use of language at the recruitment and data collection stages, because if they identified metaphor as the object of their investigations it might cause the therapist to change their natural style. Generally if there is a possibility that information is to be withheld, then this needs careful consideration by the researcher, their research supervisor, and the appropriate ethics committee. The value of the findings should outweigh the initial deception and there should not be any possibility of harm for the participants. The participant should, of course, always be fully debriefed at the end of the research process.

The second form of deception is omission—where the researcher fails, through anxiety, inefficiency, a fear of a lack of recruits, or some other inhibition, to inform the participant fully about the research study. Most often this is due to a lack of prior planning and discussion with supervisors or colleagues, and ought to be avoidable.

ANONYMITY

As part of the information giving the degree of anonymity should be agreed. This includes the person themselves and any third parties who may be involved, including organizations and institutions. For some participants complete anonymity is essential. However, it should not be assumed, as some participants, especially in qualitative forms of research where they may have disclosed personal narratives or information, may want their name to be recorded by the researcher. For example, they might wish their name to be directly connected to their data or to be included in the research acknowledgements. If they have fully participated in the research process as co-researchers they would usually be acknowledged as co-authors. If participants want to be acknowledged by name, any physical, psychological, or social risk that may arise from this preference should be assessed and fully considered. There may be situations of serious risk to participants where the researcher and their advisors advise against any form of identification.

ONLINE RESEARCH

With the advancement of online media, new means of recruiting large numbers of participants from a wide geographical area and at low cost have evolved (Eastham, 2011). These methods of recruitment are an exciting development and are making a very positive contribution to research. However, some research using online means has involved the collection of personal data without the individuals concerned being consulted or their permission gained. Facebook, blogs, Twitter, and other online media have all been utilized by researchers to collect data about people's lives, and ethical concerns have been raised. These concerns involve consent, anonymity, and privacy. Discussions have revolved around whether it is acceptable to collect data from blogs, Facebook, Twitter, and so on, without the express permission of the people involved. The issue here is the confusion of public and private boundaries. Is it similar to observational research as argued by Bruckman et al. (2010) or is it an intrusion into privacy? Attempts to anonymize these kinds of data have not always been successful and individuals have been identified despite researchers' best efforts to maintain anonymity (Zimmer, 2010). Zimmer recommends being mindful of people's dignity when embarking on online data gathering. This is a rapidly developing area and at present the Association of Internet Researchers' Ethics guide (2012) provides the most useful information and guidance.

RESEARCH METHOD, ANALYSIS, AND REPORTING FINDINGS

An important aim of ethical research is to explore the chosen topic as effectively as possible. This means that when the area to be researched has been decided upon the next step is to choose the most effective method to research the subject. The choice of research method would not usually be the first priority. Salmon (2003) warns against "methodologism," where commitment to a particular method and its application become the central concern of the researcher. The primary focus should be how can the fullest, most useful results be obtained? This may involve the researcher in extra work in familiarizing themselves with a new research method. The reward is the knowledge that the best possible results have been achieved.

There can be ethical pitfalls in data analysis. External pressures to produce positive or interesting results may exist and timescales may be short. At worst these kinds of pressures have caused people to invent data. More commonly they result in a partial or selective analysis, which produces a biased result. Finding the best data analysis methods and thoroughly interrogating the data is all part of ethical research practice. Raw data, within the constraints of anonymity and confidentiality, should always be available for inspection if requested.

There has been a tendency only to submit papers and make public research that shows a positive outcome. A particular topic may have been researched many times with negative results but only the few positive results are released. This kind of bias is a form of deception, and all negative data should be made equally available so that the context of the positive results is clear.

AFTERCARE OF PARTICIPANTS

Is it ethical for data collection to be the endpoint of contact with participants? The general opinion is that some form of aftercare is necessary. It may be in the form of debriefing, including seeking feedback on the process. If a sensitive area has been explored there is a duty to ensure that the participant has information about where they can obtain further support if they feel it is needed. Some researchers argue for the opportunity for continuing contact to be offered to participants. Oakley (1981) has written about her continuing contact with a group of female participants that she interviewed on their experience of childbirth. "Four years after the final interview I am still in touch with more than a third of the women I interviewed" (Oakley, 1981, p. 46). For Oakley it felt unethical to cut off contact with women who had shared one of their most profound life experiences with her if they still wanted to be in contact with her.

Feedback on the research process itself gives the participants an opportunity to describe what the process was like for them and it also provides valuable information for the conduct of future research projects. Feedback can be obtained after data collection verbally when there is face-to-face contact with participants or, if appropriate, by questionnaire. Newman, Willard, Sinclair, and Kaloupek (2001) have devised a useful questionnaire "The Reactions to Research Participation Questionnaire." This kind of questionnaire is especially helpful when new research areas or new research methods are being explored. Detailed feedback can contribute to the refining and development of researchers' skills and the methods that they use.

DISSEMINATION AND THE RESEARCH AFTERLIFE

In Chapter 21 I refer to the view that counselling psychologists should stand by their clients rather than taking the position of bystanders. The same concept applies to researchers. Participants have given their valuable time and possibly participated at some emotional and/or material cost to themselves.

This places a duty on researchers to disseminate their findings and to think creatively about how the findings can best be used to achieve positive change. This may be through the usual methods to inform colleagues: academic papers, books, and presentations at conferences. When findings have a wider public value, creativity may be needed in finding ways of conveying the information. Dissemination via articles in the press, radio, and television can ensure that findings are conveyed to a large and varied audience. Public talks or arts events can also be involved. Keen and Todres (2007) say that researchers often feel that these kinds of engagements are beyond their remit, but they argue that this is a vital part of the research process and urge researchers to be creative. They cite the theatre work of Gray (2000), Gray, Fitch, Phillips, Labrecque, & Greenberg (2003), and Mienczakowski (2003), who have used drama to disseminate information about the lived experiences for people and their families of breast cancer, prostate cancer, and psychoses.

Ethical responsibility for research does not completely end with dissemination. Research has an afterlife and the researcher has a duty to ensure that it is not misquoted or misrepresented. Research is at times misused or exaggerated by the media (Sumner, Boy, & Chambers, 2011). There are also concerns that politicians do not always consult research or use it in a balanced way when promoting particular policies (Chambers et al., 2015). If research is particularly relevant to an organizational or political policy, it can be argued that researchers have a duty to make sure that the relevant people are aware of their findings. Occasionally academics themselves can cause a distortion in the understanding of a subject to occur that impacts on practice. A powerful example of this, described by Jarrett (2007), occurred in relation to bereavement counselling where the findings from a student dissertation were cited in increasingly influential publications. Researchers should check from time to time who is citing their research and rebut any forms of misrepresentation or misuse of their data and findings.

RESEARCHER SELF-CARE

This chapter has focused to a large extent on the ethical duties relating to participant care, and ensuring the accurate analysis and reporting of findings. In essence: the ethical duty to others. There is a further ethical duty and that is the researcher's duty towards themselves. If you are not in good physical and mental condition, then it is difficult to produce your best work. Research can be a demanding endeavour. Physical safety and avoiding secondary traumatization are equally important. Safety measures are all part of a well-managed research project. In addition to establishing measures to protect personal safety, exploring some subject areas in depth can open the researcher to a form of secondary traumatization (Coles, Dartnall, Limjerwala, & Astbury, 2010; Coles and Mudaly, 2010; Fontes, 2004). Listening to trenchant narratives has an impact.

> When you gaze long into an abyss the abyss also gazes into you.

> (Nietzsche, 1990, p. 102)

At times research discoveries and findings evoke painful parts of the researcher's past history. Forethought is needed to ensure that resources such as debriefing, counselling, and/or additional research supervision are in place to counter the probability of such traumatization.

Finally, researchers sometimes report feelings of guilt that they have "left their participants in difficult situations." Making efforts to have research findings heard in places that will assist in changing attitudes and influencing policy making for the benefit of people in similar situations to the participants can help to reduce these kinds of feelings.

RESEARCHER SAFETY CHECKLIST

- Do you understand the extent of your own connections to the subject you are researching?
- Have you had adequate training to deal with sensitive or emotional material?
- Have you arranged to meet participants in a safe environment?
- Do you need another person to accompany you?
- Do you need to have an alarm system?
- Have you told a reliable person about your whereabouts?
- Do you have some form of debriefing in place?
- Can you contact a supportive person as and when needed?
- Will your research be disseminated in a way that will address your participants' issues?

(Danchev & Ross, 2014, pp. 19–20)

CONCLUSION

There are almost no absolutes when it comes to ethical practice. There is, however, general agreement about best practice at any point in time, and it is often enshrined in our codes of research ethics. Best practice is subject to change as research processes and methods, and ethical understanding develop. With any ethical decision that might be controversial the key thing is to have ensured that there has been adequate discussion with colleagues and supervisors, and to have developed a sound argument in support of the decision that has been made.

In this chapter I have discussed some of the issues that most frequently are associated with ethical decisions in research. I hope that the message that all stages of the research process involve ethical decisions will lead to an increased ethical interest and mindfulness when you embark on your next research project.

SUGGESTED FURTHER READING

Danchev, D., & Ross, A. (2014). *Research ethics for counsellors, nurses and social workers.* London: Sage.
   This book covers research ethics from the perspective of people who work therapeutically.

Mertens, D. M., & Ginsberg, P. E. (Eds) (2009). *The handbook of social research ethics*. London: Sage.
A comprehensive collection of views on research ethics, including a useful chapter by Barnes on disability research.

Wiles, R. (2012). *What are qualitative research ethics?* London: Bloomsbury.
A succinct and accessible review of the field of qualitative research ethics.

REFERENCES

Annas, G. J., & Grodin, M. A. (2008). The Nuremburg Code. In E. J. Emanuel, C. Grady, R. A. Crouch, R. K. Lie, F. G. Miller, & D. Wendler. *The Oxford textbook of clinical research ethics* (pp. 136–140). Oxford: Oxford University Press.

Ashcroft, R. E. (2008). The Declaration of Helsinki. In E. J. Emanuel, C. Grady, R. A. Crouch, R. K. Lie, F. G. Miller, & D. Wendler. *The Oxford textbook of clinical research ethics* (pp. 141–148). Oxford: Oxford University Press.

Association of Internet Researchers (2012) *Ethics guide*. Retrieved from http://aoir.org/ethics/ (accessed July 23, 2015).

BPS (British Psychological Society) (2010). Code of human research ethics. Retrieved from http://www.bps.org.uk/sites/default/files/documents/code_of_human_research_ethics.pdf (accessed March 17, 2017).

Bruckman, A., Karahalios, K., Kraut, R. E., Poole, E. S., Thomas, J. C., & Yardi, S. (2010). Revisiting research ethics in the Facebook era: Challenges in emerging CSCW research. *CSCW 2010*, February 6–10. Savannah, GA: CSCW.

Cahill, C. (2007). The personal is the political: Developing new subjectivities through participatory action research. *Gender, Place and Culture: A Journal of Feminist Geography, 14*(3), 267–292.

Cameron, H. (2005). Asking tough questions: A guide to ethical practices in interviewing young children. *Early Child Development and Care, 175*(6), 597–610.

Chambers, C., Lawrence, N., Kythreotis, A., Chambers, J., O'Grady, G., & Bestmann, S. (2015). Citizen science in action: Can we forge a smarter democracy? Retrieved from www.theguardian.com/science/blog/2015/may/06/citizen-science-in-action-can-we-forge-a-smarter-democracy (accessed November 13, 2015).

Christensen, P., & Prout, A. (2002). Working with ethical symmetry in social research with children. *Childhood, 9*, 477.

Coles, J., Dartnall, E., Limjerwala, S., & Astbury, J. (2010). *Researcher trauma, safety and sexual violence research. Briefing Paper: Sexual violence research initiative*. Retrieved from http://www.svri.org/trauma.htm (accessed July 12, 2015).

Coles, J., & Mudaly, N. (2010). Staying safe: Strategies for qualitative child abuse researchers. *Child Abuse Review, 19*(1), 56–69.

Danchev, D., & Ross, A. (2014). *research ethics for counsellors, nurses and social workers*. London: Sage.

Dona, G. (2007). The microphysics of participation in refugee research. *Journal of Refugee Studies, 20*(2), 210–229.

Eastham, L. A. (2011). Research using blogs for data: Public documents or private musings? *Research in Nursing and Health, 43*, 353–361.

Fontes, L. A. (2004). Ethics in violence against women research: The sensitive, the dangerous, and the overlooked. *Ethics and Behaviour, 14*(2), 141–174

Grafanaki, S. (1996). How research can change the researcher: The need for sensitivity, flexibility and ethical boundaries in conducting qualitative research in counselling/psychotherapy. *British Journal of Guidance and Counselling, 24*(3), 329–338.

Grant, R. W., & Sugarman, J. (2004). Ethics in human subjects research: Do incentives matter? *Journal of Medicine and Philosophy, 29*(6), 717–738.

Gray, R. (2000). Graduate school never prepared me for this: Reflections on the challenges of research-based theatre. *Reflective Practice, 1*(3), 377–390.

Gray, R., Fitch, M., Phillips, C., Labrecque, M., & Greenberg, M. (2003). Managing the impact of illness: The experiences of men with prostate cancer and their spouses. *Journal of Cancer Education, 18*(4), 223–229.

Jarrett, C. (2007). *How a student dissertation destroyed bereavement counselling's reputation.* Retrieved from http://bps-research-digest.blogspot.co.uk/2007/08/how-student-dissertation-destroyed.html (accessed July 13, 2015).

Keen, S., & Todres, L. (2007) Strategies for disseminating qualitative research findings: Three exemplars. *Forum: Qualitative Social Research, 8*(3), 17.

Mechanical Turk (nd). Mechanical Turk. Retrieved from https://www.mturk.com/mturk/welcome (accessed March 17, 2017).

Mienczakowski, J. (2003). The theatre of ethnography: The reconstruction of ethnography theatre with emancipatory potential. In N. Denzin, & Y. Lincoln (Eds.), *Turning points in qualitative research: Tying knots in a handkerchief* (pp. 218–237). Thousand Oaks, CA: AltaMira Press.

Munhall, P. L. (1988). Ethical considerations in qualitative research. *Western Journal of Nursing Research, 10*(2), 150–162.

Nelson, G., & Prilleltensky, I. (Eds.) (2010). *Community psychology: In pursuit of liberation and well-being* (2nd ed.). Basingstoke: Palgrave Macmillan.

Newman, E., Willard, T., Sinclair, R., & Kaloupek, D. (2001). *The reactions to research participation questionnaire revised.* Retrieved from http://www.personal.utulsa.edu/~elana-newman/RRPQ-Rforpdf.pdf (accessed July 11, 2012).

Nietzsche, F. (1990). *Beyond good and evil.* London: Penguin.

Oakley, A. (1981). Interviewing women: A contradiction in terms. In H. Roberts (Ed.), *Doing feminist research* (pp. 30–61). London: RKP.

Salmon, P. (2003). How do we recognise good research? *The Psychologist, 16*(1), 24–27.

Sumner, P., Boy, F., & Chambers. C. (2011). Riot control: How can we stop newspapers distorting science? *The Guardian.* Retrieved from http://www.guardian.co.uk/science/blog/2011/aug/22/riot-control-newspapers-distorting-science (accessed July 13, 2015).

The Nuremberg Code (1947). The Nuremberg Code. Retrieved from http://www.hhs.gov/ohrp/archive/nurcode.html (accessed July 3, 2015).

Tufford, L., & Newman, P. (2012). Bracketing in qualitative research. *Qualitative Social Work, 11,* 80.

West, W. (2002). Some ethical dilemmas in counselling and counselling research. *British Journal of Guidance and Counselling, 30*(3), 261–268.

World Medical Association (n.d.). WMA Declaration of Helsinki—Ethical principles for medical research involving human subjects. Retrieved from www.wma.net/en/30publications/10policies/b3/index.html (accessed March 17, 2017).

Zimmer, M. (2010). "But the data is already public": On the ethics of research in Facebook. *Ethics and Information Technology, 12,* 313–325.

Qualitative Research in Counselling Psychology

JOHN MCLEOD

CHAPTER OUTLINE

INTRODUCTION 395

EPISTEMOLOGIES: WAYS OF KNOWING 395

GUIDING PRINCIPLES 397

WHAT QUESTIONS CAN BE ASKED
IN QUALITATIVE PSYCHOLOGICAL
RESEARCH? 398

KEY RESEARCH METHODS 399

SAMPLING 400

APPROACHES TO ANALYSING DATA 402

CONCLUSION 405

LEARNING OUTCOMES

BY THE END OF THIS CHAPTER YOU SHOULD BE ABLE TO ANSWER THE FOLLOWING KEY QUESTIONS:

1. What are the main philosophical and methodological perspectives underpinning qualitative research in counselling psychology?

2. What are the main issues and challenges associated with the use of qualitative methodologies?

3. What are the main ways in which knowledge from qualitative enquiry can inform the theory and practice of counselling psychology?

Counselling Psychology: A Textbook for Study and Practice, First Edition. Edited by David Murphy.
© 2017 John Wiley & Sons Ltd. Published 2017 by John Wiley & Sons Ltd.

INTRODUCTION

Qualitative research is concerned with the exploration of how meaning is constructed in people's lives, and how choices and actions are shaped by these meanings. Given that language is the primary means through which meaning is conveyed within a culture, qualitative research is therefore primarily based on an analysis of what people have to say. However, some research topics also call for attention to be paid to other forms of meaning-making, for example, through ritual and art objects. Because the practice of counselling psychology is closely tied to psychotherapeutic interventions that involve finding out about what events mean to people, and enabling them to construe these events in other ways, many practitioners regard qualitative research as having considerable relevance for practice.

Historically, the discipline of psychology has oriented itself towards experimental and quantitative methodologies. In contrast to psychology, where qualitative methodologies have only achieved acceptance within the past 20 years, qualitative approaches have been more influential and fully developed within allied disciplines such as sociology, social anthropology, education, and management, As a professional community that is committed to diversity and pluralism, counselling psychology has been one of the sub-disciplines of psychology within which the concept of methodological pluralism gained early support (Slife & Gantt, 1999). Methodological pluralism is a position within philosophy of science that acknowledges the potential value of both qualitative and quantitative methodologies. The social justice orientation of counselling psychology also finds a ready form of expression in qualitative inquiry. Counselling psychology has therefore represented one of the fields of applied psychology in which a tradition of qualitative enquiry has been most fully articulated.

Training in counselling psychology usually takes place following completion of a first degree in psychology, in which students may have been provided with intensive training in quantitative research design and statistics, and only minimal exposure to qualitative research. Some counselling psychology trainees and practitioners may therefore find it hard to appreciate the value of qualitative research, and may feel some awkwardness around aspects of qualitative methodology such as small sample sizes and the inevitable lack of precision arising from research designs that involve the interpretation of potentially ambiguous verbal data.

EPISTEMOLOGIES: WAYS OF KNOWING

Ultimately, qualitative and quantitative research methodologies are grounded in contrasting ways of knowing (McLeod, 2010). Quantitative research seeks to identify causal relationships between "variables" or "factors." For example, within the field of psychotherapy research, there have been many quantitative studies that have demonstrated that the establishment of a strong working alliance by the third session of therapy predicts eventual outcome. This kind of causal association comprises a general, law-like, if-then statement that can be further tested and refined in subsequent studies.

By contrast, qualitative research is grounded in a way of knowing that characterizes individuals and groups as purposeful human agents who are actively involved in making things happen. This is an important distinction. In quantitative research, it is the variables that have explanatory power. In qualitative research, people themselves (and the products of collective action, such as discourses) are regarded as possessing powers. Qualitative research around the topic of the therapist–client relationship does not seek to measure the strength or presence of an abstract entity such as an "alliance." Instead, qualitative researchers have engaged in studies that have looked at such topics as the ways in which clients make sense of the therapist–client relationship (Bachelor, 1995), therapist actions that clients regard as contributing to the development of a productive relationship (Bedi, Davis & Williams, 2005), or therapist strategies to build relationships with their clients (Oddli & McLeod, 2017).

The distinctive epistemological position expressed in qualitative research has been described and understood in different ways by various groups of researchers: constructivist, social constructionist, phenomenological, postmodern, and poststructuralist (Ponterotto, 2005). Although each of these philosophical stances has interesting and important things to say, they all share a concept of the person as a being who is a creative, storytelling meaning-maker who exists within a network of relationships, a culture, a historical tradition, and a language community. A further crucial aspect of this epistemological stance is its acknowledgement that people are reflexive beings, with the capacity to be aware of their own motivations and intentions.

These conceptual footings have significant implications for the way in which qualitative enquiry is conducted. Quantitative research is closely aligned with everyday, common-sense notions of objectivity, facticity, and truth. Qualitative research, on the other hand, goes against the grain of common sense, in its insistence that in human affairs, foundational objective truth is not possible. In its focus on language (slippery and ambiguous) rather than numbers, qualitative research runs the risk of entering the territory of fiction, conjecture, and anecdote. To be able to negotiate these challenges, it is necessary for qualitative researchers to be philosophically informed to an extent that is not required in quantitative research.

The most straightforward way to make sense of these ideas is through an appreciation that human beings have always been involved in debates around the meaning of events and ideas, and have developed strategies for facilitating this process. Three key strategies, which have existed for many hundreds of years, are hermeneutics, phenomenology, and rhetoric (McLeod, 2010, 2013). Hermeneutics refers to guidelines for achieving a comprehensive and convincing interpretation of the meaning of a text, such as the Bible, legal case papers, or a Shakespeare play. These guidelines are equally applicable to interpreting the meaning of an interview transcript in a qualitative research study.

Phenomenology is a philosophical method that refers to the process of arriving at the essential, hidden, or implicit meaning of an experience, through the activity of "bracketing-off" assumptions, leading to the possibility of constructing a richly nuanced description of an experience. Applied to qualitative research, a phenomenological perspective enables a researcher to identify multiple implicit meanings in an interview transcript. The analysis of rhetoric (how language is used to persuade people of the truth of an argument) represents a further ancient philosophical tradition that is highly relevant to contemporary qualitative research. For example, an understanding of language structures might make it possible for a researcher to see that a research informant was not merely trying to report on their experience of recovering from depression, but was doing so in a way that made use of a cultural narrative about the meaning of being a man (or woman) in a particular culture.

GUIDING PRINCIPLES

The epistemic stance that informs qualitative research can be seen as generating a number of underlying principles that guide the work of qualitative researchers. Some of the main guiding principles are shown in the text box below.

Naturalistic enquiry: studying real-world phenomena in as unobtrusive a manner as possible, with a sense of open-ness to whatever emerges.

Inductive analysis: allowing conclusions to arise from a process of immersion in the data, rather than imposing categories or theories decided in advance. A willingness on the part of the researcher to "bracket-off" his or her assumptions about the phenomena being studied.

Human agency: research participants are viewed as purposefully involved in co-creating their social worlds.

Awareness of uniqueness: willingness to respect the particular configuration of individual cases even when developing general conclusions.

Contextual awareness: findings can only be understood within a social, cultural, historical, and environmental context.

Design flexibility: within a study, methods and procedures are adapted in response to new circumstances and experiences.

Reflexivity: the idea that the researcher is his or her primary instrument, and as a result must be aware of the assumptions, expectations, and needs that his or her participation introduces to the research process.

In any particular study, the relative salience of each of these principles will depend on the goals of the research, and the particular qualitative methodology that is being adopted.

In practice, it has been found useful to translate these guiding principles into procedures for assessing the validity of qualitative research studies. Within the quantitative tradition in psychological research, it is relatively straightforward to determine the robustness and credibility of the data yielded by a measure; for example, by drawing on well-understood statistical procedures for analysing different types of validity and reliability. Establishing the plausibility and practical utility of qualitative research requires the application of specific criteria and procedures, relevant to this form of enquiry (Elliott, Fischer, & Rennie, 1999;

Stiles, 1993). For example, in order to demonstrate that the principle of inductive analysis has been followed, it is usual in qualitative reports to supply the reader with sufficient examples of qualitative data (e.g., segments of interview transcript) to allow them to arrive at their own interpretation of the material. To demonstrate the principle of reflexivity, it is usual for a qualitative article to include a section in which the researcher (or all members of the research team) provides information about their own pre-expectations and their experience of conducting the study.

WHAT QUESTIONS CAN BE ASKED IN QUALITATIVE PSYCHOLOGICAL RESEARCH?

Qualitative research is primarily exploratory, descriptive, and discovery-oriented, rather than seeking to test or confirm hypotheses (McCaslin & Scott, 2003; McLeod, 2014). As a result, the questions that can be asked in qualitative psychological research need to reflect this epistemological stance. For example, a quantitative study into the effectiveness of therapy might be framed in terms of the impact of cognitive-behavioural therapy (CBT) on depression, or a prediction that therapy would be expected to be more effective than a waiting list condition. By contrast, qualitative research into the effectiveness of therapy is based on a more open-ended question, such as exploring the experiences of clients who have received CBT for depression, or the metaphors used to describe the experience of being on a waiting list.

Qualitative methods can be applied to a wide range of research topics. It can be helpful to consider the process of psychotherapy in terms of three units of scale: macro, mid-range, and micro. Macro-level studies explore the social, cultural, and historical context within which therapy takes place. Examples of this type of study include the analysis into the emergence of psychotherapy in the USA through the 19th and early 20th centuries (Cushman, 1995) and the study by McGivern and Fischer (2012) of the strategies used by therapists in the UK for dealing with government regulation of the profession. Mid-range studies examine the experience of therapy for participants. This type of research includes interview-based explorations of the experience of either clients or therapists, and has contributed the largest proportion of qualitative studies in the psychotherapy literature. Typical questions that have been pursued at this level of analysis include: What do clients find helpful/unhelpful in the therapy they receive? How do clients experience various aspects of the therapeutic relationship? What have therapists learned from working with a particular client group? What do therapists find helpful or unhelpful in clinical supervision? Micro-level investigations consider moment-by-moment processes. Some micro-level studies involve the use of structured interviews that focus on specific therapy processes, such as the research carried out by Angus and Rennie (1988) into the client's experience of metaphor. Other micro-level studies are based on detailed analysis of patterns of language within therapy session transcript data, such as the study carried out by Fitzgerald and Leudar (2010) into active listening in solution-focused therapy. Each of these units of analysis presents distinctive opportunities and challenges for qualitative therapy researchers, and is associated with the use of specific methods for gathering and analysing data.

KEY RESEARCH METHODS

It is possible to identify four main approaches to collecting qualitative data: interviews that explore the experience of therapy; written documents; observation; and reflection of personal experience.

Many studies have used semi-structured interviews, based on an interview guide that allows the informant to explore different facets of their personal lived experience of a particular topic. This methodology represents a flexible approach to data collection that can yield rich data. The disadvantage of interview methods is that they are time consuming, in respect of not only needing to meet with informants, but also in relation to transcribing audio recordings of interviews. The information provided in an interview is always to a greater or lesser extent shaped by the quality of the relationship between interviewer and interviewee, around such factors as trust, gender, status difference, and ethnicity. An alternative approach to data collection is to collect written texts, in the form of client diaries, letters and autobiographies, responses to open-ended questionnaires, and material shared online through internet chatrooms. Such data come "ready to analyse." An advantage of textual data is that, other than diaries kept for research purposes, they are less reactive to researcher influence. On the other hand, the absence of opportunity to seek clarification through questioning means that it can be hard to interpret the meaning of the data that have been collected.

A further source of qualitative data comprises observation of therapy, through audio or video recordings of sessions, or ethnographic participant observation of the lives of clients or therapists. This approach represents a highly time-intensive and complex methodological choice. For example, an hour of audio recording might take at least 8 hr to transcribe. However, there are a numerous session transcripts that are available in the public domain that can be used for research purposes. Video observation of therapy sessions yields material that is fascinating and impactful, but difficult to analyse because of the complexity of the interactional processes that become apparent. Examples of ethnographic observational studies of psychotherapy, and the possibilities associated with this approach, can be found in McLeod (2010).

The use of personal experience as data has emerged in recent years as an increasingly influential mode of data collection. Autoethnography is a form of qualitative enquiry that uses *auto*biographical investigation and writing on the part of the researcher to explore wider cultural themes (*ethnography*) (Muncey, 2010). The advantage of autoethnography is that it allows a topic to be explored in much depth, through the process of opening up and articulating the experience of a person whose life experience has allowed them to be a powerful witness to at least some aspects of that topic. A good example of the potential of this approach can be found in the analysis of the experience of pregnancy loss written by Scheach Leith (2009), which arguably goes well beyond anything that could be generated through the application of an interview methodology. The limitations of autoethnography are that it is emotionally demanding to carry out, and personally exposing in what is written, and that it is hard to achieve a narrative balance that description of personal experience (as in a novel) alongside academic rigour.

Different qualitative data collection approaches can be combined in a variety of ways. Strong and Turner (2008) observed therapy interaction using video, analysed the video in order to identify key moments when client strengths and resources were mobilized, and then interviewed clients and therapists about what they had been thinking and feeling during these segments of the sessions. There are also valuable possibilities around mixed-method research that combines qualitative and quantitative approaches to data collection. On the basis of prior analysis of quantitative outcome data, Hansen, Lambert, and Vass (2015) were able to identify a particular therapist who achieved exceptionally positive outcomes with clients. Qualitative interviews were then conducted with some of the clients of that therapist, to explore the attributes that enabled such unusual outcomes to be achieved.

SAMPLING

One of the most striking differences between qualitative and quantitative approaches to research lies in the domain of sampling. In general, in statistical analysis, the larger the sample size, the better. Large samples make it easier to argue that the sample that has been collected is representative of the total population of cases, and also allow for the application of more sophisticated and powerful forms of statistical analysis. In recent years, data mining analyses of real-world data sets have made use of samples of several thousand clients. By contrast, most qualitative research is based on samples of between one and 15 cases. The key methodological rationale for this difference is that qualitative methods aim to carry out *intensive* analysis of patterns that occur within individual cases, whereas quantitative studies are predominantly oriented towards *extensive* analysis of specific variable across large numbers of cases, for example, through group comparisons. However, there are also practical considerations: it is extremely hard for a researcher to handle the complexity entailed by intensive analysis. In qualitative research, there is a risk that reports based on large samples lose the nuanced and detailed representation of individual experience.

Qualitative research tends to be based on the recruitment of a sample of individuals who are able to report on a particular type of lived experience, such as being a client in psychodynamic therapy, or being a therapist who has experiences of impasse with clients. Within that sample, it then makes sense to try to recruit informants who might tell different stories—for instance, clients who vary in their satisfaction with psychodynamic therapy, or therapists from different theoretical orientations. In many qualitative studies, sampling is theoretically informed. For example, if the aim is to explore client experiences of the helpfulness of psychodynamic therapy, it is necessary to interview those who have benefitted from it alongside other who have been disappointed. On the other hand, if a similar study was motivated by an interest in cultural factors, it would be necessary to recruit informants from different ethnic groups. Sometimes, theoretical sampling can emerge during the course of a study. For instance, if early interviews reveal that educational level makes a difference to client receptiveness to psychodynamic therapy, then it may be worthwhile to find another one or two informants who have theoretically interesting profiles in respect of this.

In a qualitative study, the issue of sampling is also associated with considerable practical challenges around actually finding the sample. If the design of the study requires participants to make a time commitment, through being interviewed or keeping a diary, not everyone will be willing to do this. If the design is shaped by theoretical considerations (such as educational level), how does the researcher find participants with the necessary backgrounds? Some qualitative studies use a snowballing recruitment technique, where the first interviews are carried out with individuals who are available within the social or professional network of the researcher, who are then asked to nominate other potential informants. In some studies, a general call for participants is made through email, leaflets, or posters, and then those who respond are screened through a brief pre-interview or questionnaire. In some therapy clinics, all clients may be asked at intake if they are in principle willing to be contacted after the end of their therapy, to be invited for interview.

Decisions around sample size and participant attributes may also reflect the approach to data analysis that has been adopted. Interpretative Phenomenological Analysis (IPA; Smith, Flowers, & Larkin, 2009) is a methodology for analysing interview data that has the aim of identifying individual difference and diversity, as well as common themes. By contrast, similar methodologies such as grounded theory (Charmaz, 2013), and Consensual Qualitative Research (CQR) (Hill, 2012) are more focused on arriving at general themes. As a result, IPA studies tend to be based on smaller sample sizes (one to six informants), to allow individual cases to be reported in some detail in the analysis. By contrast, grounded theory and CQR tend to use larger samples, in which contrast between individual informants gets washed out. Conversation Analysis (CA; Perakyla, Antaki, Vehvilainen, & Leudar, 2008) is a qualitative methodology that enables micro-analysis of interactional processes and language use in conversation, such as therapist–client discourse. This type of analysis yields highly detailed accounts of quite brief segments of transcript data. It is not feasible to conduct such analyses on large samples, and even if it were, the resulting report would not be readable. As a consequence, the methodological assumptions that underpin CA lead to studies that use relatively small numbers of cases.

It is not easy to use qualitative methodologies to carry out comparative studies; for example, investigating differences in how male and female clients make sense of therapy. Clearly, comparison group studies represent a central focus of quantitative research, because it is a straightforward matter to compare groups in terms of their quantitative scores on a measure, and determine whether the difference is significant. In qualitative research, it is much harder to know, when making comparisons, whether verbal descriptions and themes generated by different groups have the same meaning. For example, if male interviewees talk about their therapy is terms of "winning the battle against depression," while female clients talk about "learning to accept my own needs," are they talking about different things, or can both of these ways of talking be understood as referring to an underlying similar theme of helpful therapy? Comparative qualitative research therefore requires very careful sampling and analysis. A good example of how this can be achieved can be found in Nilsson, Svensson, Sandell, and Clinton (2007).

A key take-home message, in relation to the issue of sampling in qualitative research, is that some degree of pragmatic compromise is always necessary. An important implication of this insight is that it is necessary, when writing a qualitative dissertation or research article, to pay close critical attention to the possible ways in which the recruitment of participants has shaped the findings that emerged from the study, and to be highly cautious in making generalizations based on findings. In qualitative research, it is only possible to make limited inferences around the likely frequency of occurrence of a finding. For example, interviewing 12 clients who have received psychodynamic therapy and finding that 10 of them were satisfied with treatment does not provide solid grounds for concluding that this form of therapy is successful 83% of the time. However, if the same interviews have identified a pattern in which even a relatively small proportion of clients report a mix of disappointment and satisfaction (von Below & Werbart, 2012), then the existence of the phenomenon of client disappointment has been established—how extensively this pattern is found within the overall population of psychodynamic clients requires a different type of study. In other words, qualitative research is a relatively powerful approach in respect of producing generalizable themes, patterns, and concepts, but a relatively weak (but nevertheless not wholly worthless) approach in relation to determining extent or frequency of occurrence.

APPROACHES TO ANALYSING DATA

The aim of qualitative enquiry is to contribute to building an understanding of how the meaning and significance of some aspect of social life is constructed. The notion of "making a contribution" represents a crucial aspect of qualitative research, in serving as an acknowledgement that some degree of understanding will always exist before the study, and further layers of understanding will inevitably be added at some future time. In addition, it is highly likely that other persons, groups, and cultural traditions will contribute additional understandings. A qualitative research study can therefore be viewed as comprising one statement or one voice within an ongoing multi-person conversation.

In building an understanding of an aspect of the experience or activity of therapy, it can be helpful to think in terms of three distinct yet overlapping ways of working with data: description, analysis, and interpretation. A common thread across all of these activities is the notion of "condensation." In the end, any way of making sense of qualitative data requires the condensation of perhaps hundreds of pages of text into some kind of much briefer summary representation of what that text has to say to us.

Qualitative description seeks to convey what is there, or what was said, with as few assumptions as possible (Sandelowski, 2000). Methodological approaches that focus primarily on description include qualitative content analysis (Hsieh & Shannon, 2005) and empirical phenomenology (Churchill, 2013). In the context of qualitative research, analysis consists of finding or identifying patterns of meaning, in terms of recurring themes or categories. There are many methodological approaches that have the goal of producing analytic accounts of interview transcripts or other forms of qualitative data. In the field of psychotherapy and counselling psychology, the most widely utilized of these are grounded theory (Charmaz, 2013), CQR (Hill, 2012), and thematic analysis (Braun & Clarke, 2006).

Beyond description and analysis, it is also possible to apply an interpretative frame, and make sense of qualitative data in relation to an existing theoretical perspective such as psychoanalysis or linguistic theory. Most qualitative research that incorporates a theoretical dimension tends to follow the rule that discussing the data in theoretical terms needs to follow, rather than precede, description and analysis. This kind of methodological sequence can be found in IPA (Smith, Flowers, & Larkin, 2009). A limited role for theory in the early stages of working with data can be found in CQR (Hill, 2012) in the form of using prior concepts and research as sensitizing constructs. The rationale for being cautious around using pre-existing theory is that it can lead to results that look suspiciously as though the researcher found what he or she expected to find, rather than giving a sense of genuine open-ness to new meanings. However, CA (Perakyla et al., 2008) provides many examples of ways in which pre-existing concepts (in this instance, from linguistic theory) can be used to open up new understandings of the co-construction of meaning and action within therapy discourse.

An important aspect of the process of working with qualitative data consists of the position taken by the researcher in relation to reflexivity (Finlay & Gough, 2003). Some researchers pay minimal attention to the ways in which their subjectivity shapes their understanding of data, while others embrace their personal response to data as a potential route toward arriving at a deeper and more nuanced analysis. At the present time, there is no consensus within the qualitative research community around how to handle the issue of researcher reflexivity.

In practical terms, qualitative analysis requires a willingness to become immersed in the data, in order to allow different meanings to emerge. The procedures for data description, analysis, and interpretation that are associated with different qualitative methodologies, such as grounded theory, IPA, and other approaches, can be regarded as alternative structures for ensuring that a sufficiently disciplined form of immersion takes place. Some qualitative researchers find it helpful to use software packages such as NVivo to assist in this process (Leech & Onwuegbuzie, 2011), while others prefer to work with paper documents or display techniques such as post-it notes.

The process of making sense of qualitative data needs to be informed by, and go hand-in-hand with, a process for evaluating the validity, rigour, or credibility of the findings that are being generated. Increasingly, qualitative researchers use independent external auditors, such as colleagues or research participants, to read their findings and check whether they are consistent with the data. Another useful validity check involves carrying out an analysis then conducting one or two additional interviews to test whether they yield the same themes. In some forms of qualitative research it may be possible to make large segments of the data, such as interview transcripts, available to readers of the research, so they can make up their own minds whether the findings match the data.

AN EXAMPLE OF A QUALITATIVE RESEARCH STUDY

A study by Pugach and Goodman (2015) provides a good example of the potential value of qualitative research within the field of counselling and psychotherapy. In this piece of research, Pugach and Goodman (2015) interviewed 10 low-income women in the USA about their experience of therapy, with a particular focus on what they had found helpful or unhelpful. This is a beautifully written study that is easy to follow and theoretically interesting, as well as opening up further reflection on implications for training and practice. It is also, in giving voice to the views of a disadvantaged group, a study that supports the commitment of counselling psychology to the promotion of social justice.

While the structure of the Pugach and Goodman (2015) study follows standard APA style, it illustrates some of creative ways in which that format can be adapted for the purpose of reporting qualitative findings. The introduction to the paper invites the reader to reflect on the experience of being a low-income woman, before moving on to consider some of the ways in which feminist theory can form a bridge between the life challenges faced by such women, and the practice of therapy. This introductory material creates a context in which it is readily appreciated that it is both necessary and possible to learn from the experiences of low-income women who have received therapy.

The conduct of the study reflects an informed sensitivity to the needs of the research participants, for example, in respect of such matters as where interviews were conducted, how participants were recruited, and the design of an interview guide. The reflexive involvement of the researchers is carefully explained, both in terms of their professional identity and pre-understandings, and their way of working together to make sense of the data.

A form of qualitative description was used, in order to stay close to the experiences of participants. This approach to data condensation produced eight clusters of meaning, within three broad descriptive domains (*awareness*, *practices*, and *relational quality*). The key findings of the study were summarized as:

within the domain of Awareness, participants found therapy to be meaningful and effective when the therapist: (1) was aware of the nature of poverty and poverty-related stressors, and (2) had some sort of direct exposure to poverty. Within the domain of Practices, participants described therapy as useful when the therapist: (3) demonstrated flexibility, (4) provided instrumental support, and (5) emphasized building strengths. Within the domain of Relational Quality, participants found therapy to be meaningful when the therapist: (6) really listened to the clients—without judgment, (7) attempted to share power, and (8) demonstrated authenticity.

(Pugach and Goodman, 2015, p. 403).

Within the Results section of the paper, each of these areas was presented through a descriptive account of clients' experiences, illustrated by excerpts from interviews.

The Pugach and Goodman (2015) study offers an example of the kind of research that could be achieved by a postgraduate student or a group of practitioners. It is clear that it provides a sensible, insightful, and balanced contribution to evidence-based training and practice in this area of work.

CONCLUSION

The experience of conducting qualitative research can reinforce skills, such as empathic engagement and interpretation of unclear meaning, that are central to therapy practice (Thorpe, 2013). Qualitative research also represents an effective way to carry out good-quality small-scale studies on topics that are of interest to clinicians and trainees. Within the overall landscape of psychotherapy research, qualitative methodologies are able to explore topics that are not readily accessible to quantitative approaches, and offer a critical counter-balance to prevailing theory and practice, in ways that enable the profession to be open to new perspectives. A crucial aspect of the role of qualitative enquiry is associated with its capacity to give voice to the experience of marginalized and silenced individuals and communities, and draw attention to power dynamics within professional practice.

The growing acceptance of qualitative methodologies in the field of counselling psychology, and allied disciplines, means that researchers can access a rich array of learning resources, and can publish their work in a wide range of journals. Relevant current developments in qualitative research are highlighted in two main journals: *Qualitative Research in Psychology* and *Qualitative Psychology*. The expansion in the number of qualitative articles that are published has meant that qualitative meta-analysis or meta-synthesis has emerged as a crucial area for recent and further development. In the domain of quantitative outcome research over the past 30 years, the publication of meta-analytic reviews has had the effect of establishing quality standards for research that is carried out, while at the same time providing policy makers with robust knowledge updates that they could use to inform evidence-based practice. Until recently, the reach of qualitative research has been fragmented and patchy, with the result that it has been hard to promote this kind of knowledge as a reliable source of knowledge that could feed into policy decisions. However, this situation is beginning to change, with the consequence that systematic qualitative enquiry is beginning to have more of an impact in terms of shaping the future of the profession.

SUGGESTED FURTHER READING

Fischer, C. T. (Ed.) (2006). *Qualitative research methods for psychologists: Introduction through empirical examples.* New York: Academic Press.
Leading qualitative researchers go "behind the scenes" to explain their work.

McLeod, J. (2010). *Qualitative research in counselling and psychotherapy* (2nd ed.). London: Sage. Comprehensive overview of how different qualitative approaches can be applied in the development of new knowledge in counselling and psychotherapy.

Minichiello, V., & Kottler, J. A. (Eds.) (2010). *Qualitative journeys: Student and mentor experiences with research.* Thousand Oaks, CA: Sage.
What it is like to carry out a qualitative study—students and their supervisors share their experience of using different qualitative methodologies.

REFERENCES

Angus, L. E., & Rennie, D. L. (1988). Therapist participation in metaphor generation, collaborative and noncollaborative styles. *Psychotherapy, 25,* 552–560.

Bachelor, A. (1995). Clients perception of the therapeutic alliance, a qualitative analysis. *Journal of Counseling Psychology, 42,* 323–337.

Bedi, R. P., Davis, M. D., & Williams, M. (2005). Critical incidents in the formation of the therapeutic alliance from the client's perspective. *Psychotherapy: Theory, Research, Practice, Training, 41,* 311–323.

Braun, V., & Clarke, V. (2006). Using thematic analysis in psychology. *Qualitative Research in Psychology, 3,* 77–101.

Charmaz, K. (2013). *Constructing grounded theory* (2nd ed.). Thousand Oaks, CA: Sage.

Churchill, S. D. (2006). Phenomenological analysis: Impression formation during a clinical assessment interview. In C. T. Fischer (Ed.), *Qualitative research methods for psychologists: Introduction through empirical examples* (pp. 79–110). New York: Academic Press.

Cushman, P. (1995). *Constructing the self, constructing America: A cultural history of psychotherapy.* Reading, MA: Addison-Wesley.

Elliott, R., Fischer, C. T., & Rennie, D. L. (1999). Evolving guidelines for the publication of qualitative research studies in psychology and related fields. *British Journal of Clinical Psychology, 38,* 215–229.

Finlay, L., & Gough, B. (Eds.) (2003). *Reflexivity: A practical guide for researchers in health and social sciences.* Oxford: Blackwell.

Fitzgerald, P., & Leudar, I. (2010). On active listening in person-centred, solution-focused psychotherapy. *Journal of Pragmatics, 42,* 3188–3198.

Hansen, B., Lambert, M., & Vass, E. (2015). Sudden gains and sudden losses in the clients of a "supershrink": 10 case studies. *Pragmatic Case Studies in Psychotherapy, 11,* 154–201.

Hill, C. E. (Ed.) (2012). *Consensual qualitative research. A practical resource for investigating social science phenomena.* Washington, DC: American Psychological Association.

Hsieh, H., & Shannon, S. (2005). Three approaches to qualitative content analysis. *Qualitative Health Research, 15,* 1277–1288.

Leech, N. L., & Onwuegbuzie, A. J. (2011). Beyond constant comparison in qualitative data analysis: Using NVivo. *School Psychology Quarterly, 26,* 70–84.

McCaslin, M. L., & Scott, K. W. (2003). The five-question method for framing a qualitative research study. *The Qualitative Report, 8,* 447–461.

McGivern, G., & Fischer, M. D. (2012). Reactivity and reactions to regulatory transparency in medicine, psychotherapy and counseling. *Social Science and Medicine, 74*, 289–296.

McLeod, J. (2010). *Qualitative research in counselling and psychotherapy* (2nd ed.). London: Sage.

McLeod, J. (2013). Qualitative research: Methods and contributions. In M. J. Lambert (Ed.), *Bergin and Garfield's handbook of psychotherapy and behavior change* (5th ed, pp. 49–84). New York: Wiley.

McLeod, J. (2014). *Doing research in counselling and psychotherapy* (2nd ed.). London: Sage.

Muncey, T. (2010). *Creating autoethnographies*. London: Sage.

Nilsson, T., Svensson, M., Sandell, R., & Clinton, D. (2007). Patients' experiences of change on cognitive-behavioral therapy and psychodynamic therapy: A qualitative comparative study. *Psychotherapy Research, 17*, 553–566.

Oddli, H. W., & McLeod, J. (2017, in press). Knowing-in-relation: How experienced therapists integrate different sources of knowledge in actual clinical practice. *Journal of Psychotherapy Integration*.

Perakyla, A., Antaki, C., Vehvilainen, S., & Leudar, I. (Eds.) (2008). *Conversation analysis and psychotherapy*. Cambridge: Cambridge University Press.

Ponterotto, J. G. (2005). Qualitative research in counseling psychology: A primer on research paradigms and philosophy of science. *Journal of Counseling Psychology, 52*, 126–136.

Pugach, M. R., & Goodman, L. A. (2015). Low-income women's experiences in outpatient psychotherapy: A qualitative descriptive analysis. *Counselling Psychology Quarterly, 28*, 403–426.

Sandelowski, M. (2000). Whatever happened to qualitative descriptive? *Research in Nursing and Health, 23*, 234–340.

Sheach Leith, V. M. (2009). The search for meaning after pregnancy loss: An autoethnography. *Illness, Crisis and Loss, 17*, 201–221.

Slife, B. D., & Gantt, E. E. (1999). Methodological pluralism: A framework for psychotherapy research. *Journal of Clinical Psychology, 55*, 1453–1465.

Smith, J. A., Flowers, P., & Larkin, M. (2009). *Interpretative phenomenological analysis: Theory, method and research*. London: Sage.

Stiles, W. B. (1993). Quality control in qualitative research. *Clinical Psychology Review, 13*, 593–618.

Strong, T., & Turner, K. (2008). Resourceful dialogues: Eliciting and mobilizing client competencies and resources. *Journal of Contemporary Psychotherapy, 38*, 185–195.

Thorpe, M. R. (2013). The process of conducting qualitative research as an adjunct to the development of therapeutic abilities in counselling psychology. *New Zealand Journal of Psychology, 42*, 35–43.

von Below, C., & Werbart, A. (2012). Dissatisfied psychotherapy patients: A tentative conceptual model grounded in the participant's view. *Psychoanalytic Psychotherapy, 26*, 211–229.

Quantitative Research in Counselling Psychology

DUNCAN CRAMER

CHAPTER OUTLINE

INTRODUCTION 409

WHY USE QUANTITATIVE RESEARCH METHODS? 409

GUIDING PRINCIPLES AND CORE METHODOLOGICAL ASSUMPTIONS 411

MAJOR TYPES OF EXPERIMENTAL DESIGNS 412

QUESTIONS THAT CAN BE ASKED IN QUANTITATIVE PSYCHOLOGICAL RESEARCH 413

KEY RESEARCH METHODS 414

SAMPLING 416

SAMPLE RESEARCH STUDY EXAMPLE 420

CONCLUSION 422

Counselling Psychology: A Textbook for Study and Practice, First Edition. Edited by David Murphy.
© 2017 John Wiley & Sons Ltd. Published 2017 by John Wiley & Sons Ltd.

LEARNING OUTCOMES

BY THE END OF THIS CHAPTER YOU SHOULD BE ABLE TO ANSWER THE FOLLOWING KEY QUESTIONS:

1. What are the main objectives that the quantitative research approach to counselling psychology is trying to achieve?

2. What are the key ideas underlying the quantitative research approach to counselling psychology?

3. What are the major considerations for determining the empirical validity of therapeutic processes underpinning counselling psychology?

INTRODUCTION

You may be interested in studying counselling psychology because you want to help people who have psychological problems. Initially you may have expected that there would have been general agreement on how to do this and that you would be taught what this was. However, you may soon have realized that there does not appear to be any such consensus and that there is a variety of different approaches which at first sight do not seem to be easily reconcilable. For example, in some approaches, such as the person-centred one, the counsellor appears to be nondirective in that they do not tell the client or patient what they should do, whereas others, such as cognitive-behavioural ones, seem to be directive in that the counsellor instructs the client or patient on what they should do. How do we decide which approach we should follow? Do we adopt what our instructors recommend we do if they do indeed recommend a particular approach? Do we simply choose that approach which makes most sense to us or which we feel most comfortable with? Do we select the approach that seems to have the most advocates or practitioners? Or do we attempt to make a decision in terms of which approach seems to have the most and the strongest empirical support? If we decide that this last option is the best procedure to take, then we need to know what empirical support is and how to evaluate it. One kind of empirical support is quantitative research.

WHY USE QUANTITATIVE RESEARCH METHODS?

Research on counselling psychology (and relevant topics) aims to help further our understanding of the processes that underlie them. Most of this research is quantitative rather than qualitative. In order to understand the results of this substantial body of work and to be able to critically evaluate its contribution to this field, it is essential to have as sound a knowledge of the nature of quantitative research as possible. Ideally, you need to be able to understand the method and results sections of research papers in order to determine whether the aims of the research have been appropriately met by the way the research had been conducted and reported, and, if not, whether it could have been done, and if so, how this should have been done.

Quantitative research is generally concerned with answering two main types of question. One type of question is how common one or more characteristics are in a particular defined population of units such as people. For example, we may wish to know what percentage of psychotherapists and counsellors working in the UK are female or what are the most common counselling psychology approaches used. This kind of research is relatively uncommon because it requires obtaining a random or representative sample of the designated population, a process that is usually time-consuming and costly. The second type of question concerns whether one characteristic or variable is related to one or more other characteristics or variables. For example, we may want to know whether patients or clients who feel more understood by their counselling psychologist are more likely to show greater psychological improvement than those who feel less well understood. Or we may wish to determine whether patients or clients who receive psychotherapy or counselling demonstrate greater psychological improvement than those who receive a drug treatment. Most quantitative research is of this second kind in which a convenient, and not a random or representative, sample of individuals is chosen to participate but where it is assumed that the findings obtained generally apply to the population in question. If the findings are not considered to be representative of the population, then the reason or rationale for this needs to be stated and ultimately tested.

Ideally and importantly, this second kind of quantitative research should test relationships of theoretical interest. It should not be sufficient to justify your research by saying that you were simply interested in whether two or more variables were related to one another. For instance, it should not suffice to state merely that you wanted to see whether patients or clients who felt better understood by their counselling psychologist were more likely to show greater psychological improvement. It is essential to provide a strong theoretical rationale as to why this may be the case. For example, it may be proposed, as Rogers (1959) has done, that individuals who are psychologically distressed do not understand themselves. Being understood by significant others helps them to understand themselves better and so become less psychologically disturbed. It may be useful to contrast a particular theoretical perspective, such as this one, with other psychological approaches, such as the behavioural approach, which seemingly puts less emphasis on the patient or client feeling understood because a change in behaviour does not require a corresponding change in self-understanding. Providing a careful theoretical rationale for what you do should suggest what other variables should be measured. For example, if it is thought that how much the patient or client understands themselves is an important part of the process, then it is important to assess this variable. In other words, quantitative research should not be "mindless empiricism."

Nonetheless, quantitative research that may appear to be primarily undertaken for its practical value may be of considerable theoretical interest. For example, clinical evaluation studies of the relative effectiveness of systematic desensitization compared with implosion or flooding (e.g., Gelder et al., 1973) have helped to question whether the theoretical principle of reciprocal inhibition (Wolpe, 1990) is necessary for phobias to be extinguished.

The findings of any well-conceived and conducted study are generally held to be valid. If there are problems with the study's design or its execution, these problems should be corrected and the study rerun. Further studies should usually seek to answer questions that the original study did not address. There is little point in simply repeating a study as it was originally conducted because the results will be either the same or different. Either outcome will not by itself tell us why the particular results occurred. So, simple replication is of itself not very informative other than to let us know how replicable the findings are. The results of studies using similar designs and variables often vary. Where a number of such studies have been carried out, it may be possible to combine their results in a meta-analysis to give a better estimate of the size and likelihood of a particular finding and to determine to what extent this finding may be affected by other factors that have also been measured in these studies, such as the mean age of the samples.

GUIDING PRINCIPLES AND CORE METHODOLOGICAL ASSUMPTIONS

Surprisingly, one of the main difficulties for researchers new to quantitative research in carrying out such research is not the quantitative analysis of the data but is not having a clear idea of the idea they are trying to test. Without a good grasp of what the main research questions are, it is difficult to design, analyse, and write up a study appropriately. Consequently, it is essential to state in writing at or near the outset of the research what the main research questions are and how they are to be answered by the research. As you conduct the research and continue to think about it, the research questions will most probably need to be revised and modified as they become clearer to you. Formulating quantitative research is a creative process where what you are trying to do may not always be immediately obvious. You also need to make sure that the research questions can be justified in terms of the previous literature on the topic and to be quite clear what the original contribution is that the research is trying to make to the theoretical understanding of the topic or to the practice of counselling psychology. Any contribution is usually a modest one that builds in a small way on similar previous research. Ideally, it is a good idea to write down what you are thinking of doing in the form of a research proposal. This proposal should remind you of what your original ideas were and should help you to write the final report once the research has been completed as much of the work has already been done.

The recommended way of formulating a research question is to state it in terms of a hypothesis. The hypothesis describes the relationship between the variables that are being tested. It is often referred to as the prediction of what you expect the results to be if certain theoretical assumptions hold. In order to better understand and to evaluate a quantitative research report, it is important to know what the research hypotheses are. These should be briefly stated in the report summary or abstract, and outlined more fully in the introduction section of the report. In a formal description of the statistical analysis, the research hypothesis is contrasted with the null hypothesis, which simply postulates there is no relationship between the variables. As the null hypothesis is not very informative, there is no need to state it explicitly. In most quantitative research you should have a clear idea of the direction the results should take if certain theoretical assumptions hold and which way they should go if those theoretical assumptions do not hold or other theoretical assumptions hold.

A theoretical explanation usually implies that one variable affects or causes another variable or that both variables affect each other. For example, Rogerian person-centred theory postulates that the patient's or client's perception of the counselling psychologist as understanding them leads to greater self-understanding, which in turn leads to greater psychological improvement (Rogers, 1959). Whether or not the hypothesis is stated in a causal or a noncausal way should strictly speaking depend on the design of the study. Hypotheses should only be stated in a causal fashion if the design is a true or randomized experiment (Campbell & Stanley, 1963; Shadish, Cook & Campbell, 2002).

MAJOR TYPES OF EXPERIMENTAL DESIGNS

A true or randomized study is one in which only the presumed causal variables are manipulated; all other major variables are held constant and participants are randomly assigned to either the different conditions in a between-subjects design, or to the different orders of those conditions in a within-subjects design. A between-subjects design is one in which each subject or participant is randomly assigned to only one of the conditions. A within-subjects design is one in which each subject or participant undergoes all the conditions and is randomly assigned to one of the possible orders of those conditions. If there is a statistically significant difference between conditions, then this difference is most likely due to the manipulated variable as all other factors have been held constant. Caution should always be exercised in interpreting a particular observed difference as this difference may be due not to what was intended to be the manipulation, but to one or more other variables that were inadvertently manipulated at the same time.

Designs other than true or randomized ones are known as nonexperiments or quasi-experiments. The most common kind of nonexperiment is a cross-sectional study, where all variables are measured at a similar point in time. Causality cannot be determined in these designs because any assumed causal variables have not been manipulated independently of other variables. Authors of non- or quasi-experiments sometimes describe their study as if they had carried out a true or randomized experiment but doing this is incorrect and misleading.

QUESTIONS THAT CAN BE ASKED IN QUANTITATIVE PSYCHOLOGICAL RESEARCH

There are many questions that can be asked in quantitative psychological research. In this brief section only a few of these can be discussed and illustrated. These questions partly build on what has already been outlined. The kind of question that can be asked depends on the nature and design of the study. In representative surveys, the incidence and prevalence of various behaviours (such as psychological disorders and their treatment) occurring in a specified population (such as the USA) can be estimated (e.g., Stinson et al., 2007).

In cross-sectional and longitudinal studies the direction and size of the association between two or more variables can be assessed, such as the relation between presumed therapeutic factors and psychological health and improvement (e.g., Rogers, Gendlin, Kiesler, & Truax, 1967). The extent to which the direction and size of any association is statistically related to other variables, such as the degree to which the association between therapeutic factors and psychological adjustment at a later point in therapy may be related to or affected by earlier psychological adjustment (e.g., Murphy & Cramer, 2014), may also be investigated. Statistically controlling for other variables may affect the size and possible direction of any association. Controlling for other variables may increase the size of an association, implying that the original relationship may be suppressed or hidden due to the variable or variables being statistically controlled. Alternatively, statistically controlling for other variables may decrease the size of an association, suggesting that the original association may be partly or wholly spurious and due to the variable or variables being statistically controlled. Under some circumstances the direction of the association itself may be reversed making interpretation of the association difficult (Cramer, 2003).

The extent to which variables (such as putative therapeutic factors) are related to an outcome (such as psychological adjustment), independently of one another, may be examined. The degree to which one variable may be moderated by another variable may also be investigated. Controlling other variables and testing for mediating and moderating variables may be analysed using statistical techniques such as multiple regression (e.g., Baron & Kenny, 1986). Whether apparently similar constructs such as therapist empathy and acceptance can be distinguished from each other can be determined using statistical techniques such as exploratory or confirmatory factor analysis (e.g., Murphy & Cramer, 2014). The degree to which different informants (such as client and therapist) perceive the same behaviour (such as the therapeutic relationship) as being similar can be established as can the correspondence between what these informants report and what may be observed as having occurred (e.g., Rogers et al., 1967). Whether physiological measures are related to verbally reported behaviour may also be assessed (e.g., Leitenberg, Agras, Butz, & Wincze, 1971). The degree to which one therapeutic approach may be more effective than another or to no treatment may also be investigated (e.g., Gelder et al., 1973) as may the potential differential effects of the separate components of a therapeutic treatment (e.g., Jacobson et al. , 1996).

KEY RESEARCH METHODS

Various research methods have already been briefly referred to, such as the representative survey and the true or randomized study. Some of these methods will be expanded upon in this section. In quantitative research the variables being investigated have to be measurable. This may be done in numerous ways. The variables may be rated (e.g., Rogers et al., 1967) or counted (e.g., Piper, Azim, Joyce, & McCallum, 1991) from observed, or typically recorded, behaviour. The extent to which different observers, judges, or raters agree on what has been observed needs to be assessed. If agreement is low, attempts should be made to increase it. Open-ended questions may be asked where the content of the answers has to be coded. Closed questions may be used in which respondents are provided with set answers from which they have to choose. The extent to which closed questions actually assess what they are designed to measure can be determined by factor analysis. The degree to which respondents answer similar questions in a similar direction can be assessed through Cronbach's (1951) alpha measure of internal reliability. The alpha reliability of a set or scale of questions may be increased by dropping questions or items that lower it. Alpha reliability may also be increased by using items of similar meaning, but this typically limits the comprehensiveness of the scale. Physiological measures, such as heart rate, may be employed to assess what are thought to be the physiological reflections of a psychological construct such as anxiety. Different measures, such as closed and open-ended questions, may both be included in the same study provided that participants are not overburdened with assessment. The degree to which measurement may affect the outcome of a study can be assessed in the same study by varying the amount of measurement and seeing whether this has any effect on outcome.

A longstanding interest in the field of counselling psychology, psychotherapy, and counselling has been the question of whether one theoretical approach is more effective than another and more effective than a no treatment control condition and what has sometimes been referred to as an attention-control condition. The methodological requirements for a well-designed randomized clinical trial of a therapeutic approach have increased since the earlier studies were published and are now generally agreed. They include the following conditions: clients or patients should be those typically seeking therapy so that the results of any study are more likely to apply to this group of people. The term "efficacy" has been recommended to be used to describe the therapeutic outcome of studies that meet more of these conditions in actual clinical practice, and the term "effectiveness" for studies that do this to a lesser extent (e.g., Nathan,

Stuart, & Dolan, 2000). This distinction will not be upheld in this chapter as it may be difficult to make without providing considerable justification for its usage for a particular study. Consequently, both terms will be used interchangeably.

Participants should be restricted to a specific diagnostic group, such as patients with anorexia nervosa or unipolar depression because a particular treatment may be better suited to dealing with one problem than another. The more severe the problem, the more sensitive the study is in measuring the effectiveness of the approach as all approaches may be equally effective with less severe problems. The number of patients or clients in each condition should be large enough so that a clinically significant difference should be statistically significant (e.g., Jacobson & Truax, 1991).

Patients or clients should be randomly assigned to treatments, or to the order of treatments if a cross-over or within-subjects design is used. Although more experienced therapists have not been shown to be more effective than less experienced ones, therapists should be well trained and should carry out all treatments to rule out a therapist effect. Treatment manuals should be prepared and followed for all treatments, and at least some treatment sessions should be assessed to ensure the appropriate treatment is being carried out. The treatments should be as similar as possible to each other in all other respects, such as the length, number, and spacing of sessions, and whether patients are treated in groups or individually. The comparison treatments should ideally include the most commonly used or the most effective known treatment to determine whether the treatment being evaluated should replace these. A waiting list no treatment control condition should also be included to see if the treatments are indeed better than no treatment. This requirement may be considered unethical in denying clients or patients a treatment that is thought to be effective, and unnecessary in view of some previous studies that have shown some form of treatment to be more effective than no treatment. However, because of the relatively few studies that have included a waiting list condition it is important to establish that treatment is indeed generally more effective than no treatment in most circumstances. Furthermore, in many situations it is not possible to treat immediately all clients or patients thought to be of equal urgency and so some of them will inevitably have to wait before being treated, which may perhaps be best determined randomly.

The psychological well-being of patients or clients should be assessed immediately prior to treatment to determine they start off at a similar point and to assess the extent of any change that occurs. Outcome should be assessed as soon as treatment has ended to evaluate its immediate effectiveness. Ideally its longer term effectiveness should also be evaluated after a period of, say, 3 months or more to determine whether any effects persist after treatment has ended. Any further treatment received during this time should be recorded, as those receiving additional treatment may fare better.

Various reliable and valid measures of psychological well-being should be used, including ones assessed by the patient or client and those assessed by a trained clinical observer, who ideally should be blind to the treatment received by the patient or client. Outcome should be presented in terms of clinical improvement and deterioration (e.g., Jacobson & Truax, 1991). Patients or clients not completing treatment or any of its assessments should be statistically analysed (e.g., Ten Have et al., 2008).

It should be clear from this list of requirements that conducting randomized clinical trials is not easy, although some researchers have done so with seemingly little financial support (e.g., Emmelkamp, Visser, & Hoekstra, 1988). Because most psychological treatments involve many variables, it is difficult to tell from randomized clinical trials which of their components were primarily responsible for any therapeutic improvement. The effects of what are thought to be the main explanatory principle underlying a theoretical approach, such as reciprocal inhibition in Wolpe's (1990) behaviour therapy need to be investigated (e.g., Gelder et al., 1973). Manipulating the relevant therapeutic principle may be difficult when the principle depends on the interaction between client and therapist, such as in Rogers' person-centred approach, where it is the client's perception of the therapist that is thought to be important. However, it would appear to be possible to compare in a randomized clinical trial an approach, such as Rogerian person-centred therapy, with one that puts far less emphasis on therapist qualities, such as behaviour therapy or a placebo drug condition. Such a study may require fewer therapists and clients than a longitudinal one in which therapist qualities are simply assessed and no attempt is made to manipulate them. Furthermore, it may be easier to interpret in such a study whether the therapist qualities facilitate psychological improvement. If the Rogerian approach is shown to be more effective than the comparison condition of behaviour therapy or a drug placebo, then this design provides stronger evidence than nonexperimental ones that these qualities are therapeutically important.

SAMPLING

Most research in the psychological sciences, including psychotherapy and counselling, involve what is called convenience sampling in which participants whom the researcher has ready access to are asked to take part. These participants are generally assumed to be similar to people in the population to be generalized to, although this may not be the case. Where such data exist, you can see how similar your sample is to other samples of the assumed population by comparing them on certain readily obtained characteristics (such as age, biological sex, and any psychological measures). Convenience samples may be contrasted with simple random samples in which every member of the population at a particular time has a known probability of being selected. Obtaining a simple random sample from a population is not done for various reasons, including the difficulty of defining what the population refers to, such as its time and location, ensuring that most of the people approached actually participate in the study, and the potentially prohibitive effort of obtaining such a sample. Taking a simple random sample of patients or clients in a particular setting is possible, but generally this is also not done as people meeting the inclusion criteria are simply included until a sufficient number of participants has taken part. It may be useful to make a note of the number of people who declined to take part or who agreed to take part but did not attend or did not complete all of the measures.

When it is not possible to code or to rate a whole recorded therapy session, it is usual and practical to select a sample at random. This procedure increases the likelihood that what is being observed is not confined to an arbitrarily selected point in the session.

Up to a certain size the larger the sample is, the more likely it is that the same size of statistical association or difference will be statistically significant. So, for example, a correlation of $\pm.20$ will be statistically significant (at the one-tailed .05 probability level) for a sample of 70 or more but not for one less than this. A correlation of this size is what may be typically expected between two different psychological constructs that are related, such as the Rogerian therapeutic core conditions and psychological well-being. If a correlation of this kind of magnitude is anticipated, then it would be prudent to select a slightly larger sample in case the actual correlation is a little smaller than this. However, having a much larger sample than this (say, twice or more this size) is generally not worthwhile, as a larger sample will not change the size of the correlation.

APPROACHES TO ANALYSING DATA

Often some data for some participants may be missing. For example, a participant may forget to record their age, or what they have written down may not be legible. They may omit to answer one or more questions on a set or scale of questions, which need to be added together to form an overall score for some psychological construct. The way in which such missing data is handled is often not described in research papers. If there is much incomplete data for a participant, this may indicate that the participant does not understand what is being requested of them or may not be fully engaged with the research. In this case it may be best to omit them from the analysis. If, however, there is only a small amount of missing data, then it would be wasteful to leave out that participant from the analysis.

For scales or measures that consist of a number of questions, you need to set up a cut-off point that determines whether the score for that scale is to be computed or not. There is no set or agreed cut-off point for doing this but a not unreasonable one is where more than 10% of the data are missing. So, this may represent one missing answer for scales of up to 15 items, two missing answers for scales of between 16 and 25

items, and so on. When an analysis is to be based on a set of three or more variables, it may be better to select those participants who have no missing total scores on those variables, otherwise the size and the nature of the sample may vary from one analysis to another making interpretation more difficult.

It is worth checking the shape of the distribution of scores for any variable. If the scores of a variable do not differ, then the variable is in effect a constant as it does not vary. Consequently, such measures should be omitted from any analysis. Other things being equal, variables that have a restricted variance or distribution of scores will be less strongly related to other variables that are not so restricted. When calculating a correlation between two variables, it is worth examining the scattergram of their values to see whether a high correlation is the result of one or more extreme scores or outliers and to determine whether a correlation close to zero may represent the presence of a nonlinear or curvilinear relationship rather than no relationship.

The most commonly used statistical tests for assessing statistical significance are called parametric tests as they are based on certain assumptions about the characteristics or parameters of the distribution of the variables in the population, such as their scores being normally distributed and their variances being similar (see Table 27.1). However, the distributions of many variables in the field of counselling psychology are skewed. Nonetheless, parametric tests are still often used because they are more versatile than nonparametric ones and because the parametric assumptions on which these tests are based have not always been found to be necessary for their interpretation. But if this problem is a concern it may be possible to transform the distribution of these variables so that they better meet these assumptions. You could also carry out both parametric and nonparametric tests to see if the results differ substantially. If they do, a choice has to be made as to which results to present.

The internal reliability and factorial validity of questionnaire scales chosen for these qualities should be checked in any new study to see if they hold. If they do not, then a decision has to be made whether to use them as they were originally scored or to revise the scoring for the new sample. Of course, the results of both procedures may be compared to see if the results actually differ substantially. If they do differ, then a choice has to be made as to which to present. Factorial validity refers to whether the items comprising a particular scale such as empathy do go together as a group or factor that can be distinguished from the items which make up another scale such as genuineness.

Multivariate analysis of variance is used to determine whether the variances in the scores of two or more outcomes or dependent variables differ significantly for one or more independent variables such as the different treatment conditions. If the scores immediately prior to treatment differ significantly, then these scores can be made to be statistically equal by covarying or controlling them through a multivariate analysis of covariance. A repeated measures analysis is applied to determine whether there are any differences in therapeutic change at different points in the different treatments.

At least three kinds of analysis can be carried out with multiple regression. One is to determine what percentage of the variance in outcome is significantly and uniquely explained by a set of predictor variables. Another is to examine whether the relationship between two variables, such as the therapist core conditions and therapeutic outcome, is mediated by one or more other variables, such as the client's self-acceptance and self-understanding. A third is to see if the relationship between two variables, such as the therapist core conditions and therapeutic outcome, is moderated by or differs according to one or more other variables, such as the client's psychological mindfulness. A mediating variable is one in which one variable, the antecedent variable, is thought to affect a second variable, the mediating variable, before affecting a third variable, the consequent variable. This mediating effect may be total in that all the influence of the antecedent variable on the consequent variable works through the mediating variable. Alternatively, it can be partial in which part of the influence of the antecedent variable on the consequent variable works indirectly through the mediating variable and the other part of it works directly on the consequent variable without influencing the mediating variable. A moderating variable, on the other hand, is one in which the assumed influence of one variable, the antecedent variable, on the other variable, the consequent variable, depends on the values of another variable, the moderating variable. For example, there may be no influence of the antecedent variable on the consequent variable for one value of the moderating variable, a positive influence for another value of the moderating variable, and a weaker positive or even negative influence for a third value of the moderating variable.

Table 27.1 *Some Suggested Parametric Statistical Tests for Particular Types of Analysis*

Parametric statistical tests	Types of analysis
Cronbach alpha (α) internal reliability test	To assess the extent to which a measure is internally reliable in that all its component parts contribute substantially to the overall score
Principal components factor analysis (PCA)	To determine if the components making up a measure are best assessed as a single measure or as more than one measure (or factor)
Confirmatory factor analysis	To determine if the components of a measure are associated with that measure as they are expected to be associated
Pearson's product-moment (*r*) correlation	To determine the linear relationship between two continuous variables, two binomial variables, or one continuous and one binomial variable
Scattergram	To determine if there is a nonlinear relationship between two continuous variables as well as to see if the scatter of values appears to be roughly similar above and below the line of best fit
Unrelated *t* test	To determine if the mean scores of two unrelated or different groups of people differ
Related *t* test	To determine if the mean scores of the same measure on the same group or two related groups of people differ
One-way analysis of variance (ANOVA)	To determine if the variances of one measure on two or more unrelated or different groups of people vary
Two- (or more) way analysis of variance	To determine if the variances of one measure on two (or more) unrelated variables differ
Analysis of covariance (ANCOVA)	To determine if the variances of one measure on two or more unrelated groups of people differ if one or more correlated variables are controlled
Repeated measures of analysis	To determine if the variances of one measure on two or more related samples of people differ
Mixed analysis of variance	To determine if the variances of one or more unrelated variables and one or more related variables differ
Multiple analysis of variance (MANOVA)	To determine if the variances of two or more measures differ on two or more unrelated variables

(continued)

Table 27.1 *(Continued)*

Parametric statistical tests	Types of analysis
Multiple analysis of covariance (MANCOVA)	Like MANOVA except that it controls for other variables that are correlated with the dependent or outcome variables
Standard or simultaneous multiple regression	To determine how much variance in a continuous dependent variable can be accounted for by two or more predictor variables all of which individually whose values can be at least ordered according to size
Hierarchical multiple regression	Like standard multiple regression except that the predictor variables are put into a particular sequence

SAMPLE RESEARCH STUDY EXAMPLE

One well-known study, aspects of which have been described in various papers, is the National Institute of Mental Health Treatment for Depression Collaborative Research Program (e.g., Elkin et al, 1989). The main aim of this large multisite randomized clinical trial was to compare the effectiveness of the four treatments of Beck's cognitive-behavioural therapy, interpersonal psychotherapy, an antidepressant, and a drug placebo condition on 250 patients diagnosed with major depression, of whom 239 started treatment and 162 completed it. To be included in the study patients had to be aged between 21 and 60, to be currently having a major depressive episode (as defined by research criteria) lasting for at least the previous 2 weeks, and to have scored above a certain level on a depression scale as rated by an independent clinician. Criteria for excluding patients from the study included having other specific psychiatric disorders, being currently treated, having physical conditions incompatible with the drug treatment, and feeling actively suicidal. This study was a mixed between- and within-subject design in which four unrelated groups of participants (i.e., between-subjects design) were followed up on two or more occasions (within-subjects design) using a convenience sample.

Patients in all four treatments were generally seen once a week for about 16 weeks with 50-min sessions for those in the two psychotherapy conditions and 20–30-min sessions for those in the two drug conditions, which also included providing support, encouragement, and, when necessary, advice. Follow-up assessments at 6, 12, and 18 months after treatment had ended were carried out on 192, 187, and 191 patients, respectively. Cognitive-behavioural therapy was conducted by 8 experienced cognitive-behavioural therapists, interpersonal psychotherapy by 10 experienced interpersonal psychotherapy therapists, and both drug treatments by the same 10 experienced therapists. Therapists had a mean average of about 11 years of clinical experience, ranging from 2 to 27 years. Manuals were prepared for the two psychotherapy conditions and these two treatments were monitored by experts to ensure they were carried out as prescribed.

The main outcome measures were the Beck Depression Inventory and the Hopkins Symptom Checklist as completed by the patient, and the Hamilton Rating Scale for Depression, the Global Adjustment Scale, and the Social Adjustment Scale based on interviews by and assessed by a clinical evaluator. Outcome was measured at 4-weekly intervals during treatment and at the three follow-up points. There were no statistically significant clinically significant differences between the four treatments at the end of treatment for the two depression scales (Ogles, Lambert, & Sawyer, 1995). However, there were some statistically significant differences in clinically significant improvement in the Hopkins Symptoms Checklist, which assesses general symptom severity. Significantly greater improvement was shown for the drug than for the placebo treatment and for interpersonal psychotherapy than for cognitive-behavioural therapy. No more than three patients in any condition showed significant deterioration on any of these measures.

Other measures included in this study have been analysed in relation to outcome by other authors. For example, the Barrett-Lennard Relationship Inventory, which assesses the client's perception of the four Rogerian core therapeutic conditions of level of regard, empathy, congruence, and unconditionality of regard, was used after the second session and at the end of treatment (Blatt, Zuroff, Quinlan, & Pilkonis, 1996). A principal components factor analysis of the four scales assessed after the second session found that three of the four scores formed a single factor, so the scores for these three scales were added together to form a single score for each of the 149 participants for whom scores were available. A factor analysis of the scores for the inventory's 64 questions rather than its four scales would have determined whether the four core therapeutic conditions were distinguished by clients. The two psychotherapy groups did not differ significantly in their overall score of their perception of the therapist. This score was significantly higher for the 18 therapists in these two psychotherapy groups than for the 10 therapists in the two drug treatments.

Clients who saw their therapist as being altogether more accepting, understanding, and genuine after the second session were more likely to complete treatment. In fact clients who saw their therapist as positive were 75% more likely to complete treatment than those who saw their therapist as average. Client's perception of the therapist after the second session was also significantly negatively related to all of the outcome measures apart from the Hamilton Rating Scale for Depression. The correlations ranged from $-.11$ for this scale to $-.26$ for the Social Adjustment Scale. So clients who saw their therapist as being more accepting, understanding, and genuine after the second session generally showed greater improvement. This relationship was moderated by the client's need for perfection. It was strongest for those with a moderate need for perfection, suggesting the three core conditions may be most important for these clients.

CONCLUSION

The primary aim of quantitative research is to propose and to appropriately test empirically explanations for human behaviour. Without a clear idea of what the explanation is that is being tested, it is not possible to design a suitable test for it. Thinking about how to test an explanation may, in turn, help to further develop and refine that explanation. Explanations that do not seem convincing are unlikely to be seen as worth testing. In psychotherapy and counselling we are primarily interested in explaining how psychological problems develop and how they can be overcome, although we may also be interested in other relevant issues, such as how to ensure that people initially turn up for treatment and to continue doing so. Quantitative research in psychotherapy and counselling is also concerned with determining whether one approach is more effective than another and more effective than no treatment. This kind of research can be seen as testing an overall explanation of treatment rather than the particular assumptions that comprise it. As well as providing evidence for whether these treatments should be sought and supported, this research may also throw light on the plausibility of their underlying explanations. For example, the finding that the behavioural treatment of flooding may generally be as effective as systematic desensitization casts doubt on whether the principle of reciprocal inhibition underpins all effective forms of psychological treatment. The fact that many of the treatments that to date have been adequately compared do not appear to differ substantially in their effectiveness or efficacy suggests we need to develop and to test better explanations of how these treatments work.

SUGGESTED FURTHER READING

Howitt, D., & Cramer, D. (2017). *Understanding Statistics in psychology with SPSS* (7th ed.). Harlow: Prentice Hall.
This is one of many statistics texts that should be helpful in explaining the rationale behind many statistical tests and showing how they are calculated.

Howitt, D., & Cramer, D. (2017). *Research methods in psychology* (5th ed.). Harlow: Prentice Hall.
One of a smaller number of research method books that should be useful in elaborating many important issues in quantitative as well as qualitative research, including how to write up a research report.

Howitt, D., & Cramer, D. (2014). *Introduction to SPSS in psychology: For version 22 and earlier* (6th ed.). Harlow: Prentice Hall.
This book provides a step-by-step description of how to carry out, interpret, and write up a wide range of procedures and statistical tests employing the most widely used statistical package for the social sciences (SPSS). The 7th edition does not include as many procedures as this edition.

REFERENCES

Baron, R. M., & Kenny, D. A. (1986). The moderator-mediator variable distinction in social psychological research: Conceptual, strategic, and statistical considerations. *Journal of Personality and Social Psychology, 51*, 1173–1182.

Blatt, S. J., Zuroff, D. C., Quinlan, D. M., & Pilkonis, P. A. (1996). Interpersonal factors in brief treatment of depression: Further analyses of the National Institute of Mental Health Treatment of Depression Collaborative Research Program. *Journal of Consulting and Clinical Psychology, 64*, 162–171.

Campbell, D. T., & Stanley, J. C. (1963). *Experimental and quasi-experimental designs for research.* Boston, MA: Houghton Mifflin.

Cramer, D. (2003). A cautionary tale of two statistics: Partial correlation and standardised partial regression. *Journal of Psychology, 137*, 507–511.

Cronbach, L. J. (1951). Coefficient alpha and the internal structure of tests. *Psychometrika, 16*, 297–334.

Elkin, I., Shea, M. T., Watkins, J. T., Imber, S. D., Sotsky, S. M., Collins, J. F., . . ., & Parloff, M. B. (1989). National Institute of Mental Health Treatment of Depression Collaborative Research Program: General effectiveness of treatments. *Archives of General Psychiatry, 46*, 971–982.

Emmelkamp, P. M. G., Visser, S., & Hoekstra, R. J. (1988). Cognitive therapy vs exposure in vivo in the treatment of obsessive-compulsives. *Cognitive Therapy and Research, 12*, 103–114.

Gelder, M. G., Bancroft, H. J., Gath, D. H., Johnston, W., Mathews, A. M., & Shaw, P. M. (1973). Specific and non-specific factors in behaviour therapy. *British Journal of Psychiatry, 123*, 445–462.

Jacobson, N. S., Dobson, K. S., Truax, P. A., Addis, M. E., Koerner, K., Gollan, J. K., Gortner, E., & Prince, S. E. (1996). A component analysis of cognitive-behavioral treatment of depression. *Journal of Consulting and Clinical Psychology, 64*, 295–304.

Jacobson, N. S., & Truax, P. (1991). Clinical significance: A statistical approach to defining meaningful change in psychotherapy research. *Journal of Consulting and Clinical Psychology, 59*, 12–19.

Leitenberg, H., Agras, S. Butz, R., & Wincze, J. (1971). Relationship between heart rate and behavioral change during the treatment of phobias. *Journal of Abnormal Psychology, 78*, 59–68.

Murphy, D., & Cramer, D. (2014). Mutuality of Rogers' therapeutic conditions and outcome in the first three therapy sessions. *Psychotherapy Research, 24*, 651–661.

Nathan, P. E., Stuart, S. P., & Dolan, S. L. (2000). Research on psychotherapy efficacy and effectiveness: Between Scylla and Charybdis? *Psychological Bulletin, 126*, 964–981.

Ogles, B. M., Lambert, M. J., & Sawyer, J. D. (1995). Clinical significance of the National Institute of Mental Health Treatment of Depression Collaborative Research Program data. *Journal of Consulting and Clinical Psychology, 63*, 321–326.

Piper, W. E., Azim, H. F., Joyce, A. S., & McCallum, M. (1991). Transference interpretations, therapeutic alliance, and outcome in short-term individual psychotherapy. *Archives of General Psychiatry, 48*, 946–953.

Rogers, C. R. (1959). A theory of therapy, personality, and interpersonal relationships, as developed in the client centered framework. In S. Koch (Ed.), *Psychology: A study of a science* (pp. 184–256). New York: McGraw-Hill.

Rogers, C. R., Gendlin, E. T., Kiesler, D. J., & Truax, C. B. (Eds.) (1967). *The therapeutic relationship and its impact: A study of psychotherapy with schizophrenics.* Madison, WI: University of Wisconsin Press.

Shadish, W. R., Cook, T. D., & Campbell, D. T. (2002). *Experimental and quasi-experimental designs for generalised causal inference*. New York: Houghton Mifflin.

Stinson, F. S., Dawson, D. A., Chou, S. P., Smith, S., Goldstein, R. B., Ruan, W. J., & Grant, B. F. (2007). The epidemiology of DSM-IV specific phobia in the USA: Results from the National Epidemiology Survey on alcohol and related conditions. *Psychological Medicine, 37*, 1047–1059.

Ten Have, T. R., Normand, S.-L. T., Marcus, S. M., Brown, C. H., Lavori, P., & Duan, N. (2008). Intent-to-treat vs. non-intent-to-treat analyses under treatment non-adherence in mental health randomized trials. *Psychiatric Annals, 38*, 772–783.

Wolpe, J. (1990). *The practice of behaviour therapy* (4th ed.). Oxford: Pergamon Press.

28 Hermeneutic Single Case Efficacy Design for Counselling Psychology

ROBERT ELLIOTT AND MARK WIDDOWSON

CHAPTER OUTLINE

INTRODUCTION 426

EPISTEMOLOGIES: WAYS OF KNOWING 426

GUIDING PRINCIPLES AND ASSUMPTIONS 428

RESEARCH QUESTIONS ADDRESSED 429

KEY RESEARCH METHODS 430

SAMPLING 432

APPROACHES TO ANALYSING DATA 432
    Rich Case Record 432
    Affirmative Case 433

Sceptic Case 433
Adjudication 434

HSCED EXAMPLES 434

CONCLUSION: STRENGTHS AND LIMITATIONS OF HSCED 435
    Strengths 435
    Limitations 436

LEARNING OUTCOMES

BY THE END OF THIS CHAPTER YOU SHOULD BE ABLE TO ANSWER THE FOLLOWING KEY QUESTIONS:

1. What distinguishes Hermeneutic Single Case Efficacy Design from other approaches to single case research?

2. What are the key ingredients in a Rich Case Record?

3. How can counselling psychologists make use of HSCED to support their practice?

INTRODUCTION

This chapter focuses on a mixed-methods approach to case study research. Within the chapter we will consider the importance of conducting case study research and the specific in-depth knowledge that can be gained from studying individual cases. We suggest that case study research illuminates key information about process that can be related to outcome which is not possible in large scale outcome-based trials. We will present the key features of Hermeneutic Single Case Efficacy Design (HSCED) and provide an outline step-by-step guide to conducting such case studies. We also present a brief example.

EPISTEMOLOGIES: WAYS OF KNOWING

There has been a growing unease amongst psychotherapy researchers about the dominance of randomized controlled trials (RCTs) in researching the efficacy of psychological therapies (Elliott, 2002; Vossler, Moller, & Cooper, 2015). Although RCTs provide convincing demonstrations that a particular therapy has been generally effective in a particular situation, they suffer from several critical difficulties: First, they are carried out in situations that often bear little resemblance to the day-to-day realities of routine practice, and provide little basis for justifying inferences about routine practice (Cartwright & Hardie, 2012). Second, RCTs ignore therapy change processes, relying instead on an empty definition of causal influence rather than seeking a substantive understanding of how change actually takes place. They thus cannot answer questions about how or why treatments were effective. Third, in an RCT, even when a therapy has been shown to be responsible for client change in general (because randomly assigned clients in the active treatment condition show outcomes superior to those of control clients), this overall result does not necessarily apply to particular clients. After all, for any specific client, factors other than therapy might actually have been the source of observed or reported changes, or the client's apparent change might have been illusory. Fourth, RCTs typically cast clients as passive recipients of standardized treatments rather than as active collaborators and self-healers (Bohart & Tallman, 1999). Thus, the fundamental presuppositions of RCTs are at variance with core values regarding personal agency and person-to-person relationships, values that hold across a wide range of theoretical approaches.

For these reasons, counselling psychologists need alternatives to RCTs, and as luck would have it, we are in the midst of a growing wave of interest in the utility of case study research for answering questions about how or why a therapy was beneficial for a particular case, alongside a growing interest in developing robust methods of conducting case study research (Fishman, 1999; Iwakabe & Gazzola, 2009). In fact, the past 15 years have seen a renaissance of systematic case study research (see McLeod, 2010). In this chapter, we present a sketch for one such alternative, HSCED (for others, see McLeod, 2010)

Traditionally, systematic case studies have been classified under the traditional design rubric of *single-case pre-post designs* and have been designated as *nonexperimental*; that is, causally uninterpretable (Cook & Campbell, 1979). However, Cook and Campbell (1979), following Scriven (1974) also described the use of retrospective "modus operandi" designs that can be interpreted under certain conditions; that is, when there is rich contextual information and *signed causes*. Signed causes are influences whose presence is evident in their effects. For example, if a bumper-shaped dent with white paint in it appears in your new car after you have left it parked in a car park, then the general nature of the causal agent can be readily inferred, even if the offending vehicle has long since left the scene. Mohr (1993) went further, arguing that the single case is the *best* situation for inferring generalizable causal influence.

Furthermore, standard suspicions about systematic case studies ignore the fact that skilled practitioners and laypeople in a variety of settings continually use effective but implicit practical reasoning strategies to make causal judgements about single events, ranging from medical illnesses, to crimes, to aeroplane crashes (Schön, 1983). For example, forensic and medical practice are both fundamentally systems for developing and testing causal inferences in naturalistic situations.

It is worth noting that words like *explanation* and *cause* can be perceived as reductionistic or dehumanizing. However, thinking causally and searching for explanations is part of what makes us human (Cook & Campbell, 1979), like telling each other stories. When we describe therapy as *responsible for, bringing about*, or *influencing* change on the part of our clients, we are speaking in explicitly causal terms. Even language such as *facilitating* and *empowering* is implicitly causal. However, in discussing causal influence processes in humans, it is clear that we are not talking about anything like mechanical forces; rather, we are talking about *narrative causality*, which employs a range of modes of explanation including who did something (agentic explanation), what the person's purpose was in acting (intentional explanation), what plan, role, or schema the person was enacting (formal explanation), and what situation allowed the action (opportunity explanation) (Elliott, 1992; cf. Cartwright, 2007). At the same time, it is very important for counselling psychologists to be very careful with their language so as not to fall into the common trap of treating psychological processes as if they involve mechanical causes like those that run cars or computers. Most strikingly, counsellors do not "cause" their clients to change;

rather, clients make use of the therapeutic opportunities offered them by their counsellors in order to *cause themselves to change*: they are the active agents in their change process (Bohart & Tallman, 1999).

GUIDING PRINCIPLES AND ASSUMPTIONS

Thus, the challenge is to explicate a convincing practical reasoning system for judging the influence of psychotherapy/counselling on client change. HSCEDs attempt to explicate a set of practical methods that are transparent, systematic, and self-reflective enough to provide an adequate basis for making inferences about therapy efficacy in single cases. The approach outlined here makes use of rich networks of information ("thick" description rather than elegant design) and descriptive-interpretive (rather than experimental) procedures to develop probabilistic (rather than absolute) knowledge claims. Such an approach is hermeneutic in the sense that it attempts to construct plausible understandings of the influence processes in complex ambiguous sets of information about a client's counselling.

HSCED is also dialectical in that it uses a mixture of positive and negative, quantitative and qualitative evidence to create a rich case record that provides the basis for systematic construction of affirmative and opposing positions on the causal influence of psychotherapy on client outcome. As outlined here, it involves a set of procedures that allow counselling psychologists to make a reasonable case for claiming that a *client very likely improved* and that the client *very likely used therapy* to bring about this improvement. Making these inferences requires two things. First, there is an *affirmative case* consisting of two or more types of positive evidence linking therapy to observed client change, for example, client change in long-standing problems and a self-evident association linking a significant within-therapy event to a shift in client problems. Second, a *sceptic case* is also required, marshalling the evidence that plausible nontherapy explanations might be sufficient to account for apparent client change. The collection and presentation of negative evidence requires good-faith efforts to show that nontherapy processes can explain apparent client change, including systematic consideration of a set of *competing explanations* for client change (cf. Cook & Campbell's 1979 account of internal validity).

In short, we can sum up the basic epistemological and methodological position of HSCED with the following six guiding principles:

1. *Use thick description:* it is useful to employ multiple data collection methods (mixed quantitative-qualitative) to construct a rich data record of what happened in a psychotherapy case.

2. *Apply a hermeneutic approach:* in order to make sense of the complex, often ambiguous array of evidence and possible causes, it is a good idea

to systematically and carefully weigh and interpret the available evidence in order to develop explanations for client change. For example, we can use qualitative and quantitative data to complement, clarify, and interrogate each other, thus deepening our understandings of the case.

3. *Adopt a critically reflective stance:* it is important to consciously work against our general human tendency to preferentially seek confirming rather than disconfirming evidence (Nickerson, 1998). Therefore, in confronting apparent client change over the course of psychotherapy, we will want to work against our belief that psychotherapy is effective by making good-faith efforts to find evidence that the client did not change, and that if they did change, therapy was not responsible for this change.

4. *Be practical:* in carrying out HSCED studies, there is a preference for easily implemented, off-the-shelf and preferably free measures. This helps researchers not get distracted from HSCED's focus on reflective consideration of evidence.

5. *Borrow from the legal system:* As HSCED has developed over time, it has increasingly adopted various quasi-judicial procedures, including actively adopting affirmative vs. sceptic positions to clarify evidence and using sets of judges external to the study to evaluate evidence and opposing arguments.

6. *Be flexible:* HSCED studies rely on creative adaptation of methods to a particular situation. For example, it is common to rely on a relaxed standard of proof closer to the legal standard of "reasonable assurance" ($p < .2$) rather than "beyond a shadow of doubt" ($p < .05$ or $p < .01$). Similarly, HSCED studies adopt a broad definition of causality, including intentions and the offering of opportunities.

RESEARCH QUESTIONS ADDRESSED

A HSCED study draws conclusions about the efficacy of a particular therapy in relation to a specific case. Furthermore, both client factors and aspects of the therapeutic process that have contributed towards this outcome are considered. Originally, HSCED emphasized two main types of research question (Elliott, 2002). First, it addressed therapy outcome questions: *Did the client change over the course of therapy?* Second, it looked at whether therapy was causally implicated in client change: *Was the therapy effective in this case?* That is, *did therapy bring about client change?* Over time, a third type of question considering therapeutic change processes emerged as increasingly important: *What factors were associated with client change this case?* (Stephen & Elliott, 2011).

One area where HSCED studies are particularly useful is in determining the outcome of cases where the picture of change is somewhat ambiguous, or where the client made some changes, but did not completely resolve their problems (e.g., Elliott et al., 2009).

In addition, over time the research questions have been refined: thus, in more recent HSCED studies by Elliott and associates (e.g., MacLeod & Elliott, 2014), researchers have begun specifying degree of client change and therapy causality;

that is, that it be substantial rather than trivial or minor. As a result, the outcome question has become, *did the client change **substantially** over the course of therapy?*, and the causality question has become, *did therapy contribute **substantially** to client outcome?*

Furthermore, the change process research question has been elaborated, so that HSCED researchers are now urged to consider two types of change processes, mediators and moderators. *Mediators* are in-therapy processes that contribute substantially to client outcome, such as the quality of the therapeutic relationship or the use of Empty-Chair work in emotion-focused therapy (EFT). *Moderators* are pre-existing extra-therapy factors that contribute substantially to client outcome, such as client motivation or supportive others (Shearer, 2015). Mediating and moderating factors are now considered to be important in HSCED research because they provide the basis on which results from HSCED studies can be generalized to other clients.

Thus, the use of qualitative data in a HSCED study provides detailed information about mediating factors, that is, the actual therapy process, using client and therapist questionnaires and session recordings; specifically, this allows researchers to examine the different aspects of the therapy that the client experienced as most helpful, and as most facilitative to their process of change. Furthermore, rich case records that include an account of the therapist's use of interventions provide technical information about the implementation of the therapeutic process. Other details, such as demographic data about both client (age, gender, nature and onset of problems, and so on) and therapist (age, gender, experience level) can be useful as potential moderating factors, especially when aggregating cases to examine the potential impact of these factors on therapeutic outcomes.

In outlining the requirements for a therapy to be designated as an *empirically supported therapy*, Chambless and Hollon (1998) stated that nine different single-case experimental design studies (comprising a series of three cases conducted by three independent research groups) was sufficient. This provides currently marginalized or emerging psychotherapies (MEPs; see Stiles, Hill, & Elliott, 2015) with an opportunity to build an effective argument for their effectiveness by using case study research. The systematic and rigorous process of the HSCED method provides an ideal framework for investigating the efficacy of MEPs, and for identifying the change processes (both mediators and moderators) in these approaches—information that can be used to enhance their effectiveness.

KEY RESEARCH METHODS

As noted, the first step in HSCED research is assembling a rich, comprehensive collection of information about a client's therapy. This includes background information, as well as data on therapy process and outcome, using multiple sources (client, therapist, observers) and instruments (qualitative and quantitative). Elliott (2002) recommended the following:

1) *Basic facts* about client and therapist, including demographic information, diagnoses, presenting problems, therapeutic approach, or orientation.

2) *Quantitative outcome measures.* Therapy outcome has both descriptive/qualitative (*how* the client changed) and quantitative (how *much* the client changed) aspects. Thus, standard, off-the-shelf quantitative self-report questionnaires such as the CORE Outcome Measure (Barkham et al., 2001) and the Inventory of Interpersonal Problems (Horowitz, Rosenberg, Baer, Ureño, & Villaseñor, 1988) can be used. At a minimum, at least one of these measures should be given at the beginning and end of therapy, but it is also a good idea to give them periodically during therapy, every 8–10 sessions.

3) *Change Interview.* The Change Interview (Elliott, Slatick, & Urman, 2006) is a semi-structured interview that provides: (a) qualitative outcome data, in the form of client descriptions of changes experienced over the course of therapy; and (b) client descriptions of their attributions for these changes, including helpful aspects of their therapy (information on negative aspects of therapy and on medications is also collected). The Change Interview takes about an hour and is best carried out by a third party, every 8–10 sessions, at the end of therapy, and at follow-up.

4) *Weekly outcome measure.* A key element in HSCED is the administration of a weekly measure of the client's main therapy-related problems or goals. The Personal Questionnaire (Elliott et al., 2016), an individualized target complaint measure consisting of roughly ten 7-point distress rating scales, is useful for this purpose.

5) *Helpful Aspects of Therapy (HAT) Form* (Llewelyn, 1988) is a frequently employed postsession qualitative measure of client perceptions of significant therapy events. This open-ended seven-item questionnaire is administered to clients after therapy sessions. In HSCED, HAT data are used to pinpoint significant therapeutic processes that may be associated with change on the weekly outcome measure or to corroborate change processes referred to in the Change Interview. Descriptions from the HAT provide a summary narrative of what the client considered at the time to be the most helpful events in therapy.

6) *Records of therapy sessions.* Therapist process notes or recordings of therapy sessions are collected in case they are needed to pinpoint, corroborate, or clarify issues or contradictions elsewhere in the data.

A recent systematic review of HSCED studies (Benelli, De Carlo, Biffi, & McLeod, 2015) analysed 13 articles according to their stringency and rigour, and developed a series of recommendations for future HSCED research.

SAMPLING

Little has been written about the sampling or selection of cases for HSCED studies. The Benelli et al. (2015) review revealed various strategies for recruiting and selecting clients, but paid little systematic attention to this issue. HSCED research lends itself to investigations of new kinds of treatment or extension of existing treatments to new client populations, such as EFT with panic/phobia (Elliott et al., 2009) or transactional analysis with emetophobia (Kerr, 2013). However, as soon as there are two or more cases available of a given client × treatment combination, the issue of sampling becomes relevant and issues of selection bias emerge. Possibilities for addressing this problem include:

1) With case series of two or more clients, the researcher could select one case at *random*. The problem is, few researchers would consider a sample of one to be an adequate representation of the large set of cases.

2) With a short case series of two to six cases, the researcher (or a team of researchers) could avoid the sampling issue altogether by selecting *all* cases for HSCED analysis (e.g., Widdowson, 2012a, b, c, 2013).

3) With longer case series, where sampling all cases is impractical, the researcher could *randomly* select two or three cases. However, this strategy could plausibly lead to accidental undersampling of good or poor outcome cases, or cases that might be considered unrepresentative of the larger sample (e.g., on gender or severity of presenting difficulties)

4) Thus, an alternative to complete or random sampling of cases from a larger case series is to adopt a *stratified sampling* approach of deliberately and explicitly selecting cases based on outcome or some other relevant variable. For example, MacLeod and colleagues carried out four HSCED studies contrasting good and poor outcome in person-centred and EFT for social anxiety (MacLeod & Elliott, 2012, 2014; MacLeod, Elliott, & Rodgers, 2012; Stephen, Elliott, & MacLeod, 2011).

APPROACHES TO ANALYSING DATA

Rich Case Record

The first stage of data analysis in an HSCED study is the construction of a rich case record, which begins with a description of both client and therapist. Scores on quantitative outcome measures are calculated and summarized in a table in order to provide information about the nature and magnitude of the client's change on these. Qualitative data on outcome and change process from postsession feedback forms and posttherapy Change Interview are also included to provide a rounded picture of the therapy. There may also be a narrative summary of the course of therapy, constructed by the researcher.

The case is then subjected to a hermeneutic analysis using a quasi-legal framework. Typically within HSCED studies, a single researcher, or alternatively two teams of researchers, take two opposing stances with regards to analysis and interpretation of the case, analogous to the legal framework of a case with a defence and a prosecution. The affirmative case identifies data that support an argument that the client changed and that these changes were clearly due to the therapy. The sceptic case provides a good-faith argument that the client did not change, or, if they did, that any observed changes were not due to therapy and could be attributed to other factors.

Affirmative Case

The affirmative team (or researcher working in an affirmative role) seeks to find clear evidence of at least two of the following:

1) Changes in long-standing or stable problems.
2) Client attribution of changes directly to therapy.
3) Outcome to process mapping, whereby specific posttherapy changes have plausible links with specific aspects of or episodes within the therapy.
4) Event-shift sequences, where reliable client session-to-session improvements appear to follow on from specific significant events within therapy.

(A fifth form of evidence, process-outcome correlation, was originally proposed but has consistently proven to be unproductive.)

Sceptic Case

At the same time the sceptic team (or researcher enacting the sceptic position) examines the rich case record and makes a good-faith effort to find evidence for each of eight alternative explanations for the results in the rich case record. Four of these are nonchange explanations and four are nontherapy explanations. The nonchange explanations are:

1) That any apparent client pre-post change was either trivial or negative (i.e., deterioration), and did not meet criteria for clinically significant change and/or reliable change.
2) That the apparent change was due to statistical problems such as measurement error, regression to the mean, or experiment-wise error.
3) That the apparent change was due to relational artefacts such as the client trying to please or impress the therapist.
4) That the apparent change was due to client expectancy ("placebo") effects or scripts for therapy outcome.

The nontherapy change explanations are:

1) That any actual client change was due to spontaneous remission or natural self-correcting processes including self-help efforts.

2) That any actual client change is due to extra-therapy events, such as a new relationship, job, or improved financial circumstances.

3) That any actual client change is due to psychobiological causes, such as recovery from illness or medication.

4) That any actual client change is due to the impact of participating in the research, such as a sense of altruism from contributing to research or greater self-reflection from completing research procedures.

Adjudication

A crucial aspect of an HSCED study is the adjudication process, whereby expert psychotherapists act as judges in examining the rich case record and the affirmative and sceptic cases, and drawing conclusions about the extent to which the client changed, whether or not the changes were due to therapy, what factors influenced the outcome, and which data they used to form their conclusions. This procedure provides additional stringency to the research process. The adjudication process can be facilitated by the use of structured formats or pro forma, such as the one used by MacLeod and Elliott (2014).

Within the legal framework, different standards and burdens of proof are applied to judgments. HSCED generally follows the example of civil law in using a more relaxed standard of evidence than in criminal law: "reasonable assurance" (estimated at 80% probability of avoiding being wrong) vs. "beyond a shadow of a doubt (estimated at 95% probability of avoiding being wrong).

HSCED EXAMPLES

In this section, we briefly describe two studies conducted by the authors, which have each been significant in providing *prima facie* evidence for EFT for panic/phobia and for transactional analysis therapy for depression, respectively. We invite the reader to read these two cases in their entirety, to get a deeper sense of the HSCED process.

The first is the case of "George," who received EFT for panic and specific phobia of crossing bridges (Elliott et al., 2009). He also had a number of interpersonal difficulties. George received 23 sessions of EFT. At the end of therapy, he experienced reliable change on sub-scales of the SCI-90-R relating to hostility and phobic anxiety, whereas some other measures used demonstrated some deterioration at the end of therapy (although not at the level of reliable deterioration). In his posttherapy Change Interview, George reported having made four major changes: being able to cross bridges, an improved relationship with his wife, more tolerance of other people, and reduced fear of flying.

The expert judges concluded unanimously that George had indeed changed and that this change had at least in part come about due to therapy. They attributed change to the presence of a strongly positive therapeutic relationship and the use of therapeutic work that facilitated emotional processing (= mediator variables), although they disagreed about the theoretical interpretation of that emotional processing (e.g., chair work vs. exposure vs. transference). Likely moderator variables included high client motivation coupled with high psychological reactance, plus anxiety difficulties embedded a history of trauma. This case is particularly interesting in that it provided some evidence that EFT can be an effective treatment for panic and phobias, thus challenging the dominance of cognitive-behavioural therapy. In fact, the three judges concluded unanimously that George had indeed changed and that this change could be attributed to therapy. This study illustrates the usefulness of HSCED with cases in which the data present a conflicting picture of change and where the outcome is ambiguous.

The second example is the case of "Peter," who was treated with transactional analysis for depression (Widdowson, 2012a). Peter was a part-time carer for his disabled father and was relatively socially isolated. Peter's mother had died when he was a child, and he recalled not being allowed to grieve openly. He was a bright young man who had actively sought out therapy. He received 16 sessions of transactional analysis psychotherapy with the author of the case. Peter experienced reliable change on the Beck Depression Inventory by the end of therapy, and moved into nonclinical range during the follow-up period, thus achieving clinically significant change. He also obtained clinically significant change as measured by both CORE-OM and the Personal Questionnaire. Peter described five changes in his Change Interview, which included changes in his outlook on life, an increased sense of hope and optimism, changes in how he felt about himself and how he related to others, and increased self-awareness.

The three judges concluded that the case was a good outcome case, and that this was largely due to therapy, although they did note that Peter had not resolved all of his problems. Moderator factors included Peter's motivation for therapy and his determination to overcome his initial discomfort, which the judges concluded had contributed to the outcome. The mediator factors identified were that the therapist had clearly engaged well with Peter on an emotional level and had been highly active throughout the therapy.

CONCLUSION: STRENGTHS AND LIMITATIONS OF HSCED

Strengths

HSCED procedure is detailed and well-documented, with a clear and systematic process of data collection and analysis. The clarity and robustness of the method means that it can be used by both novice researchers and those who are more experienced. Participating in a HSCED study can be a powerful learning tool for both students and qualified practitioners who are interested in research. Learning how to collect data, write up and present cases, conducting a detailed analysis of session notes and quantitative and qualitative data, and developing affirmative or sceptic case arguments can all provide rich sources of learning. Furthermore, learning how to critically evaluate the outcome of a case and the factors that seem likely to have influenced the outcome can play an important role in the development of researcher-practitioners.

Another major strength of HSCED is its use of expert opinion in determining the outcome of the case. Although it is not necessary to have judges from a different theoretical orientation to the therapist and researcher, it is desirable. The use of judges who are therapists from a different modality goes some way to mitigate against the potential for research allegiance bias, particularly when making claims about the effectiveness of a particular therapeutic approach. Typically, detailed information about the researcher, therapist, analysis team, and judges, including any existing relationships between them is declared in a HSCED paper, adding transparency to the data analysis process and allowing readers to draw their own conclusions about the potential for bias in each case.

Finally, HSCED studies are efficient in that they only require one case, and are relatively cost-effective means of conducting rigorous process and outcome research.

Limitations

One drawback of HSCED studies, however, is that they are resource intensive. In particular, therapists in such studies require frequent support to ensure that they are collecting all the required data. Missing or incomplete data present difficulties in completing the case analysis and can undermine claims about the effectiveness of the case. If analysis teams are being used, they need to be trained, case analysis meetings need to be arranged, and the affirmative and sceptic cases need to be written up. The judges also undertake a complex task, which requires them to read and evaluate a lot of material, which takes time.

Although HSCED enables researchers to make clear statements about the outcome of a case, and to develop hypotheses about the factors that contributed to the outcome, the method does not allow for a fine-grained analysis of micro-processes operating within the therapy.

Finally, as with all case study research methods, HSCED does not allow for generalization from single cases, although it is possible to generalize if multiple case series are conducted in different contexts, and if the moderator and mediator variables can be specified, as these provide a powerful basis for generalizing results.

SUGGESTED FURTHER READING

Benelli, E., De Carlo, A., Biffi, D., & McLeod, J. (2015). Hermeneutic Single-Case Efficacy Design: A systematic review of published research and current standards. *TPM: Testing, Psychometrics, Methodology in Applied Psychology, 22,* 97–133.

Elliott, R. (2002). Hermeneutic Single Case Efficacy Design. *Psychotherapy Research, 12,* 1–20.

Elliott, R., Partyka, R., Wagner, J., Alperin, R., Dobrenski, R., Messer, S. B., Watson, J. C., & Castonguay, L. G. (2009). An adjudicated Hermeneutic Single-Case Efficacy Design of experiential therapy for panic/phobia. *Psychotherapy Research, 19,* 543–557.

REFERENCES

Barkham, M., Margison, F., Leach, C., Lucock, M., Mellor-Clark, J., Evans, C., . . ., & McGrath, G. (2001). Service profiling and outcomes benchmarking using the CORE-OM: Toward practice-based evidence in the psychological therapies. *Journal of Consulting and Clinical Psychology, 69,* 184–196.

Benelli, E., De Carlo, A., Biffi, D., & McLeod, J. (2015). Hermeneutic Single-Case Efficacy Design: A systematic review of published research and current standards. *TPM: Testing, Psychometrics, Methodology in Applied Psychology, 22,* 97–133.

Bohart, A. C., & Tallman, K. (1999). *How clients make therapy work: The process of active self-healing.* Washington, DC: American Psychological Association.

Cartwright, N. (2007). *Hunting causes and using them: Approaches in philosophy and economics.* New York: Cambridge University Press.

Cartwright, N., & Hardie, J. (2012). *Evidence based policy: A practical guide to doing it better.* New York: Oxford University Press.

Chambless, D. L., & Hollon, S. D. (1998). Defining empirically supported therapies. *Journal of Consulting and Clinical Psychology, 66,* 7–18.

Cook, T. D., & Campbell, D. T. (1979). *Quasi-experimentation: Design and analysis issues for field settings.* Chicago, IL: Rand McNally.

Elliott, R. (1992). *Modes of explanation in psychotherapy research.* Unpublished manuscript, University of Toledo.

Elliott, R. (2002). Hermeneutic Single Case Efficacy Design. *Psychotherapy Research, 12,* 1–20.

Elliott, R., Partyka, R., Wagner, J., Alperin, R., Dobrenski, R., Messer, S. B., Watson, J. C., & Castonguay, L. G. (2009). An adjudicated Hermeneutic Single-Case Efficacy Design of experiential therapy for panic/phobia. *Psychotherapy Research, 19,* 543–557.

Elliott, R., Slatick, E., & Urman, M. (2006). Qualitative change process research on psychotherapy: Alternative strategies. In J. Frommer and D. L. Rennie (Eds.), *Qualitative psychotherapy research: Methods and methodology* (pp. 69–111). Lengerich: Pabst Science Publishers.

Elliott, R., Wagner, J., Sales, C. M. D., Rodgers, B., Alves, P., & Café, M. J. (2016). Psychometrics of the personal questionnaire: A client-generated outcome measure. *Psychological Assessment, 28,* 263–278.

Fishman, D. B. (1999). *The case for pragmatic psychology.* New York: New York University Press.

Horowitz, L. M., Rosenberg, S. E., Baer, B. A., Ureño, G., & Villaseñor, V. S. (1988). Inventory of interpersonal problems: Psychometric properties and clinical applications. *Journal of Consulting and Clinical Psychology, 56,* 885–892.

Iwakabe, S., & Gazzola, N. (2009). From single-case studies to practice-based knowledge: Aggregating and synthesizing case studies. *Psychotherapy Research, 19,* 601–611.

Kerr, C. (2013). TA treatment of emetophobia – a systematic case study – "Peter." *International Journal of Transactional Analysis Research, 4,* 16–26.

Llewelyn, S. (1988). Psychological therapy as viewed by clients and therapists. *British Journal of Clinical Psychology, 27,* 223–238.

MacLeod, R., & Elliott, R. (2012). Emotion-focused therapy for social anxiety: A Hermeneutic Single-Case Efficacy Design study of a low-outcome case. *Counselling Psychology Review, 27*, 7–22.

MacLeod, R., & Elliott, R. (2014). Person-centred therapy for social anxiety: A Hermeneutic Single-Case Efficacy Design study of a good outcome case. *Person-Centered and Experiential Psychotherapies, 13*, 294–311. DOI: 10.1080/14779757.2014.910133

MacLeod, R., Elliott, R., & Rodgers, B. (2012). Process-experiential/emotion-focused therapy for social anxiety: A Hermeneutic Single-Case Efficacy Design study. *Psychotherapy Research, 22*, 67–81. DOI: 10.1080/10503307.2011.626805

McLeod, J. (2010). *Case study research in counselling and psychotherapy*. London: Sage.

Mohr, L. B. (October, 1993). *Causation and the case study*. Paper given at meeting of the National Public Management Research Conference, University of Wisconsin, Madison, WI.

Nickerson, R. S. (1998). Confirmation bias: A ubiquitous phenomenon in many guises. *Review of General Psychology, 2*, 175–220.

Schön, D. A. (1983). *The reflective practitioner: How professionals think in action*. New York: Basic Books.

Scriven, M. (1974). Maximizing the power of causal investigations: The modus operandi method. In W. J. Popham (Ed.), *Evaluation in education* (pp. 85–93). Berkeley, CA: McCutchan.

Shearer, J. (2015). *Emotion-focused therapy for social anxiety: An investigation into client factors, from a client perspective*. Unpublished MSc dissertation, Counselling Unit, University of Strathclyde.

Stephen, S., & Elliott, R. (2011). Developing the adjudicated case study method. *Pragmatic Case Studies in Psychotherapy, 7*(1), 230–241. Available online at: http://pcsp.libraries.rutgers.edu.

Stephen, S., Elliott, R., & MacLeod, R. (2011). Person-centred therapy with a client experiencing social anxiety difficulties: a hermeneutic single case efficacy design. *Counselling and Psychotherapy Research, 11*, 55–66.

Stiles, W. B., Hill, C. E., & Elliott, R. (2015). Looking both ways. *Psychotherapy Research, 25*, 282–293. DOI: 10.1080/10503307.2014.981681

Vossler, A., Moller, N., & Cooper, M. (2015). Setting the scene: Why research matters. In A. Vossler, & N. Moller (eds.), *The counselling and psychotherapy research handbook* (pp. 3–16). London: Sage.

Widdowson, M. (2012a). TA treatment of depression—a hermeneutic single-case efficacy design study—"Peter." *International Journal of Transactional Analysis Research, 3*, 1–11.

Widdowson, M. (2012b). TA treatment of depression—a hermeneutic single-case efficacy design study—"Denise." *International Journal of Transactional Analysis Research, 3*, 3–14.

Widdowson, M. (2012c). TA treatment of depression—a hermeneutic single-case efficacy design study—"Tom." *International Journal of Transactional Analysis Research, 3*, 15–27.

Widdowson, M. (2013). TA treatment of depression—A hermeneutic single-case efficacy design study—"Linda"—a mixed outcome case. *International Journal of Transactional Analysis Research, 4*, 3–15.

29 Theory-Building Case Studies for Counselling Psychology

WILLIAM B. STILES

CHAPTER OUTLINE

INTRODUCTION 440

HOW THEORY-BUILDING
RESEARCH WORKS 440

FACT-GATHERING RESEARCH AND ENRICHING
RESEARCH 441
    Fact-gathering Research 441
    Enriching Research 441

WHAT IS A THEORY? 442

HOW DOES RESEARCH BUILD THEORIES? 443

OBSERVATIONS PERMEATE THEORIES 443

UNIQUE FEATURES OF CASES CAN INFORM
THEORY 444

HYPOTHESIS TESTING VERSUS
CASE STUDY 444

HOW TO DO THEORY-BUILDING CASE
STUDIES 445

FAMILIARITY WITH THE THEORY AND
COURAGE TO CHANGE IT 445

SELECTING A CASE 446

RICH CASE RECORD 446

ANALYSING CASE STUDY MATERIALS 447

APPLY THE CASE TO THE THEORY RATHER
THAN THE THEORY TO THE CASE 448

SOME WRITING TIPS 449

CASE STUDIES DON'T YIELD ONE-SENTENCE
CONCLUSIONS 450

CONCLUSION 451

Counselling Psychology: A Textbook for Study and Practice, First Edition. Edited by David Murphy.
© 2017 John Wiley & Sons Ltd. Published 2017 by John Wiley & Sons Ltd.

LEARNING OUTCOMES

BY THE END OF THIS CHAPTER YOU SHOULD BE ABLE TO ANSWER THE FOLLOWING KEY QUESTIONS:

1. How do explanatory theories differ from treatment theories?

2. How does theory-building research differ from fact-gathering research?

3. How do case study observations change theories?

INTRODUCTION

Theory-building is a purpose of research, not a method. Theory-building research seeks to test, correct, elaborate, and extend a particular theory by comparing and reconciling it with observations, working towards a unified best account within the domain of the theory. It begins with the best available account and seeks to make it better. Any method of research can be used for theory-building purposes, but in this chapter, I focus on case study research. I have written about theory-building case study research before (e.g., Stiles, 2005, 2007, 2009, 2010, 2016), and this chapter reiterates much of what I have said previously, making it applicable to counselling psychologists.

HOW THEORY-BUILDING RESEARCH WORKS

In any scientific research, observations change theories. The observations may strengthen the theory if they correspond to expectations, or they may weaken the theory if they don't. Sometimes the changes involve refining, qualifying, modifying, elaborating, or extending the theory. Thus, through research, the theoretical ideas change to fit observations.

Theory-building is a creative process, but theory-building research (as I am using the term) almost never involves inventing a new theory. Instead, it builds on the theory, expertise, and lore that have accumulated within a field of study. Thus, it requires familiarity with the theory and with previous observations, explanations, and methods within the field. Theory-building research is what Thomas Kuhn (1970) called *normal science*. That is, it is what most scientists do most of the time in most scientific fields.

Theories say to what they apply. In this way, they specify their own generality or range of convenience. Theory-building researchers typically examine only small derived facets of the larger theory. Observations consistent with the theory increase confidence in the theory, but the findings themselves are seldom meant to be generalized. Instead, they are meant to increase confidence in the theory, supporting whatever generality the theory specifies.

Fact-gathering Research and Enriching Research

Theory-building may be contrasted with two other research purposes, which I call *fact-gathering* and *enriching*. One way to distinguish these different purposes is to consider their alternative versions of generality; that is, their alternative strategies for extending research results beyond the confines of the study itself.

Fact-gathering Research

In the absence of an accepted explanatory theory—what Thomas Kuhn would call a paradigm—scientists often focus on finding facts rather than interpreting them within a larger framework. Fact-gathering research may just show what is possible. But to get published, it often seeks results that can be generalized. In our field, this generalizability is often described as external validity—the range of populations and settings to which the conclusions may be expected to apply. (This is a very familiar idea in quantitative psychotherapy research, which was highlighted by Duncan Cramer in Chapter 27, this volume.)

External validity seems derived from the statistical idea that observations that are based on a random sample from a population can be generalized to the population with some specifiable level or confidence. Fact-gathering case studies run into problems at this point.

Enriching Research

Enriching research seeks to deepen and enrich people's appreciation or understanding of a phenomenon by considering it in alternative perspectives and unpacking the explicit and implicit meanings involved. While theory-building research focuses on a particular theory, enriching research may consider many theories as alternative, potentially useful viewpoints. Note that enriching *people* rather than enriching theories is a key feature.

Enriching research does not aim to describe broader populations but trusts its audience to find ways to transfer the observations and interpretations to their own contexts. Transferability, the enriching analogue of generality, thus encompasses imaginative transformations of the investigators' observations and interpretations.

Another activity that is not theory-building research is clinical case studies (such as the Hermeneutic Single Case Efficacy Design (HSCED) that was covered in Chapter 28). These often use one or more theories to understand the case at hand (or demonstrate the therapist's approach or competence), and they may serve an enriching function. But they do not aim to build a particular theory; this point is discussed later.

Clarity about the purposes of the research is important. Readers who expect a study addressed to one purpose but encounter research addressed to a different purpose are likely to find it confusing or wrongheaded. Detailed descriptions and examples of enriching and fact-gathering research are beyond the scope of this chapter, but are available elsewhere (Stiles, 2015).

What is a Theory?

A theory is a system of statements, formulas, diagrams, and the like. That is, a theory is a semiotic construction, made of words, numbers, and other *signs*. Signs have a concrete presence in the world (e.g., marks on a page or a screen, vibrations in the air) but they also refer to people's experience of objects or events. The experience to which a sign refers may be called the *meaning* of the sign. For example, a word's meaning is the experience that a person has upon speaking or writing or hearing or reading the word. Of course, any word's meaning to its author (e.g., speaker, writer) may be different from the meaning to its addressee (e.g., hearer, reader). A word's meaning also varies across time and contexts (Stiles, 2009, 2011).

As a semiotic construction, a theory has a concrete presence in the world and a meaning for each person who encounters it. Ideally, scientific theories have very similar meanings for different people.

Ideally, all parts of a theory should be logically consistent and interconnected so that observations bearing on a statement derived from the theory can affect people's confidence in the whole theory. If the theory were not logically interconnected to some degree, then research on one part of the theory (e.g., a hypothesis) would not bear on the rest of the theory; there would be no point in doing the research.

In speaking of theory-building, I'm referring to *explanatory theories*; that is, logically coherent accounts that aim to be precise and realistic as well as general. In psychotherapy research, we have to distinguish explanatory theories from *treatment theories*. Explanatory theories describe how the world works, for example, how psychotherapy works, whereas treatment theories are meant for clinicians to use to guide their practice. These two types of theories are often confused in psychotherapy research, I think, because some of our most familiar theories (e.g., psychoanalytic theory, person-centred theory, cognitive theory) aspire to be both. These serve as explanatory theories when they seek to describe psychopathology and the process of therapy, and as treatment theories when therapists use them in practice. But particularly for these theories, distinguishing whether the theory is being used as an explanatory theory or a treatment theory is important, because the two types of theory are evaluated by different types of research. While explanatory theories are evaluated by how general, precise, and realistic they are, treatment theories need not be general, precise, or realistic if they enable therapists to be effective in working with clients. Evaluation of treatment theories therefore takes the form of product-testing research, for example, evaluating the outcomes obtained by using a particular treatment approach, a kind of fact-gathering. Product-testing studies include clinical trials, which assess the acceptability, efficacy, and effectiveness of alternative treatment packages.

How Does Research Build Theories?

Theory-building research makes systematic observations and assesses how well they correspond to what the theory says. If the theory is a good one, a person's experience of the world (observations) should correspond to his or her experience of the theory (the theory's meaning to that person). If an observation does correspond to theory, an increment of confidence in the theory is justified. If an observation does not correspond to the theory: (a) the observation may be mistaken, so the method and interpretation must be checked; and/or (b) the theory (or the person's understanding of the theory) may be mistaken, in which case the theory (or the person's understanding of the theory) must be modified. In this way, theory-building research seeks to improve the theories' goodness of fit; that is, to ensure that the theories correspond to the phenomena they seek to explain. If the theory cannot be modified to accommodate a valid observation, then the theory must be abandoned; however, this is rare in psychotherapy research.

Theory-building research thus provides quality control on theories by making observations of the world and adjusting the theory as needed. Through successive adjustments, a theory can correct previous errors and expand to encompass new or unexpected observations. Importantly, the adjustments have to be logically consistent with the rest of the theory. They have to respect observations made in previous studies, just as future adjustments will have to respect the observations made in the current study. Further, any change in one part of a theory may have logical ramifications throughout the theory and may entail additional adjustments, which also must respect previous observations. Thus, theory-building researchers can change the theory to fit their data, but the changes are strongly constrained to ensure that results are cumulative and the theory remains coherent.

Observations Permeate Theories

As a way of describing how observations change theories, I like to say that the observations *permeate* the theory (Stiles, 1993, 2009). This is a diffusion metaphor, suggesting that particles of observation spread through the interstices of the theory. Aspects of the new observations actually enter and become part of the theory. For example, the theory may be explained differently, using words that accommodate the new observations along with the previous ones, or the new observations may be used as illustrations.

Research observations accumulate in theories. New observations permeate the theory while earlier thinking and results are retained. The diffusion metaphor offers an alternative to the brick wall metaphor for how science is cumulative. It suggests that understanding grows not by stacking fact upon fact, but by infusing observations that expand the theory.

Thus, a theory is not a fixed formula but a growing and changing way of understanding. This is a flexible view of theory, looking at the process from the perspective of investigators who may change the theory, rather than from the perspective of students who may see a theory as a static version of what other people have said.

Unique Features of Cases Can Inform Theory

Theories in counselling psychology are meant to encompass more than is encountered in any single case. Each case is different, and a good explanatory theory should encompass all of them.

This point can be drawn from the old Indian parable of the blind men and the elephant: six blind men had heard about elephants and decided to visit one to see what an elephant was really like. The man who felt its side said the elephant is like a wall. The man who felt its tusk said the elephant is like a spear. The man who felt its trunk said the elephant is like a snake. The man who felt its leg said the elephant is like a tree. The man who felt its ear said the elephant is like a fan. And the man who felt its tail said the elephant is like a rope. Each observation was valid to some degree, but each inference was different, yet all described the same animal.

In the parable, each of the blind men maintained his own interpretation of what the elephant was like and did not accept or accommodate the others' observations. The analogue in the field of counselling psychology is familiar. However, the relevant point here is that the elephant has many aspects, just as counselling psychology encompasses many cases. Each case can reveal something new, and these new observations must be reconciled with the theory, whether they confirm previous understandings or add something unexpected. Investigators who restrict themselves to the themes that are common across cases may overlook the most interesting parts. The unique aspects of cases can show where theories need to grow, and case studies can use them to inform theory (Rosenwald, 1988; Stiles, 2009).

Hypothesis Testing Versus Case Study

Both hypothesis testing and case study research can be used to build theories and both can provide scientific quality control on theory. In contrast to hypothesis testing, however, case studies address many theoretical issues in the same study rather than focusing on only one or a few.

The familiar statistical hypothesis testing strategy is to derive one statement from a theory and compare that statement with many observations. That is, we test a hypothesis by seeing if it holds across cases. If the observations tend to correspond to the statement, then people's confidence in the statement is substantially increased. We say the hypothesis was confirmed, or at least the null hypothesis was rejected. This yields a *small* increment of confidence in the theory as a whole (see Chapter 27 for a more detailed discussion of the quantitative approach to counselling psychology research).

The case study strategy is to compare each of many theoretically based statements with one or a few observations. It does this by describing the case in theoretical terms. Each case is different and may address different aspects of the theory. At issue is the correspondence of theory and observation, or how well the theory describes details of the case. Because each detail may be observed only once, the change in confidence in any one theoretical statement is small. However, there are lots of details, and each can be described in theoretical terms. Because many statements are examined, the gain in confidence in the theory, though still small, may be as large as from a statistical hypothesis testing study. The key is multiple theoretically relevant observations. This is accomplished through rich case descriptions and detailed links between theory and case observations. Campbell (1979) described such multiple observations as analogous to degrees of freedom in a statistical hypothesis testing study; that is, he suggested that the power of the test depends on the number and richness of theoretically relevant observations.

HOW TO DO THEORY-BUILDING CASE STUDIES

I address this part of the chapter to students who would like to do theory-building case studies. There is no one correct method for doing case studies. Therefore, I have not given step-by-step instructions but merely offered some suggestions about some broader considerations and requirements.

Familiarity with the Theory and Courage to Change It

First, you need to know the theory. You must be able to put your observations in the context of what has gone before, to recognize what converges with others' observations and what is new. You must recognize what aspects of the theory your observations agree or disagree with, and understand the logical implications of making adjustments in the theory. Thus, like most scientific and scholarly activity, theory-building case research requires a good deal of background reading.

In addition to familiarity with the theory and previous research on the theory, you will need the confidence and courage to change the theory—to make adjustments in light of your own observations. You must be brave enough to comment on which aspects of the theory seem to fit your observations and which must be amended. Investigators who lack this confidence may adhere to previous theory and ignore observations that fail to fit. They may cite authority rather than observation—what Freud thought, for example, rather than what actually happened. Simultaneously, however, you must be humble enough to accept the possibility that your own observations and thinking are mistaken.

Selecting a Case

At the current stage of development of explanatory theories of psychotherapy, any case can teach something new, interesting, and theoretically relevant. On the other hand, you may not know what it will teach until you have finished the study. In contrast to statistical hypothesis testing studies, case studies do not require representative sampling. An unusual case can be as informative as a typical case (if any case is typical). At worst, the case will show what is possible, and its rich details will either confirm and strengthen the theory, or show something of how it needs to be elaborated if it is to account for the phenomena for which it is supposed to account.

However you decide, one requirement is to be explicit in your report about your reasons for deciding to write about a particular case. Interest and accessibility are often salient considerations. Other considerations may be what data are available on the case (see next section) and whether sufficient permissions can be obtained to make necessary details of the case public. (The ethics of conducting case studies are beyond the scope of this chapter. McLeod, 2010, has a very useful chapter on this topic; see also Bond, 2004 or Chapter 25 of this volume on research ethics).

Rich Case Record

The data needed to conduct a theory-building case study depend, of course, on the theory and your interests, but generally case studies benefit from a rich collection of information about the client and the treatment. Elliott (2002) has provided a valuable list of possible sources, from which I have borrowed in what follows.

1. Basic facts about client and therapist, including demographic information, diagnoses, presenting problems, treatment approach or orientation.

2. Recordings of treatment sessions. Audio or video recordings, and particularly verbatim transcriptions, can provide strong grounding for inferences.

Therapists' process notes may also be useful, though these have been filtered through the therapist's attention and memory, with possible attendant selectivity and distortions.

3. **Session-by-session assessments.** Repeated measurement of the client's problems, goals, symptoms, evaluations of sessions, and strength of the client–therapist relationship can help track process and progress.

4. **Outcome assessments.** Treatment outcome has both descriptive qualitative (how the client changed) and quantitative (how much the client changed) aspects, and measures of both are helpful.

5. **Posttreatment interviews.** Sometimes clients can be interviewed after they have finished treatment, to gather their impressions.

6. **Other personal documents,** such as personal journals or diaries, poetry, artwork, letters, or email messages can be useful.

There are no firm rules about what information must be used. Useful studies may sometimes be based on only one or a few of the sources listed here. The point of a rich case record is to permit multiple links to theory, facilitate trustworthy inferences, and provide a source of evidence for presentation to your readers.

A hint: Cases drawn from clinical trials typically offer data on (or prescribe) details of diagnosis, initial distress, progress through treatment, treatment approach, therapist qualifications, and so forth. They can show relative standing of a case with respect to, for example, degree of initial distress or degree of improvement across treatment within the trial sample. Such details may or may not be important theoretically, but they can help put the case in a context for readers and reviewers.

Analysing Case Study Materials

There are many ways to go about qualitative analysis of case materials, but I have found it useful to think of the work in three phases:

1) Gaining familiarity with the case. This includes listening to or watching recordings, reading transcripts, and reviewing other available materials. Typically, researchers review case materials many times, perhaps taking different perspectives or asking different questions and making notes about the case and their thoughts. There is value in systematically attending to each item (e.g., each passage in a transcript) and temporarily suspending judgement about whether it is important. This is in addition to familiarity with the theory and previous research, addressed earlier.

2) Selecting and focusing. The goal of this phase is deciding what the focus of the study will be. It also includes selecting materials (e.g., passages in a transcript) that are relevant to the focal theoretical topic or theme.

3) Interpreting. This conceptual analysis phase requires explicit linking of observations to theoretical concepts and ideas, and making sense of what has happened in terms of the theory.

Throughout this process, the goal is to establish connections between theory and observation, for example, making explicit links between particular theoretical concepts and specific passages of therapeutic dialogue. Some investigators use forms that list observations (e.g., quotes from a text, summaries of observed patterns) in one column and corresponding theoretical concepts or relations in another column. The question is whether the observed events recognizably correspond to the theoretical concepts and the theoretical relations among them. The points of contact need not be observations that fit the theory; it is just as valuable to record observations that are contrary to theory or observations that the theory should account for but doesn't (yet). In the interpretation phase, these alternatives can be reconciled; investigators may need to modify or elaborate the theory in order to encompass the new observations.

Much research in counselling psychology is collaborative. It is valuable—some would say essential—to involve multiple people in observing and reporting. It is important that each such collaborator understands the theory that is being built, so each can independently become familiar with case materials and identify theoretically relevant observations. Having more than one person considering the material can inject new ideas into everyone's understanding of the case, and smooth the rough edges of each individual's interpretations. Consensus among multiple observers can help make the product more convincing to others. It may also be more fun to have collaborators.

Apply the Case to the Theory after Applying the Theory to the Case

Theory-building case studies are meant to support or change the theory, not just to understand the case. Of course, applying the theory to the case is an essential first step in theory-building—seeing how the theory corresponds to the new observations. But investigators then must turn the observations back on the theory in order to evaluate and improve it. This is the major difference between clinical case studies and theory-building case studies. It is why investigators must have enough confidence to modify the theory if the observations justify it—to extend its scope, to change its expression, and so forth.

A respectful attitude towards theory has a place in clinical applications. Clinical theories often point to subtle or counterintuitive phenomena, so crediting the theory or esteemed theorists above one's own initial impressions may reveal things that would otherwise be overlooked. Originators of psychotherapy theories are esteemed because they recognized and articulated nuances that others had missed. But case studies that merely apply theories, without putting them at risk of alteration, do not make a scientific contribution.

Some Writing Tips

A first step in learning to report case studies is to see how others have done it. Some journals that have published theory-building case studies include *Psychotherapy Research, Counselling and Psychotherapy Research, Person-Centered and Experiential Psychotherapies, Counselling Psychology Quarterly, Psychology and Psychotherapy: Theory, Research, and Practice, Journal of Clinical Psychology: In Session,* and *Pragmatic Case Studies in Psychotherapy*. And there are more. For some years, I and others have been involved in theory-building case studies on a theory called the assimilation model (e.g., Brinegar, Salvi, Stiles, & Greenberg, 2006; Goodridge & Hardy, 2009; Humphreys, Rubin, Knudson, & Stiles, 2005; Leiman & Stiles, 2001; Meystre, Kramer, Roten, Despland, & Stiles, 2014; Osatuke et al., 2005; Stiles et al., 2006).

The instructions to authors on the website of *Pragmatic Case Studies in Psychotherapy* (http://pcsp.libraries.rutgers.edu/index.php) offer a detailed list of information to include in case studies. In my view, this list is oriented to a specific fact-gathering purpose: it envisions a database of cases from which future theorists might draw to construct their theories. Theory-building studies aimed at assessing and improving a particular theory may require different information and may not require some of the information on the list (e.g., some theories do not use conventional diagnostic categories and may not require the indicated diagnostic details). Nevertheless, this list is a valuable source of ideas to consider in constructing a theory-building case report.

Here are a few suggestions for writing journal articles about theory-building case studies, based on my experience:

1. Pick the one or two most interesting things you have learned from the case and focus on those. Do not attempt to include everything you know about the case.

2. Begin with the main point of the study, stating the main theoretical topic, the fact that it is a theory-building case study, and a phrase about the nature of the case.

3. Early in the introduction, summarize the relevant parts of the theory. Incorporate (and explain that you are incorporating) any changes you have made to the theory as a result of this case study. An introduction is meant to quickly provide your readers with the best possible conceptual framework for understanding what was done and what was observed, including the additions to the framework. Do not make readers go back to where you started.

4. Selectively review other research about your main topic, linking what others have said with your current understanding. How would you explain their observations?

5. Depending on the journal to which you intend to submit your report, you may need to explain briefly what is meant by a theory-building case study.

6. At the end of the Introduction, summarize the purpose and design of your study and your reasons for writing about this case.

7. In the Method, describe the client, the therapist, the treatment, the co-investigators (including yourself), any measures you used, and your procedures (including how you gathered the data and how you and your

co-investigators dealt with the material and came to your interpretations), in that order.

8. Case studies require particular sensitivity to ethical issues of anonymity and informed consent (see discussion of research ethics by Bond, 2004). This can be briefly described in your description of the client or the procedure.

9. In the Results section, the central goal is to link observations with theoretical concepts. Make the links between observation and theory explicit and detailed. The case observations should be linked to the theory in many ways, not just in one way.

   Interpretations—the theoretical points you make—should be *grounded* in observations. This can be accomplished by presenting verbatim passages from sessions or interviews or other sorts of records. Show readers why you made those interpretations.

10. In reporting results, state your theoretical interpretation first and then describe the evidence that led you to it. For example, state the conceptual conclusion of your paragraph in the initial topic sentence. Begin each section with the main point of that section. Do not ask readers to keep all the pieces of evidence in mind, waiting until the end of the paragraph or the section to learn your conclusion.

11. In your Discussion, focus on the theoretical contribution—what you have learned, how you have supported or changed the theory. Acknowledge limitations. Note that criteria for evaluating qualitative work are somewhat different from criteria for evaluating statistical hypothesis testing studies (see, e.g., Elliott, Fischer, & Rennie, 1999; Stiles, 1993, 2003).

12. Be persistent. In submitting any manuscript for journal publication, you must be prepared for criticism. Expect reviewers to be as critical as you would be if you read their ideas. They will find faults and ask for changes. Almost every manuscript has to be revised, usually several times. Expect the journal to reject your first version. If you are offered a chance to revise and resubmit, do so. If one journal rejects your manuscript, consider revising and submitting it to another journal. If you are not experienced in journal publication, take the editor's letter to a more experienced colleague and ask for an interpretation. Take the revisions seriously. Consider reviewers as representative readers; if they did not understand what you meant, then many other readers won't either. If you want to be understood, then criticism is just what you need. As you revise, prepare a cover letter that describes what you have done. If you do not agree with some of the suggestions, then use the cover letter to explain your reasons. Resubmit only after you have made all of the revisions you feel you can make.

Case Studies Don't Yield One-sentence Conclusions

Typically, case studies do not test hypotheses or answer simple research questions. Hypotheses and questions narrow the study to a single statement, and, as discussed earlier, case studies typically don't change confidence in single statements very much. This lack of hypotheses and conclusions can make case studies profoundly puzzling to people used to hypothesis testing research. There is typically no one sentence that captures a case study's results. When someone asks what was found, there is no sentence to summarize it. You may have to explain how to generalize from theory-building case study research when you talk to researchers.

CONCLUSION

The main point of scientific research is quality control on theory. In case studies, investigators compare many detailed case observations to details of the theory. In this way, distinctive as well as common features of each case can permeate the theory and confirm or improve it. Conducting and reporting case studies requires patience and persistence. But it offers a way to bring clinical relevance to research on psychotherapy.

SUGGESTED FURTHER READING

Kuhn, T. S. (1970). *The structure of scientific revolutions*. Chicago, IL: University of Chicago Press.
A landmark essay on how science works.
McLeod, J. (2010). *Case study research in counselling and psychotherapy*. Thousand Oaks, CA: Sage.
Detailed descriptions of the logic and method of a variety of types of case studies.
Stiles, W. B. (2009). Logical operations in theory-building case studies. *Pragmatic Case Studies in Psychotherapy, 5*(3), 9–22. Retrieved from http://jrul.libraries.rutgers.edu/index.php/pcsp/article/view/973/2384 (March 20, 2017).
A more extended discussion of topics addressed in this chapter.

REFERENCES

Bond, T. (2004). *Ethical guidelines for researching counselling and psychotherapy*. Rugby: British Association for Counselling and Psychotherapy.
Brinegar, M. G., Salvi, L. M., Stiles, W. B., & Greenberg, L. S. (2006). Building a meaning bridge: Therapeutic progress from problem formulation to understanding. *Journal of Counseling Psychology, 53*, 165–180.
Campbell, D. T. (1979). "Degrees of freedom" and the case study. In T. D. Cook, & C. S. Reichardt (Eds.), *Qualitative and quantitative methods in evaluation research* (pp. 49–67). Beverley Hills, CA: Sage.
Elliott, R. (2002). Hermeneutic single-case efficacy design. *Psychotherapy Research, 12*, 1–21.
Elliott, R., Fischer, C., & Rennie, D. (1999). Evolving guidelines for publication of qualitative research studies in psychology and related fields. *British Journal of Clinical Psychology, 38*, 215–229.

Goodridge, D., & Hardy, G. E. (2009). Patterns of change in psychotherapy: An investigation of sudden gains in cognitive therapy using the assimilation model. *Psychotherapy Research, 19*, 114–123. DOI: 10.1080/10503300802545611

Humphreys, C. L., Rubin, J. S., Knudson, R. M., & Stiles. W. B. (2005). The assimilation of anger in a case of dissociative identity disorder. *Counselling Psychology Quarterly, 18*, 121–132.

Kuhn, T. S. (1970). *The structure of scientific revolutions*. Chicago, IL: University of Chicago Press.

Leiman, M., & Stiles, W. B. (2001). Dialogical sequence analysis and the zone of proximal development as conceptual enhancements to the assimilation model: The case of Jan revisited. *Psychotherapy Research, 11*, 311–330. DOI: 10.1080/713663986

McLeod, J. (2010). *Case study research in counselling and psychotherapy*. Thousand Oaks, CA: Sage.

Meystre, C., Kramer, U., Roten, Y., Despland, J. N., & Stiles, W. (2014). How psychotherapeutic exchanges become responsive: A theory-building case study in the framework of the Assimilation Model. *Counselling and Psychotherapy Research: Linking research with practice, 14*, 29–41. DOI: 10.1080/14733145.2013.782056

Osatuke, K., Glick, M. J., Stiles, W. B., Greenberg, L. S., Shapiro, D. A., & Barkham, M. (2005). Temporal patterns of improvement in client-centred therapy and cognitive-behaviour therapy. *Counselling Psychology Quarterly, 18*, 95–108.

Rosenwald, G. C. (1988). A theory of multiple case research. *Journal of Personality, 56*, 239–264.

Stiles, W. B. (1993). Quality control in qualitative research. *Clinical Psychology Review, 13*, 593–618.

Stiles, W. B. (2003). Qualitative research: Evaluating the process and the product. In S. P. Llewelyn, & P. Kennedy (Eds.), *Handbook of clinical health psychology* (pp. 477–499). London: Wiley.

Stiles, W. B. (2005). Case studies. In J. C. Norcross, L. E. Beutler, & R. F. Levant (Eds.), *Evidence-based practices in mental health: Debate and dialogue on the fundamental questions* (pp. 57–64). Washington, DC: American Psychological Association.

Stiles, W. B. (2007). Theory-building case studies of counselling and psychotherapy. *Counselling and Psychotherapy Research, 7*, 122–127.

Stiles, W. B. (2009). Logical operations in theory-building case studies. *Pragmatic Case Studies in Psychotherapy, 5*(3), 9–22.

Stiles, W. B. (2010). Theory-building case studies as practice-based evidence. In M. Barkham, G. Hardy, & J. Mellor-Clark (Eds.), *Developing and delivering practice-based evidence: A guide for the psychological therapies* (pp. 91–108). Chichester: Wiley-Blackwell.

Stiles, W. B. (2011). Coming to terms. *Psychotherapy Research, 21*, 367–384.

Stiles, W. B. (2015). Theory-building, enriching, and fact-gathering: Alternative purposes of psychotherapy research. In O. Gelo, A. Pritz, & B. Rieken (Eds.), *Psychotherapy research: General issues, process, and outcome* (pp. 159–179). New York: Springer-Verlag.

Stiles, W. B. (2016). La validité scientifique de l'étude de cas [The scientific validity of case study]. In V. Pomini, Y. de Roten, F. Brodard, & V. Quartier (Eds.). *L'étude de cas en psychologie clinique: Dialogue entre recherche et pratique [The case study in clinical psychology : Dialogue between research and practice]* (pp 75–94). Lausanne: Éditions Antipodes.

Stiles, W. B., Leiman, M., Shapiro, D. A., Hardy, G. E., Barkham, M., Detert, N. B., & Llewelyn, S. P. (2006). What does the first exchange tell? Dialogical sequence analysis and assimilation in very brief therapy. *Psychotherapy Research, 16*, 408–421.

Index

c.p. is counselling psychology

ableism, 203, 207
abuse, 83, 92, 252, 272, 383
　children, 180, 217, 218, 223
　sexual, 92, 223, 287, 334
　SND, 193–194
Academy of Psychological Clinical Science
　　(APCS), 372
acceptance and commitment therapy (ACT),
　　18, 20, 107, 109, 114, 116, 151
accreditation standards, 363, 370, 372
adjudication, 434
affirmative case, 428, 429, 433, 434, 436
age, 258, 289, 293, 335, 384
　children and young people, 172–173,
　　176–177, 179–180, 182
　discrimination, 266
　SND, 188, 189, 192, 195
alcohol *see* substance misuse (including alcohol)
Alliance for Counselling and
　　Psychotherapy, 337
American Psychological Association (APA),
　　11, 23, 404
　training, 367, 369–370
anarchism, 334
anonymity, 387, 450
　research ethics, 384, 386–389
anorexia nervosa, 415
anxiety, 178, 319, 322, 414
　autism, 205, 206, 208–209
　case examples, 83, 97–98, 114–116,
　　143–146, 276–277
　CBT, 107–109
　death, 64, 66
　existential c.p., 57, 61–62, 64
　gender, 282, 289
　HSCED, 432, 434–435
　psychodynamic c.p., 91, 94, 99, 100

research ethics, 380, 387
sexualities, 242, 243
SND, 186, 189, 190–191, 195–196
social class, 252, 259
supervision, 349, 352
trauma and emergency services,
　　217–218, 220, 225
asexuality, 232
Asperger syndrome, 6, 200–209
assimilation model, 449
assimilative integration, 154–155, 159
Association for Humanistic Psychology
　　(AHP), 336
Association for Psychological Science
　　(APS), 372
attachment theory, 18, 93
attitudes to SND, 186, 187–191
auditory hallucinations, 62
autism, 6, 189–190, 191, 195, 200–209
autoethnography, 399–400

bad faith, 48, 60, 68
Beck, Aaron, 106, 110–111, 113, 117, 340, 420–421
　Depression Inventory, 421, 435
behaviourism, 10, 40, 75–76, 158, 195
bereavement and grief, 177, 292, 303, 307, 435
　existential c.p., 62–63, 65–68
　pluralistic c.p., 141, 142
　research ethics, 383, 390
　SND, 186, 195
　trauma and emergency services,
　　215–216, 218, 223
Bernays, Edward, 340
bias, 64, 154, 258–260, 269–270
　HSCED, 432, 436
　race and ethnicity, 267, 268, 269–270
　research ethics, 382–383, 389
　sexualities, 233, 235, 239
　social class, 256, 258–260

Binswanger, Ludwig, 58–59, 63, 65
biomedical model, 25, 26, 61, 336, 381
bisexuality, 239, 241, 243–244, 291
   defined, 235
black minority ethnic (BME) groups,
      266, 268, 269
   see also race and ethnicity
bond domain, 110, 112–113
bondage, dominance and sadomasochism
      (BDSM), 233
Bordin, Ed, 110, 349, 350
Boss, Medard, 59, 65
Bowlby, J., 90, 93
bracketing, 63–64
British Association of Behavioural and
      Cognitive Psychotherapy (BABCP), 305
British Association for Counselling (BAC), 13
British Association for Counselling and
      Psychotherapy (BACP), 305
   politics, 331, 335, 336, 338
British Psychological Society (BPS), 3, 9, 12–17,
      37–38, 121
   children and young people, 179–180
   codes of practice and ethics, 302–305,
      307–309, 320
   Division of Counselling Psychology, 4,
      13–17, 26, 43–44
   politics, 335–338
   qualifications, 4, 13–14
   research ethics, 381
   supervision, 353, 355
   training, 42–43, 363–364, 372, 373
   trauma and emergency services, 221
Buber, Martin, 63, 121
Buddhism, 114, 124
bullying, 177, 193, 239–240, 286, 308
   case example, 277–278
burnout, 216, 218, 225, 349

Canadian Psychological Association (CPA),
      370
case study research, 6–7, 368, 425–436, 439–451
Change Interviews, 431, 433, 434, 435
child abuse, 180, 217, 218, 223
children and young people (CYP), 6, 84, 142,
      171–182, 259
   case example, 180–181
   legal and ethical issues, 172, 179–180
   online counselling, 174–175
   research ethics, 384
   SND, 186, 188–195

cisgender people, 282, 286–288, 289, 291, 293
   case example, 288
Civil Rights, 27, 234
Clark, David, 333, 335
Clarkson, Petruska, 316, 322
classical client-centred therapy, 73
classism, 250–256, 258, 260, 339
codes of practice, 300, 302–304, 305,
      306–309, 320
cognitive behavioural c.p., 5–6, 29, 31, 104–117
   case example, 114–116
cognitive behavioural therapy (CBT),
      16–20, 104–117
   autism, 206
   case examples, 114–116, 143–144, 272, 276
   children and young people, 178
   existential c.p., 62, 65
   integrative c.p., 151, 153, 154, 155
   online counselling, 324
   person-centred experiential c.p., 84
   philosophy, 40–41
   pluralistic c.p., 117, 137, 141, 142
   politics, 333, 338
   research, 111, 113–114, 398, 409,
      420–421, 435
   seven challenges, 116–117
   SND, 194, 195
   training, 29, 31, 116, 117, 372
collaborative empiricism, 106
collaborative pragmatism, 106
common factors approach, 154
compassion, 124, 125
compassion-focused therapy (CFT), 20,
      106, 114, 116
conditioning, 113, 125
confidentiality, 272, 334, 363
   children and young people, 179–181
   ethics awareness in training, 303, 306–309
   online counselling, 323–324
   practice ethics, 317, 319–325
   research ethics, 386, 389
conflict of interests, 304
congruence, 79, 80, 160, 303, 305, 311, 421
   gender, 285
Consensual Qualitative Research
      (CQR), 401, 403
consent, 308–309, 385–387, 450
   children and young people, 179
   research ethics, 380, 383–388
constructivism, 96, 99, 107, 136
contracts, 180, 350

ethics awareness in training, 304, 308, 311
    online counselling, 323–324
    practice ethics, 316–317, 323–324, 326–327
Conversation Analysis (CA), 401, 403
Cooper, Mick, 65, 135, 140, 141, 146
CORE-Outcome Measure, 143, 431, 435
Council for Healthcare Regulatory Excellence
    (CHRE), 337
Counselling for Depression (CfD), 84
countertransference, 92–96, 160, 161, 305
    case example, 97–98
creative therapy, 141, 176, 178
Cronbach's alpha reliability, 414, 419
Crossley, Rosemary, 190
culture, 46, 106, 130, 141, 332, 354
    case examples, 273–274, 277
    ethics, 301, 306
    gender, 283, 285–288, 290–291, 293
    integrative c.p., 152, 155, 162, 164
    qualitative research, 395–399, 401–402
    race and ethnicity, 266, 267, 274–276
    sexualities, 232, 235–239, 243–244
    social class, 251, 253, 254, 258
    training, 363, 371–372
    see also multiculturalism
cyclical psychodynamics, 158

data analysis, 432, 435–436, 447–448
    qualitative research, 402–404
    quantitative research, 411, 413, 417–420
data collection, 399–400, 380, 387–389
    HSCED, 430–431, 435–436
debriefing, 220, 221–222
deception, 380, 387, 389
depression, 18, 20, 61–62, 84, 99, 146, 162
    case examples, 96–98, 162–163, 243–244,
        272, 276–277
    death, 65, 67
    gender, 282, 287, 289
    qualitative research, 398, 401
    quantitative research, 398, 415, 420–421
    sexualities, 242, 243–244
    SND, 186
    social class, 252, 259
    supervision, 352
    transactional analysis, 434, 435
    trauma and emergency services, 217–218,
        220, 224–225
developmental stages, 176–177, 182, 188
diagnosis, 24–25, 46, 61, 77, 268, 415
    autism, 189, 195, 201–203

children and young people, 177
gender, 282, 287
integrative c.p., 156, 157, 162
medical model, 23–25, 27, 30–31
sexualities, 233
social class, 258, 260
theory-building, 446, 447, 449
trauma and emergency services, 216, 217
dialectical behaviour therapy, 151
dialogical person-centred therapy, 73, 82
DiClemente, Carlo, 153
dimension of self, 60
disability, 6, 282, 293, 335
    online counselling, 323
    see also special needs and disabilities (SND)
discrimination, 335, 337–338, 382
    age, 266
    case example, 277–278
    gender, 251, 266, 282, 286, 291
    race and ethnicity, 266–271
    sexualities, 232–238, 240, 242–243
distress and dysfunction, 6, 18–19, 28,
        44–45, 307, 322
    autism, 203, 204–205
    case example, 82–83
    children and young people, 172–173, 176–177
    CBT, 108–109, 111–114
    existential c.p., 61–62
    formulation, 31
    gender, 282, 287, 291
    integrative c.p., 158–159
    medical model, 23, 25, 26–27
    PCE c.p., 77–78, 79, 81, 82–83
    pluralistic c.p., 138–139, 146
    politics, 332, 333, 339
    psychodynamic c.p., 92–93
    sexualities, 237, 238, 242
    SND, 191–194
    social class, 251–253, 254, 255
    theory-building, 447
    transpersonal c.p., 124–125
    trauma and emergency services, 216, 220, 223
diversity, 27, 29, 130, 232, 255, 293, 354
    autism, 207, 209
    philosophical issues, 43, 46
    pluralistic c.p., 136–137, 139, 140, 142
    qualitative research, 395, 401
    race and ethnicity, 255, 266, 268, 269
    training, 363, 374
Division of Counselling Psychology, 4,
        13–17, 26, 43–44

Down's syndrome, 186, 191
dreams, 90, 98, 123, 124, 128–129
    case example, 130–131
drive theory, 90, 96
drugs *see* substance misuse (including alcohol)
duty of care, 307, 309, 310, 311
    trauma and emergency services, 215, 218–220

eating disorders, 99, 162, 242–243, 415
    case example, 196
eclecticism, 5, 17, 19, 29, 74, 135, 138
    integrative c.p., 151, 152–153, 156–157, 162
    technical, 152–153
Elliott, Robert, 82, 431, 432, 446
Ellis, Albert, 106, 107, 110, 113, 117
emergency services, 6, 215–226
emotion-focused couples therapy, 151–152
emotion-focused therapy (EFT), 73, 82, 430,
    432, 434–435
empathy, 110, 140, 190, 381, 405, 413
    autism, 207, 209
    case example, 83
    integrative c.p., 159, 160, 163
    online counselling, 324
    PCE c.p., 73, 75, 79, 80, 83
    psychodynamic c.p., 93, 94, 98
    trauma and emergency services, 216
empiricism, 41, 107, 108, 155
employment, 13, 16, 28–29, 68, 139, 373
    autism, 205, 207
    children and young people, 180
    emergency services personnel, 215–226
    ethics awareness in training, 308, 309–312
    gender, 288, 289
    politics, 335, 337–338
    race and ethnicity, 269
    sexualities, 233, 237, 239–240
    SND, 191
    social class, 254, 255
enactments, 91, 307
    case example, 97–98
encounter groups, 11, 332, 340
enriching research, 441–442
Epictetus, 107
ethics, 6, 79, 136–137, 450
    awareness in training, 6, 299–313
    children and young people, 172, 179–180,
        182
    codes of practice, 300, 302–304, 305,
        306–309, 320
    dilemmas, 318–322, 327
    gender, 282

marginalized and oppressed groups, 334
online counselling, 323–325
philosophical issues, 39, 46, 300, 305, 382
practice, 6, 315–327
race and ethnicity, 266, 269
research, 6, 379–391
sexualities, 233
SND, 195
training, 6, 299–313, 363, 370
supervision, 316, 319–321, 325–327, 348
ethnicity *see* race and ethnicity
Europe, 14, 58, 235–236, 240, 371
existentialism and existential c.p., 5, 14,
    18, 20, 55–70
    case examples, 62–63, 65–68
    medical model, 25, 27, 28, 32
    philosophical issues, 37–38, 40, 45, 49,
        59, 61, 69–70
    pluralistic c.p., 69, 135, 136, 142, 146
expectations, 190, 193, 216, 217,
    224–225, 240, 293
experiential c.p., 72–84, 155
    case example, 82–83
explanatory theories, 442
eye contact, 190, 204
Eye Movement Desensitization and
    Reprocessing (EMDR), 222
Eysenck, Hans, 338–339, 340

fact-gathering research, 441, 442, 449
factor analysis, 112, 413, 414, 419, 421
Fairbairn, R.D., 90, 93, 98
false assumptions, 125, 127
family issues, 10–11, 26, 160, 240–241, 334
    CBT, 114, 115–116
    children and young people, 177, 178, 181
    gender, 288, 289
    race and ethnicity, 272, 274, 277
    sexualities, 236–238, 240–241, 243
    SND, 186, 191–193, 196
    social class, 254–255, 257, 259
Fausto-Sterling, A., 284, 285
fees for counselling, 333, 337–338, 341
feminism, 27, 285, 318, 382, 404
    politics, 333–334, 339
femininity, 283–288, 293
Ferenczi, S., 92, 93, 96
Fine, C., 283, 285
focusing-oriented therapy, 73, 81, 194
Foley-Nicpon, M. and S. Lee, 186, 194
formulation, 30–31, 61, 218
Foucault, Michel, 334, 341

Freud, Sigmund, 3, 46, 89–93, 96, 98–99, 446
  existentialism, 58, 63
  politics, 334, 336, 339–341
Fromm, Erich, 334, 339, 340, 93
gay people, 132, 235, 237–240, 242, 243, 335
  see also LGBT community
gender, 6, 25, 46, 255, 281–293, 348
  autism, 202
  case examples, 274, 277, 288, 290, 292–293
  cisgender people, 282, 286–288, 289,
    291, 293
  discrimination, 251, 266, 282, 286, 291
  dysphoria, 292
  identity, 232, 234–235, 237–238, 240
  marginalization, 282, 289–290, 334–335
  non-binary people, 286, 290–293
  politics, 331, 334–335
  qualitative research, 399, 401–402
  race and ethnicity, 266, 271, 282,
    286, 289, 293
  sexualities, 232–244, 282–283, 286,
    289, 291, 293
  social class, 251, 258, 282, 286
  stereotypes, 253, 283–284, 285, 287
  transgender men and women, 234–235, 282,
    286, 288–293
  trauma and emergency services, 222
genetics, 25, 202
Gestalt therapy, 68, 141, 154, 244, 340
Gilbert, Paul, 106, 114
Gillick competence, 179
Greenberg, Les, 82
grief *see* bereavement and grief
Grof, Stanislav, 121, 124
grounded theory, 20, 401, 403
Guntrip, H., 90, 93

Hamilton Rating Scale for
  Depression, 421
Health and Care Professions Council (HCPC),
  68, 302, 304–308, 336–337, 341
  supervision, 353
  training, 362–364, 371–372
Heidegger, Martin, 37, 44, 58–59, 63
Helpful Aspects of Therapy (HAT), 431
Helsinki Declaration, 381
hermeneutics, 6, 396
hermeneutic single case efficacy design
  (HSCED), 6–7, 425–436
  case examples, 434–435
  compared with theory-building, 441
  key research methods, 430–432

Hillman, James, 124, 125
HIV, 242
Hobsbawm, Eric, 341
homophobia, 239–240, 251
Hopkins Symptom Checklist, 421
Houston, Jean, 124, 128
humanistic approach, 4, 13, 15, 18–19, 305
  autism, 209
  children and young people, 178
  existential c.p., 58, 68
  integrative c.p., 153, 155
  medical model, 25, 27–29, 31–32
  pluralistic c.p., 135, 136, 142, 146
  politics, 332, 336, 338, 339
  training, 362, 364
human rights, 75, 305, 380
hypothesis testing, 444–446, 450–451

imagery, 115, 123, 128
immigration, 235, 236, 237
Improving Access to Psychological Therapies
  (IAPT), 16–17, 68, 333, 341
  supervision, 352–353
incentives, 380, 384–385
Independent Practitioner Network (IPN), 336
inductive analysis, 397, 398
integration and integrative approach, 5–6,
  19–20, 150–164
  Asperger syndrome, 208
  case examples, 162, 163
  pluralistic c.p., 135, 138, 142, 155
  SND, 194
  training, 164, 366
  varieties, 152–155
internships, 369–370
interpersonal approach, 4, 93–95, 98,
  110, 153, 332
  children and young people, 176
  ethics awareness in training, 302–303,
    305–306, 308
  HSCED, 434
  psychoanalysis, 89, 90, 92
  quantitative research, 420–421
  race and ethnicity, 267
  research ethics, 385
  sexualities, 233
  social class, 250, 252, 258
Interpretative Phenomenological Analysis
  (IPA), 401, 403
intersectionality, 235, 237, 282, 293
  race and ethnicity, 266, 268, 227–279
intersex, 234, 284, 285

intersubjectivity, 60, 70, 129, 136, 362, 365
    psychodynamic c.p., 89, 95, 97
intuition, 38, 122, 128
James, Oliver, 333, 339
Jung, Carl, 19, 94, 96, 100, 122–124, 126

Keats, John, 122
Kierkegaard, Søren, 47, 58
kinkiness, 233
Kitchener, K.S., 300, 317, 318
Kohut, H., 93, 96
Kuhn, Thomas, 440, 441

Layard, Professor Lord Richard, 333, 335
Lazarus, Arnold, 110, 117, 152–153
learned helplessness, 192
learning disability (intellectual impairment), 187–190, 194–196
    autism, 201, 202, 206
    legal issues, 195, 320–321, 322, 363
        children and young people, 172, 179–180, 182
        online counselling, 324
lesbians, 234–237, 239, 241–243
Levinas, Emmanuel, 316, 322
LGBT community, 233–244, 282, 291, 335
    mental health, 242–243
    physical health, 241–242
linguistic theory, 403
Liu, W.M., 250–252, 258

Maguire, Kate, 130
malpractice, 325
marginalization, 46, 238, 334–335, 405
    gender, 282, 289–290, 334–335
    race and ethnicity, 275, 335
    sexualities, 232, 238, 240, 335
    SND, 186, 191, 335
marginalized or emerging psychotherapies (MEPs), 430
Marxism, 331–334, 338, 339, 341
masculinity, 283–288
Maslow, Abraham, 340
McIntosh, Peggy, 270
medical model, 4–5, 14, 16, 18, 26, 31–33, 362
    assumptions of c.p., 23, 24–27
    autism, 203, 204–205
    challenges to c.p., 28–31
    children and young people, 177
    PCE c.p., 77, 84
    philosophical issues, 38, 44–46
    sexualities, 235

metatherapeutic communication, 139–140
    nine principles, 140
methodological pluralism, 395
mindfulness, 41, 151, 206, 391
    CBT, 18, 107, 114, 116, 151
mistakes, 325
modernism, 9, 12, 16, 90
motivational interviewing, 18
movement and exercise, 47–48
Mujica, President José, 334
Mulhauser, G.R., 323, 324
multiculturalism, 27, 332, 335, 354
    race and ethnicity, 266, 275
    sexualities, 235–239, 243–244
    social class, 250, 258, 260
multimodal therapy, 153
Multiple Intelligences, 188–189
multiple regression, 413, 418, 419–420
mutuality, 82, 95
mysticism, 124

National Health Service (NHS), 12, 14, 16–18, 20, 28, 32
    autism, 206
    CBT, 117
    ethics awareness in training, 308–310
    existential c.p., 69
    PCE c.p., 84
    politics, 331, 333, 337, 338
    supervision, 352
    training, 367, 372–373
    transpersonal c.p., 121
National Institute for Health and Care Excellence (NICE), 68, 84, 352
    trauma and emergency services, 221, 222
negligence, 325
neurobiology, 90
neuroconstructivism, 188
neuroplasticity, 188, 285
neuropsychology, 10, 19, 90, 365, 370, 373
neutrality, 382
Nietzsche, Friedrich, 58, 390
non-binary people, 286, 290–293
nondirectivity, 18, 27, 79, 311, 409
Nuremberg Code, 380–381

object relations theory, 89, 90, 93
observations, 440–441, 443–444, 445–446, 448–450
Oedipus complex, 92, 96
online counselling, 174–175, 316–317, 323–325
online research, 380, 384, 388

oppression, 46, 138, 142, 334–335
   race and ethnicity, 266–268, 275–276
   SND, 194, 203
organismic valuing, 77–78
pansexuality, 235
parametric statistical tests,
      417–418, 419
personal development, 38, 78,
      307–308, 364, 365
personal ethics, 6, 300, 312
personality development, 77, 90, 93, 95
Personal Questionnaire, 431, 435
person-centred approach (PCA), 4–6, 18,
      72–84, 339
   autism, 206
   case example, 143
   ethics, 305, 322
   existential c.p., 68
   HSCED, 432
   integrative c.p., 155
   medical model, 27–31
   pluralistic c.p., 137
   quantitative research, 409, 412, 416
   SND, 190, 194–195, 196
person-centred experiential (PCE) c.p.,
      72–84, 195
phenomenology, 14, 17–19, 32, 136
   existential c.p., 59, 62, 63, 65, 68–69
   PCE c.p., 73, 75, 76
   philosophical issues, 38, 40, 41, 43, 45, 48
   qualitative research, 396–397, 403
philosophy and philosophical issues,
      36–49, 89, 373
   case example, 48
   ethics, 39, 46, 300, 305, 382
   existential c.p., 37–38, 40, 45, 49,
      59, 61, 69–70
   qualitative research, 395–397
phobias, 163, 195, 410, 432, 434–435
physical dimension of existence, 60
Piaget, Jean, 188
placements, 326, 367, 369, 374
   ethics awareness in training, 308, 309
play therapy, 194–195
pluralism and pluralistic c.p., 5–6, 17,
      19–20, 134–147
   case examples, 143–145
   CBT, 117, 137, 141, 142
   existential c.p., 69, 135, 136, 142, 146
   integrative c.p., 135, 138, 142, 155
   medical model, 29–30, 32
   PCE c.p., 74, 82

qualitative research, 395
   training, 145, 366, 369
politics, 6, 330–341
positive psychology, 32, 48, 84
positivism, 12, 90, 99
postmodernism, 17, 19, 43, 89, 99, 135–136
posttraumatic stress disorder (PTSD), 217–218,
      221–222, 324
poverty, 191, 205, 237, 385, 404
   politics, 333, 337–338
   social class, 250–251, 253, 256–259
pragmatism, 73, 82, 107, 137, 146, 155
prayer, 125
pre-therapy, 81, 194
Prochaska, James, 153
projection, 91, 93
projective identification, 91, 93, 94
psychiatry, 13, 20, 44, 61, 82, 336
   medical model, 23, 25–30
psychoanalysis, 19, 23, 27, 89–92, 94, 96, 99
   children and young people, 178
   integrative c.p., 153, 158
   PCE c.p., 74
   philosophical issues, 40, 44, 46
   politics, 332–333, 336, 339–340
   practice ethics, 322
   qualitative research, 403
psychodynamics ad psychodynamic c.p., 5–6,
      88–100, 400–402
   autism, 206
   case examples, 96–98
   ethics, 305
   history, 12, 14, 18–19
   integrative c.p., 154, 158
   pluralistic c.p., 137, 139, 142
   politics, 338, 339
   training, 29, 31, 100
psychological first aid (PFA), 220–221
psychological theory, 38, 59, 64, 365–366
psychopathology, 37, 45, 93, 158–159, 442
   existential c.p. 57, 59, 61
psychopharmacology, 19
psychosis, 61, 62, 81–82
Psychotherapists and Counsellors for Social
      Responsibility (PCSR), 337

Qualification in Counselling Psychology
      (QCoP), 4, 302, 364, 373
qualifications, 4, 11–14, 326, 331, 369, 371, 447
   change in working ethics, 300, 306–312
   existential c.p., 68
   PCE c.p., 73

qualitative research, 6, 383, 394–405, 409
case examples, 404–405
HSCED, 428–432, 436
key methods, 399–400
theory-building, 447, 450
quantitative research, 6, 383, 408–422, 445
case examples, 420–422
compared with qualitative, 395–398,
400–401, 405, 409
HSCED, 428–431, 436
key methods, 414–416
theory-building, 441, 445, 447

race and ethnicity, 6, 25, 236, 265–279, 282
case examples, 272–274, 276–279
discrimination, 266–271
diversity, 255, 266, 268, 269
gender, 266, 271, 282, 286, 289, 293
marginalization, 275, 335
qualitative research, 399, 401
sexualities, 235, 236, 239, 243–244, 266
social class, 258
stereotypes, 253, 270–271, 275, 276
racism, 250–251, 267, 268, 271, 275
case example, 243
politics, 335, 339
randomized clinical trials (RCTs), 16–17, 68,
99, 426–427
quantitative research, 410, 412, 414–416, 420
Rational Emotive Behaviour Therapy
(REBT), 105–108
case example, 114–115
reality, 10, 39, 42, 66, 75
record-keeping, 319–320, 321, 324
online counselling, 324
recruitment, 400–401, 402, 432
research ethics, 384–385, 387, 388
referrals for children and young people,
174, 182
reflective practice and reflexivity, 366,
368, 370, 429
ethics awareness in training, 300, 307, 310
qualitative research, 396–399, 403
research ethics, 382, 383
supervision, 351–352
rehabilitation, 12, 15, 186, 220, 224
Reich, Wilhelm, 338, 339, 340
relational theory, 90–96, 99
case example, 96–98
religion and religiosity, 10–11, 19, 61,
236–237, 266, 332

case example, 162, 272–274, 277
integrative c.p., 152, 162
marginalization, 335
sexualities, 235–237, 238, 335
transpersonal c.p., 124–125, 130, 132
representative survey, 400, 410, 413
Republic of Ireland, 350, 353, 370–371
research, 5–7, 12, 15, 367–369, 379–391
assumptions, 24–25
CBT, 111, 113–114, 398, 409, 420–421, 435
ethics, 6, 379–391
ethics awareness in training, 308–309
existential c.p., 66, 69
HSCED, 6–7, 425–436
integrative c.p., 152, 154, 155–157
online, 380, 384, 388
online counselling, 323, 324
PCE c.p., 79, 82
philosophical issues, 37–38, 41–43
pluralistic c.p., 136, 138–140, 142, 146
practice ethics, 316, 322
psychodynamic c.p., 89, 99–100
supervision, 349, 354, 356, 398
theory-building, 7, 439–451
training, 367–369, 370
transpersonal c.p., 130, 131
see also qualitative research; quantitative research
respect, 17, 38, 79, 95, 116, 226, 236
Asperger syndrome, 201, 209
ethics, 302–308, 310, 311
for nature, 47
pluralistic c.p., 136, 137
race and ethnicity, 268, 273, 275
responsibility, 322–323
rhetoric, 339, 396–397
Rice, Laura, 82
rich case record, 142, 428, 430,
432–434, 446–447
risk assessment, 218–220
Rogers, Carl, 3–4, 10–11, 14, 17, 45
CBT, 110
existential c.p., 58
integrative c.p., 159
medical model, 26, 27, 28
PCE c.p., 73–81
politics, 336, 339, 340
quantitative research, 410, 412, 416–417, 421
six conditions of therapeutic relationship, 79
transpersonal c.p., 122
rule of description, 64

rule of epoche, 63–64
rule of horizontalization, 64

safety, 78, 109, 155, 180, 191
  case example, 143
  research ethics, 384, 385, 390, 391
sampling, 400–402, 416–417, 432, 446
  convenience, 416, 420
  qualitative research, 395
  quantitative research, 410–411, 416–417, 420
  size, 417
Sartre, Jean-Paul, 57, 58, 60, 68
scattergrams, 419
sceptic case, 428–429, 433–434, 436
schema therapy, 108
schizophrenia, 62
Schmid, P.F., 74, 80
schools, 173, 177, 178, 180–181, 332
  sexualities, 239–240
  SND, 191–193, 195–196
screening and surveillance, 218–220, 222–223
second wave CBT, 113–114
self, 76–77
self-determination, 5, 58, 74, 79
self-direction, 74
self-esteem, 91
  case example, 96, 276–277
  SND, 192, 194
  social class, 251, 252, 258
self-identity, 177
Seligman, Martin, 333
sexism, 251, 339
sexualities, 6, 25, 37, 46, 231–244, 266
  case example, 243–244
  discrimination, 232–238, 240, 242–243
  gender, 232–244, 282–283, 286, 289, 291, 293
  marginalization, 232, 238, 240, 335
shared decision making, 135, 139–140
signed causes, 427
Social Adjustment Scale, 421
social class, 6, 25, 249–260, 266, 331, 335
  classism, 250–256, 258, 260, 339
  gender, 251, 258, 282, 286
social dimension, 60
social factors, 176, 177, 178
social justice, 27–28, 138, 142, 395, 403
  Asperger syndrome 205
  SND, 186, 187, 194
social model, 187, 203, 205, 335
social processes, 23, 26–28

socioeconomic status (SES), 235, 237
  social class, 250–252, 254–259
Socrates, 39, 40, 46, 48, 64, 66–67
soul, 123–124, 126–127
special needs and disabilities (SND), 6, 185–196, 282, 293
  autism, 6, 189–190, 191, 195, 200–209
  case example, 195–196
  marginalization, 186, 191, 335
  online counselling, 323
spina bifida, 186
Spinelli, Ernesto, 37, 38, 65, 69
spirituality, 19, 60, 61, 106, 136, 152, 162
  transpersonal c.p., 123–126, 129–131
stage models, 238–239
Standards of Education and Training (SETS), 363
Standards of Proficiency (SOPS), 363
statutory regulation, 336–337, 362–363, 398
stereotypes, 253
  gender, 253, 283–284, 285, 287
  race and ethnicity, 253, 270–271, 275, 276
stigma, 175, 191, 203, 233, 236, 242
stress, 250, 252, 350
  gender, 289, 292
  sexualities, 232, 238, 241, 242
  trauma and emergency services, 215–226
subjectivity, 43, 70, 89, 91
substance misuse (including alcohol), 24, 99, 131, 142, 162, 333
  case examples, 66–68, 163
  emergency services personnel, 220, 223
  gender, 287
  sexualities, 241, 242, 243–244
  social class, 259
suicide and suicidal ideation, 216, 242–243, 287, 291, 319, 420
  case example, 162
suitability for short-term CBT (SSCT), 112
Sullivan, H.S., 90, 93, 94, 95, 96
supervision, 6, 325–327, 346–356
  autism, 207, 208
  children and young people, 180
  ethical dilemmas, 319–321
  ethics, 316, 319–321, 325–327, 348
  ethics awareness in training, 300, 303–305, 308–313
  psychodynamic c.p., 95, 98, 100
  research, 349, 354, 356, 398
  training, 4, 347–355, 367, 370

supervisory relationship, 348, 349–350
Support Post Trauma (SPoT), 221
systems-based therapy, 29, 31

technical eclecticism, 152–153
thematic analysis, 403
theory–building, 7, 439–451
  case examples, 444–448, 450–451
therapeutic goals, 135, 140–142, 146–147
  case example, 143–145
  children and young people, 174, 177
therapeutic methods, 135, 140, 141,
      142, 146–147
therapeutic relationship, 4, 17, 331, 332, 447
  autism, 206
  case examples, 65–68, 98, 162–163,
      243–244, 273–274
  CBT, 110–111, 112–113
  children and young people, 174, 175, 181, 182
  ethics awareness in training, 309, 310
  existential c.p., 62–64
  integrative c.p., 154, 156, 159–161
  mirror of supervision, 326
  PCE c.p., 74, 78, 79, 80, 82
  philosophical issues, 38, 43–44
  pluralistic c.p., 135, 139–140, 146
  practice ethics, 316–317
  psychodynamic c.p., 89, 91, 93–94, 95
  qualitative research, 396
  quantitative research, 395, 410, 413, 416, 421
  race and ethnicity, 271–272
  sexualities, 243–244
  six conditions, 79
  SND, 190, 194, 196
  transgender people, 289–290
  transpersonal c.p., 125–127, 129
therapeutic tasks, 135, 140–142, 146–147
  case example, 144
third wave CBT, 114
training, 6, 13–19, 37–38, 299–313, 353–
      354, 361–374
  autism, 207
  CBT, 29, 31, 116, 117, 372
  core domains, 364–369
  demands by employers and funders,
      28–29
  different therapeutic approaches, 29–33
  emergency services personnel, 215–218,
      220, 222
  existential c.p., 56, 61, 68
  gender, 282

integrative c.p., 164, 366
PCE c.p., 73
philosophical issues, 37, 42–43
pluralistic c.p., 145, 366, 369
politics, 331, 335, 337, 338
practice ethics, 325, 326
psychodynamic c.p., 29, 31, 100
qualitative research, 395
quantitative research, 395, 404
race and ethnicity, 269–270
social class, 254, 255
supervision, 4, 347–355, 367, 370
transactional analysis, 18, 127, 432, 434, 435
transference, 91–92, 94–96, 318
  case example, 97
transgender people, 20, 234–235, 282,
      286, 288–293
  case example, 290
Transpersonal 1 (subtle), 123–126, 128, 130
Transpersonal 2 (causal), 123–126, 130
transpersonal c.p., 6, 19, 120–132
  case example, 130–131
trauma, 6, 20, 84, 214–226, 435
  case example, 222–225
  four types of exposure, 217
  impact of events scale, 224, 225
  psychodynamic c.p., 92, 93
  research ethics, 383, 390–391
trauma-focused cognitive-behavioural therapy
    (TF-CBT), 222
trauma-focused therapy, 218–219, 222
  case example, 222–225
trauma risk management (TRiM) protocol,
    221
treatment theories, 442
true or randomized study, 412, 414
trust, 316–317, 399
  children and young people, 175
  ethics awareness in training, 309, 311
  PCE c.p., 74–76, 80, 84
  practice ethics, 316–317, 319
  race and ethnicity, 268, 271, 277
  therapeutic relationship, 110, 113, 125, 208,
      271, 309, 316–317

unconditional positive regard, 78, 334–335
United Kingdom Counselling and
    Psychotherapy (UKCP), 305, 336
universal values, 301
upward mobility bias (UMB), 258–260
urbanity, 235, 237–238

van Deurzen, Emmy, 37–38, 40, 42, 49, 60, 65
variables, 19, 99, 241, 253, 266
    integrative c.p., 159, 160, 161
    quantitative research, 395–396, 400, 410–420
    supervision, 355, 356
variance, 160, 253, 418, 419
Veterans Administration (VA), 369
violence, 238, 251, 253, 384
    gender, 286, 287, 291
    SND, 193–194

Wachtel, Paul, 153, 158
Wilber, Ken, 123, 127
Winnicott, D.W., 90, 93
Woolfe, Ray, 9, 12, 368
working alliance theory, 110, 111, 112
World Health Organization (WHO), 232

Yalom, Irvin, 62, 63, 65